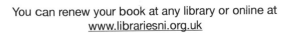
y Book from CGP

GCSE Foundation Spanish.

*doing it's the same
facts and you've just got
anish is no different.*

*you all that important
concisely as possible.*

*It's also got some daft bits in to try and make the whole
experience at least vaguely entertaining for you.*

What CGP is all about

*Our sole aim here at CGP is to produce the highest quality
books — carefully written, immaculately presented and
dangerously close to being funny.*

*Then we work our socks off to get them out to you
— at the cheapest possible prices.*

Contents

SECTION 5 — HOME AND ENVIRONMENT

SECTION 6 — EDUCATION AND WORK

SECTION 7 — GRAMMAR

Published by CGP

Contributors:
Simon Cook
Taissa Csáky
Heather Gregson
Gemma Hallam
Katherine Stewart
Jennifer Underwood
Gillian E Wallis
James Paul Wallis
Emma Warhurst

With thanks to Emma Warhurst and Raquel Montes for the proofreading.

No corny clichés about Spanish people were harmed in the making of this book.

ISBN: 978 1 84762 359 1

Groovy website: www.cgpbooks.co.uk
Jolly bits of clipart from CorelDRAW®
Printed by Elanders Ltd, Newcastle upon Tyne.

Based on the classic CGP style created by Richard Parsons.

Numbers and Amounts

Five, four, three, two, one. We have <u>lift-off</u>…

Uno, dos, tres — *One, two, three…*

0	cero
1	uno (un), una
2	dos
3	tres
4	cuatro
5	cinco
6	seis
7	siete
8	ocho
9	nueve
10	diez

1 11 to 15 all end in '<u>ce</u>'. But 16, 17, 18 and 19 are '<u>ten and six</u>', etc.

11	once
12	doce
13	trece
14	catorce
15	quince
16	dieciséis
17	diecisiete
18	dieciocho
19	diecinueve

21	veintiuno
22	veintidós
23	veintitrés
31	treinta y uno

2 All <u>twenty-something</u> numbers are rolled into one — "<u>veintiuno</u>" etc.

After <u>30</u>, numbers are joined by "<u>y</u>" (and), but written <u>separately</u> — "<u>treinta y uno</u>" etc.

20	veinte	60	sesenta
30	treinta	70	setenta
40	cuarenta	80	ochenta
50	cincuenta	90	noventa

When you put "<u>one</u>" in front of a <u>masculine</u> word, "uno" <u>drops</u> the "<u>o</u>" — e.g. veintiún caballos = 21 horses, treinta y un caballos = 31 horses. …And before a <u>feminine</u> word, the "<u>o</u>" changes to "<u>a</u>" — e.g. veintiuna galletas = 21 biscuits.

3 Most 'ten-type' numbers end in 'nta' (except '<u>veinte</u>').

4 When you get to hundreds and thousands, just put ciento, doscientos, mil (etc.) before the number. A <u>year</u> is <u>written</u> like an ordinary number.

100	ciento (cien)
101	ciento uno
200	doscientos/as
500	quinientos/as
923	novecientos veintitrés
1000	mil
1,000,000	un millón

Ciento becomes "<u>cien</u>" unless it's followed by a number — e.g. cien pájaros = 100 birds.

mil novecientos cuarenta y siete	= 1947

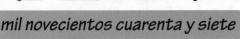

1000 900 40 7

First, second, third — *they're a bit different…*

These always end in "o" for <u>masculine things</u> or "a" for <u>feminine things</u>.

1st	primero, primera	6th	sexto/a
2nd	segundo/a	7th	séptimo/a
3rd	tercero/a	8th	octavo/a
4th	cuarto/a	9th	noveno/a
5th	quinto/a	10th	décimo/a

NB When "<u>primero</u>" or "<u>tercero</u>" appear in front of a masculine word, they always drop the "o" — "el <u>primer</u> baile" = the first dance.

Tome la segunda *calle a la izquierda.*

= Take the <u>second</u> street on the left.

¿Cuánto? — *How much?*

These words for how many or how much are <u>important</u>.
Write each one out in different sentences — make sure you don't cheat and skip any.

Tengo todas las *manzanas.* = I have <u>all the</u> apples.

all the (masc. plural):	todos los
all the (fem. plural):	todas las
other:	otros/as

many:	muchos/as
few:	pocos/as

Cada plátano es amarillo.

= <u>Every/Each</u> banana is yellow.

all the (singular): todo el / toda la

Your days are numbered — *today's the 20th…*

You're bound to know a bit about numbers already — which is cool. And it means you can spend more time checking that you know the rest of the page. Learn <u>all</u> of these words about amounts. The <u>best</u> way to check is to cover up the page, and then try to write them down — right now.

Times and Dates

Time — it's one of the most <u>precious</u> things... especially if you want to do well in your Spanish GCSE.

¿Qué hora es? — What time is it?

There are <u>loads</u> of ways of saying the time in English, and there are in Spanish too.

| ¿Qué hora es? | = What time is it? |

Use 'es' for <u>one</u> o'clock, something to one or something past one, and '<u>son</u>' for all the other hours.

1) **Something <u>o'clock</u>:**

It's 1 o'clock:	Es la una
It's two o'clock:	Son las dos
It's 8pm:	Son las ocho de la tarde

2) **<u>Quarter</u> to and past, <u>half</u> past:**

(It's) quarter past two:	(Son) las dos <u>y cuarto</u>
(It's) half past two:	(Son) las dos <u>y media</u>
(It's) quarter to three:	(Son) las tres <u>menos cuarto</u>

3) **'... <u>past</u>' and '... <u>to</u>':**

(It's) twenty past seven:	(Son) las siete <u>y veinte</u>
(It's) twelve minutes past eight:	(Son) las ocho <u>y doce minutos</u>
(It's) ten to two:	(Son) las dos <u>menos diez</u>

4) **The <u>24-hour clock</u> :**

20.32:	(Son) las veinte horas treinta y dos minutos
03.14:	(Son) las tres horas catorce minutos
19.55:	(Son) las diecinueve horas cincuenta y cinco minutos

You use 'el' for all the days of the week

Without these words you <u>won't</u> be able to <u>understand</u> when anything's <u>happening</u>.

DAYS OF THE WEEK

Monday:	lunes
Tuesday:	martes
Wednesday:	miércoles
Thursday:	jueves
Friday:	viernes
Saturday:	sábado
Sunday:	domingo

Voy **el martes** .   = I'm going <u>on Tuesday</u>.

Voy de compras **los martes** .

= I go shopping <u>on Tuesdays</u> (every Tuesday).

Days of the week are all <u>masculine</u>. <u>Don't</u> put capital letters on days.

SOME USEFUL WORDS ABOUT THE WEEK

today:	hoy
tomorrow:	mañana
yesterday:	ayer
week:	la semana
weekend:	el fin de semana
on Monday:	el lunes
on Mondays:	los lunes

Hoy es mi cumpleaños.   = <u>Today</u> is my birthday.

Tengo un examen **mañana** .

= I've got an exam <u>tomorrow</u>.

Fui al cine **ayer** .   = I went to the cinema <u>yesterday</u>.

¿Qué hora es? Time you got a watch...

Times and dates are really <u>handy</u> for your writing and speaking tasks to say <u>when</u> things happen, and they're pretty likely to crop up in the <u>listening</u> and <u>reading</u> exams too. You need to know the <u>days of the week</u> and things like '<u>tomorrow</u>' or '<u>weekend</u>'. So find the time... and <u>get down to it</u>.

Times and Dates

Knowing how to say dates is really useful. If you learn all this, then you'll have no problem saying when you're going on holiday, when your birthday is... that kind of thing.

Enero, febrero, marzo, abril...

Spanish month names bear a striking resemblance to the English ones

January:	enero	July:	julio
February:	febrero	August:	agosto
March:	marzo	September:	septiembre
April:	abril	October:	octubre
May:	mayo	November:	noviembre
June:	junio	December:	diciembre

— make sure you learn what's different.

Va en julio . = He's going in July.

in March:	en marzo	in summer:	en (el) verano
in October:	en octubre	in autumn:	en (el) otoño
in spring:	en (la) primavera	in winter:	en (el) invierno

Months are all masculine.
They don't start with capital letters.

You say "the 3 of May" instead of "the 3rd of May"

Here's how you say the date. It could come in handy in your assessments.

1) In Spanish, they don't say "the third of May" — they say "the three of May". Weird, huh.

Llego el tres de octubre. = I arrive on the 3rd of October.

Check out page 1 for help with the numbers, and pages 10 and 11 for how to write letters.

2) And this is how you write the date in a letter:

Londres, 5 de marzo de 2009. = London, 5th March 2009.

3) And here are some other useful bits:

in the year 2000: en el año dos mil
in 2001: en (el) dos mil uno — **NOT** 'dos mil y uno'

Mañana — Tomorrow... Ayer — Yesterday

Use these with the stuff on page 2 — great for sorting out your social life.

Voy a esquiar a veces . = I sometimes go skiing.

always: siempre
seldom: pocas veces

tomorrow:	mañana
yesterday:	ayer
this morning:	esta mañana
this afternoon/evening:	esta tarde
this week:	esta semana
next week:	la semana que viene
last week:	la semana pasada
every fortnight:	cada quince días
every day:	todos los días
at the weekend:	el fin de semana

See page 105 for how to say you never do something.

¿Qué haces esta noche ? = What are you doing tonight?

Dates are nice if they're stuffed with marzipan...

It doesn't come much more crucial than this. Throwing a few time expressions into your speaking and writing tasks will get you more marks. It's not that hard, either. Just learn a few phrases like '¿Qué haces esta noche?', and the different words you can slot into them.

Asking Questions

You might have to ask questions in your speaking tasks or understand them in your listening exam. And before you ask, "What's the Spanish for hello?" won't cut it.

1) Make it a question with ¿ ? or tone of voice

To turn a statement into a question, just add an upside down question mark to the beginning and a normal question mark to the end of the sentence. When you're speaking, raise your voice at the end to show it's a question. Peasy.

¿Tus pantalones son negros?

= Are your trousers black?

(Literally: Your trousers are black?)

See the grammar section for more on endings.

¿Tienes un coche?

= Do you have a car?

(Literally: You have a car?)

2) 'What' questions — stick '¿Qué...?' at the start

If your question starts with "What...", use "¿Qué...".

¿Qué comes por la mañana?

= What do you eat in the morning?

¿Qué quieres hacer?

= What do you want to do?

3) ¿Cuándo? – When? ¿Por qué? – Why? ¿Dónde? – Where?

There are loads of other question words you can slot into a sentence at the start instead of 'qué'. Look at these question words — then cover 'em up and learn 'em.

when?:	¿cuándo?
why?:	¿por qué?
where?:	¿dónde?
how?:	¿cómo?
how much?:	¿cuánto?
how many?:	¿cuántos/as?
at what time?	¿a qué hora?
who?:	¿quién?
which?:	¿cuál?
what?:	¿qué?
is...?:	¿es...?

¿Cuándo vuelves a casa?

= When are you coming home?

¿Quién rompió la ventana?

= Who broke the window?

¿Cuánto dinero tienes?

= How much money do you have?

I can't read this — it's upside down...

This page is full of question words — start by learning them all. Shut the book and write down all the question words. Look back for the ones you missed and try again till you get them all.

Being Polite

You'll lose marks (and sound <u>rude</u>) if you don't stay polite in your speaking assessment — it's <u>dead important</u>.

Por favor — Please... Gracias — Thank you

Easy stuff — maybe the first Spanish words you ever learnt. Don't ever forget them.

por favor = please

gracias = thank you

thank you very much: muchas gracias

¡Muchas gracias!

Es muy amable = That's very nice of you *(formal)*

If you're talking to a friend:
<u>Eres</u> muy amable

de nada = you're welcome

Lo siento = I'm sorry ← *I'm really sorry:* lo siento mucho

Excuse me! (e.g. wanting to ask the way, or attract attention): Por favor / Perdone señor(a)
Excuse me! (e.g. wanting to get past someone): Con permiso

Quisiera — I would like

As my mum always says, "I want never gets". It's the same in Spanish —
it's much more polite to say '<u>quisiera</u>' (I would like) than '<u>quiero</u>' (I want).

Here's how to say you would like <u>a thing</u>:

Quisiera *un zumo de naranja.* = I would like an orange juice.

Here's how to say you would like <u>to do</u> something:

Quisiera hablar. = I would like to talk.

¿Puedo sentarme **?** = May I sit down?

go to the toilet: ir al baño
have something to drink: beber algo

Sorry's not the hardest word in Spanish...

These little phrases are just the ticket for becoming a social butterfly in Spain... oh yes, and
they'll help masses when it comes to your <u>speaking tasks</u>. These charmers really are <u>vital</u>.

Being Polite

You'd like a page on handy meeting and greeting phrases? Your wish is my command.
The thing about Spanish is if you can say stuff politely, you're bound to pick up more marks.

¡Buenos días! ¿Qué tal? — Hello! How are you?

Good day / Hello:	Buenos días
Good evening:	Buenas tardes
How are you? (informal):	¿Qué tal?
How are you? (formal):	¿Cómo está?
Good day (to a man):	Buenos días, señor
Good day (to a woman):	Buenos días, señora/señorita
Hello:	Hola
Goodbye:	Hasta luego / Adiós

Bien , gracias.   = (I am) fine thanks.

Very well: muy bien   *Not bad:* así así
Not good: no muy bien   *Terrible:* fatal

To reply to 'Buenos días', just say 'Buenos días' back. Do the same with 'Buenas tardes'.

Buenos días

See page 22 if you're not well and you need to explain why.

Le presento a Nuria — May I introduce Nuria?

My life's such a social whirl — parties, introductions...
oh, have we met before...

If you're a girl: Encantada

Esta es María   = This is María

Encantado   = Pleased to meet you

For a man: Este es ...

Mucho gusto   = Pleased to meet you

Pasa. Siéntate.   = Come in. Sit down. *(Informal, singular)*

Pase. Siéntese.   = Come in. Sit down. *(Formal, singular)*

Pasad. Sentaos.   = Come in. Sit down. *(Informal, plural)*

Pasen. Siéntense.   = Come in. Sit down. *(Formal, plural)*

You say adiós and I say hola...

It's a bit boring, I know. But grin, bear it, and most of all learn it, and you'll be fine. It'll be worth it when you show off your excellent manners in your speaking assessment. It's worth the effort.

Opinions

It pays to have an opinion, in more ways than one. Learn how to say what you think, or stay dull.

¿Qué piensas de...? — **What do you think of...?**

All these nifty phrases mean the same thing — 'What do you think of ...?'. Look out for them.
If you can use all of them, then your Spanish will be more interesting — and that means more marks.

FINDING OUT SOMEONE'S OPINION

What do you think?:	¿Qué piensas?
What do you think of...?:	¿Qué piensas de...? / ¿Qué te parece...?
What's your opinion of...?:	¿Cuál es tu opinión de...?
Do you find him/her nice?:	¿Le encuentras simpático/a?
	¿Te parece simpático/a?

AGREEING AND DISAGREEING

I agree:	Estoy de acuerdo
I disagree:	No estoy de acuerdo
That's true:	Es verdad
That's not true:	No es verdad

¿ _Qué piensas de_ mi novio?   = What do you think of my boyfriend?

Creo que está loco.   = I think he's mad.

Juan _me parece_ muy simpático.   = I think Juan's very nice.

I THINK...

I think that ... :	Pienso que ...
	Creo que ...
I think ... is ... :	... me parece ...

Say what you think — it's impressive

Being able to say you like or dislike something is a good start,
but make the effort to learn something a bit more expressive too.

Me gusta el tenis de mesa, pero _no me gusta_ el fútbol.

= I like table tennis, but I don't like football.

LIKING THINGS

I like... :	Me gusta (singular)...
	Me gustan (plural)...
I like... a lot:	Me gusta(n) mucho...
I love:	Me encanta(n)...
I'm interested in... :	Me interesa(n)...
I find... great:	Encuentro ... fantástico/a

DISLIKING THINGS

I don't like... :	No me gusta...(singular)/ No me gustan...(plural)
I don't like at all... :	No me gusta nada...(singular)/ No me gustan nada...(plural)
...doesn't interest me:	... no me interesa
I find ... awful:	Encuentro ... horrible/muy mal

When you like more than one thing, remember to add the "<u>n</u>".

Me gustan los deportes.   = I like sports.

Table tennis or football?

OTHER USEFUL PHRASES

I prefer... :	Prefiero...
It's fine:	Está bien

An opinion — a prickly onion...

Never underestimate the power of opinions. It might seem hard to believe, but they really do want
you to say what you think. Make sure you learn one way to say 'I like' and 'I don't like' first.
They're the absolute basics — you'll get nowhere without them. Then add all the fancy bits.

Opinions

Don't <u>just</u> say that you like or hate something. Really go to town by explaining <u>why</u> you think the way you do — you're sure to pick up marks if you use some of these handy descriptions.

Use words like 'bueno' (good) to describe things

Here are a juicy bunch of words to describe things you <u>like</u> or <u>don't like</u>.
They're rather easy to use, so it really is worth learning them.

good:	bueno/a	*perfect:*	perfecto/a	*nice (person):*	simpático/a
great:	estupendo/a	*fantastic:*	fantástico/a	*nice / kind:*	agradable
great:	fenomenal	*brilliant:*	magnífico/a	*marvellous:*	maravilloso/a
great:	genial	*fabulous:*	fabuloso/a	*bad:*	malo/a
beautiful:	precioso/a	*incredible:*	increíble	*awful:*	horrible
friendly:	amable	*interesting:*	interesante	*ridiculous:*	ridículo/a
excellent:	excelente	*entertaining:*	entretenido/a	*strange:*	raro/a

Owen **es** estupendo .

= <u>Owen</u> is <u>great</u>.

Los niños **son** horribles .

= <u>The children</u> are <u>awful</u>.

To say 'because' say 'porque'

Congratulations — you have an opinion, so you're officially not <u>dull</u>. But to reach the coveted rating of '<u>interesting</u>', you need to know how to back it up with '<u>porque</u>'.

'porque' is <u>ultra-important</u> — forget it at your peril.

Me gusta esta película **porque** los actores son muy buenos.

= I like this film <u>because</u> the actors are very good.

Pienso que esta película es horrible **porque** la historia es aburrida.

= I think this film is awful <u>because</u> the story is boring.

Don't mix up 'por qué', and 'porque'

Be careful not to <u>mix up</u> 'why' and 'because'. They're almost the same — but not quite:

WHY? = ¿POR QUÉ?   BECAUSE = PORQUE

Poor Kaye? What's wrong with her...

It's not much cop <u>only</u> knowing how to ask someone else's opinion, or how to say 'I think', without being able to say <u>what</u> you think and <u>why</u>. All these phrases are easy — just <u>stick them together</u> to get a sentence. Just make sure you don't say something <u>daft</u> like 'I like it because it's awful'.

What Do You Think of...?

Giving <u>opinions</u> is one of those things that will <u>definitely</u> get you marks in the exam.
Learn these <u>general phrases</u> and you'll be able to give your opinions on a zillion different topics.

Use 'Creo que...' or 'Pienso que...' to give your opinion

¿Qué piensas de este grupo?   = What do you think of <u>this band</u>?

Creo que este grupo es bueno.   = I think <u>this band</u> is <u>good</u>.

this team:	este equipo
this magazine:	esta revista
this music:	esta música
this novel:	esta novela
this actor:	este actor
this actress:	esta actriz
this film:	esta película
this newspaper:	este periódico

bad:	malo/a
excellent:	excelente
boring:	aburrido/a
quite good:	bastante bueno/a
fantastic:	fantástico/a

You can use any of the <u>opinion words</u> from p. 8.

Use 'Estoy de acuerdo' to agree

No me gusta este libro. Creo que es aburrido. ¿Estás de acuerdo?

= I don't like this book. I think it's boring. <u>Do you agree?</u>

These are <u>linked</u>. If <u>the thing you're talking about</u> is <u>masculine</u>, then the <u>description</u> has to be masculine too.

Estoy de acuerdo.   = I agree.

No, no estoy de acuerdo. A mí me encanta este libro.

= No, <u>I don't agree.</u> I love this book.

You can also use '<u>¿Y tú?</u>' after giving your opinion
to find out what the other person thinks.

Creo que esta película es ridícula. ¿Y tú?

= I think this film is ridiculous. <u>How about you?</u>

Let's just agree to disagree...

Giving your <u>opinion</u> about things gets you <u>big marks</u> in the exams. It's all a matter of having the
vocab at your fingertips, ready to use. And the best way to have that is, yep, lots of <u>practice</u>.

Writing Informal Letters

You might need to write a letter to a friend or pen pal for one of your Spanish writing tasks.
Just remember the secret to writing a good letter in any language is knowing the rules.

Learn this layout for starting and finishing

Here's an incredibly short letter — it shows all the key bits you need for letter-writing.

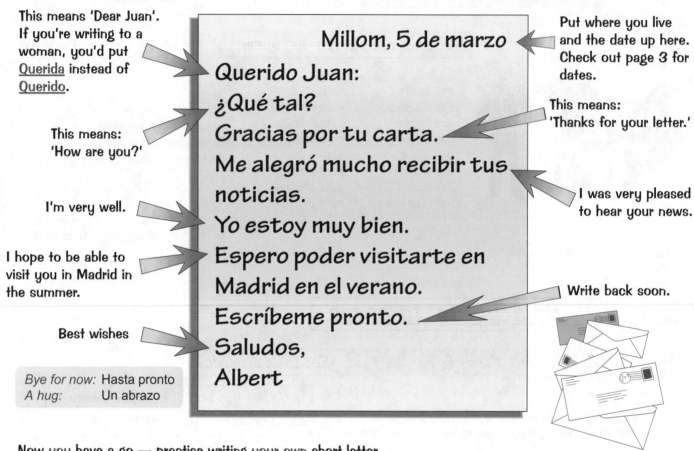

This means 'Dear Juan'. If you're writing to a woman, you'd put Querida instead of Querido.

This means: 'How are you?'

I'm very well.

I hope to be able to visit you in Madrid in the summer.

Best wishes

Bye for now: Hasta pronto
A hug: Un abrazo

Millom, 5 de marzo
Querido Juan:
¿Qué tal?
Gracias por tu carta.
Me alegró mucho recibir tus noticias.
Yo estoy muy bien.
Espero poder visitarte en Madrid en el verano.
Escríbeme pronto.
Saludos,
Albert

Put where you live and the date up here. Check out page 3 for dates.

This means: 'Thanks for your letter.'

I was very pleased to hear your news.

Write back soon.

Now you have a go — practise writing your own short letter.

Use plenty of common phrases in your letters

Learning the layout is all very well, but it's only the start. Writing good letters means using lots of nice clear Spanish phrases and vocab. They don't need to be complicated — just right.

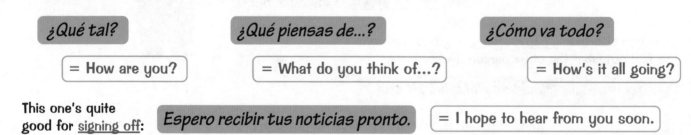

¿Qué tal?
= How are you?

¿Qué piensas de...?
= What do you think of...?

¿Cómo va todo?
= How's it all going?

This one's quite good for signing off:
Espero recibir tus noticias pronto.
= I hope to hear from you soon.

Informal letters — they keep you informed...

Think you've got it sussed? Then cover up the page and practise writing a few short letters — it's the only way to make sure. And always use plenty of nice simple phrases — and get 'em right.

Writing Formal Letters

Sigh... Formal letters are sooo boring. They've got even more rules than informal ones. You might need to know how to write one if you do a job application or a letter of complaint for one of your writing tasks.

Get the layout and language right

The name and address of who you're writing to goes here.

If you don't know the person's name, write here "Muy señor mío: / Muy señora mía:". Remember to follow the greeting with a colon (:) and not a comma (,). If you do know the person's name, write "Estimado señor García:" or "Estimada señora García:".

Yours faithfully

Hotel Gobi
Calle Altamirano 220
Granada
Spain

Rebecca Horwich
16 Peel Street
Guildford
Reino Unido
3 de agosto de 2009

Muy señor mío:

Pasé diez días en su hotel en junio, y tuve muchos problemas. La televisión en mi habitación no funcionaba. No había agua caliente y el cuarto de baño estaba sucio. Además, la recepcionista era antipática. No quiero pagar la cuenta porque estoy decepcionada.

Le saluda atentamente

R Horwich

Rebecca Horwich

Put your name and address up here.

Put the date over here.

This lot means: I spent ten days in your hotel in June, and I had lots of problems. The television in my room wasn't working. There was no hot water and the bathroom was dirty. Also, the receptionist was unfriendly. I don't want to pay the bill because I'm disappointed.

Use 'usted' instead of 'tú' in formal letters

The best way to make your letters sound more formal is to use 'usted' — it's the polite way of saying 'you'. It's a bit tricky but it's bound to turn your letters from drab to fab.

For more about 'usted' see page 91.

Use 'su' instead of 'tu' to talk about something that belongs to the person:

Gracias por su respuesta.

= Thank you for your reply.

La comida en su hotel es fatal.

= The food in your hotel is awful.

If you're saying 'to you' in your letter, you'll need 'le' instead of 'te':

Le escribo para informarle de un problema.

= I'm writing (to you) to tell you about a problem.

How to end a formal letter — just stop writing...

Practice, practice, practice — that's what GCSE Spanish is all about. You'll pick up lots of marks if you can write in a formal style without sounding like you've just learnt a few stock phrases. So get going now — the more letters you write, the more natural the phrases are going to sound.

Revision Summary

This section is all the absolute basics. You need to know all this backwards by the time you get into the exams. All the bits on your opinions, and on times (including today, tomorrow, every week, on Mondays, etc.) can make a huge difference to your marks. The best way to check you know it all is to do all these questions — if you get stuck or get it wrong, go back over the section and have another try at the questions until you get them right every time.

1) Count out loud from 1 to 20 in Spanish.

2) How do you say these numbers in Spanish? a) 22 b) 35 c) 58 d) 71 e) 112

3) What are these in Spanish? a) 1st b) 2nd c) 5th d) 10th

4) What do these words mean? a) muchos   b) cada

5) Ask 'What time is it?' in Spanish.
   Look at your watch, and say what time it is, out loud and in Spanish.

6) How could you say these times in Spanish? a) 5.00 b) 10.30 c) 13.22 d) 16.45

7) Say all the days of the week in Spanish, from Monday to Sunday.

8) How do you say these in Spanish? a) yesterday b) today c) tomorrow

9) Say all of the months of the year, from January to December in Spanish.

10) How do you say the <u>date</u> of your birthday in Spanish?

11) '¿Qué haces <u>esta noche</u>?' means 'What are you doing <u>tonight</u>?'
    How would say 'What are you doing   a) this morning?'   b) this afternoon?'   c) next week?'

12) 'Practico <u>pocas veces</u> el deporte' means 'I <u>seldom</u> do sport.'
    How would you say: a) 'I do sport every day.' b) 'I often do sport.'
                          c) 'I sometimes do sport.'

13) 'Cantas' means 'You sing' or 'You are singing'. What do these questions mean?
    a) ¿Por qué cantas?   b) ¿Dónde cantas?   c) ¿Qué cantas?
    d) ¿Cantas bien? e) ¿Cuándo cantas?   f) ¿Cantas?

14) How do you say these in Spanish? a) Please b) Thank you c) You're welcome

15) How would you ask someone what they think of Elvis Presley? (In Spanish.)
    Give as many ways of asking it as you can.

16) How would you say these things in Spanish? Give at least one way to say each of them.
    a) I like this film.   b) I don't like this newspaper.   c) I find this novel interesting.
    d) I love this magazine.   e) I find this music awful.   f) I think that this team is fantastic.

17) To win this week's star prize, complete the following sentence in
    10 words or less (in Spanish):   'I like Big Brother (Gran Hermano) because...'

18) To win last week's rotten eggs, complete the following sentence
    in 10 words or less (in Spanish):   'I don't like Big Brother because...'

19) a) How would you start a letter to your friend Elena?
    b) How would you end it? Give two options.

20) How would you end a letter in Spanish to the manager of a hotel?

Food

This page is guaranteed to get your tummy rumbling. Any of this stuff could come up in your GCSE.

La carnicería, la tienda de comestibles — Butcher's, grocer's

Meats: la carne y el pescado

beef:	la carne de vaca
pork:	la carne de cerdo
chicken:	el pollo
lamb:	el cordero
sausage:	la salchicha
ham:	el jamón
steak:	el filete
burger:	la hamburguesa
fish:	el pescado
seafood:	los mariscos
squid:	los calamares

Vegetables: las legumbres

potato:	la patata
carrot:	la zanahoria
tomato:	el tomate
onion:	la cebolla
cauliflower:	la coliflor
bean:	la judía
mushroom:	el champiñón
cabbage:	la col
lettuce:	la lechuga
peas:	los guisantes

Fruit: la fruta

apple:	la manzana
banana:	el plátano
strawberry:	la fresa
lemon:	el limón
orange:	la naranja
peach:	el melocotón
pineapple:	la piña
pear:	la pera

Las bebidas y los postres — Drinks and desserts

Mmm, my favourite vocab — this is more like it...

Drinks: las bebidas

beer:	la cerveza
tea:	el té
coffee:	el café
white coffee:	el café con leche
wine:	el vino
red/white wine:	el vino tinto / blanco
orange juice:	el zumo de naranja
mineral water:	el agua mineral

Desserts: los postres

cake:	la tarta / el pastel
biscuit:	la galleta
ice cream:	el helado
chocolate:	el chocolate
sugar:	el azúcar
cream:	la nata
pancake:	el crep
yogurt:	el yogur
honey:	la miel
jam:	la mermelada

Otros alimentos — Other foods

Some absolute basics here — and some Spanish specialities that could just pop up.

bread:	el pan	salt:	la sal	
milk:	la leche	pepper:	la pimienta	
egg:	el huevo	rice:	el arroz	
butter:	la mantequilla	pasta:	la pasta	
cheese:	el queso	soup:	la sopa	
sandwich:	el bocadillo			
breakfast cereals:	los cereales			
chips:	las patatas fritas			
crisps:	las patatas			

Spanish specialities: las especialidades españolas

cold tomato soup:	el gazpacho
snacks eaten in cafés and bars:	las tapas
rice dish with chicken, seafood and vegetables:	la paella
omelette:	la tortilla
spicy sausage:	el chorizo, el salchichón
cured ham:	el jamón serrano
thick hot chocolate with fritters:	chocolate con churros
set custard dessert:	el flan

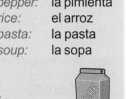

There's some food for thought on this page...

A lot of foods are similar to the English words — like el café, el chocolate, el limón, but a lot of them aren't. You'll just have to learn them — any of them could easily come up in your reading or listening exam. Have a good look at those Spanish specialities too — they might turn up.

Food

You probably have some foods you <u>can't stand</u>, and others you <u>love</u> — well, here's <u>how to say so</u>.

Me gusta / Me gustan... — I like...

You can use '<u>me gusta</u>' and '<u>no me gusta</u>' to talk about <u>anything</u> you <u>like</u> or <u>dislike</u> — including <u>food</u>.

(No) me gusta **la nata** . = I (don't) like <u>cream</u>.

coffee: el café

(No) me gustan **las manzanas** . = I (don't) like <u>apples</u>.

bananas: los plátanos
vegetables: las verduras

No **como** **queso** . = I <u>don't</u> eat <u>cheese</u>.

never: nunca

chocolate: chocolate
meat: carne
squid: calamares
nuts: nueces

Soy **vegetariano/a** . = I'm a <u>vegetarian</u>.

vegan: vegetariano/a estricto/a

See page 13 for the names of <u>foods</u>.

¿Puedes...? — Can you...?

Here's a <u>dead nifty</u> phrase to <u>learn</u>. Use it <u>properly</u> and you'll be the essence of politeness.

¿Puedes pasarme **la sal** , por favor? = Can you pass me <u>the salt</u>, please?

the sugar: el azúcar
the cream: la nata
the milk: la leche
the pepper: la pimienta

¿Tienes hambre o sed? — Are you hungry or thirsty?

Of course, it won't do you any good to be able to say what you like if you can't tell people you're <u>hungry</u> first...

¿Tienes **hambre** ? = Are you <u>hungry</u>?

very hungry: mucha hambre
thirsty: sed
very thirsty: mucha sed

Tengo **hambre** . = I'm <u>hungry</u>.

thirsty: sed

No gracias, no tengo **hambre** . = No thanks, I'm not <u>hungry</u>.

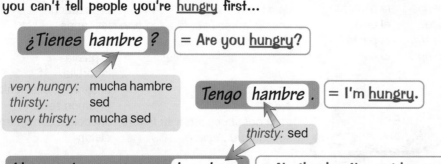

Are you hungry or thirsty? Or Bashful or Doc...

Make sure you can say what you <u>like</u> and <u>don't like</u> — it comes up in loads of different situations, so it's dead important. And if you say you're <u>vegetarian</u> or <u>vegan</u>, <u>don't</u> say you like sausages.

Mealtimes

A lot of this is useful in <u>different</u> situations — <u>not just</u> in conversations at the dinner table. There's a pretty good chance it'll come up in the listening exam, so it's the sort of stuff you <u>really need to know</u>.

¿Te gusta la cena? — Do you like the dinner?

You'll get asked for an opinion in <u>most Spanish restaurants</u>.

La comida estaba **buena**.

very good:	muy rico/a
bad:	malo/a
very bad:	muy malo/a

= The meal was <u>good</u>.

La comida no estaba buena.

= The meal wasn't good.

El desayuno estaba **delicioso**, gracias.

= Breakfast was <u>delicious</u>, thanks.

¿Quisieras...? — Would you like...?

Remember: '<u>Quisiera</u>' means 'I would like' and '<u>Quisieras</u>' means 'you would like' or 'would you like?'

¿Quisieras tomar **sal**?

= Would you like <u>salt</u>?

the water: el agua
the butter: la mantequilla

pepper: pimienta
wine: vino

¿Te puedo pasar **una servilleta**?

= Can I pass you <u>a napkin</u>?

If you only want a <u>little</u>, ask for 'un poco'

These amount words are dead <u>useful</u>, and not just here...

Quisiera **mucho** azúcar, por favor.

= I would like <u>lots of</u> sugar, please.

a bit: un poco de

Quisiera **una porción grande** de tarta.

= I would like <u>a big piece</u> of cake.

He comido **bastante**, gracias.

= I've eaten <u>enough</u>, thanks.

a lot: mucho

Tengo suficiente.

= I've got enough.

For more <u>quantities</u> info, look at page 1.

Tasty words — plenty to get your teeth into...

There's <u>loads of really useful stuff</u> on this page. There are <u>zillions</u> of situations where you'll need to say 'lots', 'not much', 'a little', etc. Scribble down those words and <u>learn</u> them — and don't forget the <u>rest</u> of the page. Spend some time <u>practising</u> a few sentences — it'll make all the difference.

Daily Routine

You might find it hard to imagine that anyone would ever care what time you get up, have your breakfast and have a shower. You've got to be able to talk about it though, so don't just skip it.

¿Cuándo comes...? — When do you eat...?

¿Cuándo cenas ?

= When do you eat dinner? *(singular)*

¿Cuándo cenáis ?

= When do you eat dinner? *(plural)*

¿A qué hora almuerzas?

= What time do you eat lunch? *(singular)*

See page 2 for more times.

Almuerzo a la una.

= I eat lunch at one.

I eat breakfast: Desayuno
I eat dinner: Ceno

Cenamos a las siete.

= We eat dinner at seven o' clock.

We eat breakfast: Desayunamos
We eat lunch: Almorzamos, Comemos

¿A qué hora te levantas?— What time do you get up?

¿A qué hora te despiertas ?

= What time do you wake up?

get up: te levantas   *go to bed:* te acuestas

Me despierto a las siete y media.

= I wake up at half past seven.

I get up:	Me levanto	*I go to bed:*	Me acuesto
I have a shower:	Me ducho	*He / She wakes up:*	Se despierta
I get dressed:	Me visto	*They wake up:*	Se despiertan

See p. 104 for more on how to use these verbs.

¿Ayudas en casa?— Do you help at home?

Lavo los platos en casa.

= I wash up at home.

I tidy my room: Arreglo mi cuarto
I vacuum: Paso la aspiradora

Tengo que lavar los platos .

= I have to wash up.

lay the table: poner la mesa

I get up at 8am — and I wake up at about 11...

There's lots to learn on this page, but it's all really useful if you need to talk about your daily routine. These phrases are great if you do a "day in the life" task for your writing assessment too.

About Yourself

Talking about yourself — well, it's my favourite subject. There are <u>all sorts of things</u> they could ask about — it's a good idea to have a think about <u>how to answer</u> some of these questions <u>now</u>.

Háblame de ti — *Tell me about yourself*

¿Cómo te llamas? = What are you called?   Me llamo Angela. = I'm called <u>Angela</u>.

¿Cuántos años tienes? = How old are you?   Tengo quince años. = I'm <u>15</u> years old.

¿Cuándo es tu cumpleaños?   Mi cumpleaños es el doce de diciembre.
= When is your birthday?   = My birthday is on the <u>12th December</u>.

¿Dónde vives? = Where do you live?   Vivo en Lancaster. = I live in <u>Lancaster</u>.

¿Qué te gusta? = What do you like?   Me gusta el fútbol. = I like <u>football</u>.

¿Cómo eres? — *What are you like?*

Soy alto/a. = I am <u>tall</u>.   Tengo los ojos azules. = I have <u>blue</u> eyes

small: pequeño/a fat: gordo/a
slim: delgado/a short (in height): bajo/a

brown: marrones
green: verdes

Tengo el pelo largo. = I have <u>long</u> hair

short: corto dark: moreno blonde/fair: rubio
shoulder-length: a media melena black: negro straight: liso
quite long: bastante largo light brown: castaño curly: rizado

I'm red-haired: soy pelirrojo/a

For more <u>colours</u> see page 35.

¿Cómo se escribe? — *How do you spell that?*

Here's how to <u>pronounce</u> the letters of the Spanish <u>alphabet</u>. Practise going through it <u>out loud</u> — yes, you'll sound daft, but you'd sound dafter getting it <u>wrong</u>.

A—a (like 'c<u>a</u>t') H—**ach**ay ('ch' like '<u>ch</u>ild') Ñ—**en**yay U—ooh
B—bay I—ee (like 'm<u>e</u>') O—o (like 'p<u>o</u>t') V—**ooh**bay
C—thay* (like '<u>th</u>ink') J—**ho**ta ('h' like 'lo<u>ch</u>') P—pay W—**ooh**bay **do**blay
D—day K—ka (like 'c<u>a</u>t') Q—koo X—**ek**is
E—ay (like 'd<u>ay</u>') L—**el**ay R—**er**ay Y—ee gree-**ay**ga
F—**ef**ay M—**em**ay S—**ess**ay Z—**thay**ta*
G—hay ('h' like 'lo<u>ch</u>') N—**en**ay T—tay

*In southern Spain and Latin America, they say these as C — <u>s</u>ay and Z — <u>s</u>ayta.

Enough about me, let's talk about... me again...

<u>Talking about yourself</u> isn't a chore — it's a matter of <u>practice</u>. The alphabet's a bit of a pain though.

Family, Friends and Pets

Zzzzz... Families and pets... How boring... Still — there are marks to be won I suppose.

Tengo una hermana — I have one sister

This is pretty easy — just learn the words for different family members and then slot in their names.

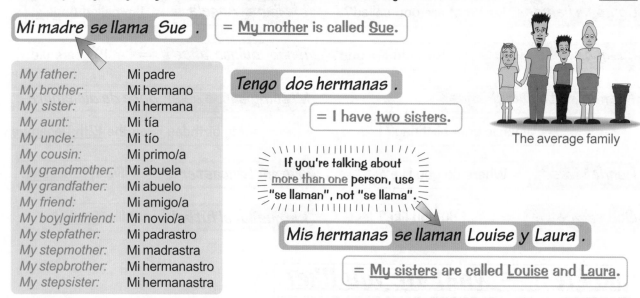

| Mi madre se llama Sue . | = My mother is called Sue. |

My father:	Mi padre
My brother:	Mi hermano
My sister:	Mi hermana
My aunt:	Mi tía
My uncle:	Mi tío
My cousin:	Mi primo/a
My grandmother:	Mi abuela
My grandfather:	Mi abuelo
My friend:	Mi amigo/a
My boy/girlfriend:	Mi novio/a
My stepfather:	Mi padrastro
My stepmother:	Mi madrastra
My stepbrother:	Mi hermanastro
My stepsister:	Mi hermanastra

Tengo dos hermanas .

= I have two sisters.

The average family

If you're talking about more than one person, use "se llaman", not "se llama".

Mis hermanas se llaman Louise y Laura .

= My sisters are called Louise and Laura.

Have a bash at describing some of your family members too:

Tiene doce años.　= He/She's 12 years old.

Son bajos .　= They are short.

Tiene el pelo liso .

= He/She has straight hair.

Tiene los ojos azules .

= He/She has blue eyes.

¿Tienes animales? — Do you have any pets?

Even if you don't have any pets, you still need to learn this stuff.
Otherwise you'll kick yourself if you get a question on it in your listening or reading exam.

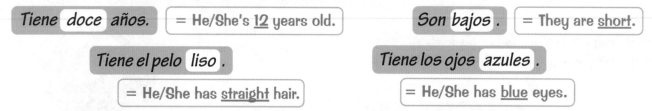

Tengo un perro .　= I have a dog.

Es amarillo .　= He is yellow.

a cat:	un gato
a bird:	un pájaro
a rabbit:	un conejo
a mouse:	un ratón
a horse:	un caballo
a guinea pig:	una cobaya

Mi perro se llama Enrique .

= My dog is called Enrique.

Practise using different descriptive words.

See page 35 for colours and page 17 for things like fat and thin.

My dog's called Rocky — he's a Boxer...

Questions about family can get you some easy marks — if you know your stuff, that is. Learning this stuff will give you a big headstart — practising it will make your chances of doing well even better.

Personality

The more <u>description</u> you can give about people's personality in Spanish, the better.
Just writing "My mum is nice. My dad is nice. My friend is nice..." is too <u>boring</u> for words.

¿Cómo es ...? — What's ... like?

Mi mejor amiga **es** inteligente. = <u>My best friend</u> *(female)* is <u>intelligent</u>.

My best friend (male):	Mi mejor amigo	*very intelligent:*	muy inteligente
My mum:	Mi mamá	*creative:*	creativo/a
My dad:	Mi papá	*outgoing:*	extrovertido/a
My Spanish teacher:	Mi profesor(a) de español	*funny:*	gracioso/a

Mis padres **son** responsables. = <u>My parents</u> are <u>responsible</u>.

My brothers and sisters:	Mis hermanos
My aunt and uncle:	Mis tíos
My grandparents:	Mis abuelos
My friends (male and female):	Mis amigos
My friends (female only):	Mis amigas

strict:	estrictos/as
friendly:	amables

La personalidad — Personality

GOOD QUALITIES: LAS CUALIDADES

friendly:	amable	*optimistic:*	optimista	*brave:*	valiente
nice:	simpático/a	*honest:*	sincero/a	*ambitious:*	ambicioso/a
cheerful:	alegre		honesto/a	*strong:*	fuerte
	feliz	*honourable:*	honrado/a	*sporty:*	deportivo
funny:	cómico/a	*patient:*	paciente	*active:*	activo/a
	gracioso/a	*affectionate:*	cariñoso/a	*independent:*	independiente
generous:	generoso/a	*talkative:*	hablador(a)	*intelligent:*	inteligente
polite:	formal	*tolerant:*	tolerante	*creative:*	creativo/a
	bien educado/a	*responsible:*	responsable	*outgoing:*	extrovertido/a
good-looking:	guapo/a	*sensible:*	prudente	*reserved:*	reservado/a
understanding:	comprensivo/a	*serious:*	serio/a	*shy:*	tímido/a

BAD QUALITIES: LOS DEFECTOS

aggressive:	agresivo/a	*lazy:*	perezoso/a	*highly strung:*	nervioso/a
impatient:	impaciente	*selfish:*	egoísta	*arrogant:*	orgulloso/a
unfriendly:	antipático/a	*pessimistic:*	pesimista	*weak:*	débil

I've got a great personality — and 4 horrid ones...

You don't need to be able to say <u>all</u> these words in Spanish — just the ones that fit in with your
writing and speaking tasks. Make sure you can <u>recognise</u> and <u>understand</u> everything though.

Relationships and Future Plans

Here's your chance to talk about who you <u>get on with</u> and who you could happily <u>throw down a well</u>.

Me llevo bien con ... — I get on well with ...

"<u>(No) me llevo bien con...</u>" is a really handy phrase if you're asked to talk about <u>relationships</u> with your family and friends. For <u>extra marks</u>, say <u>why</u> you do or don't get on with them.

Me llevo **bien** con mi madre porque es muy **simpática**.

= I get on <u>well</u> with my mother because she's very <u>nice</u>.

very well:	muy bien		*funny:*	graciosa
badly:	mal		*generous:*	generosa
dreadfully:	fatal		*cheerful:*	alegre

No me llevo bien con **mi padre** porque es **estricto**.

= I don't get on well with <u>my father</u> because he's <u>strict</u>.

my stepfather:	mi padrastro		*impatient:*	impaciente
my grandfather:	mi abuelo		*lazy:*	perezoso
my brother:	mi hermano		*pessimistic:*	pesimista

Planes para el futuro — Plans for the future

Use '<u>me gustaría</u>' to say what you'd like to do in the future.

Dentro de diez años **me gustaría** casarme.

= <u>In ten years</u> I'd like to <u>get married</u>.

In fifteen years:	Dentro de quince años
In the future:	En el futuro

have a child: tener un hijo

Algún día me gustaría alquilar un apartamento.

= One day I'd like to rent a flat.

Me gustaría vivir en una casa grande.

= I'd like to live in a big house.

No quiero casarme nunca. = I never want to get married.

I don't like relationships — I get sea sick...

Saying who you don't get on with and why is pretty <u>satisfying</u>. The stuff about future plans is tricky, but you'll look <u>super clever</u> if you manage to use the future <u>correctly</u> in the speaking or writing tasks.

Social Issues and Equality

Talking about this kind of thing can seem <u>daunting</u> enough in English, let alone in Spanish.
They <u>love</u> social issues though, so learning all this stuff could earn you a <u>whole heap</u> of marks.

El paro / el desempleo — Unemployment

Unemployment is rubbish, but you might have to <u>talk</u> about it or at least <u>understand</u> it.   Here goes...

Hay [mucha gente] en paro en [la ciudad].   = There are <u>lots of</u> unemployed people in <u>the town</u>.

not many: poca gente   *the area:* la región   *the village:* el pueblo

El desempleo en Gran Bretaña es un gran problema.   = Unemployment in Britain is a big problem.

Nadie tiene problemas en encontrar trabajo.   = Nobody has a problem finding work.

La igualdad de derechos — Equal Rights

This is your chance for a good <u>rant</u>, in Spanish of course.

Creo que la igualdad de derechos [es muy importante].

are unimportant: no es muy importante   = I think equal rights <u>are very important</u>.

Hay discriminación contra [los extranjeros].   = There's <u>discrimination</u> against <u>foreign people</u>.

sexist: sexista
unfair: injusto

women: las mujeres
immigrants: los inmigrantes

Me parece [racista].   = It seems <u>racist</u> to me.   Eso me molesta.   = That annoys me.

La presión del grupo — Peer Pressure

Peer pressure now — the fun <u>never ends</u> on this page, does it?

Hay presión para estar delgada en mi instituto.

= There's pressure to be thin at my school.

Uno siempre tiene que llevar ropa de moda y es muy cara.

= You always have to wear fashionable clothing and it's really expensive.

If you want to avoid peer pressure, stop peering...

Maybe you'll be <u>lucky</u> and you won't actually need any of this stuff for any of your exams. There's
a good chance you'll be unlucky though, so you'd better <u>learn it</u> to be on the safe side. Sorry.

Feeling Ill

If your speaking or writing task's about <u>being ill</u> on holiday, then this is the page for you. Even if you're not doing it for a speaking or writing task, this stuff is still <u>useful</u> for reading and listening.

¿Estás bien? — Are you OK?

If you're <u>feeling ill</u> (or pretending to for one of your speaking tasks) you need to be able to <u>say so</u>.

Estoy **enfermo/a** .   = I am <u>ill</u>.

Me siento **mal** .   = I feel <u>ill</u>.

Necesito ir **al médico** .   = I need to go <u>to the doctor's</u>.

to the hospital: al hospital
to the chemist's: a la farmacia

¿Dónde tienes dolor? — Where does it hurt?

Use '<u>tengo dolor de</u>...' to say <u>which bit hurts</u> — you don't even need to use '<u>el</u>' or '<u>la</u>' before the body part. Good times...

Tengo dolor de **dedo** .   = I have a sore <u>finger</u>.

head: cabeza
ears: oídos

Estoy resfriado/a.   = I have a cold.

Tengo **gripe** .   = I have <u>flu</u>.

sunstroke: una insolación
a temperature: fiebre *(fem)*

You can use '<u>tengo dolor de</u>' with <u>any</u> part of your body that's hurting.

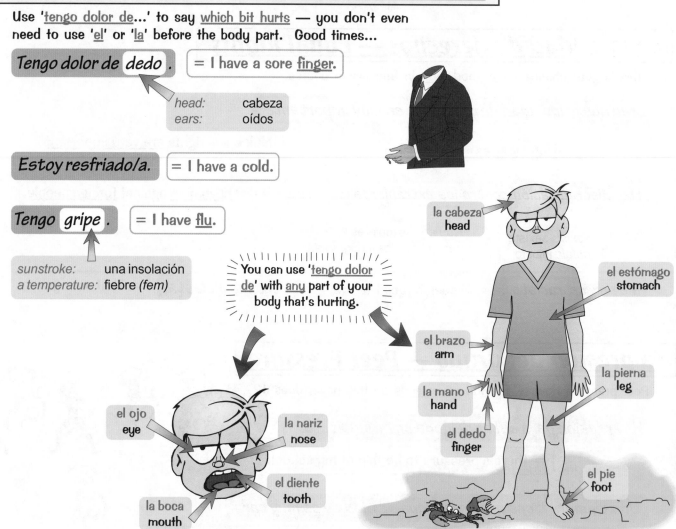

la cabeza
head

el estómago
stomach

el brazo
arm

la pierna
leg

la mano
hand

el dedo
finger

el pie
foot

el ojo
eye

la nariz
nose

el diente
tooth

la boca
mouth

Going to the doctor's — it's a pain in the neck...

You know the score — <u>practise</u> using these phrases as much as you can. If you know 'em well, you <u>won't</u> get 'em wrong. This stuff's all really useful for if you ever actually feel ill on <u>holiday</u> — unless of course you're in Germany or France or somewhere, in which case it'll be no use at all.

Health and Health Issues

¡Qué bueno! — PSHE in Spanish, you lucky, lucky thing.

La dieta — Diet

No, I'm not talking about any ridiculous <u>lettuce-only</u>, weight loss diet.
This is about your normal everyday diet and how <u>healthy</u> it is, or isn't.

¿Comes bien? = Do you eat well?   **Sí, como mucha fruta.** = Yes, I eat lots of fruit.

No, como patatas fritas todos los días. = No, I eat chips every day.

El ejercicio — Exercise

It doesn't matter if you don't do any, just be able to <u>say so</u>.

¿Qué haces para mantenerte en buena salud? = What do you do to stay healthy?

Juego al fútbol y al tenis a veces.   **No hago nada. Nunca hago ejercicio.**

= I sometimes play football and tennis.   = I don't do anything. I never exercise.

Problemas de salud — Health problems

¿Qué piensas del fumar? = What do you think of smoking?

Creo que el fumar es un hábito horrible. = I think smoking is a horrible habit.

No fumo porque no quiero ser **adicto/a** .

= <u>I don't smoke</u> because I don't want to be <u>an addict</u>.

I don't drink alcohol: No bebo alcohol
I don't take drugs: No tomo drogas

an alcoholic: alcohólico/a
ill: enfermo/a

El alcohol puede dañar **el cuerpo** . = <u>Alcohol</u> can damage <u>your body</u>.

drugs: Las drogas (pueden)
junk food: La comida basura
smoking: El fumar

your heart: el corazón
your lungs: los pulmones

Doesn't lots of revision cause health problems...

There is loads you might want to say about these <u>exciting</u> things, but learning the stuff on this page
is a <u>good</u> start. <u>Think</u> about what else you might want to say, write it down, and <u>practise</u> it.

Revision Summary

Phew, there's a lot to learn in this section. All the vocab lists might seem daunting, but vocab's the most straightforward thing to learn — just keep testing yourself until you're sure of everything. Boring but effective. Once you think you've got everything, have a go at these delightful questions — that's sure to cheer you up.

1) How do you say these foods in Spanish? Don't forget 'el' or 'la'.
   a) ham   b) potato   c) orange   d) wine   e) ice cream   f) egg   g) rice

2) Name two typical Spanish foods.

3) How would you ask your Spanish friend Miguel if he likes carrots? (Miguel doesn't speak English).

4) Miguel offers you a burger. How would you say:
   a) Thank you, I like burgers.
   b) I'm a vegetarian.
   c) No thanks, I'm not hungry.

5) How would you tell Miguel that you would like:
   a) lots of milk in your coffee.
   b) a big portion of omelette.

6) ¿A qué hora cenas?

7) Describe your daily routine in Spanish. Mention at least three things that you do and say when you do them.

8) ¿Cómo te llamas?

9) ¿Cuántos años tienes?

10) You get a letter from your Mexican pen pal Susana. She includes this description of herself:
    Soy baja y delgada. Tengo el pelo largo y negro. Tengo los ojos marrones.
    Write out the description of Susana in English.

11) Describe yourself in Spanish.

12) Say (out loud) how to spell your name in Spanish.

13) What do these Spanish words mean?   a) el hermano   b) la abuela   c) el padrastro

14) Make a list of five good qualities in Spanish, and three bad qualities.

15) How do you say 'I get on well with my sister' in Spanish?

16) Write a sentence about unemployment in Spanish. Any sentence you like.

17) Write out the following body parts in Spanish: a) head   b) stomach   c) nose.

18) What do the following words mean?   a) el brazo   b) la boca   c) la pierna

19) How do you say 'I've got a sore hand' in Spanish?

20) ¿Qué haces para mantenerte en buena salud?

Sports and Hobbies

I was never much cop at sport — I could never remember the vocab. OK, maybe you <u>don't</u>
need to know it <u>perfectly</u>, but you've got to be able to <u>recognise</u> these words if they turn up.

¿Practicas deportes? — **Do you play sports?**

NAMES OF SPORTS

football:	el fútbol
basketball:	el baloncesto
swimming:	la natación
tennis:	el tenis
table tennis:	el tenis de mesa,
	el ping pong
squash:	el squash
hockey:	el hockey
athletics:	el atletismo
boxing:	el boxeo
skating:	el patinaje
skateboarding:	el monopatinaje

VERBS FOR SPORTS

to run:	correr	to go climbing:	hacer alpinismo
to cycle:	hacer ciclismo	to do aerobics:	hacer aerobic
to swim:	nadar	to go for a walk:	dar un paseo
to play football:	jugar al fútbol	to go fishing:	ir de pesca
to play tennis:	jugar al tenis	to ski:	esquiar,
to jog:	hacer footing		hacer esquí

PLACES YOU CAN DO SPORTS

sports centre:	el polideportivo	gym:	el gimnasio
swimming pool:	la piscina	park:	el parque
sports field:	el campo de deportes	ice rink:	la pista de hielo

MORE SPORTY WORDS

ball:	la pelota
match:	el partido

Mi deporte preferido es el boxeo .

= My favourite sport is <u>boxing</u>.

Me gusta hacer alpinismo . = I like <u>going climbing</u>.

¿Tienes un pasatiempo? — **Do you have a hobby?**

Strewth — more flippin' lists. This time it's <u>hobbies</u>. Same thing applies — you <u>won't</u> need them all,
but <u>any one</u> of them <u>could</u> turn up...

GENERAL BUT VITAL

hobby:	el pasatiempo
interest:	el interés
club:	un club (de...)
member:	el/la miembro

OTHER IMPORTANT NOUNS

film:	la película
showing (of film):	la sesión
play (in a theatre):	la obra de teatro
game:	el juego

VERBS FOR OTHER ACTIVITIES

to dance:	bailar
to sing:	cantar
to collect:	coleccionar
to read:	leer
to play (an instrument):	tocar

MUSICAL INSTRUMENTS

violin:	el violín
flute:	la flauta
clarinet:	el clarinete
guitar:	la guitarra
trumpet:	la trompeta
piano:	el piano
cello:	el violoncelo

MUSICAL WORDS

band, group:	el grupo	instrument:	el instrumento
CD:	el CD, el disco	concert:	el concierto
	compacto	stereo:	el estéreo

Toco la guitarra *en un grupo.* = I play <u>the guitar</u> in a band.

My hobby is revising Spanish...

<u>Sport</u> and <u>hobbies</u> are common enough topics, so learn as much of this vocab as you can. Even
if you <u>hate sport</u>, you still need to have a <u>good idea</u> of what things mean — you'll kick yourself if
you skip it and then end up getting a question on sport in your <u>reading</u> or <u>listening</u> exam.

Sports and Hobbies

<u>Free time activities</u> are bound to come up one way or another at GCSE. You have to be able to say what <u>you</u> get up to, and give <u>opinions</u> on other hobbies. It's <u>must-learn</u> stuff.

¿Qué haces en tu tiempo libre?

Practise <u>writing</u> some of <u>your own</u> sentences about your free time.

— What do you do in your free time?

| Los fines de semana | juego | al fútbol |. = I play <u>football</u> <u>at weekends</u>.

Every day: Todos los días
Every week: Todas las semanas

badminton: al bádminton
tennis: al tenis

\\\\\\ | | | | | ///////
'To play' is '<u>jugar a</u>' for sports
and '<u>tocar</u>' for instruments.
//////// | | | \\\\\\

Toco | el piano |. = I play <u>the piano</u>.

the guitar: la guitarra
the trumpet: la trompeta

Soy miembro de un | club de tenis |.

\\\\\\ | | | | | ///////
'<u>Miembro</u>' stays <u>the same</u>
whether you're a girl or a boy
— <u>don't</u> change it to 'miembra'.
//////// | | | \\\\\\

squash club: club de squash
football team: equipo de fútbol

= I'm a member of a <u>tennis club</u>.

¿Te gusta el fútbol? — Do you like football?

Here's how to say what you <u>think</u> of different hobbies — good phrases to know even if you don't really <u>care</u>.

Creo que | el fútbol | es | aburrido |. = I think <u>football</u>'s <u>boring</u>.

the cinema: el cine
hiking: el alpinismo

exciting: emocionante
interesting: interesante

Sí, me encanta el fútbol. = Yes, I love football.

No me gusta correr porque es cansado. = I don't like running because it's tiring.

Does biting your nails count as a hobby...

I don't know about you, but whenever anyone asks me what my hobbies are, my mind just goes <u>completely blank</u>. Learn all this stuff and you <u>won't</u> have the same embarrassing problem.

TV and Films

Everyone likes TV, so it <u>shouldn't</u> be too dull to talk about it in Spanish.

Tipos de programas — Types of programmes

¿Qué tipo de _películas_ te gusta ver? = What type of <u>films</u> do you like to watch?

programmes: programas

Me gusta ver películas _de ciencia ficción_. = I like watching <u>science fiction</u> films.

crime: policíacas   *adventure:* de aventura
romantic: románticas   *action:* de acción

Confessions of a
Bunsen Burner

Me gusta ver _comedias_. = I like watching <u>comedies</u>.

game shows: programas concursos
cartoons: dibujos animados
soaps: telenovelas

¿Tienes un programa preferido?
— Do you have a favourite programme?

favourite film: película preferida

¿Cuál es tu _programa preferido_? = What's your <u>favourite programme</u>?

Mi programa preferido es _Gran Hermano_. = My favourite programme is <u>Big Brother</u>.

¿Te gusta _Dragon's Den_? = Do you like <u>Dragon's Den</u>?

Sí, me encanta. = Yes, I love it.   **No, no me gusta nada.** = No, I don't like it at all.

¿A qué hora empieza _el programa_? = What time does <u>the programme</u> start?

the film: la película

WATCH OUT — it's <u>el</u> programa <u>NOT</u> la... <u>Don't</u> get it wrong.

El programa empieza a _las ocho_ y termina a _las nueve y media_. = The programme starts at <u>eight</u> and finishes at <u>half past nine</u>.

I like watching soaps — good clean fun...

Whether you're always glued to <u>Home and Away</u>, or you're more of a <u>Newsnight</u> fan, you need to be able to say it in Spanish. Don't forget that TV could crop up in <u>reading</u> and <u>listening</u> too.

Talking About the Plot

If you've got to talk about a <u>film</u>, <u>play</u> or <u>book</u> in your writing or speaking assessment, you <u>won't</u> have much to say if you don't learn this lovely lot.

¿Qué películas has visto últimamente? — What films have you seen recently?

Half the fun of going to the pictures is <u>telling your mates</u> about it:

Hace poco vi 'Volver'. = <u>I saw 'Volver'</u> <u>recently</u>.

Last week:	La semana pasada
Two weeks ago:	Hace dos semanas
A month ago:	Hace un mes

I read: leí

the new Spielberg film:
la nueva película de Spielberg
the new novel by Jodi Picoult:
la nueva novela de Jodi Picoult

¿De qué se trata la película? — What's the film about?

'<u>Se trata de...</u>' means '<u>it's about...</u>'. You can use it to talk about <u>what happens</u> in the film.

La película se trata de una fiesta de Nochevieja. = The film is about <u>a New Year's Eve party</u>.

a car accident: *un accidente de tráfico*

En la película, un francés va a Argentina para estudiar español.

the novel: la novela

three friends rob a bank:
tres amigos roban un banco
a waiter kills his boss:
un camarero mata a su jefe

= In <u>the film</u>, <u>a French man goes to Argentina to study Spanish</u>.

La historia es triste. = The story is <u>sad</u>.

funny:	graciosa
exciting:	emocionante
romantic:	romántica

Al final, Susana gana mucho dinero en la lotería.

= At the end, <u>Susana wins a lot of money on the lottery</u>.

the team loses the match:	el equipo pierde el partido
the police discover the missing child:	la policía descubre al niño desaparecido
the singer and the actress get married:	el cantante y la actriz se casan

I think I'm starting to lose the plot...

<u>Talking about films</u> in Spanish isn't quite as much fun as <u>watching them</u>, but at least it's not pollution or unemployment. Watching films in Spanish is <u>great revision</u> for the listening exam too.

Music

If you're a <u>music fan</u>, you've come to the right page.

¿Cómo escuchas música? — How do you listen to music?

Tengo un reproductor de mp3. = I have an mp3 player.

In Spanish, <u>mp3</u> is pronounced "emay pay tres".

Escucho música en mi iPod® . = I listen to music <u>on my iPod</u>®.

on a stereo: en un estéreo
on the internet: por internet
on the radio: en la radio

iPod® is pronounced "ee pod".

Me gusta escuchar música cuando hago footing . = I like listening to music when <u>I'm jogging</u>.

I'm on the train: estoy en el tren
I'm on the bus: estoy en el autobús

Gasto mi dinero en ir a conciertos . = I spend my money on <u>going to concerts</u>.

buying CDs: comprar CDs
downloading mp3s: descargar mp3

¿Te gusta la música? — Do you like music?

Me encanta la música clásica . = I love <u>classical</u> music.

Three blind mice,
see how they run...

rock: rock
pop: pop

Me gusta todo tipo de música . = I like <u>all kinds of music</u>.

rock: el rock
jazz: el jazz
rap: el rap

jazz music: la música jazz
modern music: la música moderna
Spanish music: la música española
Coti's music: la música de Coti

Mi tipo de música preferida es el flamenco . = My favourite type of music is <u>flamenco</u>.

No me interesa la música pop . = I'm not interested in <u>pop music</u>.

How do I listen to music? With my ears...

Make sure you can say what <u>type</u> of music you like in case you get asked. Don't forget that even though mp3 and iPod® are <u>spelt the same</u> in English and Spanish, they're <u>pronounced differently</u>.

Famous People

We're all <u>obsessed</u> with <u>celebrities</u> these days — even the exam boards, it seems.

¿Admiras a los famosos? — Do you admire celebrities?

Creo que Cheryl Cole es maravillosa. = I think Cheryl Cole is brilliant.

Es una cantante famosa del norte de Inglaterra. Canta muy bien.

= She is a famous singer from the north of England. = She sings really well.

Cheryl lleva siempre ropa de moda. = Cheryl always wears fashionable clothes.

La vida de los famosos — Celebrity lifestyles

¿Qué hacen los famosos? = What do celebrities do?

¿Cómo es la vida de los famosos? = What are celebrities' lives like?

Ganan mucho dinero y son muy ricos. = They earn lots of money and they're very rich.

Salen en programas de televisión. = They appear on TV programmes.

Van a fiestas todas las noches. = They go <u>to parties</u> every night.

shopping: de compras   *concerts:* conciertos

Tienen que hacer entrevistas. = They have to do <u>interviews</u>.

La influencia de los famosos — The influence of celebrities

¿Crees que los famosos son un ejemplo positivo para los jóvenes?

= Do you think celebrities are a positive example for young people?

Tienen mucho éxito. = They're very successful.

Los admiro. = I admire them.   No son normales. = They're not normal.

I admire celebrities' taste in baby names...

Seriously, they come up with some of the <u>weirdest</u> names ever — it's almost a <u>talent</u> in itself.
If you're doing a "<u>day in the life of a celebrity</u>" task, make sure you learn this page really well.

New Technology

Here's almost everything you could ever want to say about <u>technology</u> in Spanish, on one handy page.

¿Tienes un ordenador? — Do you have a computer?

Tengo un ordenador en casa.   = I have <u>a computer</u> at home.

a laptop:	un ordenador portátil
broadband internet:	internet de banda ancha
a mobile phone:	un (teléfono) móvil

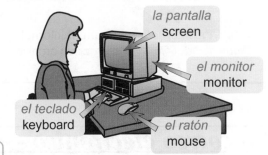

la pantalla screen

el monitor monitor

el teclado keyboard

el ratón mouse

Navego por la red todos los días.   = I surf <u>the web</u> every day.

the internet: por internet

He creado una página web sobre mi club de tenis .   = I've made <u>a web page</u> about <u>my tennis club</u>.

a website:	un sitio web
a blog:	un blog

my life:	mi vida
my family:	mi familia
my favourite films:	mis películas favoritas

¿Te gusta la nueva tecnología?
— Do you like new technology?

Creo que el internet es útil.   = I think the internet is useful.

Uso el internet para hacer mis deberes.   = I use the internet to do my homework.

Creo que los videojuegos son una pérdida de tiempo .   = I think <u>video games</u> <u>are a waste of time</u>.

the internet is: el internet es

fun: entretenido/a/os/as

This has to <u>agree</u> with the <u>noun</u> — e.g. 'entrenid<u>os</u>' for '<u>los</u> videojuegos, but 'entrenid<u>o</u>' with '<u>el</u> internet'.

Me gusta chatear con mis amigos.   = I like chatting (online) with my friends.

I can't use a computer — I'm afraid of mice...

Phew, my head's <u>spinning</u> after all this <u>techno-talk</u>. Why not take a 10-minute break from the revision and go and check your emails or update your blog or do a <u>podcast</u> or something.

Email and Texting

Emails and texts aren't too tricky — just learn the vocab on this page and you're away.

En el cibercafé— In the cybercafe

¿Puedo enviar un correo electrónico ?

= Can I send an email?

surf the internet: navegar por internet
download a file: descargar un archivo

Necesito guardar este archivo.

= I need to save this file.

Un correo electrónico — An email

Even if you don't have to write an email for a writing task, one might crop up in your reading exam.

= To

= From

Para: Charo <charo@correo.com>
De: Sonia <sonia@correo.com>
Asunto: Una invitación

= Subject:
An invitation

¡Hola Charo! ¿Cómo estás? El mes pasado, fui a Méjico. Lo pasé muy bien. Es un país encantador. Comí platos típicos de Méjico, como las fajitas y las quesadillas. ¿Te gustaría venir a mi casa para cenar este sábado? Voy a invitar a Conchi y a Marga también. Quiero contaros sobre mi viaje, y voy a preparar una cena mejicana.
Un abrazo,
Sonia

Hi Charo! How are you? Last month I went to Mexico. I had a really good time. It's a lovely country. I ate typical Mexican food, like fajitas and quesadillas. Would you like to come to my house for dinner this Saturday? I'm going to invite Conchi and Marga too. I want to tell you about my trip, and I'm going to make a Mexican dinner.
Love from Sonia

If you're writing a formal email, like a job application or a letter of complaint (see p. 11), remember to use "usted" instead of "tú".

Un mensaje de texto — A text message

Exam boards like to bring in new technology to show that they're "down with the kids", so don't be surprised if you have to read a text message from one of those imaginary Spanish friends in your reading exam.

17:23

Hola Bea. Voy a llegar tarde a la fiesta porque tengo que lavar los platos antes de salir. ¿Qué te vas a poner? Creo que voy a llevar mi vestido azul. Hasta pronto, Mari.

Hi Bea. I'm going to be late to the party because I have to wash the dishes before I leave. What are you going to wear? I think I'm going to wear my blue dress. See you soon, Mari.

Doesn't anybody write letters any more...

In my day, imaginary Spanish friends in exams used to write you a nice letter or card that you had to reply to. Now they just send you a rubbishy email or a text. That's progress for you.

Shopping

Whether you <u>love it</u> or <u>hate it</u> in real life, you need to know about shopping for your Spanish GCSE.

¿Dónde está...? — Where is...?

A <u>dead handy</u> question, this one.

¿Dónde está el supermercado , por favor? = Where is <u>the supermarket</u>, please?

The word order's <u>the same</u> in English and Spanish.

butcher's:	la carnicería	*book shop:*	la librería
baker's:	la panadería	*cake shop:*	la pastelería
grocer's:	la tienda de comestibles,	*sweet shop:*	la confitería
greengrocer's:	la frutería	*stationer:*	la papelería
chemist's:	la farmacia	*fishmonger's:*	la pescadería
newsagent:	el quiosco	*market:*	el mercado
department store:	los grandes almacenes	*hypermarket:*	el hipermercado
shopping centre:	el centro comercial	*library*	la biblioteca

Remember that '<u>la librería</u>' means book shop and '<u>la biblioteca</u>' means library. How confusing.

Ask when shops open using '¿Cuándo...?' — 'When...?'

All very well going shopping, but let's not forget Spain is the land of <u>siesta</u> — opening times <u>vary</u>...

¿Cuándo está abierto el supermercado ? = When is <u>the supermarket</u> <u>open</u>?

open (fem.): abierta
shut: cerrado/a

hairdresser's: la peluquería
greengrocer's: la frutería

¿Cuándo cierra el supermercado? = When does the supermarket <u>close</u>?

open: abre

El supermercado cierra a las siete . = The supermarket <u>closes</u> at <u>7 pm</u>.

¿Compras por internet? — Do you shop online?

Prefiero comprar ropa por internet porque es más barato . = I prefer to buy <u>clothes</u> on the internet because <u>it's cheaper</u>.

it's faster: es más rápido
I live far away from the shops: vivo lejos de las tiendas

Prefiero ver las cosas antes de comprarlas.

= I prefer to see things before I buy them.

Me parece inseguro comprar por internet con una tarjeta de crédito.

= It seems unsafe to me to shop online with a credit card.

Shop 'til you drop...

OK, start by learning that list of lovely <u>shops</u> — cover 'em up, scribble 'em down and check 'em. You need to be able to recognise as many as possible — don't forget <u>opening</u> and <u>closing</u> too.

Shopping

OK, this is a page to get you started with the vocab for <u>buying things</u> — especially <u>saying what you want</u>. It's pretty darn <u>essential</u>, if you ask me.

La moneda española — Spanish money

Spanish money's easy. There are <u>100 cents</u> in a <u>euro</u>, like there are 100 pence in a pound.

This is what you'd <u>see</u> on a Spanish <u>price tag</u>: → **€5,50**

For <u>numbers</u>, see <u>page 1</u>.

This is how you <u>say</u> the price: → **'Cinco euros, cincuenta céntimos'** | = 5 euros, 50 cents

¿En qué puedo servirle? — How can I help you?

First you've <u>got to</u> be able to <u>ask</u> if the shop has what you want.

¿Tiene **pan** *, por favor?* | = Excuse me, do you have any <u>bread</u>?

Quisiera **quinientos gramos** *de azúcar, por favor.* | = I'd like <u>500g</u> of sugar, please.

1kg: un kilo

¿Algo más? = Anything else? | *No, gracias.* = No, thank you.

Sí, por favor, también quisiera **una patata** *.* | = Yes, I'd like <u>a potato</u> as well, please.

Tiendas de ropa — Clothes shops

Quisiera unos pantalones. | = I'd like a pair of trousers.

¿Qué talla tiene usted? | = What (clothes) size are you?

Mi talla es la **cuarenta y dos** *.* | = I'm a size <u>42</u>.

Mi número de zapato es el **treinta y nueve** *.* | = I'm a (shoe) size <u>39</u>.

CONTINENTAL SIZES

size: la talla
shoe size: el número de zapato
dress size 10 / 12 / 14 / 16...:
38 / 40 / 42 / 44...
shoe size 5 / 6 / 7 / 8 / 9 / 10...:
38 / 39 / 40 / 41 / 42 / 43...

Show me the money...

Saying what you want is an absolutely <u>vital</u> thing to learn. The sizes are a bit of a <u>hassle</u>, but they're essential if you want to <u>buy clothes</u> in Spain, and they might come up in your <u>GCSE</u> too.

Shopping

Ah the roar of the crowds, the push of the queues — we all have to shop sometime... _often_ in the exams.

¿De qué color? — What colour?

Colours go after the noun, and agree with it (most end in 'a' if the noun's feminine and 's' or 'es' if it's plural).

COLOURS — LOS COLORES					
black:	negro/a	_brown:_	marrón	_light blue:_	azul claro
white:	blanco/a	_grey:_	gris	_dark blue:_	azul oscuro
red:	rojo/a	_orange:_	naranja	_pale blue:_	azul pálido
yellow:	amarillo/a	_pink:_	rosa	_bright blue:_	azul vivo
green:	verde	_purple:_	morado/a		
blue:	azul	_violet:_	violeta		

Quisiera una falda roja.

= I'd like _a red skirt_.

some blue trousers:
unos pantalones azules
a yellow jacket: una chaqueta amarilla

Watch out — if you use colours like '<u>light</u> blue' or '<u>bright</u> pink', they <u>always</u> stay in the <u>masculine singular</u>.

Estoy buscando unos zapatos azul claro. = I'm looking for _some light blue shoes_.

a bright purple skirt: una falda morado vivo
a pale yellow dress: un vestido amarillo pálido
some dark brown trousers: unos pantalones marrón oscuro

¿Lo quiere? — Do you want it?

To buy or not to buy — that is the question... and here are the <u>answers</u>...

Lo quiero. = I want _it_.

It _(feminine):_ La

Me lo quedo. = I'll take _it_.

it _(feminine):_ la

No lo quiero. No me gusta el color. = I don't want it. <u>I don't like the colour.</u>

It's too small for me: Me queda pequeño/a.
It's too long for me: Me queda largo/a.
It's too expensive: Es demasiado caro/a.

Me queda bien. = It fits me.

Me encanta. = I love it.

Quiero devolver esta falda — I want to return this skirt

Know your rights — here's how to return <u>faulty items</u>.

Falta un botón en la camisa. = There's a button missing on the shirt.

Quisiera un cambio. = I'd like an exchange.

¿Tiene el recibo? = Do you have the receipt?

This doughnut has a hole in it — I want a refund...

The trick with shopping is <u>knowing the basic vocab</u> first — it's a nightmare trying to bluff your way through your GCSE if you don't know the words. <u>Practise</u> these phrases with <u>different vocab</u>.

Shopping

More vocab, I'm afraid — but it's all everyday stuff that turns up frequently. Apart from clothes, there's a bit of vocab for pocket money and sales... Oh the thrills...

La ropa — Clothing

Me gusta este vestido . = I like this dress.

Los vaqueros están de moda . = Jeans are fashionable.

Tracksuits: Los chándals

out of fashion: pasados de moda

el sombrero

la chaqueta

los pantalones

los zapatos

MORE CLOTHES

shirt:	la camisa	*socks:*	los calcetines	*coat:*	el abrigo
trousers:	los pantalones	*hat:*	el sombrero	*jeans:*	los vaqueros
dress:	el vestido	*T-shirt:*	la camiseta	*tracksuit:*	el chándal
skirt:	la falda	*jacket:*	la chaqueta	*gloves:*	los guantes
jumper:	el jersey, el suéter	*tie:*	la corbata	*shoes:*	los zapatos

Las rebajas — The sales

Advanced shopping vocab for advanced shoppers — and for picking up extra vocab cred.

Hay rebajas en los grandes almacenes . = There's a sale on in the department store.

Los zapatos tienen un veinte por ciento de descuento. = There's 20% off shoes.

Compré un vestido a mitad de precio. = I bought a dress for half price.

El dinero de bolsillo — Pocket money

Recibo cinco libras de dinero de bolsillo por semana . = I get £5 pocket money a week.

£3: tres libras
£10: diez libras

month: mes

Gasto mi dinero de bolsillo en CDs . = I spend my pocket money on CDs.

clothes: ropa   *computer games:* juegos de ordenador
books: libros   *sweets:*   caramelos

My pocket money's never in my pocket for long...

Never forget your clothes — it's common sense really. Fortunately, some of them are dead easy — el jersey, el sombrero, etc. Others need a bit more effort to learn — but they'll come in handy.

Inviting People Out

A brief guide to having fun: 1) get someone to <u>agree</u> to do <u>something fun</u>, 2) decide <u>when</u> and <u>where</u> to meet. The tricky bit is you <u>have</u> to do it in <u>Spanish</u>...

¿Quieres salir? — *Do you want to go out?*

Here's <u>one way</u> to <u>suggest</u> a trip out:

Vamos **a la piscina** . = Let's go <u>to the swimming pool</u>.

to the theatre: al teatro   *to the park:* al parque

Sí, me encantaría . = <u>Yes, I'd love to.</u>   *No, gracias.* = No, thank you.

It's always good to give a <u>reason</u> if you say no:

Good idea: Buena idea.
Great!: ¡Estupendo!

I'm sorry:	Lo siento.
I can't swim:	No sé nadar.
I don't have enough money:	No tengo bastante dinero.
I have to do my homework:	Tengo que hacer mis deberes.

You can also use '<u>prefiero</u>' to say what you <u>prefer</u> to do instead:

Prefiero **jugar al fútbol** . = I prefer to <u>play football</u>.

¿Dónde nos encontramos? — *Where shall we meet?*

You <u>might decide</u> to meet in front of the town hall:

Nos vemos **delante del ayuntamiento** . = Let's meet <u>in front of the town hall</u>.

at your house: en tu casa
beside the church: al lado de la iglesia

For other <u>places</u>, see pages <u>25</u>, <u>33</u> and <u>56</u>.

Meet me at the ...

burger bar.

¿A qué hora nos encontramos? = What time shall we meet?

Nos encontramos a **las diez** . = We'll meet at <u>10 o'clock</u>.

For more about <u>times</u>, see pages <u>2–3</u>.

half past two: las dos y media
quarter past three: las tres y cuarto

¡Hasta **el martes** *!* = See you <u>on Tuesday</u>!   *¡Hasta* **las diez** *!* = See you <u>at ten o'clock</u>!

on Monday: el lunes
on Saturday: el sábado

¡Hasta luego! = See you later!

at one o'clock: la una
at half past five: las cinco y media

Where shall we meet? At the butcher's...

<u>Arranging a meeting</u> looks like a tricky topic. There's quite a bit of vocab to get to grips with. Then it's <u>practising sentences</u>, I'm afraid. Remember to <u>give reasons</u> and say what you <u>prefer</u>.

Going Out

Heading out? Then <u>buying tickets</u>, <u>opening times</u> and finding <u>where things are</u> is essential stuff.

Ask how much it costs — '¿Cuánto cuesta?'

¿Cuánto cuesta una sesión **de natación** ? = How much does a <u>swimming</u> session cost?

tennis: de tenis
cycling: de ciclismo

Cuesta **un euro** . = It costs <u>1 euro</u>.

2 euros per hour: dos euros la hora

¿Cuándo está abierto? — When is it open?

¿Cuándo está **abierta** **la piscina** ? = When is the <u>swimming pool</u> <u>open</u>?

open (masc.): abierto   *sports centre:* el polideportivo
closed: cerrado/a   *ice rink:*   la pista de hielo

Abre a **las nueve y media** y cierra **a las cinco** . = It opens at <u>half past nine</u> and closes at <u>five o'clock</u>.

Quisiera **una entrada** , por favor. = I'd like <u>one ticket</u>, please.

two tickets: dos entradas

For more <u>times</u> and <u>numbers</u> see pages <u>1–3</u>.

¿Hay un cine por aquí? — Is there a cinema near here?

¿Hay **un teatro** por aquí? = Is there <u>a theatre</u> near here?

a sports field: un campo de deportes
a bowling alley: una bolera

play tennis: jugar al tenis
go for walks: pasear

Theatre

I wonder if there's a theatre around here.

¿Se puede **nadar** por aquí? = Can people <u>swim</u> near here?

Is there a Laurel and Hardy museum near here...

Nothing too problematic here — provided you <u>learn</u> your stuff that is... A lot of this vocab could turn up in <u>different situations</u> — especially in the listening exam. It's <u>worth</u> learning really well.

Going Out

Blimey — lots to say here about <u>going to the cinema</u> or a <u>sports match</u>. Some of it's a bit <u>dull</u>, I'm afraid, but that's the price you have to pay if you want to <u>do well</u>. It's up to you, really.

¿Qué hicíste el fín de semana? — What did you do at the weekend?

Yep, <u>opinions</u> again — you've <u>got</u> to be able to give your thoughts.

Fui al cine y vi la nueva comedia de Jennifer Aniston. = I went to the cinema and saw <u>Jennifer Aniston's new comedy.</u>

a horror film: una película de miedo

¿Era buena la película? = Was the film good?

Era bastante buena. = It was <u>quite good</u>.

Me encantó la película. = <u>I loved</u> the film.

| *I (really) liked:* | Me gustó (mucho) |
| *I didn't like (at all):* | No me gustó (nada) |

very good:	muy buena
bad:	mala
boring:	aburrida
awful:	horrible

Un partido de fútbol — A football match

Fui al estadio para ver el partido de fútbol. *rugby:* rugby

= I went to the stadium to see the <u>football</u> match.

Vi el partido en la televisión. = I watched the match on television.

El Hull City **jugó contra el** Liverpool **en** la final **de la copa.**

semi-final: la semifinal

= <u>Hull City</u> played <u>Liverpool</u> in the cup <u>final</u>.

Daniel Cousin marcó un gol.

two goals: dos goles

= <u>Daniel Cousin</u> scored <u>a goal</u>.

El Hull City **ganó el campeonato.**

= <u>Hull City</u> won the championship.

El partido fue muy emocionante. = The match was <u>very exciting</u>.

boring: aburrido

My electricity goes out more than I do...

Even if you <u>didn't</u> do anything at the weekend apart from sit around in your pyjamas eating ice-cream, you can make something up and <u>impress</u> everyone with your Spanish knowledge.

Revision Summary

Now for the fun part — a chance to practise all the amazing stuff you've learnt in this section. Answer these questions without looking at the pages, then go back over the bits you're not sure of. Spanish revision's just one big party...

1) How do you say these sports in Spanish?   a) football   b) swimming   c) tennis

2) Your Uruguayan friend Gustavo asks you, "¿Qué haces en tu tiempo libre?".
   What does the question mean, and how would you answer it in Spanish?

3) Your friend Nigel tells you, "En mi tiempo libre, juego al tenis, leo libros y toco la guitarra."
   What does this mean in English?

4) ¿Cuál es tu programa preferido? Answer in Spanish.

5) Think of a film you've seen recently and describe the plot in Spanish.
   (You don't need to translate the title into Spanish.)

6) How would you say in Spanish: a) I have an mp3 player   b) I listen to music on the radio.

7) Write 2 sentences in Spanish about Paris Hilton and her lifestyle.

8) Carmen and Eleni are having an argument about the internet. Carmen thinks that the internet
   is a waste of time, but Eleni thinks that it's very useful because she can chat online with her
   friends in Argentina every day. Write down their conversation in Spanish.

9) In an email, what are the following in Spanish: a) To   b) From   c) Subject?

10) You get the following text message from your friend Paulina:
    "Hola. ¿Qué tal? ¿Quieres ir al parque mañana? Creo que va a hacer sol. Hasta pronto."
    Write out the message in English.

11) Write a reply to Paulina's text message in Spanish.

12) Ask when the chemist's opens in Spanish.

13) Write out the following conversation in English:
    "Quisiera un vestido amarillo."
    "¿Qué talla tiene usted?"
    "Mi talla es la treinta y ocho."

14) Soledad has bought a shirt, but it's missing a button and she wants to exchange it.
    What should she say in Spanish?

15) What are these clothes in English? a) los pantalones   b) la corbata   c) la camiseta

16) Ana has just found out that there's 30% off clothes in the department store.
    How could she tell her friend Leticia about the sale in Spanish?

17) Kormi wants to see '¡Ay, Carmela!' at the cinema, but Bernard says he wants to see
    'Cría cuervos'. They arrange to meet in front of the cinema at 7.30pm. Write down
    their conversation in Spanish.

18) Ask in Spanish what time the swimming pool closes, and say you would like two tickets.

19) Will asks Javier "¿Qué hiciste el fin de semana?" Javier says "Fui al estadio para ver un partido
    de rugby. Después vi una película en la televisión." Write down their conversation in English.

Holiday Destinations

First things first — if you're going to talk about <u>holidays</u>, you need to know the names of the <u>countries</u>.

Los países — Countries

Names of <u>countries</u> come in handy for saying where you've been on holiday, or where you'd like to go.

Learn these <u>common</u> countries:

Spain:	España (fem.)
England:	Inglaterra (fem.)
Scotland:	Escocia (fem.)
Wales:	País de Gales (masc.)
Ireland	Irlanda (fem.)
Northern Ireland:	Irlanda del Norte (fem.)
Great Britain:	Gran Bretaña (fem.)
United Kingdom:	Reino Unido (masc.)
France:	Francia (fem.)
Germany:	Alemania (fem.)
Italy:	Italia (fem.)
Portugal:	Portugal (masc.)
Austria:	Austria (fem.)
Holland:	Holanda (fem.)
USA:	los Estados Unidos (masc.)
Belgium:	Bélgica (fem.)
Denmark:	Dinamarca (fem.)
Switzerland:	Suiza (fem.)
Russia:	Rusia (fem.)
Greece:	Grecia (fem.)
Mexico:	México / Méjico (masc.)

Don't forget the <u>continents</u>:

Europe:	Europa (fem.)
Africa:	África (fem.)
North America:	América del Norte (fem.)
South America:	América del Sur (fem.)
Australia:	Australia (fem.)
Asia:	Asia (fem.)

For the <u>nationalities</u> that go with these countries, see p. 58.

Las regiones de España — Regions of Spain

If you want to be <u>really fancy</u>, you can say which <u>region</u> of Spain you've visited.

Andalusia:	Andalucía
Aragon:	Aragón
Castile:	Castilla
Catalonia:	Cataluña
Galicia:	Galicia
Basque Country:	el País Vasco
Rioja:	La Rioja
Canary Islands:	las Islas Canarias

Andalucía **está en el sur de España.**

= <u>Andalusia</u> is in the <u>south</u> of Spain.

north:	norte
east:	este
west:	oeste

País de Gales — no wonder it's so windy...

Knowing <u>countries</u> in Spanish is a good idea even if you're rubbish at geography. Look at an <u>atlas</u> and see <u>how many</u> of the countries you know in Spanish. With the ones where the Spanish word is <u>a bit like the English</u>, like <u>Holland</u> and <u>Holanda</u>, check you've got the <u>spelling</u> right too.

Catching the Train

Trains, planes and automobiles... Well, just <u>trains</u> for now. Learn how to <u>talk about trains</u> — not like a parrot, but so you can actually <u>use</u> the vocab.

Quisiera tomar el tren — I'd like to take the train

¿Hay un tren para Madrid ?   = Is there a train to <u>Madrid</u>?

Toledo: Toledo   Seville: Sevilla
Malaga: Málaga   Valencia: Valencia

Un billete sencillo para Madrid, por favor.   = <u>One</u> <u>single</u> to Madrid, please.

Two: Dos   single(s): billete(s) sencillo(s) / billete(s) de ida
Three: Tres   return(s): billete(s) de ida y vuelta

Quisiera un billete de primera clase .   = I'd like a <u>first class</u> ticket.

second class: de segunda clase

¿Cuánto cuesta un billete de ida y vuelta ?

= How much does <u>a return ticket</u> cost?

¿Cuándo quiere viajar? — When do you want to travel?

This is more <u>complicated</u>, but <u>important</u>. You won't <u>get far</u> (in Spain or your exams) without it.

Quisiera ir a Santander el sábado .   = I would like to go to Santander <u>on Saturday</u>.

today: hoy   next Monday: el lunes que viene   on the tenth of June: el diez de junio

¿Cuándo sale el tren para Santander?   = When does the train for Santander leave?

¿Cuándo llega el tren a Santander?   = When does the train arrive in Santander?

¿De qué andén sale el tren?   = Which platform does the train leave from?

¿Dónde está el andén cuatro ?   = Where is platform <u>four</u>?

When does the midnight train to Georgia leave...

Learning about how to buy train tickets isn't just useful if you're <u>on holiday</u> in Spain or Mexico or Argentina or somewhere — it could come up in your <u>reading</u> and <u>listening</u> exams. So make sure you learn this stuff and you'll be able to handle <u>anything</u> they throw at you in your exam.

Catching the Train

Taking the train's one thing, but catching the <u>metro</u>'s a whole different kettle of fish...

En la estación de metro — At the metro station

¿Qué línea necesito tomar para ir al Museo del Prado ?

= What line do I need to take to go <u>to the Prado Museum</u>?

to the Royal Palace:	al Palacio Real
to the Plaza Mayor (main square):	a la Plaza Mayor
to the airport:	al aeropuerto

Necesita tomar la línea dos . Baje en la estación de metro 'Banco de España' .

5: cinco
7: siete

= You need to take line <u>2</u>. Get off at '<u>Banco de España</u>' station.

¿Te gusta viajar en tren?
— Do you like travelling by train?

Not a great <u>chat-up line</u>, I admit. Here's how to give your <u>opinion</u> on train travel.

Me gusta viajar de Sevilla a Madrid en tren porque el AVE es muy rápido.

= I like to travel from Seville to Madrid by train because the AVE* is very fast.

*El **AVE** and el **TALGO** are Spanish high-speed train services.

No me importa viajar en tren, pero prefiero viajar en avión porque es más cómodo.

= I don't mind travelling by train, but I prefer to travel by plane because it's more comfortable.

Learn this train vocab

More <u>vocab</u> I'm afraid... Yes, it's <u>dull</u>, but it's also <u>vital</u> to know as <u>much</u> as you <u>can</u>.

to depart:	salir	to arrive:	llegar	timetable:	el horario
departure:	la salida	arrival:	la llegada	to change (trains):	cambiar
the waiting room:	la sala de espera	ticket:	el billete	platform:	el andén / la vía
Spanish rail network:	la RENFE	to get on:	subir a	ticket office:	la taquilla
the railway:	el ferrocarril	to get off:	bajar de	left luggage:	la consigna

Trains are OK, but I prefer to travel by private jet...

In real life, discussing whether or not you <u>enjoy travelling</u> by train is a clear sign of a very bad conversation. But Spanish GCSE isn't <u>real life</u> (well OK, it is, but you know what I mean) so there's nothing for it but to learn <u>everything</u> on this page. So what are you waiting for...

All Kinds of Transport

Here's what you need to <u>know</u> about other forms of <u>transport</u>. This is one of those topics that you'll need to know <u>really well</u> — and you need to know loads of <u>vocab</u> for it too.

¿Cómo vas? — How do you get there?

You need to say how you <u>get about</u>. For '<u>by</u>' (e.g. 'by car'), use '<u>en</u>'. The only one that's <u>different</u> is '<u>on foot</u>' ('a pie').

Voy al centro *en autobús* .

= I go <u>into town</u> <u>by bus</u>.

to school: al colegio
to the park: al parque
to the swimming pool: a la piscina

on the underground: en el metro
by bike: en bici (bicicleta)
by car: en coche
by motorbike: en moto (motocicleta)
by coach: en autocar
by boat: en barco
by plane: en avión
by train: en tren
on foot: a pie

La salida y la llegada — Departure and arrival

Questions like this are really handy when you're <u>travelling</u>.

¿Hay *un autobús* para Córdoba?

= Is there <u>a bus</u> to Cordoba?

a plane: un avión
a coach: un autocar

¿A qué hora sale *el próximo autobús* para Almería?

= When does <u>the next bus</u> to Almería leave?

the bus: el autobús
the coach: el autocar

the next coach: el próximo autocar
the next boat: el próximo barco

¿Cuándo llega *el avión* a Barcelona?

= When does <u>the plane</u> arrive in Barcelona?

¿Qué autobús...? — Which bus...?

No doubt about it — you need to be able to ask <u>which bus</u> or <u>train</u> goes <u>where</u>. Just learn this.

¿ *Qué autobús* va *al centro* , por favor?

= <u>Which bus</u> goes <u>to the town centre</u>, please?

Which train: Qué tren
to the airport: al aeropuerto

I'm a Spanish GCSE student, get me out of here...

This stuff's pretty straightforward, really. Learn the example phrases and then you can just <u>slot</u> the transport vocab in to make <u>loads</u> of different sentences. Remember that 'on foot' is '<u>a pie</u>' and all the other modes of transport are just '<u>en</u>' followed by 'coche' or 'tren' or 'bicicleta' or whatever.

Planning Your Holiday

This is the kind of thing that could easily come up in your <u>listening exam</u> — conversations in the <u>tourist</u> <u>office</u> or the <u>bureau de change</u>. It could come in pretty handy if you go to Spain on holiday too.

La oficina de turismo — *The tourist office*

Here's how you <u>find out</u> what a town's got to offer.

Necesito información sobre el zoo .   = I need information about <u>the zoo</u>.

the sights of Madrid:	los lugares de interés turístico de Madrid
the museum:	el museo
this region's typical food:	la comida típica de esta región

¿Tiene unos folletos sobre excursiones por Sevilla ?   = Do you have any leaflets about <u>excursions around Seville</u>?

the museums in Toledo: los museos de Toledo

Quisiera visitar Aranjuez .   = I'd like to <u>visit Aranjuez</u>.

go to a museum: visitar un museo
see the castle: ver el castillo

¿Cuánto es?   = How much is it?

Son treinta euros por persona.   = It costs 30 euros per person.

El autocar sale del ayuntamiento a la una y media .   = The coach leaves <u>from the</u> <u>town hall</u> <u>at half past one</u>.

from the church: de la iglesia
from the market: del mercado

at 2 o'clock: a las dos
at quarter past 3: a las tres y cuarto

La oficina de cambio — *The bureau de change*

¿Puedo cambiar cien libras en euros , *por favor?*   = Can I change <u>100 pounds</u> to <u>euros</u>, please?

50:	cincuenta
150:	ciento cincuenta
200:	doscientas / doscientos

dollars: dólares

Quisiera cambiar cincuenta libras *en cheques de viaje.*

= I'd like to change <u>50 pounds</u> to traveller's cheques.

Can I change this old tissue to euros, please...

It seems a bit mean to go on and on about <u>holidays</u> when you can't go on holiday because you've got your GCSEs. That's exam boards for you — <u>mean</u>. Oh well, you'll just have to grin and bear it.

Holiday Accommodation

Holidays are an exam favourite. This page has all the words you need to know about hotels, hostels, and camping. GCSEs are always full of this sort of thing, so you'd better get learning...

Las vacaciones — Holidays

Booking the right kind of room in the right kind of hotel is darned important — best learn how to do it.

General vocabulary.

holiday:	las vacaciones
abroad:	el extranjero
person:	la persona
night:	la noche

Verbs used in hotels.

to reserve:	reservar
to stay:	alojarse / quedarse
to cost:	costar
to leave:	irse

Things you might want to ask for.

room:	la habitación
double room:	la habitación doble
single room:	la habitación individual
double bed:	la cama de matrimonio
full board:	la pensión completa
half board:	la media pensión

What kind of accommodation.

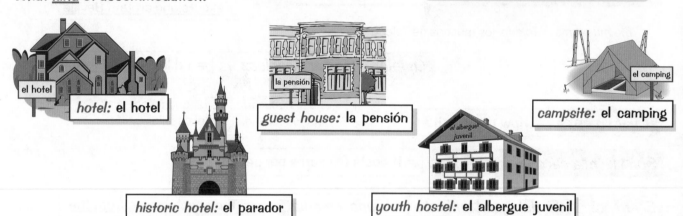

hotel: el hotel

guest house: la pensión

campsite: el camping

historic hotel: el parador

youth hostel: el albergue juvenil

More holiday vocab to learn

You may need to ask about your room, where things are in the hotel... oh, and paying the bill.

Parts of a hotel.

restaurant:	el restaurante
dining room:	el comedor
lift:	el ascensor
stairs:	la escalera
car park:	el aparcamiento
lounge:	el salón

Things about your room.

key:	la llave
balcony:	el balcón
bath:	el baño
shower:	la ducha
washbasin:	el lavabo

Paying for your stay.

bill:	la cuenta
price:	el precio

Extra words for camping.

tent:	la tienda
sleeping bag:	el saco de dormir
caravan:	la caravana
to camp:	acampar
drinking water:	el agua potable

You'll need a holiday after this lot...

OK, I admit this is just a load of vocabulary. If you want to really learn these words, you need to keep testing yourself until you've got it all — you need to understand this stuff if it crops up.

Booking a Room / Pitch

Learn this page if you don't want to end up sharing a room in Spain with two sweaty, cycling Swedes — or if you do. Oh and asking about rooms could come up in the exams as well.

¿Tiene una habitación libre? — Do you have a room free?

Quisiera una **habitación individual** . = I'd like a single room.

If you want to talk about different kinds of bookings, use the vocab you've just learned on p. 46.

double room: habitación doble
room with a bath: habitación con baño
room with a balcony: habitación con balcón

Quisiera quedarme *dos noches* . = I'd like to stay for two nights.

one night: una noche
one week: una semana
a fortnight: quince días

¿Cuánto es por noche para **una persona** ? = How much is it per night for one person?

two people: dos personas
four people: cuatro personas

Vale. = OK. Lo siento, es demasiado caro. = I'm sorry, it's too expensive.

¿Se puede acampar aquí? — Can I camp here?

Even if you're not into the outdoor life these phrases might be useful in your exams.

Quisiera acampar aquí para una noche . = I'd like to camp here for one night.

a shop: una tienda
a telephone: un teléfono

two nights: dos noches
a week: una semana
a fortnight: quince días

¿Hay **agua potable** aquí? = Is there drinking water here?

¿Puedo hacer un fuego aquí? = Can I light a fire here?

¿Dónde está el teléfono ? = Where is the telephone?

the shop: la tienda

¿Dónde están los servicios? = Where are the toilets?

Yep, tent and shop are both 'tienda' in Spanish...

That must get confusing. I wonder if people who ask the way to the shops end up being directed to the nearest campsite. Anyway, learn everything on the page — you'll be glad you did.

Where / When is...?

Here's how to <u>ask</u> people <u>where things are</u> and how to <u>get yourself fed</u>. Pretty important stuff.

Ask where things are — use '¿Dónde está... ?'

Knowing how to ask <u>where</u> things are is very important — get these <u>learnt</u>.

¿Dónde está el comedor , por favor? = Where is <u>the dining room</u>, please?

the car park:	el aparcamiento
the games room:	la sala de juegos
the telephone:	el teléfono

See <u>p. 46</u> for more things you might need to ask about.

Excuse me, where's the dining room?

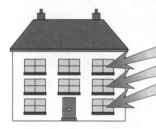

Está en el tercer piso . = It's on the <u>third floor</u>.

fourth floor:	cuarto piso
second floor:	segundo piso
first floor:	primer piso
ground floor:	la planta baja

For higher floor numbers, see <u>p. 1</u>.

Está al final del pasillo . = It's <u>at the end of the corridor</u>.

outside:	fuera
on the left / right:	a la izquierda / derecha
straight on:	todo recto
upstairs:	arriba
downstairs:	abajo

¿Cuándo es... ? — When is... ?

Questions galore — you've met 'when?' on <u>page 4</u>, this is just <u>one instance</u> where you'll need it.

¿Cuándo se sirve el desayuno , por favor? = When is <u>breakfast</u> served, please?

lunch:	el almuerzo / la comida
evening meal:	la cena

Se sirve a las ocho . = It is served at <u>eight o'clock</u>.

¿Hasta qué hora se sirve la cena ? = What time is <u>dinner</u> served until?

For more <u>times</u>, see p. 2.

Se sirve hasta las diez y media . = It is served until <u>half past ten</u>.

Actually, when is lunch? I'm starving...

The best way to check you <u>know this stuff</u> is to <u>cover up</u> the page and try to <u>scribble</u> the words down. After you can write the words down fine on their own, <u>get on</u> with writing down <u>full</u> sentences using them. The bits about 1st floor, 2nd floor etc. are <u>useful</u> for any tall buildings...

Problems with Accommodation

Holidays don't always run <u>smoothly</u> — even in Spanish GCSE exams.

Tengo un problema con mi habitación
— I've got a problem with my room

If your luxury hotel suite turns out to be more of a <u>flea pit</u>, here are the phrases you need to complain.

El aire acondicionado no funciona.   = <u>The air conditioning</u> doesn't work.

The key:	La llave
The shower:	La ducha
The telephone:	El teléfono
The television:	La televisión
The heating:	La calefacción

No hay **agua caliente**.   = There's no <u>hot water</u>.

electricity:	luz
towels:	toallas

El desayuno está frío.   = <u>The breakfast</u> is cold.

The coffee:	El café

La habitación **está sucia**.   = The room <u>is dirty</u>.

is too small:	es demasiado pequeña
has no window:	no tiene ventana

See <u>p. 11</u> for an example of a <u>complaint letter</u> to a hotel.

En la comisaría — At the police station

If it's a proper <u>holiday from hell</u>, you might even need to go to the police station.

Perdí **mi bolso**.   = I lost <u>my bag</u>.

my passport:	mi pasaporte
my purse:	mi monedero
my money:	mi dinero
my credit card:	mi tarjeta de crédito
my keys:	mis llaves
my watch:	mi reloj
my earrings:	mis pendientes

¿Dónde perdió **su bolso**?   = Where did you lose <u>your bag</u>?

Perdí **mi bolso** en **la estación**.   = I lost <u>my bag</u> in <u>the station</u>.

the museum:	el museo
the cathedral:	la catedral
the shopping centre:	el centro comercial

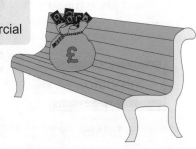

Alguien me robó el bolso.   = Someone stole <u>my bag</u>.

my necklace:	el collar
my credit card:	la tarjeta de crédito

Someone's stolen my favourite paper clip...

Complaining and reporting crimes is quite <u>fun</u> if you get to do it in your <u>speaking assessment</u> — it's a bit more dramatic than just talking about the <u>weather</u> or something. And if you ever do get your bag stolen on holiday, at least you can impress the <u>police</u> with your knowledge of Spanish.

At a Restaurant

Going to a <u>restaurant</u> in Spain or Latin America is no end of fun...

¿Tiene una mesa libre? — Do you have a table free?

Don't forget — it's all about being <u>polite</u>.

Una mesa para `cuatro`, por favor.

two: dos
three: tres

= A table for <u>four</u>, please.

Somos `cuatro`.

two: dos
three: tres

= There are <u>four</u> of us.

Queremos sentarnos `fuera`.

on the terrace: en la terraza

= We want to sit <u>outside</u>.

You might see these <u>signs</u> <u>in a</u> <u>restaurant</u>

 **Abierto**

= Open

 Cerrado

= Closed

Horario:
Lunes a sábado
19.30 - 23.00

= Opening hours:
Monday to Saturday
7.30pm - 11pm

Especialidades de la casa:
calamares, paella
Plato del día: tortilla

= Specialities of the house:
squid, paella
Dish of the day: omelette

 **Carta**

Menú del día

= À la carte menu,
fixed price menu

Reservado

= Reserved

 *Espere aquí por favor*

= Please wait here

 **Prohibido fumar**

= No smoking

Servicio incluido

= Service included

Servicios

= Toilets

 *Propinas*

= Tips

I'm sorry, this page is reserved...

I love <u>restaurants</u> — a chance to show off your language skills, order some exotic foods and be ill for weeks. Well, not that last one, maybe. You might have to <u>recognise signs</u> in your reading exam, so make sure you know them — especially the difference between '<u>servicio</u>' and '<u>servicios</u>'...

At a Restaurant

Phew — it's <u>hungry work</u>, all this talking about <u>dinners</u> and <u>restaurants</u>... Might be a good time to have a bar of chocolate or an apple... You wouldn't want your rumbling belly distracting you.

Quisiera... — I'd like...

¿Tiene **paella** ? = Do you have <u>paella</u>?

bread: pan
bananas: plátanos

the omelette: la tortilla
the dish of the day: el plato del día

salad: ensalada
rice: arroz
carrots: zanahorias

Quisiera **el filete** con **patatas fritas** . = I'd like <u>the steak</u> with <u>chips</u>.

Para mí, **una hamburguesa** , por favor. = I'll have <u>a burger</u>, please.

Quisiera probar... — I'd like to try...

You'd never learn <u>all</u> the different types of food — there are squillions.
So here's a handy sentence for when you don't know what something tastes like.

¿A qué sabe **el conejo** ? = What does <u>rabbit</u> taste like?

spicy sausage: el chorizo

No estoy satisfecho/a — I'm not satisfied

Make sure you know how to kick up a fuss if you're not happy with your meal.

El filete **está** **poco hecho** . = <u>The steak</u> is <u>underdone</u>.

The pork: La carne de cerdo
The coffee: El café

too hot: demasiado caliente
too cold: demasiado frío/a

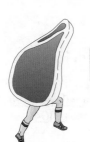

No puedo comerlo. = I can't eat it.

El servicio fue lento. = The service was slow.

¿Ha terminado? — Have you finished?

¿Puedo pagar? = Can I pay? La cuenta, por favor. = The bill, please.

I want to complain — this gazpacho's cold...

Another '<u>must-learn</u>' page, I'm afraid. Some of this stuff is useful in <u>all sorts of situations</u> — not just in a restaurant. There's a lot to remember — start by <u>scribbling</u> it down, <u>covering</u> and <u>learning</u>.

Talking About Your Holiday

Everyone wants to bore people by telling them all about their holidays. Yes, you too...
By the time you've finished this page you'll be able to bore people in Spanish all day long.

¿Adónde fuiste? — *Where did you go?*

Fui | a los Estados Unidos | hace dos semanas . = I went to the USA two weeks ago.

to Spain: a España
to France: a Francia

a month ago: hace un mes
in July: en julio
in the summer: en el verano

¿Con quién fuiste? — *Who did you go with?*

Answer this question or there'll be all sorts of gossip.

Fui de vacaciones con | mi familia | por | un mes . = I went on holiday with my family for a month.

my brother: mi hermano
my friends: mis amigos/as

a fortnight: quince días
a week: una semana

Hice un intercambio en España . = I went on an exchange to Spain.

Fui a Alemania para visitar a | mi amigo por correspondencia .

my cousins: mis primos
my grandparents: mis abuelos

= I went to Germany to visit my penfriend.

¿Qué hiciste? — *What did you do?*

You need to be able to say what you did on holiday — learn it well.

Fui | a la playa . = I went to the beach.   Me relajé. = I relaxed.

to the disco: a la discoteca
to a museum: a un museo

I enjoyed myself: Lo pasé muy bien
I played tennis: Jugué al tenis

This is a reflexive verb — see p. 104.

¿Cómo viajaste allí? — *How did you get there?*

Remember the little word 'allí', which means 'there' — it's a useful one (see page 89 for more on this).

Fuimos en | coche . = We went by car.

plane: avión   boat: barco

For more types of transport, see p. 44.

I went to London — the beach was lovely...

You need to understand other people talking about their holidays and talk about your own holidays.
Cover the page, scribble, look back, etc. Keep going till you've learnt everything on the page.

Talking About Your Holiday

Details are what it's all about. So plough on and learn this stuff as well...

¿Cómo fue el viaje? — *How was the trip?*

You can never have too many opinions as far as Spanish GCSE is concerned.

¿Cómo fueron tus vacaciones? = How was your holiday?

Me gustaron. = I liked it.   No me gustaron. = I didn't like it.

¿Adónde te gustaría ir? — *Where would you like to go?*

Mi sueño es ir a Rusia. = My dream is to go to Russia.

Me gustaría viajar a Italia. = I'd like to travel to Italy.

For more countries see p. 41.

Me gusta ir a lugares con mucha historia. = I like going to places with a lot of history.

a beach: playa
lots of shops: muchas tiendas

¿Adónde irás? — *Where will you go?*

You've got to be able to understand the future — what you or someone else will be doing...
You might need to talk about it too.

For more info about the future tense, see p. 98.

¿Adónde irás? = Where will you go?

Voy a ir a México dentro de dos semanas. = I'm going to go to Mexico in two weeks.

¿Con quién irás de vacaciones? = Who will you go on holiday with?

Voy a ir de vacaciones con mi familia por un mes.

= I'm going to go on holiday with my family for a month.

¿Cómo irás? = How will you get there?   Voy a ir en coche. = I'm going to go by car.

¿Qué harás? = What will you do?   Voy a ir a la playa. = I'm going to go to the beach.

My dream is to go to Milton Keynes...

More details = more marks. Simple. You can always make up a holiday you didn't have, or invent
things you did, as long as you know the Spanish words for it. Smile — it could be worse. Just.

Weather

You might talk about the <u>weather</u> in your <u>speaking</u> assessment. Or you might have to listen to a <u>weather forecast</u> in your <u>listening</u> exam. Or you might be in Spain planning a picnic...

¿Qué tiempo hace? — *What's the weather like?*

These <u>short sentences</u> are the ones you definitely <u>can't do without</u> — and they're <u>easy</u>.

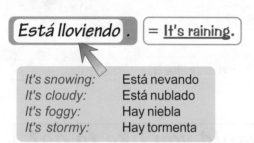

Está lloviendo . = It's raining.

It's snowing:	Está nevando
It's cloudy:	Está nublado
It's foggy:	Hay niebla
It's stormy:	Hay tormenta

Of course, it doesn't <u>always</u> rain, so here are a few others you could use:

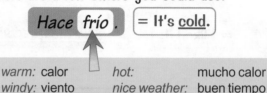

Hace frío . = It's cold.

warm: calor	*hot:*	mucho calor
windy: viento	*nice weather:*	buen tiempo
sunny: sol	*bad weather:*	mal tiempo

¿Qué tiempo hará mañana?
— *What will the weather be like tomorrow?*

This is quite easy, and it sounds <u>dead impressive</u>:

Mañana lloverá / va a llover . = It will rain tomorrow.

Next week:
La semana que viene
On Tuesday: El martes

It'll snow:	nevará / va a nevar
It'll be hot:	hará calor / va a hacer calor
It'll be cold:	hará frío / va a hacer frío
It'll be windy:	hará viento / va a hacer viento
It'll be cloudy:	estará nublado / va a estar nublado

Tomorrow it'll be wet.

See p. 2–3 for more on <u>times and dates</u>, and p. 98 for the <u>future tense</u>.

¿Qué tiempo hacía? — *What was the weather like?*

This is really <u>handy</u> for saying what the weather was like <u>on holiday</u> and that kind of thing.

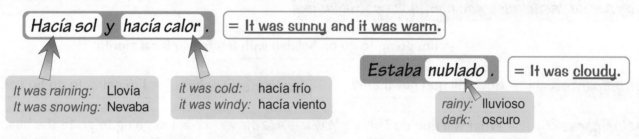

Hacía sol y hacía calor . = <u>It was sunny</u> and <u>it was warm</u>.

| It was raining: | Llovía |
| It was snowing: | Nevaba |

| it was cold: | hacía frío |
| it was windy: | hacía viento |

Estaba nublado . = It was <u>cloudy</u>.

rainy: lluvioso
dark: oscuro

It's raining, it's pouring...

This stuff on weather could come up in the <u>exams</u> — so you've got to do it. Still, all you need to do is <u>learn</u> the <u>main sentences</u> on this page and the <u>bits of vocab</u> — and you'll be working for the Met Office in no time. Well, maybe not, but at least you'll be able to do well in your GCSE if you learn this stuff.

Revision Summary

Phew — I don't know about you but I think I need a holiday after all that. There's loads to learn in this section, and unfortunately you can't just absorb it all by touching the pages (I know — I've tried). So go over everything as many times as it takes, and then when you're ready have a go at these questions and see how well you've really remembered everything.

1) How do you say these countries in Spanish?
   a) England   b) France   c) Spain   d) Germany   e) USA   f) Denmark   g) Greece

2) Write down the names of three different regions of Spain, in English and Spanish.

3) Mrs Powell is taking her class on a school trip to Spain, and she wants to buy 18 return tickets to Madrid. What should she say?

4) You're at the train station and you want to know what time the train to Bilbao leaves. How would you ask this in Spanish?

5) Your Spanish penfriend Rosalía asks you "¿Te gusta viajar en tren?" What does the question mean, and how would you answer in Spanish?

6) Say in Spanish that you walk to school, but your friend goes on the bus.

7) You're in the tourist office in Barcelona. Ask for leaflets about excursions around Barcelona.

8) How would you ask in Spanish to change 200 pounds to euros?

9) What do these mean?   a) las vacaciones   b) la habitación individual   c) la media pensión

10) You're booking a hotel in Spain. Ask for a single room, and say that you want to stay for one week.

11) Once you've booked your room, the hotel receptionist tells you "Su habitación está en el cuarto piso, al final del pasillo." What does this mean?

12) When you get to your room, you find that the television doesn't work. How would you tell the receptionist this in Spanish?

13) You've lost your passport. Tell the police in Spanish, and say that you lost it in the cathedral.

14) What do these signs mean?   a) cerrado   b) plato del día   c) prohibido fumar   d) propinas

15) You're in a restaurant with your friend Rocío. She says "Quisiera la tortilla con ensalada." What has she ordered? Say that you would like a burger with chips.

16) You're writing a letter to your penfriend Alicia. Tell her that you went on an exchange to Spain, you went to the beach and you enjoyed yourself.

17) ¿Adónde te gustaría ir? Answer in Spanish and give a reason.

18) ¿Qué tiempo hace hoy? Answer in Spanish.

Names of Buildings

You need to know the names for buildings for all sorts of things — arranging to meet people, asking for directions and talking about your town for a start. Yes, it's a bit dull, but you absolutely <u>have</u> to learn them.

Learn all these edificios — buildings

These are the basic, bog-standard '<u>learn-them-or-else</u>' buildings.

the bank: el banco

the butcher's:
la carnicería

the church: la iglesia

the theatre: el teatro

the railway station:
la estación (de trenes)

the post office:
Correos (masc.)

the baker's:
la panadería

the cinema: el cine

the supermarket:
el supermercado

the market:
el mercado

the castle: el castillo

the library:
la biblioteca

Otros edificios — Other buildings

OK, I'll come clean. There are absolutely <u>loads</u> of buildings you need to <u>know</u>. Like these:

MORE SHOPS

the shop:	la tienda
the chemist's:	la farmacia
the cake shop:	la pastelería
the newsagent, sweet shop:	el quiosco
the department store:	los grandes almacenes
tobacconist's:	el estanco
(where you can buy stamps)	

TOURISTY BITS

the hotel:	el hotel
the youth hostel:	el albergue juvenil
the restaurant:	el restaurante
the tourist information office:	la oficina de turismo
the museum:	el museo
the zoo:	el zoo

OTHER IMPORTANT PLACES

the town hall:	el ayuntamiento
the cathedral:	la catedral
the park:	el parque
the airport:	el aeropuerto
the university:	la universidad
the swimming pool:	la piscina
the sports ground:	el campo de deportes
the bull ring:	la plaza de toros
the leisure centre:	el polideportivo
the stadium:	el estadio
the secondary school:	el instituto, el colegio
the primary school:	la escuela
the hospital:	el hospital

What about the candlestick maker's...

OK, so learning vocab's not the most exciting thing you could be doing right now. But you'll be a bit <u>stuck</u> when it comes to asking for <u>directions</u> if you don't know the word for the place you're trying to get to. So <u>turn over</u> the page and keep writing the words down till you've got them all.

Asking Directions

You might get a question about <u>directions</u>.
It's not too complicated — but it's worth getting straight in your mind now.

¿Dónde está... ? — Where is... ?

It's dead easy to ask <u>where</u> a place is — say '¿Dónde está...?' and stick the <u>place</u> on the end.

¿Dónde está la estación , por favor?   = Where is <u>the station</u>, please?

¿Hay una biblioteca por aquí?   = Is there <u>a library</u> near here?

See <u>p. 56</u> for more <u>buildings</u>.

¿Está lejos de aquí? — Is it far from here?

If the place you're looking for is miles away, you don't just want to set off walking there.

¿ Está el cine lejos de aquí?   = Is <u>the cinema</u> far from here?

the tourist office: la oficina de turismo
the park: el parque
the museum: el museo

Está a dos kilómetros .   = It's <u>two kilometres away</u>.

a hundred metres away: a cien metros
nearby: cerca
far away: lejos

Use '¿para ir a...?' to ask the way

Directions could easily come up in the listening exam, so you need to be able to understand them.

Por favor, señor , ¿para ir al banco ?   = Excuse me <u>sir</u>, how do I get to <u>the bank</u>?

(to a woman): señora

<u>Important bit:</u> Replace this with any place, using 'al' for 'el' words and 'a la' for 'la' words. See p. 89.

to the station: a la estación
to the library: a la biblioteca
to the castle: al castillo

Look at <u>p. 1</u> for more stuff on <u>1st, 2nd</u>, etc.

straight on, past the church: todo recto, pasando la iglesia
take the first road on the left: tome la primera calle a la izquierda

You'll need <u>all</u> this vocab to <u>understand</u> directions.

go right: vaya a la derecha
go left: vaya a la izquierda
go straight on: siga todo recto
on the corner: en la esquina

'Vaya' is the <u>polite command</u> of '<u>ir</u>' and '<u>siga</u>' is the <u>polite command</u> of '<u>seguir</u>'. For more see <u>p. 107</u>.

So, tell me again how to get to the library.

Is this the way to Amarillo...

Cover it up, scribble it down, check what you got wrong, and try it again. That's the way to learn this stuff. Keep at it until you know it <u>all</u> — then you'll be really ready for your exams. Just reading the page once <u>isn't</u> enough — you wouldn't remember it tomorrow, never mind in an exam.

Where You're From

You're a foreigner in Spain so you need to be able to say what country you're from and what your nationality is. It'll be handy to know some others too as they may well come up in your exams.

¿De dónde eres? — Where do you come from?

Some useful phrases here — and so easy to learn. There's no excuse to forget them, is there...
If the country you're from isn't somewhere here, look it up in a dictionary.

Soy de Inglaterra . Soy inglés/inglesa .   = I come from England. I am English.

Wales:	(del país) de Gales
Ireland:	de Irlanda
Northern Ireland:	de Irlanda del Norte
England:	de Inglaterra
Scotland:	de Escocia

Welsh:	galés/galesa
Northern Irish:	norirlandés/norirlandesa
English:	inglés/inglesa
Scottish:	escocés/escocesa
British:	británico/a

For women and girls, add an 'a' on the end of nationalities ending in '-és' and drop the accent.

¿Dónde vives?   = Where do you live?   Vivo en Inglaterra .   = I live in England.

Las nacionalidades — Nationalities

And now for a lovely list of nationalities. Any of these could come up in the reading or listening exams, so don't ignore them just because you don't know anyone from Portugal or Austria or wherever.

Irish	irlandés/irlandesa	Austrian:	austríaco/a
European:	europeo/a	Dutch:	holandés/holandesa
Spanish:	español/a	North American:	norteamericano/a
French:	francés/francesa	South American:	sudamericano/a
Italian:	italiano/a	Latin American:	latinoamericano/a
Portuguese:	portugués/portuguesa	Mexican:	mexicano/a
German:	alemán/alemana		mejicano/a

For the countries to go with these nationalities, see p. 41.

IMPORTANT: Don't use a capital letter for inglés, francés etc.

¿Dónde vives? — Where do you live?

Vivo en Haxby .   = I live in Haxby.   Haxby está cerca de York .   = Haxby is near York.

Haxby es un pueblo con nueve mil habitantes.   = Haxby is a town with 9000 inhabitants.

Haxby está en el noreste de Inglaterra .   = Haxby's in the north-east of England.

north:	norte	south:	sur	south-east:	sureste
east:	este	west:	oeste	north-west:	noroeste

El paisaje alrededor de Haxby es bonito y verde.   = The landscape around Haxby is beautiful and green.

Isn't holandés the sauce you put on salmon...

All this stuff is really useful if you're meeting new people and you want to tell them where you're from and find out where they're from. Most of the nationalities are simple if you know the words for the countries in Spanish because they're similar — Alemania and alemán, España and español, etc.

Talking About Where You Live

Once you've said <u>where</u> you live, you need to be able to talk about what it's <u>like</u> there too.

En mi ciudad — In my town

This is another subject that comes up <u>all the time</u> — you need to <u>understand</u> what other people say about where they live, even if you don't have to talk about your own town.

¿Qué hay en tu **ciudad** ?   = What is there in your <u>town</u>?

small town / village: pueblo

Hay **un mercado** .   = There's <u>a market</u>.

a cinema:	un cine
a park:	un parque
a shopping centre:	un centro comercial
a university:	una universidad

¿Cómo es Birmingham? — What's Birmingham like?

If you want a <u>really good</u> mark, make sure you're ready to give more <u>details</u>.

La ciudad es **muy interesante** .   = The town is <u>very interesting</u>.

boring:	aburrida
great:	estupenda
dirty:	sucia
clean:	limpia
quiet / peaceful:	tranquila

Hay mucho **que hacer.**   = <u>There's lots</u> to do.

There's not much:	No hay mucho
There's always something:	Siempre hay algo
There's nothing:	No hay nada

> If you live in a <u>village</u> or <u>small town</u> it's 'el pueblo' so any adjectives you use with it will need to <u>end in</u> an '<u>o</u>' not an '<u>a</u>'.

¿Te gusta vivir en **Birmingham** ?

= Do you like living in <u>Birmingham</u>?

Me encanta vivir en **Birmingham** .

I like:	Me gusta
I don't like:	No me gusta

= <u>I love</u> living in <u>Birmingham</u>.

Put them all <u>together</u> and make <u>longer</u> sentences — you'll get <u>extra marks</u> if you get it right.

Me gusta vivir en **Birmingham** porque siempre hay algo que hacer.

= I like living in <u>Birmingham</u> because there's always something to do.

No me gusta vivir en **Swampville** porque no hay nada que hacer.

= I don't like living in <u>Swampville</u> because there's nothing to do.

In my town there's... um... not much...

Lots of places can seem boring when you haven't got much pocket money, you can't drive and you're not old or dull enough to enjoy things like gardening, tearooms or DIY. Still, chances are there's <u>something</u> to say about where you live, but if it's truly dull then just make something up.

Talking About Where You Live

Describing things — I reckon that's what it's all about. The more info you give,
the more marks you're gonna get for it. Stands to reason, really...

¿Cuál es tu dirección? — What's your address?

Vivo en la calle de Lime número cuarenta y cuatro, en Lancaster.

= I live at 44 Lime Street, in Lancaster.

Mi código postal es LA25 ONH.

= My postcode is LA25 ONH.

If you're saying your postcode out loud, you'll need to say all the numbers and letters in Spanish. See p. 1 for numbers and p. 17 for the alphabet.

En tu casa — At your home

Vivo en una casa .

= I live in a house.

a flat: un piso, un apartamento

See p. 84 for where to put adjectives.

Vivo en una casa pequeña y nueva .

= I live in a small, new house.

big:	grande	old:	vieja
pretty:	bonita	cold:	fría
green:	verde	modern:	moderna

Mi apartamento está cerca de un parque .

= My flat is near a park.

My house: Mi casa

the town centre:	del centro de la ciudad
the motorway:	de la autopista
the shops:	de las tiendas
a shopping centre:	de un centro comercial
a bus stop:	de una parada de autobús
a train station:	de una estación de trenes

Me gustaría vivir más cerca del centro de la ciudad .

= I would like to live nearer to the city centre.

nearer to the train station:	más cerca de la estación de trenes
in a bigger house:	en una casa más grande
in a house with a garden:	en una casa con jardín

Where do I live — at home, mostly...

Where you live is a great topic cos you don't have to find out any new information. All you've got
to do is work out how to describe your home. Start by scribbling down this page and learning it.

Inside Your Home

Luckily you won't need to give a full house tour — you just need a few things to say about your home.

¿Cómo es tu casa? — What's your house like?

¿Cómo es la cocina ? = What's the kitchen like?

La cocina es grande .

the living room: el salón
the bathroom: el cuarto de baño
the dining room: el comedor
the bedroom: el dormitorio

small: pequeño/a
tiny: muy pequeño/a

= The kitchen is big.

Las paredes son azules . = The walls are blue.

¿Qué muebles hay en tu dormitorio ? = What furniture is there in your bedroom?

En mi dormitorio hay una cama ,
dos sillas y una mesa pequeña .

= In my bedroom there is a bed,
two chairs and a small table.

armchair: un sillón
sofa: un sofá
lamp: una lámpara
table: una mesa
shelf: un estante

chair: una silla
mirror: un espejo
bed: una cama
double bed: una cama de matrimonio
wall: una pared

wardrobe: un armario
cupboard: un armario
curtains: cortinas
carpet / rug: una alfombra
fitted carpet: una moqueta

Mi casa tiene un jardín. = My house has a garden.

My flat: Mi piso
Mi apartamento

Tenemos flores en nuestro jardín.

a tree: un árbol
a lawn: césped

= We have flowers in our garden.

¿Tienes tu propio dormitorio? — Do you have your own room?

Tengo mi propio dormitorio. = I have my own room.

Comparto un dormitorio con mi hermano . = I share a room with my brother.

I love: Me encanta
I don't like: No me gusta

my sister: mi hermana

No me importa compartir un dormitorio. = I don't mind sharing a room.

Me gustaría tener mi propio dormitorio. = I'd like to have my own room.

I share a room with some mice...

This is all stuff that could come up in the exams. If the list of things in your room looks a bit scary, start off with just a few — but make sure you understand all the words if you read or hear them.

Celebrations

Ooh, birthdays and Christmas and Easter — this might be the most exciting page so far...

¿Qué celebras? — What do you celebrate?

En Gran Bretaña celebramos la Navidad en diciembre .

= In Great Britain we celebrate Christmas in December.

Christmas Eve: la Nochebuena
New Year: el Año Nuevo

January: enero
winter: invierno

La Semana Santa tiene lugar en primavera .

= Easter takes place in spring.

New Year's Eve: La Nochevieja

autumn: otoño
December: diciembre

Mi cumpleaños es el diez de abril .

= My birthday is on the tenth of April.

3rd: tres
15th: quince
27th: veintisiete

February: febrero
August: agosto
November: noviembre

For more dates and months, see p. 3.

¿Cómo celebras tu cumpleaños?

— How do you celebrate your birthday?

Celebro mi cumpleaños con mi familia .

= I celebrate my birthday with my family.

Christmas: la Navidad
New Year's Eve: la Nochevieja
Epiphany: el Día de Reyes

my friends: mis amigos
my boyfriend: mi novio
my girlfriend: mi novia

Cuando cumplí dieciséis años, tuve una fiesta grande con mis amigos.

= When I turned 16, I had a big party with my friends.

En mi cumpleaños , recibo regalos de mis amigos.

= On my birthday, I get presents from my friends.

At Christmas: En Navidad
At Easter: En Semana Santa

cards: tarjetas
chocolate eggs: huevos de chocolate

En Navidad , es tradicional comer pavo .

= At Christmas, it's traditional to eat turkey.

On New Year's Eve: En Nochevieja

to sing carols: cantar canciones de Navidad
to eat 12 grapes: comer doce uvas

I like to celebrate with a nice bit of revision...

This is quite a nice little topic. You might get people talking about traditions in their country in the listening exam, or an article on it in the reading, so learning it all would probably be a wise move.

The Environment

The environment's one of those topics you either <u>love</u> or <u>hate</u>. Whether you think it's a chance to say what you <u>think</u> about something real and <u>important</u>, or you're <u>bored silly</u> with the whole thing, you've got to learn it.

El medio ambiente — ¿es importante para ti?

Is the environment important to you?

A question like this <u>has</u> to be answered with a <u>yes</u>, or a <u>no</u>, so remember to <u>always</u> listen out first for that in a listening exam... then try to figure out the <u>reason</u>.

No, no me interesa nada.
= No, I'm not interested in it at all.

Sí, creo que el medio ambiente es muy importante.
= Yes, I think the environment is very important.

Give opinions and arguments

If you're really up on '<u>green</u>' matters then you could get well stuck into this, but if you're not then say so. You'll get as many marks for saying <u>why</u> you're not interested as you would for <u>hugging trees</u> at lunchtime.

Los problemas medioambientales son la responsabilidad del gobierno.

= The problems with the environment are the government's responsibility.

Me preocupa la contaminación industrial. = I'm worried about <u>industrial</u> pollution.

air: del aire

Las flores y la naturaleza son aburridas. Prefiero los juegos de ordenador.

= Flowers and nature are boring. I prefer computer games.

Creo que la contaminación causa problemas muy graves. = I think pollution causes <u>very serious problems</u>.

the extinction of animals: la extinción de los animales
the destruction of nature: la destrucción de la naturaleza

> **ESSENTIAL ENVIRONMENT VOCAB**
>
> | | | | |
> |---|---|---|---|
> | pollution: | la contaminación | air pollution: | la contaminación del aire |
> | emissions: | las emisiones | nature: | la naturaleza |
> | to damage: | dañar | ozone layer: | la capa de ozono |
> | extinction: | la extinción | destruction: | la destrucción |
> | to pollute: | contaminar | to disappear: | desaparecer |

I'm mad about the environment — I'm environ-mental...

There's quite a bit to learn here (especially that big horrible vocab list) but you can do it — just keep <u>covering</u> the page, <u>writing</u> down what you can remember and then <u>checking</u> it, like always.

The Environment

Here's how to show off about how <u>environmentally-friendly</u> you are, and talk about the future of the planet.

¿Qué haces para proteger el medio ambiente?
— What do you do to protect the environment?

Reutilizo las bolsas de plástico.   = I re-use plastic bags.

Apago las luces cuando dejo una habitación.   = I turn off <u>the lights</u> when I leave a room.

the television: la televisión

Compro productos ecológicos.   = I buy environmentally-friendly products.

No voy al extranjero porque los aviones producen muchas emisiones.

= I don't go abroad because planes produce lots of emissions.

Reciclo periódicos.   = I recycle <u>newspapers</u>.

magazines:	revistas	*plastic:*	plástico
bottles:	botellas	*paper:*	papel
tins:	latas	*cardboard:*	cartón

Voy al instituto a pie en vez de ir en coche.   = I go to school <u>on foot</u> instead of going by car.

by bus: en autobús

¿Qué crees que va a pasar en el futuro?
— What do you think will happen in the future?

En el futuro, vamos a tener más problemas medioambientales.

= In the future, we're going to have more environmental problems.

Creo que vamos a producir más emisiones tóxicas.   = I think we're going to produce more toxic emissions.

Más gente va a reciclar papel.   = More people are going to <u>recycle paper</u>.

protect the environment: proteger el medio ambiente
use public transport: usar el transporte público

I recycle dog hair...

Yes, I collect it from the carpet and then knit it into scarves. Environmentally friendly *and* stylish. Anyway, this is the <u>last page</u> of the section so learn it well and then it's Revision Summary time.

Revision Summary

That was a nice section. Short and sweet. There's nothing too tricky apart from the environment pages, but make sure you learn as much of the vocab as you can so that you'll be prepared for anything in the exams. If you can answer all these questions then you'll win the prize of a lifetime — the chance to move onto Section 6.

1) What are these buildings in English?   a) la iglesia   b) Correos   c) el mercado

2) What are these buildings in Spanish?   a) the bank   b) the castle   c) the library

3) Make a list of eight more buildings in English and Spanish.

4) You're in Spain and you want to go to the cinema. Ask a passer-by how to get there.

5) The passer-by gives you the following directions: "Siga todo recto, pasando la plaza de toros. El cine está en la esquina." What has she told you?

6) You make a new friend at the cinema. He asks you "¿De dónde eres?" What does the question mean, and how would you answer it in Spanish?

7) Think of five nationalities and write them out in English and Spanish.

8) Write three sentences about where you live. (Don't forget you can make something up if you can't think of anything to say.)

9) Your penfriend Gabriela sends you this email about her home:
    Vivo en un apartamento. Es pequeño pero muy bonito y moderno.
    Está cerca de las tiendas. Me gusta mucho mi apartamento.
What does the message mean?

10) Write two sentences in Spanish describing one of the rooms in your house.

11) Gabriela asks you "¿Tienes tu propio dormitorio?" Write a reply in Spanish.

12) ¿Cómo celebras tu cumpleaños? Write two sentences.

13) You read this sentence in an article about traditions in Spain:
    En Nochevieja es tradicional comer doce uvas a medianoche.
What does the sentence mean?

14) Pablo and Nerea are discussing the environment. Pablo thinks that the environment is boring and not important. Nerea thinks that air pollution is a serious problem, and she's worried about the ozone layer. Write out their conversation in Spanish.

15) What are these environment words in English?
    a) las emisiones   b) la naturaleza c) la capa de ozono

16) Write out a list in Spanish of three things you do to help the environment.
    (It's fine if they're made up, as long as they make sense.)

School Subjects

School subjects — as if you don't get <u>enough</u> of that at school. This is <u>really important</u> stuff though.

<u>¿Qué asignaturas estudias?</u> — <u>What subjects do you study?</u>

<u>Write out</u> your timetable in Spanish and <u>learn it all</u>.

Estudio **español** . = I study <u>Spanish</u>.

> You don't need the '<u>el</u>' or '<u>la</u>' when you're saying what you study.

LANGUAGES

French:	el francés
German:	el alemán
Spanish:	el español
Italian:	el italiano
English:	el inglés

ARTS AND CRAFTS

art:	el dibujo
music:	la música
drama:	el arte dramático
food technology:	
	la cocina

HUMANITIES

history:	la historia
geography:	la geografía
philosophy:	la filosofía
religious studies:	la religión
literature:	la literatura

NUMBERS AND STUFF

maths:	las matemáticas
IT:	la informática
business studies:	el comercio
economics:	las ciencias económicas

SCIENCES

science:	las ciencias
physics:	la física
chemistry:	la química
biology:	la biología

PHYSICAL EDUCATION

PE: la educación física

<u>¿Cuál es tu asignatura favorita?</u>

Or your <u>least hated</u> subject if that's how you feel about it all...

<u>What's your favourite subject?</u>

¿Cuál es tu asignatura favorita / preferida? = What's your favourite subject?

Mi asignatura preferida es **el español** . = My favourite subject is <u>Spanish</u>.

Prefiero **la biología** . = I prefer <u>biology</u>.

Me gustan **las matemáticas** . = <u>I like</u> <u>maths</u>.

I love:	Me encantan
I don't like:	No me gustan

> There's more on how to say what you like and don't like on <u>p. 7–8</u>.

No me gusta nada **la informática** . = I don't like <u>IT</u> at all.

Odio **la educación física** . = I hate <u>PE</u>.

<u>I'm subjected to school every day...</u>

School subjects are bound to come up in your exams one way or another. Make sure you can <u>say</u> all the subjects you do, and at least <u>understand</u> the ones you don't do when you hear them.

School Routine

Not the most exciting of pages ever, but it's <u>worth</u> all the effort when you're talking about <u>school routine</u>. Go for <u>short</u> snappy sentences — that way they're easier to <u>remember</u>.

¿Cómo vas al instituto? — How do you get to school?

Voy al instituto **en coche** .   = I go to school <u>by car</u>.

on foot: a pie
by bus: en autobús
by bike: en bicicleta

El viaje dura **veinte minutos** .

= The journey takes <u>twenty minutes</u>.

Una clase — a lesson

Write out all these sentences and practise slotting in the <u>right times</u> and <u>numbers</u> for <u>your school</u>.

Las clases comienzan **a las nueve** .   = School starts <u>at 9 o'clock</u>.

at twenty to nine: a las nueve menos veinte
at half past eight: a las ocho y media

For more on times,
see <u>p. 2</u>.

Las clases terminan **a las tres y cuarto** .   = School ends <u>at quarter past 3</u>.

Tenemos **ocho** clases por día.   = We have <u>8</u> lessons per day.

Cada clase dura **cuarenta minutos** .   = Each lesson lasts <u>40 minutes</u>.

half an hour: media hora
an hour: una hora
an hour and a half: una hora y media

El recreo es a **las once** .   = <u>Break</u> is at <u>11 o'clock</u>.

Lunch break: El descanso para almorzar

Hacemos **una hora** de deberes por día.   = We do <u>one hour</u> of homework every day.

Una clase — let that be a lesson to you...

Don't forget the phrases for your exciting <u>school routine</u>, and the sentences for saying how you <u>go</u> to school. Remember the handy phrase '<u>por día</u>' — you can stick it in loads of sentences.

School Routine

School is still about <u>99%</u> of your life so it makes sense that you're going to be expected to read, write, talk or hear about it in Spanish.

¿Cómo es tu instituto? — What's your school like?

This is all a bit more <u>tricky</u> and also fairly random, but if you want a <u>top mark</u>, you need to <u>learn it</u>.

Tenemos seis semanas de vacaciones en el verano .   = We have <u>six weeks'</u> holiday <u>in the summer.</u>

eight weeks: ocho semanas
five days: cinco días

at Christmas: en Navidad
at Easter: en Semana Santa

Hay tres trimestres.   = There are <u>three</u> terms.

Las reglas son estrictas.   = The rules are strict.

Los profesores se enfadan si no hacemos los deberes.

= The teachers get angry if we don't do our homework.

¿Tienes que llevar uniforme?
— Do you have to wear a uniform?

Llevamos uniforme en el instituto.   = We wear a uniform at school.

Nuestro uniforme es un jersey rojo , pantalones grises , una camisa blanca y una corbata verde .

= Our uniform is a <u>red</u> jumper, <u>grey</u> trousers, a <u>white</u> shirt and a <u>green</u> tie.

Es optativo llevar uniforme.   = Wearing a uniform is <u>optional</u>.

compulsory: obligatorio

See <u>p. 35</u> for more on colours and <u>p. 36</u> for clothes.

No me gusta llevar uniforme porque es muy feo.

= I don't like wearing a uniform because it's really ugly.

No me importa llevar uniforme porque es cómodo.

= I don't mind wearing a uniform because it's comfortable.

School rules — not as far as I'm concerned...

You know all this stuff in English, so you're over the first <u>hurdle</u> already. It's just a case of learning how to say it all in Spanish. <u>Close the book</u> and see how much you can <u>remember</u>.

Classroom Language

We all have our 'off' days, so it's really <u>useful</u> to be able to ask someone to <u>repeat</u> something, or <u>spell out</u> a word you're not sure about.

¡Siéntate! — Sit down!

<u>Learn</u> these three short phrases to avoid the wrath of a scary teacher.

¡Levántate! = Stand up!

Stand up! (plural): ¡Levantaos!

¡Siéntate! = Sit down!

Sit down! (plural): ¡Sentaos!

¡Silencio! = Be quiet!

If you don't understand say "No entiendo"

These phrases can be <u>vital</u> in your <u>speaking assessment</u>. Even if the worst happens, it's far better to say 'I don't understand' <u>in Spanish</u> than to just shrug or say something in English.

¿Me puedes explicar esta palabra? = <u>Can you</u> (informal) explain this word?

Can you (formal): puede

(No) entiendo / comprendo. = I (don't) understand.

¿Qué quiere decir eso? = What does that mean?

No lo sé. = I don't know.

¿Puedes repetir eso, por favor? = Can you (informal) repeat that, please?

¿No es correcto? = Is that wrong?

No es correcto. = That's wrong.

Eso es. = That's right.

¿Cómo se dice en español? = How do you say that in Spanish?

En mi mochila — In my school bag

Here's a handy list of things you might find in your <u>school bag</u>.

a pen:	un bolígrafo / un boli	scissors:	unas tijeras
a pencil:	un lápiz	a calculator:	una calculadora
a rubber:	una goma	a pencil case:	un estuche
a ruler:	una regla	a book:	un libro
a pencil sharpener:	un sacapuntas	an exercise book:	un cuaderno
pencil crayons:	unos lápices de colores	a dictionary:	un diccionario

Mind your classroom language...

You can <u>save</u> yourself from an embarrassing silence in your speaking assessment if you learn these <u>dead useful</u> phrases. Just remember, bouts of forgetfulness happen to everyone so <u>don't panic</u>.

Problems at School

School isn't all <u>fun and games</u>, you know (is it ever...?). You need to know about school-related <u>problems</u> too.

¿Te gusta ir al instituto? — Do you like going to school?

Sí, los profesores son muy simpáticos.

= Yes, the teachers are really nice.

No me importa ir al instituto porque puedo ver a mis amigos.

= I don't mind going to school because I can see my friends.

See p. 92 for more about the <u>personal 'a'</u>.

No me gusta ir al instituto porque saco malas notas.

= I don't like going to school because I get bad marks.

¿Cuáles son los problemas en el instituto? — What problems are there at school?

Now's the chance to get all your school and exam <u>woes</u> off your chest.

Tengo muchos exámenes y no quiero suspenderlos.

= I have lots of exams and I don't want to fail them.

Mis padres son estrictos. No puedo salir con mis amigos porque tengo que estudiar.

= My parents are strict. I can't go out with my friends because I have to study.

Si no apruebo los exámenes, no podré **ir a la universidad** .

= If I don't pass my exams, I won't be able to <u>go to university</u>.

be a doctor:	ser médico/a
go on holiday:	ir de vacaciones

Algunos estudiantes **golpean** a otros durante el recreo.

insult:	insultan
intimidate:	intimidan

= Some students <u>hit</u> others at breaktime.

Los profesores me castigan por hablar en clase.

= The teachers put me in detention for talking in class.

The best days of your life...

This is your chance to have a good moan (in Spanish) about school, and get marks for it. All this stuff could come up in the exams, so you need to be <u>prepared</u> and learn as much of it as you can.

Work Experience

Everyone's got to do <u>work experience</u> at some time or another. Even if your time hasn't come yet, you could still have to listen to people rambling on about their placements in the listening exam, so <u>pay attention</u>.

¿Qué hiciste como experiencia laboral?
— What did you do for work experience?

Como experiencia laboral, trabajé en una oficina .

a hospital: un hospital
a shop: una tienda

= For work experience I worked in <u>an office</u>.

Trabajé allí durante una semana y media .

= I worked there for <u>a week and a half</u>.

¿Cómo fue el trabajo? — How was the work?

More <u>opinions</u> wanted — own up, did you or did you not like it...?

comfortable: cómodo/cómoda
at home: en casa
isolated: aislado/aislada

El trabajo fue duro .

= The work was <u>hard</u>.

difficult: difícil
interesting: interesante

Me sentí muy solo/sola .

= I felt very <u>lonely</u>.

Mis compañeros de trabajo no eran simpáticos .

were very friendly: eran muy simpáticos
were interesting: eran interesantes

= My work colleagues <u>weren't friendly</u>.

Tengo un trabajo a tiempo parcial — I have a part-time job

Make these easier by choosing <u>easy</u> jobs and <u>simple</u> values — if only the rest of life was like that.

Tengo un trabajo a tiempo parcial.

= I've got a part-time job.

Soy recepcionista .

= I am a <u>receptionist</u>.

Gano cinco libras por hora .

= I earn <u>£5 per hour</u>.

£4.00 per hour: cuatro libras por hora
£15 per week: quince libras por semana

For work experience I did photocopying, mainly...

A friend of mine asked for a work experience placement with <u>animals</u> because she was thinking of becoming a vet, and she ended up getting sent to an abattoir for two weeks. <u>Be warned</u>.

Plans for the Future

As if you didn't have enough on your mind with all your exams and revision, those pesky exam boards want you to make your mind up about what you want to do in the <u>future</u> too — and say it in <u>Spanish</u>.

¿Qué quieres hacer después del instituto?
— What do you want to do after school?

Quiero estudiar para el bachillerato y luego estudiar geografía en la universidad.

'El bachillerato' is the Spanish equivalent of A levels.

= I want to do A levels and then study <u>geography</u> at university.

Quiero tomar un año libre.   = I want to take a year out.

Quiero empezar a trabajar.   = I want to start working.

You're fired!

Quiero estudiar música porque quisiera ser músico/a.

French: francés
maths: matemáticas

teacher: profesor/a
accountant: contable

= I want to study <u>music</u> because I'd like to be <u>a musician</u>.

¿En qué te gustaría trabajar?
— What job would you like to do?

Me gustaría ser agente de viajes.   = I would like to be <u>a travel agent</u>.

Give a short and simple <u>reason</u> for why you want to do a particular job.

Quiero ser dentista, porque el trabajo me parece interesante.

plumber: fontanero/a
chef: cocinero/a

fun: divertido
easy: fácil

= I want to be a dentist because the work seems interesting.

En mi trabajo, quiero resolver problemas.   = In my job I would like to <u>solve problems</u>.

meet new people: conocer a gente nueva
work with numbers: trabajar con números

help people: ayudar a la gente
earn a lot of money: ganar mucho dinero

After school I want to have my tea and watch Hollyoaks...

Valuable stuff. Saying what you want to do with your life is pretty <u>essential</u>. If the truth's too hard to say, then say something simpler. This is the kind of thing they just love to slip into <u>listening</u> and <u>reading</u> exams too, so don't skip it unless you're prepared to deal with the consequences...

Section 6 — Education and Work

Types of Job

There are more jobs here than you can shake a stick at — and <u>any</u> of them could pop up in your Spanish <u>exams</u>. The jobs you and your family do are <u>extra</u> important.

Muchos trabajos — Lots of jobs

You'll need to be able to <u>say</u> and <u>write</u> any of the jobs you and your family do — and <u>recognise</u> the rest when you see or hear them.

I've been soliciting for 20 years now, and it hasn't got me anywhere.

OUTDOOR JOBS

mechanic:	el/la mecánico/a
electrician:	el/la electricista
plumber:	el/la fontanero/a
labourer:	el/la obrero/a
carpenter:	el/la carpintero/a
farmer:	el/la granjero/a
gardener:	el/la jardinero/a
soldier:	el/la militar
firefighter:	el/la bombero/a
policeman/woman:	el/la policía
postman/woman:	el/la cartero/a

OFFICE JOBS

accountant:	el/la contable
engineer:	el/la ingeniero/a
lawyer/solicitor:	el/la abogado/a
businessman:	el hombre de negocios
businesswoman:	la mujer de negocios
receptionist:	el/la recepcionista
secretary:	el/la secretario/a
journalist:	el/la periodista
interpreter:	el/la intérprete
translator:	el/la traductor/a

ARTY JOBS

actor/actress:	el actor, la actriz
musician:	el/la músico/a
writer:	el/la escritor/a
painter:	el/la pintor/a

MEDICAL JOBS

dentist:	el/la dentista
nurse:	el/la enfermero/a
doctor:	el/la médico/a
vet:	el/la veterinario/a

A LOAD MORE JOBS

teacher:	el/la profesor/a
hairdresser:	el/la peluquero/a
flight attendant (female):	la azafata
flight attendant (male):	el auxiliar de vuelo
chef:	el/la cocinero/a
waiter/waitress:	el/la camarero/a
shopkeeper:	el/la comerciante
shop assistant:	el/la dependiente/a
baker:	el/la panadero/a
butcher:	el/la carnicero/a

ALTERNATIVES

student:	el/la estudiante
part-time worker:	el/la trabajador/a a tiempo parcial
housewife:	el ama de casa (fem.)

Female versions of jobs can be tricky

There <u>are</u> <u>rules</u> to how the female version of a job is formed, <u>but</u> there are also <u>exceptions</u> to every rule. The <u>only</u> way to be sure you get the female version right is to <u>learn it</u>.

MASCULINE/FEMININE

el ingeniero ⟹ la ingeniera	(an 'o' ending becomes 'a')
el pintor ⟹ la pintora	('or' becomes 'ora')
el contable ⟹ la contable	('e' just stays the same)

> Watch out for words like <u>dentista</u> and <u>recepcionista</u> — the endings of these words <u>don't change</u> depending on the gender.

I used to know two Spanish firemen — José and Hose B...

None too nice, but start with the jobs you find the <u>easiest</u> — then <u>learn</u> the rest. <u>Female</u> versions of each job need learning, so don't forget those tricky <u>odd</u> ones. There's no word for '<u>househusband</u>' in Spanish either — Spanish vocab hasn't quite caught up with the feminist movement...

Pros and Cons of Different Jobs

You might need to say what you think are the <u>good</u> and <u>bad points</u> of different jobs. It's simple enough, as long as nobody asks you about the good points of being a <u>sewer cleaner</u> or something...

¿Cuáles son las ventajas de ser profesor?

— What are the advantages of being a teacher?

Una de las ventajas de ser **profesor** es que **las vacaciones son muy largas**.

= One of the advantages of being <u>a teacher</u> is that <u>the holidays are very long</u>.

doctor:	médico/a
flight attendant:	azafata (female)
	auxiliar de vuelo (male)
gardener:	jardinero/a

they earn a lot of money:	ganan mucho dinero
they travel all over the world:	viajan por todo el mundo
they stay fit:	se mantienen en forma

Lo mejor de ser **veterinario** es **trabajar con animales**.

= The best thing about being <u>a vet</u> is <u>working with animals</u>.

| hairdresser: | peluquero/a |
| interpreter: | intérprete |

'Lo' plus an adjective means '<u>the ... thing/bit</u>', e.g. 'lo interesante' means 'the interesting thing'. See <u>p. 84</u> for more on this.

| chatting to customers: | charlar con los clientes |
| meeting people: | conocer a gente |

¿Y las desventajas? — What about the disadvantages?

Una desventaja de ser **profesor** es **tener que corregir muchos deberes**.

= One disadvantage of being a <u>teacher</u> is <u>having to mark lots of homework</u>.

Lo peor de ser **cartero** es **tener que levantarse muy temprano**.

= The worst thing about being a <u>postman</u> is <u>having to get up very early</u>.

Me gustaría ser bombero porque quiero ayudar a la gente, pero es un trabajo muy peligroso.

= I'd like to be a firefighter because I want to help people, but it's a very dangerous job.

Me gustaría ser camarero porque me gusta conocer a gente nueva, pero los camareros no ganan mucho dinero.

= I'd like to be a waiter because I like meeting new people, but waiters don't earn a lot of money.

Being a prison warden involves a lot of cons...

There's quite a lot of thinking involved in this page, but giving <u>opinions</u> and <u>reasons</u> for them will get you loads of <u>marks</u>. Advantages and disadvantages vocab is handy for all sorts of things too.

Working Abroad

Gap years are all the rage now, so you need to know how to talk about them in Spanish.

¿Te gustaría trabajar en el extranjero?
— Would you like to work abroad?

Me gustaría hacer una práctica en España. = I'd like to do a work placement in Spain.

study at university: estudiar en la universidad

Después de hacer el bachillerato, me gustaría tomar un año libre en Méjico.

= After doing my A levels, I'd like to take a gap year in Mexico.

Este verano voy a trabajar en una oficina de turismo en Burgos.

an ice-cream parlour: una heladería
a baker's: una panadería

= This summer I'm going to work in a tourist office in Burgos.

Tomé un año libre en España — I took a gap year in Spain

Trabajé en un museo en Barcelona durante nueve meses. = I worked in a museum in Barcelona for nine months.

a souvenir shop: una tienda de recuerdos
a hotel: un hotel

six months: seis meses
a year: un año

Lo pasé muy bien.

good: bien
dreadful: fatal

= I had a really good time.

Creo que mi español ha mejorado.

= I think my Spanish has improved.

El trabajo era aburrido, pero mis compañeros eran amables.

difficult: difícil

= The work was boring, but my colleagues were friendly.

No podía viajar por España porque no me pagaron.

= I couldn't travel around Spain because they didn't pay me.

go out with my friends: salir con mis amigos
go shopping: ir de compras

I'd take a gap year, but I'm afraid of falling...

This is another pretty challenging page, but these pages are perfect if you're talking about your future plans or past experiences abroad in your writing or speaking assessment.

Getting a Job

The first step to finding a job is understanding the job advert.
Then you've just got to convince someone to employ you...

Ofertas de empleo — Job Vacancies

Buscamos un camarero/una camarera con un mínimo de un año de experiencia, para trabajar en un restaurante chino en Marbella, seis tardes por semana. Salario 7€ por hora. Llámanos al 665443221.

= We're looking for a waiter/waitress with a minimum of one year's experience to work in a Chinese restaurant in Marbella, six evenings a week. Wages 7€/hour. Call us on 665443221.

Se busca recepcionista de hotel que hable inglés y español. Experiencia necesaria. Solicitudes por correo electrónico: empleos@hotelxyz.es.

= Wanted: hotel receptionist who speaks English and Spanish. Experience necessary. Applications by email: empleos@hotelxyz.es.

Estoy buscando trabajo — I'm looking for a job

Estoy buscando trabajo en una oficina de turismo .

= I'm looking for a job in a tourist information office.

a cinema: un cine

Tengo un año de experiencia como camarero .

= I've got one year of experience as a waiter.

waitress: camarera
shop assistant: dependiente/a

Hablo español . = I speak Spanish.

Soy una persona trabajadora y cortés .

= I am a hard-working and polite person.

honest: honrada *well-mannered:* bien educada

¿Por qué quiere usted este trabajo?

— Why do you want this job?

Business: El comercio

El turismo me interesa mucho. = Tourism interests me a lot.

animals: animales

Quisiera mejorar mi español. = I'd like to improve my Spanish.

Me gusta trabajar con niños . = I like working with children.

Wanted: time lord. Must have own time machine...

Learn all this and you'll be well on your way to becoming a high-flying executive in Spain.

Getting a Job

A lot of the stuff in your GCSEs uses the informal 'tú' form but for job applications you'll need to be super-polite and use the 'usted' form.

Una carta de solicitud — A letter of application

Sra. Guerrero,
C/ Goya, 123,
28030 Madrid

Hannah Osborne,
12 Crabtree Lane,
Cambridge CB5 0NH

Cambridge, el 12 de mayo de 2009

Estimada señora Guerrero:

Ayer leí su anuncio de trabajo para el puesto de intérprete.

Tengo dos años de experiencia como secretaria en España, y hablo inglés y español. Me gustaría trabajar como intérprete porque me gusta conocer a gente nueva. Además, soy trabajadora y bien educada.

Le envió una copia de mi curriculum.

Le saluda atentamente,

Hannah Osborne

Yesterday I read your job advertisement for the position of interpreter.

I have two years of experience as a secretary in Spain, and I speak English and Spanish. I would like to work as an interpreter because I like meeting new people. Also, I am hard-working and well-mannered.

I am sending you a copy of my C.V.

Yours sincerely,

Un curriculum — A C.V.

CURRICULUM

Hannah Osborne

12 Crabtree Lane, Cambridge CB5 0NH
Teléfono: 02 02 24 25 36

EDUCACIÓN

2007: Licenciatura en Español

2002: A levels (equivalentes al bachillerato)
Español (A), Historia (B), Comercio (B)

EXPERIENCIA LABORAL

Desde 2007: Secretaria, 'Mundo de Negocios',
Barcelona.

2002-2003: Dependienta, 'Soap by Sue', Cambridge.

MÁS INFORMACIÓN

Idiomas: inglés, español
Carnet de conducir

EDUCATION

2007: Spanish degree

2002: A levels (equivalent to *bachillerato*)
Spanish (A), History (B),
Business Studies (B)

WORK EXPERIENCE

Since 2007: Secretary,
'Mundo de Negocios',
Barcelona.

2002-2003: Sales Assistant,
'Soap by Sue',
Cambridge.

FURTHER INFORMATION

Languages: English, Spanish
Driving licence

I'd be ideal because I'm a perfecshonist...

Most of this stuff isn't new, but get used to dealing with it in this context. So if one of the speaking tasks is about pretending you're applying for a job as a barber in Seville, it won't throw you.

Telephones

You could quite easily get a phone call to listen to in your listening exam.
If you <u>learn</u> this stuff and <u>practise</u> using it <u>now</u>, it could come in pretty handy.

Una llamada telefónica — A phone call

¿Cuál es tu número de teléfono?   = What's your telephone number?

If you need to be more formal, use <u>su</u>.

Mi número de teléfono es el veintiocho, diecinueve, cincuenta y seis .

Put your phone number in groups of 2,
i.e. <u>twenty-eight</u> rather than <u>two eight</u>.

= My telephone number is <u>281956</u>.

Answering the phone

Here are a few phrases that you might hear in <u>phone calls</u>.

This is how you <u>answer</u> the phone: ¡Dígame!   = Hello?

¡Dígame!

And here's how to say <u>who you are</u>:   Hola, soy Louise .   = Hello, it's <u>Louise</u>.

¿Puedo hablar con Laura ?   = Can I speak to <u>Laura</u>?

¡Dígame!

¿Está Laura ?   = Is <u>Laura</u> there?

This little gem means '<u>on the line</u>' or '<u>speaking</u>':   Hablando.   = Speaking.

¿Puede Laura llamarme a las siete?   = Could <u>Laura</u> ring me back at seven?

Quisiera dejar un mensaje — I'd like to leave a message

Leaving a message is pretty similar to making a <u>phone call</u> — except that there's nobody at the other end.

Este mensaje es para Claudio.   = This message is for Claudio.

Hola, soy Paula. Mi número de teléfono es el cincuenta y nueve, dieciocho, cuarenta y siete. ¿Puede llamarme Claudio a las ocho? Gracias. Hasta luego.

= Hello, it's Paula. My telephone number is 591847. Could Claudio ring me back at 8 o'clock? Thank you. Bye.

Phoning is my vocation — I felt called to it...

Time to <u>cover up</u> the page and <u>write down</u> the key phrases. Then, yep, it's <u>learn</u> and <u>practise</u>.

The Business World

The <u>Spanish fun</u> doesn't end once you've got a job — it goes on and on and on...

¿Le interesa comprar un bolso?
— Are you interested in buying a handbag?

These little phrases could be really <u>useful</u> for your exams —
and also if you ever go on the Spanish version of <u>The Apprentice</u>.

¿Le interesa comprar **un microondas**? = Are you interested in buying <u>a microwave</u>?

some gloves: unos guantes
a wardrobe: un armario

Son de alta calidad. = They're high quality.

Vienen en **cinco** colores y en **dos** tamaños. = They come in <u>five</u> colours and <u>two</u> sizes.

El precio es muy razonable. = The price is very reasonable.

Hay un problema... — There's a problem...

If you've got an <u>unhappy customer</u>, it's always good if you can understand what it is they're so annoyed about.

Pedí un ordenador hace tres semanas pero no ha llegado.

= I ordered a computer three weeks ago but it hasn't arrived.

He pagado demasiado. = I've paid too much.

Tengo el color equivocado. Pedí un jersey azul, pero el jersey que tengo es marrón.

= I've got the wrong colour.
I ordered a blue jumper, but the jumper that I've got is brown.

Pedí dos bolsos y un paraguas, y falta el paraguas.

= I ordered two handbags and an umbrella, and the umbrella is missing.

Lo siento, voy a arreglar el problema ahora.

= I'm sorry, I'm going to sort out the problem now.

Learn this page — and that's an order...

Don't forget that <u>absolutely anything</u> could come up in your reading and listening exam, and that includes this little lot. The <u>problem</u> phrases are useful for letters of complaint too (see p. 11).

Revision Summary

That's the end of another section. And that means that you're just one section away from the end of the book. Don't get too excited though because it's the grammar section. Make sure you can answer all these questions without looking back at the pages, and then it's grammar time.

1) Say what all your GCSE subjects are in Spanish (or as many as possible).

2) Your friend Ana asks you "¿Cuál es tu asignatura preferida?"
What does the question mean, and how would you reply in Spanish?

3) How would you say that your lunch break is at 12.45?

4) Sukia has to wear a uniform at school, but she doesn't like it because it's ugly. Her uniform is a yellow skirt, a green shirt and a pink tie. How would she say all this in Spanish?

5) What do these classroom phrases mean?
   a) ¡Siéntate!   b) No entiendo   c) No lo sé   d) ¿Puedes repetir eso, por favor?

6) Are you worried about your exams? Why? Answer in Spanish.

7) Your friend Noelia is telling you about her work experience placement: "Como experiencia laboral, trabajé en un hospital. El trabajo fue interesante y mis compañeros de trabajo eran simpáticos." What does this mean?

8) Write three sentences in Spanish about your plans for the future. (If you're not sure what you want to do in the future, just invent something believable.)

9) A Carlos le gustaría ser cocinero porque le gusta la comida y el trabajo le parece divertido.
¿Cómo se dice esto en inglés?

10) What are these jobs in English?
   a) el veterinario b) el periodista c) el carnicero   d) el fontanero

11) Choose any job (that you know the name for in Spanish) and write down one advantage and one disadvantage of that job.

12) Write down in Spanish that you'd like to do a work placement in Spain after doing your A levels.

13) You see this job advert in a newspaper:
   Se busca un/una enfermero/a con un mínimo de dos años de experiencia.
   Salario 700€ por mes. Solicitudes por correo electrónico.
What does the advert mean?

14) You are doing work experience for a mail-order sock company in Bilbao. One morning when you arrive in the office, this message is on the answer machine:
   "Hola, soy Faviola Conuve. Pedí unos calcetines rojos, pero los calcetines que tengo son verdes. ¿Puede llamarme alguien a las once de la mañana?
   Mi número de teléfono es el cuarenta y seis, veintidós, diecisiete. Gracias. Adiós."
Write out the message in English.

Words for People and Objects

NOUNS

Stop — before you panic, this stuff is a lot <u>less scary</u> than it looks.
It's all <u>pretty simple</u> stuff about words for <u>people</u> and <u>objects</u> — nouns. This is <u>really important</u>.

Every **Spanish noun is** <u>masculine</u> **or** <u>feminine</u>

Whether a word is <u>masculine</u>, <u>feminine</u> or <u>plural</u> affects a lot of things. All 'the' and 'a' words change,
and as if that weren't enough, the adjectives (like big, red, shiny) change to fit the word.

> **Examples**
> *a small dog:* <u>un</u> perro pequeñ<u>o</u> *(masculine)*
> *a small house:* <u>una</u> casa pequeñ<u>a</u> *(feminine)*

For more on this, see
p. 82 and 83.

It's no good just knowing the Spanish words for things, you have to know
whether each one's <u>masculine</u> or <u>feminine</u> too.

> **THE GOLDEN RULE**
> Each time you <u>learn</u> a <u>word</u>, remember the <u>el</u> or <u>la</u> to go with it
> — don't think 'dog = perro', think 'dog = <u>el</u> perro'.

EL, LA, LOS AND LAS
An <u>el</u> in front usually
means it's <u>masculine</u>.
<u>La</u> in front = <u>feminine</u>.

These rules help you guess what a word is

> **Rules of Thumb for Masculine and Feminine Nouns**
>
> MASCULINE NOUNS:
> most nouns that end:
> -o   -l   -n   -r   -s
> -ma   -pa   -ta   -aje
> also: male people, languages,
> days, months, seas, rivers,
> oceans, and mountains.
>
> FEMININE NOUNS:
> most nouns that end:
> -a   ción   -sión   -tad
> -tud   -dad   -umbre
> also: female people,
> letters of the alphabet.

You can't tell whether a noun
ending in 'e' or 'ista' is
<u>masculine</u> or <u>feminine</u>, **e.g.**

> *the car:* <u>el</u> coch<u>e</u>
> *the people:* <u>la</u> gent<u>e</u>
> *the tourist (man):* <u>el</u> tur<u>ista</u>
> *the tourist (woman):* <u>la</u> tur<u>ista</u>

Making Nouns Plural

1) Nouns in Spanish are usually made plural by adding an '<u>s</u>' when
   they end in a vowel and '<u>es</u>' when they end in a consonant.

   e.g. one orange: una naranja
   two oranges: dos naranjas

2) <u>Family surnames</u> and nouns which finish in an <u>unstressed syllable</u> ending in '<u>s</u>' stay the same in the plural.

   e.g. the Simpsons (family): Los Simpson   *e.g. Tuesday:* el martes   *Tuesdays:* los martes

3) You may need to <u>add</u> or <u>remove</u> an <u>accent</u> when nouns become plural to keep the pronunciation.

   e.g. one young man: un j<u>o</u>ven   *e.g. one Englishman:* un inglés
   two young men: dos j<u>ó</u>venes   *two Englishmen:* dos ingl<u>es</u>es

4) Nouns ending in '<u>z</u>' change the '<u>z</u>' to a '<u>c</u>' before adding '<u>es</u>'.

   e.g. one pencil: un lápi<u>z</u>   *two pencils:* dos lápi<u>c</u>es

   TOP TIP FOR PLURALS
   Each time you <u>learn</u> a <u>word</u>, learn
   how to make it into a plural too.

5) When you make a masculine noun plural, instead of '<u>el</u>' you
   have to use '<u>los</u>' to say '<u>the</u>'. For feminine nouns '<u>la</u>' becomes
   '<u>las</u>' when it's plural — see <u>p. 82</u>.

Masculine words — butch, hunky, stud...

The bottom line is — <u>every time</u> you learn a word in Spanish, you <u>have</u> to learn whether it's <u>el</u> or
<u>la</u>, and you have to learn what its <u>plural</u> is. So start as you mean to go on — get into <u>genders</u>.

'The' and 'A'

'The' and 'a' are a bit tricky in Spanish, because they're different for masculine, feminine or plural words.

'The' — el, la, los, las

1) Spanish 'the' changes for masculine, feminine or plural:

Masculine singular:	**el**	e.g. el chico (the boy)	Masculine plural:	**los**	e.g. los chicos (the boys)
Feminine singular:	**la**	e.g. la chica (the girl)	Feminine plural:	**las**	e.g. las chicas (the girls)

2) But remember 'el' is used before feminine nouns which start with a stressed 'a':   e.g. The water is cold. El agua está fría.

'El', 'la', 'los' and 'las' are definite articles.

3) You can't say 'a el', 'de el', so you say 'al' (a + el) and 'del' (de + el) instead.

e.g. I went to the park. Fui al parque.   e.g. He's the president's son. Es el hijo del presidente.

4) Sometimes you need a definite article in Spanish when you wouldn't use one in English.

a) with nouns used in a general sense:
e.g. I don't like coffee. No me gusta el café.

b) in front of days of the week and times:
e.g. Every Monday at five o'clock.
Todos los lunes a las cinco.

c) in front of weights and measurements:
e.g. 2 euros a kilo. Dos euros el kilo.

d) when you talk about a person and give their title:
e.g. How is Mr Jiménez?
¿Cómo está el señor Jiménez?

5) There's also a neuter article 'lo' for things that aren't masculine or feminine.
You'll mostly come across it in phrases: the best/worst thing = lo mejor/peor   what/that which = lo que
I don't know what he wants. = No sé lo que quiere.

'A' — un, una

Masculine:	**un** e.g. tengo un hermano (I have a brother)	Feminine:	**una** e.g. tengo una hermana (I have a sister)

1) 'A' is left out: a) after the verb 'ser' when talking about someone's occupation or nationality: e.g. I'm a student: Soy estudiante

b) after a negative word: e.g. I haven't got a cat. No tengo gato.

'Un' and 'una' are indefinite articles.

c) in front of 'otro/a':   e.g. Do you want another coffee? ¿Quieres otro café?

2) When you make 'un' or 'una' plural, they mean 'some' or 'a few'.

I spent a few days at the beach.
Pasé unos días en la playa.

I have some very good photos.
Tengo unas fotos muy buenas.

Any, each, all and another

1) Here's something worth knowing — you don't need a special word for 'any':

Have you got any apples?   ¿Tienes manzanas?   Juan doesn't want any bread.   Juan no quiere pan.

2) Use 'otro' or 'otra' for 'another' — remember it's not 'un otro' or 'una otra'.

He's going to come another day. Va a venir otro día.   I wrote another letter. Escribí otra carta.

3) 'All' is 'todo/toda/todos/todas'.

He studies all day.   Estudia todo el día.   I bought all the books. Compré todos los libros.

4) Use 'cada' to say 'each' — it stays the same for masculine and feminine words, and you can only use it with singular words.   Each dress has a unique design. Cada vestido tiene un diseño único.

La la la la, I'm not listening...

Blimey, am I glad I speak English — just one word for 'the', and no genders. This stuff might be dull but it's important — you won't get very far with Spanish unless you get to grips with genders.

Words to Describe Things

Gain <u>more marks</u> and show what an interesting person you are by using some <u>juicy describing</u> words.
Make sure you <u>understand</u> what you're saying as well.

Adjectives _must 'agree'_ with the thing they're describing

1) In <u>English</u>, you can use the <u>same</u> describing word (adjective) for whatever you like —
like tall sunflower, tall sunflowers, tall man, tall woman, tall women...

2) In <u>Spanish</u>, the describing word has to <u>change</u> to <u>match</u> whether what it's describing is <u>masculine or feminine</u>, <u>singular or plural</u>. Even if the adjective <u>isn't</u> next to the word it's describing in the sentence, it <u>still</u> needs to agree. Look at these examples where 'pequeño' has to change:

Masculine Singular	Masculine Plural	Feminine Singular	Feminine Plural
el chico <u>pequeño</u>	los chicos <u>pequeños</u>	la chica <u>pequeña</u>	las chicas <u>pequeñas</u>
(the small boy)	_(the small boys)_	_(the small girl)_	_(the small girls)_

"You stink!"   "I agree."

1 When you look an adjective up in the <u>dictionary</u> it's listed in the <u>masculine singular</u> form. If the word being described is <u>feminine</u> (see p. 81), change the '<u>o</u>' at the end of the adjective to an '<u>a</u>'.

2 Add an '<u>-s</u>' or an '<u>-es</u>' to the describing word if the word being described is <u>plural</u> (see p. 81). If it's <u>feminine plural</u>, it'll end up with '<u>-as</u>' on the end.

3) Some colours <u>never change</u> at all, because they are actually the names of things, and are not real adjectives. The most common ones are:

orange:	naranja
pink:	rosa
violet:	violeta

_e.g._ Three orange hats.
Tres sombreros naranja.

See <u>p. 35</u> for more <u>colours</u>.

Some handy _describing words_

Here are some really important <u>describing words</u> —
they're the ones you really <u>have</u> to know.

SIZE WORDS

big:	grande
small:	pequeño/a
tall:	alto/a
short:	bajo/a
long:	largo/a
fat:	gordo/a
thin:	delgado/a

POSITIVE WORDS

good:	bueno/a
happy:	feliz
nice (character):	simpático/a
pretty/nice:	bonito/a
handsome/pretty:	guapo/a
interesting:	interesante
easy:	fácil

NEGATIVE WORDS

bad:	malo/a
sad:	triste
boring:	aburrido/a
strange:	raro/a
difficult:	difícil

A FEW MORE WORDS

old:	viejo/a
young:	joven
new:	nuevo/a
fast:	rápido/a
slow:	lento/a

Mi vecino es simpático .

= My neighbour is <u>nice</u>.

Tengo una bicicleta nueva .

= I have a <u>new</u> bike.

Las flores son bonitas .

= The flowers are <u>pretty</u>.

Compré unos libros interesantes .

= I bought some <u>interesting</u> books.

This page is interesting, don't you agree...

Aaaargh — more tables to learn, but then that's the nature of Spanish grammar. For these
endings to be of any <u>use</u> to you, you need to learn the <u>genders</u> of the nouns in the first place.
You have to know <u>what</u> your adjective needs to <u>agree</u> with. To get it right — <u>get learning</u>.

ADJECTIVES
Words to Describe Things

Once you've learned some describing words, you need to know <u>where</u> to put them.

<u>Most</u> describing words go after the word they describe

It's the opposite of English — in Spanish <u>most</u> describing words (adjectives) <u>go after</u> the word they're describing (the noun).

Es un vestido horrible .   = It's a <u>horrible</u> dress.

Occasionally you might see some adjectives <u>before</u> the word they describe, but it's <u>not</u> very common:

No voy a comprar ese horrible vestido.   = I'm not going to buy that <u>horrible</u> dress.

<u>Some</u> describing words <u>always</u> go in front of the word they're describing. These are the most common ones:

each, every:	cada	*other:*	otros/as	*so many:*	tantos/as
a lot of:	mucho/a	*little (not much):*	poco/a	*first, second...:*	primero/a, segundo/a...
lots of:	muchos/as	*few:*	pocos/as		
another:	otro/a	*so much:*	tanto/a		See <u>p. 1</u> for more <u>numbers</u>.

<u>Some</u> adjectives change if they're before masculine nouns

1) Some adjectives <u>lose</u> the final '<u>o</u>' when they go in front of a <u>masculine noun</u>:

good:	bueno/a	*some:*	alguno/a
first:	primero/a	*none:*	ninguno/a
third:	tercero/a	*bad:*	malo/a

Un buen día.   = A <u>good</u> day.

2) '<u>Alguno</u>' and '<u>ninguno</u>' both drop an '<u>o</u>' and add an <u>accent</u>:

No hay ningún taxi libre.   = There's <u>no</u> taxi free.

3) <u>Grande</u>' is the only adjective that drops '<u>de</u>' in front of both <u>masculine</u> and <u>feminine</u> words.

Una gran señora.   = A <u>great</u> lady.

4) '<u>Ciento</u>' drops '<u>to</u>' when it comes in front of <u>anything</u> that isn't another number (except 'mil' or 'millón').

Cien euros.   = <u>One hundred</u> euros.

<u>Some</u> change their meaning depending on their position

Some adjectives <u>change their meaning</u> according to whether they are <u>before</u> or <u>after</u> the noun. Here are some important ones — learn them <u>carefully</u>.

adjective	meaning if it's <u>before</u> the noun	meaning if it's <u>after</u> the noun
grande	great un <u>gran</u> hombre (a <u>great</u> man)	big un hombre <u>grande</u> (a <u>big</u> man)
mismo	same el <u>mismo</u> día (the <u>same</u> day)	self yo <u>mismo</u> (I <u>myself</u>)
nuevo	new (different) tengo un <u>nuevo</u> coche (I have a <u>new</u> [to me] car)	(brand) new tengo un coche <u>nuevo</u> (I have a <u>brand new</u> car)
viejo	old (longstanding) un <u>viejo</u> amigo (an <u>old</u> friend)	old (elderly) un amigo <u>viejo</u> (an <u>elderly</u> friend)

Add '<u>ito</u>' or '<u>ísimo</u>' to make adjectives smaller or stronger

You can add '<u>ito</u>' to almost any adjective to make things seem smaller or cuter, or '<u>ísimo/a</u>' to make the meaning stronger.

El bebé está enfermito .   = The baby is <u>poorly</u>.

La película es malísima .   = The film is <u>really awful</u>.

'<u>Lo</u>' with an adjective means '<u>the ... thing</u>'

'<u>Lo</u>' and <u>any masculine adjective</u> means '<u>the</u> good/bad/best/worst/funny... <u>thing</u>'.

Lo malo de la película es que es muy larga.   = <u>The bad thing</u> about the film is that it's very long.

Can adding 'ísimo' make people stronger...

It'd be a lot simpler than all that weightlifting. This page isn't too taxing — make sure you're clear on <u>which</u> adjectives go <u>where</u>, and don't get tripped up by the ones that <u>change</u> their meaning.

Words to Describe Things

Ooh — a lovely page all about belonging words. Cool.

My, your, our — who things belong to

You have to be able to use and understand these words to say that something belongs to someone:

You have to choose masculine, feminine, singular or plural
to match the thing it's describing, not the owner.

	masculine singular	feminine singular	masculine plural	feminine plural
my	mi	mi	mis	mis
singular familiar your	tu	tu	tus	tus
his/her/its/ singular polite your	su	su	sus	sus
our	nuestro	nuestra	nuestros	nuestras
plural familiar your	vuestro	vuestra	vuestros	vuestras
their/ plural polite your	su	su	sus	sus

Mi hermano es alto.

= <u>My</u> brother is tall.

> Make sure you have the right
> masculine or feminine ending when
> you use 'nuestro' and 'vuestro'.

Nuestra cocina es más grande que vuestra cocina.

= <u>Our</u> kitchen is bigger than <u>your</u> kitchen.

Tus zapatos son bonitos.

= <u>Your</u> shoes are nice.

Mine, yours, ours — other belonging words

These words are also used to show possession, especially if you want to make doubly sure who owns what.
Don't worry about using them though — you only have to understand what they mean. Yippee.

These words are a type of adjective. They always come after the noun in a sentence.

	masculine singular	feminine singular	masculine plural	feminine plural
mine	mío	mía	míos	mías
yours (informal)	tuyo	tuya	tuyos	tuyas
his/hers/yours/theirs	suyo	suya	suyos	suyas

¿Esa casa es tuya *?* = Is that house <u>yours</u>?

¿Esos guantes son suyos *?*

= Are those gloves <u>hers</u>?

Ese sombrero es mío *.*

= That hat is <u>mine</u>.

'Nuestro' means 'ours' and 'vuestro' means 'yours (plural)':

¿Ese hotel es vuestro *?*

= Is that hotel <u>yours</u>?

No, nuestro *hotel está cerca de la playa.*

= No, <u>our</u> hotel is near the beach.

My, this stuff's certainly worth learning...

This page is full of things you really need to know — belonging words come up <u>all the time</u> in
Spanish GCSE. Make sure you know the difference between '<u>my</u>' and '<u>mine</u>' and you'll be fine.

ADVERBS — Making Sentences More Interesting

The pages before this are about describing <u>objects</u> (e.g. the bus is <u>red</u>). This page is about describing things you <u>do</u> (e.g. I speak Spanish <u>well</u>) and adding <u>more info</u> (e.g. I speak Spanish <u>very</u> well).

Make your sentences _better_ by saying _how_ you do things

1) In <u>English</u>, you don't say 'We talk slow', you have to <u>add</u> a '<u>ly</u>' on the end to say 'We talk slow<u>ly</u>'.

2) In <u>Spanish</u>, you have to <u>add</u> a '<u>mente</u>' on the end, but first you have to make sure the describing word is in the <u>feminine</u> form (see p. <u>83</u>).

> The Spanish word for 'slow' is '<u>lento</u>', but the feminine form is '<u>lenta</u>'. Add '<u>mente</u>' and you get '<u>lentamente</u>' = slowly.

Habla **lentamente** .   = He speaks <u>slowly</u>.

quickly: rápidamente
normally: normalmente

3) <u>Unlike</u> normal describing words (see p. <u>83</u>) you <u>don't</u> ever have to <u>change</u> these words — even if what it's about is <u>feminine</u> or <u>plural</u>.

Hablamos **lentamente** .   = We speak <u>slowly</u>.

Learn these _odd ones out_ off by heart

Just like in English there are <u>odd ones out</u> — for example, you <u>don't</u> say I sing '<u>goodly</u>'...

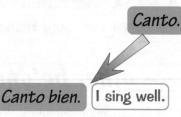

Canto. | I sing.

Spanish Odd Ones Out	
ENGLISH	**SPANISH**
good → well	bueno/a → bien
bad → badly	malo/a → mal

Canto bien. | I sing well.

Canto mal. | I sing badly.

Say _when_ and _where_ you do things

Here are some more handy little words you can stick into sentences to say <u>when</u> and <u>where</u> things happen:

here: aquí   *now:* ahora
there: allí   *already:* ya

Mi tía trabaja **aquí** .   = My aunt works <u>here</u>.

Ya tengo un reloj.   = I <u>already</u> have a watch.

Vamos a cenar **ahora** .

= We're going to have dinner <u>now</u>.

Use these _four words_ to give _even more detail_

Stick one of these <u>four</u> words in <u>front</u> of the <u>describing word</u> in a sentence to add extra detail and impress the examiners.

very: muy   *almost:* casi
quite: bastante   *too:* demasiado

Ella habla **casi** perfectamente el español.

= She speaks Spanish <u>almost</u> perfectly.

Bob está **muy** feliz.

= Bob is <u>very</u> happy.

Revise this lot really well, right here, right now...

Alrighty — this is <u>a bit like</u> English — you have a set ending (-<u>mente</u>) to learn and stick on, and it's not too tricky either. Make sure you <u>really know</u> the standard <u>rule</u> and all the <u>exceptions</u>.

Comparing Things

Saying something's <u>good</u> is easy enough, but what if you want to say it's <u>better</u>, or the <u>best thing ever</u>...

How to say 'more ...' and 'the most ...'

In Spanish you can't say 'stranger' or 'strangest', it's gotta be 'more strange' or 'the most strange':

Esta falda es cara .	*Esta falda es* más cara .	*Esta falda es* la más cara .
= This skirt is <u>expensive</u>.	= This skirt is <u>more expensive</u>.	= This skirt is <u>the most expensive</u>.

fat: gordo ⟹ *fatter:* más gordo ⟹ *fattest:* el más gordo
tall: alto ⟹ *taller:* más alto ⟹ *tallest:* el más alto
big: grande ⟹ *bigger:* más grande ⟹ *biggest:* el más grande

You can do this with almost any <u>describing word</u>. Don't forget to change the '<u>o</u>' ending to '<u>a</u>' for feminine and add '<u>s</u>' or '<u>es</u>' for plural.

To say '<u>the most...</u>' you have to use '<u>la</u> más' or '<u>los/las</u> más' if the word you're describing is feminine or plural.

Liz es la más alta .	= Liz is <u>the tallest</u>.	*Ed y Jo son* los más altos .	= Ed and Jo are <u>the tallest</u>.

BUT, just like in English, there are <u>odd ones out</u>:

good: bueno ⟹ *better:* mejor ⟹ *best:* el mejor
bad: malo ⟹ *worse:* peor ⟹ *worst:* el peor
old: viejo ⟹ *older:* mayor ⟹ *oldest:* el mayor
young: joven ⟹ *younger:* menor ⟹ *youngest:* el menor

El gorro azul es el mejor .

= The blue cap is <u>the best</u>.

More and most with adverbs is pretty much the same...

When you're saying that someone <u>does</u> something <u>more</u> or <u>most ...ly</u>, you follow the <u>same pattern</u> as above, but instead of <u>adjectives</u> (describing words — see p. 83-85), you use <u>adverbs</u> (see p. 86).

Penélope trabaja alegremente .	*Anita trabaja* más alegremente .
= Penélope works <u>cheerfully</u>.	= Anita works <u>more cheerfully</u>.

Esteban es el que *trabaja* más alegremente .

= Esteban works <u>the most cheerfully</u> /
Esteban is <u>the one who</u> works <u>the most cheerfully</u>.

For a <u>woman</u>, change 'el que' to '<u>la que</u>', and for <u>groups</u> change to '<u>los que</u>' (or '<u>las que</u>' if everyone in the group is female).

There are two <u>odd ones out</u> you need to know:

well: bien ⟹ *better:* mejor   *badly:* mal ⟹ *worse:* peor

Learn these three great ways of comparing things

Use '<u>más...que</u>' ('more...than'), '<u>menos...que</u>' ('less...than') and '<u>tan...como</u>' ('as...as') to compare things.

Ed es más joven que *Tom.*	*Ed es* menos joven que *Tom.*	*Ed es* tan joven como *Tom.*
= Ed is <u>younger than</u> Tom.	= Ed is <u>less young than</u> Tom.	= Ed is <u>as young as</u> Tom.

Wow, this is just super(lative)...

Make sure you learn how to say big<u>ger</u> or big<u>gest</u>, and how to say big<u>ger than</u>, <u>as</u> big <u>as</u> and <u>less</u> big <u>than</u>. And don't just learn the rule, <u>learn all</u> those <u>exceptions</u> to it as well.

There's loads more about it on p. 8.

CONJUNCTIONS — *Joining Words — Longer Sentences*

Everyone knows <u>long</u> sentences are <u>clever</u> — and examiners <u>like</u> clever people. So learn these joining words to <u>help</u> you make longer sentences, and get <u>more marks</u> for being smart.

Y = And

Me gusta jugar al fútbol. **AND** Me gusta jugar al rugby. **=** Me gusta jugar al fútbol **y** al rugby.

= I like playing football.   = I like playing rugby.   = I like playing football <u>and</u> rugby.

BUT: if 'y' comes in front of a word beginning with 'i' or 'hi' it changes to 'e'.

Hablo español *e* inglés.   = I speak Spanish <u>and</u> English.

O = Or

Juega al fútbol todos los días. **OR** Juega al rugby todos los días. **=** Juega al fútbol **o** al rugby todos los días.

= He plays football every day.   = He plays rugby every day.   = He plays football <u>or</u> rugby every day.

BUT: when 'o' comes in front of a word beginning with 'o' or 'ho' it changes to 'u'.

Cuesta siete *u* ocho libras.   = It costs seven <u>or</u> eight pounds.

Pero = But

Don't confuse 'pero' with 'perro' (dog).

Me gusta jugar al fútbol. **BUT** No me gusta jugar al rugby. **=** Me gusta jugar al fútbol **pero** no me gusta jugar al rugby.

= I like playing football.   = I don't like playing rugby.   = I like playing football <u>but</u> I don't like playing rugby.

When '<u>but</u>' means 'on the contrary' it becomes '<u>sino</u>':

Mi amigo no es americano **sino** australiano.   = My friend isn't American, <u>but</u> (on the contrary) he's Australian.

Porque = Because

This is a really important one you need to use to explain yourself. There's loads more about it on p. 8.

Me gusta el tenis **porque** es divertido.   = I like tennis <u>because</u> it's fun.

Other joining words to understand

You don't have to use all of these, but you should <u>understand</u> them if you see or hear them.

well, then:	pues, entonces
if:	si
with:	con
as, like:	como
so, therefore:	por lo tanto, así (que), de manera (que)
while, during:	mientras
when:	cuando

Puedes salir **si** quieres.   = You can go out <u>if</u> you want.

Tengo hambre, **así que** voy a comer.   = I'm hungry, <u>so</u> I'm going to eat.

Es **como** su hermano.   = He's <u>like</u> his brother.

Va a la playa **cuando** hace sol.   = She goes to the beach <u>when</u> it's sunny.

I'd prefer a reduced sentence...

You use '<u>and</u>', '<u>or</u>', '<u>but</u>' and '<u>because</u>' all the time when you're speaking English — if you <u>don't</u> use them when you speak <u>Spanish</u>, you'll sound a bit <u>weird</u>. But don't confuse '<u>si</u>' (if) and '<u>sí</u>' (yes). It's good if you can <u>recognise</u> all the <u>extra</u> words in the last bit too, and even better if you can <u>use</u> them.

Sneaky Wee Words

You've got to <u>learn</u> these if you want tip-top marks. They're really useful words anyway.

TO — *a, hasta*

For 'the train <u>to</u> London' use 'the train <u>for</u> London' — see next page.

'To' is usually '<u>a</u>':

| Va *a* Madrid. | = He's going <u>to</u> Madrid. |

| Voy *a* casa. | = I'm going (<u>to</u>) home. |

Or use '<u>hasta</u>' when '<u>to</u>' means '<u>as far as</u>':

| Sólo va *hasta* York. | = He's only going <u>to</u> York. |

ON — *sobre, en*

For 'on top of', it's '<u>sobre</u>' or '<u>en</u>':

| Sobre la mesa. | = <u>On</u> the table. |

When it's <u>not</u> 'on top of', it's usually '<u>en</u>':

| Lo vi *en* la tele. | = I saw it <u>on</u> TV. |

For days of the week, it's <u>left out</u>:

| Me voy el lunes. | = I'm leaving on Monday. |

IN — *en, dentro de*

'<u>En</u>' is just 'in', 'inside' is usually '<u>dentro de</u>'.

| Está *en/dentro de* la caja. | = It's in(side) the box. |

If it's in a town, it's '<u>en</u>':

| Vivo *en* Málaga. | = I live <u>in</u> Malaga. |

Don't forget to add '<u>en</u>' when going into a place:

| Entra *en* la tienda. | = She enters (<u>into</u>) the shop. |

FROM — *de, desde* **or** *a partir de*

Where we use 'from', they usually use '<u>de</u>':

| Soy *de* Cardiff. | = I come <u>from</u> Cardiff. |

'<u>Desde</u>' is used where there is a starting and finishing point:

| Desde Londres hasta Madrid. | = <u>From</u> London to Madrid. |

For dates, it's '<u>a partir de</u>':

| A partir del 4 de junio. | = <u>From</u> the 4th of June. |

OF — *de*

Where we use 'of', they usually use '<u>de</u>':

| Una botella *de* leche. | = A bottle <u>of</u> milk. |

'Made of' is '<u>de</u>':

| Es un cinturón *de* cuero. | = It's a leather belt. |

WATCH OUT: sometimes it's hard to spot the <u>de</u> in a sentence, because <u>de</u> + <u>el</u> = <u>del</u>.

| Salgo *del* supermercado. | = I go out <u>of the</u> supermarket. |

AT — *en, a*

Most English phrases with '<u>at</u>' in them use '<u>en</u>' in the Spanish — a few use '<u>a</u>'.

| A *las seis.* | = <u>At</u> six o'clock. |

| Ella está *en* la escuela. | = She is <u>at</u> school. |

| En *casa.* | = <u>At</u> home. |

Don't forget — <u>a</u> + <u>el</u> = <u>al</u>. Sometimes it can be tricky to spot.

Learn these words for saying <u>where something is</u>

You need these little words a lot, for saying where things are in your <u>town</u> or your <u>house</u>.

| El banco está *enfrente del* hotel. | = The bank is <u>opposite the</u> hotel. |

next to:	al lado de	*on / upon:*	en, sobre	*at the back of:*	al fondo de
behind:	detrás de	*above:*	encima de	*here:*	aquí
in front of:	delante de	*against:*	contra	*there:*	allí, ahí, allá
between:	entre	*in / into:*	en	*inside:*	dentro de
under / below:	bajo/debajo de	*at the end of:*	al final de	*outside:*	fuera de

Don't forget to use está / están for describing where things are.

Of, at, in, from, shake it all about...

Prepositions have loads of <u>different</u> meanings in English — it's important to remember they do in Spanish <u>too</u>, just <u>not</u> the same ones. You have to learn the words from a <u>Spanish perspective</u>.

'Por' and 'Para'

'POR' & 'PARA'

'Por' and 'para' are two <u>nightmare words</u> for English speakers because they both mean 'for' — but in different ways. This bit's going to be tricky I'm afraid, but it's really important — it's <u>worth</u> learning.

Use <u>Para</u> for...

1) Saying <u>who</u> something is <u>for</u>: **Este dinero es para ti.** = This money is <u>for</u> you.

2) Talking about <u>destination</u>: **El tren para Buenos Aires.** = The train <u>to</u> Buenos Aires.

3) When you want to say '<u>to</u>'/<u>in order to</u>':
Trabajo para ganar dinero. = I work <u>in order to</u> earn money.

4) When you want to say '<u>by</u>' in <u>time phrases</u>: **para mañana** = <u>by</u> / <u>for</u> tomorrow   **para entonces** = <u>by</u> / <u>for</u> then

5) 'For' in sentences like '<u>for X days</u>' when you're talking about the <u>future</u>:
Quiero el coche para tres días. = I want the car <u>for</u> three days.

6) 'In (my / your...) <u>view</u>':
Para mí, ella es la chica más atractiva de todas. = <u>In my view</u>, she's the most attractive girl of all.

7) '<u>About to</u>': **Está para llover.** = It's <u>about to</u> rain.   Confusingly, in <u>Latin America</u> they use '<u>por</u>' for 'about to'.

Use <u>Por</u> for...

1) 'For' in time sentences, like '<u>for X months / years</u>' in the <u>past</u> or <u>future</u>:
Vivió en Málaga por un año. = He lived in Malaga <u>for</u> a year.

2) 'In' to talk about <u>parts of the day</u>: **por la mañana** = <u>in</u> the morning

3) When you say '<u>through</u>': **El tren va por el túnel.** = The train goes <u>through</u> the tunnel.

4) '<u>Per</u>' in <u>number</u> phrases:
dos veces por día = twice <u>a</u> day   **veinte por ciento** = twenty <u>percent</u>

5) <u>Exchange</u>: **Pagó diez euros por el libro.** = He paid 10 euros <u>for</u> the book.

6) <u>On behalf of</u>: **Lo hizo por ti.** = He did it <u>for</u> you.

7) When you say '<u>gracias</u>': **Gracias por todos los peces.** = Thanks <u>for</u> all the fish.

Por and para — wish I knew what they're for...

This is possibly the <u>trickiest</u> thing in the whole of GCSE Spanish — in fact it might be the hardest thing to get your head around in Spanish full stop. All you can do is learn and apply the <u>rules</u> — learning the <u>examples</u> will really help you to understand the <u>difference</u> between 'por' and 'para'.

I, You, Him, Them...

Pronouns are really handy words that save you from having to keep repeating nouns all the time.

Yo, tú, él, ella... — I, you, he, she...

Pronouns are words that replace nouns — like 'you' or 'them'.

> _Kelly has a new job at the wig factory._
> _She likes making wigs._

'She' is a pronoun. It means you don't have to say 'Kelly' again.

'I', 'you', 'he', etc. are not usually needed in Spanish — unless you want to emphasise or make it clear exactly who you're talking about. You need to know them though — or you'll end up getting seriously confused.

THE SUBJECT PRONOUNS

_I:_	yo	_we:_	nosotros/as
you (informal singular):	tú	_you (informal plural):_	vosotros/as
_he / it:_	él	_they (masculine or mixed masculine_	
she / it:	ella	_and feminine):_	ellos
you (formal singular):	usted	_they (all feminine):_	ellas
one:	se	_you (formal plural):_	ustedes

THE FOUR 'YOU's

Remember — there are 4 ways of talking to 'you'. 'Tú' is for one person who's your friend, a member of your family or about your age. For a group of people you know, use 'vosotros/as'. You use 'usted' to be polite to one person (for older people who aren't your family or friends), or 'ustedes' if there's more than one of them.

Me, te, lo... — me, you, him...

These are for the person / thing in a sentence that's having the action done to it (the direct object).

Dave lava **el perro** . ⟶ Dave **lo** lava.

= Dave washes the dog.   = Dave washes it.

THE DIRECT OBJECT PRONOUNS

_me:_	me	_us:_	nos
you (informal singular):	te	_you (informal plural):_	os
him / it / you		_them / you_	
(formal singular masculine):	lo	_(formal plural masculine):_	los
her / it / you		_them / you_	
(formal singular feminine):	la	_(formal plural feminine):_	las

Lucky for you, you don't need to use object pronouns — but you do have to understand them if they crop up.

There are special words for _to me, to her, to them_

For things that need 'to' or 'for' — like writing to someone — there are indirect object pronouns. You don't need to use these either but you do need to recognise them.

El perro da el cepillo **a Dave** .   = The dog gives the brush to Dave.

El perro **le** da el cepillo.   = The dog gives the brush to him.

THE INDIRECT OBJECT PRONOUNS

_to me:_	me
to you (inf. sing.):	te
to him / her / it / you (form. sing.):	le
_to us:_	nos
to you (inf. plu.):	os
to them / you (form. plu.):	les

These pronouns usually come before the verb, but when it's a command they're tacked on to the end of the verb.

¡Llámame !   = Call me!

Spanish speakers need these pronouns for saying they like something. They have to say 'it is pleasing to me' etc. It doesn't matter if the person is singular or plural — you'll hear 'gusta' if the thing they like is singular, or 'gustan' if it's plural.

No nos gusta el pulpo.   = We don't like octopus.

¿ Te gustan los árboles?   = Do you like trees?

Four yous — you should see a therapist about that...

This stuff is really worth learning. If you skip it, you'll end up with sentences like: "Harry went to the pet shop and Harry saw a dog and Harry liked the dog so Harry bought the dog" — not ideal.

More on Pronouns

Sometimes you'll need the pronouns on the first bit of this page — they can be a bit confusing, so learn them.

Special words for me, you, him, her...

There are some pronouns that change when they come after a preposition like 'a' (to), 'para' (for), or 'sobre' / 'de' (about):

El regalo no es para ti *, es para* ella *.*

= The present isn't for you, it's for her.

PREPOSITIONAL PRONOUNS			
me:	mí	us:	nosotros/as
you (informal singular):	ti	you (informal plural):	vosotros/as
him/it:	él	them (masc. or mixed):	ellos
her/it:	ella	them (all feminine):	ellas
you (formal singular):	usted	you (formal plural):	ustedes

'With me' and 'with you' (familiar singular) have their own special words: with me: conmigo with you: contigo

The personal 'a'

You need to put an extra 'a' in before the word for any human being after every single verb except 'tener'. It sounds confusing but it isn't:

Estoy buscando a *Juan.*   = I'm looking for Juan.   BUT   *Estoy buscando un taxi.*   = I'm looking for a taxi.

Que — that, which, who

'Que' is a special kind of pronoun (a relative pronoun). It can mean 'which', 'who', or 'that'.

Fui a Menorca, que *es una isla preciosa.*   = I went to Menorca, which is a lovely island.

For ideas rather than objects, Spanish speakers use 'lo que' and for people after prepositions they'd use 'quien'. You only need to recognise these two though, so don't lose sleep over them.

Van a venir, lo que *es maravilloso.*   = They're going to come, which is wonderful.

el hombre a quien *vimos*   = the man whom we saw

Pronoun order can change

1) Pronouns usually go before the verb — though you might see them on the end of an infinitive or a present participle:

   Estamos mirándolo.   = We're watching it.

   ...and they always go after commands: *Deme su pasaporte.*   = Give me your passport.

2) Whenever there are two object pronouns in the same sentence, the indirect ones always go first:

   Te la enviaré.   = I'll send it to you.   *Me los da.*   = He gives them to me.

3) 'Le' and 'les' change to 'se' when they come before lo, la, los or las.

   Se lo regalé.   = I gave it to him / her / them / you.

A's back — and this time it's personal...

There's loads of lovely stuff to learn on this page. Have fun learning it all.

This & That, Something & Someone

This page is about <u>pointing things out</u>, and generally making it clear <u>which</u> thing you're on about.

How to say this, that or that over there

Use 'este', etc. for saying things like '<u>this man</u>', '<u>these apples</u>'
(when you're using 'this' as a <u>describing</u> word).

	Masculine singular	Feminine singular		Masculine plural	Feminine plural
THIS	este	esta	**THESE**	estos	estas
THAT	ese	esa	**THOSE**	esos	esas
THAT (further away)	aquel	aquella	**THOSE** (further away)	aquellos	aquellas

este pájaro	aquella casa	estas manzanas	esos bolis
= <u>this</u> bird	= <u>that</u> house	= <u>these</u> apples	= <u>those</u> pens

Use the neuter when you're <u>not</u> talking about a <u>particular thing</u>:

¿Qué es esto? = What's <u>this</u>?   ¡Eso es! = <u>That</u>'s it!

	Neuter
THIS	esto
THAT	eso / aquello

It's different when you use 'this' or 'these' as a noun

When you say things like '<u>this</u> is mine', you're using 'this' as a <u>noun</u>. That means you need to <u>stick an accent</u> on the 'this' word: e.g. <u>éstos</u>, <u>ése</u>, etc.

Tengo dos perros: éste es simpático, pero ése es malo.

= I've got two dogs: <u>this one here</u> is nice, but <u>that one</u> is nasty.

Aquella casa es más grande que ésta. = <u>That</u> house <u>over there</u> is bigger than <u>this one</u>.

Algo — Something   Alguien — Someone

There's nothing particularly special about these, you just need to be able to <u>understand</u> and <u>use</u> them:

Hay algo en mi bolso.

= There's <u>something</u> in my bag.

¿Quiere algo?

= Do you want <u>something</u>?

Buscan a alguien con el pelo largo.

See p. 92 for more on the personal 'a'.

= They're looking for <u>someone</u> with long hair.

Alguien ha llevado el dinero.   = <u>Someone</u> has taken the money.

So, what are you studying? Oh, this and that...

This stuff isn't too hard — as long as you're absolutely one hundred percent <u>sure</u> you've got it clear. Remember — '<u>este</u>', '<u>esa</u>' and the others <u>always</u> go with another word, like '<u>este hombre</u>'. If they're <u>on their own</u>, they must have <u>accents</u> ('<u>éste</u>', '<u>ésa</u>', etc.) — <u>don't</u> forget 'em.

VERBS, TENSES AND THE INFINITIVE	# The Lowdown on Verbs

Oh boy — you just <u>can't</u> get away from this stuff, I'm afraid.
But think about this — if you <u>learn it now</u>, it'll make the <u>whole</u> of Spanish GCSE easier...

Verbs <u>are</u> action words — they tell you <u>what's going on</u>

Ethel [plays] football every Saturday.

These are <u>verbs</u>.

Alex [wished] his grandma [preferred] knitting.

And so is this.

There's a <u>load</u> of stuff you need to know about verbs, but it all boils down to these <u>two things</u>...

1) The verb is different for <u>different times</u>

You say things differently if they happened <u>last week</u>, or aren't going to happen till <u>tomorrow</u>.

HAS ALREADY HAPPENED
I went to Tibet last year.
I have been to Tibet.
I had been to Tibet.
I used to go to Tibet.

PAST

HAPPENING NOW
I go to Tibet.
I am going to Tibet.

PRESENT

HASN'T HAPPENED YET
I am going to Tibet on Monday.
I am going to go to Tibet.
I will go to Tibet.
I will be going to Tibet.

FUTURE

These are all different <u>tenses</u>, in case you're interested.

2) The verb is different for <u>different people</u>

You'd say 'he <u>plays</u>', but <u>never</u> 'I plays' — it'd be daft. The verb <u>changes</u> to fit the person.

HAPPENING TO ME
I am miserable.

HAPPENING TO YOU
You are miserable.

HAPPENING TO HER
She is miserable.

OK, you get the picture — verbs are dead important. You use them all the time, after all.

The <u>infinitive</u> means '<u>to...</u>'

When you look up a verb <u>in the dictionary</u>, this is what you get:
(to) give: dar
(to) go: ir

In Spanish, infinitives always end in 'r'.

Most of the time, you won't want the verb in its <u>raw state</u> — you'll have to <u>change</u> it so it's right for the <u>person</u> and <u>time</u> you're talking about.

BUT: if you want to use two verbs together, the <u>second one</u> usually needs to be <u>infinitive</u>.

Quiero [comer]. = I want <u>to eat</u>.

Preferimos [bailar]. = We prefer <u>to dance</u>.

So I guess you could call action films 'verb films'...

I'm not kidding — this is <u>mega-important</u> stuff. Over the next few pages I'll give you <u>loads of stuff</u> on verbs because there's loads you <u>need to know</u>. Some of it's easy, some of it's tricky — but if you <u>don't understand</u> the things on <u>this page</u> before you start, you'll have <u>no chance</u>.

Verbs in the Present Tense

Sadly, this is nothing to do with Christmas gifts — it's the easiest of the <u>verb forms</u> in Spanish. That <u>doesn't mean</u> you can skip it though — you've <u>still</u> got to get it <u>right</u>.

The <u>present tense is</u> <u>what's happening now</u>

You'll use it more than anything else, so it's <u>really important</u>.
It's all about sticking 'endings' onto something (the 'stem').

Example of Present Tense Stems			
Infinitive	hablar	comer	vivir
Stem	habl	com	viv

Formula for Present Tense Stems

stem = infinitive – last two letters

For the present tense, the 'stems' that you stick the endings onto are dead easy.

Endings for -ar verbs

To form the present tense of <u>regular</u> '-ar' verbs, add the following <u>endings</u> to the verb's <u>stem</u> — e.g.:

HABLAR = TO SPEAK

I speak:	habl**o**	*we* speak:	habl**amos**
you (informal singular) speak:	habl**as**	*you* (informal plural) speak:	habl**áis**
he / she / it speaks:	habl**a**	*they* speak:	habl**an**
you (formal singular) speak:	habl**a**	*you* (formal plural) speak:	habl**an**

See <u>p. 91</u> for when to use which form of '<u>you</u>'.

So if you want to say something like 'He <u>talks</u> a lot', it's dead easy:

1) Start by <u>knocking off</u> the '<u>ar</u>':
   habl~~ar~~

2) Then <u>add on</u> the <u>new ending</u>:
   habl◄ a

3) And — <u>ta da</u>... *Habla* mucho.
   = <u>He talks a lot.</u>

Endings for -er verbs

To form the present tense of <u>regular</u> '-er' verbs, add the following <u>endings</u> to the verb's <u>stem</u> — e.g.:

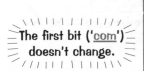
The first bit ('<u>com</u>') doesn't change.

COMER = TO EAT

I eat:	com**o**	*we* eat:	com**emos**
you (informal singular) eat:	com**es**	*you* (informal plural) eat:	com**éis**
he / she / it eats:	com**e**	*they* eat:	com**en**
you (formal singular) eat:	com**e**	*you* (formal plural) eat:	com**en**

Endings for -ir verbs

To form the present tense of <u>regular</u> '-ir' verbs, add the following <u>endings</u> to the verb's <u>stem</u> — e.g.:

<u>He</u>, <u>she</u>, <u>it</u> and <u>you</u> (usted) always have the <u>same</u> ending.

VIVIR = TO LIVE

I live:	viv**o**	*we* live:	viv**imos**
you (informal singular) live:	viv**es**	*you* (informal plural) live:	viv**ís**
he / she / it lives:	viv**e**	*they* live:	viv**en**
you (formal singular) live:	viv**e**	*you* (formal plural) live:	viv**en**

<u>They</u> and <u>you</u> (formal plural) always have the <u>same</u> ending.

Present tense — the gift that keeps on giving...

All you have to do is learn the endings for '<u>-ar</u>', '<u>-er</u>' & '<u>-ir</u>' verbs. They aren't too bad, really, because a lot of the '<u>-er</u>' and '<u>-ir</u>' endings are <u>the same</u>. <u>Learn</u> them all and <u>practise them</u>.

Verbs in the Present Tense

OK, on the last page you got the nice regular verbs. Now you get the horrible irregular ones. Enjoy.

Some Spanish Verbs are almost Irregular

1) Some verbs change their spelling in the present tense. These are called stem or radical changing verbs.
2) They change the 'e' in their stem to an 'ie' or the 'o' or 'u' to a 'ue'.
3) Stem changing verbs don't change in the 'nosotros' (we) and 'vosotros' (you — informal plural) forms.
4) The person endings are regular, even though the stem is irregular.

Example of 'e' to 'ie' verbs:

QUERER = TO WANT

I want	= quiero
you want	= quieres
he / she / it wants / you (formal singular) want	= quiere
we want	= queremos
you (informal plural) want	= queréis
they / you (formal plural) want	= quieren

INFINITIVE	'I' PERSON
cerrar (to close)	cierro
comenzar (to begin)	comienzo
empezar (to begin)	empiezo
pensar (to think)	pienso
preferir (to prefer)	prefiero
sentarse (to sit down)	me siento
sentir (to feel)	siento
tener (to have)	tengo (tú tienes)
venir (to come)	vengo (tú vienes)

These two are irregular in the 'I' part too.

Example of 'o' to 'ue' verbs:

PODER = TO BE ABLE TO

I can	= puedo
you can	= puedes
he / she / it / you (formal singular) can	= puede
we can	= podemos
you (informal plural) can	= podéis
they / you (formal plural) can	= pueden

INFINITIVE	'I' PERSON
almorzar (to have lunch)	almuerzo
costar (to cost)	cuesta (it costs)
doler (to hurt)	duele (it hurts)
dormir (to sleep)	duermo
jugar (to play)	juego
llover (to rain)	llueve (it rains)
morir (to die)	muero
volver (to return)	vuelvo
acostarse (to go to bed)	me acuesto

For more info on reflexive verbs see p. 104.

Some of the most Useful Verbs are totally Irregular

Here are three irregular verbs. They happen to be three of the most important Spanish verbs ever — typical.

SER = TO BE

I am	= soy
you are	= eres
he / she / it is / you (formal singular) are	= es
we are	= somos
you (informal plural) are	= sois
they / you (formal plural) are	= son

ESTAR = TO BE

I am	= estoy
you are	= estás
he / she / it is / you (formal singular) are	= está
we are	= estamos
you (informal plural) are	= estáis
they / you (formal plural) are	= están

There are two different verbs for 'to be' in Spanish. Weird or what? You can find out all about them on the next page.

IR = TO GO

I go	= voy	we go	= vamos
you go	= vas	you (informal plural) go	= vais
he / she / it goes / you (formal singular) go	= va	they / you (formal plural) go	= van

A secret blend of verbs makes this book taste great...

Irregular verbs might be a bit more difficult than regular ones, but they're still learnable.

'Ser' and 'Estar'

Here's where things get even more <u>complicated</u>. One verb for '<u>to be</u>' just isn't enough for Spanish speakers, so they've got <u>two</u> — the greedy things.

Ser and Estar both mean To Be

'<u>Ser</u>' and '<u>estar</u>' both mean '<u>to be</u>' in Spanish, but they're used <u>differently</u> — you <u>can't</u> just use whichever one you prefer.
It can be <u>difficult</u> to know which one to use when, but there are a few <u>rules</u> to help.

Use Ser for Permanent things

Use <u>ser</u> to talk about things that <u>don't change</u>.

1) <u>Nationalities</u>:

> *Somos españoles.*　　= <u>We are</u> Spanish.　　*Clare es de Escocia.*　　= Clare <u>is</u> from Scotland.

2) Saying <u>who</u> someone is (names, family relationships, etc.):

> *Ese chico es mi primo.*　　= That boy <u>is</u> my cousin.　　*Soy Julieta.*　　= <u>I'm</u> Julieta.

3) <u>Jobs</u>:

> *La señora Mitchell es profesora de español.*　　= Mrs Mitchell <u>is</u> a Spanish teacher.

4) <u>Physical characteristics</u>:

> *Mis ojos son verdes.*　　= My eyes <u>are</u> green.　　*Sois altos.*　　= <u>You (plural) are</u> tall.

5) <u>Personality</u>:

> *Eres muy inteligente.*　　*Mis hermanas son alegres.*

> = <u>You are</u> very intelligent.　　= My sisters <u>are</u> cheerful. (i.e. they are cheerful people)

Use Estar for Temporary things and Locations

Use <u>estar</u> to talk about things that are true <u>at the moment</u>, but might <u>change</u> in the future:

> *Está enfermo.*　　= <u>He is</u> ill.　　*Estás muy guapa.*　　= <u>You look</u> very beautiful.

> *Mi profesor está alegre hoy.*　　= My teacher <u>is</u> cheerful today (but he might not be tomorrow).

> 'Eres muy guapa' would mean 'you are (<u>always</u>) very beautiful'.

<u>Estar</u> is also used to say <u>where</u> someone or something is:

> *Madrid está en España.*　　= Madrid <u>is</u> in Spain.　　*Estamos en casa.*　　= <u>We are</u> at home.

"To be or to be" — that's the real question...

Yep, it's a bit of a <u>pain</u> having two ways of saying 'to be', but the difference is actually quite <u>straightforward</u> — use '<u>ser</u>' if it's <u>permanent</u> and '<u>estar</u>' if it's <u>temporary</u> or a <u>place</u>, and you won't go too far wrong. Just keep going over the <u>examples</u> on this page until it all becomes clear.

Talking About the Future

You'll need to talk about things that are <u>going to happen</u> at some point in the <u>future</u>.
There are <u>two ways</u> you can do it — and the first one's a <u>piece of cake</u>...

You can use 'I'm going to' to talk about the future

Saying you're <u>going to</u> do something is pretty much <u>the same</u> in Spanish as in English. You just need the bit
of '<u>ir</u>' (to go) that goes with the person you're talking about, then '<u>a</u>' and a verb in the <u>infinitive</u>. It's called
the <u>immediate future</u> tense, but you <u>don't</u> have to be talking about something that's about to happen.

> Immediate future tense = 'ir' in the present tense + a + infinitive

IR = TO GO

I am going	voy
you (inf. sing.) are going	vas
he / she / it is going	va
you (form. sing.) are going	va
we are going	vamos
you (inf. plu.) are going	vais
they / you (form. plu.) are going	van

Ella **va a leer** un libro. = She <u>is going to read</u> a book.

El sábado, **vamos a ir** a Francia.

= On Saturday, <u>we are going to go</u> to France.

Put in phrases to say when you're
going to do it (see p. 2–3).

You need to recognise the Proper Future Tense too

Spanish speakers use the proper future tense to say '<u>I will</u> do something' rather than '<u>I'm going to</u> do it'.
The future endings are the <u>same</u> for all verbs so you'll be able to spot them a mile away...

FUTURE TENSE ENDINGS

I:	**-é**	we:	**-emos**
you (informal):	**-ás**	you (inf. plu.):	**-éis**
he / she / it / you (form. sing.):	**-á**	they / you (form. plu.):	**-án**

These endings go on the end of a '<u>stem</u>'. The 'stem' is pretty easy too —
it's usually just the <u>infinitive</u> (p. 94):

Jugaré al tenis. = <u>I will play</u> tennis. *Dormirás*. = <u>You will sleep</u>.

Cogerá el autobús. = <u>He will take</u> the bus. *Venderemos* el perro. = <u>We will sell</u> the dog.

There are a few <u>sneaky</u> ones that don't follow
the pattern. And, surprise surprise, they're
some of the really <u>common</u> ones:

VERB	'I' PERSON	VERB	'I' PERSON	VERB	'I' PERSON
decir	diré	poner	pondré	salir	saldré
haber	habré	querer	querré	poder	podré
hacer	haré	saber	sabré		
tener	tendré	venir	vendré		

Look into my crystal ball...

OK, so the top one's easier, because you only have to <u>learn the words</u> for <u>times in the future</u> and
bung them in a sentence. The <u>proper future tense</u> is harder — but at least you don't need to
actually use it. Make sure you <u>understand</u>, in case it crops up in your <u>reading</u> or <u>listening</u> papers.

Conditional

Now it's time to talk about what <u>you would like to happen</u> in the future.

Use 'gustar' to say you like something

In the <u>present tense</u>, if you want to say that you like one thing you say '<u>me gusta</u>'.
If you like more than one thing you say '<u>me gustan</u>'.

Me gusta la casa. = I like the house.   *Me gustan las flores.* = I like the flowers.

Or someone might ask you a question:

¿Te gusta comer queso?   *¿Te gustan mis gafas?*

= Do you like eating cheese?   = Do you like my glasses?

For more on using '<u>gustar</u>' with negatives and other words, see page 7.

The Conditional — What would you like?

The <u>conditional</u> is for saying what '<u>would</u>' happen.
You only need to use it to say what you <u>would like</u>, so it's easy peasy.

So, instead of saying '<u>I like</u>' something, you need to say '<u>I would like</u>' something.
It's handy if you're talking about your <u>future hopes</u> and <u>dreams</u> or if you want to be a bit more <u>polite</u>.
It works in the same way as the present tense — the only part of the verb that changes is the <u>ending</u>:

GUSTAR

I like:	Me gusta(n)	*I would like:*	Me gust**aría(n)**
you (inf.sing.) like:	Te gusta(n)	*you (inf.sing.) would like:*	Te gust**aría(n)**
he/she likes:	Le gusta(n)	*he/she would like:*	Le gust**aría(n)**
you (form.sing.) like:	Le gusta(n)	*you (form.sing.) would like:*	Le gust**aría(n)**
we like:	Nos gusta(n)	*we would like:*	Nos gust**aría(n)**
you (inf.plu.) like:	Os gusta(n)	*you (inf.plu.) would like:*	Os gust**aría(n)**
they like:	Les gusta(n)	*they would like:*	Les gust**aría(n)**
you (form.plu.) like:	Les gusta(n)	*you (form.plu.) would like:*	Les gust**aría(n)**

Remember to <u>add</u> the '<u>n</u>' if you're saying someone would like <u>more than one thing</u>.

You might hear it in a restaurant or use it in a shop to sound <u>more polite</u>.
The '<u>gustar</u>' part has to agree with the thing you want so watch out for those <u>endings</u>.

Me gustaría una botella de agua, por favor. = <u>I would like</u> a bottle of water, please.

¿Te gustarían estas manzanas? = <u>Would you like</u> these apples?

If it's used with another <u>verb</u> (which it often is in the conditional tense), it's always <u>singular</u>.

Me gustaría ser profesor(a). = <u>I would like</u> to be a teacher.

¿Te gustaría ir al parque? = <u>Would you like</u> to go to the park?

Shampoo and conditional — for softer, silkier verbs...

You only need to use the conditional with '<u>gustar</u>' so there's no excuse for getting it wrong.

PERFECT TENSE — Talking About the Past

Uh oh, it's the first of several past tenses now. The main thing is you need to make sure you can tell it apart from the <u>future</u> (p. 98) and the <u>present</u> (p. 95) tenses. You don't want to be stuck not knowing whether something has happened, is happening or is going to happen.

¿Qué has hecho? — What have you done?

You have to be able to make and <u>understand</u> sentences like this:

There are <u>two</u> important bits.

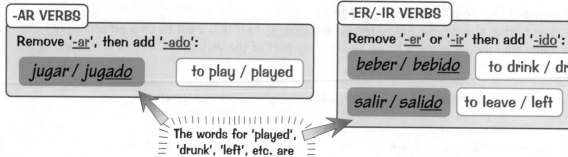

He | jugado | al tenis.   = I have played tennis.

This is the <u>Perfect Tense</u>.

1) You always need a bit to mean '<u>I have</u>' — see the next page.

2) This bit means '<u>played</u>'. It's a <u>special version</u> of 'jugar' (to play). In English, most of these words end in '-ed'. They're called <u>past participles</u>. See below for how to <u>form</u> the past participle.

Jugado = played: special past tense words

Learn the <u>patterns</u> for making the special past tense words like 'jugado' (played).

-AR VERBS

Remove '<u>-ar</u>', then add '<u>-ado</u>':

jugar / jug<u>ado</u> | to play / played

-ER/-IR VERBS

Remove '<u>-er</u>' or '<u>-ir</u>' then add '<u>-ido</u>':

beber / beb<u>ido</u> | to drink / drunk

salir / sal<u>ido</u> | to leave / left

The words for 'played', 'drunk', 'left', etc. are the <u>past participles</u>.

Some verbs <u>don't</u> follow the patterns. It's dead annoying, because a lot of the <u>most useful</u> verbs are <u>irregular</u> — you just have to <u>learn</u> them off <u>by heart</u>:

Verb	Past tense version (past participle)	English
abrir:	abierto	*opened*
decir:	dicho	*said*
escribir:	escrito	*written*
hacer:	hecho	*done / made*
poner:	puesto	*put*
romper:	roto	*broken*
ver:	visto	*seen*

That's all perfectly clear...

OK, this page isn't easy — no sireee. But it's dead important — in the exams, you'll need to <u>talk</u> <u>or write</u> about something that's <u>happened in the past</u> if you want a top grade. Scribble down the table of <u>past participles</u> and <u>learn</u> it really well — they'll come in handy for <u>other verb forms</u> too.

Talking About the Past

Now that you can form past participles, you can use them to say what you <u>have done</u>.

He hecho — I have **done**

You use the perfect tense to say <u>you have done</u> something. You need the present tense of '<u>haber</u>' to make up the 'have' part and the <u>past participle</u> to say what it is you've done.

> Perfect tense = present tense of 'haber' + past participle

The <u>past participle</u> (like 'jugado' or 'hecho') <u>always</u> stays the <u>same</u> — you <u>don't</u> need to make it feminine or plural. Only the '<u>haber</u>' part <u>changes</u> depending on who's doing the action.

HABER = TO HAVE...

I have...	he
you (inf. sing.) have...	has
he / she / it has...	ha
you (form. sing.) have...	ha
we have...	hemos
you (inf. plu.) have...	habéis
they / you (form. plu.) have...	han

He *ido al cine.* = <u>I have</u> been to the cinema.

Han *jugado al tenis.* = <u>They have</u> played tennis.

¿ **Has** *roto el vaso?* = <u>Have you</u> broken the glass?

Hemos *visto el programa en la televisión.* = <u>We have</u> seen the programme on the television.

Using <u>negative words</u> with the perfect tense <u>shouldn't</u> cause you too much trouble — just make sure you don't <u>separate</u> the part of haber and the past participle (see <u>p. 105</u> for more on negatives).

<u>No</u> *he tocado <u>nunca</u> el piano.* = I have never played the piano.

<u>No</u> *ha comido <u>nada</u>.* = He hasn't eaten anything.

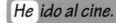

Working out <u>pronouns</u> with the perfect tense is a piece of cake...they always go <u>before</u> the part of haber.

<u>Lo</u> *he comprado.* = I have bought it.

<u>Me</u> *han dado la carta.* = They have given me the letter.

For more on object <u>pronouns</u>, have a look at <u>page 91</u>.

The perfect tense — you can't get better than that...

The <u>perfect</u> tense is really handy for talking about the past, and it's pretty <u>straightforward</u> once you get the hang of all those pesky <u>irregular past participles</u>. Then make sure you learn the <u>present</u> form of '<u>haber</u>' really well, and soon there'll be no stopping you. Perfect, you could say.

PRETERITE	# Another Past Tense: 'Did'

The <u>preterite tense</u> (<u>I went</u>, etc.) is the most useful tense for talking about what happened in the past, but, guess what, it's the one with the most irregular bits. Make sure you learn this page <u>carefully</u> — you'll <u>need it</u>.

¿Qué hiciste después? — _What did you do next?_

This means '<u>I did</u>', rather than 'I have done' — knock the <u>-ar</u>, <u>-er</u> or <u>-ir</u> off the infinitive, and add these <u>endings</u>:

PRETERITE ENDINGS FOR '-AR' VERBS			
_I_	**-é**	_we_	**-amos**
you (inf. singular)	**-aste**	_you_ (inf. plural)	**-asteis**
he / she / it /		_they /_	
you (form. singular)	**-ó**	_you_ (form. plural)	**-aron**

PRETERITE ENDINGS FOR '-ER'/'-IR' VERBS			
_I_	**-í**	_we_	**-imos**
you (inf. singular)	**-iste**	_you_ (inf. plural)	**-isteis**
he / she / it /		_they /_	
you (form. singular)	**-ió**	_you_ (form. plural)	**-ieron**

Pasó _toda la vida aquí._   = <u>He spent</u> all his life here.

Nací _en Portsmouth._   = <u>I was born</u> in Portsmouth.

Bailamos _hasta medianoche._   = <u>We danced</u> until midnight.

The <u>accents</u> are really important. They can <u>change the meaning</u> of words:

Hablo _con Susana._   = <u>I speak</u> to Susana.

Habló _con Susana._   = <u>He spoke</u> to Susana.

There are four _vital irregular verbs_ in the _preterite_

Typical — the words you'll need <u>most often</u> are the irregular ones. Make sure you get them <u>learnt</u>:

Ser — to be / Ir — to go (they have the same preterite)			
I was	fui	_we were_	fuimos
you (inf.) _were_	fuiste	_you_ (inf.) _were_	fuisteis
he / she / it was /		_they /_	
you (form.) _were_	fue	_you_ (form.) _were_	fueron

Estar — to be			
I was	estuve	_we were_	estuvimos
you (inf.) _were_	estuviste	_you_ (inf.) _were_	estuvisteis
he / she / it was /		_they /_	
you (form.) _were_	estuvo	_you_ (form.) _were_	estuvieron

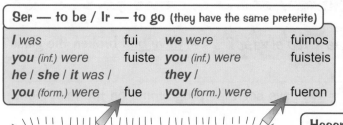

These Spanish words can also mean '<u>I went</u>', '<u>you went</u>', '<u>he went</u>' etc. — you can tell whether it's '<u>ir</u>' or '<u>ser</u>' by the <u>context</u>.

Hacer — to do or make			
I did / made	hice	_we did / made_	hicimos
you (inf.) _did / made_	hiciste	_you_ (inf.) _did / made_	hicisteis
he / she / it /		_they /_	
you (form.) _did / made_	hizo	_you_ (form.) _did / made_	hicieron

Here are some other common <u>irregular</u> ones that change their <u>stem</u> in the preterite:

Infinitives	yo	él/ella/usted
dar	di	dio
decir	dije	dijo
poder	pude	pudo
poner	puse	puso
querer	quise	quiso
tener	tuve	tuvo
traer	traje	trajo
venir	vine	vino

_No_ **vino** _al cine._   = <u>He didn't come</u> to the cinema.

Dijiste que **te gustó** .   = <u>You said</u> that <u>you liked it</u>.

¿Adónde **fuiste?**   = Where <u>did you go</u>?

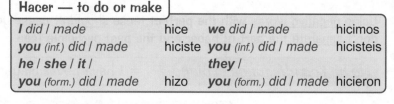

Hang on a second — I thought 'vino' was wine...

Yes, the word for 'he / she / it came' is exactly <u>the same</u> as the one for '<u>wine</u>' in Spanish. It's a bit weird if you ask me, but at least it might help you <u>remember</u> the irregular preterite of 'venir'.

'Was Doing' and 'Had Done'

There's two past tenses for the price of one on this page — you lucky thing.
For most of this stuff you only need to know it, <u>not</u> use it, so don't worry.

What you <u>were doing</u> or <u>used to do</u>

The imperfect is for <u>old past habits</u> (things you used to do regularly), <u>describing</u> things in the past and talking about <u>unfinished actions</u>. You can spot the imperfect tense a mile away by looking at those <u>endings</u>. They're stuck onto the 'stem' (the infinitive without the -ar, -er or -ir).

Imperfect Tense Endings for '<u>-ar</u>' verbs			
I	-aba	*we*	-ábamos
you (inf. sing.)	-abas	*you (inf. plu.)*	-abais
he / she / it / you (form. sing.)	-aba	*they / you (form. plu.)*	-aban

Imperfect Tense Endings for '<u>-er</u>' / '<u>-ir</u>' verbs			
I	-ía	*we:*	-íamos
you (inf. sing.)	-ías	*you (inf. plu.)*	-íais
he / she / it / you (form. sing.)	-ía	*they / you (form. plu.)*	-ían

Only 3 verbs don't follow the pattern — <u>ser</u>, <u>ir</u>, and <u>ver</u>. If you see '<u>había</u>', that means '<u>there was</u>' or '<u>there were</u>'.

Ir = to go	
I	iba
you	ibas
he / she / it	iba
you (form. sing.)	iba
we	íbamos
you (inf. plu.)	ibais
they / you (form. plu.)	iban

Ser = to be	
I	era
you (inf. sing.)	eras
he / she / it	era
you (form. sing.)	era
we	éramos
you (inf. plu.)	erais
they / you (form. plu.)	eran

Mi padre era médico.

= My father <u>was / used to be</u> a doctor.

The <u>only</u> time you'll actually have to <u>use</u> the imperfect is to talk about the <u>weather</u> in the past.

Hacía frío.   = <u>It was</u> cold.

Estaba lluvioso.   = <u>It was</u> rainy.

There are more <u>weather phrases</u> on page 54.

Había hecho — I had <u>done</u>

1) It's <u>similar</u> to the perfect tense (see p. 100-101), but it's for what you <u>had</u> done, not what you <u>have</u> done.
2) It's still made of a bit of <u>haber</u> and a <u>past participle</u>, but the bit of <u>haber</u> is in the <u>imperfect tense</u>.

> Pluperfect tense = imperfect tense of 'haber' + past participle

IMPERFECT OF HABER	
I had...	había
you (inf. sing.) had...	habías
he / she / it had...	había
you (form. sing.) had...	había
we had...	habíamos
you (inf. plu.) had...	habíais
they / you (form. plu.) had...	habían

Habían comprado una casa.

= <u>They had bought</u> a house.

Sue había llegado.   = Sue <u>had arrived</u>.

Don't worry too much about the <u>pluperfect tense</u> — you don't need to be able to use it in the exam. You do need to <u>recognise</u> it though, so make sure you know what it <u>looks</u> and <u>sounds</u> like.

The imperfect and pluperfect — they're in-tense...

Don't be put off by all this — these tenses actually aren't too <u>tricky</u> and they're <u>easy</u> to spot.

REFLEXIVE VERBS

REFLEXIVE VERBS — Myself, Yourself, etc.

Sometimes you'll have to talk about things you do to <u>yourself</u> — like 'washing yourself' or 'getting yourself up' in the morning. It sounds weird in English, but in Spanish they do it <u>all the time</u>.

Talking about yourself — me, te, se...

'<u>Se</u>' means '<u>oneself</u>'. Here are all the different ways to say 'self':

myself:	me	yourself (form. sing):	se
yourself (inf.):	te	ourselves:	nos
himself:	se	yourselves (inf. plu.):	os
herself:	se	themselves, each other:	se
oneself:	se	yourselves (form. plu.):	se

You can tell <u>which</u> verbs need 'self' by checking in the <u>dictionary</u> — they always end in '<u>se</u>', e.g. if you look up '<u>to get washed</u>', it'll say '<u>lavarse</u>'.

Reflexive verbs are really useful for talking about <u>daily routine</u> stuff... getting up, getting washed, etc. All you've got to do is <u>learn</u> the pattern — e.g. 'lavarse' = to get washed (literally 'to wash oneself'):

I get washed:	**me** lavo	we get washed:	**nos** lavamos
you get washed (informal singular):	**te** lavas	you get washed (informal plural):	**os** laváis
he / she / it gets washed:	**se** lava	they get washed:	**se** lavan
you get washed (formal singular):	**se** lava	you get washed (formal plural):	**se** lavan

There are lots of these verbs, but here are the ones you <u>should know</u>:

IMPORTANT REFLEXIVE VERBS			
to go to bed:	acostarse	to wake up:	despertarse
to get up:	levantarse	to go away:	irse
to feel:	sentirse	to get dressed:	vestirse
to be called:	llamarse		

Me despierto temprano.

= <u>I wake up</u> early.

¿*Te sientes* mal? = <u>Do you feel</u> ill?

¿Se habla español aquí? — Is Spanish spoken here?

You can talk about people in general by using '<u>se</u>' followed by the '<u>he/she/it</u>' part of the verb — this means '<u>one does</u>' something rather than talking about a specific person.

¿ *Se puede* comer aquí? = <u>Can one</u> eat here?

Se dice que es verdad. = <u>They say</u> (that) it's true.

It literally means '<u>one says</u>' but we'd say '<u>they say</u>' in English.

Se necesita estudiar más. = <u>They need</u> to study more.

This uses '<u>se</u>' because it's about people <u>in general</u> — it's not talking about one <u>specific</u> person.

Talk about myself — don't mind if I do...

There's <u>loads</u> to learn on this page, but it's all incredibly <u>useful</u>, so make sure you learn <u>everything</u>.

How to say 'No', 'Not' & 'Nobody' | NEGATIVES

You need to know how to say 'no' and 'not' and things in Spanish. You'd be in big trouble if a Mexican knife thrower asked you to be his assistant and you could only say yes...

Use 'no' to say not

In English you change a sentence to mean the opposite by adding 'not', e.g. 'I am Bob' ⟹ 'I am not Bob'. In Spanish, you have to put 'no' in front of the action word (verb).

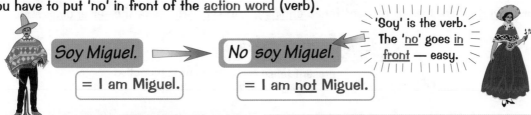

'Soy' is the verb. The 'no' goes in front — easy.

Soy Miguel. ⟹ No soy Miguel.

= I am Miguel.　　= I am not Miguel.

You do the same with all the tenses:

No voy a leer el periódico. 　= I'm not going to read the newspaper.

No fuimos al parque. 　= We did not go to the park.

No harán sus deberes. 　= They will not do their homework.

Ella no ha llegado. 　= She has not arrived.

No, I don't...

'No' in Spanish means both 'no' and 'not', so if you're answering a question, you may need to say 'no' twice:

No, no quiero pulpo, gracias. 　= No, I don't want any octopus, thanks.

No, prefiero no ver la película. 　= No, I'd prefer not to see the film.

Even more negatives...

There are more negatives you need to understand, and for top marks you should use them too.

not any more:	ya no
not anybody (nobody):	no ... nadie
not ever (never):	no ... nunca
not anything (nothing):	no ... nada
neither ... nor:	no ... ni ... ni
not any, not one:	no ... ningún/ninguna

Ya no voy a York. 　= I don't go to York any more.

No voy nunca a York. 　= I never go to York.

No voy ni a York ni a Belfast. 　= I don't go to York or to Belfast.

No hay nadie aquí. 　= There isn't anybody here.

Aquí no hay nada. 　= There isn't anything here.

No hay ningún plátano. 　= There aren't any bananas.

Just say no — and nobody and nothing and never...

Good news — it's nowhere near as bad as it looks. It seems confusing because you need 'no' with everything — but it actually makes life a lot easier when you're trying to spot negative sentences. Have a go at writing sentences using all the negative phrases here — it's the best way to learn 'em.

Subjunctive

OK, I won't lie...this stuff is a bit tricky but you're almost at the end of the grammar section. Hooray.

Present subjunctive phrases use different endings

You'll be able to spot the present subjunctive endings because they use the opposite endings from the normal present tense, stuck onto the end of the 'I' form stem of the present tense.

So, -er or -ir verbs take the -ar present tense endings, and -ar verbs take the -er endings:

$$decir \Rightarrow digo \Rightarrow diga$$

infinitive $\Rightarrow$ present tense 'I' part $\Rightarrow$ present subjunctive 'I' part

The present subjunctive is used in some set phrases

The present subjunctive isn't a new tense — it's just a different version of the present tense. It's pretty complicated but luckily you only need to understand it in a few special situations. Watch out for the present subjunctive:

(1) For some exclamations of future hope:

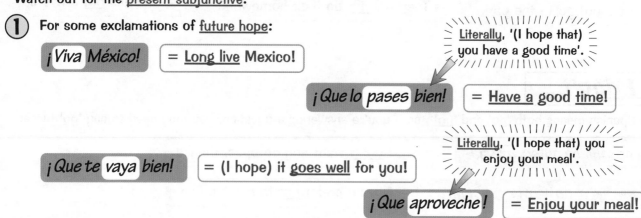

¡Viva México! = Long live Mexico!

¡Que lo pases bien! = Have a good time!

Literally, '(I hope that) you have a good time'.

¡Que te vaya bien! = (I hope) it goes well for you!

Literally, '(I hope that) you enjoy your meal'.

¡Que aproveche! = Enjoy your meal!

(2) In some set expressions that use commands:

Some commands use the same form as the present subjunctive so you'll come across it there too. See p. 107 for more on commands.

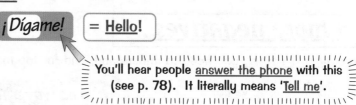

¡Dígame! = Hello!

You'll hear people answer the phone with this (see p. 78). It literally means 'Tell me'.

Quisiera — I would like

'Quisiera' is the imperfect subjunctive of 'querer' — it's used loads in Spanish to say 'I would like' in polite situations, like in a restaurant or asking for something in a shop.

Quisiera más pan, por favor. = I'd like more bread please.

You can use it with verbs to talk about what you'd like to do in the future too:

Quisiera ir a la playa mañana. = I'd like to go to the beach tomorrow.

My mum always says 'I want' never gets...

Shame. Oh well — there's only one thing for it and that's to learn everything on the page.

Ordering People Around

Of course you need this stuff — otherwise people will never do what you tell them to...

You need this stuff for bossing people about

Luckily, the singular informal (tú) bit is <u>dead easy</u>. It's just the same as the 'tú' part of the normal <u>present tense</u>, but <u>without</u> the '<u>s</u>' at the end.

hablas = you speak   *bebes* = you drink   *escribes* = you write.   *¡Escucha esto!*

¡Habla! = Speak!   *¡Bebe!* = Drink!   *¡Escribe!* = Write!   = <u>Listen</u> to this!

There are a few <u>common</u> <u>irregular</u> ones:

decir	hacer	ir	oír	poner	salir	tener	venir
di	haz	ve	oye	pon	sal	ten	ven

To tell <u>several people</u> what to do in an <u>informal</u> way, take the <u>infinitive</u> and <u>change</u> the final '<u>r</u>' to a '<u>d</u>'.

hablar ⟹ *¡Hablad!*   *salir* ⟹ *¡Salid!*   *hacer* ⟹ *¡Haced!*   *escribir* ⟹ *¡Escribid!*   *beber* ⟹ *¡Bebed!*

¡Terminad los deberes! = <u>Finish</u> your homework!

And for politely telling people what to do

To <u>politely</u> tell someone what to do, you use the <u>formal 'you'</u> part of the <u>present subjunctive</u> (see p. 106).

habla ⟹ *¡Hable!*   *escribe* ⟹ *¡Escriba!*

come ⟹ *¡Coma!*   *entra* ⟹ *¡Entre!*

The main <u>exceptions</u> are:

dar	haber	ir	saber	ser
dé	haya	vaya	sepa	sea

Siga todo recto. (seguir ⟹ siga)   *Coja la primera calle a la derecha.* (coger ⟹ coja)

= <u>Continue</u> straight on.   = <u>Take</u> the first street on the right.

At least the <u>polite plural</u> is easy — just add an '<u>n</u>' as usual: *¡Hablen!*   *¡Coman!*   *¡Escriban!*   *¡Entren!*

Add 'no' for saying what not to do

For telling someone <u>not</u> to do something, you <u>always</u> use the <u>subjunctive</u> (see p. 106).

¡No escuches! = Don't listen!   *¡No salgas!* = Don't leave!

¡No hables! = Don't talk!   *¡No mires!* = Don't look!

You're not the boss of me...

Brilliant — now you can order absolutely <u>anyone</u> around in Spanish. This stuff is <u>dead handy</u>.

'SABER', 'CONOCER' AND 'PODER'	# 'Know' and 'Can'

Here are <u>three really useful verbs</u> that people are always getting <u>wrong</u> — make sure <u>you don't</u>.

'To know information' is 'Saber'

1) <u>Saber</u> means '<u>to know</u>', in the sense of knowing <u>information</u> (like what time the bus leaves).

Have a look at these examples:

Ella sabe la respuesta.	She knows the answer.
No sé si tenemos plátanos.	I don't know if we have any bananas.
¿Sabe usted cuándo llega el tren?	Do you know when the train arrives?

2) <u>Saber</u> followed by an <u>infinitive</u> means '<u>to know how to do something</u>', in the sense of a skill, e.g.:

Sabe esquiar. *No sabe leer.* *Sé conducir.*

= He/She knows how to ski. = He/She can't read. = I can drive.

IMPORTANT: '<u>saber</u>' is a regular verb, except for the '<u>I</u>' <u>person</u>, which is '<u>sé</u>'.

'To be familiar with' is 'Conocer'

Conocer means <u>to know</u> a person or place — to '<u>be familiar with</u>'.
If someone asks you if you know their mate Gertrude, this is the one to use.

Conozco la luna.

Conozco Madrid. = I know Madrid.

No conoce esta ciudad. = He/She doesn't know this town.

¿Conoces a mi amigo? = Do you know my friend?

IMPORTANT: like 'saber', '<u>conocer</u>' is also a <u>normal verb</u> with an <u>odd</u> '<u>I</u>' <u>person</u> = '<u>conozco</u>'.

You need the <u>personal 'a'</u> (see p. 92) when talking about knowing <u>people</u>.

'Poder' means 'to be able to'

Poder (<u>to be able to / can</u>) has three very important meanings:

1) Being <u>able</u> to do something (<u>not</u> knowing <u>how</u> to do it, but just being able to — like 'Yes, I can come tomorrow').

Si quieres, puedo llevar el equipaje. = I can carry the luggage if you like.

2) <u>Permission</u> to do something. *Se pueden sacar fotos aquí.* = You can take photos here.

3) <u>Possibility</u> — something <u>could</u> be the case. *Eso puede pasar.* = That can happen.

But can you can-can...

Three mega-handy verbs that you need to sort out. Don't forget the difference between <u>saber</u> and <u>conocer</u>, and make sure that you know the three meanings of <u>poder</u>. Wonderful stuff...

'How Long', '-ing' & 'Just Done'

Three more bits to learn — you may come across them in the listening or reading papers.

¿Cuánto tiempo hace que...? — How long...?

This is a handy phrase that Spanish speakers use to find out how long someone's been doing something. You'll hear or see it followed by a verb in the present tense.

| ¿Cuánto tiempo hace que aprendes español? | = How long have you been learning Spanish? |

This is how someone would answer the question:

| Aprendo español desde hace tres años. | = I've been learning Spanish for three years. |

Don't worry about using it, but make sure you know what it means.

Present participles say what you're doing right now

Most of the time you'd translate things like 'I am doing' with the present tense — 'hago'.

But sometimes Spanish speakers want to stress that something is happening at the moment. Then, they'll use the '-ing' form to show that they're in the middle of something:

e.g.:
| Estoy almorzando. | = I'm having my lunch. |

| Está leyendo un libro. | = He is reading a book. |

You'll easily recognise it because it's made up of two bits:

a) the correct part of 'estar' (to be) in the present, and

b) the special word for the 'ing' bit — called the present participle.

'-ar' verbs e.g. hablar	'-er' verbs e.g. comer	'-ir' verbs e.g. vivir
stem (e.g. habl) + ando	stem (e.g. com) + iendo	stem (e.g. viv) + iendo
hablando	comiendo	viviendo

There are only a few irregular ones you need to know:

caer ⟹ cayendo   leer ⟹ leyendo

servir ⟹ sirviendo   pedir ⟹ pidiendo

dormir ⟹ durmiendo   morir ⟹ muriendo

seguir ⟹ siguiendo

Acabo de... — 'I have just...'

To say what's just happened, use the present tense of 'acabar' + 'de' + the verb you want in the infinitive.

I:	acabo	we:	acabamos
you (inf.sing.):	acabas	you (inf.plu.):	acabáis
he / she / it / you (form.sing.):	acaba	they / you (form.plu.):	acaban

| Acabo de ducharme. | = I have just taken a shower. | Acaba de salir. | = She has just left. |

The end of grammar — you deserve a medal...

Phew. Just the revision questions on the next page to go now, and then you're done — hurray.

Revision Summary

Hurray! Hurray! It's the end of the book! Hurray! Hurray! Before you get too carried away, do all these lovely revision questions. You know the drill by now — do the questions without looking back at the pages, and if there are any you can't do, go back over those pages and revise them (or re-revise them, or re-re-revise them, or whatever) until you know it all forwards, backwards, standing on your head and doing cartwheels. One more time, here we go...

1) What are all the Spanish words for   a) a   b) the?
2) How do you say the following in Spanish?
   a) the big dog   b) the small cat   c) the small dogs   d) the black cats
3) What's the difference between these two phrases in Spanish?
   a) Pablo es un gran hombre.   b) Pablo es un hombre grande.
4) What do these endings do to adjectives?   a) ito   b) ísimo
5) How do you say these in Spanish?   a) my flower   b) his flower   c) our flower
6) Meg asks Ben "¿El perro es tuyo?", and he replies "No, mi perro está en la casa."
   Write out their conversation in English.
7) 'Tranquilo' means 'calm' in Spanish — how would you say 'calmly'?
8) How do you say 'I sing well' in Spanish? How about 'I sing very badly'?
9) How would you say these in Spanish?   a) Helen is the tallest   b) this dress is the best
10) How would you say 'the cheese is more expensive than the milk' in Spanish? How about 'the cheese is as expensive as the milk'?
11) What do these joining words mean?   a) o   b) porque   c) pero   d) si
12) What do these little words mean? a) de   b) sobre   c) a   d) en   e) detrás de
13) Give three situations where you would use 'por', and three where you would use 'para'.
14) 'Jane compra la falda' means 'Jane buys the skirt'. What does 'Jane la compra' mean?
15) How do you say 'Do you want to come with me?' in Spanish?
16) Say whether these sentences are right or wrong:
    a) Estoy buscando a una tienda.   b) Estoy buscando a mi hermano.
    c) Estoy buscando Susana.   d) Tengo dos hermanas.
17) How do you say 'this house' in Spanish? What about 'that house'?
    And 'that house over there'?
18) What does 'Alguien está en la casa' mean?
19) How do you say these in Spanish?   a) you live   b) he talks   c) we eat
20) What is the 'I' form of these verbs?   a) pensar   b) tener   c) sentarse   d) preferir
21) Write out two sentences with 'ser', and two with 'estar'.
22) What does 'Voy a ir a la playa' mean?
23) What's the past participle of these verbs?   a) abrir   b) hablar   c) tener   d) decir
24) What do these mean?   a) he ido   b) habéis ido   c) han ido   d) has ido
25) How do you say 'I ate a burger' in Spanish? How about 'he ate a burger'?
26) What do these mean?   a) tuvo   b) dijo   c) dieron   d) pusiste
27) What does 'Iba a la playa todos los veranos' mean in English?
28) 'Lavarse' is 'to get washed' in Spanish. How do you say 'I get washed'? What about 'they get washed'? And 'you (sing.) don't get washed'?
29) What do these mean?   a) ¡Que lo pases bien!   b) ¡Que aproveche!
30) How do you say 'Speak!' a) politely to one person b) informally to a group?
31) Translate these phrases: a) I know how to swim.   b) I know Jenny.   c) Can you repeat it?
32) What does 'estoy comiendo' mean?
33) What does 'acabo de llegar' mean?

Do Well in Your Exam

Here are some little gems of advice, whichever exam board you're studying for.

Read *the* Questions *carefully*

<u>Don't</u> go losing <u>easy marks</u> — it'll break my heart. Make sure you <u>definitely</u> do the things on this list in the <u>listening</u> and <u>reading exams</u>:

1) <u>Read all the instructions</u> properly.
2) <u>Read the question</u> properly.
3) <u>Answer the question</u> — don't waffle.
4) Use the time to <u>plan</u> your answers.

Don't *give up if you don't* Understand

If you don't understand, <u>don't panic</u>. The <u>key thing</u> to remember is that you can still <u>do well</u> in the exam, even if you <u>don't understand</u> every Spanish word that comes up. Look at the words and see if there are any that seem <u>familiar</u>:

If you're reading or listening — look for lookalikes

1) Some words <u>look</u> or <u>sound</u> the <u>same</u> in Spanish and English — they're called <u>cognates</u>.

2) These words are <u>great</u> because you'll recognise them when you see them in a text.

3) Be careful though — there are some <u>exceptions</u> you need to watch out for. Some words <u>look</u> like an English word but have a totally <u>different meaning</u>:

la nota:	*mark*	la ropa:	*clothes*	fatal:	*awful*
el pie:	*foot*	la librería:	*bookshop*	la sopa:	*soup*
el campo:	*countryside*	la dirección:	*address*	el éxito:	*success*

Words like these are called 'falsos amigos' — false friends.

Make use of the Context

You're likely to come across the odd word that you don't know, especially in the <u>reading exam</u>. Often you'll be able to find some <u>clues</u> telling you what the text is all about.

1) The <u>type of text</u>, e.g. newspaper article, advertisement, website
2) The <u>title</u> of the text
3) Any <u>pictures</u>
4) The <u>verbal context</u>

Say you see the following in the reading exam, and don't know what any of these words mean:

"...ropa hecha de poliéster , de lana , de cuero y de nylon ."

1) Well, the fact that this is a list of things, all starting with '<u>de</u>' coming after the Spanish word for 'clothes' suggests they're all <u>things</u> that <u>clothes</u> can be <u>made out of</u>.

2) You can guess that '<u>poliéster</u>' means '<u>polyester</u>', and '<u>nylon</u>' means '<u>nylon</u>'. Obviously.

3) So it's a pretty good guess that the two words you don't know are different types of <u>fabric</u>. (In fact, '<u>lana</u>' means '<u>wool</u>' and '<u>cuero</u>' means '<u>leather</u>'.)

4) Often the questions <u>won't</u> depend on you understanding these more difficult words. It's important to be able to understand the <u>gist</u> though, and not let these words <u>throw</u> you.

Exams are important — failing can be fatal...

Don't get caught out by words that <u>look</u> like English words, but in fact mean something <u>different</u>. Generally speaking, if a word <u>doesn't</u> seem to <u>fit</u> into the context of the question, have a <u>re-think</u>.

Do Well in Your Exam

These pages could <u>improve</u> your grade — they're all about exam technique. No learning in sight...

Look at how a word is made up

You may read or hear a sentence and not understand <u>how the sentence works</u>. You need to remember all the <u>grammary bits</u> in Section 7 to give you a good chance at <u>piecing it all together</u>.

1) A word that ends in '<u>-ado</u>' or '<u>-ido</u>' may well be a <u>past participle</u> (see p. 100).
Look for a bit of '<u>haber</u>' nearby to work out who's done what.

2) A word that ends in '<u>-ar</u>', '<u>-er</u>' or '<u>-ir</u>' might be an <u>infinitive</u>. If you take off the last two letters it might look like an English word, which may tell you what the verb means.

> e.g. 'confirmar' = to <u>confirm</u>

3) If you see '<u>-mente</u>' at the end of a word, it could well be an <u>adverb</u> (see p. 86).
Try replacing the '-mente' with '<u>-ly</u>' and see if it makes sense.

> e.g. 'especialmente' = <u>especially</u>

4) When a word ends in '<u>-dad</u>', it's often replaced with '<u>-ty</u>' in English.

> e.g. 'sociedad' = <u>society</u>

5) Don't forget to look at the <u>beginning</u> of the word too. There is sometimes a sneaky '<u>e-</u>' added to the start of a few nouns that begin with an '<u>s-</u>' in English.

> e.g. 'estéreo' = <u>stereo</u>   'estación' = <u>station</u>

6) '<u>In-</u>' or '<u>des-</u>' at the beginning of a word makes it negative.

> e.g. 'inútil' = '<u>in</u>+<u>útil</u>' = <u>useless</u>

Take notes in the listening exam

1) You'll have <u>5 minutes</u> at the start of the exam to have a <u>quick look</u> through the paper. This'll give you a chance to see <u>how many questions</u> there are, and you might get a few clues from the questions about what <u>topics</u> they're on, so it won't be a horrible surprise when the CD starts playing.

2) You'll hear each extract <u>twice</u>. Different people have different strategies, but it's a good idea to jot down a few details that you think might come up in the questions, especially things like:

> Dates
> Numbers
> Spelled-out names

3) But... don't forget to <u>keep listening</u> to the gist of the recording while you're making notes.

4) You won't have a <u>dictionary</u> — but you probably wouldn't have time to use it anyway.

Estop trying to escare me about estupid exams...

The examiners aren't above sticking a few tricky bits yond pieces into the exam to see how you <u>cope</u> with them. Using all your expert knowledge, you should stand a pretty good chance of working it out. And if you can't make an <u>educated</u> guess, make an <u>uneducated</u> guess... but try <u>something</u>.

How To Use Dictionaries

Don't go mad on dictionaries — it's the path to ruin. However, you're allowed to use one in the writing tasks and to prepare for the speaking task, so it's good idea to make the most of it.

Don't translate Word for Word — it DOESN'T work

If you turn each word of this phrase into English, you get rubbish.

Me gusta nadar. Me it pleases to swim.

NO!

I have finished. Tengo terminado.

It's the same the other way round — turn English into Spanish word by word, and you get balderdash — don't do it.

If it Doesn't make Sense, you've got it Wrong

Some words have several meanings — don't just pick the first one you see.
Look at the meanings listed and suss out which one is what you're looking for.

If you read this... Me duele el ojo derecho.

...you might look up 'derecho' and find this:

So the sentence could mean:

My straight eye hurts. ✗

My right eye hurts. ✔ ← This is the only one that sounds sensible.

My law eye hurts. ✗

derecho, a
adj straight; upright;
// right, right-hand
// adv straight // nm law; justice
tener derecho a hacer algo:
to have the right to do something
derecho de paso: right of way
// derechos; rights; taxes; duties

Verbs change according to the person

When you look up a verb in the dictionary, you'll find the infinitive (the 'to' form, like 'to run', 'to sing' etc.). But you may need to say 'I run', or 'we sing' — so you need to change the verb ending.

Say you need to say 'I buy'.

For the lowdown on verbs and all their different endings, see the grammar section.

1) If you looked up 'buy', you'd find the word 'comprar', meaning 'to buy'.
2) But 'comprar' is the infinitive — you can't put 'yo comprar'.
3) You need the 'I' (yo) form of the verb — 'compro'.
4) Check the tense too — e.g. you don't want 'compré' (I bought).

If you're looking up a Spanish verb, look for its infinitive (it'll end in 'ar', 'er' or 'ir'). If you want to know what 'tocamos' means, you'll find 'tocar' (to touch, or to play) in the dictionary. So 'tocamos' must mean 'we touch' or 'we play', depending on the context.

Dictionaries — useful for holding doors open...

Don't get put off dictionaries by this page. They're lovely really. Just make sure your writing technique isn't to look up every single word and then bung them down in order. Cos it'll be rubbish.

Hints for Writing

Here are a few <u>general hints</u> about how you should approach the writing tasks.

Write about what you <u>know</u>

1) You <u>won't</u> be asked to write about nineteenth century Spanish novelists.

2) You will <u>need</u> to cover certain specific things that the question asks you to, but there'll be plenty of scope to be <u>imaginative</u>.

3) Usually the writing tasks will give you some <u>flexibility</u> so you can base your answer on something you know about.

No sé nada...

You need to say <u>When</u> and <u>Why...</u>

1) Saying <u>when</u> and <u>how often</u> you did things gets you big bonus marks. Learn <u>times</u>, <u>dates</u> and <u>numbers</u> carefully (p. 1–3).

2) Make sure you talk about what you've done <u>in the past</u> (see p. 100–103) or what you're going to do <u>in the future</u> (p. 98).

3) Give <u>descriptions</u> where possible, but keep things <u>accurate</u> — a short description in <u>perfect Spanish</u> is better than a longer paragraph of nonsense.

4) Examiners also love <u>opinions</u> (p. 7–8). Try to <u>vary them</u> as much as possible.

So, if I add one more drop we'll go back in time two hours...

...two hours later...

...and <u>Where</u> and <u>Who With...</u>

Examiners really are quite nosy, and love as many details as you can give. It's a good idea to ask yourself all these 'wh-' questions, and write the bits that show your Spanish off in the <u>best light</u>. Also, it doesn't matter if what you're writing is strictly true or not — as long as it's <u>believable</u>.

Don't worry too much about the length — your teacher should tell you how much to write.

Use your dictionary, but <u>sparingly</u>

1) The time to use the dictionary is <u>NOT</u> to learn a completely new, fancy way of saying something.

2) Use it to look up a particular word that you've <u>forgotten</u> — a word that, when you see it, you'll <u>know</u> it's the right word.

3) Use it to check <u>genders</u> of nouns — that's whether words are <u>masculine</u> (el/un) or <u>feminine</u> (la/una).

4) Check any <u>spellings</u> you're unsure of.

> Most importantly, don't use the dictionary to <u>delve into the unknown</u>.
> If you don't <u>know</u> what you've written is <u>right</u>, it's <u>probably wrong</u>.

Take your <u>time</u>

1) Don't <u>hurtle</u> into writing about something and then realise half-way through that you don't actually know the Spanish for it.

2) <u>Plan</u> how you can cover all the things that the task mentions, and then think about the extra things you can slip in to show off your Spanish.

Take me.

And lastly, don't forget your pen...

I suppose the key is <u>variety</u> — lots of different <u>tenses</u>, plenty of meaty <u>vocabulary</u> and loads of <u>details</u>. This is your only chance to show what you can do, so don't waste all your <u>hard work</u>.

Hints for Writing

<u>Accuracy</u> is really important in the writing assessment. Without it, your work will look like <u>sloppy custard</u>.

Start with the Verb

1) Verbs really are the <u>cornerstone</u> of every Spanish sentence.
    If you get the verb right, the rest of the sentence should <u>fall into place</u>.

> Verbs are <u>doing words</u>.
> **See p. 94.**

2) Be careful that you get the <u>whole expression</u> that uses the verb, not just the verb itself.

> <u>EXAMPLE</u>: Say you want to write the following sentence in Spanish:
>
> *If I am in a hurry, I take the bus to school.*
>
> > Don't see 'I am' and jump in with 'ser' or 'estar'.
> > The expression for 'to be in a hurry' is 'tener prisa'.
>
> > You know that 'to take the bus' is 'coger el autobús'.
>
> Make sure your <u>tenses</u> and the <u>endings</u> of the verbs are right, then piece it all together:
>
> *Si tengo prisa, cojo el autobús para ir al instituto.*

Check and re-check

No matter how careful you think you're being, <u>mistakes</u> can easily creep into your work.

Go through the <u>check-list</u> below for every sentence <u>straight after</u> you've written it.

1) Are the verbs in the right <u>TENSE</u>?

    Ayer, <u>juego</u> al fútbol en el parque. ✖   Ayer, <u>jugué</u> al fútbol en el parque. ✓

2) Are the <u>ENDINGS</u> of the verbs right?

    Mi hermano no <u>quieren</u> salir. ✖   Mi hermano no <u>quiere</u> salir. ✓

3) Do your adjectives <u>AGREE</u> as they should?

    La profesora es <u>alto</u>. ✖   La profesora es <u>alta</u>. ✓

4) Do your reflexive verbs and pronouns <u>AGREE</u>?

    A las siete, <u>me levantamos</u>. ✖   A las siete, <u>me levanto</u>. ✓

5) Do your adjectives come in the <u>RIGHT PLACE</u>?

    Una <u>blanca</u> falda ✖   Una falda <u>blanca</u> ✓

6) Have you used <u>USTED/USTEDES</u> correctly?

    Señor, <u>puedes</u> ayudarme, por favor? ✖   Señor, <u>puede usted</u> ayudarme, por favor? ✓

Then when you've finished the whole piece of work, have <u>another</u> read through with <u>fresh eyes</u>.
You're bound to pick up one or two more mistakes.

Do nothing without a verb...

I know there's loads to remember, and Spanish verbs are a pain, but checking over your work is a real
<u>must</u>. Re-read your work <u>assuming there are errors</u> in it, rather than assuming it's fine as it is.

Hints for Speaking

The speaking assessment fills many a student with dread. Remember though — it's your chance to show what you can do. It won't be nearly as bad as you think it's going to be. Honest.

Be Imaginative

There are two tricky things about the speaking assessment — one is what to say, and two is how to say it. No matter how good your Spanish is, it won't shine through if you can't think of anything to say.

Say you're talking about your daily routine (or imagining someone else's daily routine). It would be easy to give a list of things you do when you get in from school:

> "Hago mis deberes. Veo la televisión. Como la cena. Me acuesto."

> = I do my homework. I watch television. I eat dinner. I go to bed.

It makes sense, but the problem is, it's all a bit samey...

1) Try to think of when this isn't the case, and put it into a DIFFERENT TENSE:

> "Normalmente hago mis deberes, pero mañana voy a jugar al hockey después del instituto."

> = Normally I do my homework, but tomorrow I'm going to play hockey after school.

2) Don't just talk about yourself. Talk about OTHER PEOPLE — even if you have to imagine them.

> "Vi la televisión con mi hermano, pero no nos gustan los mismos programas."

> = I watched television with my brother, but we don't like the same programmes.

3) Give loads of OPINIONS and REASONS for your opinions.

> "Me gusta hacer ejercicio antes de comer. Luego puedo relajarme más tarde."

> = I like to do exercise before eating. Then I can relax later on.

A couple of 'DON'T's...

1) DON'T try to avoid a topic if you find it difficult — that'll mean you won't get any marks at all for that bit of the assessment. You'll be surprised what you can muster up if you stay calm and concentrate on what you do know how to say.

2) DON'T make up a word in the hope that it exists in Spanish unless you're really, really stuck and you've tried all the other tricks on this page. If it's your last resort, it's worth a try.

Have Confidence

1) Believe it or not, your teacher isn't trying to catch you out. He or she wants you to do well, and wants to be dazzled by all the excellent Spanish you've learnt.

2) Speaking assessments can be pretty daunting. But remember it's the same for everyone.

3) Nothing horrendous is going to happen if you make a few slip-ups. Just try and focus on showing your teacher how much you've learnt.

Imagine there's no speaking assessment...

It's easy if you try. But that's not going to get you a GCSE. The main thing to remember is that it's much better to have too much to say than too little. Bear in mind the 3 ways to make your answers more imaginative. This will give you an opportunity to show off your beautiful Spanish.

Hints for Speaking

Nothing in life ever goes completely according to plan. So it's a good idea to prepare yourself for a few <u>hiccups</u> in the speaking assessment. (Nothing to do with glasses of water.)

Try to find another way of saying it

There may be a particular word or phrase that trips you up. There's always a <u>way round it</u> though.

1) If you can't <u>remember</u> a Spanish word, use an <u>alternative</u> word or try <u>describing it</u> instead.

2) For example, if you can't remember that '<u>grapes</u>' are '<u>las uvas</u>' and you really need to say it, then describe them as 'the small green or red fruits', or 'las frutas pequeñas que son verdes o rojas'.

3) You can <u>fib</u> to avoid words you can't remember — if you can't remember the word for '<u>dog</u>' then just say you've got a <u>cat</u> instead. Make sure what you're saying makes <u>sense</u> though — saying you've got a <u>pet radio</u> isn't going to get you any marks, trust me.

4) If you can't remember the word for '<u>bedroom</u>' (el dormitorio) in your speaking assessment, you could say a '<u>room</u>' (el cuarto) instead — you'll still make yourself <u>understood</u>.

If the worst comes to the worst, ask for help in Spanish

1) If you can't think of a way around it, you <u>can</u> ask for help in the speaking assessment — as long as you ask for it in <u>Spanish</u>.

2) If you can't remember what a chair is, ask your teacher; "¿Cómo se dice 'chair' en español?" It's <u>better</u> than wasting lots of time trying to think of the word.

You may just need to buy yourself some time

If you get a bit <u>stuck</u> for what to say, there's always a <u>way out</u>.

1) If you just need some <u>thinking time</u> in your speaking assessment or you want to check something, you can use these useful sentences to help you out:

Este...	*Um...*	¿Puede repetir, por favor?	*Can you repeat, please?*
Pues...	*Well...*	No entiendo.	*I don't understand.*
No estoy seguro/a.	*I'm not sure.*	Ésa es una buena pregunta.	*That's a good question.*

2) Another good tactic if you're a bit stuck is to say what you've <u>just said</u> in a <u>different way</u>. This shows off your <u>command of Spanish</u>, and also it might lead onto something else, e.g.:

Comemos juntos. *No como solo,* *excepto cuando mis padres trabajan hasta tarde.*

Saying the same thing a different way... leading on to another idea.

We eat together. <u>I don't eat on my own</u>, <u>except when my parents work late</u>.

And don't be afraid to make mistakes — even native Spanish speakers make 'em. Don't let a silly error shake your <u>concentration</u> for the rest of the assessment.

One last thing — don't panic...

Congratulations — you've made it to the end of the book. And without accident or injury, I hope — paper cuts hurt more than people think... Anyway, enough of this idle chit-chat. <u>Read</u> these pages, <u>take on board</u> the information, <u>use it</u> in your GCSE, <u>do well</u> and then <u>celebrate</u> in style.

A

a prep *at, to*
a diario ad *daily*
a eso de prep *at around*
a fines de prep *at the end of*
a la plancha a *grilled*
a mediados de prep *in the middle of*
a menudo ad *often*
a mitad de precio a *half-price*
a partir de prep *from*
a pesar de prep *in spite of*
a pie ad *on foot*
¿A qué hora? *What time?*
a tiempo ad *in time*
a tiempo completo a *full-time*
a tiempo parcial a *part-time*
a un paso (de) prep *a short distance (from)*
a veces ad *sometimes*
abajo ad *down, downstairs, below*
el abanico m *fan*
abierto a *open*
el/la abogado/a mf *lawyer*
el abrigo m *overcoat*
abril m *April*
abrir v *to open*
la abuela f *grandmother*
el abuelo m *grandfather*
aburrido a *bored, boring*
aburrirse vr *to be/get bored*
acabar v *to finish, end*
acabar de v *to have just… (done something)*
acampar v *to camp*
el acceso m *access, entrance*
el accidente m *accident*
el aceite m *oil*
la aceituna f *olive*
el acento m *accent*
aceptable a *acceptable*
aceptar v *to accept*
acoger v *to receive*
acompañar v *to accompany*
aconsejar v *to advise*
acordarse (de) vr *to remember*
acostarse vr *to go to bed*
la actividad f *activity*
activo a *active*
el actor m *actor*
la actriz f *actress*

actuar v *to act*
adelante ad *forward*
además ad *in addition*
adictivo a *addictive*
el adicto m *addict*
¡Adiós! interj *Goodbye!*
admirar v *to admire*
adolescente a *adolescent*
el adolescente m *teenager*
¿Adónde? ad *Where (to)?*
adoptar v *to adopt*
adoptivo a *adopted*
adorar v *to adore/worship*
la aduana f *customs*
el/la adulto/a mf *adult*
el aeropuerto m *airport*
afectar v *to affect*
la afición f *hobby*
el/la aficionado/a mf *fan*
afortunado a *lucky*
afuera (de) ad *outside*
las afueras fpl *outskirts*
la agencia de viajes f *travel agency*
agosto m *August*
agradable a *pleasant*
agradecer v *to thank*
agresivo a *aggressive*
el agua f *water*
el agua mineral (con/sin gas) f *mineral water (sparkling/still)*
el agujero m *hole*
ahí ad *there*
ahora ad *now*
ahorrar v *to save*
el aire m *air*
el aire acondicionado m *air conditioning*
aislado a *isolated*
el ajedrez m *chess*
el ajo m *garlic*
al aire libre a *outdoor*
al aparato interj *speaking (answering the telephone)*
al final (de) prep *in the end/at the end (of)*
al lado de prep *next to*
al mismo tiempo ad *at the same time*
el albergue juvenil m *youth hostel*
alcanzar v *to reach*
el/la alcohólico/a mf *alcoholic*
la aldea f *village/hamlet*
alegrarse vr *to be happy*
alegre a *happy*

alemán a *German*
el/la alemán/ana mf *German man/woman*
Alemania f *Germany*
la alfombra f *carpet*
algo pron *something*
el algodón m *cotton*
alguien pron *someone*
algunas veces ad *sometimes*
algún/alguno/alguna a *any*
el alimento m *food*
allá ad *there*
allí ad *there*
el alojamiento m *accommodation*
alojarse vr *to stay, to lodge*
el alpinismo m *mountain climbing*
alquilado a *rented*
alquilar v *to rent, to hire*
alrededor (de) ad *around, about*
alto a *high, tall*
la altura f *height*
el/la alumno/a mf *pupil*
el ama de casa f *housewife*
amable a *kind*
amarillo a *yellow*
la ambición f *ambition*
ambicioso a *ambitious*
ambiente m *atmosphere*
América del Sur f *South America*
el/la amigo/a mf *friend*
el/la amigo/a por correspondencia mf *penfriend*
el amor m *love*
ancho a *wide*
anciano a *old*
el/la anciano/a mf *old man/woman*
Andalucía f *Andalusia*
andar v *to walk*
el andén m *platform*
el anillo m *ring*
animado a *lively, animated*
el animal doméstico m *pet*
el aniversario m *anniversary*
anoche ad *last night*
anteayer ad *the day before yesterday*
antes (de) ad *before*
antiguo a *old, antique*
antipático a *unpleasant*
anular v *to cancel*

el anuncio m *advert*
añadir v *to add*
el año m *year*
el Año Nuevo m *New Year*
apagar v *to turn out, to put out, to switch off*
el aparcamiento m *car park*
aparcar v *to park*
el apartamento m *flat*
aparte de ad *apart from*
el apellido m *surname*
apetecer v *to feel like*
el apoyo m *support*
apoyar v *to lean, to support*
apreciar v *to like, to value*
aprender (a) v *to learn (to)*
el/la aprendiz mf *apprentice*
aprobar v *to pass (exam)*
apropiado a *suitable*
aprovecharse (de) vr *to take advantage*
aproximadamente ad *approximately*
apto a *suitable, capable*
los apuntes mpl *notes*
aquel a *that*
aquí ad *here*
Aragón f *Aragon*
el árbol m *tree*
el archivo m *file*
el armario m *cupboard, wardrobe*
arreglar v *to arrange/repair*
arrepentirse vr *to be sorry, regret*
arriba ad *upstairs, up*
arriba de prep *above*
la arroba f *@*
el arroz m *rice*
arruinar v *to ruin*
el arte dramático m *drama, theatre*
el artículo m *article*
el/la artista mf *artist*
asado a *roast*
el ascensor m *lift*
los aseos mpl *toilets*
así así a *so-so*
así que conj *so*
el asiento m *seat*
la asignatura f *school subject*
el aspecto m *aspect, appearance*

atacar v *to attack*
el atasco m *traffic jam*
la atención f *attention*
atentamente ad *sincerely*
el/la atleta mf *athlete*
el atletismo m *athletics*
la atmósfera f *atmosphere*
atrás ad *behind*
el atún m *tuna fish*
el aula f *classroom, lecture room*
aun (si) conj *even (if)*
aunque conj *although*
ausente a *absent*
Austria f *Austria*
austríaco a *Austrian*
el autobús m *bus*
el autocar m *coach*
la autopista f *motorway*
el auxiliar de vuelo m *flight attendant (male)*
el AVE m *high-speed train service*
la avenida f *avenue*
la avería f *breakdown*
el avión m *aeroplane*
el aviso m *notice, warning*
ayer ad *yesterday*
la ayuda f *help*
ayudar v *to help*
el ayuntamiento m *town hall*
la azafata f *air hostess*
el azúcar m *sugar*
azul a *blue*

B

el bacalao m *cod*
el bachillerato m *higher certificate (A level)*
bailar v *to dance*
el baile m *dance*
bajar v *to take/go down*
bajo a *low, short*
el balcón m *balcony*
el balón m *ball*
el baloncesto m *basketball*
el banco m *bank*
la banda ancha f *broadband*
la bandeja f *tray*
el bañador m *swimming costume*
bañar(se) vr *to bathe*
el baño m *bath, bathroom*
barato a *cheap*
la barba f *beard*
el barco m *boat, ship*
la barra f *slash (in internet address)*

la barra (de pan) f
loaf (of bread)

el barrio m *district, neighbourhood*

¡Basta! interj *That's enough!*

bastante a/ad *enough, quite a lot*

bastar v *to be enough*

la basura f *rubbish*

la batería f *drums*

el bebé m *baby*

beber v *to drink*

la bebida f *drink*

Bélgica f *Belgium*

beneficiar v *to benefit*

el beneficio m *benefit*

besar v *to kiss*

el beso m *kiss*

la biblioteca f *library*

el/la bibliotecario/a mf *librarian*

la bicicleta/bici f *bicycle/ bike*

bien ad *well/good*

bien educado a *well mannered*

bien hecho a *well done*

¡Bienvenido/a! interj *Welcome!*

el bigote m *moustache*

el billar m *snooker*

el billete m *ticket/banknote*

el billete de ida / el billete sencillo m *single ticket*

el billete de ida y vuelta m *return ticket*

la biología f *biology*

el bistec/bisté m *steak*

blanco a *white*

el blog m *blog*

el bloque m *block*

la blusa f *blouse*

la boca f *mouth*

el bocadillo m *sandwich*

la bolera f *bowling alley*

el bolígrafo/el boli m *ballpoint pen*

la bolsa de plástico f *carrier bag*

el bolso m *bag, handbag*

el bombero m *fireman*

el bombón m *chocolate, sweet*

bonito a *pretty, nice*

borracho a *drunk*

borrar v *to rub out, delete*

el bosque m *wood*

la bota f *boot*

el bote m *boat*

la botella f *bottle*

el botón m *button*

el boxeo m *boxing*

el brazo m *arm*

breve a *brief*

británico a *British*

broncearse vr
to get a suntan, sunbathe

buen/mal tiempo m
good/bad weather

¡Buen viaje!
Have a good trip!

¡Buena suerte!
Good luck!

Buenas noches interj
Good night

Buenas tardes interj
Good afternoon/evening

bueno a *good*

Buenos días interj
Good day/Hello

la bufanda f *scarf*

buscar v *to look for, fetch*

la butaca f *armchair, seat (in cinema, theatre)*

el buzón m *post box*

C

c/ (= calle) f *street*

el caballo m *horse*

la cabeza f *head*

cada a *each, every*

caerse vr *to fall, fall over*

el café m *coffee*

el café con leche m
white coffee

la cafetería f *coffee shop/ café*

la caja f *box, till*

el/la cajero/a mf *cashier*

los calamares mpl *squid*

los calcetines mpl *socks*

la calculadora f *calculator*

la calefacción f *heating*

la calidad f *quality*

caliente a *hot*

la calificación f *grade, mark*

calificado a *qualified*

callado a *quiet/silent*

callar(se) v(r)
to say nothing

la calle f *street*

el calor m *heat*

caluroso a *warm, hot*

calvo a *bald*

la cama f *bed*

la cama de matrimonio f
double bed

la cámara f *camera*

el/la camarero/a mf *waiter/ waitress*

cambiar v *to change*

el cambio m *change, bureau de change*

caminar v *to walk*

el camino m *road, track, route*

el camión m *lorry*

la camisa f *shirt*

la camiseta f *T-shirt*

la campaña f *campaign*

el/la campeón/a mf
champion

el campeonato m
championship

el camping m *campsite*

el campo m *field, country*

el campo de deportes m
sports field

las (Islas) Canarias fpl
Canary Islands

el canario m *canary*

la cancha (de tenis) f
(tennis) court

la canción f *song*

el candidato m *candidate*

cansado a *tired*

el/la cantante mf *singer*

cantar v *to sing*

la cantidad f *quantity*

la cantina f *canteen*

la capa de ozono f
ozone layer

la cara f *face*

el carácter m *character/ personality*

el caramelo m *sweet*

la caravana f *caravan*

cargar v *to load/charge*

el cariño m *affection*

cariñoso a *affectionate*

la carne f *meat*

el carnet m *pass*

el carnet de conducir m
driving licence

el carnet de identidad m
ID card

la carnicería f *butcher's*

el/la carnicero/a mf
butcher

caro a *expensive*

la carpeta f *folder, file*

el/la carpintero/a mf
carpenter

la carrera f *race/profession*

la carretera f *road*

la carta f *letter, menu*

las cartas fpl *playing cards*

el/la cartero/a mf *postman/ postwoman*

el cartón m *cardboard/ carton*

la casa f *house*

la casa adosada f
semi-detached house

casado a *married*

el casamiento m *marriage, wedding*

casarse vr
to get married

el casco m *helmet*

casi ad *almost*

castaño a
chestnut brown

las castañuelas fpl
castanets

castellano a *Spanish, Castilian*

castigar v *to punish*

el castigo m *punishment*

Castilla f *Castille*

el castillo m *castle*

Cataluña f *Catalonia*

la catedral f *cathedral*

causar v *to cause*

el CD m *CD*

la cebolla f *onion*

celebrar v *to celebrate*

la cena f *dinner, evening meal*

cenar v *to have dinner*

el centímetro m *centimetre*

el céntimo m *cent*

céntrico a *central*

el centro m *centre*

en el centro de prep
in the centre of

el centro comercial m
shopping centre

el cepillo m *brush*

la cerámica f *ceramics/ pottery*

cerca (de) ad/prep
near (to)

los cereales mpl *cereal*

cerrado a *closed*

cerrar v *to shut*

la cerveza f *beer*

el césped m *lawn*

el chalet/chalé m
detached house

los champiñones mpl
mushrooms

el chándal m *tracksuit*

la chaqueta f *jacket*

charlar v *to chat*

chatear v *to chat (online)*

el cheque m *cheque*

el cheque de viaje m
traveller's cheque

la chica f *girl*

el chicle m *chewing gum*

el chico m *boy*

la chimenea f *chimney, fireplace*

el chocolate m *chocolate/ hot chocolate*

el chorizo m
spicy pork sausage

el chubasco m
heavy shower

la chuleta f *chop, cutlet*

los churros mpl
flour fritters

el cibercafé m *cybercafe*

el ciclismo m *cycling*

el cielo m *sky, heaven*

la ciencia ficción f
science fiction

las ciencias fpl *science*

las ciencias económicas fpl
economics

cierto a *true, certain, sure*

la cifra f *figure, digit*

el cigarrillo m *cigarette*

el cine m *cinema*

el cinturón m *belt*

el cinturón de seguridad m
seat belt

la cita f *appointment, date*

la ciudad f *city, large town*

el clarinete m *clarinet*

claro a *clear, obvious, light (coloured)*

claro que ad *of course...*

¡Claro! interj *Of course!*

la clase f *class, lesson*

clásico a *classical*

el/la cliente mf *customer, client*

el clima m *climate*

la clínica f *clinic*

el club m *club*

el club de jóvenes m
youth club

la cobaya f *guinea pig*

la cocaína f *cocaine*

el coche m *car*

la cocina (de gas/eléctrica) f *(gas/electric) oven*

la cocina f *kitchen, cookery, food technology*

cocinar v *to cook*

el/la cocinero/a mf *cook*

el código postal m
postcode

coger v *to take, pick, catch*

la col f *cabbage*

la colección f *collection*

coleccionar v *to collect*

el colegio m *school, college*

la coliflor f *cauliflower*

el collar m *necklace*

el color m *colour*

la comedia f *comedy, play*

el comedor m *dining room*

comenzar v *to begin*

comer v *to eat*

el/la comerciante mf *shopkeeper*

el comercio m *business studies/commerce/shop*

cómico a *funny*

la comida f *food, meal, lunch*

la comida basura f *junk food*

la comida rápida f *fast food*

el comienzo m *start*

la comisaría f *police station*

como ad *how, like, as, about*

¿Cómo? interj *Pardon?*

¿Cómo está(s)? *How are you?*

cómodo a *comfortable, convenient*

el/la compañero/a mf *companion, classmate*

la compañía f *company*

comparar v *to compare*

compartir v *to share, divide*

competente a *competent*

completo a *complete/full*

el comportamiento m *behaviour*

comprar v *to buy*

las compras fpl *shopping*

comprender v *to understand*

comprensivo a *understanding*

con prep *with*

con permiso interj *excuse me*

el concierto m *concert*

el concurso m *competition*

las condiciones de trabajo fpl *working conditions*

conducir v *to drive, lead*

la conducta f *behaviour*

el/la conductor/a mf *driver, motorist*

conectar v *to connect*

el conejo m *rabbit*

la confitería f *sweet shop*

el conflicto m *conflict*

el congelador m *freezer*

conocer v *to know, meet*

el consejo m *advice*

la consigna f *left-luggage office*

la construcción f *construction*

construir v *to build*

el/la contable mf *accountant*

contactar v *to contact*

la contaminación f *pollution*

contaminar v *to pollute*

contar v *to count, tell*

el contenedor m *container*

contento a *happy/pleased*

contestar v *to reply, answer*

continuar v *to continue*

contra prep *against*

la contraseña f *password*

el contrato m *contract*

contribuir v *to contribute*

la conversación f *conversation*

conversar v *to talk/chat*

la copa f *cup, trophy, wine glass*

el corazón m *heart*

la corbata f *tie*

correcto a *correct*

corregir v *to correct*

el correo m *post*

el correo basura m *junk mail*

el correo electrónico m *email*

Correos m *post office*

correr v *to run*

la correspondencia f *post/correspondence*

la corrida (de toros) f *bullfight*

cortar v *to cut*

cortés a *polite*

la cortina f *curtain*

corto a *short*

la cosa f *thing*

la costa f *coast*

costar v *to cost*

la costumbre f *custom*

creativo a *creative*

creer v *to think, believe*

crema a *cream (colour)*

la crema solar f *suntan lotion*

el crep m *pancake*

el cristal m *glass, crystal*

el cruce m *junction (road)*

cruzar v *to cross*

el cuaderno m *exercise book*

cuadrado a *square*

¿Cuál(es)? pron *Which/What?*

la cualidad f *quality*

cuando ad *when*

¿Cuándo? ad *When?*

¿Cuánto/a? a/ad *How much?*

¿Cuánto cuesta(n)? *How much does it/do they cost?*

¿Cuánto es? *How much is it?*

¿Cuánto vale(n)? *How much does it/do they cost?*

¿Cuántos/as? a *How many?*

¿Cuántos años tiene(s)? *How old are you?*

cuarto a *fourth*

el cuarto m *room, quarter*

el cuarto de baño m *bathroom*

cubrir v *to cover*

la cuchara f *spoon*

el cuchillo m *knife*

el cuello m *neck*

la cuenta f *bill, sum, account*

el cuero m *leather*

el cuerpo m *body*

¡Cuidado! interj *Careful!*

cuidadoso a *careful*

cuidar v *to look after, take care of*

la cultura f *culture*

el cumpleaños m *birthday*

cumplir años v *to have a birthday*

el curso m *course*

D

dado que conj *give that/since*

dañar v *to harm, damage, spoil*

el daño m *harm, damage*

dar v *to give*

dar a v *to look onto*

dar de comer v *to feed*

dar igual v *to not matter*

dar las gracias v *to thank*

darse prisa vr *to hurry*

de prep *of, from*

de...a prep *from...to*

de acción a *action*

de aventura a *adventure*

de cerdo a *pork*

de cordero a *lamb*

¿De dónde? ad *Where from?*

de momento ad *at the moment*

De nada interj *You're welcome*

de nuevo ad *again*

de primero *for the first course*

¿De qué color? *What colour?*

¿De quién? pron *Whose?*

de repente ad *suddenly*

de ternera a *veal*

de vaca a *beef*

deber v *to owe, must, should*

los deberes mpl *homework*

débil a *weak*

decepcionado a *disappointed*

decepcionante a *disappointing*

decepcionar v *to disappoint*

decidir v *to decide*

décimo a *tenth*

decir v *to say*

el dedo m *finger*

el defecto m *defect/fault*

dejar v *to leave, allow*

dejar castigado v *to put in detention*

dejar de (hacer) v *to stop (doing)*

delante (de) prep *in front (of)*

delgado a *thin, slim*

delicioso a *delicious*

los/las demás mfpl *the others*

demasiado ad *too, too much*

el/la dentista mf *dentist*

dentro (de) ad/prep *inside*

dentro de... (horas) ad *in... (hours)*

el/la dependiente/a mf *shop assistant*

el deporte m *sport*

los deportes acuáticos mpl *watersports*

los deportes de invierno mpl *winter sports*

deportista a *sporty*

deportivo a *sports*

la depresión f *depression*

a la derecha ad *on the right*

(todo) derecho ad *straight ahead*

los derechos mpl *rights*

desafortunadamente ad *unfortunately*

desagradable a *unpleasant*

desaparecer v *to disappear*

el desastre m *disaster*

desayunar v *to have breakfast*

el desayuno m *breakfast*

descansar v *to rest*

el descanso m *rest, break*

descargar v *to download*

desconectar v *to disconnect*

describir v *to describe*

la descripción f *description*

el descuento m *discount*

desde prep *from*

desde hace prep *since/for*

desear v *to wish, desire*

el desempleo m *unemployment*

desobediente a *disobedient*

desordenado a *untidy*

despacio ad *slowly*

despejado a *clear*

despertarse vr *to wake up*

después (de) ad *after, later on*

el destino m *fate/destiny*

la destrucción f *destruction*

destruir v *to destroy*

la desventaja f *disadvantage*

el detalle m *detail, small gift*

detener(se) v(r) *to delay/stop*

detestar v *to detest, hate*

detrás (de) ad/prep *behind*

devolver v *to give back, return*

el día m *day*

el Día de Reyes m *Epiphany/6th January*

el día festivo m *bank holiday*

el día laborable m *working day*

diariamente ad *daily*

dibujar v *to draw*

el dibujo m *drawing, art*

los dibujos animados mpl *cartoons*

el diccionario m *dictionary*

diciembre m *December*

la dieta f *diet*

la diferencia f *difference*

diferente a *different*

difícil a *difficult*

la dificultad f *difficulty*

¡Dígame! interj *Hello (when answering the telephone)*

Dinamarca f *Denmark*

el dinero m *money*

la dirección f *direction/ address/management*

directo a *straight, direct*

el/la director/a mf *director, head*

el disco (compacto) m *disk/CD*

el disco duro m *hard disk*

la discoteca f *disco/ nightclub*

la discriminación f *discrimination*

la discusión f *argument*

discutir v *to argue, discuss*

diseñar v *to design*

el diseño m *design*

disfrutar v *to enjoy*

la distancia f *distance*

distinto/a (de) a *different (from)*

la diversión f *fun/hobby*

divertido a *fun, funny, amusing*

divertirse vr *to enjoy oneself*

divorciado a *divorced*

divorciarse vr *to get divorced*

el DNI = documento nacional de identidad m *ID card*

el divorcio m *divorce*

doblar v *to turn, to fold*

el doble m *double*

la docena f *dozen*

la documentación f *papers/documents*

el documental m *documentary*

el documento m *document*

doler v *to hurt*

el dolor m *pain, ache*

el domingo m *Sunday*

¿Dónde? ad *Where?*

¿Dónde está? *Where is it?*

dormir(se) v(r) *to (go to) sleep*

el dormitorio m *bedroom*

Dr(a). = doctor(a) mf *doctor*

la droga (dura/blanda) f *(hard/soft) drug*

drogarse vr *to take drugs*

la droguería f *chemist's/ drugstore*

la ducha f *shower*

ducharse vr *to have a shower*

dudar v *to doubt*

dulce a/ad *sweet, soft, gentle*

durante prep *during*

durar v *to last*

duro a *hard*

E

echar de menos v *to miss*

ecológico a *environmentally-friendly*

económico a *economic, cheap*

la edad f *age*

el edificio m *building*

la educación física f *PE*

educar v *to educate*

educativo a *educational*

EEUU = Estados Unidos mpl *USA*

egoísta a *selfish*

el ejemplo m *example*

el ejercicio (físico) m *(physical) exercise*

el ejército m *army*

la electricidad f *electricity*

el/la electricista mf *electrician*

eléctrico a *electric, electrical*

elegante a *stylish*

elegir v *to choose*

emborracharse vr *to get drunk*

emocionante a *moving, exciting*

empezar v *to begin*

el/la empleado/a mf *employee*

el empleo m *employment, work, job*

la empresa f *company*

en prep *in, on*

en/por todas partes ad *everywhere*

en este/ese momento ad *at the moment/at that time*

en las afueras ad *on the outskirts*

en paro a *unemployed*

en punto ad *on the dot*

en seguida ad *immediately*

enamorarse (de) vr *to fall in love (with)*

encantado a *delighted / pleased to meet you*

encantador a *delightful*

encantar v *to delight*

encender v *to light, turn on, ignite*

encima (de) ad/prep *on, above, over*

encontrar v *to find*

encontrarse vr *to meet/be situated*

encontrarse bien/mal vr *to feel well/ill*

la encuesta f *survey*

la energía f *energy*

enero m *January*

enfadado/a a *angry*

enfadarse vr *to get angry*

la enfermedad f *illness*

el/la enfermero/a mf *nurse*

enfermo a *ill*

enfrente (de) ad/prep *opposite, in front (of)*

¡Enhorabuena! interj *Congratulations!*

la ensalada f *salad*

enseñar v *to teach, show*

ensuciar v *to dirty, get dirty*

entender v *understand*

entonces ad *then, after*

la entrada f *entry, entrance, ticket*

entrar v *to enter*

entre prep *between, among*

el entrenamiento m *training*

entrenarse vr *to train*

entretenido a *entertaining*

la entrevista f *interview*

el entusiasmo m *enthusiasm*

enviar v *to send*

el equipaje m *luggage*

el equipo m *team*

la equitación f *horse riding*

equivocado a *mistaken*

el error m *mistake*

es decir conj *that is (to say)*

la escalera f *stairs, ladder*

escocés a *Scottish*

Escocia f *Scotland*

escoger v *to choose*

escribir v *to write*

el/la escritor/a mf *writer*

escuchar v *to listen (to), hear*

la escuela f *(primary) school*

ese a *that*

el espacio m *space*

los espaguetis mpl *spaghetti*

la espalda f *back*

España f *Spain*

español a *Spanish*

el español m *Spanish (language/ school subject)*

especial a *special*

la especialidad f *speciality*

el espectáculo m *show, performance*

el espejo m *mirror*

esperar v *to hope, expect, wait*

espléndido a *splendid*

el esquí m *skiing*

esquiar v *to ski*

la esquina f *corner*

esta noche ad *tonight*

estable a *stable*

la estación f *station*

la estación (del año) f *season*

la estación de autobuses f *bus station*

la estación de metro f *metro station*

la estación de servicio f *service station*

la estación de trenes f *train station*

el estadio m *stadium*

el estado m *state (marital)*

los Estados Unidos mpl *the USA*

el estanco m *tobacco/ cigarette shop*

el estante m *shelf*

la estantería f *bookcase*

estar v *to be*

estar a x kilómetros de v *to be x kilometres away from*

estar a x minutos de v *to be x minutes away from*

estar a favor v *to be in favour*

estar de acuerdo v *to agree*

estar de moda v *to be in fashion*

estar de vacaciones v *to be on holiday*

estar en contra v *to be against*

estar en forma v *to be in shape*

estar en paro v *to be unemployed*

estar equivocado v *to be mistaken*

estar harto/a de v *to be fed up of*

estar situado/a v *to be located*

este/esta a *this*

éste/ésta/esto pron *this*

el este m *the East*

el estéreo m *stereo*

estimado a *dear (to start formal letters)*

el estómago m *stomach*

estrecho a *narrow*

la estrella f *star*

estricto a *strict*

el estuche m *case (for pencils etc.)*

el/la estudiante mf *student*

estudiar v *to study*

los estudios mpl *studies*

estupendo a *wonderful*

estúpido a *stupid*

el euro m *euro*

Europa f *Europe*

europeo a *European*

evitar v *to avoid*

exactamente ad *exactly*

exacto a *exact*

el examen m *exam*

excelente a *excellent*

el éxito m *success*

la experiencia laboral f *work experience*

la explicación f *explanation*

explicar v *to explain*

el exterior m *the outside*

la extinción f *extinction*

extranjero a *foreign*

el extranjero m *abroad*

el/la extranjero/a mf *foreigner*

extraordinario a *extraordinary*

extrovertido a *outgoing*

F

la fábrica f *factory*

fabuloso a *fabulous*

fácil a *easy*

la falda f *skirt*

falso a *false, fake*

la falta f *error*

faltar v *to lack, be missing, need*

la familia f *family*

la familia adoptiva f *adoptive family*

famoso a *famous*

el/la famoso/a mf *celebrity*

fantástico a *fantastic*

la farmacia f *chemist's*

fascinante a *fascinating*

fascinar v *to fascinate*

fastidiar v *to annoy*

fatal a *awful*

favorable a *favourable*

favorito a *favourite*

febrero m *February*

la fecha f *date*

la fecha de nacimiento f *date of birth*

¡Felices Pascuas! *Happy Easter!*

¡Felices vacaciones! *Happy holidays!*

la felicidad f *happiness*

¡Felicidades! interj *congratulations!*

¡Felicitaciones! interj *congratulations!*

feliz a *happy*

¡Feliz Año Nuevo! *Happy New Year!*

¡Feliz cumpleaños! *Happy Birthday!*

¡Feliz Navidad! *Merry Christmas!*

¡Feliz santo! *Happy Saint's Day!*

femenino a *feminine*

fenomenal a *great*

feo a *ugly*

el ferrocarril m *railway*

la ficha f *file, counter, token*

la fiebre f *fever, temperature*

la fiesta f *party, holiday, festival*

la fiesta de cumpleaños f *birthday party*

el filete m *fillet/steak*

el fin de semana m *weekend*

al final ad *in the end*

finalmente ad *finally*

firmar v *to sign*

la física f *physics*

físico a *physical*

el flamenco m *flamenco*

el flan m *crème caramel*

la flauta f *flute*

la flor f *flower*

el folleto m *brochure*

en el/al fondo (de) ad/prep *in/at the back*

el/la fontanero/a mf *plumber*

el footing m *jogging*

la forma f *shape, way, method, form*

formal a *polite*

formar parte v *to be part*

la foto f *photo*

fracasar v *to fail*

el fracaso m *failure*

la frambuesa f *raspberry*

francés a *French*

el/la francés/esa mf *Frenchman/woman*

Francia f *France*

frecuente a *frequent*

el fregadero m *sink*

fregar los platos v *to wash up*

la fresa f *strawberry*

fresco a *fresh, cool*

el frigorífico m *refrigerator*

el frío m *cold*

frito a *fried*

la fruta f *fruit*

la frutería f *fruit shop, greengrocer's*

el fuego m *fire*

fuera (de) ad/prep *outside (of)*

fuerte a *strong*

el/la fumador/a mf *smoker*

fumar v *to smoke*

funcionar v *to function*

el fútbol m *football*

futuro a *future*

el futuro m *future*

G

las gafas fpl *(eye)glasses*

las gafas de sol fpl *sunglasses*

la galería (de arte) f *(art) gallery*

Gales m *Wales*

el/la galés/esa mf *Welshman/woman*

Galicia f *Galicia*

la galleta f *biscuit*

las gambas fpl *prawns*

ganar v *to earn, win*

el garaje m *garage*

la garganta f *throat*

la gasolina f *petrol*

la gasolina sin plomo f *unleaded petrol*

gastar v *to spend (money), wear away*

el gato m *cat*

el gazpacho m *cold tomato soup*

el/la gemelo/a mf *twin*

la generación f *generation*

generalmente ad *generally*

el género m *gender*

generoso a *generous*

genial a *brilliant, great*

la gente f *people*

la geografía f *geography*

el gerente m *manager*

la gimnasia f *gymnastics, P.E.*

el gimnasio m *gymnasium, gym*

glotón a *greedy*

el gobierno m *government*

el gol m *goal*

golpear v *to hit*

la goma f *glue, rubber*

gordo a *fat*

la gorra f *cap*

grabar v *to record*

gracias interj *thank you*

gracioso a *funny*

el grado m *degree, grade*

el gramo m *gramme*

Gran Bretaña f *Great Britain*

Gran Hermano m *Big Brother*

grande a *big, great*

los grandes almacenes mpl *department store*

la granja f *farm*

el/la granjero/a mf *farmer*

la grasa f *fat, grease*

gratis a/ad *free, for nothing*

gratuito a *free*

grave a *serious*

Grecia f *Greece*

gris a *grey*

grueso a *thick, stout, fat*

el grupo m *group*

los guantes mpl *gloves*

guapo a *beautiful, handsome*

guardar v *to save*

el/la guía mf *guide*

la guía (turística) f *guidebook*

el guión bajo m *underscore*

los guisantes mpl *peas*

la guitarra f *guitar*

gustar v *to like*

H

haber v *to have...*

la habitación f *room, bedroom*

la habitacftión doble f *double room*

la habitación individual f *single room*

el/la habitante mf *resident*

el hábito m *habit*

hablador a *talkative, chatty*

hablando interj *speaking (answering the telephone)*

hablar v *to talk, speak*

hace (dos semanas) que v *for (two weeks)*

hacer v *to do, make*

hacer aerobic v *to do aerobics*

hacer cola v *to line up*

hacer ejercicio v *to do exercise*

hacer falta v *to need, lack*

hacer frío v *to be cold (weather)*

hacer la(s) compra(s) v *to do the shopping*

hacer prácticas v *to practise, train*

hacer un aprendizaje v *to do an apprenticeship*

hacerse vr *to become*

hacia prep *towards, about*

la hamburguesa f *burger*

la hamburguesería f *burger stand*

hasta prep *until, up to*

hasta el (lunes) prep *until (Monday)*

hasta luego interj *see you later*

hasta mañana interj *see you tomorrow*

hasta pronto interj *see you soon*

hay v *there is, there are*

hay que v *it is necessary to*

la heladería f *ice-cream parlour*

el helado m *ice-cream*

helar v *to freeze*

el/la hermano/a mf *brother/sister*

el/la hermanastro/a mf *stepbrother/sister*

hermoso a *beautiful*

el hielo m *ice*

el hígado m *liver*

el/la hijo/a mf *son/daughter*

el/la hijo/a único/a mf *only child*

el hipermercado m *hypermarket*

la historia f *story, history*

histórico a *historical*

el hockey m *hockey*

el hogar m *home, hearth*

¡Hola! interj *Hello!*

Holanda f *Holland*

el/la holandés/esa mf *Dutchman/woman*

el hombre m *man*

el hombre de negocios m *businessman*

el hombro m *shoulder*

honesto a *honest*

honrado a *honourable, honest*

la hora f *hour*

el horario m *timetable*

el horario de trabajo m *working hours*

las horas de trabajo flexibles fpl *flexible working hours*

el horno m *oven*

horrible a *horrible/awful*

horroroso a *dreadful, horrible*

hoy ad *today*

el huevo m *egg*

húmedo a *damp*

el humo m *smoke*

I

ideal a *ideal*

la identidad f *identity*

el idioma m *language*

la iglesia f *church*

igual que a *equal to, just like*

la igualdad f *equality*

impaciente a *impatient*

el impermeable m *raincoat*

importante a *important*

imposible a *impossible*

impresionante a *impressive*

imprimir v *to print*

el incendio m *fire*

incluido a *included*

incluir v *to include*

incluso ad *even*

increíble a *incredible*

la independencia f *independence*

independiente a *independent*

la industria f *industry*

nouns — **m**: masculine **f**: feminine **pl**: plural **v**: verb **vr**: reflexive verb **a**: adjective

industrial a *industrial*

la influencia f *influence*

la información f *information*

informar(se) v(r) *to inform (oneself)*

la informática f *computing, IT*

el/la ingeniero/a mf *engineer*

Inglaterra f *England*

el inglés m *English (language)*

el/la inglés/esa mf *Englishman/woman*

injusto a *unjust, unfair*

inmediatamente ad *immediately*

el/la inmigrante mf *immigrant*

inmigrar v *immigrate*

inseguro a *insecure*

la insolación f *sunstroke*

insolente a *rude*

las instalaciones fpl *facilities*

el instituto m *secondary school, college*

el instrumento m *instrument*

insultar v *to insult*

inteligente a *intelligent*

la intención f *intention*

intentar v *to try*

el intercambio m *exchange*

interesante a *interesting*

interesarse en vr *to be interested in*

el interior m *interior*

el internet m *internet*

el/la intérprete mf *interpreter*

intimidar v *intimidate*

introvertido a *introverted*

inútil a *useless*

el invierno m *winter*

la invitación f *invitation*

el/la invitado/a mf *guest*

invitar v *to invite*

la inyección f *injection*

el iPod® m *iPod®*

ir v *to go*

ir a + infinitive v *to be going to (Future Tense)*

ir al extranjero v *to go abroad*

ir de compras v *to go shopping*

ir de vacaciones v *to go on holiday*

Irlanda f *Ireland*

irlandés a *Irish*

irse vr *to leave*

la isla f *island*

las Islas Canarias fpl *Canary Islands*

Italia f *Italy*

italiano a *Italian*

el IVA (impuesto sobre el valor añadido) m *VAT*

(a) la izquierda f *(on) the left*

J

jamás ad *never*

el jamón (de york) m *ham (boiled ham)*

el jamón serrano m *cured ham*

el jardín m *garden*

el/la jardinero/a mf *gardener*

el/la jefe/a mf *boss, head, manager*

el jersey m *jumper*

joven a *young*

el/la joven mf *young man/woman*

la joyería f *jewellery, jeweller's shop*

jubilado a *retired*

jubilarse vr *to retire*

las judías verdes fpl *green beans*

el juego m *game, play*

el juego de ordenador m *computer game*

los Juegos Olímpicos mpl *Olympic Games*

el jueves m *Thursday*

el/la jugador/a mf *player*

jugar v *to play*

el juguete m *toy*

la juguetería f *toy shop*

julio m *July*

junio m *June*

juntos ad *together*

justificar v *to justify*

justo ad *just, exactly, fair*

la juventud f *youth*

K

el kilo m *kilogramme*

el kilómetro m *kilometre*

L

laboral a *industrial*

el laboratorio m *laboratory*

al lado de prep *next door, at the side of*

el lado m *side*

el ladrón m *thief*

el lago m *lake*

la lámpara f *lamp*

la lana f *wool*

los lápices de colores mpl *colouring pencils*

el lápiz m *pencil*

largo a *long*

la lata f *tin, can*

latinoamericano a *Latin American*

el lavabo m *washbasin, washroom*

la lavadora f *washing machine*

el lavaplatos m *dishwasher*

lavar v *to wash*

la lección f *lesson*

la leche f *milk*

la lechuga f *lettuce*

la lectura f *reading*

leer v *to read*

las legumbres fpl *vegetables, pulses*

lejos (de) ad/prep *far, far away (from)*

la lengua f *language, tongue*

lento a *slow*

la letra f *letter*

levantar la mano v *to put up one's hand*

levantarse vr *to get up*

la libertad f *freedom*

la libra (esterlina) f *pound (sterling)*

libre a *free, available*

la librería f *bookshop, bookcase*

el libro m *book*

la licenciatura f *university degree*

el limón m *lemon*

la limonada f *lemonade*

limpiar v *to clean*

limpio a *clean*

la línea f *line*

liso a *smooth, straight*

la lista f *list*

la lista de precios f *price list*

la literatura f *literature*

el litro m *litre*

la llamada f *call*

llamar por teléfono v *to call, phone*

llamarse vr *to be called*

la llave f *key*

la llegada f *arrival*

llegar v *to arrive*

lleno a *full*

llevar v *to wear, carry, take*

llevar puesto v *to wear*

llevarse bien/mal con vr *to get on well/badly with*

llorar v *to cry*

llover v *to rain*

la lluvia f *rain*

lo siento *I'm sorry*

loco a *mad*

Londres m *London*

los (lunes) *on (Mondays)*

la lotería f *lottery*

luego ad *then, after*

el lugar m *place*

el lunes m *Monday*

la luz f *light/electricity*

M

la madera f *wood, timber*

la madrastra f *stepmother*

la madre f *mother*

magnífico a *brilliant*

mal ad *badly, ill*

mal educado a *impolite, rude*

la maleta f *suitcase*

malgastar v *waste*

malo a *bad, wrong, ill, naughty*

maltratar v *to mistreat*

el maltrato m *ill-treatment*

la mamá f *mum, mummy*

mandar v *to send/order/be in charge*

la mano f *hand*

la manta f *blanket*

mantenerse en forma vr *to keep fit*

la mantequilla f *butter*

la manzana f *apple, block of houses*

mañana ad *tomorrow*

la mañana f *morning*

el mapa m *map*

la máquina f *machine*

la máquina de fotos f *camera*

el mar m *sea*

marcar (un gol) v *to score (a goal)*

el marido m *husband*

los mariscos mpl *seafood*

marrón a *brown*

el martes m *Tuesday*

marzo m *March*

más (que) ad *more (than)*

la mascota f *pet*

masculino a *masculine*

matar v *to kill*

las matemáticas fpl *maths*

el matrimonio m *marriage*

mayo m *May*

mayor a *older*

la mayoría f *the majority*

el/la mecánico/a mf *mechanic*

la media hora f *half an hour*

la media pensión f *half board*

mediano a *medium, average*

la medianoche f *midnight*

las medias fpl *tights, stockings*

el/la médico/a mf *doctor*

la medida f *measure, measurement*

medio a *half*

en el medio a *in the middle*

el medio ambiente m *environment*

medioambiental a *environmental*

el mediodía m *midday*

medir v *to measure*

el Mediterráneo m *the Mediterranean*

mejicano a *Mexican*

Méjico m *Mexico*

mejor a *better, best*

mejorar v *to improve*

mejorarse vr *to get better*

el melocotón m *peach*

menor a *younger, youngest, smaller*

menos (que) ad *less (than)*

menos cuarto (time) a *quarter to*

el mensaje m *message*

mentir v *to lie*

la mentira f *lie*

mentiroso a *untruthful, lying*

el menú del día m *menu of the day*

el menú turístico m *tourist menu*

el mercado m *market*

la merienda f *teatime snack*

la merluza f *hake*

la mermelada f *jam*

el mes m *month*

la mesa f *table*

el metro m *metre, underground (train)*

mexicano a *Mexican*

México m *Mexico*

la mezquita f *mosque*

el microondas m *microwave*

la miel f *honey*

el/la miembro mf *member*

mientras (que) conj *while, meanwhile*

mientras tanto conj *meanwhile*

el miércoles m *Wednesday*

el militar m *soldier*

mínimo a *minimum*

el minuto m *minute*

mirar v *to look at, look, watch*

mismo a *same*

la mitad f *half*

mixto a *mixed*

la mochila f *backpack, rucksack*

la moda f *fashion*

moderno a *modern*

mojarse vr *to get wet*

molestar v *to trouble, disturb*

el momento m *moment*

la moneda f *coin*

el monedero m *purse*

el/la monitor/a mf *instructor, coach*

el monopatín m *skateboard*

la montaña f *mountain*

montañoso a *mountainous*

montar v *to ride, put together*

montar a caballo v *to ride a horse*

el monumento m *monument*

la moqueta f *fitted carpet*

morado a *purple*

moreno a *dark-haired*

morir v *to die*

mostrar v *to show*

la moto(cicleta) f *motorbike*

el motor m *engine, motor*

el (teléfono) móvil m *mobile phone*

el/la muchacho/a mf *boy/ girl*

mucho a *a lot, many*

mucho gusto interj *it's nice to meet you*

mucho tiempo m *a long time*

mudarse de casa vr *to move house*

los muebles mpl *furniture*

muerto a *dead*

la mujer f *woman, wife*

la mujer de negocios f *businesswoman*

mundial a *worldwide*

el mundo m *world*

la muñeca f *doll, wrist*

el museo m *museum*

el/la músico/a mf *musician*

muy ad *very*

N

nacer v *to be born*

nacido a *born*

el nacimiento m *birth*

la nacionalidad f *nationality*

nada pron *nothing, not at all*

nada más pron *nothing more*

nadar v *to swim*

nadie pron *nobody*

naranja a *orange*

la naranja f *orange*

la naranjada f *orangeade*

la nariz f *nose*

la nata f *cream*

la natación f *swimming*

la naturaleza f *nature*

navegar v *to surf*

Navidad f *Christmas*

necesario a *necessary*

la necesidad f *necessity*

necesitar v *to need*

negativo a *negative*

negro a *black*

nervioso a *nervous*

nevar v *to snow*

la nevera f *refrigerator*

ni...ni conj *neither...nor*

la niebla f *fog*

el/la nieto/a mf *grandson/ daughter*

la nieve f *snow*

ningún a *none/not any*

el/la niño/a mf *boy, girl*

el nivel m *level*

no ad *no, not*

no fumador m *non smoker*

la noche f *night*

Nochebuena f *Christmas Eve*

Nochevieja f *New Year's Eve*

el nombre m *name*

el noreste m *northeast*

normal a *normal*

normalmente ad *normally*

el noroeste m *northwest*

el norte m *north*

norteamericano a *North American*

la nota f *note, mark, grade*

las noticias fpl *news*

la novela f *novel*

noveno a *ninth*

noviembre m *November*

el/la novio/a mf *fiancé(e), boy/girlfriend*

la nube f *cloud*

nublado a *cloudy, overcast (sky)*

nuboso a *cloudy*

nuevo a *new*

la nuez f *walnut*

el número m *number*

nunca ad *never*

O

o/u conj *or*

el objetivo m *aim*

obligatorio a *compulsory*

la obra de teatro f *play*

el/la obrero/a mf *workman/ woman*

obtener v *to obtain*

el ocio m *leisure*

octavo a *eighth*

octubre m *October*

ocupado a *occupied, engaged*

ocurrir v *to happen, occur*

odiar v *to hate*

el oeste m *west*

ofender v *to offend*

ofenderse vr *to take offence*

la oferta f *offer*

la oficina f *office*

la oficina de cambio f *bureau de change*

la oficina de turismo f *tourist office*

oír v *to hear, to listen*

¡Ojo! interj *Look out!*

el ojo m *eye*

¡Olé! interj *Hooray!*

oler v *to smell*

olvidar v *to forget*

la ONG f (Organización No Gubernamental) *NGO (Non-governmental Organisation)*

la opción f *option*

opinar v *to think, give your opinion*

la oportunidad f *opportunity*

optar v *to choose*

optativo a *optional*

optimista a *optimist*

el ordenador m *computer*

el ordenador portátil m *laptop*

la oreja f *ear (outer)*

organizar v *to organise*

orgulloso a *proud*

el oro m *gold*

oscuro a *dark*

el otoño m *Autumn*

otro a *another*

otra vez a *again*

el oxígeno f *oxygen*

P

paciente a *patient*

el padrastro m *stepfather*

el padre m *father*

los padres pl *parents*

la paella f *paella (rice dish)*

la paga f *pay, wages, pocket money*

pagar v *to pay*

pagar bien/mal v *to pay well/badly*

la página f *page*

la página web f *web page*

el país m *country*

el paisaje m *landscape*

el País Vasco m *Basque Country*

el pájaro m *bird*

la palabra f *word*

el palacio m *palace*

pálido a *pale*

el pan m *bread*

la panadería f *bakery*

el/la panadero/a mf *baker*

el panecillo m *bread roll*

la pantalla f *screen*

el pantalón m *trousers*

el pantalón corto m *shorts*

el papá m *daddy*

Papá Noel m *Father Christmas*

el papel m *paper*

el papel higiénico m *toilet paper*

la papelera f *wastepaper basket/bin*

la papelería f *stationer's, stationery*

el paquete m *packet, parcel*

el par m *pair, couple*

para prep *for, in order to, so that*

¿Para/Por cuánto tiempo? *How long for?*

la parada f *stop*

parado a *stopped, still, unemployed*

el parador m *(state-run) hotel*

el paraguas m *umbrella*

parar v *to stop*

parecer v *to seem, appear, look like*

parecerse a vr *to look like*

parecido a *similar*

la pared f *wall*

la pareja f *couple, partner*

el parking m *car park*

el paro m *unemployment, stoppage*

el parque m *park*

el parque de atracciones m *funfair*

el parque infantil m *playground*

el parque temático m *theme park*

la participación f *participation*

participar v *to participate*

el partido m *match/game, party (political)*

pasado a *past, last*

el pasado m *the past*

pasado de moda a *out of fashion/unfashionable*

pasado mañana ad *the day after tomorrow*

el/la pasajero/a mf *passenger*

el pasaporte m *passport*

pasar v *to pass, spend (time), happen*

pasar (por) v *to go past, through*

pasar la aspiradora v *to vacuum*

pasarlo bien/mal v *to have a good/bad time*

el pasatiempo m *hobby, pastime*

pasear (el perro, etc.) v *to take (the dog, etc.) for a walk*

pasearse vr *to go for a walk/stroll*

el paseo m *walk, stroll*

el pasillo m *corridor*

el paso m *step, way*

(dar un) paso v
(to take) a step

el paso subterráneo m
subway

la pasta f *pasta, paste*

el pastel m *cake, pie*

la pastelería f *baker's,
cake shop*

la patata f *potato*

las patatas fritas fpl *chips,
crisps*

el patinaje m *skating*
patinar v *to skate*

el patio m *courtyard*

las pecas fpl *freckles*

el pedazo m *piece*

pedir v *to order, ask for*
pedir permiso v
to ask permission

peinarse vr
to comb your hair

la película f *film*

el peligro m *danger*

peligroso a *dangerous*

pelirrojo a *red-haired*

el pelo m *hair*

la pelota f *ball*

la peluquería f
hairdresser's

el/la peluquero/a mf
hairdresser

los pendientes mpl
earrings

pensar v *to think*

la pensión f *guest house*

la pensión completa f *full
board*

el pepino m *cucumber*

peor a *worse, worst*

pequeño a *small, little*

la pera f *pear*

perder v *to lose*

perdón interj *sorry!
pardon me*

perdonar v *to forgive*

perdone interj *sorry!
forgive me*

perezoso a *lazy*

perfecto a *perfect*

la perfumería f
perfume shop

el periódico m *newspaper*

el periodismo m *journalism*

el/la periodista mf
journalist

el periquito m *parakeet*

permanente a
permanent

el permiso m *licence,
permit*

el permiso de conducir m
driving licence

permitir v *to allow*

pero conj *but*

el perrito caliente m
hot dog

el perro m *dog*

la persona f *person*

la personalidad f
personality

pesado a *heavy*

pesar v *to weigh*

la pesca f *fishing*

la pescadería f
fishmonger's

el pescado m
fish (dead, for eating)

pescar v *to fish*

pesimista a *pesimistic*

el peso m *weight*

el petróleo m *oil, petroleum*

el pez m *fish*

el piano m *piano*

picante a *hot, spicy*

el pie m *foot*

la piel f *skin, leather*

la pierna f *leg*

la pila f *battery*

la pimienta f *pepper
(spice)*

el pimiento m *pepper
(vegetable)*

el ping-pong m *table tennis*

pintado a *painted*

el/la pintor/a mf *painter*

la piña f *pineapple*

la piscina f *swimming pool*

el piso m *flat, floor*

la pista f *court, track,
piste (ski)*

la pista de hielo f *ice rink*

la pizarra f *blackboard*

el plan m *project*

planchar v *to iron*

el planeta m *planet*

el plano m *plan, map*

la planta f *floor, plant*

la planta baja f *ground
floor*

el plástico m *plastic*

la plata f *silver*

el plátano m *banana*

el plato m *plate, dish,
course*

el plato combinado m
one course set meal

el plato del día m
dish of the day

la playa f *beach*

la plaza f *square*

la plaza de toros f *bullring*

pobre a *poor*

la pobreza f *poverty*

poco a *little, few*

un poco a *a little*

poco sano a *unhealthy*

pocas veces ad *rarely*

poder v *to be able, can*

el policía m *policeman*

el policíaco m *detective,
crime (film)*

el polideportivo m
sports centre

el pollo m *chicken*

poner v *to put*

poner la mesa v
to lay the table

ponerse vr *to become*

ponerse a vr *to begin to*

ponerse de acuerdo vr
to agree

el pop m *pop music*

por prep *for, through, by,
along*

por año ad *per year*

por anticipado ad
in advance

¿Por dónde? ad *Where?*

por ejemplo conj *for
example*

por eso ad *therefore*

por favor interj *please*

por fin ad *finally*

por lo general ad *in
general*

por lo tanto ad *therefore*

¿Por qué? ad *Why?*

por supuesto ad *of
course*

por un lado/por otro lado
conj *on one hand/
on the other hand*

por una parte/por otra
parte conj *on one hand/
on the other hand*

la porción f *portion*

porque conj *because*

portugués a *Portuguese*

el porvenir m *future*

la posibilidad f *possibility*

posible a *possible*

positivo a *positive*

la postal f *postcard*

el postre m *sweet, dessert*

practicar v *to practise*

las prácticas laborales fpl
work experience

práctico a *practical*

el precio m *price*

precioso a *lovely*

la preferencia f *priority,
preference*

preferido a *favourite*

preferir v *to prefer*

la pregunta f *question*

preguntar v *to ask*

el prejuicio m *prejudice*

el premio m *prize*

la preocupación f *worry*

preocupado a *worried*

preocuparse vr *to worry*

preparar v *to prepare*

la presentación (oral) f
presentation

presente a *present*

prestar v *to lend*

primario a *primary/basic*

la primavera f *spring*

la primera clase f
first class

primero a *first*

el/la primo/a mf *cousin*

el principio m *beginning*

privado a *private*

probar v *to try, test,
prove, taste*

probarse vr *to try on*

el problema m *problem*

producir v *to produce*

los productos químicos mpl
chemicals

el/la profesor/a mf *teacher*

profundo a *deep,
profound*

el programa m *programme*

el/la programador/a mf
computer programmer

prohibido a *prohibited*

prohibir v *to prohibit, ban*

prometer v *to promise*

el pronóstico m *forecast*

pronto ad *soon/early/
ready*

la propina f *tip*

propio a *own*

proteger v *to protect*

la provincia f *province*

próximo a *next*

prudente a *sensible*

la prueba f *proof, test*

la publicidad f *publicity,
advertising*

el público m *public,
audience*

el pueblo m *village, people*

el puente m *bridge*

la puerta f *door, gate*

el puerto m *port*

pues conj *well, then*

el puesto m *job/position*

los pulmones mpl *lungs*

el punto m *dot, point, spot,
place*

puntocom m *dotcom*

Q

que conj *that, who,
which*

¡Qué...! ad *How...!*

¿Qué? pron *What?,
Which?*

¡Que aproveche! interj
Enjoy your meal!

¡Qué asco! interj
How disgusting!

¡Qué bien! interj *That's
great!*

¿Qué día? *What day?*

¿Qué fecha? *What date?*

¿Qué hay?
How's it going?

¿Qué hora es?
What time is it?

¡Qué horror! interj
How awful!

¡Qué lástima! interj
What a shame!

¡Que lo pase(s) bien!
interj *Have a good time!*

¿Qué pasa?
What's happening?

¡Qué pena! interj
What a shame!

¿Qué tal?
How's it going?

¡Qué va! interj *As if!*

(el mes, etc) que viene ad
next (month, etc.)

quedar v *to suit
(clothing)*

quedar en v *to agree*

quedarse vr *to stay*

quejarse vr *to complain*

querer v *to want, love*

querer decir v *to mean*

el queso m *cheese*

¿Quién? pron *Who?,
Whom?*

la química f *chemistry*

químico a *chemical*

quince días mpl *fortnight*

quinto a *fifth*

el quiosco m *kiosk,
news stand*

quisiera v
I/he/she/you would like

quizás ad *perhaps*

R

la ración f *portion*

el racismo m *racism*

racista a *racist*

el radiador m *radiator*

el rap m *rap music*

rápido a *fast*

raramente ad *rarely*

raro a *strange*

el rato m *while, amount of time*

el ratón m *mouse*

la razón f *reason*

la reacción f *reaction*

las rebajas fpl *sales*

recargable a *rechargeable*

la recepción f *reception*

el/la recepcionista mf *receptionist*

recibir v *to receive*

el recibo m *receipt*

reciclable a *recyclable*

el reciclaje m *recycling*

reciclar v *to recycle*

recientemente ad *recently*

recoger v *to pick up, collect*

recomendar v *to recommend*

reconocer v *to recognise*

recordar v *to remember*

el recreo m *break, playtime*

el recuerdo m *souvenir, memory*

la red f *internet*

redondo a *round*

reducir v *to reduce/ shorten*

regalar v *to give (as a present)*

el regalo m *present, gift*

la región f *region*

la regla f *rule, ruler*

regresar v *to return*

regular a *average*

la rehabilitación f *rehabilitation*

rehabilitar v *to rehabilitate*

relajarse vr *to relax*

el relámpago m *flash of lightning*

la religión f *religion*

rellenar v *to fill up, stuff, fill in (form)*

el reloj m *watch, clock*

la Renfe f *Spanish rail network*

repartir v *to share, divide*

repasar v *to revise*

repetir v *to repeat*

el reproductor de mp3 m *MP3 player*

la reserva f *reservation*

reservado a *reserved*

reservar v *to reserve*

resfriado a *suffering from a cold*

residencial a *residential*

los residuos orgánicos mpl *organic waste*

respetar v *to respect*

el respeto m *respect*

respirar v *to breathe*

responder v *to respond, reply, answer*

la responsabilidad f *responsibility*

responsable a *responsible*

la respuesta f *reply, answer*

el restaurante m *restaurant*

el resto m *the rest*

el resultado m *result*

el resumen m *summary*

el retraso m *delay*

la reunión f *meeting*

reutilizar v *to reuse*

la revista f *magazine*

rico a *rich, wealthy, delicious*

ridículo a *ridiculous*

el río m *river*

la Rioja f *Rioja*

rizado a *curly*

robar v *to rob, steal*

el robo m *theft, robbery*

el rock m *rock music*

rojo a *red*

romántico a *romantic*

romper v *to break*

la ropa f *clothes*

rosa a *pink*

rosado a *pink*

roto a *broken*

rubio a *blonde, fair-haired*

la rueda f *wheel*

el ruido m *noise*

ruidoso a *noisy*

Rusia f *Russia*

S

el sábado m *Saturday*

saber v *to know/taste*

el sacapuntas m *pencil sharpener*

sacar v *to take out, get*

sacar buenas/malas notas v *to get good/bad marks*

sacar fotos v *to take photos*

el saco de dormir m *sleeping bag*

la sal f *salt*

la sala de chat f *chat room*

la sala de espera f *waiting room*

la sala de estar f *living room*

la sala de fiestas f *night club*

la sala de profesores f *staff room*

salado a *salty, amusing*

el salario m *salary, wage*

la salchicha f *sausage*

el salchichón m *Spanish sausage*

la salida f *departure, exit*

salir (de) v *to go out (of/from), leave, depart*

el salón m *lounge, living room*

el salón de actos m *assembly room*

la salsa f *sauce*

la salud f *health*

saludable a *healthy*

saludar v *to greet*

saludos mpl *greetings, best wishes*

salvar v *to save*

salvo prep *except*

las sandalias fpl *sandals*

la sangre f *blood*

la sangría f *sangria (drink)*

sano a *healthy*

el santo m *saint's day*

la sardina f *sardine*

satisfecho a *satisfied*

la sección f *section*

seco a *dry*

el/la secretario/a mf *secretary*

secundario a *secondary*

la sed f *thirst*

la seda f *silk*

seguir v *to follow, continue*

según prep *according to*

el segundo m *second*

segundo a *second*

seguro a *safe, certain, sure*

la selección f *selection*

seleccionar v *to choose*

el sello m *stamp*

el semáforo m *traffic lights*

la semana f *week*

la Semana Santa f *Easter*

sencillo a *simple, single*

la sensación f *feeling*

sentarse vr *to sit down*

el sentido de humor m *sense of humour*

el sentimiento m *feeling*

sentir(se) v(r) *to feel*

la señal f *sign*

el/la señor/a mf *man/woman, Mr/Mrs, sir/madam*

la señorita f *miss, young lady*

separado a *separate*

separar la basura v *to separate the rubbish*

separarse vr *to separate/ break up*

se(p)tiembre m *September*

séptimo a *seventh*

ser v *to be*

la serie f *series, serial*

serio a *serious*

el servicio m *service*

los servicios mpl *the toilets*

servir v *to serve*

la sesión f *session/ performance*

severo a *harsh/strict*

sexto a *sixth*

si conj *if*

sí ad *yes*

sí pron *himself, herself, itself*

el sida m *AIDS*

siempre ad *always*

la sierra f *mountain range*

el siglo m *century*

siguiente a *next, following*

el silencio m *silence*

la silla f *chair*

el sillón m *easy chair, armchair*

similar a *similar*

simpático a *nice, friendly*

sin prep *without*

sin duda ad *undoubtedly*

sin embargo ad *however*

sincero a *honest*

sino conj *but (rather)*

el sitio m *place, space, room*

el sitio web m *website*

situado a *situated*

el sobre m *envelope*

sobre prep *on, about, around (time)*

sobresaliente a *outstanding*

el/la sobrino/a m *nephew/ niece*

la sociedad f *society*

el/la socio/a mf *member*

¡Socorro! interj *Help!*

el sofá m *sofa*

el sol m *sun*

solamente/sólo ad *only, just*

el/la soldado mf *soldier*

solicitar v *to apply*

la solicitud f *application*

solo a *alone*

sólo ad *only*

soltero a *single, unmarried*

la sombra f *shadow, shade*

el sombrero m *hat*

la sombrilla f *parasol*

el sonido m *sound*

sonreír(se) v(r) *to smile*

la sopa f *soup*

sorprendido a *surprised*

el sótano m *basement*

el spray m *aerosol*

Sr (Señor) *Mr*

Sra (Señora) *Mrs*

Srta (Señorita) *Miss, Ms*

Sta (santa) *saint*

subir v *to go up, rise*

sucio a *dirty*

sudamericano a *South American*

el sueldo m *salary, wage, pay*

el suelo m *floor*

el suéter m *sweater*

suficiente a *enough*

sugerir v *to suggest*

Suiza f *Switzerland*

el supermercado m *supermarket*

supervisar v *to supervise*

el suplemento m *supplement*

el sur m *south*

el sureste m *southeast*

el suroeste m *southwest*

suspender v *to fail*

T

el tabaco m *tobacco*

tal vez *perhaps*

el Talgo m *inter-city express train*

la talla f *size (clothes)*

el tamaño m *size*

nouns — **m**: masculine   **f**: feminine   **pl**: plural   **v**: verb   **vr**: reflexive verb   **a**: adjective

también ad *also*

tampoco ad *neither*

tan...como ad *as...as*

tanto...como ad *as...as*

las tapas fpl *snacks*

la taquilla f *box office, ticket office*

tardar v *to take time*

tarde ad *late*

la tarde f *afternoon, evening*

la tarea f *task*

las tareas fpl *homework*

la tarjeta f *card*

la tarjeta de crédito f *credit card*

el tarro m *jar, pot*

la tarta f *cake, tart*

el taxi m *taxi*

el/la taxista mf *taxi driver*

la taza f *cup*

el té m *tea*

el teatro m *theatre*

el tebeo m *comic*

el teclado m *keyboard*

el/la técnico/a mf *technician*

la tecnología f *technology*

el tejado m *roof*

la tela f *cloth, material*

el teléfono m *telephone*

el teléfono móvil m *mobile phone*

la telenovela f *soap opera*

el teletrabajo m *telemarketing*

la tele(visión) f *TV*

el televisor m *television set*

el tema m *theme, subject*

la temperatura f *temperature*

templado a *mild, temperate*

temprano ad *early*

el tenedor m *fork*

tener v *to have*

tener (15) años v *to be (15) years old*

tener calor v *to be hot*

tener dolor de v *to have pain in/hurt*

tener ganas v *to feel like*

tener hambre v *to be hungry*

tener lugar v *to take place*

tener miedo v *to be afraid*

tener prisa v *to be in a hurry*

tener que v *to have to*

tener razón v *to be right*

tener sed v *to be thirsty*

tener sueño v *to be sleepy*

tener suerte v *to be lucky*

el tenis m *tennis*

el tenis de mesa m *table tennis*

la tentación f *temptation*

tercero a *third*

terminar v *to finish*

la terraza f *terrace*

el texto m *text*

la tía f *aunt*

el tiempo m *time, weather*

el tiempo libre m *free time*

la tienda f *shop, tent*

la tienda con fines benéficos f *charity shop*

la tienda de comestibles f *grocery shop*

la tienda de ropa f *clothes shop*

la Tierra f *Earth*

las tijeras fpl *scissors*

tímido a *shy, timid*

el tío m *uncle*

típico/a a *typical*

el tipo m *type, kind*

tirar v *to throw, throw away, pull*

el título m *university degree*

tocar v *to play (instrument)/touch*

todas las (semanas) a *every (week)*

todavía ad *yet, still*

todo a *all, every*

todo recto ad *straight on*

todos a *every*

tolerante a *tolerant*

tomar v *to take, have*

tomar el sol v *to sunbathe*

tomar un año libre/sabático v *to take a year out*

el tomate m *tomato*

tonto a *silly, stupid*

torcer v *to turn, twist*

el/la torero/a mf *bullfighter*

la tormenta f *storm*

tormentoso a *stormy*

el toro m *bull*

la tortilla f *omelette*

la tortuga f *tortoise*

la tos f *cough*

la tostada f *slice of toast*

tóxico a *toxic*

trabajador a *hardworking*

el/la trabajador/a mf *worker*

trabajar v *to work*

el trabajo m *work, job*

los trabajos manuales mpl *manual labour*

la tradición f *tradition*

tradicional a *traditional*

el/la traductor/a mf *translator*

traer v *to bring*

el tráfico m *traffic*

Tráigame... *Bring me...*

el traje m *suit*

tranquilo a *calm, quiet*

transportar v *to transport*

el transporte m *transport*

el transporte público m *public transport*

el tranvía m *tram, local train*

tratar v *to try, treat, deal with*

tratarse de vr *to be about*

travieso a *naughty*

el tren m *train*

el trimestre m *term*

triste a *sad*

la trompeta f *trumpet*

el trozo m *piece, bit*

el trueno m *thunder*

el turismo m *tourism*

el/la turista mf *tourist*

el turrón m *Spanish nougat*

el/la tutor/a mf *tutor*

U

la UE f (Unión Europea) *EU*

últimamente ad *recently*

último a *last, latest, final*

único a *only, unique*

el uniforme m *uniform*

la universidad f *university*

unos a *some*

unos (diez) a *about (ten)*

usar v *to use*

el uso m *use, function*

útil a *useful*

utilizar v *to use*

las uvas fpl *grapes*

V

las vacaciones fpl *holidays*

vacío a *empty*

vago a *vague, lazy*

la vainilla f *vanilla*

vale interj *OK, fine*

valer la pena v *to be worthwhile*

valiente a *brave*

el vandalismo m *vandalism*

los vaqueros mpl *jeans*

varios a *several*

el vaso m *glass (drinking)*

(tres) veces fpl *(three) times*

el/la vecino/a mf *neighbour*

el/la vegetariano/a mf *vegetarian*

el vehículo m *vehicle*

la vela f *candle, sailing*

el/la vendedor/a mf *vendor, seller*

vender v *to sell*

venir v *to come*

la ventaja f *advantage*

la ventana f *window*

ver v *to see, watch*

el verano m *summer*

la verdad f *truth*

verdadero a *true*

verde a *green*

la(s) verdura(s) f(pl) *vegetables*

el vestíbulo m *hall, foyer*

vestido a *dressed*

el vestido m *dress*

vestirse vr *to get dressed*

el vestuario m *clothes, wardrobe, dressing room*

el/la veterinario/a mf *vet, veterinary*

la vez f *time, occasion*

la vía f *way, lane (motorway), track*

viajar v *to travel*

el viaje m *journey*

el/la viajero/a mf *traveller*

la víctima f *victim*

la vida f *life*

la videoclub f *videoshop*

el videojuego m *video game*

el vidrio m *glass (material)*

viejo a *old*

el/la viejo/a mf *old man/woman*

el viento m *wind*

el viernes m *Friday*

el vinagre m *vinegar*

el vino (blanco/rosado/tinto) m *wine (white/rosé/tinto)*

la violencia f *violence*

violento a *violent*

violeta a *violet*

el violín m *violin*

la visita f *visit*

el/la visitante mf *visitor*

visitar v *to visit*

vivir v *to live*

vivo a *alive, lively*

el vocabulario m *vocabulary*

volar v *to fly*

el voleibol m *volleyball*

voluntario a *voluntary*

el/la voluntario/a mf *volunteer*

volver v *to return, turn*

volver a + inf v *to do again*

volverse vr *to turn round, to turn back*

la voz f *voice*

el vuelo m *flight*

W

el windsurf m *windsurfing*

Y

y/e conj *and*

y cuarto a *quarter past*

y media a *half past, and a half*

ya ad *already, yet, now*

ya (que) conj *since, as*

el yogur m *yoghurt*

Z

la zanahoria f *carrot*

la zapatería f *shoe shop*

las zapatillas de deporte fpl *trainers*

los zapatos mpl *shoes*

la zona f *zone, area*

la zona peatonal f *pedestrian precinct*

el zoo m *zoo*

el zumo m *juice*

---

ad: adverb   **pron**: pronoun   **prep**: preposition   **conj**: conjunction   **interj**: interjection

Spanish–English Dictionary

Index

AQA
A-level

Religious Studies

For A-level Year 2

John Frye
Debbie Herring
Mel Thompson

Approval message from AQA

This textbook has been approved by AQA for use with our qualification. This means that we have checked that it broadly covers the specification and we are satisfied with the overall quality. Full details of our approval process can be found on our website.

We approve textbooks because we know how important it is for teachers and students to have the right resources to support their teaching and learning. However, the publisher is ultimately responsible for the editorial control and quality of this book.

Please note that when teaching the *AQA A-level Religious Studies* course, you must refer to AQA's specification as your definitive source of information. While this book has been written to match the specification, it cannot provide complete coverage of every aspect of the course.

A wide range of other useful resources can be found on the relevant subject pages of our website: www.aqa.org.uk.

HODDER
EDUCATION
AN HACHETTE UK COMPANY

Photo and text credits can be found on page 380 of this book.

Acknowledgements

John Frye extends his thanks to Joy Frye and to Sheila Butler for proof-reading the text.

Dr Debbie Herring wishes to thank Professor Daphne Hampson for her invaluable help with the section on the Hampson–Reuther debate in Chapter 8.

Every effort has been made to trace all copyright holders, but if any have been inadvertently overlooked, the Publishers will be pleased to make the necessary arrangements at the first opportunity.

Although every effort has been made to ensure that website addresses are correct at time of going to press, Hodder Education cannot be held responsible for the content of any website mentioned in this book. It is sometimes possible to find a relocated web page by typing in the address of the home page for a website in the URL window of your browser.

Hachette UK's policy is to use papers that are natural, renewable and recyclable products and made from wood grown in sustainable forests. The logging and manufacturing processes are expected to conform to the environmental regulations of the country of origin.

Orders: please contact Bookpoint Ltd, 130 Milton Park, Abingdon, Oxon OX14 4SE. Telephone: +44 (0)1235 827720. Fax: +44 (0)1235 400401. Email: education@bookpoint.co.uk. Lines are open from 9 a.m. to 5 p.m., Monday to Saturday, with a 24-hour message answering service. You can also order through our website: www.hoddereducation.co.uk

ISBN: 978 1 4718 7400 0

Contents

Introduction

Volume 2 of the AQA Textbook for Religious Studies is intended to be read in conjunction with Volume 1. Volume 1 covers all of the material for the AS award. Volume 2 covers everything else.

As a reminder, this is the overview of the complete A-Level:

Component 1 – PHILOSOPHY OF RELIGION and ETHICS	
Section A – Philosophy of Religion	
• Arguments for the existence of God • Evil and suffering • Religious experience	
	• Religious language • Miracles • Self and life after death
Section B – Ethics and Religion	
• Ethical theories (Natural Moral Law, Situation Ethics, Virtue Ethics) • Issues of human life and death • Issues of animal life and death	
	• Introduction to meta-ethics • Free will and moral responsibility • Conscience • Bentham and Kant
COMPONENT 2 – Study of Religion and 'Dialogue'	
Section A – Study of Religion	
• Sources of wisdom and authority • God • Self, death and afterlife • Good conduct and key moral principles • Expressions of religious identity	
	• Religion, gender and sexuality • Religion and science • Religion and secularisation • Religion and religious pluralism
Section B – The Dialogue between Philosophy of Religion and Religion	
	(How religion is influenced by, and has an influence on philosophy of religion in relation to the issues studied)
Section C – The Dialogue between Ethical Studies and Religion	
	(How religion is influenced by, and has an influence on ethical studies in relation to the issues studied)

• Your Centre/teachers might do the A-Level in a *completely* different order.

• If you are doing full A-Level at the end of 2 years, you study everything in both columns and you are examined on it using the A-Level exam format, at the end of the 2 years.

The section in Volume 2 on 'The Exam: Specimen Assessment Materials' assumes that you have access to what is said on this subject in Volume 1. Volume 2 adds to this by giving exemplar material on some of the new material studied in Philosophy/Ethics and Christianity and in particular by looking at the 'Dialogues' sections.

As with Volume 1, it is recommended that students begin with the chapter summaries before working through the material.

Component 1

Philosophy of religion and ethics

1

Religious language

You will need to consider the following items for this section

1 The issue of whether religious language should be viewed cognitively or non-cognitively.

2 The challenges of the verification and falsification principles to the meaningfulness of religious language.

3 Responses to these challenges:

- Eschatological verification with reference to Hick
- Language as an expression of a *blik* with reference to Hare
- Religious language as a language game with reference to Wittgenstein.

4 Other views of the nature of religious language:

- Religious language as symbolic with reference to Tillich
- Religious language as analogical with reference to Aquinas
- The *Via Negativa*.

5 The strengths and weaknesses of the differing understandings of religious language.

Note that a considerable proportion of this material is dealt with explicitly in: *The Philosophy of Religion*: (Oxford Readings in Philosophy) edited by Basil Mitchell, Oxford University Press, 1971.

Background to the issue of religious language

For many, religious language is language about 'God', or 'the gods'. Here is the 'problem' of religious language as described in the Internet Encyclopedia of Philosophy:

The problem of religious language is worrisome to practitioners of the Abrahamic religious traditions [for example Judaism, Christianity and Islam] because it has the potential to undermine those traditions. All three faiths proclaim truths about God in written texts, commentary traditions and oral teachings. In fact, speech about God is essential to both personal religious faith and organised celebration in these traditions. Without an adequate solution to the problem of religious language, human speech about God is called into question. Without the ability to speak about God and to understand the meaning of what is spoken, the Abrahamic faiths are vulnerable to the criticism that their sacred texts and teachings are unintelligible. [Note 1]

Equally, where Hindus talk about Brahman as the Ultimate Reality in the universe, for some this might be seen as nothing more than a form of words. In simple terms, some claim that religious language is literally meaningless, because it relates to nothing in this world. How did this claim come about? Early in the twentieth century there was a widespread view that the ideal language was that of science – it was straightforward, literal and its claims were able to be checked against observable facts. This created problems for religious and moral language, because people recognised that these involve more than just statements of observable facts; but what exactly could that 'more' mean? To appreciate the different views about the nature of religious language, it is therefore helpful to look at the general ways in which the understanding of language and what it achieves changed during the twentieth century – a discussion which influenced the whole of Western philosophy.

The world is all that is the case...

Ludwig Wittgenstein (1889–1951), whose work we study later in the chapter (pages 21–24) suggested that philosophical problems would be solved if the language people used was more precise and was limited to statements for which there could be evidence. In his book *Tractatus Logico-Philosophicus* (meaning 'Logico-philosophical Treatise'), published in 1921, he set out a narrow view of what could count as a meaningful proposition. He saw the function of language as being to picture the world. Therefore every statement needed to correspond to some information about the world itself. In the opening statement of *Tractatus*, he identified the world with the sum of true propositions: 'The world is all that is the case' [Note 2] – by which he meant that whatever cannot be shown to correspond to some observable reality, cannot be meaningfully spoken about.

Wittgenstein's early approach to language presented it as a precise but narrowly defined tool for describing the phenomenal world (meaning the world as we experience it). But in the *Tractatus* he also acknowledged that there are therefore certain things of which one cannot speak. One of these is the 'subject self' (the self as a subject of experiences); another is the mystical sense of the world as a whole. So there are limits to the use of language that he describes and he famously ended with 'Whereof we cannot speak, thereof we must remain silent'. The problem – and it is one that colours the whole discussion of religious language – is that people still want to speak and they hold that their religious claims are of supreme importance, even though they cannot be supported (as would be the case with scientific language) by empirical evidence.

So the key question becomes: How can you show that religious statements are right or wrong, or even meaningful at all, if they are not simply descriptions of observed facts?

Facts about religion

Facts about religion present no problems. 'The Pope is the Bishop of Rome', or 'Muslims and Jews are not permitted by their religion to eat pork', are simple facts. The first defines what we mean by 'Pope' and the second remains true even if some followers of those religions are spotted tucking into a bacon sandwich, because moral rules, whether or not they are obeyed, are still facts.

Key terms

Supernatural Literally 'above' what is natural; that which cannot be described by science/ the laws of nature.

Metaphysics The philosophy of concepts beyond the physical. Deals, for example, with abstract questions such as: what is the nature of time/space/reality?

Key term

Logical Positivism The philosophical approach taken by the Vienna Circle: a group of philosophers who met in that city during the 1920s and 1930s. The Logical Positivists claimed that metaphysical and theological language are literally meaningless, because they are neither matters of logic nor provable by empirical evidence.

The religious claims that we are concerned with are those that are metaphysical (beyond what we can observe in the physical universe), such as:

There is a God.

Miracles happen.

There is life after death.

In other words, metaphysical claims are to do with a general interpretation of life and are not specific bits of information. Many religious claims are also about the **supernatural**: beliefs about beings and actions that cannot be accounted for in terms of the ordinary physical world. By definition, the supernatural cannot be explained in terms of the natural language of science or empirical facts. If you believe there are supernatural entities, you step outside the world of science and into the world of **metaphysics**.

Wittgenstein's ideas were taken up by the 'Vienna Circle', a group of philosophers who met in that city during the 1920s and 1930s. The approach they took is generally known as **Logical Positivism**. The 'founding father' of Logical Positivism and leader of the Vienna Circle was the German philosopher and physicist Moritz Schlick.

Moritz Schlick (1882–1936)

Schlick was seen by many as the ideal combination of philosopher and physicist, particularly after publishing a 1915 paper commenting on Einstein's theory of Special Relativity. Schlick was assassinated by a former student, Johann Nelböck, who claimed in court that his grip on morality had been loosened by Schlick's attack on metaphysics.

The Logical Positivists took their starting point from Hume's 'Fork' (a two-pronged fork). Hume argued that we can have knowledge of just two sorts of thing: i) matters of fact; ii) the relations between ideas (for example in mathematics).

The Logical Positivists therefore claimed that there are only two types of meaningful language and you will be familiar with both of these through your study of the Ontological Argument in Volume 1:

1 **Synthetic propositions.** These are propositions that are dependent upon evidence. For example, the proposition that 'the sun will rise tomorrow' is based on the evidence of seeing the sun rise every day. We therefore know exactly what that proposition means; so it is meaningful.

2 **Analytic propositions.** These are propositions that are true by definition/by the words used and these are meaningful because they are self-evident. For example:

● All bachelors are unmarried men.
● Frozen water is ice.
● 2 + 2 = 4 (you will remember that this is a tautology, because in effect it says that 4 = 4, so it is true by the terms used).

Applying this test of meaning to religious language, the Logical Positivists concluded that metaphysics and theology are meaningless, because: 1) there is no evidence to support them, therefore they are not synthetic; 2) they are not true by definition/true by the words used.

Schlick argued that the meaning of a statement is its method of verification. This became known as the '**Verification Principle**'. To put this simply, the meaning of the statement 'My car is parked on the road outside the house' is that, if you go outside the house and look towards the road you will see my car, since that is the way you can verify the statement as being true. If it is impossible to verify the truth of a statement in that way – in other words, if there is no way that you could give an account of it in terms of sense experience – then it is meaningless.

Logical Positivism was promoted by the British philosopher A.J. Ayer (1910–89) in *Language, Truth and Logic* (1936). This was a radical and controversial book, written when Ayer was young and had just returned from spending time in Vienna engaging with the Logical Positivists. In terms of religious language, he makes the point that theism and atheism are equally nonsense, since neither can be shown to be true on the basis of evidence. The statements 'God exists' and 'God does not exist' are both meaningless because there is no sensory evidence to support them. 'God' is a metaphysical being, so is not discoverable by sensory experience or describable using scientific language.

Much of the debate about the nature of religious language since then has been an attempt to avoid his conclusion by showing that religious language does have meaning, even if not the sort of factual, literal, empirical meaning that Ayer was seeking.

The issue of whether religious language should be viewed cognitively or non-cognitively

Language is '**cognitive**' if it conveys information. Most cognitive language consists of statements that may also be described as 'synthetic' – in other words, they can be shown to be true or false depending upon evidence.

Take a straightforward example:

> **Key term**
>
> **Verification Principle** The meaning of a statement is its method of verification. For example, the meaning of the statement, 'My car is parked on the road outside the house' is that, if you go outside the house and look towards the road, you will see my car, since that is the way you can verify my statement as being true. Verification is by sense experience – for example, sight.

> **Key term**
>
> **Cognitive** Language is cognitive if it conveys factual information, and most cognitive statements are synthetic (they are shown to be true or false depending upon evidence).

Key term

Non-cognitive To say that a statement is non-cognitive is to say that it is inappropriate to ask whether or not it is factual. Non-cognitive statements may convey emotions, give orders, or make moral claims, for example.

'The Houses of Parliament are located in Westminster.'

That is a cognitive statement because it claims to give factual information. It is synthetic in that its truth depends on evidence – if you go to Westminster you are either going to find the Houses of Parliament there or you are not. 'There is a green dragon eating toast in the room next to you' is a cognitive statement for the same reason: if you look next door, you are either going to find a green dragon eating toast or you are not: the statement is cognitive irrespective of whether it is true or false – it is testable by sense experience.

By contrast, a '**non-cognitive**' statement may convey emotion, give an order, make a moral claim, express a wish, or offer an insight, for example. It may be *relevant* to facts, but its truth does not *depend* upon its correspondence to empirical facts. 'I am happy because I love this place and find it beautiful' contains three non-cognitive assertions. 'With this ring I thee wed' might be the most important statement a person ever makes, but it is not proved true or false with reference to facts. Rather, it is what is called a 'performative utterance', meaning that it makes something happen.

First we need to examine two challenges to the view that religious language is cognitive.

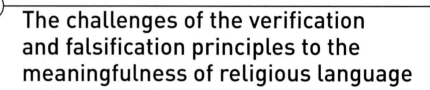

The challenges of the verification and falsification principles to the meaningfulness of religious language

Note that there are no scholars named in the specification with regard to the Verification Principle or the Falsification Principle. Nevertheless you will find it difficult to study these without coming across the work of A.J. Ayer and Antony Flew. Remember, however, that no questions can be set on Ayer or Flew.

The challenges of verification

Ayer's version of the Verification Principle appears in his 1936 book, *Language, Truth and Logic* and you can see that it follows the ideas of the Logical Positivists: A statement is meaningful if and only if it is:

i analytic (true by definition/a tautology) or

ii empirically verifiable.

(If you find any of this language difficult, refresh your memory from the work we did on the Ontological Argument – Volume 1, page 20).

Remember that the Verification Principle is NOT about whether a statement is true or false: it is about whether a statement is meaningful.

For Ayer, a statement can be meaningful either in practice or in principle.

Verification in practice happens when there is direct sense experience to support a statement; for example, 'There is a purple fire-breathing dragon next door wearing green tights and a red scarf, smoking a cigar and drinking beer' is meaningful (even though it sounds silly) because that statement can be checked by going next door and having a look.

Verification in principle happens when we know how a statement can in principle be tested empirically; for example, 'There is intelligent life elsewhere in the galaxy' is verifiable in principle, because we know what sense experience would prove it, and one day such experiences may be possible.

Ayer was mainly concerned with statements that have 'factual meaning' – in other words, if experience is not relevant to the truth or falsity of a statement, then that statement does not have factual meaning. Meaningful propositions have to say something about our experience of the world and how it is. Any statement that is not factually significant and is not a tautology he called a mere 'pseudo-proposition'.

Applying this to religious language, Ayer argued that statements like: 'God loves you'/'God is love'/'God exists', etc., cannot be verified either in practice or in principle: there is no evidence by which we could show these claims to be true or false, so they are literally meaningless: they cannot be reduced to (or given 'cash value' in terms of) a set of statements about evidence.

> [N]o sentence which purports to describe the nature of a transcendent god can possess any literal significance. [Note 3]

It is not just religious statements that Ayer dismisses in this way. The same is true about moral statements, since he thinks that these are nothing more than expressions of approval or disapproval.

> If you disapprove of stealing (for example because somebody stole your wallet) whereas I approve of it (possibly because I stole it), our disagreement cannot be solved by pointing to anything in the world ... We are both expressing moral sentiments rather than factual statements. [Note 4]

The same is true of assertions made by those who believe in God:

> Thus we offer the theist the same comfort as we gave to the moralist. His assertions cannot possibly be valid, but they cannot be invalid either. As he says nothing at all about the world, he cannot justly be accused of saying anything false, or anything for which he has insufficient grounds. [Note 5]

To appreciate the force of this, think how many religious statements are concerned with a transcendent God or some other form of spiritual being. Think of Christian statements about the Trinity, that God is Father, Son and Holy Spirit – or statements about life after death, for example that the righteous will have eternal life while sinners will suffer eternal torment (Matthew 25:46). What possible ways are there of checking whether such statements are true or false? What observations might show them to be true or false? In Ayer's view, the central claim of theism, that God exists, is neither true nor false – it is simply meaningless, and the same is true of the atheist's claim that God does not exist: all talk about God is meaningless, so the atheist also fails to say anything meaningful.

Discussion points

1 Ayer also dismisses aesthetic statements as meaningless. Is he right in this – is what you see as a beautiful tree, sunset, painting or person really beautiful, or is beauty only in the eye of the beholder?

2 Do our moral judgements boil down to expressions of approval or disapproval, or are at least some moral judgements matters of fact? For example, *discounting scenarios such as sacrificing one life to save thousands or millions*, is it factually the case that the rape and murder of a baby is always morally wrong?

3 Are historical statements meaningless?

4 Can we talk meaningfully about a transcendent being?

Strengths and weaknesses of the verificationist challenge

Here is a table of three strengths/advantages of the Verification Principle (VP) together with contrasting replies:

Strengths/advantages of the VP	Weaknesses/disadvantages of the VP
1) The VP is straightforward in what it demands: Meaningful statements are either true by definition (tautologies) or else are verifiable (in principle) by sense experience. It brackets out all questions of emotion or commitment, concentrating only on the facts.	**1) The demands of the VP are too narrow:** The VP might be straightforward, concentrating only on facts, but that does not mean that it is right. The VP in effect rules out all sorts of language as being meaningless, including moral/ethical statements, aesthetic statements (judgements about beauty), statements about ancient history and statements about religion. Yet how many people really do see these as meaningless? The VP only works as an argument when discussing matters of fact, not those of interpretation, hopes, fears or anything else that involves the complexities of human engagement with the world. Human engagement with the world is at least as important to us as matters of verifiable fact.
2) The VP is in line with science and the scientific method, since it demands that we observe the world empirically.	**2) To say that the VP is in line with science has a number of problems. Here are two:** Much of science deals with entities that *cannot* be directly observed, such as quarks and strings, so how can their existence be verified by the VP? Science does not work exclusively through verification. According to Karl Popper, it works primarily through falsification. We look at the Falsification Principle next.

Strengths/advantages of the VP	Weaknesses/disadvantages of the VP
3) The VP demands a sense of reality in what we say about the world. Whether or not we agree with the VP, it does point out one major issue with religious language, namely that people sometimes make religious statements without attempting to justify them in any way. There surely needs to be *some* justification for religious claims. Ayer gives an example by quoting at random from the scholar F.H. Bradley, who at one point says this: 'the Absolute enters into, but is itself incapable of, evolution and progress,' – a comment that seems so unrelated to any reality that we can know that Ayer suggests that Bradley 'has made an utterance which has no literal significance even for himself'. [Note 6]	**3) These are valid criticisms of some religious language, but religion makes a very clear proposition about God and the origin of the universe.** In the section on arguments for the existence of God, we made the point that either the universe explains its own existence or else its existence is explained by an external creative mind. This is a reasonable hypothesis based on our observation that minds are creative, so there could be one supremely creative Mind. Believing that such a Mind exists is no more irrational than scientific assumptions about quarks or strings, and as a hypothesis it is simple to understand.

Here are two further challenges that philosophers of religion can make to the Verification Principle:

1 Ayer's Verification Principle allows 'verification in principle' – it is enough to know how in theory a statement can be verified to render it meaningful. In that case, some argue that the Bible can supply verification in principle for religious statements, since (for example) the Gospels claim to be eyewitness accounts of the life, death and resurrection of Jesus (Luke 1:2). Many historians accept that eyewitness accounts from a particular period in a nation's history are in principle acceptable evidence to verify that history and the same can be said of eyewitness accounts from the historical period of Jesus of Nazareth. This does not show that the events recorded about Jesus are true; only that they are verifiable in principle, which is precisely what Ayer's form of the Verification Principle requires. Statements about Jesus can therefore be verified in principle as historical statements, which means that the claim that Jesus performed miracles is verifiable in principle.

2 Perhaps the most serious threat to Ayer's Verification Principle is that it is itself not verifiable in principle. The Verification Principle was presented as a way of dealing with statements that claim to be factually significant; but the Verification Principle itself fails both of its own criteria for deciding what is a factual statement – it is not a tautology and it is not verifiable in principle. By its own criteria, then, it is meaningless and cannot be used to comment on the meaningfulness of religious language.

Whether this objection disposes of the Verification Principle is a matter for debate. Ayer was forced to argue that it is a convention, or a recommendation, or a policy statement; hence it does not make a factual claim and therefore cannot be used against itself.

This does not seem to be a strong argument. Look at the possibilities:

● If the Verification Principle is a factual statement, then it is meaningless, because there are no observations that would verify it.

- It is not a logical statement, since there are no logical truths in the Principle that require it to be true.
- If it is a policy statement/a convention/a recommendation for action, then it amounts to little more than an arbitrary assumption of what Ayer thinks should be the case, which is worth nothing.

The only other possibility seems to be that it is a metaphysical assumption about the way things really are. But Ayer's main task at the start of *Language, Truth and Logic* is the *elimination* of metaphysics, hence religious language is dismissed as a collection of metaphysical utterances. If the Principle itself is a metaphysical assumption about the way things really are, then it fails, because it is an example of the very thing that it was intended to guard against.

As a final comment, perhaps the strongest aspect of the Verification Principle is that it forced philosophers of religion to consider carefully the nature of religious language. It produced decades of careful analysis and argument of the kind summarised in this chapter.

The challenges of falsification

Karl Popper (1902–94)

An Austrian-British philosopher of science, Popper disliked the 'pseudo-science' of Marxism. He advocated tolerance in society, but insisted that intolerance should not be tolerated, otherwise tolerance would be lost.

The challenge to religious language from falsification is generally considered to be stronger than that from verification. Discussions of falsification as a method of evaluating what is meaningful effectively start with the work of Popper, who argued that science works primarily through falsification rather than verification. In science, following the method known as 'induction', evidence is gathered and evaluated and from that the scientist develops a hypothesis and eventually a theory. The more evidence in favour of something, the more likely it is to be the case. This is a matter of common sense and is found in the work of David Hume, who used it as the basis for his famous criticism of miracles, which we look at in the next chapter.

But scientists do not just gather evidence to support an existing theory. They also look for evidence against that theory, something that cannot be explained by their existing ideas and therefore causes them to think again. Science makes progress by discovering evidence to prove existing theories false. In this sense, falsification is a positive and constructive approach to truth.

Popper took this a step further by saying that something can only be accepted as scientific if it is at least possible that there could be evidence to show that it is false. If you consider that nothing could ever prove your claim to be false, then it is not scientific. He used this to argue against Freudian and Marxist ideas, for example, because people holding those particular theories generally refused to allow anything to count against them, but simply re-interpreted every new fact to fit their existing theories.

> Popper: In so far as a scientific statement speaks about reality, it must be falsifiable: and in so far as it is not falsifiable, it does not speak about reality. [Note 7]

Following the principle of falsification, if you want to make a factual, cognitive claim, you should be able to specify what it is that could *falsify* that claim. Some scholars have used this approach in order to challenge the meaningfulness of religious language.

The classic argument about the use of evidence to attempt to prove the existence of God comes from the 'Parable of the Gardener' – a story, told originally by John Wisdom and developed by Flew, in which Flew applies Popper's ideas about falsification to religious language and decides that it is meaningless.

Antony Flew (1923–2010)

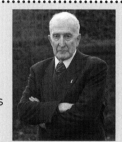

An English philosopher, Flew was, for most of his life, a 'negative atheist', following the Logical Positivist position that theological claims could not be verified or falsified. He was always concerned to submit all claims to evidence. Towards the end of his life, he acknowledged that developments in science had, in his opinion, opened up discussion about the possible existence of a god, a late change of mind much seized on by believers. His balanced view on this is included in a new introduction he wrote to the 2005 edition, by Prometheus Books, of his book *God and Philosophy*, 1966. In effect, his commitment to following where the evidence leads persuaded him of the truth of Einstein's view, that the complexity of the universe implies the existence of an intelligent creator – not a Christian/theistic God, but a deistic being.

The Parable of the Gardener

Once upon a time two explorers came upon a clearing in the jungle. In the clearing were growing many flowers and many weeds. One explorer says, 'Some gardener must tend this plot.' The other disagrees, 'There is no gardener.' So they pitch their tents and set a watch. No gardener is ever seen. 'But perhaps he is an invisible gardener.' So they set up a barbed-wire fence. They electrify it. They patrol with bloodhounds. (For they remember how H.G. Wells's 'Invisible Man' could be both smelt and touched though he could not be seen.) But no shrieks ever suggest that some intruder has received a shock. No movements of the wire ever betray an invisible climber. The bloodhounds never give cry. Yet still the Believer is not convinced. 'But there is a gardener, invisible, intangible, insensible to electric shocks, a gardener who has no scent and makes no sound, a gardener who comes secretly to look after the garden which he loves.' At last the Sceptic despairs, 'But what remains of your original assertion? Just how does what you call an invisible, intangible, eternally elusive gardener differ from an imaginary gardener or even from no gardener at all?' [Note 8]

You can see that in the parable:

- The gardener stands for God.
- The first explorer (the believer) represents theists.
- The second explorer represents those who are sceptical about the existence of God, such as atheists and agnostics.
- The garden is the world and the flowers and weeds represent what the believer sees as order and design in the world.
- By the tests of keeping watch, electrifying the fence and using bloodhounds, the explorers are using sense experience to detect the gardener: but no empirical tests show that he is present.
- For Flew the gardener's existence 'dies the death of a thousand qualifications' because every time he fails to be detected, the 'believer' qualifies what he means by his gardener.
- The gardener/God cannot be seen, so the theist says that he is invisible.
- The gardener/God cannot be touched, so the theist says that he is intangible.
- The gardener/God cannot be heard, or discovered by *any* form of sense experience, so the theist says that he is 'eternally elusive'.
- In the end, there seems to be nothing left of the original assertion that 'there is a gardener'/'there is a God', so that assertion has been 'killed by inches'.

Flew's point is simple: the believer in the parable will allow nothing to falsify his belief that there is a gardener who loves and looks after his garden. In the same way, the religious believer will allow nothing to falsify his belief that there is a God who loves and looks after the world. Statements about belief in God are therefore 'vacuous' (empty, so in effect meaningless), according to Flew. If you do not admit that there is some kind of *evidence* that could falsify your belief, then you might just as well believe any nonsense you like, because you will never admit that it is nonsense.

This, in a nutshell, is the **Falsification Principle**. It can be summed up as follows: a sentence is factually significant if and only if there is some form of evidence which could falsify it.

To see the power of such a principle, Flew asks his readers to look at utterances such as:

'God has a plan'

'God created the world'

'God loves us as a father loves his children'.

At first sight, says Flew, statements like these seem to be 'vast cosmological assertions' [Note 9], but when we look at them closely, they are not proper assertions at all, because there appear to be no instances where the believer would be prepared to admit that 'there isn't a God after all', or 'God doesn't really love us'.

Take the statement that 'God loves his children'. Flew refers to a case where a child is dying of inoperable throat cancer. [Note 10] The child's earthly father is driven frantic in his efforts to help, but its Heavenly Father appears indifferent and reveals no obvious signs of concern. The believer then qualifies his original statement by suggesting that 'God's love is not a merely human love', or it is 'an inscrutable love'. Flew asks: Just what would have to happen for the believer to say, 'God does not love us', or even,

Key term

Falsification Principle A sentence is factually significant if and only if there is some form of evidence which could falsify it.

'God does not exist'? 'What would have to occur or to have occurred to constitute … a disproof of the love of, or of the existence of, God?' [Note 11]

Strengths and weaknesses of the falsificationist challenge

Strengths

The main strength of the falsificationist challenge is that where religion makes important factual claims (such as, 'There is a God'/'God created the universe'/'God has a plan'/'God loves us'), Flew seems to show that these claims are empty, because all the evidence against such claims is ignored by the believer. They cease to be real assertions, because they die 'the death of a thousand qualifications'.

In summary, if the main criterion of a meaningful assertion is *to know what will falsify that assertion*, then believers do not appear to know what will falsify their assertions.

Weaknesses

The main weakness of the falsificationist challenge is related to the idea that something else is going on in religion other than the mere acceptance or denial of facts.

As a general argument here, we can say of the Falsification Principle what we said of the Verification Principle: it attempts to confine 'meaningfulness' to factual propositions, but there is a whole realm of human experience that cannot be confined in this way. The world of empirical facts is an utterly different world from that of fiction, poetry, drama, art, music or dance. All these are vehicles for expressing people's insights into life and its meaning – they explore emotions, moral dilemmas, hopes, fears and all the other features of human life. They are personal and engage people personally. They cannot easily be described using only facts – indeed, they create their own facts, their own worlds. For example, nothing in the world of empirical facts demands that in chess the knight's move must be two squares sideways and then one square up or down, or two squares up or down and then one square sideways: these are arbitrary rules of engagement without which the game cannot be played; nevertheless the game of chess is deeply meaningful on any number of levels: emotional, tactical and cognitive.

Ask yourself: Is religion more like a scientific and logical investigation of facts, or like a drama or piece of poetry? Is it something generated within human culture, as a way of exploring life's meaning, or is it something discovered out there in the world that is generally described using the laws of physics? The answer you come to will determine your view of the relevance of verification and falsification to religious language and beliefs.

When religious believers make claims about God, they are not making wild and unrealistic speculations. **They assume that there is a truth to be known** about the nature and origin of the universe, and that 'God' is a reasonable explanation of that truth. As a matter of fact, it is well known that in later life Flew himself came to acknowledge this, and suggested that the complexity of evolutionary biology points to the existence of a creative intelligence: a deistic kind of God. In other words, falsificationism is too rigid in its understanding of truth.

As a similar point to the last, Popper's Falsification Principle was concerned mainly with scientific statements. Statements about God are metaphysical, not scientific, so it seems inappropriate to demand that they should be empirically falsifiable.

Flew's argument that religious believers will allow nothing to falsify their assertions is not really true. For example, the extent of the problem of evil in the world has led many believers to question or reject their belief in God.

We turn, now, to the views of three scholars who have responded to the challenges from the verification and falsification principles:

● John Hick argues that the 'facts' of religion will be verified eschatologically (at the Last Judgement/when we die).
● R.M. Hare argues that religious truths are not factual assertions: rather they are non-falsifiable but deeply meaningful '*bliks*' – they are our unverifiable and unfalsifiable interpretations of the world. Since they are non-cognitive, they are not subject to attack from the falsificationist approach.
● Ludwig Wittgenstein argues that the meaning of a statement is not defined by the steps you take to verify or falsify it, but by its use: use and context govern meaning.

When you have studied these three approaches, you will be in a position:

1 To give your view as to whether religious language is cognitive or non-cognitive

2 To decide the extent of the verificationist and falsificationist critique of religion.

Responses to these challenges from verification and falsification

Eschatological verification with reference to Hick

John Hick (1922–2012)

We have come across John Hick in connection with his Irenaean-type theodicy, in the problem of evil. To remind you, Hick was a philosopher and theologian. From being an evangelical Christian with fundamentalist views, his studies led him to a more liberal approach to Christianity and he was for many years a practising member of the Presbyterian Church (later to become the United Reformed Church) before becoming a member of the Society of Friends in his final years. He was known particularly for his pluralist views, accepting that all religions offered a way towards the same goal.

Flew's article in Mitchell's *The Philosophy of Religion* is part of what is known as the 'university debate', where it is followed by contributions from Hare (which we look at shortly) and from Mitchell himself. John Hick's response

Key terms

Eschatology The doctrine of what will happen at the end of time/in the last days/at the final judgement.

Eschatological verification Refers to Hick's view that the 'facts' of the Christian religion will be verified (or falsified) at death.

follows in Chapter III of the book and its title is: 'Theology and Verification' and is a response to the challenges of the Verification Principle.

Hick's view is that the Christian concept of God is 'in principle verifiable', because it is verified eschatologically. '**Eschatology**' is the doctrine of the 'last days'/the Last Judgement/the end of time, so Hick is claiming that the 'facts' of the Christian religion will be verified (or falsified) to you after death.

Hick is thus making two important claims concerning religious language:

1 Its claims are indeed cognitive/factual;

2 Those claims are subject to **(eschatological) verification**.

Eschatological verification – The Parable of the Celestial City

Hick's parable runs in parallel to that of Flew's Parable of the Gardener, but reaches a very different conclusion. The Celestial City of course represents heaven. The interpretation of the parable should become clear as you read it.

> # The Parable of the Celestial City
>
> Two men are travelling together along a road. One of them believes that it leads to a Celestial City, the other that it leads nowhere; but since this is the only road there is, both must travel it. Neither has been this way before, and therefore neither is able to say what they will find around each next corner. During their journey they meet both with moments of refreshment and delight, and with moments of hardship and danger. All the time one of them thinks of his journey as a pilgrimage to the Celestial City, and interprets the pleasant parts as encouragements and the obstacles as trials of his purpose and lessons in endurance, prepared by the king of that city and designed to make of him a worthy citizen of the place when at last he arrives there. The other, however, believes none of this and sees their journey as an unavoidable and aimless ramble. Since he has no choice in the matter, he enjoys the good and endures the bad. … And yet when they do turn the last corner, it will be apparent that one of them has been right all the time and the other wrong. [Note 12]

The key point here is that there is no evidence, while the men are making the journey, with which to determine whether or not there is a Celestial City. However, the fact that one of them believes in the City influences the way he encounters and deals with the various events along the way. That view and commitment influences everything and is meaningful – and remains so whether it is in fact true or false. Eventually, at the end of time, it will be shown to be one or the other.

You will remember from our survey of Hick's theodicy (See Volume 1, pages 71–76) that the parable reflects Hick's own view that, beyond this life, God will continue to offer people opportunities to know him and enter into a relationship with him, so that eventually salvation will be universal. Hick is concerned to show that, however much we choose how we will see things and therefore whether we believe in God or not, and even if we dismiss all evidence to the contrary because of our commitment, *there will be, in the end, a truth one way or another*. And if we cannot get to that truth in this life, we may expect to get it after death.

Activity

If you have access to Mitchell's *The Philosophy of Religion*, read pages 62–65, which show Hick's 'replica' theory, by which he aims to show that resurrection of the body is a *logical* possibility and that the believer at least has grounds for hope.

You can also see and hear Hick discussing the theory at: **www.cleo.net.uk/resources/ displayframe.php?src=937/ consultants_resources/re/jhrt/ jhrt.html**

Explain why it is important for Hick to show that bodily resurrection is *logically* possible.

So: does Hick's argument convince us that religious language is cognitive and that it meets the criteria required by verificationists? First, an exercise:

Strengths of Hick's argument

1 Hick's claim that the Celestial City/heaven is a real *possibility* seems undeniable. The statement, 'There is life after death' *must* either be true or false.

2 In fact Hick's argument seems to show that taken as a whole, Christian truth-claims are cognitive/factual, because if we do wake up in a resurrected body, then not only will we know that Christian claims about life after death are true, but also that many other claims made by the Christian religion are true, for example that God exists, that the resurrection of Jesus really happened, and that Christian claims about how God wants us to behave are also true.

3 Hick can support this conclusion by his further argument about 'Experiencing-as', in which he tries to show that interpretation is an essential element of all factual experience. [Note 13] Hick argues that we experience things 'as' something and as soon as we try to talk about things we are interpreting them. Sometimes interpretation is straightforward – as when I see something curled on the ground that could be a snake or a rope: to find out, I need to investigate further. Sometimes it is a matter of evaluation – we experience the result of a match as either a win or a loss depending on which side we are on. Many visual tricks present images that could be either one thing or another; for example:

▲ Optical illusions

As you look at these images, there is no difference in the data received by your eyes as you switch from seeing it one way to the other: it is simply interpretation. You see them 'as' one or the other and with some of the more extreme examples it takes quite an effort to switch. This was exactly the dilemma faced by the two explorers in Flew's story; one chose to see the clearing as a garden and the other did not. Their quest to track down the supposed gardener arose simply because there was no decisive evidence in the clearing itself – each chose to interpret it in his own way. So with Hick's Parable of the Celestial City, the believer and the non-believer are interpreting the same evidence in completely different ways. Both are valid interpretations of the evidence – evidence which includes our total experience of the facts about the world – and only at some point in the future (when we die) will it be seen which is correct.

Weaknesses of Hick's argument

1 Hick writes from the perspective of the believer for whom, in the end, the Celestial City will be reached. From the perspective of the atheist, particularly the atheist who focuses on the extent of the evil in the world, the possibility of the Celestial City being verified is so remote as to be not worth considering. In other words, if the believer and the non-believer are interpreting the evidence in completely different ways, Hick's argument is no stronger than that of the atheist.

As a counter-argument to this, Hick points out that there is a body of evidence in favour of life after death. To mention two examples: near-death experiences give some support for the possibility of continued consciousness after death, as do studies of alleged reincarnational memories by children (for example in the research of Professor Ian Stevenson). Evidence such as this is considered in Chapter 3 on 'Self, death and afterlife'.

2 Hick's argument that religious claims are verifiable eschatologically is not a normal factual claim. To explain this, Hick admits that if Christian religious claims about bodily resurrection are true, then of course they will be verified when the individual 'wakes up' to bodily experience after death; but if they are false, they can never be falsified, because the individual will never wake up to *know* that they are false.

This is not how 'normal' falsification works, however. To use our earlier example: if I claim that, 'There is a green dragon eating toast in the room next to you', if I find the dragon, the statement is verified; if not it is falsified and I *know* that it is falsified.

Hick tries to solve this problem by claiming that there are other examples of statements that will be verified if they are true but can never be falsified if they are false; but the example he gives is from mathematics and is a logical rather than a factual claim. [Note 14 – if you are interested, read the footnote for further information]

It would seem, therefore, that Hick cannot show that the Christian statement 'there is life after death' is a normal factual claim, subject to falsification, since if there is no continuing experience after death you will find out nothing at all.

As a counter-argument to this, the atheist's argument that there is no life after death is not a normal factual claim either, because if there is life after death, he will know that his claim has been falsified, whereas if there is no life after death, he will not be able to verify his claim, because he will be dead.

In summary, Hick's claim that 'There is life after death' is verifiable in principle, but not falsifiable, whereas the atheist's claim that 'There is no life after death' is falsifiable in principle, but not verifiable.

Activity

Think about and discuss the following questions, and write brief notes on them:

1 Hick believes that there is evidence for the possibility of life after death. Does the atheist have evidence to the contrary? Can the argument be settled by appeal to evidence?

2 Whose position do you find most coherent: Hick's argument about eschatological verification, or the atheist's denial of any kind of existence after death?

3 Do Hick's arguments show that religious language about life after death is at least coherent?

Religious language as an expression of a *blik* with reference to Hare

Whereas Hick argues that religious language is essentially cognitive and that it can meet the criteria laid down by the Verification and Falsification Principles, Hare argues that religious language is essentially non-cognitive and non-falsifiable.

R.M. Hare (1919–2002)

An English moral philosopher. Following the traumatic experience of being captured by the Japanese after the fall of Singapore in 1942 and having to do a forced march and hard labour, Hare returned to Oxford to complete his degree, then stayed on to teach, becoming a fellow and tutor in philosophy at Balliol College in 1947. He is best known for his work on ethics and particularly the view that moral statements 'prescribe' a course of action.

Key term

Blik Hare's use of the term refers to a framework of interpretation: a view of the world that is not an assertion, but is non-cognitive and non-falsifiable.

Faced with the challenge to religious belief presented by Flew, Hare's response (in the Oxford University symposium in 1948) is to defend religion by suggesting that it actually consists of a set of assumptions about the world (he uses the term '*blik*' for these assumptions). He argues that everyone has a *blik* and that *bliks* tend to determine all that person's other beliefs. The *blik* is not negotiable in a rational debate about evidence – in some ways it is beyond both reason and evidence. It is simply the way you see things: a framework for interpreting the world, and it is essentially non-cognitive.

Like Flew and Hick, Hare provides his own parable:

Hare's Parable of the Lunatic

A certain lunatic is convinced that all dons [Oxford university lecturers] want to murder him. His friends introduce him to all the mildest and most respectable dons that they can find and after each of them has retired, they say, 'You see, he doesn't really want to murder you; he spoke to you in a most cordial manner; surely you are convinced now?' But the lunatic replies, 'Yes, but that was only his diabolical cunning; he's really plotting against me the whole time, like the rest of them; I know it I tell you.' However many kindly dons are produced, the reaction is still the same. [Note 15]

We can see, says Hare, that the lunatic is deluded. There is no behaviour by which the dons can show him that he is wrong about them: he will allow nothing to count against his theory of homicidal dons – nothing can falsify his belief about them. Dons might look friendly, but that is just a mask. They might appear harmless, but that is merely a ruse to lull you into a false sense of security.

What the lunatic has, then (according to Hare) is a *blik*, which is a view about the world. The idea of *bliks* comes from Hume, who said that we cannot decide what the world is like by observing it, because ALL observation/evidence is open to interpretation (think of what Hick says about 'Experiencing-as'); rather, we have a *blik*, a view about the world that we may get from our family or friends.

- There may be many different kinds of *blik*.
- The lunatic's blik is an insane *blik*. Alternatively, most people have sane *bliks*. For example, I might have a *blik* that the quality of steel in my car may affect its steering. I might have no evidence at all that either the steel or the steering is defective, nevertheless it is important to me, since the consequences of defective steering can be terrible. No amount of safe arrivals or tests will remove my *blik* about the steering in my car.
- A religious *blik* is a common and powerful view and if I have one and am sincere in believing it and in following where it leads, then no amount of persuasion from well-meaning philosophers (such as Flew) will make me think differently.

Now compare Flew and Hare on religious statements:

Flew	Hare
Religious statements are assertions about the world, so they are intended to be cognitive/factual.	Religious statements are *bliks*. A *blik* is not a cognitive/factual assertion – it is an *interpretation* of the world. Religious *bliks* are therefore non-cognitive/non-factual.
Religious believers allow nothing to count against their cognitive/factual assertions, so religious statements are non-falsifiable and therefore meaningless. They die the death of a thousand qualifications.	Religious *bliks* are indeed non-falsifiable, but this is because they are non-cognitive; nevertheless they are deeply meaningful. The lunatic may have an insane *blik*, but his refusal to think differently about Oxford dons shows the depth of that meaning.

Flew's reply to Hare

Flew simply rejected Hare's view that religious statements are non-cognitive *bliks*, because believers *do* see their statements about God as cognitive and not as non-cognitive.

To see what Flew means, consider the Christian assertions that 'God cares for his creation' and that 'God will resurrect believers after death.' What would be the point of a Christian making these claims if he or she did not really believe as a matter of fact that there really is a caring God and that life after death will be a reality? Unless these are cognitive/factual assertions, then they amount to what Flew calls 'dialectical dud-cheques', meaning that they have no cash value, so are worthless. Most Christians really do believe that their assertions are meaningful assertions about the cosmos, and:

'If Hare's religion really is a blik, involving no cosmological assertions about the nature and activities of a supposed personal creator, then surely he is not a Christian at all?' [Note 16]

On the same page, Flew goes on to insist that Christians do intend their assertions to be factually significant; but their assertions are non-falsifiable and therefore meaningless; so they are just doomed attempts 'to retain … faith in a loving God in face of the reality of a heartless and indifferent world'.

Strengths of Hare's theory of *bliks*

1 Hare's concept of *bliks* does explain why it is that different religions make different factual claims. The 'truths' of one religion may contradict the 'truths' of another (for example, Christianity asserts the divinity of Jesus, whereas Islam denies it), which leads some to suppose that one religion is right and the others are wrong. It seems simpler to accept Hare's view that however sincerely a believer makes his assertions about God and the world, all such assertions are expressions of non-cognitive *bliks*. They are deeply meaningful to those who have them, but their value is in that *personal* meaning and not in any factual content they might be supposed to have.

2 Hare's position explains why people are not convinced by *evidence* that appears to contradict their deeply held beliefs. Believers see the evidence through the framework of their *bliks*.

3 Hare's argument that religious people see the world in a particular way seems to be true. Within that perspective, religious people see God at work in the world in a variety of distinctive ways; for example, through the beauties of nature, through meditation – in fact through the whole range of experiences generally described as 'religious' (for more on this, see Chapter 3 on Religious experience, Volume 1). In other words, Hare's view correctly reflects the idea that religion gives a view or attitude that is used to interpret *the whole of life*.

Weaknesses of Hare's theory of *bliks*

1 As Flew says, most believers do not see their belief statements as non-cognitive: they take their assertions to express factual truths about the cosmos, otherwise they would not bother to make them. Take the claim, 'There is a God'. Believers would argue that this is not just a way of seeing the world but a factual truth.

2 Hare seems to make a very odd claim – that Christian beliefs are expressions of non-cognitive *bliks whether Christians know it or not*. Christians might be supposed to know their own minds.

3 If there are no factual truths about Christianity, its value reduces to its psychological and sociological benefits.

4 Following on from point 3, 'There is a God' is a factual claim, not a non-cognitive one. Why would believers want to believe it non-cognitively? To use the language of verification, it is verifiable in principle by the existence and qualities of the universe (as in the Design and Cosmological Arguments for the existence of God – Volume 1, pages 13 and 45); and it is falsifiable in principle by the problem of evil.

Religious language as a language game with reference to Wittgenstein

Ludwig Wittgenstein (1889–1951)

An Austrian-British philosopher, Wittgenstein taught at Cambridge 1929–47. He inherited a considerable fortune from his parents, but eventually gave it away to his brothers and sisters. For a time he was at the same school as Adolf Hitler. Wittgenstein served in the Austro-Hungarian army during the First World War and was decorated more than once for bravery.

Wittgenstein, arguably the most influential philosopher of the twentieth century, developed three different approaches to language. In his early work (The *Tractatus*) he limited the meaningful use of language to its picturing function, so that its meaning comes from its correspondence to observed reality. But by the time his ideas were being taken up by the Logical Positivists, he had already changed his view and saw the meaning of language as given by the broader context of the way it was used. His work on language games, which concerns us here, was not published in his life time, and it shows even more development in his thinking.

Wittgenstein's treatment of religious language reflects a different theory of meaning from that of the views we have looked at so far. In his approach, it is inappropriate to treat religious claims as claims about the world: religious claims are not like scientific claims. The meaning of a statement is not defined by the steps you take to verify or falsify it, but by its use: use and context govern meaning.

This approach is the central feature of Wittgenstein's later work (published in *Philosophical Investigations*): the meaning of language is found in the way it is used and language is a tool for getting something done. He expressed this in a most remarkable piece of advice coming from a philosopher:

'Don't think; look!'

In other words, if you want to understand something, it is not enough to understand the meaning of words and the way they work logically or how they are backed up by evidence. Rather, it is important to look at *how the words are used*. Meaning is given by use.

He gives the example of a builder who calls out 'beam' or 'more bricks' to his assistant. The assistant, hearing it, understands what is wanted and fetches the required items. That language is a kind of activity. You shout 'bricks' because you want some, not to give a description. And if the assistant yells back 'Yes it is!' he would not last long in the job. Exactly the same thing happens when small children first learn to use words; they test them out to see if they work. 'Yes' and 'No' are key words for exactly that reason – their context is everything!

This leads to an *internalist* account of meaning – in other words, meaning resides in *use*, not with reference to some external existing entity. This has obvious implications for the discussion of religious language. If the meaning of a religious claim can only be understood in terms of the way in which it is used, we have to pay attention and describe how religious language functions – not try to claim that it is bogus or outdated science and then dismiss it. But to appreciate this, we need to know something of a central feature of Wittgenstein's later work: the '**language game**'.

Language games

Games are fascinating because they create an enclosed, carefully defined world in which the players have to obey rules. Football would make little sense and would certainly lose its ability to generate an intense emotional response of despair or triumph, if the players simply kicked the ball around the field at random. Chess would make absolutely no sense without the rules by which each piece may be moved.

In the same way, language works by creating different games in different situations. Each game defines the way words are used and the meanings they have. Consider the following:

● Giving an order
● Making a promise
● Telling a story
● Making a joke
● Making a shopping list.

These are all valid uses of language, but they are very different activities and 'forms of life'; the words only make sense when you understand the nature and purpose of that activity.

This is the essence of Wittgenstein's 'language game' theory and it is important to recognise that the rules for the use of language are therefore neither right nor wrong: they are merely useful for the job we want them to do. You wouldn't say that a joke is factually 'wrong' – it's simply a joke, and it either works or not depending on whether it makes you laugh. You cannot criticise other people's use of language without understanding the full intention, context and meaning of that use.

> **Key term**
>
> **Language game** Wittgenstein's term for the idea that language has meaning within a particular social context, each context being governed by rules in the same way that different games are governed by different rules. The meaning of a statement is not defined by the steps you take to verify or falsify it, but by the context in which it occurs, so use and context govern meaning.

So: language is an indefinite set of social activities (language games), each serving a different kind of purpose: for example, literally playing a game such as football, chess or darts; giving orders, praying, cursing, forming and testing a hypothesis, and so on. Each of these is its own language game. All of the meaning is in the language game of those who use it. If I play chess, the world of rooks, bishops and pawns makes sense within that language game. There are points of connection with other language games (for example, chess imports some of the language of war), but chess as a language game follows its own pattern and has its own meaning.

The implications for religious language

Religious language 'is' its own language game, with its own set of rules by which the game functions, such as praying, praising, extolling, worshipping, blessing and cursing.

In fact religious language is not *a* language game – rather it contains a *multiplicity* of language games within its own context, which is the language of the believing community (think of the breadth and depth of different forms of religious expression in the world). Within that context it makes perfect sense.

Religious language regulates the believer's life. It is like a picture: you can either use it and get something out of it, or else you can leave it alone. There is no contradiction between using it and not using it, any more than there is a contradiction if you do or do not want to play a game of chess. The statements, 'I believe in God' and 'I do not believe in God' are therefore not contradictory – they are just different perspectives.

In particular, religious language is not like scientific language. In the scientific language game, using evidence is part of the game, whereas in religious language it is not. Following Wittgenstein's approach, then, verification and falsification debates are irrelevant to religious language. Scholars like Ayer and Flew are typical examples – they are locked into the view of the Logical Positivists that the only form of meaningful language is cognitive/factual/scientific/evidential, and so they conclude that religious language must be meaningless. The mistake they make is to take the language of one language game (that of science) and apply it to another (that of religion). One might as well try to apply the language of Rap to that of quantum mechanics.

In summary, then, the religious language game is meaningful to those who want to use that game by immersing themselves in the religious 'Form of Life': we should not try to separate the meaning of religious beliefs from the community of people who use them and live by them.

'God' is therefore not to be understood as a scientific hypothesis about the possible existence of *a being*, but a word used within the religious community to denote the creative power within everything. God is what 'God' means for religious people.

Strengths and weaknesses of Wittgenstein's account of religious language as a language game

Strengths

1 It avoids the confusion that results from mistaking what language is trying to do, particularly the mistakes of the verificationist and falsificationist approaches to religious language.

2 It allows a variety of meaning: artistic, poetic, musical, emotional, historical, ethical and religious (for example) rather than expecting all language to conform to an empirical or scientific norm.

3 Wittgenstein recognises the meaning behind the statement of a Christian who says, 'There is a God.' To the believer, that statement affirms that they are, as H.H. Price puts it, *believing in* God rather than *believing that* God exists (in Chapter VIII of Mitchell's volume. See also Volume 1, page 14). They are confirming belief in God as a reality in their lives, and this does seem to capture the heart of what religious belief is about.

Weaknesses

1 Wittgenstein's approach discourages debate with secular thinkers.

If we cannot understand religious language unless we engage with it and use it according to the rules of the religious language game, this isolates religion from external criticism, whereas having to engage in critical debate with secular thinkers is arguably more likely to lead to understanding rather than confrontation.

2 Many Christians are committed to dialogue with those who do not share their language game. As a 'form of life', religion *does* attempt to communicate with those outside its own community – indeed Evangelical Christianity has this as one of its primary aims. It seems unrealistic to expect the meaning of all religious assertions to be protected from external examination and criticism, whilst at the same time claiming that the Christian message is of universal significance.

3 For some, the most serious criticism of Wittgenstein's language game theory is that religious statements no longer have to be true or false, so theoretically, a group of people could construct a consistent set of belief statements based on some of the most bloodthirsty religious practices of past civilisations, and these would form a valid language game. But most believers do not assume that this is what they are doing when they make religious assertions. Believers who assert that 'there is a God', or 'God is love', or 'there is an afterlife', do not generally think of these statements in anything like the same way as Wittgenstein. Instead, they believe that they are making assertions about reality and that their assertions are true.

In other words, there is a divide between what Wittgenstein thinks believers are up to and what most believers themselves think of the matter. If Wittgenstein acknowledges that religious 'truth' is defined by those who use the language game, then he seems to ignore the fact that they disagree with him.

4 Wittgenstein's theory of meaning assumes that there can be no evidence for metaphysical beliefs. This is arguably false. 'There is a God' is the main metaphysical belief of Christian theism and is a cognitive/factual claim in so far as a creative mind is a likely hypothesis to explain the existence of the universe. Bertrand Russell's claim that the existence of the universe is an inexplicable 'brute fact' is not borne out by the scientific method. Science works on the assumption that there are discoverable natural laws by which the universe functions, such as the laws of physics. It seems arbitrary to claim on the one hand that everything in the universe is explained by the operation of natural laws and on the other that the universe itself is an exception to those laws.

Conclusions as to the issue of whether religious language should be viewed cognitively or non-cognitively

You should at this stage have an overview of the different positions on this question:

Hick argues that religious language is cognitive because it is verifiable eschatologically. Experience after death will factually verify Christian claims. Hick's argument makes sense, but we have to question it because if there is no life after death, Christians will not wake up to know that the claims of their religion have been falsified.

Hare argues that religious statements are non-cognitive: they are non-falsifiable *bliks* – views of the world by which we interpret what we experience; but Flew seems right to reject this on the grounds that most believers do indeed think of their beliefs as cognitive, otherwise they are 'dialectical dud-cheques' – worth nothing.

Wittgenstein's language-game approach is also non-cognitive, but his argument seems to insulate religious believers from dialogue with those who do not share their beliefs. A lack of dialogue in and about religion is arguably unhealthy.

The strengths of cognitivism and non-cognitivism

Strengths of cognitivism

Cognitive religious language makes factual claims that are clear and open to examination by anyone.

Most religious believers are cognitivists – they hold that their beliefs are factual, a view supported by Hick. Believers are committed to those beliefs precisely because they believe them to be factual, not because they think that they are non-cognitive *bliks*.

Strengths of non-cognitivism

It does not pretend that religious language is scientific, so it avoids the kind of challenges mounted by verificationists and falsificationists.

It reflects the distinctive views and commitments of religious people: their religious *bliks*, as Hare would put it.

It acknowledges that there can be many different ways in which language can be meaningful.

The problem is that this does not seem to get us very far, since what cognitivists see as the strengths of their position are seen as weaknesses by non-cognitivists, and vice versa.

An alternative is to combine cognitivism with non-cognitivism

We do not have to conclude that religious language is definitely cognitive or definitely non-cognitive. For a start, not all cognitivists agree on what is factual and what is not. To see the force of this, look at the section on 'Self, death and afterlife' (Chapter 8 in Volume 1), particularly the variety of interpretations of Christian beliefs about resurrection, heaven, hell and purgatory. A Christian might have a cognitive understanding of resurrection of the body but a non-cognitive understanding of hell, seeing it as a psychological condition brought about by the believer's own thoughts and actions.

In other words, Christians find little difficulty in holding both cognitive and non-cognitive beliefs at the same time.

Something of this kind can be seen in the writings of Hick:

Hick accepts that mythological language in the Bible is non-literal and non-cognitive, but myth:

> '... nevertheless tends to evoke an appropriate dispositional attitude to [the Real/God]' [Note 17]

For example, the myth of:

> '... the fall of Adam and Eve in the Garden of Eden can be seen ... as a mythic story which expresses, and thereby engraves in the imagination, the fact that ordinary human life is lived in alienation from God and hence from one's neighbours and from the natural environment.' [Note 18]

The myth has become engrained in Christian tradition and so has the power to dispose Christians to seek God.

Nevertheless the Christian belief system *as a whole* is fact-asserting: [Note 19] its truth-claims are cognitive and will be verified in the afterlife, so these claims provide:

> 'an experientially verifiable claim, in virtue of which the belief-system as a whole is established as being factually true-or-false.' [Note 20]

The central affirmations of the Christian faith therefore have a '... genuinely factual character' in which there is still:

> '... ample scope for the non-factual language of myth, symbol and poetry to express the believer's awareness of the illimitable mysteries which surround that core of religious fact.' [Note 21]

On this kind of interpretation, then, we do not have to choose between understanding religious language as cognitive or non-cognitive: it contains both elements.

Discussion points

1 How important is it for religious believers that at least some religious claims should be cognitive/factual?

2 Are some religious assertions more cognitive than others? If so, which?

3 Should an atheist see religious language as cognitive or non-cognitive?

4 Do you think that 'There is a God' is a cognitive claim?

5 Do you think that 'There is life after death' is a cognitive claim?

6 Are statements about God's nature meaningful?

Other views of the nature of religious language

So far we have been examining the nature of religious language and whether it is cognitive or non-cognitive, and in the course of this we have seen that there have been many attempts to show that religious language is not like statements of empirical fact – it has to do with:

● a particular way of seeing things (Hare)
● the possibility that one will finally know the truth about beliefs that cannot now be verified (Hick's eschatological verification)
● the meaning within the circle of people who use it (Wittgenstein).

All these have been attempts to move away from the narrow 'picturing' view of language presented by the early work of Wittgenstein and taken up by the Logical Positivists.

However, there are other thinkers who start from quite a different position. They, in different ways, start from within the experience of religion and ask what it does to the meaning of words if they are to be applied to God. The result of doing this is to recognise that the previous debate has been loaded against the religious believer, because it has assumed too narrow a view of how language refers to, and expresses insights into, the nature of reality.

This is an important recognition, because religious language does not just arrive ready made for philosophers to examine logically. It comes out of the situation in which religious people want to say things about their religion and the experience they have of it.

To do this, we shall step back in time to the thirteenth century to look at what Thomas Aquinas had to say about analogy, and then further back to the mystical writing of 'Pseudo-Dionysius' in the early sixth century about the religious claim that nothing can literally be said about God, and finally to one of the twentieth century's great theologians, Paul Tillich, who attempted to put those two earlier traditions together in his argument that all religious language is symbolic, in that it attempts to express a meaning that always transcends the literal, just as God is 'within' but transcends the world.

A 'straw man' God?

A 'straw man' argument is an argument that somebody puts forward usually because they know it is easy to knock down. An easy way of discrediting an argument is to put forward a version of it that you know your opponent does not really support. All three thinkers that we now look at recognise that 'God language' is quite different from literal descriptions of physical objects in the universe. The implication of this is that the God, whose meaningfulness was rejected by the Logical Positivists and defended by Hick, Hare and others, was little more than a straw man – a superficial caricature, presented simply in order to be knocked down in an argument.

[NB – In order to preserve the sequence of argument here, we shall study these three thinkers in a slightly different order from that given in the specification – Aquinas on analogy, then the *Via Negativa*, then Tillich on symbol.]

Religious language as analogical with reference to Aquinas

Thomas Aquinas (1225–74)

The philosophy of Aquinas is now familiar to you from his Cosmological Argument for the existence of God and from his construction of the ethics of Natural Moral Law. He also wrote extensively on the nature of religious language.

Key term

Analogy An analogy is an attempt to explain the meaning of something which is difficult to understand by comparing it with something that is more securely within our reference-frame.

An **analogy** is an attempt to explain the meaning of something which is difficult to understand by comparing it with something that is more securely within our reference-frame. You have already come across its use in theology through Paley's analogical Design Argument for the existence of God.

Aquinas' doctrine of analogy follows from his rejection of both *univocal* and *equivocal* language to describe God.

To explain these terms: if you use the same word to describe different things, its use may be:

- **univocal** – if it means exactly the same thing each time. For example, if I describe both a coat and a lump of coal as 'black' I am using that word univocally – it means exactly the same thing in each case.
- **equivocal** – if it means different things when used in the different situations. For example, we can use the word 'bat' to describe something used to hit a cricket ball; we also use 'bat' to describe a flying mammal.

So what happens when you use the same words (for example, good, loving, merciful) to talk about both a human being and God? In this situation, neither univocal nor equivocal meaning is of much use.

Univocal language will limit God, making him too much like the ordinary things to which the word generally refers.

On the other hand, if we use words equivocally nothing is going to be conveyed.

For example, if I were to claim univocally that God is loving, in exactly the same way that people are loving, then I run into all sorts of problems, because God presumably does not have a body, or the means of expressing love in an ordinary human way. On the other hand, if I claim equivocally that God is loving in a way that is nothing at all like human love, then I have said absolutely nothing about him, because it empties the word 'love' of any meaning.

Aquinas argued that language used to describe God's nature should do so analogically. In other words, the meaning of a word when applied to earthly things could be extended to be used of God, once it was recognised that it was being used as an analogy and not in a literal or univocal way.

For our purposes, we can say that Aquinas set out two different forms of analogy:

1 The analogy of attribution

God is completely different from the universe. Nevertheless there is a causal relationship between the universe and God, since God is its creator and this gives meaning to language about God.

Aquinas' explanation of analogy is not easy to understand. He talks (for example) about the relationship between a healthy body and healthy urine [Note 22], since the colour, smell (and taste) of urine were used as a diagnostic of the body's health. From this, several commentators have drawn out the following analogy, which is taken here from the account by Peter Vardy and Julie Arliss. [Note 23]

Take the statements: *The bull is healthy;* and *the bull's urine is healthy;*

The health of the bull's urine relates to its colour, smell and taste. The health of the bull is completely different; nevertheless the two are linked because the bull produces the urine.

Similarly, we can say:

God is good, wise and loving; and *Vanessa is good, wise and loving;*

God created Vanessa (just as the bull created the urine), so God is causally responsible for goodness, wisdom and love in Vanessa (and in fact in *everything* else).

This does not mean that God's goodness, wisdom and love are just magnified versions of Vanessa's goodness, wisdom and love; rather, it means that God has what it takes to produce these qualities in Vanessa.

But God's goodness is not moral goodness; rather it is simply whatever it means for God to be good and we cannot know what that is.

From the analogy of attribution, we can therefore conclude that:

1 although we have no idea what it means for God to be good, the assertion that God is good is meaningful.

2 If you look back at Section 7 ('God'), in Volume 1 (page 265) on God and the problem of using anthropomorphic language about God, Aquinas' analogy of attribution seems to solve this problem. To say that God is Love, Judge or King, for example, means that God has what it takes to produce those attributes in persons.

2 The analogy of proportionality

Both a human being and God may be described as 'powerful', but we assume that the meaning of 'powerful' in each case is *proportional* to their respective natures. Equally, an ant is remarkably powerful in being able to move a leaf, but its power does not match that of the human being who accidentally treads on it.

Hick uses an example from the Catholic theologian Baron von Hügel (1852–1925) [Note 24]:

> We can describe the quality of faithfulness in a human, and we can understand similar characteristics of faithfulness in dogs.
>
> That faithfulness is neither completely different nor the same, so the language we use to compare them is neither equivocal nor univocal – it is analogical.

The analogy is 'downwards' in the sense that there is a big difference between canine faithfulness and faithfulness in humans, since the latter is based on self-conscious deliberation (a quality that dogs do not have).

We can also make an analogy 'upwards' to the faithfulness of God, but this time the analogy is reversed: faithfulness in humans is at best a remote approximation to faithfulness or any other quality in God.

As Hick goes on to point out, the doctrine of analogy does not tell us what God's perfect attributes as such are like:

> As used by him [Aquinas], the doctrine of analogy does not profess to spell out the concrete character of God's perfections, but only to indicate the relation between the different meanings of a word when it is applied both to man and (on the basis of revelation) to God. Analogy is not an instrument for exploring and mapping the infinite divine nature; it is an account of the way in which terms are used of the Deity whose existence is, at this point, being presupposed. The doctrine of analogy provides a framework for certain limited statements about God. [Note 25]

Ramsey's view on analogy

Ian Ramsey offers a well-known clarification of analogical statements about God. Ramsey (1915–72) was an English philosopher of religion who also became Bishop of Durham.

Ramsey's views on analogy are not required in the specification, so no exam question can be set requiring knowledge of them. They are included here because they are well known, and could be used, where relevant, in response to a general question involving analogy.

Ramsey's description of the process of applying analogical terms was set out in his book: *Religious Language*. [Note 26] He uses the terms 'model' and 'qualifier'.

A *model* is a word that has a straightforward meaning when applied to ordinary things we experience, but may also be used to describe God. For example, we know what it means to be a 'creator' so, by analogy, we can use the word 'creator' as a model for describing God.

However, it is important that the model should not be misunderstood and used *univocally* of God. Hence the need for a *qualifier* – a word to show how the model is to be applied to God. So, for example, we might speak of an 'infinite' or 'perfect' creator, in which case 'creator' is the model and 'infinite' or 'perfect' are its qualifiers.

In that book, Ramsey covers other aspects of religious language, emphasizing that it expresses discernment (it tries to express something that the religious person believes they have seen or understood about reality) and also commitment (it is not simply a detached or objective description of reality). A corresponding commitment comes from God in the form of a 'disclosure', whereby everyday empirical experiences take on a new depth and meaning for believers, and the language of models and metaphors taken from these experiences is most appropriate to talk about them.

Strengths and weaknesses of the use of analogy to talk about God

Strengths

1 A literal, univocal language is going to be inadequate to talk about God, since it does not take into account God's transcendence, but tends to reduce him to the status of one *thing* among many, a possible 'thing'. Analogy avoids this.

2 In the same way, analogy avoids anthropomorphising God, because anthropomorphic language is not meant to be taken as literal.

3 Religious experience often takes a person beyond words, but in seeking to describe what they have experienced, they need to use words, but recognise that they need to push beyond their ordinary, limited meaning. Analogy does that very well.

4 Analogy uses ordinary human experience and qualities in order to express something [God] that transcends them, and because it is based on human experiences it is cognitive and allows language about God to be meaningful/to avoid non-cognitivism.

Weaknesses

1 Others disagree with the whole idea of analogy, on the grounds that in order for both the analogy of attribution and the analogy of proportionality to work effectively, you have to have prior knowledge of God. You cannot argue that God's love is analogous to human love if you do not even know what is meant by the word 'God.' Equally, you can only show a proportional relationship if you know both the things that are to be compared.

For example, Hick's account of the analogy of proportionality, based on the idea of a 'downwards' analogy from human faithfulness to faithfulness in a dog and the corresponding 'upwards' analogy to faithfulness in God, is not really proportional at all. If God's faithfulness is infinite (to use Ramsey's qualifier), then *human to God* cannot be remotely proportional to *dog to human*.

2 Some object that the analogy of attribution can be used to prove that God is evil, because if we say, 'God has what it takes to produce goodness in humans', we can also say that 'God has what it takes to produce evil in humans'.

Aquinas had an answer to this objection, which you might remember from your study of the Problem of evil in Volume 1; namely that evil is not a thing in itself, but is simply the absence of good, in the same way that darkness is not a thing in itself, but is simply the absence of light. God cannot, therefore, be accused of bringing about evil in humans. We pointed out that there are problems with this view of evil (Volume 1, page 58), so you might like to revisit that section before you make a judgement about analogy here.

(Volume 1, page 58)

Discussion points

Aquinas accepted that creation must be causally dependent upon its Creator. Aquinas also accepted that some of our ideas about God are given to us by special revelation (scripture).

For those who already believe that God exists as the Creator and that God is personal and is the source of qualities found in things in the world (the sort of God that Aquinas had argued for by his Cosmological Argument), it makes perfect sense to use analogy to explain how one might speak of God.

But those who do not already have those beliefs have no reason to say anything about God, whether analogical or univocal. Hence, analogy works best within the context of theology; that is, within the circle of those who already play the religious 'language game', to use Wittgenstein's term.

Does this mean that Wittgenstein's non-cognitive view of religious language is right after all?

Key terms

Apophatic theology (From Greek 'to deny') – the denial of a positive description of God, hence the *Via Negativa* – the 'negative way' 'by way of denial'.

Kataphatic theology Kataphatic is Greek for 'affirmation', so kataphatic theology uses positive terms about God (as opposed to apophatic theology, which uses only negative terms).

The *Via Negativa*

Kataphatic and apophatic ways

There are two different but complementary approaches to religion – the **apophatic** and the **kataphatic**.

In prayer, for example, some people think that it is appropriate to use words, describing God, asking for things, praising him and so on – that is kataphatic prayer. Others think the best approach is to sit and open the mind to silence, allowing God's presence to infuse the experience, but not in a way that can be described – that is apophatic prayer.

In theology, too, some traditions – particularly Western Christianity – place great emphasis on saying things about God, with creeds and descriptions of his qualities – kataphatic theology. Other traditions – to some extent seen in Eastern Orthodox religion, but particularly in some branches of Hinduism and Buddhism – emphasise the idea that God's reality/Ultimate Reality is beyond all description – the apophatic approach.

Mystics have generally taken the apophatic way, and Wittgenstein, who was particularly interested in mysticism, ends the *Tractatus* with a perfect definition of the apophatic way: 'Whereof we cannot speak, thereof we must remain silent.'

Think back to Volume 1, Chapter 3 on Religious experience, where we referred to those (such as Otto and Stace) who see God as being utterly transcendent and ineffable. It may be argued that God is so transcendent and therefore so beyond the ordinary meaning of the words we use to describe things, that there is *nothing* we can say about him in any positive or literal way without at the same time diminishing him. To use Ian Ramsey's language, the 'qualifiers' we need in speaking about God totally swamp out the content of the 'models'. God is somehow known, but yet remains beyond knowledge. This is called the **Via Negativa**.

If that is so, then the most we can say is what he is *not* – in other words, we can deny God the sorts of qualities and limitations that might apply to other beings.

In terms of Christianity, this tradition goes back to Pseudo-Dionysius, who lived in the fifth and early sixth century CE, and whose writings were influential through the mediaeval period.

> ### Key term
>
> *Via Negativa* The 'negative way' – to state only what may not be said about God.

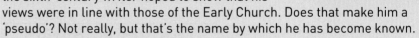

Pseudo-Dionysius the Areopagite

Be reassured, 'Pseudo' is not the saddest of first names! It refers to the fact that this unknown writer of the early sixth century presented his work as though coming from Dionysius the Areopagite, who (in Acts 17:34) was converted to Christianity by Saint Paul. According to the Church historian Eusebius, Dionysius became the first bishop of Athens. Clearly, the sixth-century writer hoped to show that his views were in line with those of the Early Church. Does that make him a 'pseudo'? Not really, but that's the name by which he has become known.

Pseudo-Dionysius was a Neo-Platonist, deeply influenced by Plato's distinction between the eternal, unchanging and perfect realm of the 'Forms', contrasted with the limited and changing material things in this world.

Pseudo-Dionysius accordingly developed the *Via Negativa* in order to emphasise the transcendence of God and therefore to separate him from any literal description which could limit him or identify him with the changeable things in this world. He was also a mystic, which means that he thought that one could experience God in a personal way that went beyond the use of language.

Pseudo-Dionysius suggested that God is nameless, and yet 'has the names of everything that is'. This follows from both the broad sense of God not just as creator (which requires no more than a deistic view of an external God) but as involved creatively within everything, and from the mystical sense of being at one with God. Language that commonly uses words to describe the 'bits and pieces' of our world cannot hope to embrace this sense of an indwelling and omnipresent God.

Support for the *Via Negativa* comes also from Maimonides.

Maimonides (c.1135–1204)

A Jewish philosopher, astronomer and physician, born in Cordova (present-day Spain). Known as 'the Great Eagle' for his expertise in the Jewish Oral Torah. Maimonides apparently despised poetry on the grounds that it was linguistic invention.

Maimonides insisted that God was not comparable to anything else, and that to say (for example) that God is the most powerful being, means that God's power can be compared with human power, which reduces God to a thing that can be measured against everything else. He therefore adopted a negative theology, which 'describes' 'God by accumulating all the negatives, such as 'God is not corporeal'/'God does not exist in space'. Consider the following passage, in which he claims that only the negative attributes bring us closer to the knowledge and understanding of God:

> I will give you … some illustrations, in order that you may better understand the propriety of forming as many negative attributes as possible, and the impropriety of ascribing to God any positive attributes. A person may know for certain that a 'ship' is in existence, but he may not know to what object that name is applied, whether to a substance or to an accident; a second person then learns that a ship is not an accident; a third, that it is not a mineral; a fourth, that it is not a plant growing in the earth; a fifth, that it is not a body whose parts are joined together by nature; a sixth, that it is not a flat object like boards or doors; a seventh, that it is not a sphere; an eighth, that it is not pointed; a ninth, that it is not round shaped; nor equilateral; a tenth, that it is not solid. It is clear that this tenth person has almost arrived at the correct notion of a 'ship' by the foregoing negative attributes … In the same manner you will come nearer to the knowledge and comprehension of God by the negative attributes … I do not merely declare that he who affirms attributes of God has not sufficient knowledge of the Creator … but I say that he unconsciously loses his belief in God. [Note 27]

What are we to make of this and of the *Via Negativa* in general?

Evaluation of the *Via Negativa*

Strengths

1 It does avoid the problem of positive language about God, where God appears to be seen as a *thing* over and against other things. If God is the

Creator and is therefore the *source* of all things, then it is reasonable to think that God cannot himself be a thing.

2 It avoids anthropomorphism, since its focus is on God's transcendence.

3 Its focus on God's transcendence is also supported by the claims of those in the mystical tradition, such as Otto and Stace, and in apophatic forms of meditation, where mystical experiences of God are said to be ineffable/indescribable/beyond sense experience.

Weaknesses

1 The *Via Negativa* claims that it is possible to approach some kind of understanding of God by saying what God is not. Brian Davies comments:

> Maimonides evidently thinks that this claim is true; but the reverse is the case. For only saying what something is not gives no indication of what it actually is, and if one can only say what God is not, one cannot understand him at all. Suppose I say that there is something in my room, and suppose I reject every suggestion you make as to what is actually there. In that case, you will get no idea at all about what is in my room. Going back to the quotation from Maimonides [quoted above] … it is simply unreasonable to say that someone who has all the negations mentioned in it 'has almost arrived at the correct notion of a "ship"'. He could equally well be thinking of a wardrobe. [Note 28]

2 To put the last point in a slightly different way, think back to Flew and the 'Parable of the Gardener', where the believer keeps qualifying his statement about the gardener, saying that the gardener is invisible, inaudible, intangible and incorporeal. You can see that this is the language of the *Via Negativa*, and Flew's complaint is that defining God in this way amounts to a definition of nothing. The concept of God 'dies the death of a thousand qualifications'.

3 Mystical tradition may support the *Via Negativa*, but if a mystic says that he or she has had an experience of God, but then cannot describe that experience, how can we tell whether it was an experience of God or simply an experience produced by the brain?

4 How practical is the *Via Negativa* for religion? Is it possible to worship a God who is described entirely in negative ways: not finite, not visible, not tangible, not limited in any way, not having parts and passions?

Clearly, most believers do want to say positive things about God and they therefore have to find appropriate ways to qualify the language they use in order to do so. Is it possible to find a form of language that is both cognitive and yet avoids the problems of literalism and safeguards the transcendence of God? One attempt to do this, which gets beyond the cognitive and non-cognitive debates outlined earlier, is Tillich's idea that religious language is based on symbols, and to this we now turn.

Religious language as symbolic with reference to Tillich

Paul Tillich (1886–1965)

A German Christian existentialist theologian, Tillich was brought up as a Protestant, was ordained and became a military chaplain to the German forces in the First World War. The experience of war led him to question traditional Lutheran theology, and for some years he taught philosophy in German universities, before being thrown out of his post by the Nazis and escaping to the United States.

His theology sought to match up the existential questions people ask about life and its meaning with the symbols offered in traditional Christian language and doctrine. He is particularly known for his argument that God is 'Being-itself' rather than a separate being, and that religion is about one's 'ultimate concern' – that which ultimately gives life value and meaning.

We have seen that debates about whether religious language is cognitive or non-cognitive, analogical or equivocal, are difficult to resolve. For Aquinas' doctrine of analogy to work, so that you can assert (for example) that 'God is loving', you have to believe: 1) that God exists; 2) that the term 'loving' can be applied analogically to God with reference to *human* experience; but – do we really know that it is appropriate to apply that term to God? Alternatively, if we prefer to use the *Via Negativa* to think of God as ineffable, infinite and indescribable, we seem to end up being able to say nothing cognitive about God at all. Paul Tillich's view of religious symbol addresses both these problems.

Here are four of the main features of symbols according to Tillich's account.

1 Symbols point to a reality beyond themselves.

2 They 'participate' in the power to which they point.

3 They open up levels of reality which would otherwise be closed to us.

4 At the same time they open up levels of the soul which correspond to those realities.

Tillich also adds:

5 Symbols cannot be produced intentionally; they grow out of the human unconscious.

6 Symbols are produced and die within a cultural context. For example, the religious systems of Ancient Greece and Rome died when the symbolism of their pantheon of gods lost its resonance and meaning.

To explain these features:

1 and 2 In his *Systematic Theology*, Tillich makes an important distinction between a sign and a symbol:

A sign is a conventional way of using an image or word to point to something other than itself. Take the example of road signs. We learn the Highway Code because we need to know what those signs stand for. Some of them picture what they signify (for example, the warning signs for a slippery road or for older people crossing); others are abstract (such as a 'no entry' sign). The key thing is that they are conventional and can be replaced if we decide to do so.

By contrast a symbol points beyond itself, like a sign, but it also participates in the power of that to which it points. [Note 29] For example, a flag is a sign of the country it represents and at the same time it participates in the power and dignity of that country:

3 and 4 For Tillich, if we want to discover the true nature of religion, then this can only arise from religious experience, and this kind of experience can be expressed only by symbolic language.

Where Tillich says (point 3) that symbols open up levels of reality which would otherwise be closed to us, he explains this by an analogy with the arts (such as poetry, art and music). The arts can put the individual in touch with another level of existence. As an example (not Tillich's), the 'Ring Cycle' ('Der Ring des Nibelungen') is a musical masterpiece that Richard Wagner constructed over a period of 26 years. It is a combination of mythological and poetic themes, not least when the Valkyrie Brünnhilde loses immortality to experience passion and death itself with Siegfried. The Ring Cycle creates its own level of reality through musical, poetical and artistic symbolism, and does so uniquely. Further, through music and art of this stature, the soul can find new perspectives on life.

Religious symbols, then, fulfil their function uniquely, so nothing else can fulfil that function. They open up a level of reality that otherwise is not opened up at all. Tillich is influenced, here, by the work of Rudolf Otto on religious experiences, which we studied in Chapter 3 of Volume 1. For Otto, the essence of religion is where the soul experiences that which is 'numinous' and 'the Holy'. You will remember his argument that numinous feelings are not just more intense versions of our normal feelings: they are *sui generis*, meaning they are unique or in a class of their own. They are a special faculty in our minds – a faculty that recognises the holy and responds to it.

Our attempts to say things about God arise out of such experiences. For Tillich, there are two essential features to the 'God' that appears through religious experience or a religious symbol:

1 God is 'Being-itself' rather than a being. In other words, an experience of God is not an experience of something that just happens to be there: it is not an experience of one object among others. Rather, it is an experience of life itself – of 'being/existence' itself: an experience which then gives meaning to everything else.

2 God is our 'ultimate concern'. For the religious believer, God demands total attention and commitment, covering all other aspects of life. This sense of God as the most important concern in life is seen in the nature of religious experience.

All this is crucially important when we talk about 'religious language'.

1 The *only* literal statement in religious language is that God is 'Being-itself'. We cannot use literal language to *describe* 'Being-itself', because asking the

question, 'What is 'Being-itself'?' is not a question about a particular being. Rather, it is to examine the question of what it means to be – to exist.

2 A symbol is 'self-transcending' – it means something in itself, but also points beyond itself to some higher or greater reality. For example, if you see a new-born baby, the significance of that experience goes beyond the physical thing you see: its meaning transcends that. As another example, for those who consume the bread and wine in a service of Holy Communion, the significance of that experience can transcend the physical experience of eating and drinking. It is this self-transcending quality of life that is key to Tillich's understanding of all religious language as symbolic, because symbolic language is the only kind of language that can express that self-transcending quality.

3 God does not exist as a separate being: God is not 'a being' among others. God is 'Being-itself'.

4 God is the name for what a religious person encounters in a way that is personal and demanding, not in any way casual or detached. This means that if we use the language of the Cosmological Argument in an attempt to prove the existence of God, for example, this is NOT religious language: it is merely about cosmology. For something to be religious, it has to reflect religious experience and/or religious practice.

To conclude:

In this way, Tillich was able to take conventional religious language and show the way in which it addresses the personal needs and questions that people have about reality and meaning. It does not give factual information about another world, or a supernatural realm, but shows the profound, religious significance of features of *this* world.

Love and God

The radical nature of the way in which the idea of the religious symbol cuts across much of the discussion of religious language can best be illustrated by taking a single example: the claim that 'God is love'.

If that claim is taken to give information about a deity inhabiting a supernatural realm, it falls under all the criticism offered by the Logical Positivists and others. There is no direct evidence for any such cognitive claim. On the other hand, if we shift to a non-cognitive approach, we end up saying that 'God is love' means little more than the personal and subjective decision to live in a loving way, or to take love as our primary motivation.

Even if we manage to define what we mean by God, we are then stuck with the problem about how an eternal, omnipresent God can be described using words whose meaning is given with reference to ordinary, limited objects in this world – hence the discussion of the use of analogy. If we despair of describing God through analogy, we may end up with the view that nothing positive can be said about God at all.

That is where symbolism comes to the rescue. Instead of starting with the idea of a separate being called 'God' and a known experience called 'love', suppose we put the two together and suggest that, in the experience of love, we encounter a reality that transcends our particular circumstances. God then becomes a name we give to the reality revealed by love. In this way, symbolic language conveys information about what is experienced, and yet it does not refer to the experience of a separate entity called 'God'. It also reflects the theological claim that God is everywhere – expressed in St Paul's idea that 'In him we live and move and have our being …' (Acts 17:28). The religious symbol is a direct consequence of that conviction about God, and of the nature of religious experience. An ordinary word becomes a symbol when it offers us insight into the nature of reality itself. That – according to Tillich– is what 'God language' is about. It is not to do with any doubtful claim about supernatural beings.

Strengths and weaknesses of the use of symbolic language to talk about God

Strengths

1 Symbolic language can relate religious ideas to ordinary/everyday experiences, such as love.

2 It allows us to make only one literal statement about what we mean when we speak of God – that God is 'Being-itself'. God is not a being who exists within this universe or in some transcendent realm, even an infinite and eternal being; so we do not have to try to say something meaningful about such a being, either through analogy or through the *Via Negativa*, for example.

3 It reflects what is known through religious experience, through which we can gain insight into issues that are central to our lives, such as guilt, sin, alienation, love, redemption, salvation, judgement and the Kingdom of God. These are understood in an existential sense: they tell us something about the meaning of our lives.

Weaknesses

1 Hick rejects Tillich's view that a symbol 'participates' in the reality to which it points and complains that Tillich does not clarify what this means. For example, if we take the symbolic statement that 'God is good':

> Is the symbol in this case the proposition 'God is good,' or the concept 'the goodness of God'? Does this symbol participate in 'Being-itself' in the same sense as that in which a flag participates in the power and dignity of a nation? And what precisely is this sense? … Again, according to Tillich, everything that exists participates in 'Being-itself'; what then is the difference between the way in which symbols participate in 'Being-itself' and the way in which everything else participates in it? [Note 30]

2 Hick also disputes Tillich's view that symbols arise from the unconscious mind:

> If we take a complex theological statement such as, 'God is not dependent for his existence upon any reality other than himself', Hick asks, 'Is it really plausible to say that [this] … has arisen from the unconscious, whether individual or collective?' [Note 31]

Hick is making the valid point that far from arising from the unconscious, many of the important things we want to say about God (such as the Cosmological and Design Arguments) arise from the *conscious* brains of philosophers and theologians.

3 Many Christians do not share Tillich's view of God as 'Being-itself'. For Tillich, God as a separate being *does not exist*, and what we call God is 'Being-itself' – the ground upon which all beings exist. This does not sit well, however, with those Christians who do see God as a separate and transcendent being who is also the ground of our existence; or with deists who see God as the Creator who made the universe and then left it to follow the laws by which it was made; or with the views of Process theologians who see 'God-and-the-universe' existing panentheistically (see Volume 1, pages 77–82).

Discussion points

1 'Using cognitive/literal language about God says nothing meaningful.' How far do you agree?

2 'All the problems about religious language disappear when we see it as symbolic.' How far do you agree?

3 To what extent is it true that religion is about the numinous/the uncanny/the 'wholly other'?

4 To what extent is religious language about value and commitment?

5 'God does not exist in any literal sense.' How far do you agree?

6 Do art, poetry, or music open up new levels of meaning for you?

Concluding synthesis

In religious studies, as in other disciplines, beware of any demands to decide *specifically* what is true and what is false, what is right and what is wrong, and what is or is not the case. There is no requirement that truth should have only one level and one descriptor.

You do not have to decide, then, whether religious language is specifically cognitive or non-cognitive, or whether it is equivocal, analogical, metaphorical, symbolic, or anything else. It is the case that religious assertions can be understood in any or all of these ways, and that each understanding says something useful to bring out the distinctive nature of religious language.

We move, now, to the study of miracles, where the central question is: What do assertions about miracles mean? This question involves both realist and anti-realist understandings of miracles and you might find that the debate offers another perspective on the nature of religious language.

Technical terms for religious language

Analogy An analogy is an attempt to explain the meaning of something which is difficult to understand by comparing it with something that is more securely within our reference-frame.

Apophatic theology (From Greek 'to deny') – the denial of a positive description of God, hence the *Via Negativa* – the 'negative way'/'by way of denial'.

Blik Hare's use of the term refers to a framework of interpretation: a view of the world that is not an assertion, but is non-cognitive and non-falsifiable.

Cognitive Language is cognitive if it conveys factual information and most cognitive statements are synthetic (they are shown to be true or false depending upon evidence).

Eschatological verification Refers to Hick's view that the 'facts' of the Christian religion will be verified (or falsified) at death.

Eschatology The doctrine of what will happen at the end of time/in the last days/at the final judgement.

Falsification Principle A sentence is factually significant if and only if there is some form of evidence which could falsify it.

Kataphatic theology Kataphatic is Greek for 'affirmation', so kataphatic theology uses positive terms about God (as opposed to apophatic theology, which uses only negative terms).

Language game Wittgenstein's term for the idea that language has meaning within a particular social context, each context being governed by rules in the same way that different games are governed by different rules. The meaning of a statement is not defined by the steps you take to verify or falsify it, but by the context in which it occurs, so use and context govern meaning.

Logical Positivism The philosophical approach taken by the Vienna Circle: a group of philosophers who met in that city during the 1920s and 1930s. The Logical Positivists claimed that metaphysical and theological language are literally meaningless, because they are neither matters of logic nor provable by empirical evidence.

Metaphysics The philosophy of concepts beyond the physical. Deals, for example, with abstract questions such as: what is the nature of time/space/reality?

Non-cognitive To say that a statement is non-cognitive is to say that it is inappropriate to ask whether or not it is factual. Non-cognitive statements may convey emotions, give orders, or make moral claims, for example.

Supernatural Literally 'above' what is natural; that which cannot be described by science/the laws of nature.

Verification Principle The meaning of a statement is its method of verification. For example, the meaning of the statement, 'my car is parked on the road outside the house' is that, if you go outside the house and look towards the road, you will see my car, since that is the way you can verify my statement as being true. Verification is by sense experience – for example, sight.

Via Negativa The 'negative way' – to state only what may not be said about God.

Summary of religious language

Background

During the early twentieth century, scientific language came to be seen as the 'ideal' language because science produces measurable results and benefits through its empirical/factual approach to the world. The Logical Positivists launched an attack on religious language through the Verification Principle (VP), claiming (following Hume's 'Fork') that language is meaningful only if it is logically true/tautological or empirically verifiable.

The challenge from the Verification Principle

Ayer in particular used the Verification Principle to argue that religious statements cannot be verified either in practice or in principle, so are literally meaningless. Religious statements, like moral statements, have no factual content. They say nothing about the world, so are neither valid nor invalid, neither true nor false; so for the same reason atheists and agnostics also fail to say anything meaningful about the world.

Strengths and weaknesses of the verificationist challenge

- One strength of Ayer's VP is that it makes a straightforward demand for verification through sense experience, but in effect he dismisses the whole range of history, morality, aesthetics, art, music and poetry as meaningless; whereas these give direction and meaning to human existence.

- The VP is in line with empirical science, but science itself deals with unobservable entities, so properly speaking the VP should dismiss science as meaningless, which of course it does not.

- The VP does make a valid demand for realism in what we say about the world, but it should recognise that religion itself does offer a reasonable hypothesis about the origin of the world through the act of a creative mind (God).

- Ayer demands verification in principle, but some philosophers of religion hold that religious statements can be verified in principle by empirical statements made by observers at the time (for example those recorded in the Gospels).

- Perhaps the most significant objection to Ayer's VP is that it appears to be a metaphysical assumption about the way things really are, but Ayer dismisses religious statements as metaphysical assumptions, so his VP is an example of the very thing it was intended to guard against.

The challenge of the Falsification Principle

This stems from Popper's argument that science makes progress by discovering evidence to prove existing theories false. Antony Flew's 'Parable of the Gardener' applied falsificationist thinking to religious statements, arguing that since the believer will allow nothing to falsify his beliefs, they are vacuous/meaningless. Statements such as 'God loves his children'/'God has a plan' seem like vast cosmological assertions, but like the explorer's belief in the gardener, they 'die the death of a thousand qualifications' and are 'killed inches at a time'.

The falsificationist approach has the strength of forcing religious believers to explain why religious 'facts' are not like ordinary 'facts'. It is difficult, for example, for believers to explain why an all-powerful God appears unable to control evil. However, as with the VP, the falsificationist approach tends to ignore the fact that life is not confined to factual understanding. Humans use art, poetry, literature and many other tools to interpret life and to give it meaning.

Falsification is too rigid in its understanding of truth: truth is not restricted to scientific truth, but can include metaphysical truths about the universe, and these cannot be analysed by falsificationism. Also, it is not true that religious believers will allow nothing to falsify their beliefs: the extent of evil in the world causes many to lose their belief.

Responses to the challenges from verification and falsification

1 Hick: Religious statements are cognitive and will be verified eschatologically

Hick claims that the Christian concept of God will be verified eschatologically, so religious language is cognitive. He attempts to show this by his Parable of the Celestial City: the traveller who believes in the celestial kingdom (heaven) has no evidence to determine whether or not it exists, but is still committed to its existence; and at the end of the journey will be shown to be right or wrong. Hick supports his argument by his Replica theory, by which he establishes that resurrection of the body is at least logically possible, so the believer has grounds for hope.

In its favour, Hick's view is a real possibility. It also makes a strong claim that religious language must be cognitive, since the claims of the Christian religion as a whole will be (after death) shown to be factually true or false. Hick's view of 'Experiencing-as' shows that interpretation is a factor in all experience and that people can and do interpret evidence in completely different ways, so our disagreements about religion are understandable. Only at death will we know which interpretation of the data is correct. Against Hick, for the atheist his views are mere wishful thinking. In particular, Hick has an 'asymmetrical' view of verification and falsification, meaning that if religion is true it will be verified, but if it is false it can *never* be falsified, because dead people can experience nothing. If people do not wake up in the resurrection, they will never know that Christianity has been falsified. However, some evidential support for Hick might come from near-death experiences and from claims about reincarnational memories.

2   Hare: Religious statements are non-verifiable/ non-cognitive *bliks*

According to Hare, religious assertions are non-verifiable/non-cognitive *bliks*. *Bliks* are assumptions about the world, and everybody has a set of *bliks* about the world which gives them a framework to understand other beliefs. *Bliks* cannot be used as evidence in a debate, so must be non-cognitive. Hare illustrates this by his 'Parable of the Lunatic'. There may be different kinds of *bliks* – insane ones (like the lunatic's); sane ones (worries about the quality of steel in your car's steering); and religious ones. Religious *bliks* are so powerful that well-meaning philosophers (like Flew) cannot make believers think differently.

Flew responds by assuring Hare that believers really do think that their religious claims are cognitive, otherwise there would be no point in making them: they would be mere 'dialectical dud-cheques'. The believer who says that God is love really means that to be a factual statement, but of course no religious claims are factual in reality, because they are non-falsifiable and meaningless, despite Hare's denial of that.

Strengths of Hare's theory of *bliks*

- It explains why different religions make different factual claims: their claims are not factual at all – they are all non-cognitive *bliks*.

- It explains why believers generally reject any *evidence* that contradicts their beliefs: they 'bend' evidence to fit their *bliks*.

- As Hick might say, for the believer, everything is 'experienced-as' having religious meaning.

Weaknesses of Hare's theory

- Most believers see their beliefs as cognitive – as making *factual* claims about the universe.

- If there are no factual beliefs in Christianity, then in effect its value just reduces to statements of psychology or sociology.

- Christians are not likely to agree with Hare that their beliefs are non-cognitive *whether they know it or not*.

- For instance, what kind of believer would really want to claim that 'there is a God' is not a factual assertion?

3   Wittgenstein: religious language as a language game

According to Wittgenstein, the use and context of a statement govern its meaning. Different activities (telling a story, playing chess, writing political slogans on a wall, etc.) are 'forms of life', and they make sense only if you understand the nature and purpose of each activity. Language is an indefinite set of social activities, each serving a different kind of purpose, each being called a Language Game [LG]. LGs are not 'right' or 'wrong' – they are merely useful for the job we want them to do. So, religious language is its own LG, with its own set of rules, such as: praying, praising, worshipping, blessing and cursing. In fact the religious LG contains a multiplicity of LGs within its own context.

Religious language regulates the believer's life; and as with games like rugby or chess, you can use it, or if you have no use for it, you can ignore it. There is no contradiction between the statements, 'I believe in God'/'I do not believe in God', since these are just different perspectives. The religious LG is not like the scientific LG, so verification and falsification debates are irrelevant to its meaning. 'God' in the religious LG is not a scientific hypothesis about a *being*, but a word within the religious community to denote the creative power within everything.

Strengths of Wittgenstein's LG theory

- It avoids the verificationist and falsificationist confusion over what religious language is trying to do.

- It allows a variety of meaning – artistic, poetic, musical, ethical, historical, emotional and religious – without demanding that everything should conform to a scientific/empirical norm.

- Wittgenstein sees that religion is about the reality of God in the life of the believing community. As H.H. Price puts it, religion is about the passionate commitment of 'belief in' God, not the intellectual statement of 'belief that' there is a God.

Weaknesses of Wittgenstein's LG theory

- How do you debate with atheists/agnostics/ secularists? Isolating religious belief from external criticism is not a good thing.

- LGs are supposedly self-contained, but many Christians (for example, evangelicals) are committed to dialogue with those outside their LG.

- Most believers do not agree with Wittgenstein about the nature of the religious LG. Religious statements no longer have to be true or false, but most believers want to make what they see as true/cognitive/factual/cosmological claims, for example that 'There is a God'.

- Wittgenstein's theory of meaning assumes that there can be no evidence for metaphysical beliefs, but the existence of the laws of nature imply a metaphysical explanation of the universe in terms of a creative mind.

Is religious language cognitive or non-cognitive?

1 Strengths of understanding religious language as cognitive

- It makes clear factual claims that can be examined by anyone.

- Most believers are cognitivists.

- Believers are committed to religion because they see their beliefs as factual, and not as non-cognitive *bliks*.

2 Strengths of understanding religious language as non-cognitive

- It avoids the view that religious language can be scientific, so avoids the verificationist and falsificationist challenges.

- It reflects the distinctive views and commitments of religious people (their *bliks*).

- It acknowledges that religious language is one of many different ways in which language can be meaningful.

BUT: the strengths of cognitivism are seen as weaknesses by non-cognitivists, and vice versa, so this doesn't get us very far. A reasonable answer is that religious language is both cognitive *and* non-cognitive. For example, some (such as Hick) hold that claims about the existence of God or life after death are cognitive claims, whereas mythological statements in the Bible are non-cognitive (for example, the myth of Adam and Eve is about alienation from God).

Other views of the nature of religious language

1 Religious language as analogical (Aquinas)

Aquinas argues that religious language is neither univocal nor equivocal: it is analogical. Although God is completely different from the universe, since God is the Creator, there must be a causal relationship between the universe and God, and that gives meaning to language about God. In the analogy of attribution, therefore, if we talk about the human attributes of goodness, wisdom and love in persons, as the Creator of humans, God has what it takes to produce these qualities in humans. In the analogy of proportionality, just as we can make a downwards analogy to the faithfulness of a dog, we can make an upwards analogy to the faithfulness of God, even though human faithfulness is only a remote approximation of faithfulness in God. Ian Ramsey uses models and qualifiers to clarify analogy: for example, to speak of an infinite and perfect Creator, where 'Creator' is the model, and 'infinite' and 'perfect' are the qualifiers.

Strengths of using analogical language about God

- It avoids using univocal language about God, and so avoids treating God as a 'thing' among other things.

- It avoids speaking anthropomorphically about God.

- It is useful in pushing words beyond their normal meaning, for example in talking about religious experiences.

- Analogy is cognitive, being based on human experiences; so it allows 'God-talk' to be meaningful.

Weaknesses of analogy

- It works only if you know both terms being compared, but we do not know God.

- If we can say that God has what it takes to produce good qualities in humans, then we have to admit that God has what it takes to produce evil qualities too (although Aquinas denies that evil exists).

2 Religious language and the *Via Negativa*

Where kataphatic theology says positive things about God, apophatic theology emphasises the belief that God is beyond all description: it is the kind of territory about which Wittgenstein famously said: 'Whereof we cannot speak, thereof we must remain silent.' The *Via Negativa* [VN] can be seen in the approach of Otto and

Stace to religious experiences of the transcendent and ineffable God. Literal language cannot describe such a being, so all positive terms about God must be denied. The VN was developed in the sixth century by Pseudo-Dionysius to emphasise God's transcendence and mystical otherness. In the twelfth century, Maimonides insisted that language about God can only say what God is not. He argued that a person who does not know what a ship is can come to that understanding by finding out what it is not.

Strengths of the VN

- As with analogy, the VN avoids seeing God as a 'thing' among other things.

- Its focus on God's transcendence also avoids anthropomorphism when talking about God.

- The focus of the VN is supported by the mystical tradition of the numinous and 'wholly other'.

Weaknesses of the VN

- As Brian Davies says, listening to someone saying what a ship is not is just as likely to lead you to think of a wardrobe as a ship.

- In Flew's Parable of the Gardener, the (theist) explorer explains God's absence from the garden/world by saying that God is invisible, inaudible, intangible and incorporeal, which takes the same approach as the VN. All that does, according to Flew, is to kill the idea of the Gardener/God by 1000 qualifications.

- Mystical experiences might support the VN, but how do we know that such experiences are of God as opposed to being produced by the brain?

- Is it possible to worship a God who is described entirely in negative ways?

3 Religious language as symbolic (Tillich)

For some, symbolic language about God solves the problem with analogy and with the *Via Negativa*.

The main features of Tillich's account include:

- Symbols point to a reality beyond themselves.

- They 'participate' in the power to which they point.

- They open up levels of reality which would otherwise be closed to us.

- At the same time they open up levels of the soul which correspond to those realities.

- Symbols cannot be produced intentionally; they grow out of the human unconscious.

- Symbols are produced and die within a cultural context.

To explain the third of these six features of Tillich's account, Tillich draws an analogy with the far-reaching effects of the arts upon our thoughts and mentality: they show us new levels of meaning. When we come to *religious* symbols, these are unique, and nothing else can fulfil their function. They come specifically from religious experience of the kind derived by Otto and Stace. Through religious experience, we learn that God is not a being, but is 'Being-itself'. Moreover, God is our ultimate concern.

The only literal statement in religious language is that God is 'Being-itself'; but we cannot use literal language to *describe* 'Being-itself', because 'Being-itself' is not about a particular being – it is about what it means to be – to exist. Where people try to show the existence of God, as through the Cosmological or Design Arguments, these miss the point, because these arguments treat God as *a* being, and not as 'Being-itself'.

Symbols are self-transcending, meaning that they point to a higher/greater reality. For example, the sight of a newborn baby transcends the physical experience of seeing; equally, the physical act of consuming bread and wine in Holy Communion is given a transcendent meaning. Symbolic language (according to Tillich) is the only kind of language that can express this self-transcending quality.

Religious symbolism does not give us factual information about another world or a supernatural realm – it shows the profound religious significance of features in this world. *To say that God is love, for example, is not to say something about a separate being; rather, 'God' becomes a name we give to the reality revealed by love in this world.*

Strengths of symbolic language

- It can relate religious language to ordinary everyday experience, such as the experience of love.

- It allows us to make one cognitive claim: that God is 'Being-itself'.

- It reflects what is known through religious experiences, and tells us the meaning of our lives.

Weaknesses of symbolic language

- Hick questions whether Tillich's view that a symbol 'participates' in the reality to which it points really means anything at all.

- Hick also rejects Tillich's idea that complex theological claims such as, 'God does not depend for his existence upon any reality other than himself', come from the *unconscious* mind. They surely come from *conscious* theological reasoning. The same is true of the kind of theology we see expressed in the Cosmological and Design Arguments for the existence of God.

- Many Christians do not share Tillich's view that God is 'Being-itself', preferring to see God as a transcendent being who is the ground of our existence (as with Aquinas).

Overall conclusion

You do not have to decide whether religious language is cognitive or non-cognitive, analogical or symbolic, or anything else. Religious assertions can be understood in any or all of the ways we have looked at, and perhaps each understanding adds something to bring out the distinctive nature of religious language.

2

Miracles

You will need to consider the following items for this section

1 Differing understandings of miracle:
- realist and anti-realist views
- violation of natural law or natural event.

2 Comparison of the key ideas of David Hume and Maurice Wiles on miracles.

3 The significance of these views for religion.

Note that these topics are not independent of each other, so their study will involve additional explanatory material.

There is no shortage of claims to miracle; and one can only think that those theologians who thought that 'modern man' can no longer believe in miracles must have had a remarkably limited range of acquaintances. [Note 1]

Introduction

This introductory material is not examinable. Its aim is to put the debate into context.

Why study miracles?

Studying what people mean by 'a miracle' is absolutely key to any Religious Studies course, because it raises fundamental questions about the nature of reality and the function of religion. Starting from Hume's argument that there is never sufficient evidence to prove a miracle, any discussion of miracles should also move outwards to consider related questions such as the nature of scientific evidence, whether the universe is predictable, whether life is fair, whether anything happens by chance, the nature of religious language and what we mean by the supernatural.

Here are some of the questions you might want to ask yourself as you approach this topic:

- If you believe that miracles are possible (in a literal, physical sense – but we'll come to that later), it follows that you believe in a God, or another spiritual force, who or which is both able to interfere with or to circumvent the workings of nature and is willing to do so. But what sort of God could that be? If people argue that nature is designed in such a way as to reflect the intentions of a loving God, does that not exclude miracles? If God needs a miracle to put something right, should he not be blamed for getting it wrong in the first place? So an understanding of miracles impinges on our understanding of 'God'. In a well-ordered world, miracles should not be necessary.

● How do miracles square with our understanding of science? Are religion and science opposed to one another? Can a scientist believe in miracles? Can a miracle be 'proved' by science and still remain a miracle?

● Are miracles morally acceptable? If one person is saved when 99 are killed, can that person claim that they were spared through a miracle? And, if they do, does that not imply that the 99 who were killed were victims of God's ill-will or indifference?

● What do we mean by 'miracle'? Is it more than a unique and unexpected event? If so, in what way?

Differing understandings of miracle

The word 'miracle' is used to describe many different types of event in this world, and has many different meanings. We have to consider **realist and anti-realist views** and the views that miracles may be **violations of natural law or natural events**.

Realist and anti-realist views

When Antony Flew (from the standpoint of an atheist) considered the miracles of the New Testament in his 1984 book *God and Philosophy*, he pointed out that a major feature of Christianity was that it was based on a particular moment in history – the life and teachings of Jesus Christ – and that its truth depended upon historical evidence. The key miracle for Christians is the resurrection of Christ, so it is important to establish whether or not this should be understood as an historical event.

His view (which is also that of a conventional Christian theologian such as Swinburne) is that the factual approach is necessary for Christianity to maintain its idea of the incarnation – in other words, that God has been revealed definitively in Jesus. This is termed a 'realist' view. The problem then, as Flew points out, is that as soon as you insist that a miracle is historical, you are faced with all the normal criteria for establishing the truth of historical claims. As Hume says, a wise man must proportion his belief to the evidence. As we shall see when we look at Hume's arguments in detail, this is an argument that undermines any realist view of miracles.

To begin with, it is clearly important to know the difference between **realism** and anti-realism. You might find these rather strange ideas, but the real/anti-real distinction is important for the study of just about anything, miracles included.

Key term

Realism Realist understandings of the world generally hold: 1) that scientific theories give us true (or approximately true) descriptions of the world; 2) that they give us knowledge of things that we believe to exist but cannot observe, such as isolated quarks; 3) that the world is mind-independent: it exists the way it is, regardless of what we think. Applied to miracles, a realist account sees them as real events brought about by God (or someone empowered by God). God exists as a real being, transcendent and unobservable, who creates and cares for the world.

Realism

1 Someone who is a realist in the scientific sense generally accepts the following:

- The best scientific theories that we now have give us true (or at least approximately true) descriptions of the world.
- These theories also give us true (or approximately true) descriptions of things that we believe to exist but which cannot be observed. For example, we have no direct observational evidence that quarks exist, since no one has seen an isolated quark, yet the indirect evidence for their existence is so overwhelming that for a realist it can be considered to be a proof. The 'Standard Model' of particle physics does not make sense without quarks, so they must exist in some manner.
- The world is mind-independent, meaning that the world exists, and is the way it is, regardless of what we think.

2 Just as scientists can be realists about the world, religious people can be realists about miracles:

- Miracles are a real part of what happens in the world.
- They are brought about by God, or by someone who is empowered by God to bring them about (for example, people like Moses and Elijah in the Old Testament), or by another spiritual force. God exists as a transcendent and unobservable being; nevertheless miracles are evidence of God's existence and of his care for the world.
- These things are true despite the fact that we do not understand everything about miracles.

When a realist informs us that a miracle has taken place, she:

- is telling us about something that has happened in the external world
- is telling us about the nature of the event
- may be making a claim about the (supernatural) cause of the event.

Realist examples of miracles

1 Miracle as an extraordinary coincidence of a beneficial nature

▲ Juliane Koepcke

Juliane Koepcke was a German-Peruvian high-school student. In 1971 she was on board flight 508 from Lima to Pucallpa when it encountered a thunderstorm over the Peruvian rainforest. The plane crashed after a free-fall of around 10,000 feet, killing all 6 crew and 85 of the 86 passengers. Juliane was the sole survivor. With various injuries, including a broken collar-bone, she survived a nine-day journey through the jungle, with maggot-infested wounds, in order to reach help.

Another (much quoted) example of a coincidence-miracle is the account of a gas explosion at West Side Baptist Church, in Beatrice, Nebraska, during 1950. The explosion demolished the church and would have killed its choir, but all 15 members were late for choir practice, each for a different reason, and so avoided certain death. [Note 2]

Note that there is no dispute about whether these events happened or not – there is good evidence that they did. Nor is there any dispute that some people identified them as miracles. However, this realist definition of miracle is limited: it only *describes* the event (it is an amazing coincidence). It does not make any claims about the involvement of God or any other supernatural power in the event: that interpretation comes from some of those who observed what happened.

In Peru, Juliane's survival was seen as a miracle brought about by God, and was subsequently produced as a film: *I miracoli accadono ancora* ('Miracles Happen Again'). The event was labelled a miracle of chance because of the extraordinary odds against her survival.

The problem with describing either of these events as a religious miracle is obvious. With Juliane Koepcke, if God helped her to survive, what about the other 91 passengers and crew who did not? Were they somehow less worthy? With the members of the church choir, in what lies the miracle? Should we believe that God manipulated the personal circumstances of each choir member so as to make them late? Why bring about their survival and not that of countless victims of explosions recorded each year throughout the world?

2 Miracle as an event brought about by the power of God or another spiritual power, working through people.

This category is obviously significant religiously, since the Bible contains numerous accounts of God acting through persons in this way, particularly Moses, whose actions in carrying out the ten plagues on Egypt (Exodus 7:8–11:10) are given through the power of Yahweh. Equally, Moses is instructed by God in how to perform 'the' great miracle of Israel's deliverance when trapped between the sea and the pursuing Egyptian chariots (Exodus 13:17–14:22). The miracles of Jesus recorded in the New Testament are also interpreted historically by many Christians.

The importance of miracles as demonstrations of divine power and compassion is particularly important in Catholic tradition. Miracles invite belief in God and strengthen faith, but are not intended to satisfy people's curiosity for magic or to abolish all evils. The Catholic Church has the 'Congregation for the Causes of the Saints', which investigates accounts of miracles performed by those people who are being considered for canonisation – in other words, to become saints. A person cannot become a Saint in the Catholic Church unless he or she has performed miracles, because they are taken as signs of God's action through that person, and therefore of his endorsement of their status. Investigations are made, witnesses interviewed and medical evidence is gathered. Something is only accepted as a miracle if there is strong evidence for it having taken place for which there is no scientific explanation, and if it was as a result of the direct action of the person being considered for canonisation, or the result of prayers inspired by that person.

3 Miracle as a violation of natural law.

If we take 'natural law' to be a statement of the way that nature works when left to itself, then 'natural law' defines what is possible, and what is not possible, for nature to do on its own. 'Miracle' then becomes the word that means something that could not have happened if nature alone was at work, so is an event brought about by the intervention of a supernatural power – which for many is God.

The 'classic' account of the view that a miracle is a violation of the laws of nature comes from David Hume. We shall look closely at Hume's definition in section 4 below, but for now, Hume had three parts to his definition:

- a miracle is a transgression of a law of nature
- by a particular volition [an act of will]
- by the Deity (God) – or by the interposition [intervention] of some invisible agent.

John Mackie also sees no issue with the *idea* of intervention into a closed system (that is one which works according to its own set of laws), but note that Mackie was an atheist, so did not believe that there is a God to intervene in the first place. However, Mackie accepts that the concept of God's intervention is conceivable.

> Even in the natural world we have a clear understanding of how there can be for a time a closed system, in which everything that happens results from factors within that system in accordance with its laws of working, but how then something may intrude from outside it, bringing about changes that the system would not have produced of its own accord, so that things go on after this intrusion differently from how they would have gone on if the system had remained closed. All we need do, then, is to regard the whole natural world as being, for most of the time, such a closed system; we can then think of a supernatural intervention as something that intrudes into that system from outside the natural world as a whole. [Note 3]

For most people today, this is the starting point for investigating the concept of miracle: the violation of natural law is needed in order to make the miracle stand out as a miracle. Most people accept that some of the more colloquial ways we speak about miracles (as a pleasant surprise or a lucky coincidence) are not sufficiently wonderful to merit being called 'miracles'. The event has to be the result of an act of God's *will*, as opposed to a completely inexplicable chance happening. Finally, the requirement for God to be the agent of the miracle acknowledges that to be a miracle, the event has to have religious significance.

There is, however, an immediate problem with this account of miracles – modern science simply does not accept this understanding of natural law, and does not accept that natural laws can be violated.

Natural law as descriptive or probabilistic

The understanding that the laws of nature cannot be violated is based on the scientific conviction that the laws of nature are *descriptive*, not *prescriptive*. In other words, a 'law of nature' cannot dictate what *must* happen; it summarises what *has been found to happen*. **Laws of nature sum up what we have observed.**

You cannot 'break' a law of nature in the way that you could disobey the law of the land. With judicial laws, you can break the law simply by disobeying it. There will probably be a penalty, depending on the severity of your crime, but there are no laws that cannot be flouted.

With the laws of nature, things are completely different. If an event does not conform to what a scientific law predicts, then there are three possibilities: the evidence for that particular event is faulty; or there is an unknown factor in play that the 'law' does not take into account; or the law is itself inadequate and needs to be adapted or expanded to take the new event into account. Scientific laws cannot be 'violated', they can only be revised.

Hick supports this conclusion: **If there appears to be an exception to a law of nature, then the law simply expands to include the exception.**

Hick's point is clear: natural laws are made by observing what has happened, so 'violation' miracles are impossible. If we observe something that appears to contradict a law of nature, then our understanding of that law has to be widened. This is the same as saying that if an event has no natural explanation at present, then that is not evidence that a supernatural explanation is required but that science still has much to learn. It is also saying that what is seen as a 'violation' is actually only a natural event.

Furthermore, Hick's studies in paranormal/parapsychological phenomena such as telepathy and psychokinesis (the ability to move objects by the power of the mind) led him to see such events as analogous to supposed miraculous happenings. Paul Badham gives an example, that

> '... an "answered prayer" might well be explained by telepathy in a more open, but still thoroughly naturalistic, world view.' [Note 4]

So, for example, what might currently be seen as miracles of healing will probably turn out to be brought about in a naturalistic way by some as-yet unknown power of the human mind. This would mean that 'God' is presently being used as an explanation to fill in the gaps in scientific understanding, but will be made redundant as an explanation by new scientific discoveries. God is a 'god of the gaps' but the gaps will soon be filled.

The present natural laws may be considered probabilistic – they show what is *likely* to happen rather than what is going to happen. For example, it is probable that if I try to walk on water I will sink, but until I try I will not know. Keith Ward argues that even in this case it is reasonable to think that some events are not produced by nature alone:

> [I]t is possible that an event, or a series of events, could be so improbable
> that even a specific set of probabilistic laws could not be formulated to
> include it. At the level of common sense observation, rare events which
> seem to be well beyond the possibilities of natural explanation available
> to us will be candidates for miraculous action … [I]t is logically possible
> that truly anomalous events could occur, and if they do, strictly scientific
> explanation will simply have to ignore them or set them on one side for the
> moment at least. [Note 5]

There are two further problems with this understanding of miracle that we will discuss later in this chapter:

- If the reported miracle is a violation of or exception to natural moral law, then the mass of evidence supporting the law counts against the claim that the miracle actually happened. That may make it unreasonable to believe in miracles.
- If God intervenes in nature when he wants to, why is there still suffering in the world? This is the problem of evil.

So far, every realist understanding of miracles suggests that they are rare or exceptional events and that the great majority of events taking place in the world are not miracles. This is not a view that all religious believers share. For them, a beautiful sunrise or sunset can be a miracle, as can the birth of a child. In short, every event may be considered miraculous. This idea brings us to an alternative perspective on miracles: the **anti-realist** view.

Anti-realism

1 Someone who has an anti-realist approach generally denies the realist positions outlined above.

An anti-realist will argue that we can have no knowledge of a mind-independent world, since the phenomena observed by our senses are *interpreted* by the mind. The mind is our only means of understanding anything.

There can be no commitment to anything unobservable (such as God as 'a being'), because an unobservable 'something' has no cognitive content: how can we talk meaningfully about 'unobservable things'?

2 Someone who is an anti-realist about miracles might make similar claims about miracles:

We can have no knowledge of a transcendent realm, so the idea of miraculous intervention in this world by a transcendent God is not a sensible idea.

Miracles are 'in the mind' – they are mental states or attitudes that are to be understood in terms of psychology and sociology: a miracle is something that lifts the spirit, or transforms a community of people.

3 When an anti-realist talks about miracles, she is informing us about her state of mind. She is NOT making a claim about the event itself.

Paul Tillich and Roy Holland both offer an anti-realist view of miracles.

Miracles as sign-events – Paul Tillich

We have looked at Tillich in connection with his view that religious language is symbolic. Within that view, Tillich does not see God as 'a being'; instead,

> **Key term**
>
> **Anti-realism** Anti-realist understandings deny that we can have knowledge of a mind-independent world, since the phenomena observed by our senses are interpreted by the mind. Any talk of God as an unobservable 'something' has no cognitive content, so 'God' cannot be discussed meaningfully. Applied to miracles, a miracle might be seen as something that lifts the spirit, or transforms a community of people.

what we call 'God' is 'Being-itself' – existence itself. Thus Tillich does not understand miracles in the realist terms of interventions in the world by a transcendent God. Instead, miracles are 'sign-events' that cannot be divorced from their religious context.

Tillich thus defines a miracle as:

> '... first of all an event which is astonishing, unusual, shaking, *without contradicting the rational structure of reality*. In the second place, it is an event which points to the mystery of being, expressing its relation to us in a definite way. In the third place, it is an occurrence which is received as a sign-event in an ecstatic experience.' [Note 6]

To be considered a miracle, then, the event first has to be astonishing, without breaking any law of nature; second, it must point to the mystery of being, relating specifically to the experiencer's existence; and third, it has to be a sign/symbol within a religious experience.

In his writing on miracles as 'epiphanies of the spirit' [Note 7], Keith Ward brings out the anti-real nature of what Tillich describes:

> What must be noted is that these three marks all stress the subjective element of the apprehension of a miracle, rather than the objective nature of the event itself. That something astonishes me, that it discloses to me the ultimate mystery of my being, and that it is received by me in a commitment of faith – these are all in the end remarks about me and my reactions. If we ask about the nature of the event itself, Tillich is quite explicit that 'miracles cannot be interpreted in terms of a supranatural interference in natural processes'. Such a thing would destroy the natural structure of events, and it is reminiscent, he thinks, of superstitious beliefs in demonism and sorcery. Tillich wishes to keep the seamless causal robe of nature intact. So miracles become patches of that robe which astonish me and cause me to re-envision and re-establish my inner relation to the ground of my being. The robe remains intact; the miracle is mainly in my mind. [Note 8]

It should be clear to you, now, why Tillich's view of miracles is anti-real:

- There is no commitment to the idea of God as 'a being' who, from a transcendent realm, intervenes to bring about a miracle.
- No law of nature is violated.
- Others would observe the same events but NOT see them as miracles.

John Hick's comment on miracles is also helpful here:

> For a miracle, whatever else it may be, is an event through which we become vividly and immediately conscious of God acting towards us. A startling happening, even if it should involve a suspension of natural law, does not constitute for us a miracle in the religious sense of the word if it fails to make us intensely aware of being in God's presence. In order to be miraculous, an event must be experienced as religiously significant. Indeed we may say that a miracle is any event that is experienced as a miracle; and this particular mode of experiencing-as is accordingly an essential element in the miraculous. [Note 9]

R.F. Holland

R.F. (Roy) Holland (1923–2013)

Holland was one of a group of philosophers called the 'Swansea Wittgensteinians'. Holland lectured in Philosophy at University College in Swansea from 1950 to 1965, where he was influenced by an American philosopher, Rush Rhees. Wittgenstein used to visit Rhees; hence the connection.

Holland was apparently fond of telling stories and anecdotes to illustrate his philosophical ideas, and the following story illustrates his approach to miracles. As you read the story you will realise that this is another 'coincidence miracle' as described in the section on realist views of miracles, but in this case Holland is saying that *there is nothing miraculous about coincidences*, except the way that they are interpreted.

A child riding his toy motor-car strays on to an unguarded railway crossing near his house and a wheel of his car gets stuck down the side of one of the rails. An express train is due to pass with the signals in its favour and a curve in the track makes it impossible for the driver to stop his train in time to avoid any obstruction he might encounter on the crossing. The mother coming out of the house to look for her child, sees him on the crossing and hears the train approaching. She runs forward shouting and waving. The little boy remains seated in his car looking downward, engrossed in the task of pedalling it free. The brakes of the train are applied and it comes to rest a few feet from the child. The mother thanks God for the miracle, which she never ceases to think of as such, although as she in due course learns, there was nothing supernatural about the manner in which the brakes of the train came to be applied. The driver had fainted, for a reason that had nothing to do with the presence of the child on the line, and the brakes were applied automatically as his hand ceased to exert pressure on the control lever. He fainted on this particular afternoon because his blood pressure had risen after an exceptionally heavy lunch during which he had quarrelled with a colleague, and the change in blood pressure caused a clot of blood to be dislodged and circulate. He fainted at the time when he did on the afternoon in question because this was the time at which the coagulation in his blood stream reached the brain. [Note 10]

It would be a confusion, according to Holland, to understand this event as involving a violation of the natural order. What makes it 'miraculous' for the mother is that it is a beneficial coincidence which she interprets in a religious fashion. The mother believes in God, and so her understanding of the event makes sense within the context of her religious life. Moreover, she continues to think this way *despite the fact that she later learns that there was nothing supernatural about how the brakes of the train came to be applied.* To that extent, Holland's account here offers an anti-real approach to miracle:

- The mother is aware that God did not cause the driver to faint.
- She offers no supernatural rationalisation of what happened.
- Nevertheless, she interprets what happened as God's response to human need.
- As Wittgenstein might say, the event belongs to a form of life to which she subscribes, and in that context it is perfectly sensible to call it a miracle.

There are obvious problems with both realist and anti-realist accounts of miracles. For now, from the anti-realist point of view, whether the event can be seen as a miracle depends on the way in which it was interpreted by those concerned. The mother sees it as a miracle, because it reflects her desperate hope that the train will stop. But what about the poor driver? Suppose, as a direct result of the blood clot reaching his brain, he becomes severely disabled or dies. Would his relatives consider that a miracle? The problem with any anti-realist interpretation is that it will vary according to the values, hopes and intentions of the people concerned.

We shall consider problems such as these in the final section on the significance of these views for religion.

▲ *Jesus Walks on the Water* from 'Illustrations of the Life of Christ', 1874

Activity

Read the account of the miracle of Christ walking on water in the Gospel of Matthew (14:22–36) and note the main features of the account. What differences of understanding might there be between a realist and an anti-realist understanding of this miracle story? Which do you think offers the best understanding, and why?

If miracles are natural events, or if they cannot be observed to be any different from natural events, does that mean that God, or another spiritual force, had nothing to do with them? The answer to that has to be 'no'. If *every* event is a miracle and God is somehow present within every event, then it is conceivable that people are divided according to how 'God-blind' they are, in a similar way to which the sighted are different from the partially sighted and the blind. God-blind people would therefore have no sense of the presence of God, partially God-sighted people would be aware of God only in the most exceptional events: those in which God is doing the equivalent of jumping up and down in front of them. Those with slightly more sight would also be aware of God in the less spectacular coincidences in which they feel God's presence. The truly God-sighted would be aware of God at all times and, for them, everything would be miraculous. In the end it is a simple matter of fact, either God is active in the world or not. It makes no difference to the truth or falsity of that statement whether I, or you, believe it or not.

Comparison of the key ideas of David Hume and Maurice Wiles on miracles

Hume's critique of miracles

> ### David Hume (1711–76)
>
> Hume was a philosopher and historian, a leading figure in the period known as the Scottish Enlightenment, and a radical critic of religious beliefs, which he believed to be contrary to reason and evidence. He was an empiricist, in that he believed all valid knowledge to be based on experience. As a historian he insisted on testing the validity of all historical documents and assessing the reliability of their authors as able to give an objective account of events.

Knowledge is based on experience

> A wise man … proportions his belief to the evidence. [Note 11]

Hume takes the empiricist's view that knowledge derives from sense experience. Hume is utterly modern – he wants to subject accounts of miracles to proper scrutiny. The more evidence we have for any event, the higher its probability. That principle is fundamental to science and Hume has therefore applied it to accounts of miracles.

Hume assumes (as do most people) that religion is based on factual claims and doctrines that (for believers) are literally true. Of course, you might want to ask whether religion is simply a matter of believing facts – and almost certainly it is not. But for Hume, the truth of a religion is the truth of the claims that it makes.

In his day, Hume was better known as a historian than a philosopher. His *History of England* was hugely popular, and in it he set to work in a way that is remarkably modern, taking all the pieces of evidence for historical claims and subjecting them to careful scrutiny, weighing up the probability that they reflected particular vested interests, and sifting contradictory accounts and interpretations of events. Hence, his approach to the issue of evidence for miracles is not simply a philosophical trick to try to disprove them, but a fundamental expression of his very modern approach to historical documents.

Hume's definition and understanding of miracle

> A miracle is a violation of the laws of nature; and as a firm and unalterable experience has established these laws, the proof against a miracle, from the very nature of the fact, is as entire as any argument from experience can possibly be imagined … The plain consequence is (and it is a general maxim worthy of our attention), 'That no testimony is sufficient to establish a miracle, unless the testimony be of such a kind, that its falsehood would be more miraculous, than the fact, which it endeavours to establish'… [Note 12]

Hume points out that people did not refer to things that happened in the ordinary course of events as miracles, but only those that went against what people would normally expect. Hence he defines a miracle as 'a violation of a law of nature'. He also believes – as an empiricist – that all knowledge depends upon experience and that the laws of nature are therefore based on the maximum amount of uniform evidence. The more evidence we have, the more certain we are about them – although, for Hume, everything is a matter of probability, not certainty.

Hume points to the consistency of our sense experience: from what we observe, all people must die; we cannot walk on water; lead cannot by itself remain suspended in the air; fire consumes wood and is extinguished by water, but:

> Nothing is esteemed a miracle, if it ever happen in the common course of nature. [Note 13]

It is not a miracle that a seemingly healthy man should die unexpectedly, because we often observe this to happen, even though it is unusual. But it would be a miracle if a dead man (really) came back to life, because that has never been observed in any age or country

> And as a uniform experience amounts to a proof, there is here a direct and full proof, from the nature of the fact, against the existence of any miracle. [Note 14]

At this point, Hume introduces his famous definition of a miracle; the italics in the quotation are his:

> A miracle may be accurately defined, *a transgression of a law of nature by a particular volition of the Deity, or by the interposition of some invisible agent.* [Note 15]

In these clauses, you can see the weight of some of the things we have been talking about:

● A miracle is a transgression (a violation) of a law of nature: it would not be appropriate to call a psychological/anti-real experience a miracle, since although these might be 'marvellous', they can never be *miraculous*.
● A miracle has to be willed by the Deity (God): only a God would have the power to bring about such an event.
● Alternatively the miracle has to be done by 'the interposition of some invisible agent'. Hume here seems to mean non-religious miracles, but this would also apply, for example, to miracles performed by any spiritual power other than God, including heavenly Buddhas.

Hume's literal view of miracles has a long history. We find it with Aquinas in the thirteenth century and Eric Mascall (Professor of Historical Theology at King's College, London) in the twentieth century. Mascall describes a miracle as:

'... a striking interposition of divine power by which the operations of the ordinary course of nature are overruled, suspended, or modified.' [Note 16]

So Hume is not playing some trick by defining a miracle in this way. He is going along with what had by then become – and has since continued to be – the majority view among religious people.

Hume's main inductive argument against miracles

Follow the logic of these four steps:

1 Witness testimony has to become more reliable in *direct proportion* to the improbability of what the witness claims to have observed. The more improbable the claim, the more reliable the witness needs to be in order to be believed.

2 The *most* improbable event would be a violation of the laws of nature, because the evidence of the 'firm and unalterable experience' on which the law is based must, by definition, contradict the claim that a miracle has happened. For example, repeated and tested experiences show that we cannot walk on water, and all that evidence contradicts any report that we can.

3 So, by definition, **the reported event is maximally improbable**.

4 **So the probability that the witnesses are lying or mistaken is always greater than the probability that a miracle has occurred**.

Hume's conclusion thus follows:

'… therefore we may establish it as a maxim, that no human testimony can have such force as to prove a miracle, and make it a just foundation for any … system of religion.' [Note 17]

Hume's strategy means that if the witness claims to have seen a miracle, then there are only *two* possibilities: either the witness was mistaken in what he saw, or the witness was lying for some reason. One of these MUST be true. Why? – because by definition, 'a miracle' is *always* the maximally improbable event – otherwise it could not *be* a miracle.

Hume's supporting arguments from psychology

● Looking back through history, we cannot find even one example of a miracle properly attested by men of sufficient good sense, integrity, education and learning. None of the miracle accounts available to us would convince us that the witnesses were not deluded, mistaken or lying.

● Humans are naturally credulous. The feeling of surprise and wonder, arising from miracles, is enough to make people of common sense less than sensible. If we then add religious spirit to our love of surprise and wonder, then 'there is an end of common sense'. [Note 18] A religious person may know that the miracle story he tells is false, but he will persevere with it because he believes his cause to be holy. The more he magnifies the story, the more his hearers believe it, and the more they believe it, the more he magnifies it.

- Most accounts of miracles come from 'ignorant and barbarous nations' and where they are found in civilised countries, that is because they had 'ignorant and barbarous ancestors'. [Note 19]
- Miracle stories are also debunked by conflicting miracle-claims among the different religions. Each religion claims that 'their' miracles were performed by their God, or brought about by karma, gods or Buddhas. Each claim cancels out another, and all arguments against the miracles of other faiths are actually arguments against your own.

Overall, Hume's complaint is that miracles are part of the psychology of belief. This psychology is a spiral of self-delusion in which belief is merit-worthy and disbelief is seen as sinful.

In *The Natural History of Religion*, Hume adds a rather cynical parting shot to the idea of miracles – one that was taken up in the twentieth century by Mackie and reflected in the title of his book *The Miracle of Theism*. Having set out his case for saying that there is never sufficient reason to believe in miracles, he has to acknowledge that the Christian religion has always required belief in them:

> … upon the whole, we may conclude, that the *Christian religion* not only was at first attended with miracles, but even at this day cannot be believed by any reasonable person without one. Mere reason is insufficient to convince us of its veracity: And whoever is moved by *Faith* to assent to it, is conscious of a continued miracle in his own person, which subverts all the principles of his understanding, and gives him a determination to believe what is most contrary to custom and experience. [Note 20]

Of course, Hume says this with his tongue firmly in his cheek! In effect he is suggesting that (given the evidence to the contrary) the real miracle is that anyone can believe that miracles happen.

How should we evaluate the effects of Hume's ideas for religious belief?

1 Hume's account of miracles is inductive, so it cannot be a 'knock-down' argument.

Hume suggested that his argument is as close to a 'proof' as we can get, but of course inductive arguments (as we saw on page 3 of Volume 1) are not 'proofs' – they deal in *probabilities*. Science cannot say that something can *never* happen, only that it is highly *improbable* that it will happen. Light, for example, goes in straight lines, but that is not an absolute rule; near a very strong gravitational force such as a planet, light rays bend. That is why Hume is careful to qualify his argument and explain that there can never be enough evidence to prove a miracle, *not* that a miracle can never occur.

In other words, scientific laws are *descriptive*, not prescriptive. They describe what we have found by experience. This means that a 'law of nature' cannot dictate what *must* happen; it summarises what *has been found to happen*. We cannot, therefore, say that miracles do not happen, however improbable they might be.

2 Hume's main inductive argument (about witness testimony) is perhaps not as strong as it looks.

Here is a counter-argument. Compare Hume's argument (on the left of the table) with that of a Christian (on the right). P stands for premise, and C for conclusion.

Hume's argument	A Christian believer's argument
P1 A miracle is a violation of a law of nature	P1 A miracle is a violation of a law of nature
P2 Violations of natural laws would have to be observed	P2 Violations of natural laws would have to be observed
P3 There are no reliable observations of such violations	P3 There are reliable observations of such violations
P4 Moreover by definition a miracle is the least probable event	P4 Moreover by definition a miracle is the least probable event
P5 The improbability defeats the idea that a miracle has happened	P5 The improbability is a necessary condition for a miracle to happen
C Therefore miracles probably do not happen	C Therefore miracles probably do happen

You can see that the structure of the argument for a Christian is identical with that of Hume. In P3 and P5, however, Hume and Christians have different ideas about reliable observations of miracles and the importance of the improbability of miracles. Those differences lead to diametrically opposed conclusions, and it is not at all clear who (if anybody) is right.

3 Hume's psychological arguments against miracles are not as strong as he thinks.

His claim that there are no properly attested miracles by men of sufficient good sense, integrity, education and learning seems to be contradicted by his own comments about the Roman historian Tacitus (54–117 CE), who reported on miracles apparently done by the Emperor Vespasian. Given that Hume describes Tacitus as,

> '... noted for candour and veracity, and withal, the greatest and most penetrating genius, perhaps, of all antiquity; and so free from any tendency to credulity ...' (§96)

Tacitus surely meets *all* of Hume's requirements for reliable testimony. Rome was neither ignorant nor barbaric (it produced Tacitus!) – so why is the testimony of Tacitus (and others like him) to be rejected?

4 Many have asked, 'What would Hume have said if he witnessed a miracle?'

His arguments seem to leave him no room for accepting any seemingly miraculous event, so by his own argument he would have to doubt the evidence of his own senses. Given that Hume had a wonderful sense of humour, he would probably have done just that.

5 Hume's critique of miracles 'sets the bar' for discussion of the topic.

Hume's definition of miracles has been the starting point for philosophers and theologians, and it is impossible to ignore what he says, even when it is rejected. Hume is surely right, when he says at the end of his argument, that

'[The Christian] religion is founded on *Faith*, not on reason' [Note 21]

which perhaps makes it ill-equipped to deal with a reasoned challenge. If you read the miracle stories in the Bible, they paint a portrait of a world very different from the present and they are written in the kind of language of 'mere human writers and historians', as the numerous contradictions, errors, questionable moral judgements and highly improbable accounts of miracles indicate. Faith may not find it difficult to overcome such problems, but reason suggests that Hume's overall judgements about miracles are closer to the truth. As ever, you will need to make up your own mind.

Hume's arguments do not compel us to reject the idea of miracle, but they do compel us to think carefully about the status of miracle claims throughout history. There is a final account of Hume at the end of section 5 below.

Wiles' critique of miracles

Maurice Wiles (1923–2005)

During the late 1960s, Maurice Wiles was Professor of Christian Doctrine at King's College London, and in the opinion of the authors of this section, JF & MT, who were both taught by him, was one of the best lecturers of his generation. He left King's to become Regius Professor of Divinity at the University of Oxford, from 1970 to 1991. Following the liberal tradition in theology, he worked to examine the meaning of Christian doctrine in the light of human reason, and to show its relevance by re-presenting it in ways that are more accessible to modern thinkers. Unlike modern philosophers who comment on religious ideas, Wiles himself was steeped in the complexities of Christian doctrine, and appreciated the way in which it had developed during the early years of the Church. Hence his views are sympathetic to a broad range of Christian experience, while trying to explore the meaning of doctrine without intellectual compromise.

1 **Wiles' main argument is that God does not act in the world through miracles.**

In *Faith and the Mystery of God* (SCM, 1982, p.26), Wiles approves of Tillich's view that miracles are sign events, and comments that:

> '...it is especially important to emphasise the symbolic character of these symbols, because they often are understood literally... [with the result that] the whole relation of God and the world becomes a nest of absurdities.'

2 **The view that God does perform miracles has happened because God has been thought of as controlling/intervening in the laws of nature.**

In the past, God has been seen as interfering in the laws of cause and effect in order to perform miracles, or else to guide human history along the best available path. For Wiles, such an idea can no longer be upheld.

3 **If God did act in this way, then God would seem to act immorally.**

Wiles means that if we think of God as *sometimes* using miracles to help people, then the whole idea of miracles becomes:

> '... not merely implausible and superfluous from the standpoint of human explanation, but religiously unsatisfactory in view of their apparently occasional and highly selective character.' [Note 22]

By 'their highly selective character', Wiles means that miracles happen very infrequently, so God would appear to be carefully selecting who is healed miraculously (for example) and who is ignored. Wiles makes this point forcefully in *God's Action in the World*:

> If the direct action of God, independent of secondary causation, is an intelligible concept, then it would appear to have been sparingly and strangely used ... it would seem strange that no miraculous intervention prevented Auschwitz or Hiroshima, while the purposes apparently forwarded by some of the miracles acclaimed in traditional Christian faith seem trivial by comparison. [Note 23]

4 **If God did intervene selectively to save some, but not others, then the problem of evil would be unsolvable, because there would be no reason why God could not intervene all the time.**

Wiles refers with approval to the writings of Brian Hebblethwaite, in whose opinion,

> '... the direct intervention of God, however rare the occasions of it, would ... have disastrous implications for our understanding of the problem of evil.'

Wiles then quotes a key passage from Hebblethwaite:

> To suppose that he does so [i.e. that God acts in the world by divine intervention] just occasionally would be to raise all the problems which perplex the believer as he reflects on the problem of evil, about why God does not intervene more often. It would also prevent him from appealing to the God-given structures of creation, and their necessary role in setting creatures at a distance from their creator and providing a stable environment for their lives, as an explanation for the physical ills which can afflict God's creatures. [Note 24]

In other words, it is not just a question of why God does not intervene to save people more often: it is much more important for us to insist that God does not intervene in this way *at all*.

5 **Instead, we should take an anti-real view of miracles: they are very much to do with our fight against evil.**

Wiles seeks to shift the argument away from Hume's question about the *evidence* for whether an event can be explained in natural terms to a debate about what an event reveals concerning God's intentions for the world. And this is clear from his view of the miracles recorded in the New Testament:

> For the critical reader today the miracle tradition is highly problematic. There can be little doubt that for the tradition to have arisen at all, Jesus must have been a remarkable exorcist and healer. Beyond that it is hard to speak with any confidence of the history that lies behind the tradition. But our concern is not simply with what happened, but with its meaning for those who developed and passed on the tradition. The healing ministry of Jesus is firmly set within the context of a conflict with evil. [Note 25]

Jesus engages in actions to oppose evil, and in Mark's Gospel, healing miracles are presented as part of that campaign, while Luke's Gospel sees them as signs of the coming kingdom and of binding the power of Satan. But a key part of Wiles' argument is that Jesus, in his temptation in the desert, expressly rejected the idea of performing miracles as signs to persuade people to believe in him as the Messiah. Jesus refuses, because to do any of these things would be to produce a miracle without a true religious context: they would be nothing more than a showman's exhibition, and would be more demonic than religious.

Hence, Wiles makes the point that Jesus refused Satan's trap of trying to use a miracle as evidence of divine power – there is no *deus ex machina* ('a god from a machine') to be summoned to put things right. Wiles means that God does not act in the world in this way. He does not intervene 'from above' to perform miracles.

The biblical accounts of miracles are also wrongly interpreted if seen as simply factual descriptions. They are myths – presented in order to express something about God; and Jesus' refusal to provide an overwhelmingly convincing miracle illustrates just how mistaken it is to try to use accounts of miracles as proof of God's power.

6 **Wiles makes one concession to the idea of a miracle being a divine action: he suggests that there is actually only one miracle, that of *creation* itself.**

Rather than seeing miracles *in* the world, we should see that the creation of the world itself is the one-and-only miracle: it is the extraordinary act by which God brings into existence the whole ongoing drama of the universe.

7 **From this, we can see that Wiles' position on miracles might suggest that he is closer to deism than to theism: God creates the universe and leaves it to work through its natural laws.**

The basic distinction between deism and theism is that deism argues for an *external* creator God who, having established the physical laws by which the universe operates, then stands back and allows the natural order to run its course, whereas theism sees God as constantly involved with everything in creation.

That distinction underlies many aspects of religious life, most obviously in terms of the 'problem of evil'. Irrespective of whether God is deistic or theistic, it is a problem to explain why God should have created a world in which there is evil (although Hick and others have attempted to answer that), but the additional problem for the theist is that a God who is active within the world could be expected to intervene, whereas an external deity could not. The fight against evil is ours to pursue. This is where the theodicies can be helpful (see Volume 1, Chapter 2 Evil and suffering).

A comparison of Hume and Wiles

Hume and Wiles could not be more different. Their assumptions are completely different. For example:

1 Hume is an atheist, whereas Wiles is a Christian. Hume therefore assumes that there is no God who is able to violate natural laws. Wiles assumes that there is a God who chooses not to intervene.

2 Hume assumes that Christianity is irrational, particularly about miracles. Hume therefore starts with the assumption that a believer is required to believe in miracles, and that his own argument that miracles are the least likely of all events shows that religious belief is fundamentally irrational. Wiles starts from within the framework of Christian belief, and suggests ways in which God can be understood which do not require him to be selectively active in the world in the way Hume's 'violation' approach to miracles suggests; so Hume's interventionist account of miracles is completely irrelevant to Wiles.

3 Hume's approach is realist; Wiles' is anti-realist.

   ● Hume assumes that accounts of miracles, in the Bible and elsewhere, are literal descriptions of (false) facts. Wiles uses biblical criticism to point out that much of the text is not literal or scientific, but symbolic and mythological.
   ● Wiles seeks to shift the argument away from Hume's question about the *evidence* for whether an event can be explained in natural terms to one in which an event reveals something of God's intention for the world.
   ● Wiles' anti-realist approach does have some advantages, since Wiles does not have to engage with the kind of argument put forward by Hume. There are no divine actions in the world that violate natural laws, so Wiles does not have to explain how natural laws can be violated.

4 Their view of the value of 'miracle' is completely different. Wiles points out that what counts as a miracle is a matter of personal interpretation – it is a symbol, not simply a matter of physical fact. The implication of this is that the sort of discussion initiated by Hume is ineffective, because it does not touch on the personal and religious elements in events that are essential if they are to be seen as miracles. Conversely, for Hume, unless a miracle is *at least* an event that is so unexpected and unexplained that it appears to be a violation of a law of nature, then there seems little point in calling it a miracle at all.

As a final comment, Maurice Wiles' approach effectively ditches Hume's idea of a miracle as a violation of the laws of nature, in favour of a more holistic view of God's activity, whether that takes the form of establishing the fundamental principles by which the world operates or of inspiring people to strive to overcome evil and suffering. By taking this approach, Wiles does not really answer Hume's challenge, but sidesteps it by re-defining the spheres of God's activity from something very specific to something more general. That may be seen as the strength of his approach, because – based on a broad consideration of Christian theology – it points to the very limited nature of Hume's eighteenth-century empiricist approach to matters of religion.

The significance of these views for religion

From all that has been said so far, you will have understood that there are major differences between realist and anti-realist approaches to miracles. Each approach involves an equally different understanding of the significance of miracles for religion.

1 Realist approaches

Biblical significance – the value of miracles for faith

The Gospels record many miracles brought about by Jesus himself. These include miracles of healing, exorcism (casting out demons), miracles over nature (for example, calming a storm) and resuscitations. The New Testament writers used a number of terms for such events – that they are *dunameis* (powerful deeds: Matthew 11:20), *terata* (wonders: John 4:48) and *semeia* (signs: John 6:2). *Dunameis* derives from the same root as 'dynamite', hence miracles as powerful deeds are seen as something extraordinary. To call them 'signs' indicates that the Gospel writers saw them as signs of the arrival of God's Kingdom.

The central miracle of the New Testament is the resurrection of Christ, and in 1 Corinthians 15:14, St Paul tells the Corinthian Christians that if Christ has not been raised, then preaching is pointless and their faith is in vain. It would be difficult to take this as a mere metaphor or figure of speech: the miracles performed by Jesus all point towards the miracle of the resurrection, which is the foundation of the Christian faith. Some Christians do of course understand the resurrection in a metaphorical or anti-real sense, but that does not seem to have been the case with the New Testament authors. Moreover Paul goes on to repeat that **if Christ was not raised, then faith is futile** (v.17), because that would mean that for humanity there can be no resurrection from the dead (vv.21–22).

God intervenes providentially as a demonstration of power and love

The doctrine of God's 'providence' means that God is believed to care for his creation. God's providence is based on his characteristics of omnipotence and omnibenevolence. As the all-powerful and all-loving Creator, God has both the power and the love to be active in the world. God intervenes through both general and special revelation. General revelation includes experiences of God given through reason and conscience. Special revelation includes Scripture, religious experiences – dreams, visions, voices, conversion experiences – and miracles. (You can remind yourself of this approach to religion by revisiting Volume 1, Chapter 6 Sources of wisdom and authority, for example page 238.)

Whereas Hume defined miracles as violations of natural laws done by a particular volition (act of will) of the Deity (God), Hume clearly believed that miracles do not occur. Many Christians accept Hume's definition but conclude that they do occur: they are demonstrations of God's power and love.

The idea of miracles as the actions of an all-loving and all-powerful God raises the problem of evil

For many Christians, the problem of evil is the greatest stumbling block to religious belief. As we saw in Volume 1, Chapter 2 Evil and suffering, for centuries theologians have racked their brains trying to explain why an all-powerful and all-loving God can allow evil to exist, and we saw above (pages 61–64) that the problem of evil led **Maurice Wiles** to reject a realist understanding of miracles.

One of the big problems with miracles is their selectivity: why would God select some to be the recipients of miracles and not others? Also, why should some humans have the power to perform miracles and not others? **Keith Ward's** answer to these questions [Note 26] is that miracles have a wider purpose than just being selective demonstrations of God's power:

- *Where God brings about a miracle*, it has universal (and not selective) significance, because it discloses to humanity something of God's intentions/plans for the universe. Miraculous events that are directly caused by God are interventions, but are also primarily *signs*: the resurrection of Jesus is a sign because it discloses God's intention that human life will have an ultimate fulfilment after death.
- When the miracle is brought about through the agency of human beings (such as the Catholic saints), this is because the power to bring about miracles is always available to human beings; but they can only make use of it if they open themselves up to God. [Note 27] Such miracles are a natural human response to God that 'open' the world in such a way.
- The power to perform miracles is therefore both natural and supernatural, but *not* interventionist.
- Ward therefore sees miracles not as God 'tinkering with his creation', but as 'Epiphanies of the Spirit'. By this he means that God intends miracles to be clues of his intentions for humanity.

2 Anti-realist approaches

By contrast with realist approaches, anti-realist understandings of miracle have a different understanding of religion

- This is particularly true of **Paul Tillich**. As we saw above (pages 52–53), according to Tillich, God is not 'a being' among others, but is 'Being-itself' – existence itself. Miracles cannot contradict the rational structure of reality, so miracles are not interventions in the world by a transcendent God. Instead, they are 'sign-events' that cannot be divorced from their religious context. They point to the 'mystery of being', and are given to us through ecstatic religious experiences. Miracles in this sense have profound personal and psychological significance.
- Think also of **Holland's** story of the child on the railway line, where the 'miracle' is not supernatural, but is an event which has deep personal significance.
- Think also of **Wiles**, who understands miracles as events that reveal something of God's intentions for the world: the New Testament miracles are about inspiring people to overcome evil and suffering.
- Looking at these interpretations of miracles, their significance for religion is personal: they do not relate to real events brought about by a real God; rather their 'reality' is in the mind of the person who experiences an event which has extraordinary *personal* significance.

3 Which approach to miracles is most significant for religion?

- If you look at Tillich's understanding of God and of miracle, to say something about them boils down to saying something about the way our minds work. Is God a real being, or does God exist only as a psychological reality?

Discussion points

1 What would have to happen for you personally to believe that a miracle had occurred?
2 Does religion depend on miracles?
3 Is the God of anti-realism really God?
4 Is the realist God really God?
5 Are miracles necessary for religious belief?

- Consider our discussion of the Cosmological Argument (Volume 1, Chapter 1.3). Do you think that God exists as the reason why the universe exists, or do you think that 'God' is just a way of looking at and explaining the world?
- For realists, miracles are real events. For anti-realists they are unusual and astonishing events within human experience. Which of these do you think most accurately describes the significance of miracles?

○——————————————————————————

Technical terms for miracles

Anti-realism Anti-realist understandings deny that we can have knowledge of a mind-independent world, since the phenomena observed by our senses are interpreted by the mind. Any talk of God as an unobservable 'something' has no cognitive content, so 'God' cannot be discussed meaningfully. Applied to miracles, a miracle might be seen as something that lifts the spirit, or transforms a community of people.

Realism Realist understandings of the world generally hold 1) that scientific theories give us true (or approximately true) descriptions of the world; 2) that they give us knowledge of things that we believe to exist but cannot observe, such as isolated quarks; 3) that the world is mind-independent: it exists the way it is, regardless of what we think about the matter. Applied to miracles, a realist account sees them as real events brought about by God (or someone empowered by God). God exists as a real being, transcendent and unobservable, who creates and cares for the world.

Summary of miracles

Realist views of miracles

Realist understandings of miracles see them as real events in the world, brought about by a transcendent being: a God who is personal, can answer prayer, and who acts in the world for a purpose, as part of his care for the world he created.

Realist examples of miracles include:

- Juliane Koepcke's 1971 survival of a plane crash and free fall over the Peruvian rainforest.
- The 1950 Nebraska church choir incident.

There are problems with describing either of these as a miracle: for example, why would God save these people but ignore others in similar situations?

- Miracles as events brought about by the power of God or another spiritual power, working through people. The Bible contains many such stories, for example those concerning Moses. Miracles as examples of God's divine power and compassion are particularly important in Catholic tradition.

- Miracles as violations of natural law: this was Hume's understanding and he defined a miracle as (1) a transgression of a law of nature (2) by a particular volition [act of will] (by) the Deity (God), or by the interposition [intervention] of some invisible agent.

There is a problem with defining miracles as violating natural laws: science does not accept such a possibility. Natural laws are generally seen as descriptive or probabilistic – they do not dictate what *must* happen; they summarise what has been *found to happen* – i.e. what we have observed. If something appears to go against a law of nature, then the law has to be revised. This was Hick's conclusion also: if there appears to be an exception to a law of nature, then the law simply expands to include the exception.

Two further problems with understanding miracles as violations of natural law are: 1) the mass of evidence supporting those laws seems to make it unreasonable to believe in miracles; 2) if God does intervene miraculously, why is there still suffering? This is the problem of evil.

Anti-realist views of miracles

Anti-realist understandings of miracles generally reject realist descriptions of miracle. There is no commitment to understanding 'God' as a transcendent 'being'. Miracles are mental states or attitudes which are 'revelatory' only in terms of human psychology or sociology: a miracle is something that transforms a community of people, or lifts the spirit, such as a beautiful sunrise or sunset, or the birth of a child; natural events such as these can be *seen as* miraculous.

Examples of those who take an anti-real approach to miracle include:

- Paul Tillich, who believes God is not 'a being', but is 'Being-itself'. Miracles are not interventions in the world by a transcendent God (because that kind of thinking would reduce them to mere superstition and sorcery). They are 1) events that are astonishing, unusual, shaking, without breaking any law of nature; 2) they point to the mystery of being, relating specifically to the experiencer's existence; 3) they are signs/symbols within a religious experience. The miracle is about my 'ultimate concern' – about the attention and commitment to religious symbols by which I make sense of my life.

- John Hick, who believes miracles are ordinary/natural events seen through the eye of faith. They are events through which we become vividly and immediately conscious of God acting towards us. *The event must be religiously significant.* A miracle is any event that is *'experienced as'* a miracle.

- R.F. Holland, whose story of the child on the railway line shows that for him an event does not have to violate a law of nature to be thought of as a miracle. What makes it 'miraculous' for the mother is that it is a 'beneficial coincidence which she interprets in a religious fashion'. She realises that there is nothing supernatural about what happened; nevertheless she interprets what happened as God's response to human need.

Comparison of the key ideas of David Hume and Maurice Wiles on miracles

Hume's critique

1 Hume's critique of miracles is based on his empirical assumptions: all knowledge comes from sense experience, a wise man proportions his belief to the evidence, and religion is based on (incorrect) factual claims.

2 Hume defines a miracle as a violation of a law of nature by God. Our experience of the consistency of these laws shows that a violation of them is the least likely of all events, and no testimony can ever overcome that.

3 His main argument is inductive: the logic of its four steps shows that it is always more likely that the witnesses are mistaken or that they are lying than that a miracle has occurred. His supporting arguments from psychology further dismiss miracles as: the product of weak education and weak integrity; the natural credulity of human

nature; the fact that miracle stories come from ignorant and barbarous nations; and the conflicting miracle-claims among the world's religions.

4 Hume's arguments have weaknesses: i) no inductive argument can ever be certain, so however improbable miracles might be, we cannot say for certain that they do not happen; ii) Christians can (if they wish) make their own counter-argument claiming first that there *are* reliable observations of violations of natural laws, and second that the improbability of a miracle is a *necessary* condition for it to happen; iii) Hume's psychological objections to miracles are not sound – not least by his own admission that Tacitus was as good a witness to miracles as we can get; iv) if Hume witnessed a miracle, could he accept it? Nevertheless, Hume's definition and critique of miracles has set the standard for discussion of miracles ever since.

Wiles' critique

1 God does not act in the world through miracles. Language about miracles is symbolic, not literal.

2 Understanding miracles as God intervening in the world has come about by thinking that God is intervening in a chain of causes, or else that God is an agent controlling the chain of causes as a whole.

3 This misunderstanding has been brought about by Hume, whose definition of miracles sees them as (causal) violations of natural laws by God.

4 But this sort of approach raises the problem of evil: miracles are highly selective, so if God does them selectively, he must be an immoral God who intervenes to save some but ignores the rest. So Hume got it wrong – God does not intervene.

5 The language of miracles, as in the Bible, is very much to do with our fight against evil; but this language is mythical, and not literal. Jesus' refusal to do miracles for Satan shows that God does not intervene to perform miracles.

6 The *only* miracle is that of creation itself.

So perhaps Wiles' God is deistic: again, God does not intervene.

A comparison of Hume and Wiles

Their starting assumptions are completely different:

1 Hume is an atheist, Wiles is a Christian, so Hume assumes that there is no God to violate anything, but Wiles assumes that there is a God who preserves human freedom by *not* intervening.

2 Hume assumes that Christianity is irrational, particularly about miracles; Hume's whole interventionist account of miracles is irrelevant to Wiles.

3 Hume's approach to miracles is realist but Wiles' is anti-realist, which at least gives him the advantage of not having to explain how natural laws can be violated.

4 Their view of the value of miracle is completely different. For Wiles, Hume ignores the real value of miracle, namely its personal and religious elements. For Hume, any idea of miracle short of a violation of natural law is not worth talking about.

Overall, Wiles' account is more holistic, underlining the very limited nature of Hume's eighteenth-century empiricist approach.

There are major differences between realist and anti-realist approaches to miracles, and each approach involves an equally different understanding of the significance of miracles for religion.

1 Realist approaches

Biblical significance – the value of miracles for faith

The Gospels record many miracles done by Jesus, including those of healing, exorcism, nature miracles and resuscitations. Miracles are *dunameis* (powerful deeds), *terata* (wonders) and *semeia* (signs – i.e., signs of the arrival of God's Kingdom). The miracles of Jesus all point towards the central miracle of God's resurrection of Jesus. For St Paul, if the resurrection is not true/real, then religious faith is vain and futile, because if Christ is not raised, then there can be no human resurrection from the dead.

God intervenes providentially as a demonstration of power and love

Being all-powerful and all-loving, God is able and willing to intervene in the world through general and special revelation, and the latter includes miracles. God's interventions match Hume's definition of miracles. Hume defined them as violations of natural laws brought about by a Deity (God). Hume expected that definition to show that they do not happen, whereas Christians believe that they do.

The idea of miracles as actions of an all-loving and all-powerful God raises the problem of evil

The problem of evil (the 'inconsistent triad') is the greatest stumbling block to religious belief, and it led Maurice Wiles to reject a realist understanding of miracle. One of the biggest problems is that miracles appear to be selective, and therefore unfair. Keith Ward answers this objection by arguing that miracles have universal (not selective) significance, because they disclose to humanity something of God's plans for the universe, including the promise of life after death: the resurrection of Jesus being God's sign of this. Where they can open themselves up to God, human beings also have the natural power to perform miracles, as with great figures such as the Catholic saints. Miracles are therefore both natural and supernatural, but they are *not* interventionist. Miracles are 'Epiphanies of the Spirit': God intends them to be clues of his intentions for humanity.

2 Anti-realist approaches

By contrast with realist approaches, these have a different understanding of religion

● This is particularly true of Tillich, who sees God not as a being, but as 'Being-itself'. Miracles cannot contradict the rational structure of reality, so are not interventions by a transcendent God. They are 'sign-events' that cannot be divorced from their religious context, which is religious experience. The significance of miracles is primarily *personal and psychological*.

● Similarly, for Holland, miracles are events with deep *personal* significance.

● For Wiles, miracles are events that reveal something of God's intentions for the world: so the miracles in the New Testament are about inspiring people to overcome evil and suffering.

● The significance of these interpretations is that miracles do not relate to events brought about by a 'real' God: rather, their reality is in the mind of the person who experiences an event which he or she judges to have extraordinary *personal* significance.

Which approach to miracles is most significant for religion?

● Tillich's approach to both God and miracle seems to boil down to saying something about the way our minds work. Is God a real being, or does God exist only as a psychological reality?

● Think of the Cosmological Argument. Does God exist as the reason why the universe exists, or is 'God' just a way of looking at and explaining the world?

● For realists, miracles are real events. For anti-realists, they are unusual and astonishing events *within human experience*. Which do you think most accurately describes the significance of miracles?

3

Self, death and afterlife

You will need to consider the following items for this section

1 The nature and existence of the soul; Descartes' argument for the existence of the soul.

2 The body/soul relationship.

3 The possibility of continuing personal existence after death.

How to study this section

- Bear in mind that only the three items listed above are examinable.
- You do not need to know *every* detail of what is in this chapter; the detail is intended to cover a broad spectrum of what might be taught.
- You need to have enough knowledge and understanding necessary to answer questions on the three areas above.
- You are advised to begin by scanning the Summary (pages 106–110), to get a feel of what will be discussed in this chapter.
- Finally, bear in mind that this topic reaches into all sorts of areas covered in the AQA specification and it is important for you to get the feel of these links in order to understand Chapter 12 and Chapter 13.

Activity

Examples of these links include: evil and suffering; religious language; free will; good conduct and moral responsibility; ethics in general and Christian views about life after death. Spend around 10 minutes in a group discussing the links with these topics.

Debates about the nature and existence of the soul are closely linked together, so it makes sense to deal with them together in the first section of this chapter. We will then go on to consider the possibility of continuing personal existence after death.

Introduction

There is a strangeness in reflecting on our mental awareness. Am 'I' seeing sense impressions in my head, or am I just seeing what I am seeing out there? Or am I interpreting what my brain deduces that I am seeing? Once we start reflecting on consciousness, we start to realise how complicated it is to explain what the mind is about, and how it relates to the body.

All this is possible because we are self-reflective beings – we are capable of looking at ourselves looking, and thinking about ourselves thinking, asking ourselves 'who or what am I?'

We start by looking at two different approaches from Plato and Aristotle, which have influenced many debates on this issue.

The nature and existence of the soul; Descartes' argument for the existence of the soul

Plato (428/427–348/347 BCE)

Plato was a dualist. He contrasted the flux and change of the empirical world of sense experience with the perfection of the world of **Forms** – the world of perfect *Ideas*. We have referred to this theory elsewhere, but here is a reminder:

In the empirical world, all things decay, but for all empirical objects, Plato reasoned that there exist metaphysical counterparts that do *not* decay or change. All things in the world are particular instances of universal Forms. The reason why we can understand that all dogs are dogs, despite the differences between the many different breeds, is that we recognise that Great Danes and Chihuahuas (for example) are particular instances of the Form, Dog. The Forms are eternal, perfect, timeless and metaphysical. The ultimate Form is the Form of the Good, because it defines all other Forms.

While the physical body is part of the world of the senses, the mind is related to that higher reality of the Forms. Plato also argues that only composite things (things made up of parts) can be destroyed or naturally disintegrate. But while bodies are composite, souls are non-material and simple (without parts), and therefore cannot be destroyed. Once created, a soul is permanent and cannot die.

This is the basis of what we term 'dualism' – the belief that reality has two aspects. For Plato there is a world of ideal Forms separate from the world of sense perception. The most well-known exposition of this is his allegory of the Cave.

> If you have not come across Plato's allegory of the Cave, you may wish to read it, for example at: **www.sparknotes.com/philosophy/republic/section7.rhtml**
>
> Note there are also simpler versions available online.

Dualism became influential by being incorporated into Christian thinking as Christianity spread through the Graeco-Roman world. Dualism was a theory that dominated the mediaeval period and was subsequently re-presented in a rather different form by Descartes (see later in this chapter).

Plato therefore presents a dualism of immaterial substance: soul (psyche), and physical body. By the time he wrote *The Republic*, however, Plato had decided that the *psyche* is more complex than he had previously presented it, and that it is composed of three parts:

1 the logical/thinking/reasoning part which seeks to learn the truth

> **Key term**
>
> **Forms** Plato's theory of Forms was that all things in the world of sense perception are particular instances of universal Forms. For example, all tables are particular instances of the universal Form of a Table. The Forms are metaphysical/perfect Ideas.

> **Key term**
>
> **Psyche** (Greek) soul, spirit, mind.

Key term

Thumos (Greek) in Plato's understanding, that part of the psyche/soul corresponding to pugnacity, righteous indignation, courage, etc. It is (or should be) subordinate to the rational part.

2 **thumos**, which means the spirited part of the psyche – for example natural pugnacity, courage, righteous indignation or righteous anger

3 the appetitive part, i.e. the appetites for sex, food and drink.

So, overall, Plato holds that the soul is separate from the body, but animates and directs it.

Aristotle (384–322 BCE)

In Aristotle's day there was no practical distinction between science and philosophy, and most of his work would today be described as science. He sorted out living things into different species and categorised them. He applied logic and demanded that evidence should be used in putting forward theories. So, as we turn to Aristotle's view of the self, remember that he represented the start of what we may now see as a 'scientific' and rational view, examining the distinctive features of human life. He accepts that it is not an easy task:

> 'To attain any assured knowledge about the soul is one of the most difficult things in the world.' *De Anima* (On the Soul). [Note 1]

You will remember from our study of Aristotle's Virtue Ethics (Volume 1, pages 164–65) that Aristotle argued that all living things have souls, and that a creature's psyche is its 'principle of life' – that which distinguishes it from a corpse or other inanimate thing. But the distinctive thing about humans is that, as well as having a psyche, they are also capable of rational thought.

Aristotle suggests that a soul is what gives something its essential nature, and illustrates what he means by various analogies:

> Suppose that the eye were an animal – sight would have been its soul, for sight is the substance of the eye which corresponds to the account [of a thing], the eye being merely the matter of seeing; when seeing is removed the eye is no longer an eye, except in name.

Then crucially, for the discussion of the soul that followed in the centuries after Aristotle, he says this:

> [A]s the pupil plus the power of sight constitutes the eye, so the soul plus the body constitutes the animal. From this it is clear that the soul is inseparable from its body, or at any rate that certain parts of it are (if it has parts) – for the actuality of some of them is the actuality of the parts themselves. [Note 2]

In other words, the soul is what makes a thing what it is – and for human beings, along with ordinary animal activity, we have the distinctive feature of rational thought. Further, on Aristotle's analysis, it is very difficult to see how body and soul could ever be separated, since the soul is expressed through the body.

Aristotle sees the psyche as the form that *organises* the material body into what it essentially is. Notice that this makes the psyche distinct from the material body, but not separate from it. You do not have the body in one place and the soul somewhere else – they are locked together, the body being given its shape and characteristics by the soul.

Notice that Aristotle goes about his work like a modern scientist. He observes that nutrition, for example, is essential to animal life. It is the soul that determines what we eat, how we move and so on. How does it do it? The soul seems to initiate movement. He notes that the soul is what enables a living thing to maintain itself in life, organising it to get what it needs.

What Aristotle is mainly doing in *On the Soul* is biology. He is looking at the characteristics of living things, as opposed to inanimate things. What he is relating when he describes the soul is what it is that makes us live. Thus we find that, **for Aristotle, the soul or mind is the essence or form of a human being, an essence that is distinct from but also inseparable from the material body.**

> ### Key term
> *Nous* (Greek) intellect.

Aristotle distinguishes rational thought from sense perception, movement, emotions and nutrition and growth, since rational thought is distinctively human, whereas sense perceptions and so on are shared with all other animals. The Greek term for the thinking mind is **nous** as opposed to the more general term *psyche*. It is debatable whether one should consider the rational mind in isolation from the broader aspects of psychology, but, for the Greeks, *nous* held a special place as *intellect*, the highest and most distinctive of human functions. Aristotle was the first serious biologist: the first to examine what enables us to live, what distinguishes us from inanimate things, and what distinguishes human beings from the rest of the animal world.

Plato v Aristotle

The views of Plato and Aristotle on the soul are very different:

- For Plato, we have a separate body, conjoined with a soul that has lived before and will go on to live again. Its real home, if you like, is the world of the Forms, not this mundane world – it is trapped in a physical body.
- For Aristotle, the self is what animates you – you are body and soul together, a living, breathing, thinking being. You live and think – that is what makes you a human being.

Both of those views have been hugely influential. The Platonic view seems to have dominated traditional western religion. The Aristotelian one is closer to the medical aspect, where we seek a more integrated view of the person.

Both seem to fit our experience of encountering death:

- Some people, looking at a corpse, feel that the 'soul' has gone and that only a shell remains. The real person is no longer here and is utterly different from the body. They might therefore tend to take a Platonic view.
- Others sense that the body expressed the person during their life, but has lost its animating principle which made it the person they knew – a more Aristotelian view.

The distinction between Plato and Aristotle on the soul may be illustrated by considering an actor performing on stage. As we watch the play, we engage with the part that the actor is playing – his or her words, actions, gestures, relationships, ambitions and everything that brings out the particular 'character' in the play. We may have seen the play before, performed by different actors, but each time we appreciate the distinctiveness of the performance – you see this *particular* Hamlet.

- If you take an Aristotelian view, the person or soul is the character that appears on stage – it is all that mixture of words and actions that leads you to guess the character's thoughts and to anticipate his reactions. The actor on stage is fully engaged in performing his part; he embodies the character whose lines he delivers.
- The Platonic view has a double focus. On the one hand there is the part being played, with all the words and actions; on the other there is the fact that this is not actually Hamlet, but my Uncle Joe performing in the local amateur dramatic performance.

Thus an Aristotelian approach sees the soul as the character that an individual displays, not some hidden actor behind that character. There is no hidden, secret you, distinct from all that you actually think and say and do. We do not have a body, with its own form and performing its own actions, to which a secondary, invisible thing called a 'soul' is added. The term 'soul' describes that which shapes and gives life to the body. By contrast, the Platonic approach sees the eternal soul as more like the actor, with an eternal and therefore ongoing life quite apart from this particular incarnation or stage performance.

Descartes' argument for the existence of the soul

We began the introduction to this chapter with the two questions, 'Who am I?' and 'What am I?' The focus in this section is on a third question: '*Where am I?*'

Where would you say that 'you' are? Are 'you' your whole body, for example, or are you something that exists inside your skull – in your brain? If you cut off your right leg, would 'you' be diminished, or would the real 'you' still be intact? If you think that 'you' are in your mind, and your mind is in your brain, then a major problem crops up when you try to explain how your mind and your brain relate to each other. How does the non-physical mind relate to the physical brain, and vice-versa?

To talk about something non-physical having a relationship with something physical appears to defy the laws of physics. This is the basis of the 'mind–body problem', and on the whole, there have been two main ways of addressing it: dualism and monism.

Monist theories hold that 'you' exist in a single substance. The main monist theory we shall be looking at is Physicalism, which holds that this substance is matter. Descartes argued for dualism: there are two substances – mind/soul and matter – and 'you'/your mind exists independently of your material body.

René Descartes (1596–1650)

Regarded as initiating what is generally termed 'modern' philosophy (to contrast it with the mediaeval world or that of the ancient Greeks), Descartes saw his work as an attempt to establish the origin of certainty in a world where sceptical doubt appeared to undermine all beliefs, and especially those of Catholic Christianity. Unable to doubt his existence as a thinking being, he argued for a radical dualism of the extended physical body and the unextended mind, a view that was to dominate the view of minds and bodies until the second part of the twentieth century.

Here is Descartes' basic argument in favour of Substance Dualism, mainly from his book, *Meditations on First Philosophy* (1641 in the Latin text):

1 **Descartes' agenda was religious,** so in his dedicatory letter to the Theology Faculty at the Sorbonne in Paris, he wrote:

> I have always thought that two topics – namely God and the soul – are prime examples of subjects where demonstrative proofs ought to be given with the aid of philosophy rather than theology. For us who are believers, it is enough to accept on faith that the human soul does not die with the body, and that God exists; but in the case of unbelievers, it seems that there is no religion, and practically no moral virtue, that they can be persuaded to adopt until these two truths are proved to them by natural reason. [Note 3]

2 **Descartes' essential argument is that mind and body are distinct substances with different essential properties:**

● Matter is *res extensa* (Latin for *extended thing*, so: 'extended substance')
● Mind is *res cognita* (Latin for 'mental substance')

In other words, Descartes is arguing for 'Substance Dualism'. He gives three 'proofs' of his argument, by which he wants to show that the soul can exist without the body. You will notice that this follows Plato's line of thinking rather than that of Aristotle.

3 First proof: **The Argument from Doubt**; *Meditation II*; also *Discourse on Method*, Part 4, which is the source of Descartes' famous dictum, *Cogito, ergo sum*: 'I think, therefore I am (I exist)'. [Note 4] Descartes supposes that there might be a 'malicious demon' who is powerful enough to make him doubt the existence of the world outside him, and the existence of other minds. So:

i I can doubt that my body exists.
ii But I cannot doubt that I exist as a thinking thing (doubt is a form of thinking).
iii Therefore (because I am a thinking thing) I am not identical with my body.

Does this work? Probably not. Most philosophers think that consciousness/mind is a product of the brain, and that the brain is simply part of what we call a 'body'. Without its body, then, mind would not exist to produce Descartes' argument. In other words, I *cannot* doubt that my body exists.

4 Second proof: **The Argument from Divisibility and Non-Divisibility**; *Meditation VI*:

> i   All bodies are extended in space, and are therefore divisible.
> ii Minds are not extended in space, and are therefore not divisible.
> iii Minds are therefore **radically** different from bodies.

To explain this further:

● To say that 'all bodies are extended in space' is true, because that is how we define a body. Descartes means that if we take any body (any object), such as a chair, a table, a book, a person or a feather, all such bodies exist in the normal three dimensions of space-time, as illustrated in the diagram.

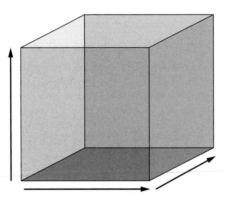

All bodies are extended in the three main dimensions (length/breadth/depth). They are therefore divisible, just like numbers or measurements

● Descartes is arguing that states of mind are indivisible. By states of mind, Descartes is referring to what we call *qualia*: your mental states, such as what it is like to smell a rose or experience redness. Smell and sight can be increased or decreased but not divided, whereas physical objects clearly can be divided, and this includes the human body:

> [T]here is a great difference between the mind and the body, inasmuch as the body is by its very nature always divisible, while the mind is utterly indivisible. For when I consider the mind, or myself in so far as I am merely a thinking thing, I am unable to distinguish any parts within myself; I understand myself to be something quite single and complete. Although the whole mind seems to be united to the whole body, I recognize that if a foot or arm or any other part of the body is cut off, nothing has thereby been taken away from the mind. [Note 5]

Does this work? The argument seems to be false. Modern **neuroscience** shows that there is a close correlation between mind and brain. When the brain is damaged, the mind can be damaged also, and to that extent it can be 'divided'.

Key term

Radical Extreme, as in 'radical dualism': the view that mind and matter are radically different: in particular, mind is not the same as the brain.

Key terms

Qualia The qualities of subjective conscious experience: for example, what it feels like in your mind to experience redness, or the smell of a rose.

Neuroscience The study of the brain and the nervous system.

5 Third proof: **The Argument from Clear and Distinct Perception**; *Meditation VI*

   i   Whatever I clearly and distinctly perceive as two different things can be created by God as two different things.

   ii I have a clear and distinct idea of *myself* as a non-extended thinking thing.

   iii I have a clear and distinct idea of my *body* as an extended non-thinking thing.

   iv So I and my body can exist apart from each other.

   v So I am distinct from my body.

Does this work? As a simple response, point i) is a strange-looking argument, because elsewhere (*Meditation V*) Descartes deduces the existence of God from clear and distinct perceptions, but now he wants to deduce the reliability of our clear and distinct perceptions from the existence of God. The argument therefore seems to be circular (and is therefore known as the 'Cartesian Circle'). Whether or not the argument is circular is a matter of debate, but the appeal to God in i) looks suspiciously like it.

> Remember that the word 'Cartesian' is made up from the second part of *Descartes'* name, so *Cartesian* simply means, 'relating to Descartes and his ideas'. It can also be used to refer to a follower of Descartes.

6 At the end of the argument, Descartes' dualism – his distinction between body and mind/soul – is at least clear:

Body/material substance	Mind/soul substance
has extension in space	is not extended in space
is located in space	is not located in space
has parts that corrupt and decay	has no parts to corrupt or decay
so cannot survive death	so is not susceptible to death
so is mortal	so is immortal

Problems with Descartes' dualism

We have already seen that Descartes' three arguments, from doubt, divisibility and 'clear and distinct perception' do not work, but there are also a number of other problems with Descartes' dualism:

The Ghost in the Machine (Gilbert Ryle)

In his book, *The Concept of Mind*, Gilbert Ryle ridiculed the Cartesian account of the body-soul relationship by calling it 'the Ghost in the Machine':

> I shall often speak of it, with deliberate abusiveness, as 'the dogma of the Ghost in the Machine'. I hope to prove that it is entirely false, and false not in detail but in principle. It is not merely an assemblage of particular mistakes. It is one big mistake and a mistake of a special kind. It is, namely, a category-mistake. It represents the facts of mental life as if they belonged to one logical type or category (or range of types or categories), when they actually belong to another. The dogma is therefore a philosopher's myth. [Note 6]

To explain a 'category mistake', Ryle used the example of someone visiting a university and seeing many different colleges, libraries and research laboratories. The visitor then asks, 'But where is the University?' The answer, of course, is that there is no university over and above all its component parts that have already been visited. The term 'university' is a way of describing all of these things together – it is a term from another category, not the same category as the individual components. [Note 7] In the same way, Ryle argued that you should not expect to find a 'mind' over and above all the various parts of the body and its actions.

Problems with the idea of soul substance

1 The idea of a 'soul substance' solves nothing.

In his essay on *The Immortality of the Soul*, Hume begins by saying that the whole idea of a 'substance' is completely confused. To argue (as Descartes does) that consciousness emerges from a non-material substance solves nothing, because that amounts to saying: 'We need to explain how a substance can think. A substance can think because soul exists as a thinking substance.' This is clearly a circular argument.

2 Thinking cannot tell us what is actually the case.

David Hume makes the point that it may well be, for example, that the cause of thought is material substance. [Note 8] This, of course, is the most common view of the mind in the twenty-first century – that ultimately, thought has a physical/material explanation.

3 According to Hume, souls cannot be counted.

If souls are not in space and are invisible, how do we know even that one body has just one soul? It is just an assumption that there is a one-to-one body/soul relationship.

4 The logic of Descartes' argument establishes only that 'there is thinking', not that there is an 'I' who thinks.

For Descartes, 'I' am something over and above the process of thinking, but many philosophers deny this, arguing that the 'self' is just an illusion – a construct derived from all of the mind's different sense experiences. The 'self' is *the flow* of these experiences, and not something that sits in the soul and looks at them. This view of the 'self' derives in large part from Hume, for whom there is no 'substantial self' to do the looking.

The body/soul relationship

We shall look at three views in this section:

- Descartes' **Interactionism**
- Physicalism: the attack on dualism through the physicalist theory of Functionalism plus a defence of dualism
- Dual-aspect Monism

Descartes' Interactionism

How, if they are radically different, can mind and body interact?
Descartes suggested that the pineal gland, a small portion of the brain that lies between the two hemispheres, was the point at which the mind controlled the body.

Key term

Interactionism (in the philosophy of mind) Descartes' (false) view that mind and body interact within the pineal gland.

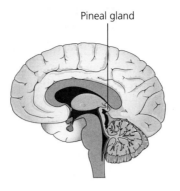
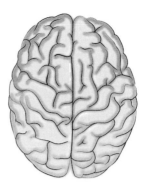

Pineal gland

▲ *Left*: the pineal gland. According to Descartes, this gland is the area of the brain in which the metaphysical soul interacts with the physical body. *Right*: the bifurcated brain – the two hemispheres of left and right brain.

How does a non-physical mind *interact* with a radically different physical body/brain? Descartes thinks he has established that mind and body are two different substances, so how can the non-physical mind interact with and direct the physical brain?

Descartes' suggestion that it does so through the pineal gland does not work, because locating mind-brain interaction *anywhere* in the brain solves nothing. It merely says, 'It interacts here', but does nothing to show *how* interaction takes place. If the self is a separate, mental thing, it is difficult to see how we could ever establish the way in which it engages with the physical world. Also, Descartes was intrigued by the pineal gland because its function was unknown, whereas modern anatomy shows it to be associated with the production of melatonin, which regulates sleep rhythms. The pineal gland is still the subject of much pseudo-science, so beware of sources that talk about its deep mysteries.

Descartes was working with seventeenth-century science, which took a mechanistic view of the physical universe. His physics required physical contact in order for one thing to affect or be the cause of another, since this was prior to Newton's discovery of fields of force, as in the effect of gravity on an apple falling from a tree. He therefore tries to find some mechanical way in which thought might make a physical difference – hence his (entirely wrong) view that the point of contact was the pineal gland.

Physicalism: there *is* no body/soul relationship

Physicalism is the philosophical position that **everything can be explained and described in terms of matter**. If everything is explained by matter, then 'soul' is not needed to explain the nature of persons. There is no body/soul relationship, for the simple reason that **there is no soul**.

Physicalism is a reductive philosophy: just as 'water' reduces to H_2O, 'mind' reduces to brain.

Physicalism seems to give an obvious explanation to common phenomena:

- As people reach old age, they tend to become forgetful, confused and, in some cases, may suffer from senile dementia. These things can be shown in terms of brain activity and progressive brain damage.
- If I take alcohol or other drugs, I may experience myself and my surroundings in a way that does not correspond to reality. Afterwards, I may accept that my senses were impaired, but at the time that is exactly how things seemed.
- If I get excited, my pulse rate increases.
- If I am ill, I feel sluggish, tired and can't think straight.

These all suggest that what we experience is related to straightforward physical causes and that science can provide answers to all the significant questions about life.

Functionalism as a physicalist theory of mind

Functionalism is an example of a physicalist theory of mind. Philosophers tend to talk of 'mind' rather than 'soul', so the body/soul problem is the mind/body problem.

Functionalism as a theory developed out of cognitive science, specifically the field of artificial intelligence, where the mind is seen as an information-processing system – as a working computer program.

To understand the idea of a function, think of your heart: its function is to pump blood around the body. The function of a mousetrap is to catch mice; the function of a kettle is to boil water; the examples are endless, but in each case, to talk about a thing's function is simply to describe the job it does.

Now think of a thermostat – the kind that you probably have in your own home: the function of the thermostat is to regulate the temperature in a room or a building. We can show this by a simple diagram of Input – Function – Output:

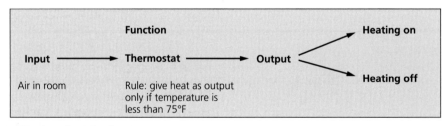

▲ The function of a thermostat

As you can see from this diagram, the *input* is the air in the room; the *function* is to follow the rule that if the temperature of the air is less than 75 °F (I get cold very easily) the heating is turned on, or if it is above 75 °F, the heating is turned off; the *output* is warmer or cooler air.

The function of the mind is what it does – it processes data inputted through the senses and generates an appropriate outcome. In a human being the platform on which it does this is the human brain, but functions can be multiply realised.

To understand the idea of '**multiple realisability**', think of a clock. Clocks work through a number of different systems: for example, they can be electric, mechanical, atomic or digital; they can run by water, by the sand in an hourglass, or by the light on a sundial. All these states are different platforms for telling the time, and you can choose which type of clock you prefer.

Applied to minds, then, the platform on which a mind might run can be equally varied. Mental states are also identified by their functional role: by what they do rather than what they are made of. Mental states can be 'multiply realised', for example through human brains or through a non-biological system such as a computer.

It is possible that a mind could run on a physical platform such as a computer. Think about this: In a human being, INPUT would be sense experience; FUNCTION would be the processing carried out by the brain; OUTPUT would be behaviour. For example, if your friend decided to liven things up by sticking a pin in your arm, that would be the input; function would be the brain's processing of the stimulus in terms of pain; output would be your behaviour, which would be interesting. A robot could be programmed to react in the same way.

In summary, then, Functionalism gives an account of mind in which the mind could be 'run' on any appropriate physical system:

- It does away with inventing 'mental substance' to explain the mind.
- Mental states consist of sensory inputs and behavioural outputs.
- Given that we are on the verge of developing quantum-mechanical computer systems that can match the power of the human brain, human minds might best be seen as powerful biological computers.

The possibility of human brain-to-computer upload

One of the most interesting things about Functionalism is that it might be possible to 'upload' the content of a human brain onto a different platform, such as a powerful computer. Given that the power of computers doubles approximately every two years, it might be possible to increase human brain-power exponentially.

We shall return to this theme in section three, on the possibility of personal existence after death.

Does Functionalism show that Cartesian Dualism is false?

1 **All physicalist theories, including Functionalism, show that there are major problems with the kind of dualism described by Descartes:**

    i   If mental substance is completely different from physical substance, then there seems to be no way that they can interact, which seems to destroy Cartesian Substance Dualism.
    ii Physicalist theories do make the fairly obvious point that mind is fundamentally linked to matter, in the sense that if there are no physical bodies, then there are no minds. Those who believe in ghosts might want to object, but there is no verifiable case on record of a public and intelligent discussion between a human and a ghost.
    iii There seems to be no doubt that drugs, for example, affect the way that the mind thinks.

2 **Nevertheless Dualism in some form is still a valid option:**

i **Most dualists today think that Dualism is 'obviously' true.** Dualists think it is obvious that matter does not control mind; rather, our minds control our thoughts and bodies. If you tell yourself to raise your right hand, then you will raise your right hand. If an external physical pressure (like a dog wanting to be stroked) pushes against your right hand, you can will your hand to be still. Mental events cause physical events and we have free will to act as we wish (an issue which we shall discuss further in Chapter 5 Free will and moral responsibility).

ii **Dualism is still the most popular religious approach to the mind.** Dualism is obviously compatible with conventional religious ideas:
   ● Many Christians believe that humans have souls, and that the soul can survive the death of its body.
   ● The soul can then be judged by God; heaven being the reward for belief and moral obedience, and hell for disbelief and disobedience.
   ● Christians believe that God thinks, but has no body, so it is logical for them to hold that the soul or thinking self can also be independent of physical matter.

iii **There is some evidence for Dualism in accounts of near-death experiences (NDEs).** This is because NDEs are most often understood by those who have them, and by some who investigate them scientifically, to be evidence for the existence of a soul that survives death. We look at near-death experiences in detail on pages 98–100 later in this chapter.

iv **The 'Hard Problem' of consciousness is nowhere near being solved** (see box).

v **The qualia argument.** This interesting term comes from the Latin *qualis*, 'of what sort'/'of what kind'. In the philosophy of mind, to refer to qualia is to ask 'what is it like' to have subjective, conscious experience? What is the quality of experiencing the redness or the scent of a rose? What is it like to experience the pain when a rose thorn pricks your finger?

Despite the fact that it seems obvious that everybody has qualia, they can never be proved to exist by describing them, precisely because they are subjective. As Wittgenstein would say, 'Try describing the smell of a cup of coffee' – nobody could experience that smell by hearing a description of it, however detailed: qualia have to be experienced.

A full description of the neurological states of the brain when someone is experiencing qualia can never explain what qualia are. The problem of trying to understand the connection between physical changes in the brain and our experience of qualia is known as the 'Hard Problem' of consciousness which is explained below.

Note that what follows is a long explanation of the 'Hard Problem' of consciousness, but it illustrates the simple point that **consciousness implies that dualism in some respect or form is true**, and that is the bit you need to remember.

The 'Hard Problem' of consciousness

The 'Hard Problem' of consciousness is the problem of how the physical brain produces consciousness when consciousness seems so different from the physical brain. This question was introduced as the 'Hard Problem' of consciousness over 20 years ago by the Australian philosopher David Chalmers, and it has tended to dominate discussions in the philosophy of mind.

Neuroscience can show that when we make a conscious decision to do something, particular physical parts of the brain are electrically active, but that does not tell us how a conscious decision is reached; for that, we still seem to need a thinking *self*. **To put that another way, the 'I' seems to be irreducible**. For a materialist/physicalist, the 'I' is just an illusion thrown up by the brain's hardware. If so, it beats any illusion performed on stage or off.

Mostly, when dealing with scientific matters, **we think as materialists but experience as dualists**. We cannot get away from the fact that our experience of ourselves experiencing the world is quite different from what we can physically examine and quantify. It is the most fundamental thing about us – so how can it be dismissed as an illusion?

If we ask how the brain produces consciousness, we hit a wall. There really seems no way of getting from neural activity to conscious experience.

The Hard Problem of consciousness is not just about consciousness; it is about life and its relationship to thought. We know what consciousness is; we recognise when someone is unconscious; we

distinguish between animate and inanimate, conscious and unconscious; we know what it is to be conscious, because we know what it is to be embedded in our world. The faculty for understanding consciousness is imagination, not analysis. To reflect on one's immersion in a world of space and time, colour and sound, is a source of wonder. It is something to be enjoyed or grieved over, but it is not something that can be 'understood' in the normal sense of that word. It is not – and I suspect it never will be – open to a full explanation in reductive, physical and rational terms.

Hence, to say that you are 'nothing but' neural activity – as though the whole personal and social fabric of life were only a result of the firing of neurons – makes little sense. What happens in the brain is intimately and necessarily linked to each and every personal and social action and trait, just as muscular and skeletal activity is linked to every movement of the body. But that does not imply that the brain is the prior or only reality and all else simply a popular or conventional way of describing brain activity; quite the opposite. What happens in the brain mirrors and continues to make possible what happens to us as persons and as social agents.

Hence any materialist approach to understanding the self, if it relies heavily on the findings of neuroscience, runs into some fundamental problems by effectively eliminating the consciousness of self of which we are all aware. (This is made very clear by the qualia argument in point v above (page 82), and by Thomas Nagel's article below: 'What Is It Like to Be a Bat?')

Activity

Read Nagel's article online at:

www2.warwick.ac.uk/fac/ cross_fac/iatl/activities/ modules/ugmodules/ humananimalstudies/ lectures/32/nagel_bat.pdf

It is quite short at just 14 pages and is worth the read.

Thomas Nagel: What Is It Like to Be a Bat?

Nagel's position is clear. All mammals have conscious experiences and those conscious experiences occur in countless different forms that are *unimaginable* to us. The 'what-it-is-like-ness' of a bat's subjective experience is alien to us: for example, we move around aided by vision, whereas bats use a kind of sonar – echolocation – and we can have no idea of what that feels like.

> But no matter how the form may vary, the fact that an organism has conscious experience at all means, basically, that there is something it is like to be that organism. [Note 9]

Whatever organism we are talking about, be it bat, human or other, what it is like to be that organism cannot be reduced to a physical description or to an account of its functional states, so no physicalist theory (even Functionalism) can explain qualia in purely physical terms.

Note that Nagel is *not* saying that Physicalism/Materialism is wrong, but he is saying that the mind-body relationship cannot be understood without characterising objective *and* subjective experience. We cannot do away with subjectivity and qualia.

Dual-aspect Monism

We have now looked at two contrasting views about the relationship between the body and the soul. For substance dualists, there are two distinct substances, body and soul, which are somehow connected. For physicalists, there is only body, and what we call 'soul' is a product of that body and dependent on it. We now go on to look at a third option: Dual-aspect Monism.

1 Dual-aspect Monism

Dual-aspect Monism is *not* dualism, since it holds that there is only *one* kind of substance.

Neither is it physicalism, which reduces mind to matter.

It is monist, meaning that there is only *one* kind of ontological entity, but that entity has two aspects, and *neither reduces to the other*. **Mind and brain are two aspects of the same substance**.

One aspect (mind) is first-person subjective awareness, so is the perspective of consciousness. If we take qualia (what it is like to smell a rose or to feel pain), we cannot know their subjective feeling – what these things are like – by observing atoms or molecules or the activity of the neurons in the brain. The other perspective is that of third-person objective experience. For example, we could put somebody in a brain-scanner to look at the brain's physical state, but however hard you look at the brain images, and even if you could see all the electrical activity going on inside the brain, this would never tell you what the brain is experiencing subjectively.

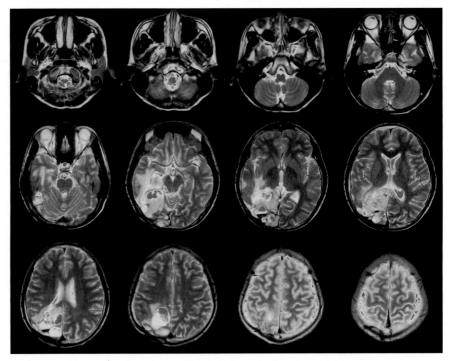

▲ MRI brain scans

Component 1 Philosophy of religion and ethics

2 Dual-aspect Monism avoids one obvious problem with substance dualism.

That is, how separate mental and physical substances can interact, because there are no separate substances: there is only one substance with two aspects – mental and physical.

3 It avoids physicalism's problem with qualia.

No matter how hard physicalism tries, it does not succeed in reducing consciousness or qualia to a purely physical description.

4 The single substance of Dual-aspect Monism is unknown.

In quantum theory (the science of the universe at its smallest levels), entities such as quarks are unobservable, yet the 'standard model' of particle physics does not make sense without quarks, so they must exist in some manner. The idea that mind and matter are underpinned by a single, as-yet unknown substance, is therefore not unlikely.

5 Dual-aspect Monism does receive powerful support from quantum theory in describing the relationship between the two aspects.

It can be described not as one of dependency but of *complementarity* [Note 10]. In quantum mechanics, the behaviour of light and electrons is sometimes wave-like and sometimes particle-like, i.e. it exhibits wave-particle duality. The wave and particle aspects cannot be observed simultaneously, yet together they provide a fuller description than either on its own. The physicist Wolfgang Pauli and the psychologist C.G. Jung applied this concept to the mind–brain relationship, theorising that the mental and the physical are complementary aspects of one psycho-physical reality. In other words, there is scientific support for Dual-aspect Monism through one of the basic principles of quantum mechanics.

> To clarify: Dual-aspect Monism holds that the fundamental reality is a single substance with mental and physical aspects. Quantum mechanics shows that reality at its basic level has a dual aspect.

6 When it comes to persons, Dual-aspect Monism becomes yet more interesting when combined with Panpsychism.

Panpsychism is the view that there is a level of consciousness/mentality in all entities in the universe, down to and including quantum particles. You can see that where Dual-aspect Monism holds that *the* fundamental reality is a single substance with mental and physical aspects, Panpsychism and Dual-aspect Monism are mutually supporting. Where even the smallest entities have a dual aspect, then their appearance in persons looks simply like one of development through increasing complexity.

This solves the problem (brought about largely by Aristotelian and Christian thinking) of the conscious states of other animals. They are conscious, but to a lesser degree, since their brain structures are less complex. It also solves the problem of finding a cut-off point for which animals are conscious and which are not: they all are.

Activity

If Dual-aspect Monism/ Panpsychism turn out to be right, what might the implications be for environmental ethics in general and for animal ethics in particular?

7 What, then, is a self?

We might describe a self as a complex psycho-physical arrangement with first-person subjective and third-person characteristics: the former being characterised by self-awareness/consciousness; the latter by the brain's physical/electrical/neuronal states. For example, imagine you can choose the chocolate you want. Bite into it. This will produce a state of your brain that has two aspects: 1) the mental aspect of the flavour, taste and texture of the chocolate and 2) the physical aspect involving electrical and chemical changes in your brain. 2) is third-person observable by science and 1) is first-person subjective and unobservable.

▲ Chocolate choice leads to a state of the brain that has two aspects: one physical and observable, the other subjective and unobservable.

8 In Dual-aspect Monism, the idea of souls becomes redundant.

In dual-aspect thinking, souls are unnecessary entities. Persons are bodies and brains, but bodies/brains are not just physical systems, they are objects with both mental and physical aspects. All forms of dualism, including substance dualism, are unnecessary, since subjective mental life can be explained as one aspect of one underlying substance.

The possibility of continuing personal existence after death

There are two related issues here: first: what, if it were to happen, would count as 'the person' surviving the death of their body? Second, is there any evidence that this occurs? To understand the idea of personal existence after death, we have to unpack the idea of personhood – of how we identify persons. In other words, what is personal identity?

As we progress through life we change radically, from being a small baby through to adulthood and old age. Along the way, things may happen to us that affect how we think of ourselves and how other people see us – for instance, a physical injury may damage my brain or render me unconscious; an emotional trauma may leave me depressed; I may lose my memory. But through all these events, I still think of myself as an individual person, so what is it that constitutes my identity through life? Unless we come to some view on that, it is difficult to know how we could even start to examine the question about whether I might be able to survive death in some form, because we need to know what constitutes the 'I' who might survive.

There are, generally speaking, three sets of ideas about personal identity:

● that it consists in the **physical** identity of body and/or brain
● that it consists in **metaphysical** identity of consciousness/the soul/pure ego
● that it consists in **psychological** characteristics of personality and of memory.

Remember that these sets of ideas are not self-contained; they are only general categories. Many people will accept parts of all three categories as being a true description of personal identity.

Personal identity as physical, involving spatio-temporal continuity of the body and brain

1 **A physicalist would argue that you cannot do without your brain and still be a person.**

If you have no brain, you have no memory, no personality and no thoughts. Whereas many of the cells in your body are replaced as you get older, the neurons in the cerebral cortex are never replaced. Moreover, no neurons are added to the cerebral cortex after birth and any cerebral cortex neurons that die are not replaced. [Note 11] At the very least, then, the brain retains its identity of the neurons in the cerebral cortex.

2 **Physicalists generally agree that to be the 'same person' throughout life depends also on the** *spatio-temporal continuity* **of a functioning body and brain.**

This cannot, of course, be the 'same body' as the one you were born with, since your current body is much larger. Although it is a popular myth that every cell in the body is replaced every 7–10 years, the rate of cell replacement in the body does mean that there is a significant discontinuity between the body's various states over the period of a life time. Also, you can lose various bodily parts through illness or accident.

Bodily 'identity' is therefore more a case of spatio-temporal *continuity*. In other words, your body/brain occupies a unique location in space and time throughout its life.

Personal identity as metaphysical, involving continuity of consciousness

1 To say that **the 'I' has metaphysical identity of consciousness** means that what is 'really real' about persons is not something physical, but their unchanged conscious awareness – hence Descartes' *cogito*: '*I* think, therefore *I* am'.

To get the flavour of what this means, the philosopher C.A. Campbell gives an illustration of the clock Big Ben striking 1 o'clock then 2 o'clock:

> Suppose I hear Big Ben striking. A moment later I – the same subject – hear it striking again … It is a pre-condition of my apprehending the second stroke *as* the second stroke that I remember having heard the first. But then I do not 'remember' having heard the first (and here is the crucial point) unless I am aware that it was *I*, the being who now hears the second stroke, who hears the first stroke; unless, in other words, I am not merely the same subject, but also conscious of my selfsameness, in the two experiences. [Note 12]

If you think about this carefully, you'll see what Campbell means:

- When Big Bang strikes 1, then 2, these two strikes are *separate* events in space–time.
- How then does an observer/listener know that the clock has struck 2?
- Because the observer/listener is conscious during both strikes of the clock.
- AND is consciously aware of being the *same self* as heard the clock strike 1 as now hears the clock strike 2.
- So memory is dependent on the 'I' being self-aware.

Now think of the objection to Descartes' Substance Dualism, on page 78 above, that the logic of Descartes' argument establishes only that 'there is thinking', not that there is an 'I' who thinks. For Campbell, mere 'thinking' could *never* relate the two strikes of the clock. To do that relation requires a conscious, self-aware mind – a 'substantial self', so perhaps Descartes was right.

Personal identity as *psychological continuity* of personality and memory

The 'Bundle' theory of identity

The 'Bundle' theory of identity is generally associated today with the work of Derek Parfit, and is set out in his 1984 book *Reasons and Persons*. Parfit argues against finding a single, definitive feature that enables a person to maintain his or her unique identity. As we pass through life, many things change, and often do so gradually. 'Identity' therefore depends on the number of features and not on some core of 'self'.

If you consider yourself as you are now, with a developed conscious awareness and a developing memory and personality, you are psychologically and spatio-temporally connected (through your brain and body) with all your past and future states of existence, but at no time is there an *identity* between different states. The neurons in your cerebral cortex will not change, but your body, memory and personality will change – perhaps drastically – over the course of your life.

Look at the diagram of the life development of a fictitious version of 'you':

Activity

Consider the claim that somebody with total memory loss would still be the 'same person'. What view do you take on this and what are your reasons for holding that view?

The continuity of temporary terminal states (TTS)									
	TTS A			**TTS B**				**TTS C**	**TTS D**	
0	10	20	30	40	50	60	70	88	
born	tonsils removed	lost an eye	had 2 children	had 2 more children	lost a leg	both parents died	2 grand-children	died	future descendants
weight 7 lbs	weight 68 lbs	weight 161 lbs	weight 165 lbs	weight 168 lbs	weight 196 lbs	weight 160 lbs	weight 149 lbs	weight 140 lbs	
continuity of body and brain, ongoing sense-impressions, memories and developing psychology									
				accident amnesia	personality change: depressive	partial memory loss	dementia		

▲ The continuity of the temporary terminal states (TTS)

In this diagram (which is not Parfit's) we can see a representation of the continuity of a person's life: her age changes, bodily changes, changes in memory and personality and the ongoing impact of sense impressions from the outside world. It is not intended to be complete in any way – we could, for example, have included her existence as a foetus, and before that her genetic inheritance from ancestors, since in Parfit's terms, these would also be part of her connectedness to the past, just as in the future her children will be connected to her in the same kinds of ways.

'TTS' here refers to a snapshot of the totality of a person's physical and psychological states *at any one particular instant in time*. [Note 13] If you apply it to yourself, your body and psychology will stay the same only for very brief fractions of time. Think of the speed of your thoughts, your continual interaction with the environment, the way in which you are constantly reacting to sense impressions (touch, taste, hearing, smell and sight), the processes of digestion and absorption: all these things form a *narrative* identity from cradle to grave, but according to Parfit there is no deeper level of 'self' that remains the same. The four vertical TTS lines (A, B, C, D) in the diagram refer to states that are far apart in time and obviously describe significantly different states of 'you', but in reality, even 'touching' TTS points, measured in micro-seconds apart, are different.

Note: If you wish to explore some of the more unusual implications of Parfit's ideas (such as brain splitting, brain fusion and teletransportation), you might like to read Part Three of his book *Reasons and Persons*. [Note 14]

Parfit concludes that we have to abandon any idea of some enduring 'identity' in persons. What matters is what Parfit calls 'Relation R' – *psychological connectedness*, including memory and personality.

On this account of a person, then, you do not survive death as the 'same person'. In Parfit's view, you have *continuity* with your ancestors through genetics and with your immediate ancestors through psychological connectedness. Equally, when you die, your children will be psychologically connected to you, but you do not survive in any deeper sense.

Personal existence after death

First of all, we should recognise that, in terms of logic, the very notion of 'life after death' is a contradiction in terms. The usual meaning of death (whether measured by cessation of activity within the brain stem or other means) is that life has stopped. Life after death suggests that what we call death is nothing of the sort, it is simply the failure of the physical body, but it allows something else (the mind, the soul) to continue, or that death is a temporary state, awaiting the possibility of a resurrection or reincarnation at a future date.

In the examples that follow, we shall be looking at two parallel issues:

- Whether the idea of life after death can be possible in some form or other, including the value of evidence such as near-death experiences.
- Whether or not what survives death can be said to be the 'same person' as the one that died.

The possibility of physical existence after death

For those who think that personal identity lies in the physical facts about the body and the brain, here are four conclusions that might be drawn concerning the possibility of continuing personal existence after death.

1 There is no continuing personal existence after death

This would be a clear conclusion for those who adopt a purely physicalist/materialist understanding of the nature of persons, since it is evident that body and brain decay after death and no longer exist in any recognisable form. For example, Bertrand Russell sees the self as bound up with what happens in the brain, so cannot entertain the idea of an existence that outlives its dissolution:

> Our memories and habits are bound up with the structure of the brain, in much the same way in which a river is connected with the riverbed. The water in the river is always changing, but it keeps to the same course because previous rains have worn a channel. In like manner, previous events have worn a channel in the brain, and our thoughts flow along this channel. This is the cause of memory and mental habits. But the brain, as a structure, is dissolved at death, and memory therefore may be expected to be also dissolved. [Note 15]

2 As an alternative to (1), science and technology may allow us to survive our death

Physicalism/materialism does not automatically entail a denial of life after death or of continuation in some form or other, but whether it is *personal* survival is another matter. For example, the developing science of cryonics deals with the low-temperature preservation of people whose lives cannot be saved by conventional medicine. Their heads (for example) can be preserved at −196 °C, waiting for resuscitation and reattachment to a body as and when science permits.

Another physicalist suggestion is provided by Daniel Dennett, for example, that the information presently stored in the brain could be uploaded onto a different platform, such as a computer (see pages 101–103).

Further views that are consistent with physicalism include resurrection of the body and Hick's Replica theory, which we look at in point 4.

3 The Christian concept of resurrection of the body

We have seen that Christians disagree concerning whether resurrection will be spiritual or bodily. You can refresh your memory of these different ideas by referring to Volume 1, pages 286–92.

Here we are considering the idea that resurrection in a bodily form is a coherent, philosophical view of continuing life after death. The obvious difficulty with such a view is that bodies rot and the material of any one body becomes part of other physical systems, including those of other human beings. If a body of some form is necessary in order to be recognised as a person, how are we to understand identity, if a body available after death is not to be physically and numerically identical to the one that dies?

The key question is, then: **'How would it be possible to establish identity in the re-embodied existence?'** One way out of this dilemma is simply to observe that an omnipotent God can do whatever he likes, and so there is no reason why God cannot allow souls to live again after the death of their bodies or be attached to another body. (This is the approach taken by Swinburne in many of his books, including *The Evolution of the Soul* (1997).) One of the best-known answers to the body problem is that of John Hick:

4 Hick's Replica theory

Hick wants to give a philosophical defence of the Christian concept of bodily resurrection. If you look back at Chapter 1 Religious language, you will remember that **Hick's view is that the Christian concept of God is 'in principle verifiable', because it is verified eschatologically** – that is, at death. Equally, if the resurrection takes place in bodily form, then bodily resurrection will also be verified at death.

Hick is a monist: he considers that there is one substance – a 'body-soul', in which body and soul are unified. Hick argues that as a psychosomatic unity, when the body-soul dies, all of it dies and is then raised by God.

Since the body clearly decays and its atoms become part of other living things, it is not possible for the individual to be resurrected with bodily *identity*, so Hick argues that what is resurrected is a *perfect replica*. He maintains that the replica retains the individual's identity as a mind-body unit.

Hick's argument is given through three related scenarios concerning 'Mr X'. The following is a summary. [Note 16]

● Scenario 1: Mr X disappears from a meeting in New York and immediately reappears at a similar meeting in Australia. He telephones his colleagues, who are mystified, but (since they are able to test his memory and identify his body) they eventually accept that he is the 'same person'.

● Scenario 2: This time, Mr X dies in the meeting in New York, so his colleagues see his corpse; but Mr X feels unwell for a moment, and then finds himself in the meeting in Australia. His friends are astonished when he phones them and they go to meet him, because his corpse is still present in New York. Nevertheless, however odd the situation, his friends will eventually accept that he is the 'same person', because he passes all the tests of his identity.

- Scenario 3: This time, Mr X dies, and a Mr X replica, complete with a set of memories that Mr X had at the last moment before his death, comes into existence in a 'resurrection world'. His new body is composed of material other than physical matter, although it looks exactly like his old body. It is obvious to him that he is in a spatio-temporal world, although it is not Earth. In these circumstances, how does Mr X know that he has been resurrected? He remembers being on his death bed and becoming weaker, until he loses consciousness. How does he know that he has not just recovered and is now somewhere else on earth? Well, he meets and recognises friends and relatives and they tell him that he has just appeared among them. Eventually, resurrected persons would be in no more doubt about their personal identity than they would have been in Scenarios 1 and 2, so they would know that they were now in a resurrection world.

Hick therefore concludes that resurrection into a *post-mortem* world is at least possible and that the person who was resurrected would indeed be the 'same person' as the one who had died.

Does the story of Mr X demonstrate the logical possibility of bodily resurrection?

Those who say 'No' argue that by definition a replica cannot be the original, so cannot be the 'same person'. In particular, they argue that God could, in principle, create any number of replicas, each believing itself to be the original, whereas in fact each one would have a different consciousness.

Those who say 'Yes' argue that this is to misunderstand Hick's idea of a replica. Hick is a monist and not a dualist, so Mr X is not something that can be copied like a page of writing: Mr X is not a body that *possesses* consciousness: he is (like all human beings) a unique mind-body unity, so there can only ever be one version of Mr X in existence.

It is not at all obvious, however, why this means that God could not create more than one replica of a unique individual, so Hick's logic is hard to follow here. It is not enough to say (as some do) that although God *could* create more than one replica he *would* not, because that is merely to admit that the replica can in fact be copied. If a replica can be copied even in principle, then the copy of the replica would have a different consciousness and would occupy a different spatio-temporal location.

Moreover, there are many further issues to deal with. For example: does the resurrected Mr X get the same body as that which died, or is it recreated at an ideal point in Mr X's life? Presumably God has the option of replacing a missing limb or of removing dementia. What happens if the pre-death body is hated by its owner – is it resurrected with all its hateful characteristics?

How likely is Hick's Replica theory to be true?

- If there is an omnipotent God, then it would be child's play for such a being to resurrect human bodies *post-mortem*. Christians believe that God resurrected Jesus, for example.
- Presumably, therefore, bodily resurrection must be *logically* possible, although Hick's argument that there could not be more than one replica of Mr X seems unlikely to say the least. If the mind-body of Mr X can be replicated once by God, then surely it can be replicated any number of times.

As a final comment on Hick, his position is to some extent consistent with the theory of reincarnation, since he suggests that humans may undergo a very lengthy process of being reborn to future lives in order, eventually, to choose freely to become 'children of God'. If you look back to Volume 1, Chapter 2 Evil and suffering, you will remember that this is part of Hick's theodicy: his explanation of evil.

As a concluding question, if bodily resurrection is possible, what would be its value? The obvious value is that of continued sense experience. Who would want to exist in a form that was incapable of experiencing the smell of a rose, the taste of food or the sight of magnificent scenery? Resurrection into a physical universe would offer endless possibilities of continued sense experience. To many people that would be preferable to a disembodied existence.

Activities

1 Discussion: would you prefer to exist as a disembodied soul or as an embodied being with full access to sense experience of the universe?

2 Read Hick's account of Mr X, which can be found online at: **http://philosophicalfragments.com/pdf/The_Philosophy_ of_Religion.pdf**

 Do you think Hick's Replica theory shows that resurrection of the body is possible?

3 If God does resurrect people's bodies, how far back in time does he start doing this? Given that humans are the product of approximately 3.8 billion years of evolution, why would God not resurrect all beings? Some animals are more intelligent than the least intelligent humans. Why would they not be resurrected? Where is the cut-off point? Would *any* cut-off point be arbitrary?

The possibility of the existence after death of a conscious self

Plato's arguments for the natural immortality of the soul

Plato – typical of dualists – holds that the soul is naturally immortal. In the *Phaedo*, he presents a number of arguments for the immortality of the soul. For example:

1 The Argument from Opposites

Everything comes to be from its opposite. Life and death are opposites, so in the same way that living bodies die, the dead must become living.

2 The Argument from Recollection

Plato believed that knowledge is recollection. He attempted to demonstrate that the principles of geometry can be recollected even by the uneducated. True knowledge is knowledge of the unchanging Forms. If we take two sticks of equal length but unequal width, we understand that they are of equal length because our knowledge of the Forms gives us an innate (built in) knowledge of the Form of Equality. To have such an understanding implies that we must have existed before birth, which implies further that the soul continues to exist after the death of the body.

These arguments suggest that after the death of the body, the soul goes to the world of Forms to contemplate their perfection and is subsequently reborn in the flesh. This follows an early Greek (religious) belief that everything is involved in an eternal cyclic process, so Plato seems to be endorsing a view of reincarnation of the soul as an automatic process.

A major problem with Plato's view of the immortality of the soul is that it rests on his theory of Forms together with some very doubtful arguments. For example, the Argument from Opposites seems, simply, to be wrong. Plato uses the analogy of sleeping and waking: clearly one does have to be asleep before one can wake up, but to say that one has to be dead before one lives is not the same thing at all. There is no space here for an extended critique of Plato, but his arguments for the natural immortality of the soul are very speculative, to say the least.

Another issue with Plato's account is its appeal to 'simplicity'. The core of Plato's argument is straightforward: the soul is immaterial, unextended and simple – i.e. it has no parts. Something can be destroyed if its parts are separated. Having no parts, the soul cannot be destroyed. But a self that is so simple it cannot be destroyed is so simple that it cannot be understood and encountered. We only recognise one another because of our distinctive complexity, and we gain that by contact with the physical environment in which we live and the world of ideas and language that we inherit and to which we contribute. We might entertain the idea of a simple, eternal soul, but we cannot imagine what such a soul would be like, and certainly not how it could have character.

In the seventeenth century, Descartes' radical dualism presented the self as a thinking entity separate from the physical body, and therefore opened up the possibility that, once established, such an entity might survive the removal of the physical body to which it was originally attached.

A twentieth-century example of this approach can be seen in the ideas of H.H. Price.

Price on disembodied souls

H.H. Price (1899–1984)

Price was a Welsh philosopher who was keen on parapsychology, which is the study of psychic phenomena and of alleged psychic abilities in humans.

Price hypothesised that the afterlife would be mind-based. Just as in a dream state we perform bodily actions, a community of disembodied, Cartesian-type souls, could perform bodily actions. Price suggested that their environment would correspond to the individual soul's deepest desires and strongest memories, from which their environment would be created. [Note 17] As with dreams, Price thought that the constructed environment would not have to conform to the laws of physics.

On the basis of his parapsychological studies, Price suggested that disembodied souls would communicate telepathically. In response to the question of how disembodied souls would recognise each other as persons in the afterlife, Price suggested that telepathic communication would allow individuals to project an image of themselves to other disembodied souls.

Ideas such as these are, perhaps, coherent, but whether or not they are true is another issue. Price's disembodied souls would seem to spend a lot of time manipulating images in order to create a substitute for sense perception. One wonders how those born blind, or those who died at birth, for example, would be able to manipulate images at all.

Price does not seek to prove the existence of a disembodied afterlife: rather he wants to show that the concept is at least coherent, primarily because parapsychological phenomena provide some support for it. For example, some people claim to be 'mediums', capable of communicating with the spirits in the afterlife. This is deeply suspect, however, since the possibility of fraud (and its clear demonstration in many cases) suggests that mediums have no real ability to communicate with the dead.

Although those who had known each other while embodied might understand each other to be the same person, the absence of bodies, brains and sense experience would seem to stretch the definition of 'same' far beyond its normal use.

Swinburne's light-bulb argument

In his book, *The Evolution of the Soul*, Swinburne says that the conscious self can continue to exist after the death of its body because all it needs is something to replace the function that the brain has in its present life. [Note 18]

Richard Swinburne (b.1934)

Swinburne is a British philosopher. He is a Christian apologist (someone who offers a defence of something controversial) and converted from the Anglican to the Orthodox Church, since the latter more specifically reflects his beliefs. He argues that God is metaphysically necessary (not logically necessary) – God is needed to explain the way things are. Swinburne also defends a form of Cartesian Substance Dualism and a libertarian concept of free will and is famous for the vigorous use of chalk while lecturing!

Swinburne is a substance dualist, so believes that there are two substances in a human being: a material body and a non-material soul. He says this about the soul:

> '[T]he human soul at death [has] a structure, a system of beliefs and desires which might be expected to be there to some degree in the soul if that soul were to be revived. If a man does survive death, he will take his most central desires and beliefs with him, which is the kind of survival for which, I suspect, most men hope.' [Note 19]

Swinburne uses an interesting analogy to explain how the soul relates to the body and how it may survive death:

> The soul is like a light bulb and the brain is like an electric light socket. If you plug the bulb into the socket and turn the current on, the light will shine. If the socket is damaged or the current turned off, the light will not shine. So, too, the soul will function (have a mental life) if it is plugged into a functioning brain. Destroy the brain or cut off the nutriment supplied by the blood, and the soul will cease to function, remaining inert. But it can be revived and made to function again by repairing or reassembling the brain – just as the light can be made to shine again by repairing the socket or turning on the current. But now, my analogy breaks down slightly (as all analogies do – else they would not be analogies). Humans can repair light sockets. But there is a practical limit to the ability of humans to repair brains; the bits get lost. Humans can move light bulbs and put them into entirely different sockets. But no human knows how to move a soul from one body to another and plug it into another; nor does any natural known force do this. Yet the task is one involving no contradiction and an omnipotent God could achieve it ... [Note 20]

Swinburne accepts that *in principle* a conscious self **could continue to exist after death in a disembodied state**, because the concept of me is the concept of a soul – an immaterial substance distinct from my body [Note 21] – so God could make it continue to exist.

The alternative is that God could connect the soul to its old body or to a new body (if its previous body had been annihilated).

- Note that the first possibility here is supported by functionalist arguments. You will remember that in principle, Functionalism could accept that minds could operate on a metaphysical platform.
- Given Swinburne's opinion that mental states are soul states, whether embodied or disembodied, a soul could in both instances retain its memories and desires, and would be the 'same person' as the one who had died.
- Note that Swinburne is careful to say that these are *possibilities*, not facts. It is logically possible that souls, as Swinburne defines them, could survive death either in an embodied or a disembodied state.
- Swinburne seems to be in no doubt that religious belief requires the soul to be embodied. In the Appendix to his conclusions concerning immortality, he refers to,

> '... the Christian emphasis on the embodiedness of men as their normal and divinely intended state.' [Note 22]

- For some Christian theists, then, (such as Swinburne himself), the argument that an omnipotent God could cause souls to exist after death in either an embodied or a disembodied state will make sense. For a 'soft materialist' Christian such as John Hick, the idea of a disembodied soul makes no sense, since for Hick a human is a psychosomatic (mind-body) unity, so God would have to resurrect the whole person.

Reincarnation of the soul

Swinburne's mention of moving a soul from one body to another brings us naturally to the concept of reincarnation. This view is generally associated with Eastern thought. Most Hindus believe that, after this life, the soul enters into another body – either that of a human being, a god or an animal – the nature of which is determined by *karma*, actions (good or bad) performed in this life. This view also assumes that a person's situation in this life has been caused, to some extent, by actions in previous lives. It assumes a single entity – the soul (*atman*) – that passes from body to body, but may aim finally at identity with divine reality itself (Brahman).

Notice the radical implication of this for issues of life and death. In the *Bhagavad Gita* (part of the Hindu scriptures), issues about bad *karma* being generated by those whose role is to be a warrior are countered by the claim that to kill the body is not really to kill the person, for that person has a soul that goes on to another life. [Note 23]

Reincarnation is compatible with physicalist/materialist views that see the self as necessarily embodied, but requires, in addition to this, the sense that the embodied self accumulates karmic character and therefore *is independent of any one particular embodiment*.

Support for reincarnation comes from past-life regression and from direct past-life recall.

Past-life regression is a technique used in hypnotherapy, where the therapist uses a variety of techniques intended to locate the causes of a patient's present mental stress in a supposed past life. The general assessment of past-life regression is that it is best explained by cryptomnesia, which is where a patient experiences a forgotten memory and does not recognise it as having been experienced before.

Direct past-life recall occurs most often in young children, who may confuse their parents, for example, by apparently remembering a different set of parents. Of particular interest here is the research of Professor Ian Stevenson.

Ian Stevenson (1918–2007)

Stevenson was a Canadian-US psychiatrist with an interest in the paranormal, particularly cases where children claimed to remember past lives. During the 1960s, he apparently left a combination lock in a file in his university department's Division of Perceptual Studies, telling his co-workers that he would try to communicate the unlocking combination from beyond the grave. Apparently the lock still remains shut. [Note 24]

In 1974, Stevenson published an account of 20 cases in which he concluded that reincarnation was strongly indicated as an explanation of the facts. [Note 25] These were from India, Ceylon, Brazil, the Tlingit Indians of Southeastern Alaska and the Lebanon. By the time of his death, Stevenson had amassed over 1,000 such cases. You can read some examples at:

https://med.virginia.edu/perceptual-studies/wp-content/uploads/sites/267/2015/11/STE1.pdf . [Note 26]

Evaluating reincarnation

In philosophical circles, reincarnation is not well received. Objections to it include:

● Weak research procedures – this was frequently alleged against Stevenson, who (it is said) had a predisposition to believe what he was told about reincarnation.
● Reincarnation is an accepted belief in most of the cases studied by Stevenson, so there is perhaps a tendency for people to encourage each other to provide testimony to support their beliefs.
● The well-known phenomenon of cryptomnesia shows that people can believe that they remember events, whereas in reality they are forgotten memories that have resurfaced.
● Philosophically, how could it be established that any individual now living is the 'same person' as a previous incarnation? There is no continuity of memory or psychology (except in the claims made by Stevenson and others) or of body and brain, so belief in the reincarnation of a non-physical soul is unverifiable. This does not disprove reincarnation, but for physicalists/materialists it is clearly not going to be an acceptable theory.

In its favour, the amount of evidence from spontaneous childhood memories of past lives cannot be dismissed so easily. For those who believe in the existence of an indestructible soul, reincarnation is the most likely explanation in many of the cases investigated by Stevenson and others.

Near-death experiences

There is some evidence for Dualism and personal survival after death in accounts of near-death experiences (NDEs). This is because NDEs are most often understood by those who have them, and by some who investigate them scientifically, to be evidence for the existence of a soul that survives death.

NDEs have been reported from all cultures and times since the days of Plato, who in Book X of *The Republic* tells the story of Er, a soldier who was killed in battle, then awoke on his funeral pyre and described his journey into an afterlife. NDEs are most commonly reported in hospitals, where the chances of resuscitation are much higher than for those who suffer cardiac arrest or a major stroke where help is not close at hand.

NDEs are structured

Near-death experiences commonly begin with an out-of-body experience, where someone sees himself from a vantage point somewhere near the ceiling, for example, and recognises his own body on a hospital bed. Some

> **Activity**
> Research Buddhist philosophical ideas concerning rebirth and the Buddha's idea of the 'self'. How do these differ from Hindu ideas?

witness resuscitation attempts on their body and are afterwards able to describe the procedure in detail. Other parts of the structure include:

- seeing a light, commonly described as being brighter than the sun but not hurting the eyes
- moving along a long dark tunnel with the light in the distance
- feelings of peace and serenity
- meeting a barrier, border or limit (symbolic of death)
- meeting a 'being of light', or just as commonly, 'three beings of light'
- an instantaneous past-life review, during which, for example, the effects of one's actions on others, negative and positive, are experienced without judgement
- meeting relatives who have died previously
- the need to return to the body, presumably through resuscitation
- the effect of the experience on the way one lives thereafter
- a different understanding of the nature of death and the afterlife.

Some people might get no further than the out-of-body experience. Others might experience some or all parts of the structure.

Most NDEs are of the 'heavenly' type; some are the 'hell' type, where the experience is generally interpreted as a warning. Some NDEs are religion-specific and culture-specific, so that Christians will see Jesus and Christian saints and those who belong to other religious traditions will see their own religious figures.

Negative interpretations of the NDE

- Neuroscientific studies of the NDE are generally 'reductive', meaning that the whole experience is understood as a product of the dying brain and as having no further or deeper meaning.
- In support of this interpretation, neuroscientists point to the fact that the NDE is culture- and religion-specific. Christians will not see Buddhist figures, and Sikhs will not see Jewish figures, so the NDE simply reflects what the person expects to see.
- By definition, those who remember a NDE did not actually die, so many would say that the NDE is not evidence for what happens after death.

Positive interpretations of NDEs

- NDEs are not popular as a source of study for any one religious group, for the simple reason that they do not give exclusive support to the claims of any one religion over another. Those who believe that the NDE is real count this in its favour. If the NDE is real, then we might expect it to be culturally and religiously relative. There would be no point giving a Buddhist a Muslim NDE, because the Buddhist would not understand it.
- One indication that the NDE is a real experience is that there have been examples of people giving detailed sighted experiences despite having been blind from birth and having no optic nerve. In a study of such cases, Mark Fox comments:

[W]hat is being claimed is that sight is not simply restored or bestowed during these special cases, but that it is sight of a kind that transcends the usual limits of perception, *even in the sighted*. [Note 27]

Fox comments also on the neuroscientific reductionism mentioned above:

> [A]t present, no total neuro-scientific 'explanation' of even the most basic and consistently encountered features of an NDE is sufficient to adequately explain them … Thus, while NDEs remain theoretically explainable by science, they are at present unexplained by it. [Note 28]

A common objection to the reality of NDEs, (made, for example, by Dr Susan Blackmore, a British psychology lecturer) is that they probably happen at the point of becoming unconscious, or else at the point of regaining consciousness, so the NDE is the product of the brain in a state where the brain is capable of constructing a fictional experience. [Note 29]

Against that, the singer-songwriter Pam Reynolds (1956–2010) is credited with having a NDE at a point when she had no blood flowing in her brain, so was clinically dead. On the basis of her experience, **some researchers argue that the NDE shows the possibility of mind-brain separation at death**, which would suggest that Dualism cannot be dismissed.

The British mathematician/physicist Roger Penrose, and the American anaesthesiologist Stuart Hameroff, have been collaborating for some years on a theory of quantum consciousness which suggests that when the brain stops functioning, some of its quantum information might not be lost or dissipated or destroyed, but could persist in some way in the fundamental level of space–time geometry, and could exist indefinitely.

The possibility of psychological continuity after death

The Bundle theory

On the face of it, the 'Bundle' theory of personal identity, as presented by Derek Parfit, gives little hope of personal survival after the death of the body. The possibility of continued personal existence after death can be described only in limited ways:

- Persons do not live after death, since the physical body and brain die, and a person's memories and personality die with him.
- There can be a psychological connectedness with children and close friends, for example, in the sense that the person's influence on them during life continues for as long as the person is remembered.
- Aside from that, there is no deeper level of self that remains the same.

Nevertheless, Bundle theory may not be inconsistent with a belief in personal survival after death. Parfit sees links between his 'Bundle' theory and Buddhist views, and presents a series of passages from Buddhist scriptures in support of his theory. Buddhism sees a person as an ever-changing combination of mental and physical energies, as Parfit does, but also teaches that this continuous process of change continues through what we regard as death. In Buddhist teaching the person who dies is neither the same as nor different from the one who is reborn because the new life arises from the last in the same way that the future arises from the past and present in this life. This does not show that rebirth is 'true', but it does suggest that a belief in some form of personal survival is consistent with the idea that the self is a 'Bundle'.

Dennett: survival by uploading brain information to a different platform

The idea that the information presently stored in the brain could be uploaded onto a different platform, such as a computer, does give a possible model for personal survival beyond death.

Daniel Dennett (b.1942)

Dennett is an American philosopher, notorious to some, but famous to others for the title of his book *Consciousness Explained*, which, if verified, would count as the greatest ever achievement in philosophy, let alone neuroscience. Dennett has a very engaging writing style, so if you have the time to read all 500 plus pages, you might find it an interesting read. Dennett is known as one of the 'Four Horsemen of New Atheism', the other three being Sam Harris, Christopher Hitchens and (of course) Richard Dawkins. [Note 30]

To see a person as a narrative self is now a fairly common view. For example, Daniel Dennett describes the self as a 'Center of Narrative Gravity' and the phenomena of consciousness as,

> '… the activities of a virtual machine realized in the astronomically adjustable connections of a human brain'.

Dennett goes on to say:

> '… then, in principle, a suitably "programmed" robot, with a silicon-based computer brain, would be conscious, would have a self. More aptly, there would be a conscious self whose body was the robot and whose brain was the computer.' [Note 31]

You should have no trouble in understanding this as being a *functionalist* approach to the mind-body problem, since Functionalism holds that minds can function on different platforms. Dennett expands on this at the end of his chapter on 'The Reality of Selves':

If you think of yourself as a center of narrative gravity … your existence depends on the persistence of that narrative (rather like the *Thousand and One Arabian Nights*, but all a single tale), which could *theoretically* survive indefinitely many switches of medium, be teleported as readily (in principle) as the evening news, and stored indefinitely as sheer information. If what you are is that organization of information that has structured your body's control system (or, to put it in its more usual provocative form, if what you are is the program that runs on your brain's computer), then you could in principle survive the death of your body as intact as a program can survive the destruction of the computer on which it was created and first run. Some thinkers (e.g. Penrose …) find this an appalling and deeply counterintuitive implication of the view I've defended here. But if it is potential immortality you hanker for, the alternatives are simply indefensible. [Note 32]

With Dennett's approach, then:

- Your experiences/memories/personality are the organisation of information: the 'program that runs on your brain's computer'.
- Immortality is in principle possible through the means of storing that information on another platform.
- What can survive, then, is the 'persistence of the narrative' that is you. This is not your body or your brain, or some metaphysical higher 'self': it is the narrative of your experience, memory and personality.
- Depending on the platform used, the stored information of your life could presumably be psychologically continuous with what went before.

To give a (very basic) contrast between Dennett's approach on the one hand and the dualism of Swinburne on the other, consider the comparison figure below, in which a person's life is shown as a series of 'temporary terminal states':

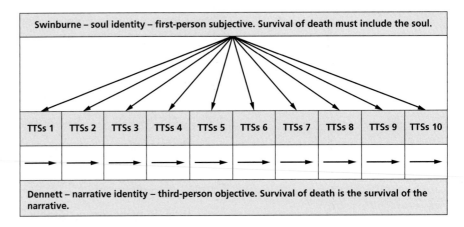

▲ Life as a series of 'temporary terminal states'

Temporary terminal states (TTS) 1–10 represent a person's temporary states over a lifetime. These include every successive experience in a person's life. If you consider all that person's physical changes, ongoing thoughts and experiences, their total number would be incalculable.

For Swinburne, the self is characterised by first-person subjective accounts of its mental states (the conscious 'I' who thinks, feels, and has qualia). For Dennett, information is third-person objective. Dennett wants a scientific approach to consciousness, and since science uses objective third-person methods, science cannot verify conscious states, so for Dennett they do not exist.

In the Dennett model, a person is the sum total of the information stream. There is nothing over and above the information itself. In the Swinburne model at the top, the person is not the information stream itself, but the subject-self – the 'I', or soul whose consciousness *processes* the information and can reflect on it. The subject-self has to exist in order for persons to understand the *sequence* of TTSs.

For Swinburne, what can survive death is the subject-self – the soul – perhaps resurrected in the same or another body, because survival makes no sense without the survival of the person's mind. For Swinburne, survival appears to need the intervention of God. For Dennett, what survives can only be the information stream of the narrative self, because there is nothing else to survive. For Dennett, his functionalist account means that a person's 'narrative' might continue on another platform, but that platform cannot be a subjective consciousness, because the narrative is merely stored information.

Who do you think is right? Dennett's critics do not think that he solves the 'Hard Problem' of consciousness or explains qualia, in other words he reduces consciousness to information and circuitry when it is so much more than that. For example John Searle writes:

> It is just a plain fact about me – and every other normal human being – that we have sensations and other sorts of conscious states... Should I pinch [Dennett] to remind him that he is conscious? Or should I pinch myself and report the results in more detail? ... The fact that many people have back pains, for example, is an **objective** fact of medical science. The existence of these pains is not a matter of anyone's opinions or attitudes. But the mode of existence of the pains themselves is **subjective**. They exist only as felt by human subjects. [Note 33]

The view of Dual-aspect Monism: persons have objective, and perhaps subjective, immortality

We met the idea of Dual-aspect Monism earlier in this chapter when we looked at the relationship between the body and the soul, and it may help you to refresh your understanding of it by re-reading this section before going any further. When associated with Panpsychism, Dual-aspect Monism is mostly associated with an objective understanding of survival after the death of the body.

The possibility of continued existence after death still exists for Dual-aspect Monism, for example in the 'objective immortality' of Process Theology. You will remember that we have looked at Process Theology fairly closely in Volume 1: Chapter 2 Evil and suffering (pages 77–84), Chapter 7 God (pages 274–77) and particularly on Objective immortality in Process thought in Chapter 8 Self, death and afterlife (pages 298–99). You should refresh your memory of this before reading on.

Process Theology has abandoned what it sees as indefensible elements within Christianity, such as God's supposed omnipotence and the idea of creation from nothing. Its revisionary agenda also includes Christian ideas about life after death. In essence, the argument below says that God is a combination of mind and all the matter of the universe; all things are a combination of mind and matter; all things therefore live on in the mind of God after death, and this includes persons.

To draw out the connections here, from Dual-aspect Monism and Panpsychism, **Process Theology has a panpsychic feature** in the thought of A.N. Whitehead, who was the main influence behind Process thinking.

Whitehead was convinced that for consciousness to be *anywhere* in nature it must be *everywhere* in nature. Follow the logic:

● Process Theology abandons the idea that God is above and beyond space–time, which means that the relationship between God and the universe needs to be defined. **God is di-polar, meaning that God is in the universe and the universe is in God**, so in a rough sense God and the universe are the mental and physical poles of what exists: **they are the two fundamental aspects of reality** (so you can see how this relates to Dual-aspect Monism).

● If this double-aspect is true of God/the universe, then it must be true of everything in the universe, so humans, animals, vegetables, rocks, water and even matter down even to the level of electrons – **all entities have a dual aspect**. This has to be the case, because all entities are literally 'in' God. All *persons*, therefore, are in God.

● **When persons die, therefore, they are objectively, and not subjectively, immortal**. Most Christians believe in subjective immortality, so that they exist as the same thinking subjects they were before death. On the Process view, immortality is objective, because persons stay forever in the mind of God, but their nature as persons is limited, since they no longer have their own self-conscious states. Only God has subjective immortality.

● **Nevertheless, some Process thinkers argue that God has the power, and possibly the wish, to give persons *subjective* immortality**. David Griffin (whose views we looked at in Volume 1, Chapter 7 God) considers the possibility that this might be granted to the extent that

'... life after death ... would allow time for souls to actualize all their potentialities, to reach a state of wholeness, and thereby to have their lives finally make a contribution to the divine life within which they can be content.' [Note 34]

● If Griffin is right about the possibility of subjective immortality, then God, even if not omnipotent, has the power to bring it about that the 'same person' remains in existence by some means or another.

There are, of course, many objections to the Dual-aspect Monism/Process Theology/Panpsychism mix, for example:

● That its God is not omnipotent or omniscient, so is not worthy of worship.
● It denies the divinity of Jesus, and does away with souls, whereas soul is a 'bedrock' item for most Christians.
● For some, objective immortality is not worth having, because 'you' are not self-aware.

Nevertheless for others:

● It is far more realistic in terms of its science. In particular, Dual-aspect Monism provides a coherent understanding of the nature of persons without having to rely on some mysterious 'soul stuff'.
● It does away with an anthropomorphic (human-centred) universe. The universe does not revolve around humans: all entities are made in the same way, with mental and physical aspects. In particular, in terms of the continuation of biological entities after death, humans have no position of special privilege.

- It leaves open the possibility that persons could survive with subjective immortality.
- It is also consistent with the functionalist idea of uploading minds onto a computer platform, since such a platform must, by the principles of double-aspect monism, already possess a mental aspect.

As a final comment on this section, 'the truth' about reality, about persons and about how they might survive death, cannot be known. We can see that within the next century, the possibility of uploading human minds onto a computer platform might become realised, and no doubt there are further possibilities. Whether the universe contains structures to bring about the reincarnation of persons, or whether God is required to resurrect beings, is largely a matter of belief (or disbelief). You do not have to look for definitive answers, because there are none. Be alive, instead, to the sea of possibilities.

Technical terms for self, death and the afterlife

Dual-aspect Monism   The view that mind and matter are two aspects of one (as yet unknown) substance. Mind is first-person subjective experience (qualia), whereas brain events are third-person objective (e.g. observable through brain scans), and neither is reducible to the other. Double-aspect theory is thought to receive support from the principle of complementarity in quantum mechanics, for example, that light manifests sometimes as a wave and sometimes as a particle.

First person   Language which uses the subjective case – 'I' and 'we', either of which can be used as the subject of a sentence. To say that mental states are experienced first person is to suggest that the 'I' is a subjective self – conscious and self-aware. By contrast with 'first person', third-person language is objective: so, for example, Daniel Dennett holds that scientific language must be third-person objective. This is because subjective entities cannot be investigated or verified; hence he argues that language about persons is objective: we cannot talk meaningfully about subjective selves. He therefore rejects the idea of Cartesian selves as absurd.

Forms   Plato's theory of Forms was that all things in the world of sense perception are particular instances of universal Forms. For example, all tables are particular instances of the universal Form of a Table. The Forms are metaphysical/perfect Ideas.

Functionalism   Functionalism conceives of the mind as a function. Mental states are identified by their functional role, by what they do rather than what they are made of. This means they can be 'multiply realised', for example through human brains or through a non-biological system such as a computer.

Interactionism   (in the philosophy of mind) – Descartes' (false) view that mind and body interact within the pineal gland.

Introspection   To examine/observe/look at one's own conscious thought processes/one's own thoughts and feelings.

Multiple realisability   In Functionalism, this is the argument that minds/mental states (like clocks) can run on a variety of different platforms, including, for example, computers, and potentially (however unlikely) on a metaphysical (Cartesian-type) platform.

Neuroscience   Study of the brain and the nervous system.

Nous   (Greek) Intellect.

Panpsychism   The view that all entities, including quantum particles, are to some extent conscious; so consciousness is not unique to humans and other animals, but is possessed even by what we normally refer to as 'inanimate objects' such as rocks.

Physicalism   The monist view that there is only one substance – physical matter (so physicalism in this sense is also called materialism). For physicalists, mind reduces to matter.

Psyche   (Greek) Soul, spirit, mind.

Qualia   The qualities of subjective conscious experience, for example, what it feels like in your mind to experience redness or the smell of a rose.

Radical   Extreme, as in 'radical dualism'; the view that mind and matter are radically different. In particular, mind is not the same as the brain.

Scepticism   In philosophy, the view that it is impossible to have certain knowledge (i.e. knowledge that cannot be doubted).

Thumos   (Greek) In Plato's understanding, that part of the *psyche*/soul corresponding to 'pugnacity', 'righteous indignation', 'courage', etc. It is (or should be) subordinate to the rational part.

Summary of self, death and afterlife

The nature and existence of the soul; Descartes' argument for the existence of the soul

- Descartes' agenda was religious, which many would see as not being helpful in a philosophical argument.

- He thinks that there are two essential substances: mind (soul) and matter. Matter is *res extensa* (extended substance); mind/soul is *res cognita* (mental substance).

- Descartes' Argument from Doubt: I can doubt that my body exists/But I cannot doubt that I am a thinking thing (doubting *is* thinking)/Therefore I am not identical with my body.

This doesn't work. Most modern philosophers think that the mind is produced by the brain, so brain and body are the same thing, so the brain *cannot* doubt its body's existence.

- The Argument from Divisibility and Non-Divisibility: All bodies are extended in space and so are divisible/Minds are not extended in space, so are not divisible/Minds are therefore radically different from bodies.

This doesn't work either: neuroscience shows that there is a close correlation between mind and brain. If the brain (which is part of the body) is damaged, the mind is damaged also, so to that extent it can be 'divided'.

- The Argument from Clear and Distinct Perception (CDP): I have a CDP of *myself* as a non-extended thinking thing/I have a CDP of my *body* as an extended non-thinking thing/So I and my body can exist apart from each other/So I am not my body.

This doesn't work either, because Descartes starts the argument by presupposing that God exists to guarantee his CDPs, but that just becomes the 'Cartesian circle' (a circular argument), because in *Meditation V* Descartes deduces God's existence by having CDPs, and now wants to use God to guarantee his CDPs.

If you find that complicated, just hold on to the fact that any *philosophical* argument that uses God as part of its logic is bound to get into trouble at some point.

- Descartes' Dualism:

However, in addition to the fact that the arguments from doubt, divisibility and CDPs don't work, problems with Descartes' Dualism include Ryle and the Ghost in the Machine/category error and Hume and the idea of soul substance:

- the idea of 'soul substance' is a circular argument because it merely says: *Soul substance can think because soul exists as a thinking substance*

- it may well be that the cause of thought is a material substance

- the problem of counting souls.

Descartes' *cogito* establishes only that 'there is thinking', not that there is an 'I' who thinks.

Descartes' dualism of body and soul	
Body	**Soul**
extended in space	not extended in space
located in space	not located in space
has parts that corrupt and decay	has no parts to corrupt or decay
so cannot survive death	so is not susceptible to death
so is mortal	so is immortal

The body/soul relationship

We looked at three theories here: Descartes' Interactionism, physicalism (for example, Functionalism) and Dual-aspect Monism:

1 Descartes' Interactionism

Descartes thought that body and soul interacted in the pineal gland, but interactionism solves nothing: saying where interaction might take place tells us nothing about *how* a non-physical mind can interact with a physical brain.

2 Physicalism, which explains everything in terms of matter

There *is* no body-soul relationship, because there is no soul. Physicalism is a reductive philosophy: 'mind' reduces to brain, and physicalism seems to give an obvious explanation to common phenomena, for example that dementia affects both brain and mind in parallel, so the brain must *be* the mind.

Functionalism is a persuasive reductive physicalist theory. A system's function can be described in terms of input/function/output, as with a thermostat, for example. It is possible, therefore, that human minds could run on a computer platform, where the input is sense experience, the function is the processing of information by the brain, and the output is the resultant behaviour. It is even possible that human mentality could at some stage in the future be 'uploaded' to super-powerful computers and massively enhanced.

Functionalists would have to admit that minds could run on a metaphysical (Cartesian-type) platform, although most functionalists see that as extremely unlikely. Does Functionalism show that the dualist account of the mind-body relationship is false? Probably not, although all physicalist theories, including Functionalism, show that Cartesian Dualism has lots of problems, for example:

- the problem of how non-physical mind can interact with physical matter
- the fact that it seems obvious to most people that matter and mind are inextricably linked: we do not find minds that are not linked to matter
- the fact that drugs clearly do affect the mind.

Nevertheless, Dualism in some form is still a valid option, for example:

- Most dualists today think it is *obviously* true that mind and matter are not the same.
- Religiously, it is still popular: having a soul that can survive death means that Christians can be judged by God and sent to heaven or hell. Also, God is thought to be bodiless, so it makes sense to believe that humans have a non-physical soul.
- There is some evidence for Dualism in accounts of near-death experiences.
- The 'Hard Problem' of consciousness is nowhere near being solved. The idea of the 'I', the thinking self, is very difficult to reduce to a physical description. We can see this from the qualia argument – what it is like to have subjective, conscious experience, for example Thomas Nagel's *What Is It Like to Be a Bat?*

3 Dual-aspect Monism (DAM)

This is not Dualism, because it holds there is only one kind of substance; neither is it physicalism, which reduces mind to matter. Mind and brain are two aspects of the same, as-yet-unknown, substance. One aspect (mind) is first-person subjective awareness/consciousness (qualia); the other is third-person objective experience. A brain scanner can see the physical states of a brain (such as someone reacting to eating chocolate), but cannot know the first-person qualia of the taste and smell of chocolate.

- DAM avoids Descartes' problem of how the two substances of non-physical mind and physical brain can interact because there are no separate substances: there is only one substance with two aspects – mental and physical.
- DAM has no problems with qualia – they are first-person subjective experiences.
- DAM gets support from the principle of complementarity in quantum physics, where light can sometimes behave as a wave and sometimes as a particle (i.e. it also has two aspects).

The possibility of continuing personal existence after death

There are two related questions here: first, what, if it were to happen, would count as 'the person' surviving the death of their body? Second, is there any evidence that this occurs?

Persons change radically over their lives through growth, injury, memory loss and so on, so what is it that constitutes my identity through life? We need to know what constitutes the 'I' who might survive before asking *how* it might survive. We can look at three sets of general ideas:

1 Personal identity as physical, involving spatio-temporal continuity of the body and brain

A physicalist would argue that you cannot do without your brain and still be a person. Having no brain means you have no memory, personality or thoughts. The brain is especially important because, unlike many of the body's cells, the neurons in the cerebral cortex are not replaced as you age, so the brain retains *identity* of neurons in the cerebral cortex.

Physicalists generally agree that to be the 'same person' throughout life depends also on the spatio-temporal continuity of a functioning body and brain. Your body/brain occupies a unique location in space and time throughout its life.

2 Personal identity as metaphysical, involving continuity of consciousness

On this view, what is 'really real' about persons is their unchanged conscious awareness. As Descartes says: '*I* think, therefore *I* am.' This is best understood by thinking of C.A. Campbell's illustration of a clock striking. There has to be an unchanging 'I' – a same self who hears each successive stroke and remembers each one – because memory depends on there being an 'I' who is self-aware.

3 Personal identity as psychological continuity of personality and memory

Parfit's account of 'psychological connectedness' follows in the general tone of Hume's 'Bundle theory' of the self, and from the Buddha's view that we are a bundle of mental events. This means that persons have a 'narrative identity' – they form the subject of a connected narrative (a series of TTSs – 'temporary terminal states') from birth to death, which gives the (false) *impression* of being a self.

Parfit uses a series of thought experiments in brain fission, brain fusion, branching and teletransportation to suggest that it is futile to ask where the conscious self or soul might go in such cases. The (lack of) evidence from these cases suggests that what matters is 'Relation R' – psychological connectedness, including memory and personality. Persons are psychologically and spatio-temporally connected (through brain and body) with all past and future states of existence, but at no time is there an identity of self that links these different states. On this account of persons, then, you do not survive death as the 'same person': you merely have psychological connectedness with your immediate ancestors and your children who survive you.

Now we turn to the second question: What are the possibilities of continuing personal existence after death?

1 The possibility of physical existence after death

Bertrand Russell states the 'common sense' view of physicalists/materialists, that persons are reducible to matter, so there is no physical existence after death.

Functionalist arguments can establish the possibility, and perhaps the probability of continued life, for example by uploading the mind into a computer. Strictly speaking, this is not a continuation after death, since the brain is uploaded before death. Nevertheless, the functionalist account allows for human immortality through human technology rather than as an act of God.

It would be difficult to show, however, that a brain uploaded to a computer would be the 'same person' as the discarded brain and body of the original person.

The Christian idea of bodily resurrection is defended by John Hick, who uses his 'replica' theory to argue that God resurrects a replica of the human body-soul. His thought experiment of Mr X perhaps shows that bodily resurrection is *logically* possible, but Hick's view does not seem to avoid the problem that God could in theory produce any number of replicas of Mr X, so it is hard to see how a replica can really be the 'same person' as the Mr X who died.

2 The possibility of the existence after death of a conscious self

H.H. Price pictures a community of disembodied, Cartesian-type souls, who would communicate telepathically and project images of themselves to other disembodied souls. It is very difficult, however, to talk of sameness in the absence of body, brain and sense experience.

Plato argued for the natural immortality of the soul, using, for example, the Argument from Opposites and the Argument from Recollection. Plato's core argument is that the soul is immaterial, unextended and simple (i.e. it has no parts), so it cannot be destroyed at death. But what would a 'simple' soul be like? How could it have a character? How could the reincarnated soul be verified as the 'same person'?

Swinburne's defence of Substance Dualism rejects the idea that the soul can be naturally immortal. He sees the soul as an evolutionary development in connection with bodies and brains, brought about by God's intervention or some other process. Mental states are states of the soul, so at the point of death the soul, which is the real person, would have character, beliefs and desires. Just as a light bulb will shine only if it is plugged into a live socket, a soul will function only if it is attached to a living, functioning brain.

In principle, souls could survive death in a disembodied state. Certainly God could bring this about. Alternatively God could reconnect a soul to its original body, or to another body if the original body had been annihilated. In either event, *since a soul has character, beliefs and desires*, the surviving person would be the 'same person' as the one who had died.

Swinburne clearly assumes that God's intervention would be needed to bring about the survival after death of disembodied souls or souls linked to existing or new bodies. For some, this is a weakness of his argument.

3 Reincarnation of the soul

In Eastern thought (Hinduism), the *atman* (soul) passes from body to body, governed by the law of *karma*, but may aim finally at identity with divine reality itself (Brahman). During successive incarnations the soul is necessarily embodied, but the law of *karma* means that the soul is independent of any one particular embodiment. *Karma* is a natural law, not a law dictated by the gods, so there is no judgement of individuals by the gods.

Support for reincarnation comes from past-life regression and from direct past-life recall, particularly by young children (documented in detail by Ian Stevenson). The evidence from both hypnotic regression and past-life recall is discounted by most philosophers, usually on the basis of weak research procedures, the tendency of those who believe in reincarnation to invent or to unconsciously 'find' evidence, and cryptomnesia.

In favour of past-life recall, some of the evidence for it is difficult to dismiss, not least because the main factor in the recall is often that the child concerned remembers a traumatic death. That appears to be an important factor in triggering past-life memory.

In terms of being the 'same person' throughout its incarnations, there is no continuity of memory or psychology, or body or brain, between incarnations, so identifying a person as the 'same person' at any stage of the process would seem to be impossible.

4 The evidence for dualism and survival after death in accounts of near-death experiences

These occur in all cultures and all times. The fact that they are highly structured suggests they are not caused by drugs or by lack of oxygen to the brain, but are real accounts of what happens at death. In particular, they appear to give support for the idea of mind-brain separation at death, and therefore for the continuation of consciousness after death. At the present moment, there is no adequate neuro-scientific explanation of NDEs. Even if one is forthcoming, there is no guarantee that explaining the physiological basis of the experience in the brain will explain the meaning and significance of the NDE.

However, there is an obvious problem with all ideas about non-physical minds, or souls: these are unobservable metaphysical entities, and so will be rejected by those who reject metaphysics and religion.

5 The possibility of psychological continuity after death

According to **Parfit's Bundle theory** there is only psychological connectedness after death.

The possibility of a person's continued existence after death can be described only in limited ways: (a) persons do not live after death, because their bodies and brains die, so their memories and personalities die also; (b) all there can be is 'psychological connectedness', such as with their children and close friends, for example. Aside from that, there is no deeper level of self that remains the 'same person'.

Parfit's reductionist account gets into difficulties when he denies that there is a 'subject of experiences'. In order to maintain this view, he has to explain what any particular thought refers to if it does not refer to a self who thinks it. His answer, that a particular thought may be *self-referring*, seems to beg the question. How can a thought refer to itself?

A more likely answer might be that thoughts require selves as thinkers: it is the self that holds together all the physical and psychological events in a person's life into a connected narrative.

For **Daniel Dennett**, your experiences/memories/personality are the organisation of information:

109

the 'program that runs on your brain's computer'. Immortality is in principle possible through the means of storing that information on another platform.

What can survive, then, is the 'persistence of the narrative' that is you. This is not your body or your brain, or some metaphysical higher 'self': it is the narrative of your experience, memory and personality. Depending on the platform used, the stored information of your life could presumably be psychologically continuous with what went before, but would not be the 'same person'.

Dennett's ideas do away with some of the difficulties of 'soul talk', but John Searle in particular shows that it is very difficult to get rid of the subjectivity of consciousness, which is what Dennett (and Parfit) want to do. Qualia are first-person subjective experiences – what it is like to feel pain because somebody has poked a needle in my leg: the pain is felt by me as a self-aware/conscious being, and no amount of scientific analysis of my brain can describe that pain.

Objective immortality: the view of Dual-aspect Monism combined with Process Theology and Panpsychism

Dual-aspect Monism holds that the fundamental reality is a single (unknown) substance with both mental and physical aspects. This matches the panpsychist view that there is no 'cut-off' point for consciousness: *all* entities have some degree of mentality/some degree of consciousness. Process thought holds that all entities are part of God, who is the ultimate psycho-physical reality.

At death, therefore, perhaps no entity goes out of existence: it remains as part of the total experience of God/the universe. Persons would, therefore, have *objective* immortality, since all experience remains within God.

Some Process theologians hold that God has the power to give persons *subjective* immortality, i.e. immortality where the thinking subject is the same conscious 'I' as the one who died.

This might appear speculative, since our understanding of the fundamental nature of mind and matter is still very limited. Nevertheless, it offers a potential model whereby continued personal life after death is a rational possibility.

Finally, remember that these are all hypotheses, not facts. You need to be *aware* of the possibilities, but do not treat them as facts.

Introduction to meta-ethics: the meaning of right and wrong

4

> **You will need to consider the following items for this section**
>
> **1** Divine Command Theory – right is what God commands, wrong is what God forbids.
>
> **2** Naturalism: Utilitarianism – right is what causes pleasure, wrong is what causes pain.
>
> **3** Non-naturalism: Intuitionism – moral values are self-evident.
>
> **4** The strengths and weaknesses of these ideas.
>
> Note that this constitutes only an introduction to meta-ethics. It is not meant to be a detailed exploration of ethics as a whole or even meta-ethics as a whole. Ethics is a vast area for discussion, and the number of different ethical positions people take is equally vast. There are some who even take a nihilistic view, and think that there are absolutely no moral facts or values at all.
>
> The 'strengths and weaknesses' of items 1–3 are considered within each section, and not as a separate section.

Introduction – why 'meta'?

Basically, there are four kinds of ethics you can do: **descriptive ethics**, **normative ethics**, **applied ethics** and **meta-ethics**.

Descriptive Ethics	Normative Ethics	Applied Ethics	Meta-ethics
Describes and compares the ethical norms in different societies.	What things are good/bad?	Applying normative principles and arguments to particular areas, for example: Medical Ethics Business Ethics Legal Ethics	What is the meaning of ethical language?
For example: What do Italians think about crime and punishment? What did the British think about slavery in the seventeenth century?	What moral behaviour is right/ wrong?		What is the meaning of the terms: 'good', 'bad', 'right', 'wrong'?
	How ought we to behave? For example, should we hang murderers?	Dealing with difficult moral questions and issues, for example: abortion euthanasia capital punishment	Are our ethical values facts or intuitions (for example)?
	Normative theories recommend how we should behave, for example: Divine Command Theory Utilitarianism Situation Ethics Kantian Ethics		
		So applied ethics is really a branch of normative ethics: recommending how we should behave	
	Questions about what we should do/ normative ethics are called first-order questions		Meta-ethical questions about the nature and purpose of morality are called second-order questions

From this table, you can see that:

Descriptive ethics describes how people behave. It is a useful way of looking at how patterns of behaviour change over time and between different cultures. What is permitted by one society may be forbidden by another, and a properly objective and detached description of social behaviour in that society does not imply that it is either right or wrong – it simply presents the facts. For example, it is a fact that at different times in history, various societies have practised cannibalism. Of course, it is always possible to use descriptive ethics to side-step moral argument entirely and simply behave in ways that are expected of you; if challenged, you can simply say, 'That's what everybody else does.'

Normative ethics, by contrast, investigates the questions that arise when considering how we ought to behave. There are various ethical theories that can help us to decide whether we consider any particular action to be right – for example, by looking at the expected results, or thinking about questions of duty, or whether the action is natural, or whether it is commanded or forbidden by God. We shall see in a moment that one of the key questions for ethics is how facts and judgements of right and wrong should be related. So, for example, to say that 'most people, if in desperate need and starving, are prepared to steal food for themselves and their families' is simply a statement of fact. It is descriptive and does not address the question of whether, in those circumstances, it would be right or wrong to steal (which would be a 'normative' question).

Applied ethics is the process of applying normative principles and arguments to particular situations. One example of this is professional ethics: the medical, nursing and legal professions draw up codes of conduct for those who practise them. Applied ethics is also a useful way of checking whether our 'normative' values and the arguments that support them produce sensible answers to practical moral questions. Thus, for example, a discussion of euthanasia will generally have a 'descriptive' input in terms of which nations have legalised euthanasia, using what procedures and safeguards, and how many people, given the option, choose to be able to decide when they judge it to be the right time to die. That discussion may also involve taking into consideration legal and professional rules – such as the 'Hippocratic Oath', taken by doctors, promising that they will always seek to benefit their patients and not cause harm. All such things inform the debate about euthanasia, but in themselves they do not start to address the question about whether euthanasia is right or wrong. To do that, we are likely to turn to various normative ethical theories (Kantian ethics, Utilitarianism, Natural Law ethics and so on) in order to establish principles by which an action can be judged right or wrong.

But there is another vital element in any moral discussion, because we can always stop and ask 'What do you mean?' or 'How do you know?' when someone pronounces that an action is good or bad, right or wrong … that of meta-ethics.

Meta-ethics is the branch of ethics that examines what moral language is about and how it can be justified. 'Meta' in Greek means something like 'beyond', so meta-ethics goes beyond our normative theories to ask the most general questions about: whether we can be certain about moral questions, what we mean by saying that something is good or bad, right or wrong; or whether all such discussion is meaningless. Is moral language just a way of expressing our own preferences or emotions? What is a moral 'value', and what is its relation to fact? Are we creating our own rules, or discovering rules that are somehow embedded in the world? And do we know what is right by a process of reasoning, or is it simply a matter of intuition?

Key terms

Descriptive ethics Describes and compares the ethical norms in different societies.

Normative ethics First-order ethical questions about how we should behave; what ethical norms we should follow.

Applied ethics Applying normative principles and arguments to particular areas, for example, medical ethics, animal ethics, business ethics, legal ethics; also to difficult specific questions about euthanasia, capital punishment, the conduct of a war, etc.

Meta-ethics The consideration of second-order questions about the nature and purpose of morality, such as: what is the meaning of 'good', 'bad', 'right' or 'wrong'?

First-order questions Questions raised by normative ethics – about how we should behave/what we should do – are called first-order ethical questions.

Second-order questions Meta-ethical questions about the nature and purpose of morality are called second-order ethical questions. In ethics, second-order questions are questions about first-order questions and the answers given to those questions.

So meta-ethical questions are of two sorts:

- Questions about what moral language **means**.
- Questions about how moral statements may be **justified**.

And, of course, you cannot really tackle one of these without considering the other: it is by trying to justify my moral claims that I discover what it is I am really doing when I use moral language, and it is by considering the meaning of my moral language that I start to understand the basis upon which I can justify its claims. Meta-ethics is therefore what we may call a second-order language. Whereas an ethical statement concerns what is right or wrong, a meta-ethical statement is about what it means to claim that something is right or wrong. Similarly, the questions we ask as part of meta-ethics are known as second-order questions.

Unless you have some idea of what it means to say that something is 'good' or 'right', how can you sort out any moral argument? Of course, you may not be able to define what you mean by 'good', or you may argue that, even if we know what it is, we cannot explain it in any other terms; in other words, is it just… well… 'good'? We shall examine this question later, particularly in the work of the philosopher G.E. Moore. But the starting point for most considerations of meta-ethics is to sort out the relationship between facts and normative judgements.

There are, broadly, three different approaches to defining what we mean by 'good' and how we judge the validity of ethical statements. They are:

- ethical naturalism
- ethical non-naturalism
- ethical non-cognitivism.

We shall clarify these approaches later, but for now, ethical naturalism and non-naturalism hold that moral claims are about facts. These are therefore both *cognitive* theories – they explain moral language in terms of what moral facts we can know. By contrast ethical non-cognitivism holds that we cannot know these things at all – and it therefore tries to find an alternative basis for moral claims. In other words, it suggests that moral claims appear to be about one thing, but in reality they are quite different: they seem to describe the world, but are actually expressions of our own wishes, intentions or prescriptions.

We begin with Divine Command Theory, for the simple reason that in Religious Studies there is an obvious concern to understand the relationship between human morality and God.

Divine Command Theory

Introduction: The difference between secular and religious ethics

1 **Divine Command Theory** is obviously a **religious theory of ethics**, because it suggests that moral commands come from God. An alternative view is that ethics is a secular affair. **Secular ethics** simply means non-religious ethics. Secular ethics is based on a moral intuition, or on a general view of the values by which people should live, and it is justified in terms of the application of those values to moral dilemmas, reasoned out in various different ways, for example: following Utilitarianism, Virtue Ethics and other theories. Secular moral arguments aim to appeal to everyone, on the basis of shared experience and reason.

2 In many cases, moral conclusions are shared by secular and religious people, partly because everyone, religious or not, shares a common experience and reason, and partly because many secular values are in line with those of one or more of the world religions. For example, thinking that it is wrong to steal or murder is common to both religious and secular thinkers. So the distinction between secular and religious ethics is not seen in the *result* of moral reasoning, nor in the *values* that underlie that reasoning.

3 The point at which religious ethics parts company with the secular variety concerns religious sources of authority which the secular ethics cannot share; for example:

● The belief that there is a God or gods whose wish it is that people should behave in certain ways. Examples of this include Jesus' response to the woman taken in the act of adultery (read this in John 7:53–8:11), or his teachings on the value of Sabbath laws (read, for example: Mark 2:23–3:6)

● Particular moral commands found in religious scriptures. In other words, the record of situations in which the implications of obedience to God's will have been set out, or in which it is believed that God set down particular rules. An obvious example is that of Moses coming down the mountain, having been instructed by God to write the law on tablets of stone.

Obedience to the will of God is therefore a key feature in deciding right or wrong for a religious believer.

4 Belief in God, or scriptural authority, may in themselves be sufficient warrant for a moral choice in the eyes of a believer, and all ethical discussion will therefore be restricted to a consideration of how God's moral law should be applied in a particular situation.

Divine Command Theory

1 At its simplest, the 'Divine Command' theory of ethics argues that whatever God commands must be good, because God is the source of all goodness, and what he forbids must be evil.

2 This is not always unambiguous, however, because it leaves open the question (even given belief in the existence of God) of how we know exactly what it is that God commands or forbids. Throughout history, different religions, and different denominations within a religion, have taken different views about what 'God' or 'Ultimate Reality' requires in terms of morality. So, for example, many Buddhists and Hindus would argue against eating meat, on the grounds that it causes unnecessary animal suffering and is therefore against the fundamental principle of *ahimsa* (non-violence), whereas other religions approve of meat eating and may have specific laws about how animals are to be treated and slaughtered for that purpose (for example, *kosher* and *halal* rules). So we should not assume that, in every situation, there is going to be a

definitive religious rule, applicable to everyone, commanded directly by God. Nevertheless, the fundamental principle of the 'Divine Command' theory of ethics is that people should act in a way that reflects the will of God for them, as they best understand it.

3 We shall be dealing specifically with **Christian Divine Command Theory**.

In Protestant Christianity, for example, Divine Command Theory has a basically straightforward rationale:

- God is the Creator of everything.
- There must therefore be an organic link between Creator and created, and this is reflected in the statement in Genesis 1:26–27, that humans are created in God's image. Most theologians take this to mean that humans are like God in having a rational and a moral character.
- It follows, therefore, that human moral behaviour should literally follow God's commands.
- For Protestants who live by the doctrine of *Sola Scriptura* ('by scripture alone' – See Volume 1, Chapter 6, Sources of wisdom and authority: the Bible, pages 228–236), God's commands are seen specifically in scripture.
- In summary, then, Divine Command Theory is based on both God's moral *character* and God's moral *commands*, and these commands are understood as statements of God's will.
- The heart of these commands includes the Ten Commandments in the Old Testament (Exodus 20) and the ethical teachings of Jesus in the New Testament, particularly those found in the 'Sermon on the Mount' (Matthew 5–7).

4 The **Divine Command Theory** has a long and influential history in Christian theology, for example in Calvin and Barth.

John Calvin

In *The Institutes of the Christian Religion*, John Calvin uses Divine Command Theory to justify his view of predestination:

> The will of God is the supreme rule of righteousness, so that everything which he wills must be held to be righteous by the mere fact of his willing it. Therefore, when it is asked why the Lord did so, we must answer, because he pleased. But if you proceed farther to ask why he pleased, you ask for something greater and more sublime than the will of God, and nothing such can be found. [Note 1]

The key theological argument here is that God cannot be 'caused' to do anything, for that would imply that there is a force external to God, whereas God is believed to be omnipotent. Also, to challenge or question God's will is to ask for something Greater (an impossibility that reminds us of Anselm's Ontological Argument for God's existence). Thus for Calvin, the Divine Command Theory is a natural result of the absolute power and sovereignty of God.

Karl Barth

Moving into the twentieth century, a similar argument was presented by Karl Barth in his *Church Dogmatics*:

> How can God be understood as the Lord if that does not involve the problem of human obedience? ...The doctrine of God must be expressly defined and developed and interpreted as that which it also is at every point, that is to say *ethics* ... It makes God's command for [a man] the judgment of what he has done and the order for his future action. [Note 2]

Barth uses this to argue that, although he is not surprised that people have always tried to understand the general ethical problem and to define what is good, this is not his concern in terms of Christian doctrine – for man's obedience to God is the answer to all questions about ethics.

In other words, the commands of God set Christian ethics totally apart from general discussions about what is good or right, and totally over-ride fallible human debate on moral issues. Christians should listen to and seek to understand secular ethical principles, but the Christian approach should be critical and:

> ... decidedly not one of compromise ... For the question of good and evil has been decided and settled once and for all in the decree of God, by the cross and the resurrection of Jesus Christ. Now that this decision has been made, theological ethics cannot go back on it. [Note 3]

These two examples (Calvin and Barth) come from the Protestant branch of Christianity, but the Catholic Church has a similar argument, although it is not generally presented as a 'divine command' theory, based on authority. As we said above, although recognising the fallibility of individual Christians, Catholics believe that Christ gave to the leaders of his Church – and particularly to the Pope, the Bishop of Rome – the authority to make pronouncements on matters of doctrine and ethics. This does not make the Pope infallible in ordinary matters (he remains a fallible human being), but special pronouncements, made on the basis of his authority as Pope, are infallible. In other words, for Catholics, they represent the will of Christ, and should not be challenged on the basis of human reason or evidence.

Details of the doctrine of papal infallibility need not concern us here. What is crucial is to see that any such structure of religious authority means that, in present-day situations, a pronouncement relevant to moral issues can be given an authority that claims to come directly from God.

Strengths and weaknesses of (Christian) Divine Command Theory

Strengths

1 For religious people, Divine Command Theory grounds their moral behaviour in the teachings of a factually-existing God. Most believers see God as all-knowing and all-loving, so they have the advantage of

believing that God's commands must be right, and that they must be the best way of promoting love in human relationships.

2 The rules are universal, and are right for all times and places. This avoids the problem of trying to sort out different moral ideas in different countries at different times.

3 The system is clear and straightforward. What God says is 'good'/'bad', 'right'/'wrong' must be 'good'/'bad', 'right'/'wrong'.

4 Most Christians link God's moral commands with the promise of life after death for those who keep them (as well as with the threat of punishment for those who do not), so there is an end-goal to morality.

5 God does not have any of the weaknesses of human judges. He is omniscient and omnipresent, and so is totally aware of people's good and bad deeds. In other words, God is a totally fair judge.

Weaknesses

1 Even if the moral commands in the Bible come from God (and not from humans), we cannot tell whether they are as God gave them. We have no 'original' version of any Old Testament book, so the texts we use today are in many cases attempts to reconstruct what might have been the original meaning. The New Testament exists only in Greek, whereas Jesus spoke Aramaic to the crowds, so we do not know what might have been lost or changed in translation.

2 **The Bible contains what most people would consider to be immoral commands**. For example:

Slavery. In the Letter of Paul to Titus, part of the moral advice given is to slaves, who must be 'submissive to their masters and … give satisfaction in every respect … to show entire and true fidelity …' (2:9–10), which appears to condone slavery by requiring slaves to put up with their situation.

Homosexual behaviour. For many, the Bible's approach to homosexuality is self-evidently immoral. Leviticus 20:13 says that: 'If a man lies with a male as with a woman, both of them have committed an abomination; they shall be put to death, their blood is upon them.'

If some commands are seen as immoral, then Divine Command Theory offers no real solution to the normative ethical question of which moral commands should be followed.

3 **The problem of autonomy**. Many, perhaps the majority, think that to be morally good, a choice has to be made freely. Divine Command Theory does not really offer a free choice, because the promise of heaven and the threat of hell mean that people will choose to follow God's commands out of self-interest. Morality should be based on reason, not on religious belief.

4 **The Euthyphro Dilemma**

For many, the biggest objection to Divine Command Theory is a logical problem, generally known as the Euthyphro Dilemma, so called because it is found in Plato's dialogue *Euthyphro*. It may be expressed in a single question:

'Is conduct right because the gods command it, or do the gods command it because it is right?'

If you accept the first option, then God loses moral goodness:
The implication of the first option is that whatever God commands must be good by definition, and you are not in a position to challenge it from your own experience or by your own reason. But that leads to the specific problem of God making immoral commands. In addition to the two examples given in (2) above, in the Old Testament there are stories in which God commands the slaughter of innocent children (as part of a policy of destroying the local inhabitants as the Children of Israel enter their Promised Land) [Note 4] – commands that appear to sanction both genocide and ethnic cleansing. But these things go against the most fundamental values expressed in secular ethics. They also go against other biblical images of God and of his requirements for justice, fairness, love of the stranger and outcast and so on. Are we then justified in calling any recorded command from God 'right' just because it appears in scripture? And, if so, do we assume that such a command applies to all people at all times, or might it be in response to a particular situation, very different from our own? How do we resolve apparent contradictions between divine commands? So – taking the first option is not without its problems.

If you accept the second option, then God loses omnipotence:
The implication of the second option is that God commands an action because it is good in itself; but this also leads to problems, because we can then ask, 'How does God know that it is good in itself?' The answer can only be that God recognises that there is a moral law external to himself, and that he has to obey it. In that case God is subject to the moral law, and loses his omnipotence.

These difficulties seem to show that Divine Command Theory must be wrong, because taking either option means that morality no longer relies on God.

Several solutions have been offered to the Euthyphro Dilemma, for example:

- William of Ockham (1287–1347) suggested a 'bite the bullet' approach by adopting the first option. God is God – omnipotent and omniscient, so even if God commands murder or genocide, those commands must be obeyed. Needless to say, that is not a popular solution to the dilemma.
- Another option is to suggest that God's nature and God's character are the same: God and goodness are identical, so God's moral commands must be good. This sounds reasonable, but it still gives no answers to why God commands genocide and murder in the Bible.
- The problem of God's immoral commands in the Bible is sometimes 'solved' by suggesting that the text of those bits of the Bible is corrupt, and does not mean what it says; but this gets us nowhere, because if some parts of the text are corrupt, then other parts can be corrupt, and if scripture is corrupt then we have no hope of knowing what God's commands might be.

Suffice it to say that there is no solution to the Euthyphro Dilemma that is universally accepted. As a meta-ethical theory, then, Divine Command ethics is not without its philosophical and practical problems. Where the supposed commands of God conflict with autonomous human ethics, or with our intuitions about right and wrong, it raises the 'problem of evil'. In other words, we are left with a key issue: If God's commands are in line with human ethical thinking and intuitions, they appear unnecessary; but if they contradict them, we have the problem of trying to reconcile them with the belief that God is benevolent.

Now that you understand Divine Command Theory, we move on to look at ethical naturalism and ethical non-naturalism, and you will see that Divine Command Theory is a non-naturalist theory, because it holds that the source of 'good' is not in nature at all, but is in a supernatural being (a being who is literally 'above nature') – God.

Naturalism: Utilitarianism – right is what causes pleasure, wrong is what causes pain

At this point, before we get to ethical naturalism and non-naturalism, it will be useful to consider an overview of the various meta-ethical positions. Consider the diagram below:

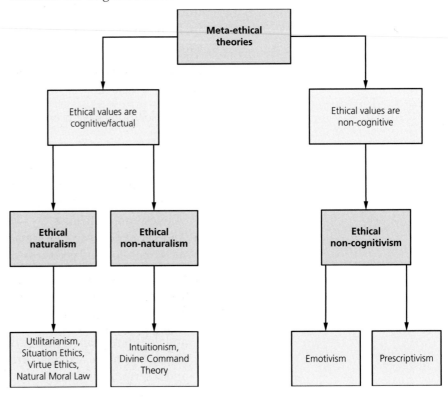

▲ Meta-ethical theories

From this diagram, you can easily see, following the arrows, that Utilitarianism is an example of a cognitivist and naturalist theory of ethics. It holds that ethical values are factual – they are about the facts of pain and pleasure. Other naturalist theories include: Situation Ethics, Virtue Ethics and Aquinas' Natural Moral Law. For Situation Ethics, the moral 'facts' are about *agape*-love; for Virtue Ethics they are about *eudaimonia*. Aquinas' Natural Moral Law is a form of ethical naturalism in that it assumes that satisfaction and fulfilment come by following one's true essence; so the right thing to do relates to what reason judges to be the natural or essential feature of an action.

You can then see that Intuitionism is also a cognitivist theory of ethics. It holds that ethical values are factual, although its facts are non-natural: in this case they are intuited.

Finally, although we have not yet covered non-cognitivism you know what non-cognitivism is from your study of religious language. Emotivism is a non-cognitivist theory of ethics, holding that morality is not about objective facts at all, but is about subjective emotions. *We shall refer to non-cognitivist ethical theories only briefly, in the context of looking at the strengths and weaknesses of naturalism and non-naturalism.*

Divine Command Theory is a non-naturalist meta-ethical theory. For the moment, hold this on one side. After we have looked at ethical naturalism and ethical non-naturalism, this should become clear.

As we go through these ideas, keep a finger in the previous page to see where each piece of the moral picture fits into the diagram.

Naturalism

1 'Naturalism' is the term we use for the view that moral values can be described in terms of natural properties (such as love or happiness). In other words, moral values are an objective part of the furniture of the universe. They exist and can be described, and it is therefore possible for us to discover and understand them.

2 So, if you think back to the discussion (in Chapter 2 Miracles) about realism and anti-realism, naturalist ethical theories are realist.

3 In essence, **naturalism is grounded in the facts of nature, or in the facts of human nature**. You can see straight away that Divine Command Theory is not a naturalist theory, because far from being grounded in the facts of nature, or human nature, morality is grounded in the commands of a transcendent God.

4 If you can look at the world and at people's behaviour, and can deduce right and wrong from them (in any way, be it social, psychological or evolutionary), then you are an ethical naturalist. So, for example, there are any number of natural facts about the world and human life, and different groups of people will discern 'the good' in a particular set of facts:

● A utilitarian will see 'the good' in the facts about pleasure and pain, happiness and misery; from which utilitarians form the normative theory that we ought to do that which brings the greatest happiness for the greatest number.
● You have looked at Aristotle's Virtue Ethics in Chapter 4.3 of Volume 1 of the textbook, so you will know that a virtue ethicist will see 'the good' in the facts about *eudaimonia* (complete well-being). Modern Virtue Ethics might see 'the good' in the facts about the environment as a whole (including plants and animals, together with the whole biological ecosystems on which all living beings are dependent).

- Naturalist theories often talk of intrinsic good, meaning the value that something has 'in itself', and holding that this good (such as *eudaimonia*) is self-evident.
- Naturalist theories do have common denominators. For example, Natural Moral Law and Virtue Ethics both emphasise the value of particular virtues, since these lead to *eudaimonia*. Situation Ethics is often seen as a religious version of Utilitarianism.

5 What people do in order to follow a naturalist ethical system is often expressed in a rule: Do the most loving thing in the situation/Do that which gives the greatest happiness for the greatest number. Those who comply with such rules and display the appropriate character traits in their behaviour (distributing love/bringing about happiness, etc.) are then described as being morally good.

6 Meta-ethically, an ethical naturalist will argue that it is vitally important to hold that there are ethical facts about the world, because otherwise we have no real justification for our actions. On this approach, a naturalist perspective is crucial for the survival and well-being of life on this planet.

Using these ideas, we can now look at a specific theory of **ethical naturalism**.

Key term

Ethical naturalism The meta-ethical view that morality is defined by facts about nature or human nature.

Utilitarianism

We shall be dealing with Bentham's approach to Utilitarianism in some detail in Chapter 7. The point here is to look at Utilitarianism as a naturalist meta-ethical theory. Here are some of the main points:

Jeremy Bentham (1748–1832)

Bentham's argument starts with what he sees as a basic feature of human life, and one that determines the way we regard right and wrong:

> Nature has placed mankind under the governance of two sovereign masters, *pain* and *pleasure*. It is for them alone to point out what we ought to do, as well as to determine what we shall do. On the one hand the standard of right and wrong, on the other the chain of causes and effects, are fastened to their throne. They govern us in all we do, in all we say, in all we think. [Note 5]

- Notice how rich this statement is meta-ethically. First of all, he identifies pain and pleasure as not only determining what in fact motivates and directs our lives, but also what ought to do so. In other words he argues that a natural feature of life determines both descriptive and normative ethics. In effect, he identifies here the origins of both a science of human behaviour, and an ethical theory.
- Pain and pleasure rule us – we observe their relationship with action as a matter of cause and effect, but we also recognise that they lie behind all claims about what we 'ought' to do. Morality is therefore linked to observation and experience – the very essence of ethical naturalism.
- For Bentham, **pleasure (or happiness) is the one intrinsic good**: it is the one thing that is good in itself, and not for some other valuable thing that it produces. Likewise, pain/unhappiness is the one intrinsic evil.

- The next logical step is to use the observable facts of pain and pleasure to determine **moral obligation** – we (and, we hope, others) seek to maximise pleasure and minimise pain. And if we ask why we should do so, Bentham would simply point to the reality of pain and pleasure in our lives. If we observe that pain and pleasure rule humankind, and that we ourselves seek to achieve pleasure and avoid pain, it is a straightforward step to see the relative promotion of pleasure and avoidance of pain as determining moral obligation. In any situation of moral choice, we are to act in such a way as to **seek the greatest happiness for the greatest number of people** – a formula (and a rule) that was originally coined in order to assess the value of different political systems, but here taken over by Bentham as a basis for ethics generally.

- And because happiness is based on our observation of it as a natural phenomenon, we are able to calculate it objectively in terms of its: intensity, duration, certainty, proximity, productiveness, purity and extent. We all know and immediately understand that a pleasure that is here and now seems to motivate us more strongly than one that is no more than a future possibility. Pleasure and pain are not just encountered in extreme situations, but pervade our lives, so that at any time they are balanced in various ways, each offering something to which we are attracted, or warning of something to be avoided. And for Bentham it does not matter whether the pleasure comes from a simple game such as push-penny or from some sophisticated cultural creation such as opera – it is all just measurable as pleasure, and the pleasure of each individual is to count equally.

- Utilitarianism is a particular example of a consequentialist approach to ethics. To remind you, in any such theory, the moral value of an action is determined by the anticipated results that it seeks to achieve. If I am concerned to know whether or not I should do some particular action, I predict the result of doing it, or of not doing it, and then compare the two results – choosing the one that is likely to maximise pleasure and minimise pain. Nevertheless moral rules are also found in Utilitarianism, and this element was introduced mainly by John Stuart Mill.

John Stuart Mill

John Stuart Mill (1806–73)
The importance of moral rules

Mill was a philosopher and political economist. He was the godson of Jeremy Bentham, and became the godfather of Bertrand Russell. His father, the Scottish philosopher, economist and 'Benthamite' James Mill, wanted to develop his intellect early, so as to produce a child who would carry on the utilitarian cause, so he was kept apart from children of his own age other than his own siblings, and 'crammed' with Greek from the age of three and Latin from the age of eight. He was a supporter of capital punishment for its deterrent effect. When capital punishment was abolished, he put it down to the effeminate mind of the country. Mill is sometimes called a 'Rule Utilitarian' because he suggested that moral rules should be followed except where they conflict, at which point people should follow the 'primary principle' of Utility, which is to do that which gives the best results in the situation.

- Mill's brand of Utilitarianism differed from that of Bentham in a number of respects: for example, he rejected Bentham's view that all pleasures are equal and measurable and insisted that there are 'higher' cultural and intellectual pleasures, and that these are to be preferred to 'lower' physical ones. This led to his well-known claim that it is better to be Socrates dissatisfied than a fool satisfied, even though the fool may not be able to appreciate that fact.

- Nevertheless, we can see that **Mill was an ethical naturalist**, because he described happiness (and therefore the good) in terms of the quality of life rather than the quantity of pleasure, and – for him – that quality is based on a view about the relative importance of different human attributes: physical, social, cultural and intellectual. For him, Utilitarianism is all about a fair and just distribution of those natural benefits. Whether the 'fool' is able to understand the primitive nature of his pleasures is quite irrelevant to that assessment.

- As well as arguing for a distinction between higher and lower pleasures, Mill also argued that, rather than considering only the anticipated results of particular actions, it was important to take into account the positive benefits offered by **general moral rules or principles**. He argued that many moral rules have developed naturally because it was found that not stealing, lying or murdering had beneficial effects on society. In other words, such principles were justified because they produce a balance of pleasure over pain/happiness over unhappiness.

Take the example of telling a lie. If everyone decided whether or not to tell the truth in each individual situation as it arose, the result could be general chaos, since the principle of truth-telling is important for general trust in society. Thus it could be argued that, in most cases, telling the truth is the **right** thing to do, because it supports a principle that offers the greatest happiness to the greatest number.

Notice, however, that Act Utilitarianism (Bentham's version of the theory) and Rule Utilitarianism are not necessarily opposed to one another. In most situations, all would agree that supporting a generally beneficial rule (like telling the truth) maximises benefit, but few would argue that one should follow that rule even when the immediate consequences are harmful. What Mill was offering was not an alternative, but a balance.

There are of course other forms of Utilitarianism, but the views of Bentham and Mill should give you a good understanding of ethical naturalism.

The strengths and weaknesses of ethical naturalism

Strengths

1 One obvious strength of ethical naturalism is that ethical propositions are true because they are **factual**. They 'reduce to' non-ethical properties about the world, such as happiness, love and well-being, and these facts are grounded in nature or in human nature.

2 Further, right and wrong are **objective** – they exist in the world outside ourselves. If there is an objective moral reality, then we can know if we are doing right or wrong.

3 Ethical propositions can give us solid **guidelines and rules** to follow, as with Rule Utilitarianism, for example.

4 We can be **judged** by our compliance with the rules. If we break the rules, then this gives us the justification for punishing offenders.

5 Most people tend to follow (knowingly or otherwise) one naturalist theory or another. It is often said, for example, that many principles of law and politics in the UK are broadly utilitarian in character.

Weaknesses

1 The claim that ethical propositions are factual does not impress **ethical non-cognitivists**, who argue that moral propositions are not factual. Briefly, we can see the non-cognitivist approach from Ayer. You will remember that Ayer argued that statements that cannot be verified or falsified are meaningless. If we take a naturalist claim such as 'Murder is wrong', this claim (according to Ayer) cannot be verified or falsified, since those who disapprove of murder will accept the claim, whereas those who do not mind murdering others (a sizeable proportion of the human race) will reject it, and there is no way that this dispute can be solved by appealing to facts or evidence. There are different forms of ethical non-cognitivism. Ayer's approach is called **Emotivism**, and for him, moral statements reduce to statements of approval or disapproval.

For emotivists and others, morality is subjective, not objective: morality is an internal feeling and not something that is objective and in the world. Rules and guidelines are largely a matter of convention, as is the issue of punishment for non-compliance. If enough people agree, they will make and enforce a rule forbidding murder.

2 **The 'naturalistic fallacy'**

The naturalistic fallacy, as defined by the philosopher G.E. Moore, is that it is a mistake to try and define the concept 'good' in terms of some natural property, such as 'pleasant', or 'desirable'.

If Moore is right, you can see straight away that there is a problem with Utilitarianism, where 'pleasure' is at the heart of Bentham's theory, which says that 'pleasure is good', so 'we ought to seek pleasure'.

Moore argued that it is not possible to derive an 'ought' from an 'is' – we cannot go from: 'Pleasure *is* good' to: 'We *ought* to seek pleasure'.

Another way of saying this is that **we cannot derive moral values from facts**. For example:
i   She **is** old and lonely (fact).
ii You **ought** to help her (moral value).
Deriving 2 from 1 is logically invalid. Something is missing in the reasoning between 1 and 2. For example, someone else could validly argue:
i   She **is** old and lonely (fact).
ii You **ought** to euthanise her (moral value).
If ethical naturalism is right, and ethical values are facts, then we should not be able to get two different values ('help her'/'euthanise her') from the same fact ('she is old and lonely'). Naturalism therefore (according to Moore) fails. We shall see later that there are good grounds for thinking that Moore might be wrong here, but at the time a lot of philosophers thought that he was right, so we shall continue with Moore's ideas.

3 **Moore argued instead that good is undefinable**, and in an attempt to show this, he used an '**Open Question**' **argument**. [Note 6]

- For example, a utilitarian will seek to maximise pleasure over pain, so that any action which gives a balance of pleasure over pain is defined as 'good'. So if you ask a utilitarian, 'This action maximises utility, but is it good?', then that would be a closed question, and she would have to answer, 'Yes', because 'maximising utility' is how she defines the good. The question is 'closed' because no other answer is possible for her. But, according to Moore, whenever we do ask questions like this, they prove to be 'open' questions, because we can *always* stand back and ask: 'But is it good to bring about more pleasure than pain?' There is nothing unintelligible about this question to the person who asks it, so there must be something wrong with Utilitarianism.
- Equally there must be something wrong with all other naturalist definitions of the good – they are all open to the same objection.

Strengths and weaknesses of Utilitarianism

The strengths and weaknesses of Utilitarianism are broadly the same as for ethical naturalism as a whole:

Strengths

1 It gives a factual basis for morality.

2 Utilitarians have guidelines and rules, for example Bentham's Pleasure Calculus, where pleasure is measured by its intensity, duration, certainty, proximity, productiveness, purity and extent. We look at this later in Chapter 7 when we look at Bentham and Kant.

3 It gives us a way of measuring the moral worth of people – whether or not they seek to maximise happiness and minimise pain.

4 Utilitarianism is a practical system, and UK politics is broadly utilitarian in character.

5 If you ask people what they want, most will say that they want happiness.

Weaknesses

1 'Happiness' varies between people, so is impossible to define. Some people derive pleasure from inflicting pain, which can hardly be called 'good' for the majority.

2 It requires us (like all consequentialist theories) to second-guess the future, but the fact is that we can never be sure of the consequences of our actions, so any decision we make may turn out to maximise pain rather than pleasure.

3 The principle of 'the greatest good for the greatest number' is assumed to be right, but it is often minorities who are right. Moreover, the principle in effect ignores the rights of the minority, and for many people there is something wrong with any ethical theory which does this.

4 Moore's objections to ethical naturalism seem to show that there is something wrong with all naturalist ethical theories, namely that they commit the **naturalistic fallacy**. However, as we shall see, there is a debate about this.

Since this objection brings us to non-naturalism, we turn now to his theory.

> **Key term**
>
> **Naturalistic fallacy** G.E. Moore's argument that it is a fallacy when people reason from facts to moral claims.

Non-naturalism: Intuitionism – moral values are self-evident

G.E. Moore (1873–1958)

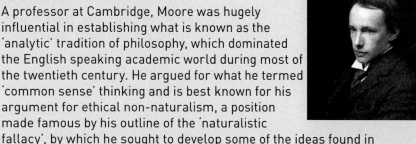

A professor at Cambridge, Moore was hugely influential in establishing what is known as the 'analytic' tradition of philosophy, which dominated the English speaking academic world during most of the twentieth century. He argued for what he termed 'common sense' thinking and is best known for his argument for ethical non-naturalism, a position made famous by his outline of the 'naturalistic fallacy', by which he sought to develop some of the ideas found in Hume, and to challenge ethical naturalism.

1 In *Principia Ethica* ('The Principles of Ethics', 1903 [Note 7], Moore followed Hume in claiming that in many ethical arguments people tended to start with facts and then slip into speaking of moral values, without making clear that they had switched the basis on which they were arguing. As we have seen in our account of the weaknesses of ethical naturalism, he called this the naturalistic fallacy – the failed attempt to derive an 'ought' from an 'is' – the failed attempt to derive values from facts.

2 In order to avoid the 'naturalist fallacy', Moore came to the conclusion that 'good' is a term that cannot be defined or explained in terms of anything more basic; hence he is described as an **ethical non-naturalist**. If you can't agree that moral values are natural properties out there in the universe to be discovered, like Moore, you may take a non-naturalist approach and argue that, although moral values and questions of right and wrong are real, and can be known, they cannot be identified with any natural properties. They are still part of the world as we experience it, but they are based on a moral sense that cannot be described literally.

3 To get the idea of the difference between naturalism and non-naturalism; **in naturalist terms, 'good' is complex and analysable**. Think, for example, of a horse:

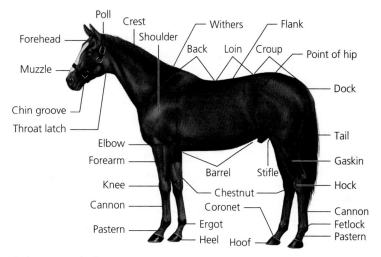

▲ Anatomy of a horse

127

A horse, like any other natural object, is analysable in terms of its parts: forehead, muzzle, elbow, heel, ergot, fetlock, hock, tail, dock, croup, flank, back, withers, crest, and so on. Ethical naturalism says the same about 'good' – it is complex and analysable in terms of natural properties such as pleasures, desires or needs.

Having rejected all this as being the 'naturalistic fallacy', **Moore wants to convince you that 'good' is non-natural, so it is simple and unanalysable**. Unlike 'horse', 'good' cannot be broken down in terms of its natural properties. He believed that 'good' was a quality that things could possess, but it was not one that could be defined – it was something that we naturally recognise, and understand. He illustrated this with reference to the colour 'yellow'.

You can point to objects that are yellow, and say that they are yellow, but that does not fully explain what yellow is. You can compare it with other colours, and explain that it can have different shades, but you cannot define or analyse 'yellow' in terms of any simpler concept. Of course, once we have some yellow things pointed out to us, we quickly develop the ability to see what they have in common and start to use the word 'yellow' to describe them, but we can do that without ever needing to define it. Wittgenstein's example was the smell of a cup of coffee: try defining that smell to somebody else. Similarly, Moore claims that we have a working sense of what goodness it, even if it always goes beyond any definition.

Moore's definition is that 'good' means 'good', and that is all there is to say about it. This is what he says in *Principia Ethica*:

> If I am asked, 'What is good?' my answer is that good is good, and that is the end of the matter. Or if I am asked 'How is good to be defined?' my answer is that it cannot be defined, and that is all I have to say about it. But disappointing as these answers may appear, they are of the very last importance. (I.§6)
>
> My point is that 'good' is a simple notion, just as 'yellow' is a simple notion; that, just as you cannot, by any manner of means, explain to anyone who does not already know it, what yellow is, so you cannot explain what good is. (I.§7) (Referenced from: www.collier.sts.vt.edu/5424/pdfs/moore_chapter1_1903.pdf)

4 **Remember that both naturalism and non-naturalism are cognitivist theories**, suggesting that there are moral facts that we can know. Non-natural facts simply cannot be defined.

5 **Intuitionism** is a non-naturalist theory, as we can now see. Divine Command Theory is another, and we shall come back to this at the end of the chapter.

Intuitionism

1 **Intuitionism argues that our knowledge of right and wrong does not come as a result of evaluating results, nor as the conclusion to a logical argument, but through our fundamental moral intuitions.** It is sometimes used of those thinkers who argue that the good cannot be defined (non-naturalism), such as Moore (although he himself rejected the term), but mostly it is a broad approach that creeps into many philosophical discussions at some point, often unnoticed. The key to knowing if someone

Key terms

Ethical non-naturalism The meta-ethical view that moral knowledge is a factual property known by intuition or by God's commands, for example.

Intuitionism As a form of non-naturalism, Intuitionism is the meta-ethical view that moral knowledge is a factual property known by intuition.

is appealing to intuitions is to watch out for phrases such as, 'It seems reasonable to assume that ...', since that is the point in an argument where an appeal is made to the listener's or reader's moral intuitions.

2   The key thing to appreciate about intuitions is that they are beliefs that are not supported by inference from other beliefs. In other words, they are 'stand-alone' beliefs, so moral judgements are self-evident to those who hold them. Intuitionism is, by the same token, a form of moral realism: moral truths exist independently of persons.

Mostly we believe things, or hold values, for reasons that we can explain – that they conform to natural law, for example, or are likely to maximise happiness. But often, when we have exhausted any such explanations, we come to the view that – quite apart from the validity of any arguments – we just sense that something *is* the case. To torture or kill an innocent person is just wrong; we sense that to be the case, even if we can produce any number of reasons why it might be advantageous to do so (such as to save a large number of other innocent people).

3   **An example: The Trolley Problem** (see the box below).

The Trolley Problem

One of the most widely discussed set of thought experiments is the 'Trolley Problem', which provides a clear example of the balance between a utilitarian and an intuitionist approach to a moral dilemma. [Note 8]

In the basic form of the problem, a runaway railway trolley (to distinguish it from the trolleys you are more used to in supermarkets!) is hurling down the track and heading towards five people, who are on the track and apparently unable to escape being killed. The only way to save them is to throw the points, diverting the wagon onto another track on which there is just one innocent person. Do you move the points and kill that one person, or do you allow the five to die?

Clearly, as presented, there would be a utilitarian case for choosing to kill one innocent person in order to save five. But many people, faced with this thought experiment, simply cannot bring themselves to take an action that will lead to the death of that innocent person.

There are, of course, many elements to unpacking that moral dilemma, which is what makes it so interesting. But at its heart there is also a clash between a utilitarian assessment and a deeply held intuition that killing the innocent is wrong, even in this situation. That intuition may be subsequently justified – with reference to an absolute prohibition of killing, for example – but it remains fundamental, or 'foundational' for the thinking of many people. Whatever the arguments presented, they are likely to find that they simply will not accept that it is right to move the points.

One of the problems for Intuitionism is the extent of moral disagreement. How can Intuitionism be true if there is so much disagreement about what is 'good', 'bad', 'right' or 'wrong'?

One answer to this is the idea that we have a number of duties that are self-evident, such as a duty to parents and a duty to care for the sick. This idea was developed particularly by W.D. Ross, who argues that **Intuitionism is how people choose between conflicting duties.** You cannot be asked questions on Ross, but his ideas will help you to understand Intuitionism.

W.D. Ross (1877–1971)

Ross was a Scottish philosopher. His ethical ideas show that he was a moral realist, an ethical non-naturalist and an intuitionist.

In *The Right and the Good* (1930) and *The Foundations of Ethics* (1939), Ross pointed out that people sometimes have conflicting duties, and that it may not be at all obvious which should take priority.

For example, a doctor sees it as her duty to keep a seriously ill person as pain-free as possible, but equally that it is her duty to avoid killing her patient. There comes a point, as the quantities of pain-killing drugs increase to meet the first duty, when it is likely to hasten death, and therefore conflict with the second duty.

Ross listed several duties that we feel instinctively we must do. We must:

1 keep our promises

2 pay back the harm we do to others

3 not injure others

4 return favours and services given to us by others

5 not harm innocent people

6 look after parents.

These duties he called *prima facie*, meaning 'at first face' or 'on the face of it'. By this he meant that if there are no conflicting circumstances between these duties, then each duty is absolute; however if there is a conflict between two or more duties, as there often is, then I have to balance them and consider what to do.

This is where moral intuition comes in. When I am forced to consider conflicting duties, then if I really do consider them as well as I can, then common sense/intuition will tell me what I ought to do. So: take the well-known problem with Kantian ethics, of the mad axe-murderer who knocks on your door and asks you the whereabouts of his victim. Kant could get no further than suggesting that you tell him an evasive truth, for example that you saw him an hour ago at a particular place (and you know that he will already have gone somewhere else). For Ross, such evasion would be unnecessary: you would simply lie to the maniac, because you have a *prima facie* duty to protect the innocent. The vast majority of people would agree with this, and Ross would argue that this is because **careful thinking about the problem reveals an intuitive truth: the intended victim's life is more important than any problem about lying.**

So, providing we have sufficient mental maturity, Ross argues that our judgements on *prima facie* duties will be intuited truth:

> The moral order expressed in these duties is just as much part of the
> fundamental nature of the universe (and, we may add, of any possible
> universe in which there were moral agents at all) as is the spatial or
> numerical structure expressed in the axioms of geometry or arithmetic.
> In our confidence that these propositions are true there is involved the
> same trust in our reason that is involved in our confidence in mathematics;
> and we should have no justification for trusting it in the latter sphere and
> distrusting it in the former. In both cases we are dealing with propositions
> that cannot be proved, but that just as certainly need no proof. [Note 9]

Discussion point

Is Ross right in arguing
that where there is moral
disagreement, mature reflection
will provide an intuitive answer?
Think out some situations to test
your reasoning.

So, for example, it might be right to break a promise in order to avoid
injuring someone, and to steal rather than to let someone die. Moreover,
what is right for particular moral situations that people encounter is unique
to that situation, and that explains why moral judgements do differ in the
way that they do.

Strengths and weaknesses of Intuitionism as a non-naturalist theory

Strengths

1 Everyone has moral intuitions, and tends to use them to underpin or
check moral arguments, whether they are recognised as such or not. For
example, many have the intuition that killing can sometimes be justified,
for example in war or self-defence, whereas murder cannot.

2 It overcomes one of the central problems of ethical naturalism, namely
the problem that there seems to be no agreement as to what the 'facts'
of ethics are. They differ for each of the normative theories such as
Utilitarianism, Situation Ethics, Natural Law and Virtue Ethics.

3 As a form of non-naturalism, Intuitionism is still a form of moral realism:
statements can still be true or false. It is realistic in admitting that moral
intuition is not perfect, which explains why we still have disagreements
in our moral intuitions. For Ross, where there are such disagreements,
this is because people's thinking about conflicting *prima facie* duties is not
clear or deep enough.

Weaknesses

1 Intuitionism does not give a satisfactory answer to the question of how it is that
we come to have intuitions about right and wrong. Is intuition some faculty
in the brain, or does it amount simply to reasoning? If we cannot observe the
presence of such a faculty, it seems more likely that it does not exist.

2 Intuitionism makes ethical discussion very difficult, since there seems
to be no fundamental, reasoned basis upon which to argue. People may
have different intuitions about what is right, but if they cannot justify
their intuitions in any way, all they can do is continue to state them. If
people have different moral intuitions, how do we choose between them?

3 It is easy to be unconsciously influenced by prevailing social norms.
Had we lived in the eighteenth century, we might have 'intuited' that
slavery is right, because that is what we had been brought up to believe.
In other words, 'intuition' might be nothing more than the unconscious
acceptance of the norms of the society we live in.

Key term

Ethical non-cognitivism The view that morality is non-cognitive, has nothing to do with facts, but reduces instead to 'emotional ejaculations' (Ayer) or to universalisable prescriptions about moral behaviour (Hare).

4 An indirect but major problem with Moore's Intuitionism is that it has led many to turn to **ethical non-cognitivism**, which claims that ethics has nothing to do with facts at all but instead is about wishes/emotions/intentions, for example. We have already mentioned Ayer's Emotivism, a non-cognitive theory, which dismisses ethical statements as mere statements of emotion. In fact for Ayer, ethical 'statements' are not even proper statements, so someone who says that 'murder is wrong' is merely making an 'emotional ejaculation', like crying, laughing or screaming, probably because they are disturbed by the sight of blood. This seems to be a deeply unsatisfactory account of the importance to us of our moral thinking. If 'killing innocent children is wrong' is just the equivalent of 'I am averse to the idea of killing innocent children', then that just begs the question of, 'Should you be averse to the killing of innocent children?' For some, then, ethical non-cognitivism is not an attractive theory of ethics, since if everybody adopted it, it would not be likely to have a beneficial effect on society.

5 In fact, Moore may have been wrong in dismissing ethical naturalism, since some ethicists dismiss his idea of the 'naturalistic fallacy'.

For example, **we can question Moore's 'Open Question' argument**: how does Moore *know* that there will never be a successful definition of 'good'? As Robin Attfield says:

> '… it is clear that Moore was assuming that no successful definition will ever be produced, and was thus actually assuming his own conclusion on the way to reaching it.' [Note 10]

As a matter of fact, there is one quite powerful naturalistic description of 'good' which might be successful: it is called 'neo-naturalism' (meaning 'new naturalism'), and it comes from philosophers such as Philippa Foot (1920–2010), Mary Midgley (b.1919), Geoffrey Warnock (1923–95) and others. Neo-naturalism holds that virtue plays a key role in ethics. According to Foot, dispositions/virtues depend on certain biological and sociological facts about humans (although this approach is not confined to humans: it is an inevitable fact of biology, for example: there are key virtues (as Aquinas might say) to being a good wolf or a good eagle). Scientific facts do not lead away from virtue, but towards it. Biology and sociology can direct us to see what is virtuous, so individuals should strive to recognise, pursue and attain the virtues that lead to human flourishing. In other words, we can see that morality does have a factual *content*, namely the flourishing of human beings. This content is not absolute, but it is objective, being really 'in' the natural world. **Neo-naturalism is therefore objectivist and cognitivist**. Moreover by insisting that morality does have an obvious factual content (the flourishing of humans), there is a criterion by which we can judge whether our values are indeed facts:

> If what we want to do contributes to human flourishing, it is good/right/factual. If it goes against it, it is bad/wrong.

6 **This reasoning also 'fills' the 'is–ought gap'.**

So, whereas we previously went from:
- 'She **is** old and lonely' (fact)

to:
- 'You **ought** to help her' (moral value)
– With a neo-naturalist approach, the gap in the reasoning between the 'is' and the 'ought' can be filled in:
- 'She is old and lonely' (fact).
- 'The content of morality is the flourishing of human beings' (socio-biological fact).
- 'Not helping her does not contribute to the flourishing of human beings' (fact).
- 'Therefore you ought to help her' (moral value).

Note that this still leaves plenty of room for ethical discussion, because it is not always clear what leads to human flourishing. There might be circumstances under which euthanasia could be a preferred option. That would be decided on the socio-biological facts relevant to each case. There is no guarantee that the right 'facts' will be appealed to, but that is an issue with all factual claims: they can be true or false.

We could argue that 'the flourishing of human beings' is too narrow to be the factual content of ethics, since humanity is simply one species within the planet's biosphere, and all species are inter-dependent. A more accurate description might therefore be that 'good' is what contributes to the flourishing of the biosphere as a whole.

Returning to Divine Command Theory

As we have pointed out before, you can see that this is a non-naturalist theory. God's moral commands are seen as being grounded in the facts of his divine nature. In effect, then, we can see that Divine Command Theory is a form of theological Intuitionism. It is either a true or a false intuition.

To see the contrast between Divine Command Theory and ethical naturalism, naturalism grounds its facts in the world – in nature or in human nature. For the non-naturalist Divine Command Theory, however, moral commands are from a supernatural source: God. For a naturalist, moral facts are discovered through observation of the world. For a Divine Command theorist, God's commands are revealed through scripture and the Church, and must be obeyed without reference to any other facts about the world.

Many Christians accept this, but for other Christians, such as John Hick, having to obey God's commands takes away the necessary freedom to respond to God, which is why there are several different kinds of Christian ethics.

133

Technical terms for meta-ethics

Applied ethics Applying normative principles and arguments to particular areas, for example, medical ethics, animal ethics, business ethics, legal ethics; also to difficult specific questions about euthanasia, capital punishment, the conduct of a war, etc.

Descriptive ethics Describes and compares the ethical norms in different societies.

Divine Command Theory Meta-ethically, the non-natural view that morality is defined by God's commands, revealed through scripture and the Church.

Ethical naturalism   The meta-ethical view that morality is defined by facts about nature or human nature.

Ethical non-cognitivism   The view that morality is non-cognitive, has nothing to do with facts, but reduces instead to 'emotional ejaculations' (Ayer) or to universalisable prescriptions about moral behaviour (Hare).

Ethical non-naturalism   The meta-ethical view that moral knowledge is a factual property known by intuition or by God's commands, for example.

First-order questions   Questions raised by normative ethics – about how we should behave/what we should do – are called first-order ethical questions.

Intuitionism   As a form of non-naturalism, Intuitionism is the meta-ethical view that moral knowledge is a factual property known by intuition.

Meta-ethics   The consideration of second-order questions about the nature and purpose of morality, such as: what is the meaning of 'good', 'bad', 'right' or 'wrong'?

Naturalistic fallacy   G.E. Moore's argument that it is a fallacy when people reason from facts to moral claims.

Neo-naturalism   'New naturalism' – a new form of ethical naturalism which argues (against G.E. Moore) that morality *does* have a factual content: 'good' is that which leads to the flourishing of human beings, or the flourishing of the entire environment.

Normative ethics   First-order ethical questions about how we should behave; what ethical norms we should follow.

Religious ethics   The approach to ethics which derives moral values from God/a divine realm: for example, Divine Command Theory.

Second-order questions   Meta-ethical questions about the nature and purpose of morality are called second-order ethical questions. In ethics, second-order questions are questions about first-order questions and the answers given to those questions.

Secular ethics   The approach which argues that ethical theories and actions are based on human faculties such as logic and reason, and not on religious values or commands given by God.

Summary of meta-ethics

Introduction

Descriptive ethics describes ethical practices in different times, places and cultures, without making any judgement about these different practices.

Normative ethics investigates the questions that arise when considering how we ought to behave, so those who develop normative ethical theories (such as Natural Moral Law, Situation Ethics, Virtue Ethics and Utilitarianism) are recommending that you ought to behave in accordance with the principles of each theory. Normative ethics is 'first-order' ethical language.

Applied ethics is the process of applying normative principles and arguments to particular situations, for example, business ethics, medical ethics, legal ethics, animal ethics.

Meta-ethics is 'second-order' ethical language. It examines what moral language is about, its origin and cause, and how it can be justified. It asks questions such as:

- What is the meaning of 'good', 'bad', 'right', 'wrong'? (Since this question needs to be answered before doing any other kind of ethics, such as the normative practice of recommending how people should behave.)

- What is a moral value, and where do moral values come from?

- Do moral facts exist, and if so, what are they?

- What motivates people to act morally? Is it pleasure, happiness, love, or what?

Meta-ethical theories. With regard to the theories you have to study:

- **Ethical naturalism** holds that morality is cognitive/factual; good is real, objective and in the world. It is to be found in the facts about nature, and/or the facts about human nature. Utilitarianism finds the facts of morality in human happiness/pleasure.

- **Ethical non-naturalism** holds that morality is cognitive/factual; good is real but cannot be defined; it is intuited (Intuitionism), or else is revealed by a supernatural source (God).

Many philosophers have abandoned both naturalism and non-naturalism in favour of **ethical non-cognitivism**, which maintains that 'good' is not a factual property at all. Our moral ideas and claims are nothing more than wishes, emotions or intentions, for example.

Divine Command Theory (DCT)

DCT is a non-naturalist approach to ethics. Moral facts are not found in nature or in human nature: rather, they are **revealed** (through scripture and the Church) by a supernatural source – God. 'Supernatural' means, literally, 'above the natural'.

DCT is clearly a religious rather than a secular ethic. It is based on belief in the existence of a divine being, God, who is the source of 'good', and whose moral commands are revealed through scripture and made clear (where necessary) by the Church. Many Protestant Christians follow DCT, believing that God's will is the only true source of moral authority.

1 DCT argues that whatever God commands must be good, and whatever he forbids must be evil.

2 People should therefore act in a way that reflects God's will.

3 DCT is grounded in the belief that God is the Creator, and humans are made in God's image, so there must be a link between Creator and created. For Protestants in particular, who live by the doctrine of *Sola Scriptura*, God's commands are revealed in scripture, particularly in the Ten Commandments and in Jesus' teachings in the Sermon on the Mount. DCT is based both on God's commands and on his ethical character.

4 Calvin argued that there is nothing more sublime than God's will, so whatever God commands must be obeyed. For Barth, all questions about good and evil were settled by the death and resurrection of Jesus.

Strengths of DCT

- For religious people, it grounds their moral behaviour in the teachings of a factually-existing God whose commands must be good and promote good.

- The rules are universal, so are the same in all times, places and cultures.

- DCT is clear: 'good', 'bad', 'right', 'wrong' are defined precisely by God's commands.

- There is an end-goal to following those commands, namely life after death.

- God is a totally fair judge.

Weaknesses of DCT

- Even if the moral commands in the Bible do come from God (and not from humans), we cannot tell that they are as God gave them: there are too many issues with the text itself.

- The Bible contains immoral commands, for example, concerning slavery and homosexuality.

- The problem of autonomy: DCT does not allow a genuinely free moral choice beyond the carrot and stick of 'obey and go to heaven' or 'disobey and go to hell'.

- Euthyphro's Dilemma seems insoluble: 'Is conduct right because the gods command it, or do the gods command it because it is right?' There is no universally-accepted solution to either 'horn' of the dilemma.

Ethical naturalism (and Utilitarianism as an example)

Ethical naturalism holds that moral values can be described in terms of natural properties such as love or happiness, so they are objective and in the world. Naturalist theories are therefore realist, and aspire to be true, although (as with other matters of fact) naturalists admit that we can be right or wrong about them. Naturalism is grounded in the facts of nature or of human nature; so utilitarians see 'the good' in terms of the facts about pleasure and happiness, whereas virtue ethicists think that the facts are about complete well-being. Naturalists often devise rules to guide behaviour, so a utilitarian who follows the rule of 'the greatest happiness for the greatest number' can be described as 'morally good'. Naturalists argue that it is vital to hold that there are ethical facts about the world, because these justify our actions.

Utilitarianism

- **Bentham's Utilitarianism** sees pain and pleasure as the 'two sovereign masters' of humanity, determining all we do, and therefore what we ought to do. We observe this to be true, so we can see these facts in human nature. Pleasure or happiness is the one intrinsic good, valued for itself, and not for some other valuable thing it produces. Likewise pain/unhappiness is the one intrinsic evil. We ought, therefore, to maximise pleasure and to minimise pain, by seeking the greatest happiness for the greatest number. Observation shows us that pleasure can be measured objectively by its intensity, duration, certainty, proximity, productiveness, purity and extent. It does not matter whether pleasure comes from a simple game or from cultural activities such as opera and philosophy. Utilitarianism is a consequentialist ethic, where the moral value of an action is measured by its results.

- **Mill's Utilitarianism** argued (against Bentham) that the 'higher' cultural pleasures are superior to lower (physical) ones (to avoid the objection to Utilitarianism that it is 'pig philosophy'). He described the good in terms of the quality of life rather than the quantity of pleasure. Further, Mill pointed out the value of moral rules, since many of the rules society uses are there because they have proved their utilitarian value over many centuries: they are justified by producing a balance of pleasure over pain, and produce a society based on justice.

Strengths of ethical naturalism

- Ethical values are seen as factual because they reduce to properties about the world, such as happiness, love and well-being, and these are seen as factual, being grounded in nature or human nature.

- Right and wrong are objective, existing in the world, outside ourselves, so we can know whether we are doing right or wrong.

- Ethical propositions give us guidelines and rules to follow.

- We can be judged by our adherence to the rules, and punished if we break them.

- Most people tend to follow one naturalist theory or another. It is often said that UK law and politics are broadly utilitarian in character.

Weaknesses of ethical naturalism

- It faces powerful and popular opposition from ethical non-cognitivism.

- Moore was considered by most philosophers at the time to have destroyed naturalism by his arguments about the 'naturalistic fallacy' – arguing that we cannot derive moral values from facts: we cannot derive an 'ought' from an 'is'.

- Moore also used his 'Open Question' argument to insist that good is undefinable.

Strengths of Utilitarianism

- It gives us a factual basis for morality.

- It gives us guidelines and rules: for example, Bentham's Pleasure Calculus.

- We can measure the moral worth of people by how far they maximise happiness.

- The success of Utilitarianism can be seen by its broad use in UK politics.

- If you ask people what they want, most people will say that they want happiness.

Weaknesses of Utilitarianism

- Happiness varies between people, so is hard to define. Some get happiness from inflicting pain on others, which can hardly be called 'good' for the majority.

- Its consequentialist basis means that Utilitarians have to guess the future.

- The principle of 'the greatest good for the greatest number' ignores the fact that minorities are often right.

- Moore's 'naturalistic' fallacy seems to show that there is something wrong with all naturalist theories of ethics, including Utilitarianism. However, there is no guarantee that Moore was right.

Ethical non-naturalism (and Intuitionism as an example)

1 Moore began by rejecting ethical naturalism on the grounds that it commits the 'naturalistic fallacy' – it attempts to derive moral values from facts.

2 To avoid the naturalistic fallacy, Moore denied that moral values can be derived from facts about the world. They are based on a moral sense that cannot be described literally.

3 Whereas in ethical naturalism 'good' is held to be complex and analysable (like the concept 'horse'), Moore held that moral facts are simple and unanalysable, like the concept of 'yellow'. Just as we recognise (but cannot describe) 'yellow', we can recognise (but cannot describe) 'good': it is known non-naturally.

4 Non-naturalism, like naturalism, is still a cognitive/factual ethical theory. There are real moral facts that we can know: we just cannot define them.

5 'Intuitionism' is a widely-known non-naturalist theory. Divine Command Theory is another.

Intuitionism

- Intuitionism argues that our knowledge of right and wrong comes through fundamental moral intuitions.

- Intuition is a well-known and well-documented concept in ethics, for example in the writings of Plato and Aristotle.

- Intuitions do not need to be justified by reference to any other beliefs – they 'stand-alone' and are (according to intuitionists) self-evident. The moral truths behind our intuitions exist independently of persons.

- The 'Trolley Problem' is a good illustration of the difference between a naturalist/utilitarian approach to a dilemma and an intuitionist approach.

- Ross clarifies the intuitionist approach by arguing that we are all aware of *prima facie* duties, such as duties to parents and the innocent, and where these duties conflict (as in the famous example of Kant and the mad axe-murderer), then when we balance one *prima facie* duty against others, moral intuition kicks in to provide an intuitive truth.

Strengths of ethical non-naturalism/Intuitionism

● Everyone has moral intuitions, and we use them to underpin our moral decisions.

● Intuitionism solves the problem faced by ethical naturalism, that there are so many conflicting definitions of the good that they cannot all be correct. For the non-naturalist, good cannot be defined, only intuited in situations.

● It is still a form of realism: statements can be true or false, and it is realistic in explaining that our moral intuitions are not perfect because every moral *situation* is different, as Ross points out.

Weaknesses of ethical non-naturalism/Intuitionism

● Intuitionism does not give a satisfactory answer as to *how* we have moral intuitions. Some call intuition a 'faculty' of the brain, but it is one that cannot be observed so might not exist.

● Intuition is a weak basis on which to argue: it stifles ethical debate, because people just pit one intuition against another.

● Intuition could in fact boil down to the unconscious influence of social norms. Had we lived in the eighteenth century, we might have 'intuited' that slavery is right.

● Non-naturalism in effect led many to turn to ethical non-cognitivism (such as Ayer's Emotivism), but: 1) non-cognitivism gives an unsatisfactory account of the importance we place on our moral views; 2) if society as a whole comes to believe that there are no factual moral values, the results are likely to be horrendous.

● Ethical naturalists argue that Moore was wrong in his assessment of ethical naturalism. Moore's 'Open Question' argument does not destroy naturalism. Neo-naturalism (new naturalism) argues that despite Moore's arguments, there is no 'naturalistic fallacy', and morality does have a factual content. Virtue plays a key role in ethics, and virtues depend on certain biological and sociological facts about humans, from which we can see that morality does have an obvious factual content, namely the flourishing of human beings. Whatever does this is factually 'the good' for humans.

● 'Human flourishing' (or 'the flourishing of the entire biosphere') therefore provides us with the reasoning to fill the 'is–ought gap': 'She is old and lonely'/*helping the old and lonely contributes to human flourishing*/'you ought to help her'. This still leaves room for ethical debate, because it is not always clear what leads to human flourishing.

Returning to Divine Command Theory

This is a non-natural ethical theory, since God's moral commands are seen as being grounded in the facts of his divine nature. DCT is a form of theological Intuitionism, and is either a true or a false intuition.

To see the contrast between DCT and ethical naturalism, naturalism grounds its facts in the world – in nature or in human nature. For the non-naturalist DCT, however, moral commands are from a supernatural source: God. For a naturalist, moral facts are discovered through observation of the world. For a Divine Command theorist, God's commands are revealed through scripture and the Church, and must be obeyed without reference to any other facts about the world. Many Christians (such as Hick) reject DCT on the grounds that it takes away the heart of morality, which is the freedom to respond to God.

5

Free will and moral responsibility

You will need to consider the following items for this section

1 The conditions of moral responsibility: free will; understanding the difference between right and wrong.
2 The extent of moral responsibility: Libertarianism, Hard Determinism, Compatibilism.
3 The relevance of moral responsibility to reward and punishment.

The conditions of moral responsibility: free will; understanding the difference between right and wrong

If you are accused of doing something wrong, there are two ways to excuse yourself. You can say that you could not help it or were forced to do it; or you can say that you did not understand that it was wrong to do it.

The whole discussion of free will and moral responsibility is centred on those two excuses, either of which would seem to absolve you of responsibility and therefore of blame.

Aristotle made the crucial point that only voluntary actions (those that you do through your own free will) qualify for praise or blame (*Nicomachean Ethics*, Book III, Chapter I). This is a fundamental feature of moral discussion; if you are forced to do something, and therefore have no option but to do it, or if you are ignorant about the significance of what you are doing, then you should not be held morally responsible.

Hence, for ethics, it is important to consider both of these two features that enable an action to be judged morally right or wrong.

Free will

To be morally responsible, people must act through their own free will. It needs to be shown that the people concerned are in fact able to make that choice. We need to exclude other possibilities, for example that they might have been hypnotised or brainwashed, in which case what they thought was their free choice was in fact forced on them.

By comparison with freely-acting people, **machines** are incapable of independent thought, so cannot be blamed for whatever they do. I may claim to hate computers or complain that my car is unroadworthy and therefore a menace to other road users, but neither car nor computer will be morally to blame if valuable data is lost or if there is a road accident. Machines, cars and computers are dependent upon those who programme or drive them, so if something goes wrong, blame lies with the conscious agents, not the unconscious machine. To take the most extreme case, acts of murder are not carried out by guns or knives, but by the people who use them.

The same is true of **non-human animals**. We may watch a wildlife film showing a predator stalking its prey. We may desperately hope that the cute little animal that is innocently finding its way will not be snapped up for a meal, but in reality we know that it is likely to happen and that it is completely natural for it to happen. The lion is not *morally* responsible for the death agony of the young wildebeest.

We speak in loose terms of a **virus** or a cancer being 'responsible' for a person's death, but that does not imply any moral responsibility, as the term 'responsible' in this case means no more than that it is the *cause* of death.

Thus, for moral responsibility, we need a free human agent. There are some situations in which, even if a person believes he or she is free to choose what to do, an observer – taking into account all the circumstances, the person's upbringing, psychological make-up and the social pressures under which the person lives – might suggest that they actually have no control over their actions.

In addition, the human agent needs to be conscious and capable of making the decision that is the subject of our moral consideration, because if you are unconscious, you are not in a position to choose what to do.

To take the most obvious example, suppose a person has a fatal heart attack while driving a car, as a result of which the car is involved in an accident and kills someone. Since the person who had been driving was dead (or even simply unconscious at the wheel) at the moment when the accident took place, he or she cannot be morally responsible for what happened, unless …

And here the situation becomes more complicated. One might need to ask:

- Did the person driving the car know about the heart condition?
- Had he or she been warned by a doctor not to drive?

If the person concerned had previously been warned about the danger by a doctor, then he or she must have taken a decision to drive in spite of the risks involved. That earlier decision was free and conscious and contributed indirectly to the death of the road accident victim, and it is therefore morally significant. But it is not at the moment when the car kills someone that the driver is to blame, but at the point at which he or she took the decision, against advice, to drive and therefore to expose others to the risk of harm.

However, one can then argue that there are situations so serious and urgent that they override any warnings about the dangers of driving in such a case. Suppose the driver was trying to get a desperately ill person to hospital.

Would it be reasonable, or morally responsible, for the person to say, in effect: 'I appreciate that without my assistance you are going to die, but I really can't rush you to the A & E department because I have been advised by my doctor not to drive'? There are clearly some situations in which the usual precautions may be set aside. In that case, would the person be morally to blame for *not* driving against advice?

This would suggest that knowing the degree of moral responsibility may be problematic because human beings (believe it or not) are human. In a thought experiment, or as part of a logical argument, it may be straightforward to define the point at which a person may be deemed to be conscious of the moral significance of his or her action; however, in real life the factors involved sometimes make it difficult to determine the *degree* of freedom and awareness involved. Again, that is simply because we are human.

Understanding the difference between right and wrong

In addition to being a free, conscious, human agent, a further requirement of moral action is that a person should be able to distinguish right from wrong.

To be able to do this, a person needs to have lived long enough to acquire some moral discretion, and cannot be hindered by some psychological or neurological disability. Specifically, there are clearly some humans, then, who cannot meet this additional requirement:

- Babies and young children, and those with severe learning difficulties, are not regarded as being able to take legal or moral responsibility for their actions.
- Those who are suffering from dementia, or other serious mental illnesses, are equally regarded as not able to distinguish right from wrong, or to understand the significance of their actions.
- Under extreme pressure, it may be argued that people are no longer able to think normally, and may therefore take actions that, with hindsight or calm reflection, they know to be wrong. People may do or say something in a fit of temper that they later regret. The question is whether or not, in that moment of anger, they were able to think rationally and therefore able to take moral responsibility.

In terms of knowledge of the good, there would therefore seem to be four exemptions:

1 those who have not yet learned it
2 those who cannot understand it.
3 those who have permanently forgotten it.
4 those who have temporarily forgotten it.

In the case of the fourth of these, of course, the circumstances of that forgetting (such as being blind drunk at the time) may not absolve you from moral responsibility – but in that case, the moral question is whether it was right or wrong to put yourself in a position, by drinking too much, in which you could no longer tell right from wrong.

Further, assuming a person is of an appropriate age, is intellectually/mentally competent, is mentally in good health and has not been provoked beyond being capable of a rational response, there remains the question of the degree and content of a person's moral awareness.

What are the sources of a person's moral awareness in telling right from wrong?

So, how does a person know right from wrong? Or, in other words, what are the sources of an individual's moral awareness?

1 Some will argue that we all have an innate moral sense.

For example, we generally feel it is right to go to the aid of someone in need or distress. This was the basis of David Hume's approach to morality – that we have a built-in 'moral sense' – a 'faculty of sympathy'. In the next chapter we shall be discussing the conscience, which some philosophers think is an *innate* faculty of this kind.

2 Another approach is to say that we learn about right and wrong from our social context.

In other words we learn them from our parents and from others in society as we grow up, and that those moral principles (often backed up by law) form the basis of our social life. In this case, we see that morality is linked to particular cultural and social traditions. In modern debate this is seen as the problem of multiculturalism, when actions that are seen as being wrong by some people are nevertheless seen as right by others – classic examples in recent debate being female circumcision and arranged marriages. Here the fundamental question concerns whether moral principles, and the practices that result from them, that are understood and accepted within any one community, culture or religion should be accepted globally. Whatever your answer to that question, the point remains that questions of right and wrong are culturally conditioned and will therefore vary from society to society and over time – in other words there appears to be moral relativism – morality is relative to the society in which you live, and where and when you were brought up.

3 In addition to the possibility of an innate moral sense and the significance of social and cultural moral education, there is the question of religious morality.

Each religion presents its followers with fundamental moral principles, and sets of practical moral rules, which serve to define the way of life of that particular religious group. Some traditions tend to define social practices in such a way that the religion 'embodies' its own culture in terms of food, dress and day-to-day behaviour, while others tend to present moral principles that are adaptable to a variety of cultures.

For a religious person, therefore, knowledge of the good is encountered at three levels: the innate, the social and the religious. Moral dilemmas arise where these come into conflict.

The extent of moral responsibility: Libertarianism, Hard Determinism, Compatibilism

Assuming a sufficient understanding of right and wrong by an adult who is mentally competent to understand and put into practice moral principles, the fundamental question remains about whether or not we have free will. That is the key question to which we now need to turn.

An early argument that highlighted this problem was made by the Greek philosopher Epicurus.

Epicurus (341–270 BCE)

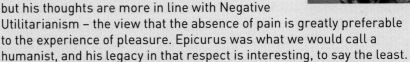

Epicurus was a Greek philosopher whose philosophy is known as 'Epicurean philosophy', which was basically the idea that philosophy can, and should, lead people to lead happy lives, as free from pain or fear as possible, in which respect Epicurus anticipated Utilitarianism. He is generally associated with living a life of rampant pleasure, but his thoughts are more in line with Negative Utilitarianism – the view that the absence of pain is greatly preferable to the experience of pleasure. Epicurus was what we would call a humanist, and his legacy in that respect is interesting, to say the least.

If you add to all this that he was the first to put forward a version of the 'inconsistent triad', which we studied in Volume 1 (The Problem of Evil); that he also put forward the atomic thesis, that matter was composed of minute particles – atoms; that he suggested the 'Epicurean hypothesis', used by Hume to attack the Design Argument for the existence of God (that given sufficient time atoms will organise themselves); and that he is credited with being the first to draw attention to the problem of free will, Epicurus was, as we say colloquially, 'a legend'. Even Nietzsche regarded him as one of the greatest human beings ever to have walked the earth, and Nietzsche was not an easy man to impress. Epicurus left a written legacy of over 300 works, but only a fragment of that output survives, which is a *real* Greek tragedy.

In terms of physics, Epicurus took the view (presented by the 'Atomists') that the world consisted entirely of atoms within a void; that it was entirely physical, and that any event was therefore theoretically predictable given its circumstances and the natural forces involved. This would mean that we have no control over the forces of nature, nor can we determine the situations in which we find ourselves – therefore we have no freedom of action, but are entirely determined by forces and circumstances outside ourselves and beyond our control.

But this was problematic for Epicurus himself, because he also believed that one should seek to maximise happiness in life by living simply and peacefully. But how could he recommend a particular way of life if there was no choice about the matter? He therefore tried to modify his physics in order to make free will possible. In attempting this, he points to a fundamental issue that continues to haunt this debate: **observation and science tend towards Determinism; personal and moral experience tend towards free will**.

In order to unpick that debate, we need to consider two fundamentally different views and two ways in which they relate to one another:

The fundamental views are:

- Hard Determinism (we are not free, but are fully determined by antecedent physical causes)
- Libertarianism (we are free).

The two ways they relate to one another:

- Incompatibilism (we are either determined or free, but cannot be both)
- Compatibilism (Scientific Determinism is compatible with our experience of freedom – this is sometimes referred to as 'Soft-Determinism', in contrast to Hard Determinism).

Hard Determinism

Determinism is the view that all events and states of affairs, including all human decisions and actions, are the necessary consequence of antecedent (previous) states of affairs. Determinism is commonly identified with **Causal Determinism**, because the laws of cause and effect in physics can be seen as a chain of antecedent causes going back to the Big Bang.

Hard Determinism is the view that because Determinism is true, no one has free will. All forms of Hard Determinism are based on the concept of 'universal causation'. According to this approach, every event in the universe has a cause. This applies, then, not just to physical events but to mental events: every thought we think, every decision we take, is merely an event in a chain of causes and effects. Taken as a whole, the network of causes and conditions that exist at any one moment is held to be sufficient to determine everything that will happen in the future. That includes the fact that I have just written this and that you are reading it at this precise second.

Most science works on the assumption that the world operates in ways that are regular and theoretically predictable. Again, we do not need to prove that we *know* every possible cause of an event; it is only necessary to show that, in general, all events have causes that are theoretically knowable.

Hard Determinism therefore governs ethical choices also. In effect, ethical choices do not exist: our moral decisions are as determined as anything else, as are all events in the brain.

We may *think* that we are free to choose what to do, but such freedom is merely an illusion created by the very complex processes that go on in the human brain. We think we are choosing, whereas in fact we are running through a very complex calculation, the outcome of which is already determined.

A Hard Determinist would argue that, since freedom is an illusion, we are not logically justified in claiming responsibility for our actions, even if we feel that we have freely chosen to do them.

Key terms

Determinism The view that all events and states of affairs, including all human decisions and actions, are the necessary consequence of antecedent (previous) states of affairs.

Causal Determinism Determinism is often identified with *Causal* Determinism, because the laws of cause and effect in physics suggest that there is a complete chain of antecedent causes going back to the Big Bang.

Hard Determinism The view that because Determinism is true, no one has free will.

Reductionism

Determinism is sometimes backed up by an approach called *Reductionism*. This is the view that, to understand a complex entity, one should analyse (or reduce) it to the smallest component parts of which it is made. With this approach, human behaviour is reduced to biology, which is then reduced to chemistry, which is then reduced to physics. What starts out appearing to be a very complex action is simply the cumulative effect of many simple ones.

On this basis, our thoughts may be seen as no more than electrical impulses in the brain, and our actions are simply the result of chemical and electrical activity. If everything is *reduced* to its simplest physical components, and those components can be shown to be determined by the laws of physics, then the complex *whole* is also thereby determined by those laws.

Whether Determinism and reductionist approaches really do explain our moral behaviour is, of course, another issue.

The possibility that our feeling of freedom is simply ignorance

Your immediate reaction to Hard Determinism might be that it is a 'bog of nonsense', because **you *know* that you are free to make choices**. Determinist philosophers, including Spinoza, insist that **this 'feeling of freedom' is merely ignorance**.

Baruch Spinoza (1632–77)

Spinoza was a Dutch rationalist philosopher of Portuguese Jewish descent. He was considered a heretic by the Jewish community, and his books were on the Catholic Church's *Index of Forbidden Books*.

Spinoza considered that everything in the world was totally determined by physical causes, and therefore there was no scope for human freedom. And this, of course, has been the approach of determinists, materialists and behaviourists, who have also tried to fit the idea of the human mind and its experience of freedom into a closed system of physical cause and effect. Spinoza suggested that we merely consider ourselves to be free because we are ignorant of all the causes operating upon us.

Thus, for example, if at some point you decided to consult a therapist or an analyst, he or she would be quick to point out the unconscious causes of your actions of which you were, naturally, quite unaware. Many influences from your past, long forgotten, may contribute to what you do in the present. If you stop and think about it, or it is pointed out to you, it may appear obvious – but you normally act without considering all those influences.

The approach taken by Spinoza is therefore reasonable as far as it goes. If you knew absolutely everything there is to know, then you would understand that there are very good reasons for every apparently 'free' decision that you make. *You think you are making a completely free choice, but that simply reflects your ignorance of the causes operating on you all the time.*

In other words, the experience of freedom is an illusion generated by our ignorance of the totality of causes acting upon us. If we could take into account everything that had ever happened to us, every experience that etched neural pathways into our brains, then we would understand that our choices are determined.

This is the point at which the determinist distinguishes between freedom itself and the apparent freedom of the will. Our experience of free will – the conviction that we are free to will something to happen over which we appear to have control – is factually incorrect (we are actually determined by physical forces), but the limited nature of human awareness of those causes means that we experience the process, by which we assess and register the infinite number of influences acting upon us, as free will.

Determinism creates a general problem in terms of the relationship between mind and body. Can the human mind make a difference to anything? If the operation of our minds is simply the experience of what is happening in our brains, and the electrical impulses in our brains are part of a closed mechanical system, then our freedom is indeed an illusion.

We shall now consider three versions of Hard Determinism: scientific, psychological and theological.

Scientific Determinism

Scientific Determinism holds that all events, including human actions and choices are determined by antecedent events and states of affairs, so there can be no freedom of the will.

Consider this picture of the cosmic microwave background (CMB):

▲ The cosmic background radiation

The CMB is the oldest light in the universe, dating from about 378,000 years after the Big Bang. This light is picked up by radio telescopes, and is strongest in the microwave region of the radio spectrum. This is a picture of the infant universe, created over nine years of very precise measurement from the Wilkinson Microwave Anisotropy Probe (WMAP). It determined that the universe is very close to 13.77 billion years old.

When we look at the WMAP image, we are actually seeing the universe as it was 13.77 billion years ago, since it has taken that amount of time for the light to reach our solar system. Time itself appears to be bivalent, however, in that the equations in physics work just as well backwards in time as they

145

do forwards. There is a complete sequence of cause and effect, beginning with the Big Bang and culminating in the present, and from the present back to the Big Bang, and an omnipotent mind would be aware of every infinitesimally minute part of that sequence.

Equally, an omnipotent mind could reverse the process back to the Big Bang, like rewinding an old movie. In other words, the equations in physics are deterministic; physics governs everything; therefore every event in the universe, physical and mental, is determined by physics.

This means that the future is also determined.

The brain itself can be analysed as a physical system, and thoughts appear to be electrical impulses in the brain. In fact, all of what we call a human being can be analysed by sciences such as anthropology, sociology, **physiology** and psychology. There seems, therefore, to be no escape from the conclusion that we do not have free will: Hard Determinism is true.

This is not a new idea. The first full expression of Determinism came in the work of the French physicist, mathematician and statistician Pierre-Simon Laplace (1749–1827):

> **Key term**
>
> **Physiology** The biology of how living organisms (and their parts) function.

> We ought then to regard the present state of the universe as the effect of its anterior state and as the cause of the one which is to follow. Given for one instant an intelligence which could comprehend all the forces by which nature is animated and the respective situation of the beings who compose it – an intelligence sufficiently vast to submit these data to analysis – it would embrace in the same formula the movements of the greatest bodies of the universe and those of the lightest atom; for it, nothing would be uncertain and the future, as the past, would be present to its eyes. [Note 1]

The 'intelligence' here is usually referred to as 'Laplace's Demon' (although Laplace did not use that term).

When we look at physical nature, then, we see a chain of causality that spreads outwards and backwards from any one physical event. Everything appears to arise in dependence upon other things, and there appear to be no 'gaps' in that chain of causation into which a 'mental' input could be inserted. In other words, the physical world appears to be a seamless interlocking whole, with no scope for human free will to make a difference.

Can we avoid Scientific Determinism?

There are two ways in which it might be possible to avoid Scientific Determinism:

1 Scientific Determinism can be avoided if the laws of nature are probabilistic.

Science generally operates by gathering experimental evidence and/or observed facts, and from them seeks the best available interpretation of them. Various hypotheses are tested experimentally, and – if the results appear to bear them out – a theory is framed to account for what has been observed. It may not be the only possible theory, but the hope is that it will be the best one available for now.

We have to recognise, therefore, that it is almost certain that our scientific theories are wrong. History shows that newer theories replace older ones as our knowledge increases, therefore in the future all that we now regard as the 'laws of nature' will, in all likelihood, be discarded and replaced.

Hence scientific laws cannot claim absolute truth, but only a degree of probability, proportional to the evidence upon which they are based.

2 Scientific Determinism might also be avoided if the quantum world is indeterminate.

If it can be shown that there are entities that are not completely governed by the laws of nature, then we might have reason to reject Scientific Determinism.

Matter at the quantum scale appears to be different from its appearance at the 'macro' scale we experience. It is a matter of debate among quantum physicists as to how Quantum Theory should be interpreted. The 'standard interpretation' is the 'Copenhagen Interpretation', devised between 1925 and 1927, mainly by Niels Bohr and Werner Heisenberg, according to which the laws governing the quantum world are indeterministic and probabilistic.

How this affects events at the macro scale is not clear, but if there is indeterminism somewhere in matter, then Determinism seems to be false. It depends, of course, where the indeterminate element is.

It also needs to be recognised that the Copenhagen Interpretation is not the only interpretation of the quantum world. There are other powerful accounts, and the 'Many Worlds Interpretation', for example, is deterministic. If you are interested in this, do an internet search: it will be rewarding.

Chaos Theory is often quoted as an example of random/chance events producing large-scale changes through the '**butterfly effect**' (for example, that a butterfly flapping its wings in Brazil can eventually cause a tornado in Texas); but this has nothing to do with quantum indeterminacy or any other kind of indeterminacy, because chaotic systems only give the *appearance* of randomness. In reality, the events described are completely deterministic. They are merely so complex that they cannot be computed – no computer system could begin to unravel such complexity – nevertheless they are still deterministic.

Key term

Psychological Determinism A form of Hard Determinism, for example that of B.F. Skinner, according to whom all behaviour is the result of genetic and environmental conditions, and all human actions are conditioned by the good or bad consequences of previous decisions; so there can be no freedom of the will.

Most of the philosophers who reject Determinism do so by locating indeterminacy in the mind, where indeterminacy at the quantum level might somehow allow for free will. There are many speculative ideas about how this might work, but for now it is probably best simply to note this possibility.

So: in answer to the question, 'Can Scientific Determinism be avoided?' – many people think so, but the simple fact is that we do not know.

Psychological Determinism

Psychological Determinism is closely associated with the work of B.F. Skinner:

Burrhus Frederic Skinner (1904–1990)

Skinner was an American psychologist and behaviourist. During World War II, Skinner proposed an interesting solution to the problem of improving missile guidance systems of the kind needed to attack large German battleships of the Bismarck class. His system involved putting pigeons into separate compartments in the nose cone of a missile. At launch, an image of the target would appear in front of each pigeon, the theory being that as each bird pecked at it, it guided the missile to the target. Skinner claimed that nobody would take the idea seriously, although tests showed some degree of success. [Note 2]

Key term

Behavioural psychology A theory of learning: that all behaviours, human and animal, are acquired through conditioning – by interaction with the environment. In B.F. Skinner's view, the good and bad consequences of previous actions dispose the brain to repeat or avoid such actions.

Activity

Research Pavlov's experiments and write a short paragraph showing how they contributed to the development of behavioural psychology.

Skinner's variation of Psychological Determinism is known as Psychological Behaviourism. According to this theory, all behaviour is a product of genetic and environmental conditions. All human actions depend on the consequences of previous actions. If an action has good consequences, then the brain becomes disposed to repeat it. If the consequences are otherwise, then the disposition becomes one of avoidance.

One of the classic experiments in **behavioural psychology** was carried out by the Russian physiologist Ivan Pavlov (1849–1936) in a set of experiments known as 'Pavlov's Dogs', and culminating in the idea of 'classical conditioning'. In common with many others working in this field, Skinner's ideas on conditioning were derived from experiments based on animals.

Skinner's approach is sometimes termed 'Radical Behaviourism' because it involves *all* aspects of mental activity. In 1971, in *Beyond Freedom and Dignity*, Skinner denied the existence of internal psychological states such as intentions and purposes, and denied the existence of free will. According to Skinner, Determinism is 'complete'.

Evaluating Skinner's Radical Behaviourism

The American philosopher and cognitive scientist Noam Chomsky (b. 1928) dismissed Skinner's proposals as an example of futile behaviourist speculation and assumption. [Note 3]

One particular criticism of Skinner's assumptions is that his application of the principles of animal behaviour to the much more complex human behaviour is unsound.

Another obvious response to Skinner is that if human behaviour in its entirety is merely a set of conditioned responses determined by genetics and the environment, then his own behavioural thesis is merely an example of a conditioned response, so why should we bother to listen to it?

Theological Determinism

Theological Determinism is a view of Hard Determinism that is rooted in the Christian idea that God is omniscient (all-knowing).

In its earliest form, Theological Determinism led the likes of St Augustine and Calvin to the doctrine of Predestation, which we studied in Chapter 9 of Volume 1. An omniscient God must know the entire past, present and future of the universe and of humanity. Calvin concluded that God's omniscience means that '... some are eternally ordained to glory, through the sheer will of God, and the rest are ordained to eternal torment' – a view which receives far less support now than it did then, since it appears to make God out as an immoral monster. A more reasonable option for God would have been not to create humanity in the first place.

Leaving aside the doctrine of predestination, the problem still remains that an omniscient God's foreknowledge must be causal, because if God knows that you will do 'x' at a specific point in the future, you cannot avoid doing 'x'. If this is the case, then free will must be an illusion, and all events in the universe, both physical and mental, are determined by God's omniscience.

Evaluating Theological Determinism

If there is no God, then Theological Determinism does not even get off the ground; but if there is a God, then of course there is a case to answer.

The issue seems to hinge on God's relationship to time.

- **A timeless God**: Aquinas' view is that God does not exist in time: rather he exists timelessly. For God, there is no today, tomorrow or yesterday: timeless God sees all times, rather like an unrolled scroll, so sees the entire history of the universe timelessly. Following this idea, some argue that God's omniscience means that God sees the results of our future free choices but does not cause them. On this view, God has the power to intervene and control, but does not – he permits human free choices.
- **A temporal God**: The alternative view is, of course, that God exists in time. If that is the case, then God cannot know the future, so Theological Determinism is false. You will remember from Volume 1 that Christian Process theologians see God and the physical universe as two aspects of one reality: God is equivalent with all the physical processes of the universe. In the physical universe, the future has not yet happened – a temporal God would not know the future, and so would not be a threat to human free will.

It seems, therefore, that Theological Determinism is false. The issue is very complicated, however, depending on your theological starting point, so Theological Determinism cannot be rejected out of hand.

Conclusions concerning Hard Determinism

There is no conclusive evidence, as yet, to show that Hard Determinism as a general theory is either true or false. For the non-religious, for example, Theological Determinism is a non-starter. For some, there is cumulative evidence in favour of Determinism, and recent studies in cognitive psychology are often seen to point in that direction, for example those of Benjamin Libet.

Benjamin Libet (1916–2007)

Libet was an American neuroscientist. During the 1980s, Libet conducted a series of experiments to show that unconscious electrical processes in the brain (described as the brain's 'readiness potential') *precede* the brain's conscious decision to perform volitional acts (acts of the will).

Libet's experiments seemed to show that the brain prepares to act well before we are conscious of the urge to move. The implication of this is that the will is not under an individual's conscious control, but is the result of *determined* electrical brain processes. If that is the case, then free will is denied and mental activity is determined.

This produced a flutter of approval from determinist philosophers and scientists who assumed that Libet had proved their case; but the deterministic interpretation of the data was denied by Libet himself, who argued that the brain has the ability to *veto* pre-conscious intentions, and that the veto appears to be freely chosen, without any neurophysiological evidence for neurophysiological Determinism. [Note 4]

Where, at one point, Libet's experiments were seen as a conclusive proof of neurophysiological Determinism, clearly that is no longer the case, not least because Libet himself denies it.

Assessment of Hard Determinism.

We still do not have enough evidence to decide whether any form of Hard Determinism is true or false.

Libertarianism

1 **Libertarianism** is the view that:

- all forms of Determinism are false
- in issues of right and wrong we act as free moral agents.

2 **Most (but by no means all) libertarians are mind–body dualists.**

This follows the view of Descartes, that the mind is a separate substance from the physical body and brain, and is able to act freely in the physical world.

3 **Other libertarians claim that causality has nothing to do with free will, so human moral freedom is non-causal.**

Libertarianism The view that, despite restraints from genetics and the environment (for example), human beings are free moral agents.

This is not an easy view to understand, but basically it asserts that there are two types of events: those that are caused and those that are free, and these are ontologically distinct. This might well be true, but, as with many of the philosophical positions adopted in this debate, it cannot be shown to be true.

4 A 'moderate' libertarian

- would not deny that the external world is deterministic
- would also accept that deterministic processes affect living beings
- would accept that the personality is to a large extent governed by heredity, social situation and environment
- would accept that such influences incline us to act in certain ways rather than others.

Nevertheless, a libertarian insists that human behaviour **is not *determined* by external causes**. The usual example here is that of a kleptomaniac whose physiological, psychological and genetic disposition may dispose him to steal; nevertheless this is not a forgone conclusion, so when left unobserved in a shop, he might or might not steal.

To spell this out in a bit more detail, all our experience of decision-making and following moral principles, and even our sense of guilt when something goes wrong, suggests that we are actually free: that we can choose what to do, and that we must therefore take responsibility for our actions.

However, it is clear that nobody is *totally* free, as human behaviour is constrained by certain limitations:

- **Physical limitations**. There are some things that we are physically incapable of doing. We cannot run a mile in two minutes, and even if we would have been able to save someone's life by doing so, we cannot be blamed for having failed in the attempt. But physical limitations of that sort have little ethical significance.
- **Psychological limitations**. If we have a strong psychological motivation for one particular choice rather than another, this will have some bearing on what we choose, depending on the degree of motivation.
- **Social limitations**. We are all limited by the financial, social and political structures under which we live. The way we understand life and the choices we make are profoundly influenced by our circumstances. Naturally, we can become anti-social and rebel against the norms of our society, affirming our freedom to do so – but it takes more effort and conviction to do so rather than simply to conform to expectations.

For a libertarian, limitations such as these are acceptable, because the idea of *complete* freedom makes little sense. In fact, a libertarian could argue that complete freedom would lead to a kind of paralysis. [Note 5]

5 The most common reason for arguing for Libertarianism is that we *experience* ourselves as free, and also we have a sense of moral responsibility (including guilt if we get things wrong).

This is the 'common sense' argument from what is sometimes called 'folk psychology' – in other words the opinion of ordinary people who make day-to-day decisions without doubting that they are freely made.

The paralysis of complete freedom

Imagine this situation. You are completely free – no limitations, no rules, no bad consequences, no question of guilt, no praise or blame; in fact nothing at all to limit your choice of action.

So what do you do? You may want to satisfy some physical urge. But that would suggest that you are not free, but simply following some natural causation. So perhaps you just decide to do whatever you want. But you don't know what you want, because wants are things that your past has caused you to have. If you knew what you wanted, you'd know that you were conditioned by experiences of attraction or revulsion – in other words, that you had been conditioned to like one thing rather than another. So how do you even start to decide what to do?

The experience of complete freedom would be like being set down in the middle of a completely featureless, flat landscape and trying to decide which way to go. You'd be rooted to the spot, because the actual experience of freedom requires limitations in order to make sense.

You may be free to choose anything on the menu; but first you need the menu.

Determinists generally reject this by arguing that this 'sense of freedom' is simply an illusion, brought about by the fact that our brains are so complex, and the reasons for our actions are so varied, that (as Spinoza claimed) we simply experience the unconscious sorting out of these reasons as freedom.

The libertarian response to this is that if it is an illusion, it is a very persistent one. Moreover, if unconscious processes are so complex, then it is just as likely that they support real freedom as opposed to the imaginary kind.

6 You can see that Libertarianism is 'forward looking' by comparison with Determinism.

Where Determinism looks back to the sequence of prior causes that determine an event or a moral action, libertarians are primarily concerned with future goals, precisely because the future can be self-directed. Libertarians have no problem with the idea that they can deliberate about the likely consequences of their actions without being hamstrung by the idea that those consequences are in some way determined.

For a libertarian, the emphasis is not on what has *caused* her actions but on the *reasons* for action, particularly future action. Where moral decisions are goal-directed, the libertarian can (despite what Hume says, which we shall look at shortly) control her desires in favour of rational deliberation.

In summary, Libertarianism argues for the existence of a moral self. The moral self is able to override the personality and the demands of society, and can make a causally undetermined choice of what should be done for the best in any particular moral situation.

Evaluating Libertarianism

As with Hard Determinism, Libertarianism carries with it a set of assumptions, none of which are known to be true. The determinist claims that the mind is subject to causal laws, but the libertarian argues that this is obviously false, otherwise there would be no argument about it.

Determinists argue that there is evidence for Determinism, but no evidence for Libertarianism. Libertarians argue that the only evidence possessed by determinists is that physical systems are governed by natural laws, but there is no compelling reason to think that the mind is governed in such a way.

The most common argument for Libertarianism is that we consistently experience ourselves as being free, although determinists dismiss this as an illusion brought about by the great complexity of unconscious mental processes.

A strong argument in favour of Libertarianism is that if Hard Determinism is true, there is no point in discussing the question of whether or not we have free will. Yet discussing the question is precisely what we do, for two reasons:

i **Most of us assume that we are free.** Our feelings of moral guilt arise because we realise that we have made a wrong free choice.

ii **Those who claim that we are determined are merely making a determined statement, so why should we pay any attention to it?**

An equally powerful argument in favour of Libertarianism is its positive approach to decision-making in general, and to moral decision-making in particular, because libertarians feel that they are deliberating rationally about achievable goals, as opposed to following a predetermined and unalterable path directed by events determined in the past.

Compatibilism

First, a brief word on **Incompatibilism**. This is the view that Determinism and Libertarianism are incompatible with each other. It seems clear that if Determinism is true, then Libertarianism must be false, and vice versa. However, some philosophers think that Determinism and Libertarianism are compatible with each other.

Compatibilism is the view that human freedom and moral responsibility are compatible with Determinism. It is the view that we can be shaped by physical and other laws, and yet at the same time be sufficiently free to make moral and other choices.

The 'classic' account of the compatibilist position is given by David Hume. Note that no questions can be set on Hume's ideas, but you can of course use them to illustrate a compatibilist view.

In brief, as a summary of Hume's understanding of free will, **Hume thinks that we have 'liberty of spontaneity'** rather than 'liberty of indifference'. Liberty of indifference is freedom from necessity – being free of causal necessity – which Hume saw as a delusion. Liberty of spontaneity is that kind of liberty which is consistent with necessity, and this is **the ability to do what you desire**. The following account explains Hume's ideas in more detail.

1 Hume believed that the controversy about freedom and Determinism has been made more difficult because philosophers have not defined their terms with sufficient accuracy, so the dispute has been going on for over 2000 years and getting nowhere fast. **Hume therefore begins by giving his own definition of 'necessity'**.

2 **The kind of necessity required by Causal Determinism is not *logical* necessity**. Logical necessity is the kind that we find in mathematics, for example, where the idea that 2 + 2 = 4 is logically true. We have got into the habit of assuming that the laws of nature have this kind of necessity, but all we really see in nature is 'constant conjunction'.

3 **This is what Hume says about 'constant conjunction'**:

> Our idea … of necessity and causation arises entirely from the uniformity observable in the operations of nature, where similar objects are constantly conjoined together, and the mind is determined by custom to infer the one from the appearance of the other. These two circumstances form the whole of necessity, which we ascribe to matter. Beyond the constant *conjunction* of similar objects, and the consequent *inference* from one to the other, we have no notion of any necessity or connection. [Note 6]

Key terms

Incompatibilism The view that Determinism and Libertarianism are incompatible; a deterministic universe has no room for free will: we must choose one or the other.

Compatibilism Sometimes called 'Soft Determinism' to distinguish it from Hard Determinism: the view that human freedom and moral responsibility are compatible with Determinism.

153

What does Hume mean by this?

Wherever we look in nature, we see that (A) is constantly accompanied by (B). For example:

- Whenever (A) we throw a brick at a pane of glass, then we constantly find (B) that the glass will shatter.
- Whenever (A) water is heated to 100 °C at sea level, then we constantly find (B) that the water boils.

Since these things always happen together, the mind makes a connection between them, so that through habit we have come to assume that (A) will *always* be accompanied by (B). But this kind of conjunction is not logically necessary, because however many times a brick shatters a piece of glass, it is always possible that at some point in time a piece of glass will remain intact.

We cannot, therefore, talk about *necessary* laws of cause and effect in nature. That understanding of 'necessity' is too strong. All we really find in nature is 'constant conjunction': (B) constantly follows (A).

4 Moreover, constant conjunction is found also in *human* nature.

To explain what Hume means: if you think about the people that you know fairly well, you will probably agree with Hume that their nature is fairly consistent, so much so that we will often remark that 'people don't change'. According to Hume, people's principles and motives are as constant as the patterns of wind, rain and cloud in the weather. People in all societies depend upon each other to the extent that there is hardly anything we do that is done without reference to others. Hume points out, for example, that anybody who makes or grows something to sell, in order to feed himself and his family, expects to be able to sell his goods at a reasonable price. If somebody tries to cheat him, he expects the justice system to come to his aid. If he needs to travel to sell what he makes, then he expects to be able to get on a bus, or in a car, or train or plane.

> The mutual dependence of men is so great in all societies that scarce any human action is entirely complete in itself, or is performed without some reference to the actions of others ... [Note 7]

5 According to Hume this kind of regularity shows that liberty and necessity are compatible, and that liberty *requires* necessity.

Because constant conjunction is found in both nature and human nature, Hume therefore sees physical events and human wishes and desires as one kind of operation: the actions of the will and natural causes form one linked chain. There is a kind of regularity between human choices on the one hand, and human actions on the other. It must be, therefore, that human actions stem from human choices, and that is all that is required for free will. Freedom *requires* Determinism (in Hume's sense) because **if our wishes and desires were simply *random*, the order of human life, by which we make sense of the world and ourselves, would be lost**.

Hume thus defines freedom in the following way:

> By liberty ... we can only mean *a power of acting or not acting, according to the determinations of the will;* that is, if we choose to remain at rest, we may; if we choose to move, we also may. Now this hypothetical liberty is universally allowed to belong to every one who is not a prisoner and in chains. Here, then, is no subject of dispute. [Note 8]

Oliver McAdoo clarifies this neatly:

> Hume claims that our freedom lies in being able to carry out our desires without interference and restraint from external factors. On this basis, freedom is not only compatible with Determinism, it requires it. It is essential that our desires are not random, that they flow from our personality that is genuinely our own. And our personality or character is the sum total of the causal conditions that have created us. Freedom is the expression of this character, to act according to one's desires (rather than focus on the choice of desires). So if the cause of my action is my own desire, then I am free in the opinion of a compatibilist. If I join a club because I want to, that is free will. If I join a club because my parent's make me, that is coercion. Non-freedom for a compatibilist is not being able to do what I desire because I am forced to do something else through physical restraint or coercive threats. Thus freedom is doing the following without interference:
>
> - thinking what I like
> - saying what I like
> - doing what I like
> - meeting whom I like
> - going where I like.
>
> It is 'doing what I desire' rather than 'choosing what I desire'. This is the liberty of spontaneity popularly described as 'doing what you want.' [Note 9]

This, then, is Hume's compatibilist thesis. We are shaped by physical and other laws, and at the same time we are free to make choices, including moral choices. **We have the ability to do what we desire**.

Evaluating Hume's Compatibilism

An evaluation of Hume's concept of Compatibilism could fill several volumes, so we shall pick out a selection:

1 Hume's philosophical method is brilliant. He insists that the whole debate about freedom and Determinism is about definitions, and that once we accept his definitions, everything becomes clear. That is correct. If necessity boils down to 'constant conjunction' in nature and in human nature, then Hume seems to be right: liberty is consistent with necessity, and we have freedom to do what we desire.

2 For twenty-first-century hard determinists, however, Hume's idea of necessity and causation as 'constant conjunction' is too watered down. For the scientific determinist, Hume's 'wishes and desires' are the product of absolute causal forces, so the idea that wishes and desires can in any way be free is unscientific nonsense. 'Wishes and desires' are as determined as everything else.

For the determinist, all actions are caused, so if Determinism is true, then Hume's Compatibilism must be false.

3 For libertarians, Hume's Compatibilism ignores the very power of reason by which Hume arrives at Compatibilism. In other words, on Hume's account, human reason becomes virtually redundant, despite having led him to Compatibilism! For the libertarian, reason allows us to make *real* moral choices by which our lives become properly meaningful. For Hume, reason seems to be indistinguishable from the forces of nature. Everything is watered down to 'constant conjunction'.

Synthesis

It is not possible, at this stage of our understanding of natural laws and of the mind, to decide whether determinists, libertarians or compatibilists are in the right. There are problems with each theory.

- The problem with Determinism is that if it is true, then even the discussion or consideration of Determinism must be determined, and that seems to be counter-intuitive to say the least.
- The problem with Compatibilism is that if Determinism is true, then for a compatibilist to say that we can still perform voluntary acts – that we are free to follow our wishes and desires – makes no sense, since voluntary acts must also be determined. The defining phrase for Compatibilism is 'could have done otherwise'. Faced with a moral choice, if an individual makes a choice, but 'could have chosen otherwise', then that choice would have been free; but if Determinism is true, then this is not a possibility.
- The problem with Libertarianism is that most libertarian arguments claim that although physical systems are determined, the mind is somehow free, but although there are several accounts of how this might be the case (for example, that the brain works on quantum mechanical principles which are not deterministic), so far nobody has produced a *convincing* answer concerning how the brain manages to act freely, and exactly where and what part of the brain is involved.

Until some form of persuasive evidence comes to light, then the problem of free will remains unsolved.

The relevance of moral responsibility to reward and punishment

Reward and punishment are the appropriate response to socially acceptable and socially deviant behaviour respectively. They are justified (or not) by a society's understanding of moral responsibility.

Approaches to crime and socially deviant behaviour

In general, there are two different approaches to the treatment of crime. In broad terms, these correspond to the different approaches to free will and moral responsibility taken by determinists and libertarians.

1 Crime is a mental condition: an illness that can be treated.

This viewpoint accepts that there are determining factors in an individual's life for which they either cannot be blamed, or for which their blame is limited. For example:

The individual might have been brought up in a domestic environment of violence, sexual abuse and general ignorance.

Lack of education can mean that the individual has at best a very limited grasp of how and why people should behave in a responsible manner.

Treatment should therefore be **therapeutic** – aimed at helping/healing the criminal – rather than retributive. Corporal punishment and harsh prison regimes are inappropriate because they will lead to re-offending. Capital punishment is inappropriate, because it is the ultimate injustice for behaviour that the individual has been taught by others.

Therapy centres on reform, offering the criminal the chance to start a new life, with different values and ambitions that do not involve committing the crime for which they are being punished. Reform of this kind is in effect a reward, since the person is not so much suffering something disagreeable as having something beneficial imposed.

2 Crime is a deliberately anti-social behaviour, and should be punished.

According to this view, punishment might be carried out for one or more reasons, for example:

- Retribution. This is simple justice, because retributive punishment a) to some extent compensates the victim, and b) allows the criminal to pay for his crime.
- It signifies society's disapproval of criminal acts and acts as a deterrent for those who are thinking of committing a crime.
- It enforces the idea of responsibility. Where criminals are not punished, they re-offend, as can be seen where courts are reluctant to punish 'petty crime', with the result that the criminal can rack up hundreds of crimes before the courts impose punishment.
- Reform of the criminal is costly and ineffective. The time and money put into attempts at reform are a *reward* for criminal behaviour, and would be much better spent in compensating the victims of crime.
- Criminals cause harm to others and to society more widely; society should therefore be protected from criminals.

Key term

Therapeutic punishment
Treatment/punishment aimed at helping/healing the criminal rather than being retributive/proportional to the crime.

Discussion point

Consider the two different approaches to punishment and reward above. In your view, which is the most appropriate? Does your conclusion reflect a determinist, a libertarian or a compatibilist approach to the idea of moral responsibility?

157

Consequences of moral responsibility theory for reward and punishment

With regard to Hard Determinism, Libertarianism and Compatibilism, each approach to the problem of freedom of the will assumes different levels of moral responsibility, and these condition the different attitudes towards reward and punishment.

Hard Determinism

1 If Determinism is true, then there can be no freedom of the kind required for moral responsibility. It would be pointless punishing those who murder, rob, rape or steal, or rewarding those who do none of these things, because all such events are determined and unavoidable. If our human behaviour is determined, then so is our system of rewards and punishments: they are simply consequences we have built into the system.

2 Further, if Determinism is true, then in the religious sense, any idea of 'sin' against God becomes redundant, because nobody can be blamed by God for doing what their created/determined nature makes them do. This also means that Christianity is totally incoherent, because its central doctrine of Jesus' atonement for human sin by his crucifixion and resurrection is pointless, as is the doctrine of reward for morally good behaviour by being allowed to enter heaven after death.

In our discussion of Theological Determinism (on pages 149–150), you will remember that Augustine and Calvin believed that some are predestined for heaven and others for hell as a result of God's omniscience. This seems to be a very strange doctrine, since Theological Determinism has no convincing answer as to why a loving God would create people who are predestined to damnation. The believer who is in fact predestined to hell seems to be in a dilemma from which there is no escape, since there can be no moral behaviour, good or bad, that can change the predetermined outcome of eternal punishment.

3 B.F. Skinner believed that his work would lead to a reform of all the practices of praise and blame, reward and punishment. He argued that punishing people for antisocial behaviour is not really effective, because once the punishment is over, they will eventually go back to their original behaviour – a thief will go back to being a thief, for example. Punishment also makes people resentful and aggressive. We should therefore make sweeping changes to our traditional practices in order to keep society safe. [Note 10]

Skinner suggests further that:

> [I]t should be possible to design a world in which behaviour likely to be punished seldom or never occurs. [Note 11]

Psychological conditioning can direct what people desire or want, so even if now they desire or want to rob, rape, steal or destroy, they can be conditioned so that in future they desire to do nothing that harms society. People will be conditioned so that they do not do anything that needs punishing.

Critiques

To the libertarian, ideas such as these are completely incoherent, since for the determinist, any attempt to apply conditioning must itself be determined by existing conditions, so we might as well sit back and do nothing, because doing nothing can make no difference to what is determined. For a psychologist to engage a patient in reconditioning must therefore be a complete waste of time: the whole matrix of moral responsibility, reward and punishment, is merely what 'is', and not what 'ought to be'. In a discussion with Skinner, the libertarian would simply point out to Skinner that his recommendations about punishment and credit are an acknowledgement that people really do have the freedom to do otherwise, so Skinner is really a 'closet libertarian'.

Libertarianism

1 The libertarian must hold people responsible for their actions: hence praise and blame, reward and punishment are part of the libertarian strategy for leading people to be morally responsible.

To see people as the product of social and genetic forces, as determinists inevitably do, is to treat people as objects without dignity – as subjects for experiments in environmental engineering along the lines suggested by Skinner.

2 The law in the UK acknowledges diminished responsibility for a number of different types of people and situation such as children, those suffering from depression and the mentally unstable.

Defence lawyers will make every effort to take into account the situation, together with the defendant's social circumstances and mental state. Otherwise the law punishes those who are judged to be guilty of a crime, for the specific reason that **they could have done otherwise**: their behaviour was free, and not wholly determined by mental, social or environmental circumstances.

3 Kant insisted that '**ought implies can**', which is a libertarian point of view: we feel the moral compulsion concerning what we 'ought' to do, which strongly suggests that we are able/free to do it.

Moreover our freedom is clear from the fact that we are able to override that compulsion and do otherwise. At the same time, we can feel **guilt and remorse** when we fail to do what we ought. Such feelings are strongly indicative of moral freedom, so most libertarians are likely to agree with view 2 on page 161, that crime is a deliberately anti-social behaviour, and should be punished.

4 **Kant offers a libertarian account of punishment as retribution.**
   (Note: you might like to have a forward look at Kant's theory of ethics in Chapter 7 Bentham and Kant.)

We can be free **internally** (in our minds) to follow the moral law, and **externally** (politically) by being able to pursue our own ends. In a State of Nature (a system where there are no laws to control anybody's behaviour), we lack external freedom, because other people can enforce their own choices with violence, so we might have to be violent in return. To have external freedom, then, we have to live under the rule of law,

Activity

Do a word search on 'credit' and 'punishment' in the PDF of Skinner's *Beyond Freedom and Dignity*: **archive.org/stream/ Beyond_Freedom_and_Dignity/ Beyond%20Freedom%20&%20 Dignity%20-%20Skinner_djvu.txt**

Evaluate any one claim Skinner makes about credits/ rewards and one claim about punishments. Do you think that Skinner provides evidence for his deterministic account of reward and punishment?

where I can have the maximum amount of freedom that co-exists with the freedom of other people. To create such a society is a rational duty.

If someone in that society breaks the law, then he or she limits other people's freedom and damages the law itself, which pushes us back towards a State of Nature. Using this reasoning, theft (for example) is wrong because the criminal has a maxim ('I can steal X's property') which, if universalised, would take us back to a State of Nature.

In response to this, society must reverse the maxim on the criminal: the thief should have his property removed; the murderer should be killed, so the maxim becomes: 'Whatever underserved evil you bring upon another person must be brought upon yourself.'

The proper aim of punishment is therefore retribution. The aim cannot be *deterrence*, because that uses the criminal as a means to an end. It cannot be *rehabilitation*, because that assumes that the criminal is like an animal – incapable of reason. Only *retribution* allows the criminal to become a rational person who is responsible for her actions.

5 The weakness of the libertarian approach to reward and punishment is that if Determinism is true, then Libertarianism itself is merely another kind of determined response to moral issues.

Some people are conditioned to believe that they are causally determined; others are conditioned to believe that they are causally free. For the determinist, it just so happens that their conditioning corresponds to the truth of the matter. For the libertarian it just so happens that their conditioning does not. Whether the libertarian supports a retributive, or a deterrent, or any other approach to reward and punishment makes no difference, because all such responses are determined. There is no 'niche' in the causal world for free will to operate.

Activity

Discuss and write notes on the following questions:

1 Considering the two main approaches to crime and socially deviant behaviour with which we began this section (page 157), would all libertarians take the second approach?

2 In a notorious case that took place in 2011, David and Judith Tebbutt were captured in Kenya by Somali pirates. You can get the details of this from the online newspaper accounts. Judith's captors shot her husband dead and took her to Somalia, where she spent six months in captivity. During that time, her weight dropped to under 70 lbs, and her hair fell out in clumps.

She said that her captors saw her as a 'thing' that they were going to make money from. They had no real interest in her as a person, or as a woman. She also remarked that they had no understanding of the gravity of their actions. The only one of her captors who spoke English told her that his friend wanted to know if she thought he was a bad man. When told that her husband had been killed, their reaction to her grief was that it was 'no problem', because she could get another husband: they could not understand that some people marry for love.

How might determinists and libertarians approach questions of moral responsibility and punishment in this case?

How would *you* decide on questions of moral responsibility and punishment in this case? Which principles would guide your judgement?

Compatibilism

Remember that with Compatibilism, an action is free if the agent could have done otherwise. If I perform such an act, then I am responsible.

Notice the difference in the answer to the key question of, 'Could I have done otherwise?' For the determinist, the answer must be, 'No'; for the libertarian, it must be, 'Yes'; for the compatibilist, the answer must be:

'Yes, if I had desired to do otherwise.'

Compatibilists therefore see themselves as morally responsible/morally accountable, because:

- Their moral choices are not the results of physical restraints or coercive threats.
- They wanted/desired to act as they did despite being aware of alternative actions.

Where people's actions are done through ignorance, we can say that they are wrong, but that those concerned are not morally responsible. Basically, then, for Hume it makes no sense to punish or to reward someone when his actions are the result of factors apart from what they choose.

Thus Hume argues that people are blameworthy only where our choices come from our character. People's actions are judged only in so far as '… they are indications of the internal character, passions, and affections'. [Note 12]

Most of the kinds of behaviour that we approve of, such as sympathy and empathy, increase the general well-being of society. Hume's approach to punishment is equally taken to be utilitarian in character. Its function is to improve society. Hume's approach to punishment therefore is largely in accord with the first approach to crime and punishment that we referred to at the start of this section: punishment should be a part of social engineering through which fear of punishment helps to repress anti-social behaviour; equally, rewards stimulate a virtuous character.

Moreover, for Hume, this approach shows why the Christian idea of eternal reward in heaven and eternal punishment in hell makes little sense.

In his essay *On the Immortality of the Soul*, Hume points out that human beings do not fall into two neat categories of good and evil: the vast majority 'float between vice and virtue'. This is what we should expect if our wishes and desires reflect our human nature, so our ideas of punishment must bear some proportion to the offence.

When it comes to heaven and hell:

> Why then would there be eternal punishment for the short-term offences of a frail creature like man? Our moral ideas come mostly from our thoughts about the interests of human society. Those interests are short-term and minor; ought they to be guarded by punishments that are eternal and infinite? The eternal damnation of one man is an infinitely greater evil in the universe than the overthrow of a billion kingdoms. [Note 13]

For Hume, then, both the ultimate reward of heaven and the ultimate punishment of hell are senseless, because they are totally disproportionate either to human good or to human evil. Look at the person next to you, and then consider the wider world of international affairs. Judge whether you think that Hume has got it right or wrong.

All in all, there appear to be (at least) two major problems with compatibilist accounts of moral responsibility/reward and punishment:

1 One involves the notion of '**just deserts**'. This is a theory of punishment that sentencing should be proportionate to the severity of the crime. A book by one of its leading proponents, Andrew von Hirsch (*Doing Justice*), published in America in 1976, argued that the 'treatment' model of punishment (the first of the two options that we began with) should be replaced with a judicial system of sentencing the criminal according to his or her just deserts. 'Just deserts' theory is therefore retributive rather than therapeutic.

   Compatibilism and Determinism both lean towards the therapeutic model, but there is a strong 'common-sense' feeling among libertarians and in the thinking of the 'ordinary person' that the punishment should fit the crime. There is a strong ground-swell of public opinion that the criminal justice system is failing the victims of crime by paying more attention to the needs and rights of the criminal than those of the victim.

2 The other problem is the strong suspicion, despite the fact that the majority of philosophers are compatibilists, that Compatibilism is incoherent. Hume himself admitted that Causal Determinism may well be true (see Key quotation box below).

   It has to be said that Hume's account of 'necessity' as 'constant conjunction' is rejected by determinists and libertarians alike: by determinists because what Hume supposes *might* be the case (in the Key quotation box below) they suppose is in *fact* the case; by libertarians because they suppose that Determinism of the *will* is an incoherent idea: a will that is not free is not a will at all.

   If either the determinists or the libertarians are right, then compatibilist ideas about moral responsibility are the 'miserable subterfuge' that Kant derides.

Key term

Just deserts The view that punishment for crimes should be proportionate to the seriousness of the crime committed. The theory is often used to criticise determinist and compatibilist approaches to punishment, where responses to crime can be seen as lenient, ineffective and disproportionate.

I pretend not to have obviated or removed all objections to this theory, with regard to necessity and liberty. I can foresee other objections, derived from topics which have not here been treated of. It may be said, for instance, that, if voluntary actions be subjected to the same laws of necessity with the operations of matter, there is a continued chain of necessary causes, pre-ordained and pre-determined, reaching from the original cause of all to every single volition of every human creature. No contingency anywhere in the universe; no indifference; no liberty. [Note 14]

Technical terms for free will and moral responsibility

Behavioural psychology   The theory that all behaviours, human and animal, are acquired through conditioning – by interaction with the environment. In B.F. Skinner's view, the good and bad consequences of previous actions dispose the brain to repeat or avoid such actions.

Causal Determinism   Determinism is often identified with *Causal* Determinism, because the laws of cause and effect in physics suggest that there is a complete chain of antecedent causes going back to the Big Bang.

Compatibilism   Sometimes called 'Soft Determinism' to distinguish it from Hard Determinism: the view that human freedom and moral responsibility are compatible with Determinism.

Determinism   The view that all events and states of affairs, including all human decisions and actions, are the necessary consequence of antecedent (previous) states of affairs.

Hard Determinism   The view that because Determinism is true, no one has free will.

Incompatibilism   The view that Determinism and Libertarianism are incompatible; a deterministic universe has no room for free will: we must choose one or the other.

Just deserts   The view that punishment for crimes should be proportionate to the seriousness of the crime committed. The theory is often used to criticise determinist and compatibilist approaches to punishment, where responses to crime can be seen as lenient, ineffective, and disproportionate.

Libertarianism   The view that, despite restraints from genetics and the environment (for example), human beings are free moral agents.

Physiology   The biology of how living organisms (and their parts) function.

Psychological Determinism   A form of Hard Determinism, for example that of B.F. Skinner, according to whom all behaviour is the result of genetic and environmental conditions, and all human actions are conditioned by the good or bad consequences of previous decisions; so there can be no freedom of the will.

Scientific Determinism   A form of Hard Determinism which holds that all events, including human actions and choices, are determined by antecedent events and states of affairs, so there can be no freedom of the will.

Theological Determinism   A form of Hard Determinism according to which the future is determined by God's omniscience (God's foreknowledge), so there can be no freedom of the will.

Therapeutic punishment   Treatment/punishment aimed at helping/healing the criminal rather than being retributive/proportional to the crime.

Summary of free will and moral responsibility

The conditions of moral responsibility: free will; understanding the difference between right and wrong

If you are accused of wrong-doing, there are two ways to excuse yourself: you can say that you could not help it/were forced to do it; or you can say that you did not understand that it was wrong to do it. Hence for ethics it is important to consider both features that enable an action to be judged morally right or wrong: i) that the person acted from free will; ii) they understood the difference between right and wrong.

1 Acting with a free will requires a conscious human agent.

Machines or animals are not morally responsible; viruses are not really 'responsible' for someone's death. There are many ramifications of where responsibility lies: for example, if you suffer a fatal heart attack at the wheel of your car and kill someone, you are not responsible – unless you knew that you were not feeling well – or you had failed to take your heart medicine, etc. In other words, defining precise levels of responsibility can be problematic.

2 Being able to distinguish right from wrong is also not so clear cut as we might think, because there are at least four types of people who cannot make this distinction: those who have not yet learned it, such as babies and young children; those who are intellectually incapable of learning it; those who have permanently forgotten it, such as those suffering from dementia; and those under pressure of anger, anxiety, etc., who might temporarily forget it.

What are the sources of a person's moral awareness in telling right from wrong?

- Hume believed that we have a 'moral sense' – a faculty of sympathy. Many believe similarly that our sense of morality is in some way innate.

- Another approach is to say that we learn about right and wrong from our **social** context.

- Religions present believers with moral principles and rules. For a Christian, then, knowledge of the good is encountered at three levels: the innate, the social, and the **religious**.

The fundamental question, however, is whether or not we have free will in order to be morally responsible.

The extent of moral responsibility: Hard Determinism, Libertarianism and Compatibilism

1 Hard Determinism (HD)

The debate about HD goes back to Epicurus' view that although observation and science point to Determinism (D), personal and moral experience point to free will. Hard Determinism assumes 'universal causation', and assumes that free will is simply an illusion caused by brain processes.

Hard Determinism is supported by Reductionism, since (for example) Reductionism reduces our thoughts to caused electrical impulses in the brain.

The powerful 'feeling' that we are free is merely an illusion caused by our ignorance of the totality of causes operating on us (Spinoza).

2 HD(1): Scientific Determinism (SD)

As far as we can tell, all the physical processes in the universe operate in a sequence of causes from the Big Bang, approximately 13.77 billion years ago.

The causal sequence, which operates from present to past as well as from past to present, suggests that all physical events are determined by prior causes. The mind can be examined by the physical sciences, so is also determined, and has no free will, and no freedom of moral choice.

An omniscient 'Intelligence' (Laplace's Demon) could compute all these forces and so prove the point.

Can we avoid SD?

- Yes, if the laws of nature are probabilistic, or if it turns out that the quantum world is indeterminate (as in the 'Copenhagen Interpretation').

- Yes, if indeterminacy is located in quantum states of the mind.

- The best answer is that we simply do not know.

3 HD(2): Psychological Determinism (PD)

This is mainly associated with B.F. Skinner's Psychological Behaviourism, according to which all behaviour is the result of genetic and environmental conditions, and all human actions are conditioned by the good or bad consequences of previous decisions. We seek to avoid behaviour with bad consequences and to repeat that which has good consequences. There are no inner psychological states such as intentions and purposes; there is no free will; Determinism is complete.

Evaluating Skinner's PD

Noam Chomsky suggested that Skinner's application of laboratory experiments to complex human behaviour is superficial, amounting to 'futile speculation'.

Further, if human behaviour is nothing but a set of conditioned responses, then Skinner's radical behaviourism must itself be a conditioned response, so why should we bother to listen to it?

4   HD(3): Theological Determinism (TD)

TD is rooted in the Christian idea of God's omniscience. It leads to ideas about predestination, although as an idea, predestination seems to point to an immoral God.

The real problem with TD is that God's foreknowledge would appear to be causal, because if God knows what 'x' will do at any point in time, then 'x' cannot avoid doing it; hence Determinism must be true, and free will must be an illusion.

Possible responses include: 1) Aquinas' view that God sees the results of our future free choices, but sees them timelessly, so does not cause them; 2) If God is in time, then temporal God does not know the future, so free will is preserved. This is the conclusion of Process theologians, for example. TD seems to be false, but the issue is very complex.

TD is clearly of no interest to those who reject belief in any form of deity.

General conclusions concerning HD

We do not know whether HD is true or false, although it does have some evidential basis. Benjamin Libet's experiments in the 1980s were taken to show that the human will is determined, but Libet himself argued that the brain can veto pre-conscious intentions, so the will is not determined (a conclusion supported by recent studies of Libet's experiments).

Perhaps the strongest evidence for HD is the determination of those who have already made their minds up (one way or another). In reality there is not enough evidence to decide.

5   Libertarianism (L)

- L is the view that all forms of Determinism are false, and that we are free moral agents.

- Most libertarians are mind–body dualists, following Descartes' view that the mind is a separate substance, able to act freely in the physical world by interacting with the brain.

- Some libertarians argue (without evidence) that there are two distinct types of events: those that are caused, and those that are free, so human moral freedom is non-causal.

- Moderate libertarians would not deny that the external world is deterministic/would accept that deterministic processes affect human beings/would accept the influences of heredity, social situation and environment/would accept that such influences incline us to act in certain ways rather than others. *Complete* freedom would leave us unable to act. Nevertheless a libertarian insists that human behaviour is not *determined* by external causes, so even a kleptomaniac left alone in a shop might *or might not* steal.

- The common argument for L is the argument from 'folk psychology' that we experience ourselves as free, and also that we have a sense of moral responsibility (including guilt if we get it wrong). Determinists see this as an illusion caused by brain complexity, but libertarians see brain complexity as supporting real freedom.

- L is forward looking by comparison with D, because whereas D looks back at unavoidable past causes, libertarians look to accomplish moral and other goals, and can deliberate rationally about their decisions, putting aside wishes and desires if that is what is required. The L emphasis is not on the cause of her actions but on the reasons for action, particularly future action.

Evaluating L

- The assumptions of L are no more provable than those of HD.

- Determinists argue that there is evidence for HD but not for L, but libertarians reply that D affects physical systems but not the mind.

- The common L argument from our 'feeling' of freedom is dismissed by HD as being blissful ignorance of the totality of causes operating on us.

- A strong L argument is that given against Skinner: that those who insist that we are determined are merely making a determined statement, so why should we listen to it?

- An equally powerful L argument is its positive approach to decision-making, especially moral decision-making, because libertarians feel that they are deliberating rationally about achievable moral goals, as opposed to following a predetermined and unalterable path directed by events determined in the past.

6 Compatibilism [C]

Whereas incompatibilists hold that D and L are fundamentally opposed to each other, compatibilists hold that human freedom and responsibility are compatible with D.

The 'classic' account of C is that of Hume:

- Free will and D are held to be incompatible because philosophers have not defined their terms properly.

- What we have thought of as *necessity* in cause and effect is in fact **'constant conjunction'**.

- By *liberty*, we mean: **'a power of acting or not acting, according to the determination of the will'** – so if we choose to move, we may; and if we choose to stay at rest, we also may.'

- We find the same kind of regularity and conjunction in human affairs, so much so that if people act out of character, we assume that they are ill or peevish.

- In the natural world we infer that one thing follows from another by necessity (by which, of course, we mean 'constant conjunction'). Human affairs have the same kind of necessity. In fact they must do, or human life would be unlivable: all human affairs are interlinked. As a simple example, when someone carries his goods to market he expects (from constantly seeing it happen) that someone will buy them, so that he can use the money to support his family.

- So physical events and human actions and desires form one linked chain.

- **Freedom requires D**, because if our wishes and desires were simply random, the order of human life would be lost. Our desires flow from our personality that is genuinely our own; and our personality or character is the sum total of the causal conditions that have created us.

- Freedom is the expression of this character, to act according to one's desires.

- Non-freedom for the compatibilist is not being able to do what she desires because she is forced to do something else by physical restraint or coercive threats.

Evaluating Hume's C

- If we allow that Hume's definitions of liberty and necessity are right, then he seems to be right in his understanding of freedom.

- For twenty-first century hard determinists, Hume's idea of necessity and causation as 'constant conjunction' is too watered-down. For the scientist/hard determinist, Hume's 'wishes and desires' are the product of absolute causal forces, so cannot in any way be free. If hard D is true, then C must be false.

- For libertarians, Hume's C ignores the very power of reason by which Hume arrives at C. For the libertarian, reason allows us to make real moral choices by which our lives become meaningful; whereas for Hume, reason seems to be indistinguishable from the forces of nature. Everything is watered down to 'constant conjunction'.

Synthesis

Decisions do not have to be made between D, L and C, because until new evidence comes to light, we have insufficient information to decide.

The relevance of moral responsibility to reward and punishment

Approaches to crime and socially deviant behaviour fall under two general categories (X and Y for ease of reference):

X Crime is a mental condition that can be treated. The individual might have been brought up under conditions of domestic violence, sexual abuse, general ignorance and lack of education, in which case treatment should be therapeutic, with the focus on the reward of reform and rehabilitation rather than on pointless punishment.

Y Crime is deliberately anti-social behaviour and should be punished. The aims can include: retribution/deterrence/to enforce responsibility. Reform is costly and for most criminals is ineffective; it ignores the rights and claims of victims, and of society, which should be protected from criminals.

1 Hard Determinism

- D denies freedom of the kind needed for moral responsibility, so the **Y** approach is inappropriate.

- D makes the whole Christian idea of sin redundant. The idea of after-death rewards and punishments in heaven/hell is equally incoherent.

- As an example of D, Skinner's Psychological Behaviourism led him to argue for a version of Y in which social conditioning will eventually make a system of punishment and rewards obsolete, because crime will become obsolete. The real blame for social deviance lies with the environment. Under a perfectly conditioned social system, no one needs 'goodness'.

Skinner's ideas lack coherence, since if D is assumed, then 'deliberate' social engineering is a contradiction in terms: what happens in society will happen with complete indifference to the opinions of Skinner or anybody else. If Skinner really does believe that punishment and reward can be made obsolete, then he appears to assume that people do have the 'freedom to do otherwise', which is a libertarian viewpoint.

2 Libertarianism

- L holds people responsible for their actions, so praise and blame, regard and punishment, are part of the L strategy for leading people to be morally responsible.

- L accepts that children, depressives and others have varying degrees of diminished responsibility. For everybody else, those who commit crimes are assumed by the law to have been free to do otherwise, and so are guilty and deserve punishment.

- Kant's dictum of 'ought implies can' (backed up by feelings of remorse and guilt) is a strong indication that we do have this kind of freedom.

- Kant offers a libertarian account of punishment as retribution, in line with Y. Crime returns us to a state of nature, because the criminal wants to universalise maxims that allow them to rob or murder. In response to this, society must reverse the maxim on the criminal so that the thief's property should be removed and the murderer should be killed. The proper aim of punishment must therefore be retribution, because retribution alone (unlike deterrence or rehabilitation) allows the criminal to become a rational person who is responsible for her actions.

- L obviously fails if D is true. D insists that there is no 'niche' in the causal world for free will to operate.

3 Compatibilism

- For C, an action is free if it is caused by wishes or desires that are uncompelled. If I perform such an act, then I am free.

- In response to the key question, 'Could I have done otherwise?', a determinist must answer, 'No'; a libertarian must answer, 'Yes'; a compatibilist must answer, 'Yes, if I had *desired* to do otherwise.'

Compatibilists assume that they are morally responsible because:

- Their moral choices are not the results of physical restraints or coercive threats.

- They wanted/desired to act as they did despite being aware of alternative actions.

For Hume, it makes no sense to punish people for acts done through ignorance or coercion: their acts in such cases are wrong but the person is not morally responsible. People are blameworthy only when their choices come from their character. People's actions are judged only in so far as 'they are indications of the internal character, passions, and affections'.

For Hume, most actions that we approve of (for example, sympathy, empathy) increase public utility (they are beneficial). The aim of punishment and reward must also be to increase utility. Punishment must therefore be along the lines of social engineering through which: 1) fear of punishment helps to repress anti-social behaviour; 2) rewards stimulate a virtuous character.

We need to have sense of realism in our approach to reward and punishment. For this reason (in *On the Immortality of the Soul*) Hume rejects Christian ideas about eternal punishment in hell and eternal reward in heaven as being out of all proportion to both our human nature, which for most of us exists somewhere 'between vice and virtue', and our natural sense of justice.

There are at least two major issues with C accounts of moral responsibility/reward and punishment:

- They ignore the notion of 'just deserts': the feeling of the ordinary person that the punishment should fit the crime. The criminal justice system fails the victim by focusing on the (usually ineffective) attempt to rehabilitate the criminal.

- Hume's view that a will is 'free' if it has the liberty to follow its desires and wishes makes sense neither to determinists nor to libertarians. For D, the will is as much determined as anything else; and for L, the will is free, so for both D and L, C ideas about moral responsibility, punishment and rewards are like the rest of the theory, a 'miserable subterfuge' (Kant). Even Hume admits that D might be true.

6

Conscience

You will need to consider the following items for this section

1 Differing ideas, religious and non-religious, about the nature of the conscience.

2 The role of conscience in making moral decisions with reference to:
   ● telling lies and breaking promises
   ● adultery.

3 The value of conscience as a moral guide.

Introduction

Two health warnings!

1 Avoid the common mistake of writing 'conscious' (which hopefully you are when you read this) for 'conscience' (which you can have whether conscious or not).

2 Just to remind you, you cannot be asked to explain or examine the work of *particular* named scholars on the conscience, since none are given in the specification. The scholars named here have been selected as a representative cross-section to give you the feel of the general discussion about conscience.

A clear conscience is the sure sign of a bad memory. (Mark Twain)

You are likely to have experienced conscience, but it is a strange phenomenon. It is the inner conviction that something is right or wrong, and it is found in both secular and religious ethical discussions. It is not the result of a logical argument; you do not get persuaded that you should have a troubled conscience. In some ways it is more like an emotion and it is linked with ideas of guilt and shame.

Most often it takes the form of having a 'bad conscience' about something that you have done, implying that, in some way, you know that you did not do the right thing – even if, at the time, it was what you most wanted, or what everyone else was doing, or what you were able to justify (to yourself or others) rationally. A bad conscience produces a sense of guilt or shame, even if others try to tell you that you have no reason to feel guilty.

It is also used when thinking about, or advising others on, what should be done in the future. When there seems to be no clear moral guide about what to do, you might advise a person to follow her conscience. By that, you do not mean that she should think about all the moral arguments for or against, nor start looking up what is taught in scripture or what the law has to say. You mean something much more intuitive, personal and internal: that she should follow her own sense of what is right – even if other people argue against what she does, or shun her, or say that she is guilty.

So conscience is personal, internal, intuitive, and goes deeper than the moral principles established through ethical arguments or social conventions. But that, in itself, does not explain what conscience is and how it develops. What we do know, however, is that the brain is remarkably plastic, and that it adapts to habitual ways of thinking and acting. Every decision etches itself onto our neural pathways and suggests what our next decision should be; we train ourselves. Hence we may suggest that some people have an 'over-developed conscience', if they tend to feel badly about even the slightest thing that they may have done wrong. Equally, we may suggest that someone 'has no conscience' if she goes against what most people would feel to be the right thing, and with no apparent remorse.

It is normal to have moments when conscience troubles us. As Shakespeare said:

'Thus conscience does make cowards of us all.' [Note 1]

There are moments when we do what we think to be right, but feel emotionally troubled by it, perhaps because someone is going to feel hurt or let down, and we have a strong aversion to causing them pain. At other times our emotions tell us to do something that our rational self knows to be foolish. We may even have what we might think of as an 'old fashioned' conscience about some things – perhaps through what our parents have taught us – but feel embarrassed because it does not fit with the views of our friends, or with what we see as our lifestyle. In all these situations we can feel torn one way or another. And that is exactly why moral issues present problems, for if there was always one and only one morally correct answer to every situation, there would be no moral dilemmas.

Our word 'conscience' comes from the Latin **conscientia** and, until the seventeenth century, it encompassed broader ideas of what we now think of as *consciousness* and *self-consciousness*. In other words, it is about the fundamental awareness we have of ourselves as thinking, feeling individuals. From the seventeenth century onwards, through the Enlightenment era, there was an increased emphasis on individual moral and social responsibility. During this period, a narrower view of conscience emerged, which went hand-in-hand with an emphasis on each

Key term

Conscientia In Aquinas' system, conscientia (conscience) applies the first principles of *synderesis* to particular situations. It is the experience of realising that what the individual is about to do (or has already done) is good or evil, right or wrong.

individual as being morally independent. It was no longer just a matter of 'obey or be punished', but of a more democratic sense that each individual should play his or her part in deciding what is right and acting upon it. In particular, as we shall see, the rise of Protestantism tended to encourage personal reflection on moral issues, rather than simply making confession to a priest and accepting forgiveness and penance. This gave added significance to conscience, which had been a feature of Christian thought since the time of St Paul's letter to the Romans.

In examining the ethical significance of conscience, we shall therefore need to separate out four things:

1   Secular understandings of the nature of conscience, including its natural development.

2   Some distinctively religious understandings of conscience.

3   We can then look at the way in which conscience can be used in making moral decisions.

4   Finally, we shall need to assess the place of the conscience as a moral guide.

In considering these questions, we shall also need to examine the basic question about whether it is always right to follow the conscience, or whether the conscience may itself be wrong; and, if it is, how could we ever be convinced of that? We may also want to consider which comes first: a person's conscience or her set of moral principles. If we examine why we have a bad conscience about something, we may then come to frame principles by which – guided by our conscience – we think it right to live. But if we had no principles in the first place, how could we have a conscience?

Another important question concerns whether conscience is always a personal and individual matter, or whether it is shared within society or within the membership of a religion. If conscience rules supreme, but everyone has his or her own conscience, formed and shaped in an individual way, then that would suggest that we cannot frame general moral principles, since everyone's conscience would be free to overrule those principles whenever it seemed appropriate.

Differing ideas, religious and non-religious, about the nature of the conscience

We begin by looking at the secular/non-religious view of conscience – social and psychological.

Conscience as a behaviour developed through social interaction

Lawrence Kohlberg (1927–87)

Kohlberg was an American psychologist, whose work on child development followed from his fascination with children's ways of reasoning in their reactions to moral dilemmas.

Lawrence Kohlberg defined six stages of moral development from birth in three levels (pre-conventional, conventional, and post-conventional). In brief:

- The pre-conventional level begins with the 'punishment and obedience' stage, at which our understanding of right and wrong is that right is what we are rewarded for and wrong is what we are punished for.
- The conventional level begins with the development of good inter-personal relationships, and concludes with the decision to obey society's rules and thus avoid guilt. Many never get past this stage.
- The post-conventional level begins with a (utilitarian) recognition that where the needs of individuals and of society conflict, individual needs must give way in order to benefit society as a whole. **The final stage is the level of an individualised conscience**. The conscience directs that moral choices must be consistent and universalisable (applicable to everybody). **To go against the conscience leads to feelings of guilt**, so it will be followed even if it leads to imprisonment. Comparatively few reach this level.

Kohlberg reached and tested his conclusions by the **use of moral dilemmas**, because his method was to test the moral reasoning by which individuals reached their decisions in these dilemmas. In a typical Kohlberg dilemma, the needs of two individuals are in conflict with each other, so that either by acting or not acting, there will be a negative outcome for one of the parties in the dilemma. In solving the conflict, the individual (given little additional information) is forced to imagine the consequences of different courses of action, and Kohlberg used the data he accumulated by these tests to locate each participant in one of the levels of reasoning described above.

Probably the best known of Kohlberg's dilemmas is that of Heinz.

The dilemma of Heinz

In Europe, a woman was near death from a special kind of cancer. There was one drug that the doctors thought might save her. It was a form of radium that a druggist in the same town had recently discovered. The drug was expensive to make, but the druggist was charging ten times what the drug cost him to make. He paid $200 for the radium and charged $2,000 for a small dose of the drug. The sick woman's husband, Heinz, went to everyone he knew to borrow the money, but he could only get together $1,000, which is half of what it cost. He told the druggist that his wife was dying and asked him to sell it cheaper or let him pay later. But the druggist said, 'No, I discovered the drug, and I am going to make money from it.' So Heinz got desperate and broke into the man's store to steal the drug for his wife. [Note 2]

Somebody on stage 1 of Kohlberg's pre-conventional level might answer that Heinz should not steal the drug because stealing is wrong and he would get put in prison. On stage 5, at the post-conventional level, Heinz might take a right-to-life argument that everybody has an equal right to treatment, so Heinz should steal the drug. On stage 6, where people develop their own universal ethical principles, the individual might reason (on Kantian lines) that theft is always wrong, and so refrain from stealing the drug, with the inevitable result that the wife of Heinz would die.

In such processes of moral reasoning and decision, then, worked out in social contexts (such as that of Heinz), we can see the conscience developing and deciding.

Reactions to Kohlberg's view of conscience vary

One often-heard comment is that it is not clear that moral reasoning guides the conscience so much as 'gut-reaction' or intuition. In this comment we can see the influence of **Hume**, whose general view of ethics was that 'reason should be a slave of the passions', and not the other way round. In other words, you decide what the right thing to do is through your intuition about right behaviour, and only subsequently do you justify that rationally, or sort out how best to put your intuition into effect.

Conscience as an aspect of the *super-ego*

Sigmund Freud (1856–1939)

Freud was an Austrian neurologist, and the founder of psychoanalysis, through which he believed people could be cured of various mental ailments. Freud suggested that a person's development is determined by childhood events which may have been forgotten or repressed. Where the conscious mind is in conflict with the unconscious mind, trauma, or neurosis (mental sickness) can result. Psychoanalytic techniques can bring such events to the surface, but often at the cost of resistance by the individual concerned, who may have repressed memories of these events as a self-defence mechanism. Reactions to Freud's theories still vary widely. Karl Popper dismissed psychoanalysis as non-falsifiable pseudo-science, and the physicist Richard Feynman labelled both psychiatrists and psychoanalysts as 'witch-doctors'.

Freud produced the best-known (and certainly the most colourful) account of the **conscience as a psychological phenomenon**. It derives from his account of the mind, including that part of it termed the 'unconscious'.

He distinguished between three elements in the mind: the *id*, the *ego* and the *super-ego*.

- The *id* is the unconscious and instinctive part of the personality at the level of its basic physical and emotional needs, and includes (for example) *eros* – the instinct for love, sexuality and satisfaction; and *thanatos* – the drive for aggression, violence and death.

Key terms

Super-ego In Freud's thought, that part of the (unconscious) mind which controls the instincts that can damage society (*eros* and *thanatos*); it is the repository of parental commands delivered from infancy, together with the commands of other authority figures; it manifests through feelings of guilt, remorse and anxiety.

Eros In Freud's analysis of the mind, eros is the life instinct/the instinct for sexual gratification.

Thanatos In Freud's analysis of the mind, the instinct for aggression, violence and death.

- The *ego* is the rational self. It mediates between the desires of the *id* and what the world lets us have.
- The **super-ego** (literally 'above I') is the controlling, restraining self. It develops (according to Freud) around the age of 3–5, and it controls those impulses that can be damaging to society such as the *eros* and *thanatos* instincts.

The *super-ego* also has an important role in developing a person's morality. In particular, it acts as an 'inner parent', in the sense that it can literally be the place where your parents' moral commands delivered from infancy are stored, together with the commands of other authority figures.

On this account, then, **conscience is an aspect of the operation of the super-ego**. The rules and regulations given to us by authority figures, particularly one's parents, are internalised so that we cannot escape them. **To try to do so brings about guilt**. In this way, conscience is the repository of our parents' commands to us during childhood.

The following passage illustrates Freud's thinking here. The section in bold type is for emphasis, and is not emboldened in the original:

> Freud ... stresses that the superego is the internalization of external parental authority. Once internalised, this new psychical agency continues to carry on the functions which have hitherto been performed by the people ... in the external world: it observes the ego, gives it orders, judges it, and threatens it with punishments, exactly like the parents whose place it has taken. Thus, according to Freud, the superego functions in various ways. **Only in its judging and threatening actions is the superego identified as conscience.** So conscience appears to be a functional part of the superego: the part that judges and threatens with punishment. [Note 3]

This is why the workings of the conscience manifest themselves through feelings of **guilt**: an active conscience tends to be a guilty conscience. According to Freud, the conscience can function at both the conscious and the unconscious level. At the unconscious level, it manifests itself by feelings of shame, guilt, anxiety and remorse.

Examining Freud's views

Freud's idea of a conscience which functions at both a conscious and unconscious level has interesting implications for the role of the conscience in ethical discussions. If conscience is simply an expression of our unconscious application of rules that we have been given in our early childhood, **then it certainly does not provide some alternative source of moral authority**, since it is no more than an expression of the wishes of one's parents or other significant adults.

Also, it cannot be seen as the voice of God, or as an expression of a natural self, because – however we experience it now – it is nothing more than a left-over expression of our childhood training. Logically, therefore, we would be expected to grow out of conscience as we get a more balanced and mature view of ourselves, and as our rational *ego* asserts itself. But for Freud the *super-ego* remains as an unconscious force shaping our adult lives. If God does figure in the conscience, it is only (Freud argues) as another control mechanism – another authority figure alongside parents, other influential adults, and society's expectations of us – it does not matter whether or not God exists factually – the idea of God, for those who believe in God, is likely to give the biggest guilt-trip of all to those who break God's rules, particularly in those who have been brought up in a religious faith since childhood.

Whereas some might see conscience as giving the freedom, based on intuitions of right and wrong, to go against the rules of society, the problem with Freud's view is that it presents conscience not as an expression of personal or emotional wish to do what is right, but simply as conformity to parental expectations, whether or not one's parents are still around to keep an eye on us. Their view is internalised and experienced as conscience.

These observations do not mean that Freud was wrong about the conscience: only that his view of it reduces its value. **Is this really all that conscience amounts to?**

Conscience as sanctions or social conditioning

Émile Durkheim (1858–1917)

David Émile Durkheim was a French sociologist and social psychologist. He was one of the main figures in the development of social science.

Durkheim's view of the conscience is interesting in that he brings together both God and the conscience into a social explanation of human behaviour.

Durkheim argued that **conscience is social conditioning – the sanctions that the group brings to bear on the individual**. For Durkheim, God is Society, God does not exist but is a useful idea. God is a projection of society's powers, and a belief in God gives individuals a moral obligation to obey society's demands. When projected onto an omnipotent God, society's demands become unconditional, because to disobey them is to disobey the will of God.

Conscience is, therefore, a perception of loyalty to the group. So, for example, having a guilty conscience about the food you eat is your fear of society judging you for being too fat or too thin.

To say that someone has no conscience is simply to say that they are socially maladjusted.

Durkheim also put forward the idea of a collective conscience (or collective consciousness), which is the totality of beliefs and sentiments common to the average citizens in the same society. In other words, conscience is organic to the social group as a whole. Within this context, an act is socially bad simply because society disapproves of it: it is not that an action conflicts with the common conscience because it is criminal, but rather that it is criminal because it conflicts with the common conscience.

Durkheim's view is reinforced by an *evolutionary* perspective on the conscience, according to which conscience is a mechanism whereby the group grows stronger. Conscience is a survival mechanism developed through people adhering to shared moral values.

Evaluating this, it has to be said that a combined social, evolutionary and psychological explanation of the conscience has good explanatory power. Groups improve their survivability by individuals having a conscience that compels them to maintain group loyalty. On the other hand, what do we say about great moral teachers such as the Old Testament prophets and Jesus of Nazareth, who stood *outside* their 'group' to criticise it?

The authoritarian and the humanistic conscience

Erich Fromm (1900–80)

Fromm was a psychoanalyst, philosopher, Marxist, and much more besides. He abandoned religion (having been a rabbi) to become an atheist, believing that religion was the source of most (or all) of the disharmony and strife on the planet. Having escaped the Nazi threat by moving to America, he analysed the writings of Freud and judged them to contain fundamental inconsistency. He then denounced Freud as a misogynist (strongly prejudiced against women) who could not get beyond the patriarchal 'mould' of his time. Nevertheless, Fromm believed that Freud, like Einstein and Marx, was a prophet of the modern era. Life within the radius of Fromm could never have been boring.

Key terms

Authoritarian conscience In Fromm's view, the aspect of conscience which represents the internalised voice of a disapproving society which we are afraid to disobey.

Humanistic conscience In Fromm's view, the aspect of the conscience that has an intuitive knowledge of what is human and inhuman: of what makes life flourish and what destroys it. A common response of the humanistic conscience is disobedience, where that brings about flourishing.

According to Fromm, guilt, shame, conscience and a sense of moral responsibility may arise out of fear of being rejected by society, simply because society is based on obedience to rules and conformity to norms. In *On Disobedience and Other Essays*, Fromm pointed out that in most social systems, the supreme virtue is obedience, whereas the supreme sin is disobedience. For most people, when they feel guilty, they feel afraid because they think they have been disobedient. They are not really troubled by a moral issue (although they think they are) – rather they are troubled because they have disobeyed a command. They have an **authoritarian conscience**.

In other words, our conscience arises out of fear of being shunned and excluded from society because we have been disobedient. It would not be so much the inner voice of our own deepest nature or convictions, but the internalised voice of a disapproving society. You can see the influence of Freud's account of the conscience here. There are times, however, when obedience to the authoritative conscience needs to be over ridden.

Fromm also distinguishes between an authoritarian conscience and a more positive '**humanistic conscience**'. The humanistic conscience has an intuitive knowledge of what is human and inhuman: of what makes life flourish and what destroys it. One such destructive force was the Nazi regime in Germany, from which Fromm was forced to flee, first to Geneva and then to the USA. The end of the war saw the advent of an even more destructive force, namely nuclear weapons, and for Fromm, the humanistic conscience knows instinctively that both Nazism and nuclear weapons require civil disobedience in order to resist them, hence Fromm supported unilateral nuclear disarmament.

Key term

Innate (conscience) Inborn conscience – originating in the mind.

Fromm appears to suggest that even if we do have an **innate** sense of right and wrong, experienced as conscience, the actual forms that our pangs of conscience take are shaped by our society:

> The difference between humanistic and authoritarian conscience is not that the latter is molded by the cultural tradition, while the former is not. On the contrary, it is similar in this respect to our capacities for speech and thought, which, though intrinsic human potentialities, develop only in a social and cultural context. The human race, in the last five or six thousand years of its cultural development, has formulated ethical norms in its religious and philosophical systems toward which the conscience of every individual must be orientated. (*Man for Himself,* 1947.) [Note 4]

In other words, our existing religious, philosophical and social systems have given us an intuitive knowledge of the difference between the two forms of conscience. To reject the authoritarian form and embrace the humanistic form is to free ourselves from the fear of unjust and violent authority and to realise instead our full potential as people.

The Religious conscience – biblical and theological

Conscience as the innate voice of God

For Augustine (354–430) and others, the conscience is innate: put into human minds by God, so it amounts to an innate knowledge of God's moral laws. This follows closely St Paul's arguments in Romans 2:15 where he describes it as:

> 'a witness to the requirements of the law'.

Augustine goes beyond Paul, however, and appears to have seen conscience literally as the voice of God. For example, in his work *On the Sermon on the Mount*, Book 2, Chapter 9, verse 32, he says:

> 'For when will they be able to understand that there is no soul, however wicked ...in whose conscience God does not speak?'

This understanding of conscience is also seen in the writings of the Protestant theologian, Friedrich Schleiermacher.

Friedrich Schleiermacher (1768–1834)

Schleiermacher was a Prussian/German theologian and philosopher, and is seen as an early leader of liberal Christianity. Schleiermacher wanted to re-instate the significance of the academic study of religion, following the rationalist critiques of the Enlightenment period. See particularly his book *On Religion: Speeches to its Cultured Despisers* (1799). Despite his achievements as a theologian, he was more widely known as a brilliant and charismatic preacher. When he died, twelve of his students carried his coffin for over a mile through the streets of Berlin.

> We use the term 'conscience' to express the fact that all modes of activity issuing from our God-consciousness and subject to its prompting confront us as moral demands, not indeed theoretically, but asserting themselves in our self-consciousness in such a way that any deviation of our conduct from them is apprehended as a hindrance to life, and therefore as sin. … [C]onscience also is very markedly traced to divine causality, and, as the voice of God within, is held to be an original revelation of God; it is one of those inward experiences which we may assume to be universal in this sphere. [Note 5]

Here conscience is a source of direct revelation from God, and to go against it is sin – not because it is subsequently shown to go against established moral principles, but because to do so would be a hindrance to a Christian way of life. Conscience, for Schleiermacher, has become part of what God *does*, guiding people from within. As a direct revelation, it takes priority over all else.

The view that the conscience is the voice of God speaking to the individual causes several problems:

- The amount of evil in the world seems to suggest either that God is selective in choosing who to talk to, or else a lot of people are remarkably good at ignoring the voice of God.
- You will remember that in our discussion of Divine Command Theory in Chapter 4 Introduction to meta-ethics: the meaning of right and wrong, the big problem with that theory is that it seems to make ethical discussion and decision-making redundant.
- Following on from that, most people today would accept that being morally good requires us to make free moral decisions. Decisions that are made for us cannot be free. If conscience is the voice of God speaking to us, we cannot, therefore, be morally free.
- Throughout the history of the Christian Church, Christians have disagreed about moral principles, and all parties in these disagreements have appealed to the God-given conscience. How is it, then, that they have been given different answers?

Conscience as the God-given faculty of reason

This view is held by Thomas Aquinas (1225–74) and expressed through his teaching on Natural Moral Law. It is highly influential within Christianity.

- Aquinas begins with what he calls **the *synderesis* rule**: that **all human beings seek to do good and avoid evil**; they have a natural orientation towards the good. So: 'Good should be done and pursued and evil should be avoided' is a principle that must govern all human reasoning.

> [S]ynderesis is in the rational part of a human agent. It is a natural disposition of the human mind by which we apprehend without inquiry the basic principles of behaviour … Once the basic principles are apprehended and become part of synderesis, conscience [*conscientia*], also in the rational part, applies these first principles to particular situations. [Douglas Langston commenting on Aquinas] [Note 6]

Discussion point

In view of problems such as these, do you think that there is still a place, in modern ethical discussion, for the idea that conscience is the voice of God speaking to us?

Key term

Synderesis In Aquinas' system, synderesis is in the rational part of human agents – a natural disposition of the human mind by which we apprehend without inquiry the basic principles of behaviour. The synderesis rule is that 'good is to be done and evil is to be avoided'.

- Aquinas argues that **what is innate for humans is not the voice of God telling them what to do but the God-given faculty of reason.** Practical reason, reflecting on human nature, arrives at and understands the primary precepts of Natural Moral Law. Conscience then applies these through secondary precepts to particular situations and becomes 'activated' fully by realising that what the individual is about to do (or has already done) is good or evil, right or wrong.

- **The conscience is fallible – it can be mistaken.** There are two reasons why it may make a wrong decision. First, if it is ignorant of the moral law that should be applied to the situation, then Aquinas argues that the person is guilty of sin in this case, because they should have known the law. Second, it can go wrong if it is not informed about the facts of the case. For example, if someone sees a pile of newspapers and assumes that they are free, the conscience will allow her to take one. If, however, those papers were for sale and therefore not actually free, then the conscience has allowed her to steal them, and the conscience has made a mistake. In this second case, Aquinas would argue that the person is not responsible for such a mistake, so the 'theft' is not a sin.

- **The conscience should always be followed.** This seems rather an odd conclusion, given what we have said above. However, where one does an act that is really in accordance with one's conscience, even if the conscience is in error and the act leads to terrible misdeeds, *what the conscience dictates is true to the individual concerned, and truth must be followed.* Truth comes from God, so to go against what you think your conscience is telling you to do is to go against God.

Evaluation of Aquinas' understanding of conscience

Aquinas is realistic in his view that conscience is not infallible – it can go astray by following apparent goods rather than real goods. His emphasis on the use of reason is also a good one, since reason allows us to make a freely chosen moral decision, which to many is the essence of being a moral being.

On the other hand, Aquinas seems to ignore the fact that large numbers of people act irrationally, not just because they are blinded by their own desires, but also because their reasoning powers are limited. Equally, Aquinas thinks that we are all aware of the synderesis rule that 'good is to be done and evil is to be avoided', but if we look at the state of the world today, we might be tempted to say that many people follow the rule of self-interest.

Conscience as a God-given faculty – intuitive, reflective and autonomous

Joseph Butler (1692–1752)

Butler was an English theologian and philosopher, and was also a Bishop in the Church of England. He is seen as a 'defender of the faith', particularly in his arguments against deism. He wanted to show that morality and religion are an indispensable part of life.

For Joseph Butler, conscience is in human nature: it is a *reflective principle placed within us by God* as a natural guide and 'proper governor', so it is our duty to follow it. By a 'reflective principle', Butler means that we are able to reflect morally on what we have done in the past and what we are about to do in the future. All humans, therefore, have a reflective sense of right and wrong.

> [T]here is a principle of reflection in men, by which they distinguish between, approve and disapprove their own actions. We are plainly constituted such sort of creatures as to reflect upon our own nature. The mind can take a view of what passes within itself, its propensions, aversions, passions, affections as respecting such objects, and in such degrees; and of the several actions consequent thereupon. In this survey it approves of one, disapproves of another, and towards a third is affected in neither of these ways, but is quite indifferent. This principle in man, by which he approves or disapproves his heart, temper, and actions, is conscience … And that this faculty tends to restrain men from doing mischief to each other, and leads them to do good, is too manifest to need being insisted upon. [Note 7]

Butler's analysis of the conscience is based on the two governing principles of human behaviour – prudence and benevolence. By prudence, Butler means our natural love of self (egoism); and by benevolence, he means our natural love of others (altruism). Prudence is as necessary to the balanced self as benevolence. It is unrealistic to believe that people will behave benevolently all the time, without considering their own desires and needs. Love of self is absolutely necessary for people to be able to love others, and is not the same as selfishness. What is required in order for individuals to function morally and effectively is a *balance* between prudence and benevolence. What is required for society as a whole to function morally is the same balance.

Conscience is that part of the hierarchy of the self which judges between prudence and benevolence. In other words, conscience is a natural faculty we have for getting the conflicting elements of our lives in order.

As a judge, the conscience works intuitively. We know intuitively when we are planning or have made the decision, because we can feel the balance between self-love and love of others. Conscience is also an **autonomous** judge: there is no sense of approval or disapproval, reward or punishment for acting morally: the conscience is motivated solely by its internal criteria of what is right and what is wrong. It is a natural ability given to human beings, not the voice of God.

Key term

Autonomous Self-directing, independent, self-governing (as, for example, in Butler's view of the conscience).

> It is by this faculty [of conscience], natural to man, that he is a moral agent, that he is a law to himself, but this faculty, I say, not to be considered merely as a principle in his heart, which is to have some influence as well as others, but considered as a faculty in kind and in nature supreme over all others, and which bears its own authority of being so. [Note 8]

Butler argues that since this is a God-given faculty, it must be followed, because:

> '... it therefore belongs to our condition of being; it is our duty to walk in that path, and follow this guide' [Note 9]

Conscience *can* be put to sleep, but only by avoiding reflection through self-deceit. (Sermon VII).

Evaluation of Butler's understanding of conscience

When a person acts in a morally appropriate way, according to Butler's theory, it means that the conscience sorts out the balance between self-love and benevolence towards others, and controls the appetites and affections accordingly. In particular, he considered that the conscience is able to overcome an instinctive concern for the self, and enable people to consider the welfare of others. One driving force behind such concern is the instinctive compassion we have for those in trouble, and Butler devotes many pages to the nature of compassion in his *Sermons*.

In effect, Butler's view is that a good person is someone who has his or her priorities correctly sorted. Moral dilemmas happen when there is a conflict between our emotions, desires, and the moral principles to which we subscribe. When we are conflicted, our conscience is troubled; therefore, following conscience is a good way of ensuring that we have got the balance right.

For Butler, conscience gave an intuitive awareness of right and wrong and of the fact that God had created human beings in such a way that their flourishing would come from obeying conscience, which God has provided for their guidance. But here there is a potential problem. Natural Law suggests that everyone should seek to fulfil his or her nature, and that will involve an element of self-love, to ensure that one's basic needs are met. But if, following Butler, that self-love is to be balanced by love of others, might that not lead us to take moral decisions that actually cause us harm, in the long run, and therefore fail to enable us to fulfil our own potential? Butler's answer is that following the conscience is going to be to our long-term benefit, so that, in the long run, conscience is not going to run counter to a natural sense of self-love, since it will serve one's own good.

What do we say about those who do the most terrible things in the name of conscience? In other words, if conscience is to trump both reason and appetite, what do we do when reason suggests that conscience – either our own or someone else's – is plainly wrong? This problem was pointed out by Elizabeth Anscombe (in 'Modern Moral Philosophy', *Philosophy*, 1958), who notes that Butler assumes that conscience, having been given by God in order to direct the self, will always be good. He does not appear to consider the possibility that it may be distorted or evil.

Both Aquinas and Butler describe conscience as a faculty, but exactly what is a 'faculty' of the conscience supposed to be, and how do we observe it in the human mind? Immanuel Kant (1724–1804), one of the greatest of philosophers, was mocked by another German philosopher, Friedrich Nietzsche (1844–1900) for inventing non-existent faculties to answer questions for which he really had no answer. Nietzsche accused Kant of 'discovering a moral faculty' in humans. Being very fond of bad puns,

Nietzsche implied that this was not so much a case of *discovering* ('finden' in German) a moral faculty as of *inventing* one ('erfinden'). [Note 10] He then painted an amusing picture of all the young theologians of Tübingen University, where Kant used to teach, hunting in the bushes looking for lost 'faculties'. You can see the point: if we have to explain conscience by claiming that it exists in some undetectable 'faculty' of the mind, is this just another word for pure invention?

Conscience as *agape*-love making decisions situationally: Joseph Fletcher (1905–91)

We met Joseph Fletcher in Volume 1, Chapter 4.2 Situation ethics. Fletcher comments that there are four theories about conscience:

1 that it is an innate (built-in) faculty

2 that it is guidance by the Holy Spirit, or by an angel or by some other entity

3 that it is the internalised values of society

4 that conscience is reason making moral judgements (Aquinas).

Fletcher rejects all of these, and offers a very distinctive understanding of conscience in their place. For him, conscience is something we DO, not something we have. He writes:

> **'There is no conscience, "conscience" is merely a word for our attempts to make decisions creatively, constructively, fittingly.'** [Note 11]

According to Fletcher, conscience is not like the Roman Catholic confessional: it is not a 'review officer' judging what you have done: it is prospective, not retrospective: it is choosing what *agape*-love demands in the present situation. It is this calculation which is the conscience in situation ethics, so the conscience is not a noun – it is not something we have – it is a verb, something we do when we are deciding and calculating how love is best served in a situation.

The last three words are key here: **'in a situation'**. Conscience is your active decision 'there and then'.

The role of conscience in making moral decisions with reference to telling lies and adultery

We start by looking at ways in which people actually do use their conscience in making moral decisions, and at the type of decisions they may be called upon to make.

The role of conscience may be:

● to decide what should be done before making any decision
● to inform the moral agents whether their actions were right or wrong, for example the conscience may cause a feeling of guilt after the event
● to demand a particular course of action.

As we have seen, some people may appear to have no conscience: no sense of having to follow, for example, the norms of their society, the laws of God or the dictates of reason. Some may never feel the need to use their conscience because all the decisions they may be faced with have been made for them in advance. For many, however, conscience does play a role in their decision-making.

The use of the conscience by those who believe it is the 'voice of God' is easily described. They will listen to that voice, perhaps in prayer, and do what it instructs. Their difficulty, as we have noted elsewhere, lies in knowing that they are genuinely hearing God's voice. Two individuals may report 'hearing' contradictory commands; both may be sincere in their belief that they come from God, but both cannot be right. In Augustine's thinking, conscience has to be supported by grace for that reason. Grace, which is also a gift from God, ensures that the conscience is correctly motivated by love of God.

In *On the Morals of the Catholic Church*, Augustine defines the cardinal virtues of prudence, justice, fortitude and temperance as differing expressions of love of God. [Note 12] The Catechism of the Catholic Church, in its account of the cardinal virtues, also quotes from Augustine:

> To live well is nothing other than to love God with all one's heart, with all one's soul and with all one's efforts; from this it comes about that love is kept whole and uncorrupted (through temperance). No misfortune can disturb it (and this is fortitude). It obeys only [God] (and this is justice), and is careful in discerning things, so as not to be surprised by deceit or trickery (and this is prudence). [Note 13]

So, for example, if two people are asked to contribute to a charity, and both contribute, but the first does so through guilt or a desire to be thought well of, whereas the second does so through the love of God, then only the second person's act is morally good. Good actions without the right intention are not morally good.

For others, the way conscience may be used, or its use understood, depends on what the conscience is considered to be. You may consider the role of conscience in moral decision-making using any of the theories of conscience we have considered in the earlier part of this chapter and/or any other theories you may have studied.

The role of conscience in making moral decisions: telling lies and breaking promises

We live in a (broadly) utilitarian society, in which telling a lie or breaking a promise, if these lead to the greatest happiness for the greatest number, can be seen as morally right. For Aquinas, these acts would be seen by the conscience for what they are – as a betrayal of reason. For those who have a sociological understanding of the conscience, telling lies and breaking promises are acts which destabilise society, so they might be described as immoral for that reason only.

Lying becomes an issue either when we are tempted to lie for our own benefit or when it seems that lying would be the right thing to do to help others. Conscience may be involved in this decision-making in various ways, as illustrated below.

Example 1: Using the reason as conscience (Aquinas)

- Conscience would inform the individual that telling lies/breaking promises is not rational, because it conflicts with the synderesis rule to seek to do good and avoid evil.
- Telling lies and breaking promises violates the primary precept of living in an ordered society, since there can hardly be an ordered society where people habitually lie to each other and break their promises. If people lied in business arrangements, no property would ever be safe. If husbands or wives broke their marriage promises, no marriage would ever be safe. The principle is therefore established in Natural Moral Law: 'tell the truth: do not lie'/'keep your promises: do not break them'. You can review what Aquinas says in Volume 1, pages 185–86.
- What about exceptional circumstances? Aquinas is well aware of these, which is why he accepts that sometimes the secondary precepts of Natural Moral Law may apply differently *in specific cases*. If you are faced with the 'mad axe-murderer' situation, where you have promised to tell the maniac the truth and not to lie about the whereabouts of his victim, Aquinas says that you could tell an evasive truth; for example, if you are asked where the victim is, you could say that you saw him at a certain place some time ago, which avoids telling the axe-murderer where the victim is now. This is the point at which, for many people, Aquinas' views become too rigid, because most would instinctively break any promise to tell the truth and would lie in order to save the victim.

Example 2: Applying a sociological view of conscience

- Telling lies and breaking promises would probably be seen as socially destructive, since the stability of society depends on keeping promises and avoiding lies. Bank notes bear the legend that the Bank of England 'promises to pay the bearer, on demand', the sum of £5, £10, or whatever the bank note proclaims. To break that promise would bring social mayhem, because all banking and financial institutions would fail overnight.
- Social understandings of this principle might follow from Fromm's idea of the authoritarian conscience: the individual might not break a promise for fear of society's disapproval. Further, the humanistic conscience would inform the individual that telling lies or breaking promises would violate the ethical norms that society needs in order for life to be fruitful.

Example 3: applying Freud's psychological understanding of conscience.

- A Freudian analysis would only begin with the arrival of feelings of guilt, anxiety and remorse surfacing from the subconscious mind of the individual who tells a lie or breaks a promise. These would be the repository of parental commands (or those of some other authority) not to lie or to break one's promises, where the influence of that authority is so great that the individual cannot escape its psychological command.
- Both telling lies and breaking promises are common in modern society, so on Freud's account this would explain why the *super-ego* remains quiet in some people; presumably their parents saw no problem with such acts and made no prohibition to their children about committing them.
- There is little or no sense here of the conscience treating lying/breaking promises as a *moral* issue.

Activity

Consider again for yourselves the mad axe-murderer situation, where you have promised to tell the maniac the truth and not to lie about the whereabouts of his victim. If you would lie and break a promise in order to save the victim's life, what view of the conscience would you appeal to in reaching that decision?

The role of conscience in making moral decisions: adultery

Several of the ethicists we have referred to in this chapter explicitly discuss adultery, for example Aquinas, Fletcher and Freud.

The use of conscience as reason

For Aquinas, reason (conscience) dictated that adultery was wrong. Remember, though, that Aquinas did NOT believe that the conscience was infallible; he thought it could make mistakes. One of the examples he gave of this was about adultery.

> For instance, if erring reason tells a man that he should go to another man's wife, the will that abides by that erring reason is evil; since this error arises from ignorance of the Divine Law, which he is bound to know. But if a man's reason, errs in mistaking another for his wife, and if he wish to give her her right when she asks for it, his will is excused from being evil: because this error arises from ignorance of a circumstance, which ignorance excuses, and causes the act to be involuntary. (*Summa Theologiae* I, II, Q.19, a.5)

Imagine, for example, a man who marries a widow and has sex with her, only to discover that her husband was still alive. His conscience cleared him to have sex with her, it saw nothing wrong in it, but was mistaken. Aquinas says that while the conscience was mistaken there was no intention to do wrong and no fault in following the conscience in that situation. You may be able to think of other examples in which a genuine lack of knowledge of the true facts of the case lead the conscience to the wrong decision but do not make it wrong for the person to follow their conscience.

The use of conscience as acting with *agape*-love

Activity

In Volume 1, you will have looked at Fletcher's example of 'sacrificial adultery'. Here is Fletcher's text:

As the Russian armies drove westward to meet the Americans and British at the Elbe, a Russian patrol picked up a Mrs Bergmeier foraging food for her three children. Unable even to get word to the children, and without any clear reason for it, she was taken off to a prison camp in the Ukraine. Her husband had been captured in the Bulge and taken to a POW camp in Wales.

When he was returned to Berlin, he spent weeks and weeks rounding up his children; two (Ilse, twelve, and Paul, ten) were found in a detention school run by the Russians, and the oldest, Hans, fifteen, was found hiding in a cellar near the Alexander Platz. Their mother's whereabouts remained a mystery, but they never stopped searching. She more than anything else was needed to reknit them as a family in that dire situation of hunger, chaos, and fear.

Meanwhile, in the Ukraine, Mrs Bergmeier learned through a sympathetic commandant that her husband and family were trying to keep together and find her. But the rules allowed them to release her for only two reasons: 1) illness needing medical facilities beyond the camp's, in which case she would be sent to a Soviet hospital elsewhere, and 2) pregnancy, in which case she would be returned to Germany as a liability.

She turned things over in her mind and finally asked a friendly Volga German camp guard to impregnate her, which he did. Her condition being medically verified, she was sent back to Berlin and to her family. They welcomed her with open arms, even when she told them how she had managed it. When the child was born, they loved him more than all the rest, on the view that little Dietrich had done more for them than anybody. [Note 14]

- Remember that for Fletcher the conscience is a verb – it is an action carried out in a specific situation, guided by *agape*-love and by reason.

- Do you think that Fletcher's example here justifies Mrs Bergmeier's adultery in this situation?

- How might Aquinas approach this situation? Do the differences of approach show that conscience can or cannot be defined accurately?

- Note that since Mrs Bergmeier's case involves adultery, **adultery is also the breaking of promises/vows** made during the marriage service.

The use of adultery: conscience as social conditioning

Sociology generally views religion as a social phenomenon, without passing judgement on the reality (or otherwise) of God. For Durkheim, you can see that he puts together a fairly convincing argument that 'God' is a mechanism (so to speak) by which society's rules are enforced. Conscience is the social conditioning – the sanctions that the group brings to bear on the individual. God is a projection of society's powers, because belief in God gives individuals a moral obligation to obey society's demands.

In Durkheim's view of the collective conscience, an act is bad simply because society disapproves of it. Adultery, seen in such a light, is merely a matter of group perception, and in nearly all western societies adultery is tolerated in a way that it never used to be. The reason for this is that the authority of God has declined as a force in the collective conscience, so religion has lost much of its authority. Marriage today is therefore seen not so much as a religious ceremony but as a social contract, and it can be broken at the will of those who contract into it. Whereas adultery used to be seen as a sin against God's laws, it is now more of a reason to terminate the marriage contract where husband and wife so desire. The only morality involved is that of keeping or breaking a contract.

You can see that this is completely different to religious views of marriage and adultery seen through the eyes of Christian scholars such as Aquinas.

The use of conscience as an aspect of the *super-ego*

In 1930, Freud published *Civilization and its Discontents*. In it, he theorised that humanity had invented civilisation in order to control its instinctive drives (*thanatos* and *eros*). To keep those ever-present drives in check, laws were made prohibiting acts such as murder, rape and adultery. This created a paradox, since having created civilisation to protect ourselves from unhappiness, this has become our greatest source of unhappiness, because it frustrates our instinctive drives for killing and for sexual gratification. [Note 15]

On this kind of analysis, then, the operation of the conscience seems to depend on nothing more than which drive is more deeply rooted in the individual's psychology: the preference for civilisation or for sexual gratification.

Since that preference in turn depends on the main influences in an individual's life, such as,

> '... racial, national and family traditions ... as well as the demands of the actual social milieu which they represent' [Note 16]

the conscience amounts to a deep-rooted *psychological compulsion* from an incalculable number of sources. This is a long way from those views of the conscience, Christian or otherwise, in which the act of adultery is seen as morally wrong in itself, either from religious reasons or from the exercise of reason.

The value of conscience as a moral guide

We can approach this by asking if the conscience is *useful* when making moral decisions, including whether it actually makes it possible to reach a decision rather than leaving us confused and stressed. However, our judgement about its value also depends on what result we are looking for once the decision is made. Below are some ideas to consider; you can suggest examples to illustrate each point.

1 The value of the conscience as the 'voice of God'

This type of conscience may not be valuable if:

- there is no way of knowing if the 'voice' you are hearing is genuinely the voice of God
- there are conflicting messages coming to people who all believe that God is speaking to them.

'Conscience' here appears to be both subjective and unreliable.

2 The value of the conscience as the internalised values of society or inner parent

On this view, the conscience naturally unites society, because its members have shared values which the conscience enforces. However, this would apply whether the society was 'good' or 'bad'. If you regard the collective morality of a particular society as 'evil', then you are not going to approve of the mechanism by which that society's values are sustained. If the role of conscience is to challenge existing values, then the collective conscience described by some thinkers has no value.

3 The value of the individualised conscience (Kohlberg)

The inner demand that moral decisions should be consistent and universalisable, as described by Kohlberg, gives a strongly rational account of conscience and it has to be asked how many are actually *capable* of such a level of thought.

4 The value of reason as conscience

The key problem here is that reason is not infallible. We have seen that Aquinas offers examples of how conscience can be mistaken, either because it does not know the moral law relating to the case in hand or because it is not in full possession of the relevant facts: for example, in the case of adultery (see page 184), it does not know that the 'widow' still has a living husband. This means that the conscience is an unreliable guide. Aquinas also admits that the conscience is influenced by the passions and by social conditioning, which means that following the conscience can lead to seriously harmful acts. We need to be able to judge what our conscience is telling us to do by some higher standard; it is not a sufficient guide on its own.

5 Feelings of guilt – are they useful?

Feelings of guilt are often associated with conscience. We can see that they may warn us when our actions are 'wrong' and that, since such feelings are unpleasant, we may want to modify our behaviour in the future to avoid them, and that sounds positive. However, *how* we may be influenced, and which behaviour we are motivated to change, will vary widely, and we may feel guilty about something that we do not need to change. For example, the conscience may make someone feel guilty about being a homosexual, whereas whether you think those feelings of guilt are appropriate or not depends on what you believe about homosexuality.

6 Can conscience 'guide' at all?

For some, the whole idea that conscience is a guide is invalid, because they believe that all behaviour, including moral conduct, is determined. That means that we are not free to choose how to behave and we have no free will that can be influenced by any guide.

7 The subjectivity of conscience

Only you know what your conscience is telling you to do. If you claim that you were 'following your conscience' when you did something that others do not approve of, only you know if that is true. As a justification to others, that will have little or no value unless, of course, what you did happens to be something they approved of. This reason for your decision may be irrelevant to whether it was right or wrong: the consequences may be the only element relevant to others and to a justification for what you did.

The problem of defining conscience

Perhaps the real problem in assessing the value of the conscience as a moral guide is that there is no agreed definition of it. Sociologists, psychologists, theologians and others tend to think within the compartments of their own disciplines, so perhaps any single definition is too narrow. A definition needs to include the following:

- Reason, because moral views ought not to be irrational.
- Social value, because the vast majority of people live in a society.
- The ability to judge and criticise society over its moral norms (for example over slavery).

- Some relation to religious values, since many are religious. Moreover, if there is a God, then in some respect the conscience must relate to God.
- An alternative source of values where religion is rejected, for example a humanistic conscience.
- A recognition of the nature of human psychology, which as Freud shows, combines human instincts that can point in different directions.

For most people, what we mean by conscience seems to include one or all of these factors: rational, judgmental, social, psychological, humanistic and religious, and there is no argument that can show that any particular view is right, or that one takes precedence over another.

The obvious issue with conscience is that something needs to 'sit outside it' in order to stop those who think that their conscience cannot make a colossal mistake from doing just that, otherwise the killing-fields of twentieth-century wars will look like skirmishes by comparison with future global conflicts.

To put that another way, perhaps what is needed is a guiding principle which most people could subscribe to. In Chapter 4 Introduction to meta-ethics: the meaning of right and wrong, we saw that a modified form of virtue ethics might offer such a principle: 'Do that which contributes to the flourishing of the whole environment'.

Conscience would then be the religious, social, psychological and other reasons through which people might come to accept such a principle. Even this would have its problems, because to be effective, it would have to be accepted by all, and of course there would always be those whose conscience would not allow them to accept it. If people on the whole act according to their own presuppositions about the world, then we might have to accept that no single understanding of conscience will be ever be accepted by all.

▲ *The Awakening Conscience* by William Holman Hunt (1853)

William Holman Hunt (1827–1910)

Hunt was an English painter and a committed Christian, and many of his paintings had religious themes, one of the most famous being *The Light of the World*, which pictures Jesus about to knock on an overgrown door, illustrating Revelation 3:20 – 'Here I am! I stand at the door and knock. If anyone hears my voice and opens the door, I will come in and eat with that person, and they with me.'

Activity

In 1853, Hunt painted *The Awakening Conscience*, which shows a young woman with her lover; so she is a 'kept' woman, not a prostitute. Her conscience has brought her to a spiritual awakening. You may find it useful to use the internet to look at the painting in more detail.

Consider the facts about the painting and then discuss and answer the following questions:

1 Given the different understandings of the conscience we have considered: rational, judgemental, social, psychological, humanistic and religious, which are likely to be the main influences at work on and in her mind?

2 Which theory (or theories) of the conscience best explains her 'awakening'?

3 Who or what is she moving towards, in her mind?

The facts of the painting (these are in no particular order):

● The man is in a social class above that of the woman.

● The man is the reason for her moral 'fall'. His authority over her is symbolised by the encirclement of his arms. She has just risen from his lap.

● She wears many rings, but no wedding ring.

● She is about to straighten up and stand.

● Her expression is of someone saying, 'No!' His is one of amused incomprehension.

● The song that has just been played reminds her of her childhood. It is a poem by Thomas Moore, *Oft in the Stilly* Night, set to music. You can check the words online.

● On the picture frame is a quotation from Proverbs 25:20:

'As he that taketh away a garment in cold weather, so is he that singeth songs to an heavy heart.'

● God/Jesus has come to her when least expected.

● Just about everything in the painting is new; nothing is worn or used.

● Red can be seen as a symbol of sin.

● There is a discarded glove on the floor, belonging to the man.

● The picture on the wall is of 'Christ and the Woman taken in Adultery' (John 8:1–11).

● There is a cat under the table who has caught a bird, and is playing with it.

● Nothing is visible of the woman's real family.

● The look on her face is where she remembers past innocence, and at that moment her conscience brings her to a complete spiritual awakening.

● She was fallen, but is now redeemed.

● Light shines on her face.

● There is an image of her in the mirror behind, in which she appears to be looking to the light of the world outside and to the beauties of nature.

● The moment of the awakening conscience is a psychological one. In this painting, Hunt was inspired by Charles Dickens' novel *David Copperfield*, in which one of the heroines, Emily, has run away with her lover, Steerforth, and is on the verge of prostitution after being abandoned by him. Hunt could have painted the moment of dramatic confrontation between Emily and her father, Daniel Peggotty, where he rescues her. Instead, he does not show the source of her change, because it would not be psychologically accurate.

Technical terms for conscience

Autonomous Self-directing, independent, self-governing (as, for example, in Butler's view of the conscience).

Authoritarian conscience In Fromm's view, the sense of guilt individuals can feel out of fear of being rejected by society, because society is based on obedience to rules and conformity to norms.

Conscientia In Aquinas' system, *conscientia* (conscience) applies the first principles of *synderesis* to particular situations. It is the experience of realising that what the individual is about to do (or has already done) is good or evil, right or wrong.

Eros In Freud's analysis of the mind, *eros* is the life instinct/the instinct for sexual gratification.

Humanistic conscience In Durkheim's view, the aspect of the conscience that has an intuitive knowledge of what is human and inhuman: of what makes life flourish and what destroys it.

A common response of the humanistic conscience is disobedience where that brings about flourishing.

Innate (conscience) Inborn conscience – originating in the mind.

Super-ego In Freud's thought, that part of the (unconscious) mind which controls the instincts that can damage society (*eros* and *thanatos*); it is the repository of parental commands delivered from infancy, together with the commands of other authority figures; it manifests through feelings of guilt, remorse and anxiety.

Synderesis In Aquinas' system, synderesis is in the rational part of human agents – a natural disposition of the human mind by which we apprehend without inquiry the basic principles of behaviour. The synderesis rule is that 'good is to be done and evil is to be avoided'.

Thanatos In Freud's analysis of the mind, the instinct for aggression, violence and death.

Summary of conscience

Differing ideas, religious and non-religious, about the nature of the conscience

The secular/non-religious view of conscience – social and psychological

1 Conscience as behaviour developed through social interaction: Lawrence Kohlberg

Kohlberg defined six stages of moral development from birth, in three levels: pre-conventional, conventional and post-conventional. The final stage is an individualised conscience where moral decisions must be consistent and universalisable. To go against the conscience leads to feelings of guilt. Kohlberg stressed the development of conscience through encountering dilemmas (for example, the dilemma of Heinz). In such processes of moral reasoning and decision, worked out in social contexts, we can see the conscience developing and deciding.

Social explanations receive negative criticism from those who see the conscience as more of a moral *intuition*: a kind of gut feeling, rather than the moral reasoning Kohlberg talks about.

2 Conscience as an aspect of the *super-ego* (Sigmund Freud)

The *super-ego* is the controlling/restraining self: it controls impulses that are potentially damaging to society (for example, the *eros* and *thanatos* instincts). The *super-ego* is the repository of parental authority (and of other authority figures), so the *super-ego* judges, and threatens punishment. The feeling of threat is the conscience. To go against the *super-ego* brings about feelings of shame, guilt, anxiety and remorse. If Freud is right, then the conscience cannot be seen as a source of moral authority for us, since it is just the internalisation of the wishes of our parents. Moreover, it has nothing to do with God, except where God is invented as another source of authority, in which case God is the source of the biggest guilt-trip we can have. On Freud's view, conscience has little or nothing to do with our desire to do what is morally right; *but is that really all that the conscience amounts to?*

3 Conscience as sanctions or social conditioning (Émile Durkheim)

Conscience, for Durkheim, is the sanctions/social conditioning that the group brings to bear on the individual, reinforced by the figure of God as the ultimate 'projection' of society's powers whose moral authority we feel compelled to obey. Durkheim argued that societies work through a collective conscience, and that an act is bad/wrong if society disapproves of it. Durkheim's ideas receive some support from evolutionary accounts of the conscience, according to which conscience is a survival mechanism, because societies feel a shared sense of responsibility.

4 Conscience as the authoritarian and the humanistic conscience (Erich Fromm)

According to Fromm, conscience is associated with guilt, shame and fear: it is a sense of moral responsibility arising out of fear of being rejected by society, simply because society is based on obedience to rules and conformity to norms. Aside from this authoritarian conscience, Fromm argues that we have a humanistic conscience that arises out of our instinctive knowledge of what destroys life and what makes it flourish, and this can make us (rightly) disobey society to bring about flourishing.

Social and psychological explanations of the conscience have good explanatory power. Groups improve their survivability by individuals having a conscience that compels them to maintain group loyalty. The authority of parents and of society is a powerful tool to compel social obedience. On the other hand, what do we say about great moral teachers who criticised their own societies?

The religious view of conscience – biblical and theological

1 Conscience as the innate voice of God (Augustine and Schleiermacher)

For Augustine, conscience is innate, put into human minds by God, and so amounts to innate knowledge of God's moral laws. This closely follows Paul's arguments in Romans 2, where he describes it as a 'witness to the requirements of the law', although for Augustine, he seems to have seen conscience as literally being the voice of God. Augustine's view has several problems: 1) if conscience is the voice of God, the amount of evil in the world suggests that God speaks to people selectively, or else they are good at ignoring his voice; 2) it makes ethical discussion redundant: all one has to do is to obey the voice; 3) this means that we cannot be morally free, yet freedom is the essence of being morally good;

4) throughout history, Christians have disagreed about morality, and have appealed to God-given conscience, so how is it that they have been given different answers?

For Schleiermacher, conscience is God-consciousness/the voice of God within/direct revelation from God. 'God-consciousness' is direct revelation from God, and to go against it is a sin; revelation takes priority over everything else, and to react in any other way is to hinder your life. This sounds fine, but has some clear weaknesses, for example, 1) What guarantee is there that the recipient of 'God-consciousness' is really receiving divine revelation as opposed to being psychologically deluded? 2) There are any number of people who claim divine inspiration as the basis for committing barbaric acts.

2   Conscience as the God-given faculty of reason (Aquinas)

Aquinas begins with the synderesis rule: 'Good should be done and evil avoided', which is implemented through the principles of Natural Moral Law. What is innate is not the voice of God but God-given reason. Conscience is reason applied to specific situations, and guided by synderesis. Synderesis can never be mistaken, but conscience can make mistakes by faulty understanding or faulty application of the synderesis rule. The conscience can err vincibly (through the individual's fault) or invincibly. Conscience is binding, because what the conscience dictates is true to the individual concerned, and God's truth must be followed. Aquinas' views are virtually flawless in their internal logic; but whether or not they are correct depends on your view of the synderesis rule and the background of Natural Moral Law.

3   Conscience as a God-given faculty – intuitive, reflective and autonomous (Bishop Butler)

For Butler, conscience is a reflective principle that works as an autonomous (self-directing) judge. Butler believes conscience is in human nature: it is a *reflective* principle placed within us by God as a natural guide and 'proper governor', so it is our duty to follow it. Conscience acts as a judge between human prudence (egoism) and benevolence (altruism). Conscience works intuitively and autonomously, and being a God-given faculty, it must be followed. However, despite being a God-given faculty, its *operation* is secular and autonomous. Moral dilemmas happen when there is a conflict between our emotions, desires, and the moral principles (particularly compassion) to which we subscribe. When we are conflicted, our conscience is troubled, therefore following conscience is a good way of ensuring that we have got the balance right. Elizabeth Anscombe pointed out that Butler assumes that conscience, having been given by God in order to direct the self, will always be good. He does not appear to consider the possibility that it may be distorted or evil.

4   Joseph Fletcher: Conscience is *agape*-love making decisions situationally

According to Fletcher, conscience is not a 'review officer' judging what you have done; rather, it is prospective, not retrospective: it is choosing what love demands *in the present situation*. It is this calculation which is the conscience in situation ethics, so the conscience is not a noun: it is not something we have; it is a verb – something we do when we are deciding and calculating how love is best served *in a situation*. If we compare this approach to that of Aquinas: for Aquinas, conscience is the application of reason, to a situation, informed by the synderesis rule. For Fletcher, conscience is the application of reason, to a situation, informed by *agape*.

The role of conscience is making moral decisions with reference to telling lies/breaking promises and adultery

The role of the conscience may be to decide what should be done before making any decision; to inform the moral agent whether their actions were right or wrong (for example, the conscience may cause a feeling of guilt after the event); and to demand a particular course of action. Some people appear not to have a conscience, so they feel no need to obey the laws of their society. For others, conscience plays an important part in their moral decision-making. How the conscience is used depends, of course, on what the conscience is thought to be: whether it is defined in terms of religion, society or psychology, for example.

1   Applied to telling lies and breaking promises (TL/BP)

A lie is a deliberate distortion of the truth; breaking a promise is the deliberate breaking of a contract.

Example 1: Using the reason as conscience (Aquinas)

- Conscience would tell the individual that TL/BP is not rational, because it conflicts with the synderesis rule to seek good and avoid evil.

- TL/BP also violates the primary precept of living in an ordered society. The effect of TL/BP on institutions such as finance and marriage would be devastating. Look at Volume 1, pages 185–86, for what Aquinas says.

- In the mad axe-murderer situation, Aquinas would say that a promise to a maniac could be met by telling an evasive truth. Many would see this as too rigid, since allowing the death of the victim would be a worse sin than lying in order to save the victim.

Example 2: Applying a sociological view of conscience

- TL/BP would be seen as socially destructive, for instance, in its effects on the banking system.

- In Fromm's idea of the authoritarian conscience, the individual might not break a promise for fear of society's disapproval. Also, the humanistic conscience would inform the individual that TL/BP would violate the ethical norms that society needs in order for life to be fruitful.

Example 3: Applying Freud's psychological understanding of conscience

- A Freudian analysis would begin with the arrival of feelings of guilt/anxiety/remorse surfacing from the subconscious mind of one who has told a lie or broken a promise. They would be the product of parental or societal conditioning.

- TL/BP are both common in modern society, so Freud's account would explain why the *super-ego* remains quiet: parents may themselves have seen TL/BP as acceptable.

- There is little or no sense of the conscience treating TL/BP as a *moral* issue.

2 Applied to adultery

The use of conscience as reason

For Aquinas, reason/conscience dictated that adultery was wrong; nevertheless the conscience is not infallible, so makes mistakes. He gave the example of a man who commits adultery with another man's wife through ignorance of the Divine Law: this reason is evil, because he should know God's law. If he commits adultery through *mistaken* reason, however, his will is excused from being evil.

The use of conscience as acting with *agape*-love

There is a clear and useful contrast between Aquinas and Fletcher. For Aquinas, the conscience condemns adultery as a sin, erring vincibly or invincibly. Fletcher's case study on 'sacrificial adultery' (Mrs Bergmeier) actually performs two roles: first, it suggests that the conscience can permit adultery in specific situations, as the requirement of *agape*-love; second, since marriage is a contract in which vows are usually explained, the case of 'sacrificial adultery' is also relevant to the issue of breaking promises.

The use of conscience as social conditioning

Sociology generally sees religion as a social phenomenon, without passing judgement on the reality or non-existence of God. Conscience is the social conditioning – the sanctions that the group brings to bear on the individual, so society might disapprove of adultery and show its disapproval by telling people that God condemns it.

In Durkheim's view of the collective conscience, an act is bad simply because society disapproves of it, so whether or not adultery is seen as wrong depends on society's perception of it, and society's perceptions change. Whereas adultery used to be seen as a sin against God's laws, it is now more of a reason to terminate the marriage contract if husband and wife so desire. The only morality is that of keeping or breaking a contract.

The use of conscience as an aspect of the *super-ego*

According to Freud, civilisation and its laws were invented to keep the warring instinctive drives of *thanatos* and *eros* in check. However, making laws prohibiting murder, rape and adultery created a paradox, because these laws frustrate our instinctive drives for killing and for sexual gratification. On Freud's view, then, conscience seems to depend simply on which drive is more deeply rooted in an individual's psychology – the preference for civilisation or for killing and sexual gratification.

That preference depends on an incalculable number of influences operating on each individual – parents, society, race, nation and social milieu. This is a long way from any view of conscience, Christian or otherwise, where adultery is seen as morally wrong in itself.

The value of conscience as a moral guide

We can approach this by asking if the conscience is *useful* when making moral decisions, including whether it makes it possible to reach a decision rather than leaving us confused and stressed. Our judgement about its value also depends on what result we are looking for once the decision is made. Here are some ideas to consider. You can suggest examples to illustrate each point.

1 The value of the conscience as the voice of God

This type of conscience may not be valuable if:

- there is no way of knowing if the 'voice' you are hearing is genuinely the voice of God

- there are conflicting messages coming to people who all believe that God is speaking to them.

This type of conscience appears to be both subjective and unreliable.

2 The value of the conscience as the internalised values of society or inner parent

On this view, conscience naturally unites society because it enforces shared values. BUT – if one society sees the values of another society as evil, then there will be antagonism and dislike between societies. If the role of conscience is to challenge existing values, then the collective conscience described by some thinkers has no value.

3 The value of the individualised conscience (Kohlberg)

The inner demand that moral decisions should be consistent and universalisable, as described by Kohlberg, gives a strongly rational view of conscience, but how many people are capable of such a level of thought?

4 The value of reason as conscience

The key problem is that reason is not infallible. Aquinas shows this by pointing out that reason may not know all the relevant facts, as with his example of adultery, where the man's conscience does not know that the 'widow' still has a living husband. Aquinas admits that conscience is influenced by the passions and by social conditioning, so following conscience can lead to harmful acts. We need to be able to judge what reason/conscience is telling us by some higher standard.

5 Feelings of guilt – are they useful?

Guilt may motivate us to change our behaviour because it has unpleasant consequences. This sounds positive, but the problem is that *how* we may be influenced, and which behaviour we are motivated to change, will vary, so we may feel guilty about something that we do not need to change. For example, the conscience may make someone feel guilty about being a homosexual, whereas whether you think those feelings of guilt are appropriate or not depends on what you believe about homosexuality.

6 Can conscience 'guide' at all?

Those who are determinists will believe that all behaviour is determined, in which case we are not free to choose how to behave morally, and we have no free will to be influenced by others.

7 The subjectivity of conscience

Only you know what your conscience is telling you to do, so if you do something that others disapprove of, only you know whether or not you are following your conscience. If you justify your actions by saying that you were following your conscience, then that is of no value to others unless you are doing something they approve of. Consequently, other people are likely to be interested only in the consequences of what you do, and not the reasons you claim to have for doing it.

The problem of defining conscience

The real problem in assessing the value of conscience as a moral guide is that we have no agreed definition of it. A useful definition needs to include:

- reason, because moral views should not be irrational

- social value, since most people live in society

- the ability to judge and criticise society over its moral norms (such as over slavery)

- some relation to religious values, since many are religious

- an alternative source of values where religion is rejected, such as a humanistic conscience

- a recognition of the nature of human psychology and its instincts.

For most people, conscience involves one or even all of these factors, but no argument can show that any one definition is right, or that it should take precedence over the others. Conscience is unquantifiable and untestable, and we cannot know whether humans have a conscience as an innate faculty. On any view of the conscience, people can act with amazing courage and love; equally they can act with unspeakable barbarity and stupidity; so those who think that they cannot be blamed for using their conscience appear to be wrong. Conscience cannot act in isolation.

Conscience therefore needs to be controlled by something that sits outside it. One possibility is that we should adopt the Neo-Naturalist view that good/right is what leads to the flourishing of humans and their entire environment. Acts of conscience that go against this principle can be deemed bad/wrong. However, there will always be some whose conscience will not let them accept any such check.

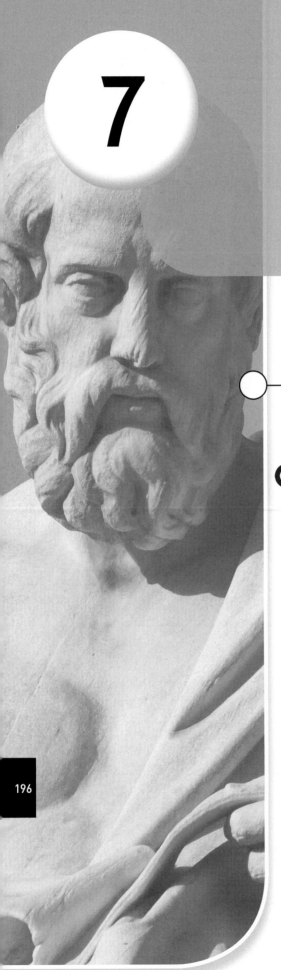

Bentham and Kant

You will need to consider the following items for this section

1 Comparison of the key ideas of Bentham and Kant about moral decision-making.

2 How far these two ethical theories are consistent with religious moral decision-making.

Some biographical details

Jeremy Bentham

Jeremy Bentham (1748–1832)

Bentham was an English philosopher and social reformer. In his will, Bentham left his body to be dissected by his friend Thomas Smith, after which the skeleton and head eventually came into the possession of University College London, who padded it out with hay, dressed it in Bentham's clothes, and then displayed it in the south cloisters of the college. In 2013 it was brought to a meeting of the College Council, where it was registered as 'present but not voting'. Since the head was in poor condition, it was early on replaced with a wax model, the original head being displayed in the same cabinet. It became a target for repeated student pranks, so it was eventually stored in a locked cupboard. [Note 1]

▲ Jeremy Bentham

▲ Jeremy Bentham in his cabinet

Jeremy Bentham and Immanuel Kant were about as different from one another as you can possibly imagine, and their ideas and arguments were shaped by their circumstances and their overall aims in life. It is one thing to know that Bentham presented a basic form of 'Utilitarianism' and that Kant argued for a 'Categorical Imperative', but *why* did they each take their particular approach? What questions were they asking themselves to which these seemed to be the answer?

Bentham was an intellectual child prodigy. He read voraciously from an early age, and in 1760, aged only 12, he was sent to Queen's College, Oxford, where he achieved his Bachelor's degree three years later and a Master's degree three years after that. He came from a wealthy family and trained in the law but, although qualified, he was frustrated by what he saw as the failure of the legal system to defend the poorest in society and so he never took up that profession. He became involved with several social and political causes, and became convinced that, in many cases, progress was frustrated by the influence of those who held power. This he declared to be 'sinister influence', where those presently in power worked to protect their own vested interests, rather than the interests of society as a whole. He worked to deal with corruption in the Port of London, and for many years tried to persuade the government to build a new kind of prison, a 'Panopticon', with cells that would be constructed around the inner walls of a circular building, so that prisoners would always be on view from the jailors placed in the centre. Keen that learning should be freed from the influence of the Church, he was indirectly involved with establishing the University of London (now University College). Overall, he was a towering figure in promoting social, legal and economic reform and in promoting equality, attacking privilege and everything that stood in the way of justice and a fair distribution of benefits among people of all classes.

Bentham was always practical in his thinking, opposed to what he saw as high-flown ideas (such as *natural law* and *natural rights*, which he famously criticised as 'nonsense on stilts'). He was always concerned to examine what would be in the interest of society as a whole, and was concerned that action should be judged by its practical results. He wanted to examine what people actually chose to do, and why they did it, and hoped that in some way this would contribute to what amounted to a science of human behaviour.

Bentham's development of Utilitarianism began as a theory of law rather than one of ethics. The law in Bentham's day was absurd in its treatment of citizens: there were around 200 offences on the statute book that were punishable by hanging, so the English Legal System was known as 'The Bloody Code'. In order to be properly grounded, Bentham said that the Law must be governed by the *Primary* Principle of **Utility** – that the greatest happiness of the greatest number is the measure of right and wrong. Laws are only *secondary* principles. A good law is, simply, one that obeys the primary principle; a bad law is one that does not.

He insisted that things like too much respect for antiquity, hatred of innovation, antipathy, sympathy, fiction, fancy and religion, should have nothing to do with making laws. Take religion, for example. The theistic religions of Judaism, Christianity and Islam have a historical antipathy for homosexual practices, and some scriptures state that it is punishable by death. Bentham thought that such attitudes were based on superstition and ignorance, and argued that all laws that criminalise homosexual acts should

Key term

Utility that property in any object, whereby it tends to produce benefit, advantage, pleasure, good, or happiness; or to prevent mischief, pain, evil, unhappiness to the party whose interest is considered (an individual or the wider community).

be thrown out. Bentham argues that homosexual acts do not 'weaken' men, or threaten the population or marriage, and he documents their prevalence in ancient Greece and Rome.

In short, Bentham spent his life campaigning for the kind of social justice that would offer the greatest possible benefit for the greatest number of people in society, and tackling the practical issues involved with doing so.

Immanuel Kant

Immanuel Kant (1724–1804)

Kant was a Prussian philosopher, born in Königsberg (which is now the Russian city of Kaliningrad). Kant believed that his paternal grandfather was Scottish, which might or might not have pleased Hume.

Kant spent his whole life in and around Königsberg, moving from school to university and then taking up a teaching post all in the same city. His output of intellectual material was enormous. We are mainly concerned with his ethics, but he also taught and contributed widely in science and in astronomy. One of his earliest works, *Universal Natural History of and Theory of the Heavens* (1755), attempted to use Newton's physical laws to explain the universe in a mechanistic way without the need for Newton's idea of an external creator God. He was a leading figure in the European Enlightenment – a general movement that sought to explore autonomous human reason, contrasted with the superstition and imposed authority of earlier periods, and he was fascinated by the development of science.

He was also the first major *professional* philosopher of modern times. In Ancient Greece, both Plato and Aristotle may be considered professional in that they established places of learning and taught students, but most of the best-known thinkers that followed them were either clergyman (for example Anselm or Aquinas) or they were aristocrats who dabbled in Philosophy alongside other positions (for example, Descartes), or general writers (for example Hume, who was best-known in his day as a historian), or like Bentham, Paine or Burke, social and political thinkers who wrote works that are of interest to philosophers. But Kant was a professional. Year by year he taught students and built up his research notes for what were to be launched as his three great critiques – the *Critique of Pure Reason* (1781), the *Critique of Practical Reason* (1788) and the *Critique of Judgement* (1790). He followed up his ethical thinking in the second critique with *Groundwork of the Metaphysics of Morals* (1785) and finally *The Metaphysics of Morals* (1797), and contributed a serious study of the economic relationships between nations and how they contribute to or avoid war, in his *Eternal Peace* (1795). In other words, he crafted a massive body of academic work, and did so with a regular lifestyle and daily work as a teacher. By all accounts, he was also extremely good company, enjoyed hosting supper parties, and laced his lectures with wit. He may have been an academic, but he certainly wasn't dry.

Kant was profoundly influenced by science, but he recognised the limitations of reaching conclusions as a result of empirical evidence. He spent years working on a system of thought that would reconcile the sort of empirical skepticism he found in David Hume's work, with his conviction that there are things we know for certain (for example that everything has a cause) that go beyond empirical evidence. His answer was that the world is a rational place, organised in time, space and causality, not because we have sufficient evidence to convince us of that fact, but because *our minds perceive it that way*. That was the basis of the switch in thinking that is loosely termed his 'Copernican Revolution' – **we see the world as we do, not because our minds conform to what is 'out there' but because our minds** *organise* **our experience**. With ethics, he concluded that morality cannot be based on the evidence of the senses, but he remained convinced that people had an inherent sense of right and wrong.

Later in this section we shall be looking at how religious people might view his ethical thinking, so it is worth noting that he was a German Protestant, influenced by the Pietist tradition, which emphasised personal experience rather than rational argument when it came to religious convictions. He was, therefore, understandably critical of the traditional 'proofs' of the existence of God, thinking that none of them were rationally sound, and instead turned to the idea of ethical thinking and religious conviction based on inner experience. He wanted to promote the kind of religion that would be fully compatible with human reason, and published *Religion within the Limits of Reason Alone* in 1793, after which the university forbade him to publish anything else on religion – he may have been an academic, but at the end of the eighteenth century there were limits to what one could make public in terms of any criticism of established religion.

So a key feature of his thinking is that, as we examine the world, we do so using fundamental ideas that interpret all we see. **We cannot know things as they are in themselves (what he called** *noumena***) but only things as we perceive them to be (the** *phenomena***)**. He found inspiration both in the wonders of the world, which he expressed as 'the starry heavens above me', and also 'the moral law within me'. Coming to Kant we should, therefore, expect to find someone who uses careful, professional arguments in order to show that there are fundamental principles of human reason that underpin our morality. And that is exactly what we find in his 'Categorical Imperative'.

Bentham's Act Utilitarianism

Bentham's is an '**Act Utilitarian**' theory, meaning that decisions about right and wrong are made in each unique situation, established on the basis of the moral choices that are *made for particular actions in particular situations*, rather than by applying general moral principles.

1 Bentham insists that people are motivated to seek pleasure and to avoid pain.

Bentham was what we would today call a 'social scientist'. He sought to look at how people behaved and what motivated them to make the choices they did. He recognised that what people actually do is to seek happiness and try to avoid pain – both for themselves and those they care about. That is reality. Whatever universal ideals you put forward, in the end people are still going to seek what will make for their own happiness or benefit. He put this starkly:

> **Key term**
>
> **Act Utilitarianism** Bentham's account of Utilitarianism: in any situation, one should choose the action that maximises utility.

> Nature has placed mankind under the governance of two sovereign masters, *pain and pleasure*. It is for them alone to point out what we ought to do, as well as to determine what we shall do. On the one hand the standard of right and wrong, on the other the chain of causes and effects, are fastened to their throne. They govern us in all we do, in all we say, in all we think. [Note 2]

2 The desire to pursue pleasure and to avoid pain leads us to the Principle of Utility.

Because he was a practical man, Bentham believed that things should be judged to be right or wrong according to whether or not they benefited the people involved. He therefore argued for the 'Principle of Utility':

> By utility is meant that property in any object, whereby it tends to produce benefit, advantage, pleasure, good, or happiness, (all this in the present case comes to the same thing) or (what comes again to the same thing) to prevent the happening of mischief, pain, evil, or unhappiness to the party whose interest is considered: if that party be the community in general, the happiness of the community: if a particular individual, then the happiness of that individual. [Note 3]

3 So in any situation, we should seek the maximum happiness, or benefit, for the maximum number of people involved.

Bentham's social conscience led him to the conclusion that everyone had an equal right to happiness or benefit, irrespective of their situation or status in life. He was always opposed to privilege, particularly where those in power claimed more than their fair share of benefit. So how might benefit be apportioned?

His argument is this: that, in any particular situation, the right thing to do is that which offers the maximum benefit/happiness to the maximum number of people involved. This appeared to have two advantages as a moral theory:

- It reflected Bentham's social and political views. It was democratic, in that it treated everybody alike. This contrasted with what he saw of conventional social and legal rules, which tended to benefit those in power.
- It offered a 'scientific' approach to morality, in that – once benefit could be quantified – it could be apportioned on that basis, with evidence that could be presented to justify the moral choice. Once the decision was taken that the right thing was to confer benefit/maximise happiness, his principle of utility seemed to offer a clear way in which that decision could be applied.

4 Pleasure (and pain) can be measured: the Hedonic Calculus.

To assist in putting his principle into practice, Bentham put forward what is termed his 'Hedonic Calculus' (alternatively called the 'Felicific Calculus' for those who prefer Latin to Greek). Bentham paraphrases 'pleasure' with other terms, such as: *benefit*, *happiness*, *advantage* and *good*.

The calculus was his scheme for assessing how pleasure could be measured. To calculate this we need to take into consideration:

- its **intensity** (how strong is the pleasure?)
- its **duration** (how long does the pleasure last? A short-term pleasure should not have the same significance as something that is longer-lasting or permanent; many people will resist present happiness in favour of some security or benefit that is considered more worthwhile in the longer term)
- its **certainty** or uncertainty (how likely or unlikely is it that the pleasure will happen?)
- its **propinquity** (closeness or remoteness – how soon will the pleasure happen?)
- its **fecundity** (people who are fecund find it easy to reproduce/have lots of offspring, so Bentham is asking how likely it is that the action concerned will produce similar pleasures in the future, or else pains)
- its **purity** (for example, if you calculate the pleasures and pains resulting from the action, to what extent would there be an overall balance of pleasure over pain, or else pain over pleasure?)
- its **extent** (how far will the pleasure or pain extend *to other people affected by the action*?).

It may sound rather clinical to examine pleasure or happiness in this way, but it fits Bentham's overall desire to establish something of a science of moral and political action. He wanted to have a rational, evidential basis for his moral, legal and political choices – a tendency that has persisted to the present day, when economists and politicians are always trying to weigh benefits and harms in order to resolve difficult political decisions.

Bentham also applied the Calculus to human infants and to animals. Since pleasure and pain are measurable, clearly they are measurable in animals, and Bentham thought that to assume otherwise is ignorance. He argued that many animals are more intelligent than the least intelligent humans, and are certainly 'more rational and conversable' than any month-old human, for example. Animals should, therefore, be treated as members of the moral community. Just as human pleasures and pains can be measured in terms of their intensity, duration, and extent, so can those of animals.

To conclude, **the Calculus is, broadly speaking, looking to establish whether an act has a balance of pleasure over pain. If it does, then the act is good/right.**

Bentham's is an 'Act Utilitarian' theory. In other words, **one should choose the action that maximises utility in any particular situation.** The theory is, as we said above, that one should seek to achieve '**the greatest good for the greatest number**' – a phrase coined by Hutcheson in trying to decide on the best sort of government. In this process, any moral law can be suspended.

The idea of the greatest good for the greatest number fitted exactly with Bentham's natural sense of justice and fairness. Whether or not following this calculation of the greatest good led people to choose an action that matched the rules laid down by those in authority was only of secondary importance. Predictably for someone who criticised the application of laws that had been framed for the benefit of those in power, he placed the benefit of the majority above imposed authoritarian rules.

In calculating happiness and pleasure: i) Bentham made no attempt to claim that some pleasures are superior to others, and ii) he maintained that one person is 'worth' the same as another person.

For i), in *The Rationale of* Reward (1830), he famously insisted that, 'Prejudice apart, the game of push-pin is of equal value with the arts and sciences of music and poetry.' (In Push-pin, two or more players put a pin (like a needle) on a table, and try to push their pin over their opponents' pins).

For ii), this means that when we calculate the greatest happiness for all those concerned in an action, 'each person is to count for one and no one for more than one.' Utilitarianism therefore is committed to the principle of equality among humans.

Moreover individuals are committed to seeking the *general* happiness, not just their own. Bentham thinks that individuals will do this because by seeking the general happiness one tends to safeguard one's own happiness.

Evaluating Bentham's Act Utilitarianism

There are many objections to Utilitarianism. We shall look at a sample of four alleged weaknesses of the theory, and in each case consider how a utilitarian might reply.

1 It puts too much emphasis on the consequences of our actions.

You can see that Act Utilitarianism is an example of a consequentialist ethical theory. It aims at producing the consequence of the greatest happiness for the greatest number. The problem with this is that requires us to second-guess the future, and it is easy to get that wrong. A classic example would be the right or wrong in saving the life of a child who then grows up to be a mass-murderer. With hindsight, you might regret what you did, although at the time it seemed to offer happiness/benefit.

Utilitarian reply: On the whole, this is not true. Act Utilitarianism does try to assess specific situations, but in reality most situations are typical of 'general classes of acts' (for example murder, theft, rape, arson). We know from experience, for example, that most acts of murder, theft and rape will lead to unhappiness, so a simple utilitarian calculation will show that we should not do them. In the case mentioned above, of the right or wrong of saving the life of a child, we know that this will probably lead to a balance of happiness over pleasure for everybody concerned. If the child happens to be Hitler, we cannot know *at the time* that he will grow up to be a genocidal maniac. A Kantian response would also be to save the life of the child.

2 It ignores motives, rules and duties.

The morality of an action is in *why* you do it. People need to have the stability of moral rules, and it is their duty to obey them.

Utilitarian reply: Rules and duties are useful only if they serve the 'primary principle' of Utility – if they generate more happiness and pleasure than unhappiness and pain. If they do not, then the rule is immoral. The motive of the utilitarian is the same as the intended consequence, which is to bring about the greatest happiness for the greatest number.

3 It ignores the rights of minorities.

In any walk of life there is no guarantee that the majority is morally right, so Act Utilitarianism can be unjust to minorities. To take an extreme example, in a situation where seven sadistic guards are raping one woman, the hedonic calculus seems to justify this because their pleasure exceeds her pleasure in the ratio of 7 to 1.

Utilitarian reply: If the rights of the minority are considered above the rights of the majority, then that is unjust to the majority, which is a far greater injustice. The accusation that the hedonic calculus justifies gang rape misunderstands the calculus. *Items 5, 6 and 7 in the calculus (fecundity, purity and extent) in effect require the calculation of pleasure and pain to be made with reference to all concerned.* If gang rape suddenly became morally right, the unhappiness of the rape would extend to all the women on the planet and to their husbands, so Utilitarianism would never justify such an act.

Note that although it seems unfair to claim that Utilitarianism can justify gang rape, there are other grounds for thinking that it can ignore the rights of minorities. Take the example of a permanently unhappy homeless person, without friends or family to care for them, who distresses everyone they come across: would it maximise utility to murder such a person, or would the long-term consequences argue against this?

4 Utilitarianism fails because it cannot bridge the 'is-ought' gap.

You will remember that we studied G.E. Moore's rejection of ethical naturalism in Chapter 4 Introduction to meta-ethics: the meaning of right and wrong. Moore argued that all naturalist theories, Utilitarianism included, commit the naturalistic fallacy of going from an 'is' to an 'ought' – from facts to moral values. We cannot go from 'happiness is what all humans desire' to 'you ought to bring about the greatest happiness for the greatest number'.

Utilitarian response: If you ask people what they want, they universally reply that they want happiness, so this is reason enough to support the claim that one *ought* to bring about the greatest happiness for the greatest number. No other explanation is possible, and no other explanation is needed.

For now we shall leave Utilitarianism and go on to look at Kant. Bear in mind, in the meantime, the *practical* nature of Utilitarianism. In many ways, utilitarian arguments go hand-in-hand with democracy (of which Bentham was totally in favour) and with a sense of the value and **autonomy** of the individual.

> **Key term**
>
> **Autonomy** The state of being self-governed/self-ruled/free from external control or influences.

Kant's Categorical Imperative

Best known for what is often termed his 'Copernican Revolution', Kant argued that space, time and causality are not 'out there' to be discovered, but are the way in which our minds organise experience. We cannot know the world as it is in itself, only the world as it appears to us. This is absolutely central to an understanding of Kant – he stands at the head of a long tradition in philosophy, in which our minds are the key to understanding the world. Unscramble our minds and the rest will fall into place.

Kant's theory of ethics, compared with Utilitarianism, expresses a similar shift towards the personal experience of the *moral will*. It was developed in his *Groundwork of the Metaphysics of Morals* (1785) and in the *Critique of Practical Reason* (1788).

1 Kant insists that there is only one thing that can be regarded as good without qualification: a good will.

Kant saw that, where empirical evidence is concerned, we can never have absolute certainty, since all our sense perceptions can be mistaken. For example, a straight stick, when put into water, will appear bent. Under sodium lighting, colours appear different.

He also thought, from reading Hume, that one could never argue logically from an 'is' to an 'ought', for facts can only show what is the case, and not what ought to be the case. Kant therefore wanted to find an entirely new starting point for morality, and found it in the idea of the 'good will'. **The good will is autonomous, and it is good without reservation.**

> **'The autonomy of the will is the sole principle of all moral laws and of the duties conforming to them...'**
>
> Kant: *Critique of Practical Reason*, Book 1, Chapter 1, Theorem 4.

Kant begins his outline of ethics with the 'good will' – knowing what it is to act morally:

> There is no possibility of thinking of anything at all in the world, or even out of it, which can be regarded as good without qualification, except a *good will*... The sight of a being who is not graced by any touch of a pure and good will but who yet enjoys an uninterrupted prosperity can never delight a rational and impartial spectator. Thus a good will seems to constitute the indispensable condition of being even worthy of happiness.
>
> (From the opening of *Groundwork for the Metaphysics of Morals*)

His aim, set out in the preface to that book was nothing less than: 'To seek out and establish the supreme principle of morality.' His moral reasoning remains central to many modern discussions of normative ethics (of how we should behave/what moral principles we should follow).

2 Alongside the good will, we are all aware of having a sense of moral obligation.

Kant's moral theory is based on the principles of the *pure practical reason*, (reason that chooses actions because they are good in themselves), and **pure reason is aware of the compulsion of the moral 'ought'**. We all know what it is to have a sense of moral obligation – to believe that there is something we *ought* to do, irrespective of the consequences it may have for us. Starting from that experience of morality, he believed that it should be possible to give a systematic account of our moral duties. The advantage of his approach was that these principles, once established, might be applied universally, since they do not depend upon particular circumstances.

3 Kant's moral theory is therefore deontological: based on duty.

Duty is always a matter of conscious choice; an internal sense of what one ought to do. Starting with the experience of a moral 'ought', Kant seeks to establish the principles/rules by which this sense of duty can conform to human reason. Notice that a sense of 'duty' implies an unqualified obligation – it gives the sense of what *ought* to be done, quite apart from the personal cost or likely result. Acknowledging moral duties means that we develop moral rules, because rules bind us to our duty.

There are, however, teleological aspects to Kant's theory, which we will arrive at below (point 5).

4 Duty gives a single focus to ethics.

Kant demands moral seriousness. He considers that you are not acting morally if you do what you enjoy, or what gives you some personal benefit. To be moral, an action must be based on the pure practical reason, following rational principles. *After you have reasoned out what you ought to do*, you should seek to do what is your duty, no matter what your inclinations or the consequences involved (contrast that with Bentham's Utilitarianism).

It is not that to benefit from what you do, or to enjoy it, is immoral in itself; it is simply that your potential enjoyment is irrelevant to the morality of an action: morality does not depend on results or inclinations. Morality is also a positive act by which we shape our world. Being kind, or helpful, may be a natural gift, but **to have a 'good will' Kant argues is not a natural gift, it is a chosen act. So the aim is not to be happy, but to be *worthy* of being happy.**

> ## Key term
> **Categorical Imperative**
> An absolute/categorical (undeniable), unconditional, moral command; for example, **Do not** murder, **do not** steal, **do not** lie.

Notice how clear-cut Kant is compared with other theories – there is no vague sense of what is to the benefit of all, nor are there arguments about the relative values of different societies or cultures. What Kant is after is a **Categorical Imperative** – an 'ought' that does not need qualification.

5 Note that the existence of this categorical 'ought' does *not* mean that we should do 'duty for duty's sake *whatever the consequences*'.

Kant's ethic is *not* 'absolutely' deontological: Kant does not ignore the consequences of our actions. The consequences have to be worked through before you can tell whether the principle you want to act on conforms to the Categorical Imperative. On his website, 'Philosophical Investigations', having referred to Keith Ward's views on the teleological aspects of Kant's ethics, Peter Baron makes the point in interesting style:

> But we can say this: in order to make the imaginative leap of universalising we have to imagine the consequences of everyone modifying their car, fitting a loud exhaust and driving at twice the speed limit through my village. One consequence, of course, is that I would be dead, as the exit from my drive is completely blind! That is a teleological leap of imagination – it's looking at ends, not rules. [Note 4]

According to Keith Ward, the content of ethics is the wants and desires that people actually have, and not some intuition that falls like corn from the sky.

Kantian morality is autonomous – people have to work out their own rules using the Categorical Imperative, which is a rational, reflective principle. There has to be an organic link with people's wants and desires, because it would be futile deciding upon principles that nobody wanted to follow! For example, there is a natural link between a person's duty to tell the truth and their natural desire not to be lied to.

6 The Categorical Imperative.

In order to get the right sense of the Categorical Imperative, Kant contrasted it with the hypothetical imperative.

The Categorical Imperative has the form: 'Do A'. **The hypothetical imperative** has the form: 'If A, then B'.

Because they use the word 'if', you can see that hypothetical imperatives are conditional. For example:

If you want to be a fighter pilot, then you need to learn engineering.

If you want to be happy, then go bungee jumping.

The good of hypothetical imperatives is clearly instrumental (done to get something out of it) and motivated by self-interest, so **they can never lead to commands that everybody ought to obey**.

Now contrast them with the force of the Categorical Imperatives. Categorical Imperatives are commands that cannot be disobeyed, because their good is intrinsic and deontological, for example:

Do not murder

Do not steal

Do not lie.

So Categorical Imperatives alone can lead us to universal maxims (principles of action) that everybody ought to follow.

7 There are three main formulations of the Categorical Imperative, each one linked to the others.

If something is an 'imperative', it is a command; so a Categorical Imperative is a command that cannot be denied/must be obeyed. To put that another way, a Categorical Imperative is simply an 'ought' – a moral command that is absolute and unconditional. But when we speak of the three formulations of Kant's Categorical Imperative, we refer to the principles he set down to establish the rational basis of that 'ought'.

Looking, now, at each of Kant's three formulations in detail:

First formulation: Universalisability

Act only according to that maxim whereby you can at the same time will that it should become a universal law.

A note on maxims

We have already introduced the term 'maxim', and you will see below that the first form of the Categorical Imperative uses it.

It can be expressed as: 'Whenever X happens, I consider it right to do Y.' It is your *maxim* that Kant says should be universalised, not the actual thing you are planning to do.

Key term

Maxim A general guideline or principle of action.

Key term

Universalisability The main formulation of the Categorical Imperative: Act only according to that maxim whereby you can at the same time will that it should become a universal law.

Keeping in mind that it is only the maxim that is universalised, this suggests that, if what I propose to do is to be considered to be right, I should be prepared for everyone else to work on the same principle. In short, this is Kant's principle of **universalisability**.

Here are **two examples given by Kant of how maxims can fail the test of universalisability**:

● **Making false promises/lying.**

I am forced to borrow money, but I know that I will not be able to pay it back. I also know that my only hope of getting the money is to promise to pay it back. If I decide to do that, then my maxim would have to be:

When I am in need of money, I will borrow it and promise to pay it back, although I know that I can never repay it.

I then ask myself: 'What would happen if my maxim became a universal law?' I can then see that such a maxim would be self-contradictory. If everybody who got into financial difficulties was able to make a lying promise, then the promise itself would become impossible, and the whole institution of 'promise-keeping', upon which much of life depends, would fall apart. Think, for a moment, about how that would affect society in general and your life in particular.

I therefore have (what Kant calls) a '**perfect duty**' (meaning one which there can never be any kind of exception to) not to act in this way.

● **Refusing to help others.**

I live in prosperity, and I see that others live in misery and wretchedness, and that I could help them. I think to myself: 'What concern is it of mine? Let others be as happy as they can. I will take nothing from them, but will contribute nothing to their welfare, and will not relieve their distress.' To do this, then my maxim would have to be:

It is permissible for me never to help those who are less well-off than myself.

Again, I then ask myself: 'What would happen if my maxim became a universal law?' There is no contradiction in my saying this (unlike with the previous example, where to universalise promise-breaking would break the whole institution of promise-keeping); nevertheless, I can never be sure that at some stage I will not need the help and sympathy of others. If that situation arises, then my maxim would deprive me of that help and sympathy.

I therefore have a duty to help others. This is an '**imperfect duty**' because there might be an exception to that rule, for example when I don't have enough money to help.

Second formulation: The Practical Imperative

Act in such a way that you always treat humanity, whether in your own person or in the person of any other, never simply as a means, but always at the same time as an end.

At its simplest, this principle excludes using other people simply as a means of achieving your own ends. That does **not** mean that you should not use somebody as a means to achieve something you want (otherwise you'd have real problems with taxi drivers, because you use them in order to get

Activity

Another of Kant's examples is that of neglecting talents. Kant thinks of a man who has a talent that could make him useful to society in many ways, but he prefers to live a life of pleasure and refuses to develop that talent.

What maxim would the man put forward for this, and why could that maxim not become a universal law?

to your destination). The clue is given in the phrase 'at the same time'. If you need to use someone as a means to your end, and society is built on people providing services for one another, you should treat them also as 'ends', in other words, as free moral agents in their own right.

This follows from the first formulation, because, if you can will that the principle upon which you act should become a universal principle of law, then you must be prepared for everyone else to make that same moral choice. In other words, you have to allow that all others are free moral agents, just as you are. But to treat people only as 'means' is to dehumanise them, and you could not want them to treat you in that way. So if you respect yourself as an autonomous moral individual, you need to allow everyone else to be their own 'end' as well.

Third formulation: The Kingdom of Ends

Act as though a legislating member in the universal kingdom of ends.

The third formulation – less well known that the first two, but logically following on from them – is that you should always act as though you were responsible for making rules in a kingdom where everyone is to be treated as an 'end' and not as a means; in other words, a society of free and autonomous human individuals.

8 The Categorical Imperative is, however, challenged by the existence of 'radical evil'.

Kant was forced by the realities of life to acknowledge that despite the rationality of the Categorical Imperative, human existence contains a great deal of moral evil. Kant's explanation of this was that radical evil happens when we subordinate the moral law to our own self-interest.

In fact, Kant suggested (for example in: *Religion Within the Bounds of Bare Reason*, 1793) that humanity has a *universal tendency* towards radical evil. Radical evil happens when people focus on a maxim of self-interest, which leads them to bend every other maxim to that one maxim.

9 Kant's theory of ethics culminates in his idea of the *summum bonum*, which is underpinned by the three 'postulates of practical reason' – God, freedom and immortality. (Beware of writing those as, 'God, freedom and immorality' – not an uncommon occurrence.)

Kant argued that one should not strive to be happy, but to be worthy of happiness, and he had no respect for those who appeared to achieve happiness without regard to the morality of their means of doing so. Thus the *highest good* (*summum bonum*) for Kant is this joining of virtue and happiness.

Virtue has to be the starting point, because it is the virtuous person who possesses the 'good will,' which is necessary for morality. Happiness is an optional bonus, but it is certainly not guaranteed, and should not be our aim.

Notice, however, that **morality is internal, in that it concerns the 'good will'.** When Kant speaks of the 'highest good', he is not referring to something 'out there', an ideal that we need to believe in before we can act morally. You do not need to believe in a 'highest good', you simply have to

---

Key terms

Summum bonum The highest/ supreme good: the culmination of Kant's ethics where virtue meets its appropriate reward of perfect happiness.

Postulate A presupposition or assumption which you must have accepted in order to make sense of your moral choices. In Kant's ethics, the three 'postulates of practical reason' are: God, freedom and immortality, and these underpin Kant's doctrine of the *summum bonum*.

Key term

'Ought implies can' Kant's view that the force of the moral 'ought' – the Categorical Imperative that we *ought* to do our moral duty – implies that we *can* do our moral duty.

will the highest good. In other words, you believe that, as an autonomous human individual, you will be worthy of happiness if you act morally.

But also, Kant argues that if you do in fact seek the *summum bonum* **you must assume that its achievement is at least possible**. If the good will tells us that we **ought** to do our moral duty, then that sense of 'ought' implies that we **can** in fact do our moral duty. This is often expressed by saying that **'ought implies can'**.

In order to make sense of this conviction, our practical reason tells us that **we must make three important assumptions about the world**. These are Kant's three **'postulates of practical reason'**. Kant refers to these postulates towards the end of his *Groundwork for the Metaphysics of Morals*. A 'postulate' is a presupposition or assumption to which you, on reflection, must have subscribed in order to make sense of your moral choices.

In other words, *if* you really believe that acting virtuously will, in the end, also be the way of achieving happiness, and *if* your mind tells you that morality is a 'Categorical Imperative' that you must follow, then that implies that you accept the following three things: God, immortality and freedom.

God and immortality

- God does not command the moral laws: they arise from reason and the good will.
- Nevertheless I feel the compulsion of the moral 'ought': I know that I ought to do my duty.
- 'Ought implies can', meaning that if I feel that I ought to do my duty, then I can do it.
- If this is the case, then I can assume that the universe is fair, so if I do my duty and become morally worthy, this implies that there must be a reward of happiness in proportion to my obedience to the moral law.
- The reward for the highest obedience is the *summum bonum* – the highest good, which is the perfect match between morality and happiness.
- Perfect happiness cannot be achieved in this life.
- Therefore, there must be immortality in which the *summum bonum* can be achieved.
- Only God can provide immortality, so God exists to guarantee the *summum bonum*.

Freedom

Freedom of the will is the core of morality. We cannot show from any kind of experience that we are free, nevertheless we know *a priori* that we are free. If we are not free, morality makes no sense, and we should have to give up on morality. Freedom for us is, therefore, an *a priori* (necessary) assumption.

Notice, however, that these are presuppositions, and not prior requirements. You cannot wait until you are certain that you are genuinely free to act before you do anything, or you would never move! Rather, by taking the decision to act, and taking it in line with what you see as your duty, you presuppose that you are free. The same is implied by the postulates of God and Immortality. What does it say about life, if you experience and respond to a moral 'ought'?

10 For those who want to go further:

Note that this level of knowledge and understanding would **not** be required in order to gain full marks in an A-Level essay. Points 10 and 11 are included here because they are important parts of Kant's ethics, and for those who would like to have that overview they are worth the trouble of getting to grips with. We have already mentioned Kant's use of the term *noumena/noumenal*. It is advisable to understand this idea, as described in the following point.

- For Kant, reality (meaning what is 'really real') has two aspects: the **noumenal** and the **phenomenal**. The phenomenal realm is what reality appears to be like according to our senses. The noumenal realm is the way reality 'really' is.

- To illustrate this from modern physics and philosophy, a good example of this difference is given in Bertrand Russell's, *The Problems of Philosophy*, in Chapter 1 on 'Appearance and Reality'. We experience the reality of objects like tables and chairs as part of our every-day experience; but if we talk about the colour of a table, that colour will appear different from different points of view and under different conditions of lighting, and since each different viewpoint has as good a right to be considered real, we are compelled to deny that the table has any one particular colour. [Note 5] If, then, we go down into the table through to the level of atoms, and then to electrons and quarks, and possibly to one-dimensional vibrating strings, physics tells us that reality appears to be completely different, and that this level is more 'fundamental' than the level of our sense experience. Appearance and reality are different aspects of the world.

- Returning to Kant, our knowledge of the phenomena is *a posteriori*, through sense experience, so is empirical. Since our senses literally tell us only of the phenomena, knowledge of the noumena would have to be *a priori* – knowledge that is independent of sense experience, of things as they really are.

- So Kant's next question is – can we have *a priori* knowledge of the noumena? He thinks that we can, and gives mathematics as an example: maths (he argues) is **synthetic *a priori***, meaning that 1) it gives us new information that is 2) necessarily true. Kant argues that the Categorical Imperative is also a synthetic *a priori* proposition, and that all our moral duties derive from the Categorical Imperative.

i Moral judgements are *a priori* because we do not know them by sense experience. If you think about it, experience tells us about the way things *are*, not about the way they *ought* to be.

ii Moral judgements have **necessary** force – rational necessity – because the force of the moral 'ought' tells us what we must do: hence we can know our **moral duties**.

iii Moral judgements are **synthetic** because we cannot establish what we ought to do by arguing about definitions (remember: analytic statements are true by definition – by the words used, for example 'Frozen water is ice'). Moral judgements must therefore be synthetic. Synthetic judgements are true by how their meaning relates to the world. As we said above (point 5), people have to work out their own rules using the Categorical Imperative, which is a rational, reflective principle which takes account of people's wants and desires.

You now have the substance of what Kant means by the 'synthetic *a priori*'.

11 Second point for those who want to go further:

Meta-ethically, Kant is an ethical non-naturalist.

You will remember from Chapter 4 Introduction to meta-ethics: the meaning of right and wrong that G.E. Moore, in his critique of ethical naturalism, decided that ethical statements are cognitive/factual but *non-natural*: they are moral *intuitions*. We also suggested that Divine Command Theory is a non-naturalist meta-ethical theory, because it holds that moral commands are from a *super*natural source – God.

Now consider the following things about Kant's theory of ethics:

- The command to obey the Categorical Imperative is a rational choice of the will. The mind is not physical, and is not governed by the laws of nature, so the will belongs to the noumenal realm.

- The noumenal realm is outside space and time, and therefore outside the realm of the natural sciences/of scientific enquiry, so knowledge of the noumena must therefore be *non*-natural.

- **Morality therefore exists in the noumenal realm, and not the world of sense experience/facts, and is known non-naturally.**

Key terms

Noumenal (realm) Reality as it 'really' is, experienced by the synthetic *a priori*.

Phenomenal (realm) The world of phenomena – the world as experienced through the senses, governed by the laws of cause and effect.

Synthetic *a priori* Synthetic *a priori* propositions (such as the Categorical Imperative) provide new information that is necessarily true. Moral judgements are **a priori** because we do not know them by sense experience. They have **necessary** force – the compulsion of the moral 'ought'. They are **synthetic** because we cannot establish what we ought to do by arguing about analytic definitions.

Evaluating Kant's Categorical Imperative

Of the making of judgements about whether Kant's theory of ethics works or not, there is no end. Here is a selection of linked arguments, in no particular order:

1 Kant's principle of the Categorical Imperative and universalisability is simple and effective.

The Categorical Imperative is expressed by the principle of universalisability, and this gives us a good tool to find out what the universal laws are. In its basic form, it can be understood even by children: if you want to murder, rob, rape, steal and lie, then you need to be happy that other people do all those things to you, whenever they feel like it.

Response:

The Categorical Imperative/universalisability principle is no more believable than Divine Command Theory. Both theories amount to non-natural guesswork. If we look at the state of the world, it is obvious that there are no agreed universal moral rules, so the idea of a Categorical Imperative is Kant's wishful thinking. Morality is in this world, and not in some imagined noumenal realm. Utilitarianism gets it right on that score.

2 Kant highlights a problem with Bentham's consequentialism.

Bentham's emphasis on consequences means that a utilitarian is justified in doing a bad act to bring about good consequences (for example killing one person to save seven). For Kant, this can never be justified.

Response:

If the consequence is good, then doesn't this make the act good? If killing one person saves the lives of seven, then there is an excess of good over bad. How many people would Kant let die in order to avoid killing one innocent person – the whole population?

3 Kant's theory cuts out emotion in favour of reason.

This is good, because if we are swayed by emotion, then we show favouritism, which is immoral.

Response:

This again shows that Kant's theory is unrealistic. As Hume shows, it is impossible for humans to ignore their emotions, because emotions are part of what it means to be human. Moreover for Hume, it is moral sentiment combined with utility that motivates us to act.

4 Kant's theory is influential today because the modern emphasis on human rights, equality and justice stems from him.

This means that humans have intrinsic value, so they cannot be enslaved, for example.

Response:

That may be so, but Kant's emphasis is completely anthropocentric (human-centred), so that humans alone have intrinsic value. According to Kant, animals are non-rational and therefore cannot be seen as members of the moral community. This justifies just about any cruelty to animals and is environmentally of no more use than the Aristotelian/Thomist conception of animals.

Kant also ignores the fact that many humans are incapable of the intellectual effort required to universalise maxims.

5 **Kant's three postulates of practical reason include two that are religious: God and immortality. This makes little sense for those who are not religious.**

Kant's views on the autonomy of reason, morality and the moral agent seem to be compromised by the undeniable religious elements in the theory. This might not be a problem for those who are religious, but it puts a question mark over the success of the theory.

Response:

The main thrust of Kant's ethical theory can be used in a secular sense, and many do use it in that way, ignoring the religious elements.

6 **Kant's theory does not make it clear what to do where there are conflicting moral duties.**

The obvious example is the dilemma of the axe murder, where there are two duties that apply: the duty to not tell the truth, and the duty to preserve innocent life. To say that the agent could give an evasive response ('I saw your victim at a football match two hours ago') seems unsatisfactory, because even an evasion is a form of untruth.

Responses:

There are a number of responses available in answer to this, for example:

i   W.D. Ross's theory of **_prima facie_ duties** (pay back the harm we do to others/do not injure others/return favours and services/do not harm the innocent/look after parents) was intended as an amendment to Kant's theory. (To remind yourself of Ross' theory, see pages 130–131.) For Ross, evasion would be unnecessary: you would simply lie to the maniac, because you have a _prima facie_ duty to protect the innocent. Ross would argue that this is because careful thinking about the problem reveals an _intuitive_ truth: the intended victim's life is more important than any problem about lying. Kant himself would probably have rejected this, because a moral _intuition_ is not the same as the _good will_; nevertheless one can still be a Kantian and modify Kant's ideas where it seems right to do so, and this seems to be just such a case.

ii In a similar way, there seems to be no reason why someone should not decide to universalise a rule to allow a white lie: 'Put your respect for life above the rule to tell the truth'. In the case of the axe murderer, the white lie would allow the agent to say, 'I do not know where your victim is'. If the axe-murderer is deranged, then it would seem the best course to tell a white lie in order to save the murderer from killing somebody else.

Key term

Prima facie duties W.D. Ross's amendment to Kantian ethics, that we have _prima facie_ ('on the face of it') duties, for example, to parents, children and the innocent; and that in cases where categorical imperatives conflict, one of these duties can take priority over another: so with the mad axe-murder, the duty to save an innocent life overrides the duty to tell the truth.

How far Bentham and Kant's ethical theories are consistent with religious moral decision-making

Christian religious decision-making is a diverse creature. For example, we have looked at three varieties of it, and you now understand the differences in how they approach moral decision-making:

● Aquinas' Natural Moral Law
● Divine Command Theory
● Fletcher's Situation Ethics.

Natural Moral Law begins with the synderesis rule: that humans aim to do good and avoid evil. It emphasises the role of reason, and the primary and secondary precepts. Divine Command Theory requires that moral decisions are consistent with the laws and principles of scripture. Situation Ethics focuses specifically on the law of love, applied situationally. In other words, religious decision-making covers a broad perspective of moral ideas. Nevertheless, all Christian theories are based on God's moral demands, expressed through the teachings of Jesus and St Paul.

How consistent are these ideas with Bentham's Utilitarianism and Kant's Categorical Imperative?

How far is Bentham's Utilitarianism consistent with religious decision-making?

For many, the answer is: 'not very':

1 Bentham's Utilitarianism was formulated independently of belief in God.

If God is irrelevant to the theory, then this suggests that Utilitarian moral decision-making is inconsistent with any religious form of moral decision-making. Bentham in fact looked forward to a future time when religion would become irrelevant in human affairs, which is one of the reasons why he left his body for dissection and display: neither he nor any God would have a further use for it.

2 For Utilitarianism, self-interest is inevitable. Christianity lacks this focus.

Bentham envisaged that a properly utilitarian society must be a secular one, because religious belief perverted the principle of utility, particularly in so far as it encouraged individuals to act against their own self-interest and that of the community as a whole. Since Christians seek to put self-interest on one side, Bentham himself clearly saw little or no consistency between Utilitarian and Christian moral decision-making.

3 Unlike Utilitarianism, religion has a spiritual dimension.

Religion emphasises the spiritual dimension to life and the relationship with a personal God. In other words, the kind of happiness that Christianity looks for is rooted in the Kingdom of Heaven, whereas for Bentham, happiness is pointless if it is not quantifiable within society as we experience it in day-to-day living.

Act Utilitarianism makes decisions for specific situations. Christianity makes decisions with regard to the will of God and the reward of life after death.

4 Christian moral decision-making has a particular focus on the weaker members of society: the meek, the poor, those who are diseased and suffering.

Bentham's Act Utilitarianism is not really compatible with this approach, since it insists that every individual's happiness counts as one.

5 Christianity in general gives greater value to rules in decision-making.

Not all forms of Christianity are rule based, but most are, so moral decisions in Divine Command Theory and Natural Moral Law are based on specific rules. In Act Utilitarianism, the 'primary principle of Utility' is more important than any rule, to the extent than any law or rule that does not maximise happiness/minimise pain is a bad law or rule.

6 In Christianity, to be truly moral, a decision must be made in the right mental state.

In Bentham's thinking, the state of mind of the individual making moral decisions cannot be known, because we cannot read minds; so the individual's task is to maximise happiness in any situation. In Christian moral decision-making, the agent's mental state matters, because God knows people's thoughts. In the 'Sermon on the Mount', Jesus reminds those around him that the law forbids adultery, but then says that any man who looks at a woman lustfully has already committed adultery in his heart (Matthew 5:27–28). In this respect, Christians and utilitarians are looking at moral decisions from different points of view.

For others, however, there is greater compatibility:

1 Jesus' actions are utilitarian because he judges people by how they respond to the needy.

When Jesus was asked by what authority he acted, he pointed to the healing of people and the feeding of the hungry as illustrating the sort of change that his ministry was bringing about. In other words, even if not done for utilitarian reasons, he sees utilitarian arguments as relevant to an assessment of moral action. In the Parable of the Sheep and the Goats (Matthew 25:31–46), he says that those who ignored strangers, those needing clothes, the hungry, the sick and those in prison, will be punished by God. People are to be judged according to their response to situations of need. The relief of need, which is at the heart of Bentham's approach (it brings about the greatest happiness for the greatest number), is also usable as a religious evaluation of behaviour.

2 Like a utilitarian, Jesus acts situationally.

The situational response is the essence of Act Utilitarianism, which aims to maximise utility *in the situation*. As an example: for both Jesus and Act Utilitarians, the situation dictates the response, and in dealing with any particular situation, laws can sometimes be irrelevant. The law of the land has to be obeyed, unless the case is extreme, but *morally*, the law can be redundant. For example, there are several incidents recorded in the Gospels (such as Matthew 12:1–14) where the Pharisees accused Jesus of breaking Sabbath laws, but Jesus responded that God's law simply required them to do what was right in the situation, such as healing the sick.

3 John Stuart Mill claimed that there is a direct link between Utilitarianism and Christianity. Jesus made decisions by means of the 'golden rule', and so do utilitarians.

As you know, Mill was Bentham's direct successor in developing utilitarian theory, and his comments here apply equally to Bentham's version of the theory. Although on the whole Mill had very little time for Christianity, he says this (where the text is in bold, this has been added for emphasis):

> I must … repeat, what the assailants of utilitarianism seldom have the justice to acknowledge, that the happiness which forms the utilitarian standard of what is right in conduct, is not the agent's own happiness, but that of all concerned. As between his own happiness and that of others, utilitarianism requires him to be as strictly impartial as a disinterested and benevolent spectator. **In the golden rule of Jesus of Nazareth, we read the complete spirit of the ethics of utility. To do as you would be done by, and to love your neighbour as yourself, constitute the ideal perfection of utilitarian morality.** As the means of making the nearest approach to this ideal, utility would enjoin, first, that laws and social arrangements should place the happiness, or (as, speaking practically it may be called) the interest of every individual as nearly as possible in harmony with the interest of the whole; and secondly, that education and opinion, which have so vast a power over human character, should so use that power as to establish in the mind of every individual an indissoluble association between his own happiness and the good of the whole … [Note 6]

4 Bentham accepted religion in his assessment of the feelings of self-interest and sympathy by which he says that we are governed.

In his *Essay on Bentham*, Mill says that Bentham thinks of 'man' as being governed by pleasures and pains, self-interest and sympathy. All of the principles that drive or restrain individuals are self-love or else love or hatred towards other sentient beings.

Bentham does not exclude religion: religion comes under 'self-interest' (because it gives us the prospect of divine rewards or punishments). It also comes under 'sympathy', as 'the devotional feeling under that of sympathy with God.' [Note 7] Having said that, for Bentham, the effect of religion on human thinking here is no more than psychological, since he believed that religion was fundamentally untrue.

As a matter of fact, Jesus does not exclude self-love from being a natural part of the human character. In his summary of the great commandment (Mark 12:28–31) Jesus brings together love of God and love of one's neighbour, the second of these being to 'Love your neighbour as yourself'. This clearly acknowledges the principle that love of self and love of others are interconnected. Unless one grows up to love the self, it would hardly be possible to love others. This principle is acknowledged by Bentham, so Utilitarianism and Christianity both acknowledge the value of self-love.

There is, of course, a difference. For Bentham, as we said above, religion, although it is classified under both self-interest and sympathy, is seen as a psychological disposition in much the same way as Freud considers it: it might bring some benefits to human life, but its doctrines are false. For Christians, love of God, together with love of self and of one's neighbour summarise the whole of the moral law. Moreover, as the theologian Vincent Taylor remarks: '[A]s Jesus presents them, they form an indissoluble unity: love for man arises out of love for God.' [Note 8]

How far is Kant's Categorical Imperative consistent with religious decision-making?

Note: by 'Categorical Imperative' here, we include the attendant 'package' of Kant's ethical theory based on the Categorical Imperative itself.

Kant's ethics are compatible with religion in several respects:

Commentators on Kant cover almost the whole range of possibilities concerning Kant's views on God, including the idea that he was an atheist. It is very difficult, however, to show that Kant was anything of the sort if one looks at the whole range of his discussion of religion. There is a clear compatibility with religion in several respects. For example:

1 Kant's concept of the good will is at least compatible with Christian ideas about virtue.

For Kant, the good will is the only thing that is good without reservation or qualification. This is (at least) compatible with the Christian idea that the virtuous man is the one who freely practises the good because that is part of his religious intentions. For Christians and Kantians, the importance of intention and will in assessing morality is crucial.

2 Kant's emphasis on the use of reason to define moral truths is similar to Aquinas' use of reason to understand the natural moral law.

For Kant, pure practical reason chooses actions because they are good in themselves. For Aquinas, reason is a God-given faculty that underpins morality.

3 Moreover, the 'end' of moral decision-making is similar for both Kant and Aquinas.

For Kant, the 'end' of moral activity is to achieve the perfect union of virtue and happiness in the *summum bonum*. For Aquinas, the end is union with God in the next life.

4 For Kant, his 'postulates of practical reason' include two religious ideas.

At the end of his *Groundwork*, Kant's moral theory assumes beliefs about human nature and the world that are rooted completely in religion rather than in unaided reason: God and immortality are both required in order to make sense of human moral nature.

5 Kant's principle of universalisability is clearly compatible with religious ideas concerning our behaviour to others.

For example, in Luke 6:31 Jesus says:

> 'Do unto others as you would have them do to you.'

This is the essence of the Categorical Imperative/the principle of universalisability, as is Jesus' statement that the second great principle of religion is to love one's neighbour as oneself (Mark 12: 31). These two Christian principles are universal in the same sense as Kant's Imperative.

However, Kant's Categorical Imperative can be seen as being more consistent with secular rather than religious ideas

1 His system is based on Enlightenment values of reason and autonomy.

In particular, his view of the Categorical Imperative, universalisability, and the value of individuals as ends in themselves, together with the ideal society as being a 'kingdom of ends', all suggest the inherent value of individuals, and the rule of human reason, without reference to religion. He is, after all, generally regarded as the leading figure of the European Enlightenment, where human reason and autonomy are seen to triumph over earlier ages of superstition and the unquestioning acceptance of authority.

2 The moral law must be autonomous, and not religious, for the agent to have a good will.

> **Key term**
>
> **Volition** Exercise of the will.

Kant insists that the only thing that is good in itself is the good will, and the good will is self-evidently a matter of **volition**. Kant, therefore, excludes all consideration of divine command in his ethics, because by definition following a divine command involves accepting the moral will of another authority.

3 Equally, Kant makes no appeal to any text or scripture as an ethical authority.

All such authority is invested in the moral agent, who has to assent to the Categorical Imperative through practical reason, and not by submitting to the dictates of any (supposedly) God-given text.

4 Kant's principle of universalisability can be used in secular ethics, for example Hare used a version of it in his meta-ethical theory of Prescriptivism; so universalisability needs no religious reference.

The foregoing points suggest that Kant's Categorical Imperative can function just as well without any religious context. If moral law and the good will are autonomous, and if moral autonomy is invested in the moral agent rather than in any text or scripture, then the religious parts of Kant's theory can be abandoned without weakening his ethical approach. In fact, his ideas about God and the *summum bonum* can be seen as being *incompatible* with his ethical approach, since they weaken his argument about moral *law* and moral *will*.

5 Kant's Categorical Imperative is an unconditional command (*do not murder; do not steal, etc.*). The unconditional nature of the command is incompatible with some versions of Christian ethics:

217

- Fletcher's Situation Ethics holds that, depending on the situation, any moral command or rule can be ignored in order to maximise love.
- Within Catholic ethics, Aquinas held that there are situations where secondary precepts are not absolute. For example, it is permissible to steal in order to save a starving man from death.

Concluding comments

Bentham and Kant: the essential difference

The essential difference between Bentham's Act Utilitarianism and Kant's Categorical Imperativism is their meta-ethical starting point. Act Utilitarianism is an example of ethical naturalism – it is a cognitivist and **naturalist** theory of ethics. It holds that ethical values are factual – they are about the facts of pain and pleasure, and those facts are really 'in the world'.

For Kant, morality is cognitivist but it is **non-naturalist** as opposed to naturalist. The command to obey the Categorical Imperative is a rational choice of the will. The mind is not physical, and is not governed by the laws of nature, so the moral will belongs to the noumenal realm, which is outside space and time and therefore cannot be investigated by the natural sciences. Moral facts are non-natural.

Bentham and Kant: the main problems

Each of these theories has its problems. Utilitarianism is often said to fail because, as a naturalist theory, it cannot bridge **the gap between the 'is' and the 'ought'** (we looked at this in detail in Chapter 4 Introduction to meta-ethics: the meaning of right and wrong). Moore argued (following Hume) that all naturalist theories, Utilitarianism included, commit the naturalistic fallacy of going from an 'is' to an 'ought' – from facts to moral values. We cannot go from 'happiness is what all humans desire' to 'you ought to bring about the greatest happiness for the greatest number'.

Kant agreed with Hume that one cannot rationally argue to an 'ought' from an 'is', so Kant concluded that morality cannot be based on the evidence of the senses/on anything we *observe* in the phenomenal realm. Hence Kant got over the problem by arguing that morality is not *in* the realm of the senses – it is in the noumenal realm – and we have synthetic *a priori* knowledge of morality. The issue that many modern philosophers have with Kant, however, is what they see as his invention of an extra **ontological** realm (a second realm of existence) – the noumenal, for which there is no evidence.

Key term

Ontology A branch of metaphysics that deals with the nature of existence/being.

Possible defences of Bentham

You will remember that in Chapter 4 Introduction to meta-ethics: the meaning of right and wrong, we suggested that there is a solution to the problem of the 'is-ought gap', namely that there really is a factual content to human morality – namely the flourishing of human beings. Humans are one part of the total biosphere, so the fact of the biosphere flourishing will automatically entail the factual flourishing of human beings. Good, then, is (factually) that which brings about the flourishing of human beings (or, better, of the biosphere as a whole), and bad is that which interferes with flourishing. If this is right, then Utilitarianism, which focuses on human and animal happiness/pleasure/benefit, is perhaps an incomplete theory: these things are necessary to human flourishing, but human flourishing is a much wider concept than just happiness/pleasure/benefit. Act Utilitarianism therefore takes us (only) part of the way.

Possible defences of Kant

Kant's postulate that there is a noumenal world does not invent a separate world: the phenomenal and the noumenal are, in his thinking, two aspects of *one* reality. You will remember that in Chapter 3 Self, death and afterlife, we discussed the theory of Dual Aspect Monism, according to which mind and matter are not distinct substances; rather they are two aspects of one underlying/unknown substance. If you also consider what we have said about the appearance of reality at the level of quantum events, Kant's idea of a noumenal realm is not as unnecessary as it might seem to some. Whether Kant shows that morality is really in a noumenal reality as opposed to the world we experience through our senses is for you to consider.

Both Utilitarianism and Categorical Imperativism are powerful accounts of the nature of human morality. You do not have to choose between them, since the simple answer is that we do not have absolute knowledge of the nature of human morality.

Technical terms for Bentham and Kant

Act Utilitarianism   Bentham's account of Utilitarianism: in any situation, one should choose the action that maximises utility.

Autonomy   The state of being self-governed/self-ruled/free from external control or influences.

Categorical Imperative   An absolute/categorical (undeniable), unconditional, moral command, for example **Do not** murder, **do not** steal, **do not** lie.

Maxim   A general guideline or principle of action.

Noumenal (realm)   Reality as it 'really' is, experienced by the synthetic *a priori*.

Ontology   A branch of metaphysics that deals with the nature of existence/being.

'Ought implies can'   Kant's view that the force of the moral 'ought' – the Categorical Imperative that we *ought* to do our moral duty – implies that we *can* do our moral duty.

Phenomenal (realm)   The world of phenomena – the world as experienced through the senses, governed by the laws of cause and effect.

Postulate   A presupposition or assumption which you must have accepted in order to make sense of your moral choices. In Kant's ethics, the three 'postulates of practical reason' are: God, freedom and immortality, and these underpin Kant's doctrine of the *summum bonum*.

***Prima facie* duties**   W.D. Ross's amendment to Kantian ethics, that we have *prima facie* ('on the face of it') duties,

for example, to parents, children and the innocent; and that in cases where categorical imperatives conflict, one of these duties can take priority over another: so with the mad axe-murder, the duty to save an innocent life overrides the duty to tell the truth.

Summum bonum   The highest/supreme good: the culmination of Kant's ethics where virtue meets its appropriate reward of perfect happiness.

Synthetic *a priori*   Synthetic *a priori* propositions (such as the Categorical Imperative) provide new information that is necessarily true. Moral judgements are *a priori* because we do not know them by sense experience. They have **necessary** force – the compulsion of the moral 'ought'. They are **synthetic** because we cannot establish what we ought to do by arguing about analytic definitions.

Universalisability   The main formulation of the Categorical Imperative: Act only according to that maxim whereby you can at the same time will that it should become a universal law.

Utility   That property in any object, whereby it tends to produce benefit, advantage, pleasure, good, or happiness; or to prevent mischief, pain, evil, unhappiness to the party whose interest is considered (an individual or the wider community).

Volition   Exercise of the will.

Summary of Bentham and Kant

Bentham's Act Utilitarianism

1 People are motivated to seek pleasure and to avoid pain.

2 Things are good/bad, right/wrong according to the principle of utility – what is beneficial confers happiness/benefit.

3 Do that which gives the greatest happiness/ benefit for the greatest number (a democratic and scientific principle).

4 This can be brought about by the Hedonic Calculus, measuring pain and pleasure to assess whether an act shows a balance of pleasure over pain.

5 Bentham's Act Utilitarianism seeks to maximise pleasure/minimise pain in a particular situation or in the community (the community meaning everyone concerned).

6 The theory does not claim that some pleasures (for example poetry) are superior to others (for example push-pin). It does claim that the happiness of each person counts exactly for 1.

Evaluating Bentham's Act Utilitarianism

1 **Objection**: it puts too much emphasis on the consequences of our acts, whereas we do not know the future. **Reply**: most moral situations we encounter are 'general classes of acts', and we know very well that acts such as murder, theft and robbery cause pain.

2 **Objection**: it ignores motives, rules and duties, and these are morally crucial. **Reply**: not so: rules are useful because they have been shown to bring happiness. Where they do not, it is right to abandon them. The motive of a utilitarian is the same as the intended consequence – to maximise happiness, and that is also the single utilitarian duty.

3 **Objection**: Utilitarianism ignores minority rights, and can even justify gang rape. **Reply**: injustice to the majority is worse than injustice to the minority, so which should you do? The allegation about gang rape misunderstands the Hedonic Calculus, which covers the interests *of all concerned*, and could never justify gang rape.

4 **Objection**: Utilitarianism fails because it cannot bridge the 'is-ought gap'. **Reply**: If you ask people what they want, they want happiness, and that justifies the utilitarian claim of the 'greatest happiness principle'. No other explanation is possible, and no other explanation is needed.

Kant's Categorical Imperative

1 Only one thing is good without qualification: the good will. The good will is autonomous.

2 We are all aware of the moral 'ought' – of having a sense of moral obligation. From this we can form an account of our moral duties.

3 Kant's account is deontological: we develop moral rules, because moral rules bind us to our duty. Kant's theory does have consequential/ teleological aspects (see point 5 below).

4 Duty gives ethics a single focus. After you have reasoned out what you should do, consequences can no longer be considered. Acting morally is not about what you enjoy, or about personal benefit: it is based on pure practical reason.

5 However, the categorical 'ought' does *not* mean that we should do 'duty for duty's sake *whatever the consequences*'. The consequences have to be worked through before you can tell whether the maxim you want to adopt conforms to the Categorical Imperative. There has to be an organic link here with people's wants and desires, otherwise you would decide upon principles that nobody wanted to follow.

6 The force of the Categorical Imperative [CI] can be seen by contrasting it with that of hypothetical imperatives [HI]. Whereas the HI has the form, 'If you want X, then do Y', the CI simply says 'Do X/ Do not do X'. Only the CI can lead us to universal maxims (principles of action) that everybody ought to follow.

7 There is only one CI expressed in three main formulations.

The first is: Universalisability: *Act only according to that maxim whereby you can at the same time will that it should become a universal law.*
(A maxim is a general guideline or principle of action.)
Kant illustrates universalisability through four examples – making false promises; lying; refusing to help others; neglecting talents. These would in each case lead to a contradiction, so could not be universalised.

The second formulation is the Practical Imperative, and the third is the Kingdom of Ends. These follow on logically from the first.

8 The CI is, however, challenged by the existence of 'radical evil'. This happens when people take a maxim of self-conceit/self-interest as their main maxim, which leads them to bend every other maxim to that one maxim.

9 Kant's ethical theory culminates in the idea of the *summum bonum* – the highest/supreme good, where virtue is rewarded by perfect happiness. If 'ought implies can', then the realisation that we ought to do our duty tells us that we can, in fact, do our duty. In order to make sense of this conviction, Kant argues that we have to make three important assumptions about the world: three 'postulates of practical reason': God, freedom and immortality. Immortality is the reward of virtue, and God is needed to bring about the immortality that individuals hope for as the reward for virtue, and to judge whose virtue is worthy of that immortality. Freedom of the will is the core of morality. Experience cannot tell us that we are free, but if we were not free, morality would be impossible. We have to assume, therefore, that we are free, and in fact this is a valid *a priori* assumption: the will knows noumenally that it is free.

10 [For those who want to go this far] In Kant's metaphysics, reality has two aspects: the phenomenal world of sense experience, and the noumenal world, which is the way reality 'really' is. The body is subject to the laws of the phenomenal world, but according to Kant, the mind can have synthetic *a priori* knowledge of the noumenal world, for example through maths and through the moral awareness of the CI.

11 [For those who want to go this far] The command (the 'ought') to obey the CI is a rational choice of the will, and since the will is not physical (it is not governed by the laws of nature), the will belongs to the noumenal realm. This is outside space and time and cannot be known by scientific enquiry. Moral facts, therefore, cannot be known naturally (through the facts about *this* world) – they can only be known non-naturally. Kant is therefore (meta-ethically) a non-naturalist.

Evaluating Kant's Categorical Imperative

1 ✓ The CI and the principle of universalisability are clear. We know what the sense of 'ought' is, and we know the principle of universalisability instinctively. **Response**: Kant has added an unnecessary layer (the noumenal) to what exists. It makes more sense to see morality as a product of this world, as in Utilitarianism. Moral disagreements happen simply because people do not agree about moral 'facts', not because they decide on the wrong maxims.

2 ✓ Kant picks out what is often seen as a major flaw in Bentham's Act Utilitarianism – it justifies bad acts to bring about consequences (for example killing 1 to save 7), and that is immoral. **Response**: How many people would Kant let die in order to save one innocent person – the entire human race? If the utilitarian *consequence* is good (saving the majority), then the *act* is good.

3 ✓ Kant's theory cuts out emotion in favour of reason. **Response**: This is unrealistic – as Hume says, it is impossible for humans to shut off their emotions. It is moral sentiment that motivates us to act. For utilitarians it is the desire for happiness/pleasure.

4 ✓ Kant's theory is influential today because of the modern emphasis on human rights, equality and justice, which stems from him. **Response**: this is yet another emphasis of a lack of realism in Kant's ethics. It is anthropocentric and ignores the rights of all other species. Contrast that with Bentham's Utilitarianism.

5 ✗ The religious parts of Kant's theory (for example the postulates of God and immortality) make no sense to those who are not religious. **Response**: The main thrust of Kant's theory can be (and is) used by secular ethicists.

6 ✗ Kant has no clear answer to what we should do where moral duties conflict. **Response**: 1) A Kantian might follow W.D. Ross's modification of Kant's theory (the idea of *prima facie* duties). *Prima facie* duties can be prioritised by your moral intuition, depending on the situation, so you could lie to the axe-murderer; 2) Another Kantian might universalise a rule to tell a white lie: 'Put your respect for life above the rule to tell the truth'. This would allow you to tell the axe-murderer that you did not know of his victim's whereabouts.

How far is Bentham's Utilitarianism consistent with religious (Christian) decision-making?

Bear in mind that Christian moral decision-making is a very varied thing, ranging (for example) from Aquinas' emphasis on reason to Divine Command Theory and Fletcher's Situation Ethics.

Incompatibility for Bentham

1 Bentham considered religion as an untrue irrelevance, inconsistent with Utilitarian moral decision-making.

2 For Utilitarianism, self-interest is inevitable. Christianity lacks this focus.

3 Unlike Utilitarianism, religion has a spiritual dimension, for example in its focus on the Kingdom of Heaven and life after death.

4 Christian moral decision-making has a particular focus on weaker members of society as requiring more attention. For Bentham, every individual counts only as 1.

5 Christianity generally gives a greater value to moral rules, which in Bentham's system are merely 'secondary principles'.

6 In Christianity, right decision-making requires the right mental state, not least because God knows people's inmost thoughts (see what Jesus says about adultery, in the Sermon on the Mount). This is not an issue for Bentham, since people's thoughts are private and God does not exist to know them anyway.

Compatibility for Bentham

1 Jesus' actions are utilitarian, because he judges people on how they respond to the needy, as in the Parable of the Sheep and the Goats.

2 Like a utilitarian, Jesus acts situationally, for example in connection with the Jewish Sabbath laws.

3 Mill insisted that 'In the golden rule of Jesus of Nazareth, we read the complete spirit of the ethics of utility. To do as you would be done by, and to love your neighbour as yourself, constitute the ideal perfection of utilitarian morality.'

4 Although Christianity is not focused on self-interest, Jesus does not exclude self-love from being a natural part of the human character; for example, in his summary of the great commandment: 'Love your neighbour as yourself'. Love of others is not possible without love of self.

How far is Kant's theory of the Categorical Imperative consistent with religious (Christian) decision-making?

Compatibility for Kant

1 Kant's concept of the good will is compatible with Christian ideas about virtue, because the virtuous Christian man *freely* practises the good.

2 Kant's emphasis on the use of reason to define moral truths has many echoes in Aquinas.

3 Moreover, the end of moral activity is similar for Kant and Aquinas: for Kant, the end is the perfect union of virtue with happiness in the *summum bonum*; for Aquinas the end is union with God in the next life.

4 Two of Kant's postulates of practical reason are religious: God and immortality.

5 Kant's principle of universalisability is compatible with religious ideas about behaviour towards others; for example, 'Do unto others as you would have them do to you' (Jesus, in Luke 6:31) is the essence of the Categorical Imperative/universalisability.

Incompatibility for Kant

1 His system is based on Enlightenment ideas of reason and autonomy, and these are secular aims needing no religious support.

2 The moral law must be autonomous for the agent to have a good will, so it does not rely on God/divine command.

3 Kant makes no appeal to scripture as a moral authority for making moral decisions.

4 His principle of universalisability can be used in secular ethics (for example R.M. Hare's Prescriptivism).

Points 1–4 above show that Kant's ethics can be divorced from any religious context without losing *any* important aspect of the theory. In fact, the religious elements stand outside his approach, and his ideas about God and the *summum bonum* are arguably *incompatible* with his stress on the autonomy of the moral law and the good will.

5 Kant's Categorical Imperative is incompatible with some versions/aspects of Christian religious ethics; for example, Fletcher's Situation Ethics, and Aquinas' view that secondary precepts are not always absolute.

Concluding comments

Perhaps the major difference between Bentham and Kant is that Bentham's Utilitarianism is, meta-ethically, a naturalist theory of morality: morality is in the *facts* about pleasure and pain *in this world*. By contrast, Kant is a non-naturalist: morality exists in the noumena, not the phenomena.

As a naturalist theory, Utilitarianism is often rejected because it fails to get over the 'is-ought gap': we can't go from: 'Happiness is what humans desire', to: 'You ought to bring about the greatest happiness for the greatest number'.

Kant accepted Hume's argument that you can't go from an *is* to an *ought*, and solved it by putting morality into a noumenal realm, as a result of which Kant is often accused of inventing an extra layer to existence.

In defence of Bentham, we can make a good case for thinking that the 'is-ought gap' does not exist. Morality really is in the facts of this world, and this closes the so-called gap. Morality is factually about human flourishing (or, more widely, about the flourishing of the biosphere of which humans are a part), so 'good' is what contributes to the flourishing of the biosphere, and 'bad' is anything that damages it. If this works, then Utilitarianism perhaps doesn't go quite far enough by saying that the good is happiness/pleasure/benefit, but nevertheless is on the right lines.

In defence of Kant, he does not describe the noumenal realm as a different reality: it is one aspect of the same reality. Dual Aspect Monism similarly sees mind and matter not as two different substances but as two aspects of one as-yet-unknown substance. Quantum physics describes a layer of reality that is completely different from what we experience at our level. Kant's description of the phenomenal and noumenal aspects of reality may possibly be correct.

In the end, we do not know the true nature of human morality, so you can decide between Bentham and Kant, or you can refuse to make a decision until further knowledge comes to light (if it ever does).

Here is a brief comparison table for Bentham and Kant. It is not meant to be all-embracing, so you can expand it as you see fit:

A quick-glance comparison table for Kantian ethics and Bentham's Act Utilitarianism	
Kant	**Bentham**
Morality is rooted in the noumenal realm	Morality is rooted in this world
Meta-ethically, Kant is a non-naturalist	Meta-ethically, Bentham is a naturalist
Morality is seen in the rational choice of the will, which is noumenal	Morality is seen in the facts about happiness/well-being in this world
The only thing that is good in itself, without reservation, is a good will	Pleasure is the sole good and pain is the sole evil
Kant's system is deontological, based on duty, rules and motive, although to follow the Categorical Imperative requires us to think through the consequences of our intended actions	Bentham's system is consequentialist, based on the greatest happiness for the greatest number. It is not without motive, since motive and consequence are the same: to maximise happiness and minimise pain
Morality is primarily in the mind	Morality is primarily in what you do in the world
Following the Categorical Imperative makes us worthy of happiness	Happiness is an end in itself
Kantian rules are absolute – they cannot be broken	Bentham's Utilitarianism is relativist, so rules are merely 'secondary principles' and are subordinate to the 'primary principle' of utility. Rules can be broken if they conflict with the primary principle of utility
People must be treated as ends in themselves (although this does not mean, for example, that we can't use taxi-drivers to get us from A to B)	People can be treated as a means to an end, for example killing 1 to save 10 (the alternative is to allow injustice to 9 rather than to 1)
Immorality is inconsistency through faulty reasoning	Immorality is a failure to maximise happiness and minimise pain
Kant starts from what is *right*	Bentham starts with what is *good*

Component 2

Christianity and dialogues

Christianity, gender and sexuality

You will need to consider the following items for this section

1 Historical and social factors that have influenced developments in Christian thinking about these issues including: The development of biblical criticism, especially in the nineteenth century, and the resulting freedom to challenge traditional readings of passages such as 1 Timothy 2:8–15; The changing roles of men and women in society outside of religion; The rights given to women by secular governments.

2 Developments in Christian thought, including feminist approaches:

- Debates about female ordination in the Church of England up to and after 1994; the continuing debate today.

- A comparison of the significant ideas of Daphne Hampson and Rosemary Radford Ruether about the patriarchal nature of Christianity including Hampson's view that Christianity is irredeemably sexist and Ruether's ideas about the androgynous Christ and her view that the female nature is more Christlike than the male.

- Different Christian views about celibacy, marriage, homosexuality and transgender issues.

Introduction

There are many debates within the Christian Churches today concerning gender and sexuality, including the ordination of women, the nature and status of marriage, the significance and value of celibacy and sexuality in life, homosexuality and transgender issues. Please remember that in the UK there are many different Churches, and groups within Churches, so any discussion of 'Christian views' is a generalisation which may not apply to large numbers of UK Christians. Much of what follows will focus on the Church of England, but other Churches may have very different views. For example, Conservative Evangelical churches often hold strict traditional

225

views about gender and sexuality, while the Society of Friends (Quakers) is very broad-minded about these issues.

Within the Christian community these debates are generally carried out between those who take a traditional or conservative approach to Christian teachings and those who would be seen as liberal or progressive. Key to this is a discussion of how the Bible should be interpreted.

So the key questions we need to start with in this section are:

1 Is it possible to express Christian beliefs in a way that is timeless, or is every expression of belief related to the social and historical setting in which it was made?

2 If Christian teachings are timeless and cannot develop or change, how do we decide where to find their authentic expression? In the New Testament texts as we have them now? In the creeds of the Early Church? In the original teachings of Jesus? If the latter, how can we know what Jesus actually said, as opposed to what people claimed he said several decades later?

3 If Christian teachings can develop and change, how can a believer judge what to believe or, if there are alternative approaches, which to take?

Influences on the place of women in the Church and society

Women in the Church before the nineteenth century

At the time when the New Testament was being written, the Christian community was expanding through the eastern Mediterranean in a culture dominated by Greek and Roman thought. From being a minority sect within Judaism, it emerged as a separate religion to which both Jews and Gentiles could belong.

The New Testament shows that some women had positions of authority in the Church. In his letter to the Romans, Paul refers to Phoebe as a 'deacon and patron of many', and describes Junia as an apostle. There is no doubt, however, that there are many passages, both in scripture and in the writings of later Church leaders, which express views that we would now regard as sexist.

Between the second and fifth centuries, these views became more pronounced in the writings of Church leaders such as Tertullian (c.155–c.240 CE), St Jerome (c.347–420 CE) and St Augustine of Hippo (354–430 CE). Augustine and others saw the world as damned because of the sin of Adam and Eve, and in the western part of the Roman Empire, Christianity developed a sense of loathing for the physical body and everything to do with it. Women were regarded as – to use an expression of Tertullian – 'the devil's gateway'.

However, by the fifth century women must already have been playing a significant role within the organisation of the Church, and one which Church authorities had come to see as a threat, since a number of Church councils forbade the ordination of women as deacons. You don't forbid something unless it is going on and having an impact that you regard as unwelcome.

Key term

Celibacy The choice to abstain from marriage and sexual relations for social or religious reasons.

Once Christian monasticism became established, **celibacy** offered similar opportunities for men and women. From the fifth century, convents offered the opportunity for women to escape the male-dominated life in society or the demands of motherhood. This offered the opportunity for study and the arts, and some rose to positions of great responsibility. One example, from the Mediaeval Church, was Hildegard of Bingen (1098–1179), who was not only an important Abbess, but also wrote poetry and music and held views that were, for her day, very progressive.

Hildegarde of Bingen (1098–1179)

Hildegarde of Bingen was a German Benedictine Abbess (leader of a convent) who wrote music, poetry and letters. Although not highly educated, she became very influential through her letters, which express views on women that would now be called feminist.

▲ Hildegarde of Bingen

Key term

Protestant Reformation The period during the sixteenth century when, as the result of protests against some beliefs and practices of the Roman Catholic Church, new churches were formed that were separate from the Roman Catholic Church.

So, although it is true that from the early days through the Mediaeval period and into the upheavals of the sixteenth-century **Protestant Reformation**, the Church and society were generally dominated by men, with women playing supplementary roles, there were many exceptions to that rule.

However, as a background to present debates we need to be aware that in Europe, following the Reformation, there were major social changes that affected the place of women in society, and therefore influenced how women saw themselves within the Church. In particular, we need to look at the place of women in the nineteenth century.

Women in the nineteenth century

For centuries, men had control of their wives' property when they married, and most men and women generally worked in or around the home or labouring for a local landowner, with women based in the home, with responsibilities for childrearing and taking on extra work for cash. In more wealthy households, women would often take responsibility for running a business, organising servants and managing accounts.

The nineteenth century was a time of radical change. Technology was transforming the world, and new ideas were taking shape. Many men now travelled to work in factories and offices, while their wives stayed at home, and single girls were often sent to work 'in service' in wealthy households. Following the Enlightenment period, there was a general emphasis on reason and evidence as ways of understanding humankind and its place within the world.

However, this new attitude did not automatically lead to the idea that men and women should be treated equally. It was generally thought that women, being physically weaker than men, should focus on the home and the education of children, while men were sent out to perform manual or military tasks.

But what was also new in the nineteenth century was the spread of education, and particularly the education of women. By 1848 Bedford College and Queen's College in London were established in order to train women to become teachers, and the 1870 Education Act provided universal primary education for both boys and girls.

The same period saw the start of the movement for women's rights. Feminist ideas spread among the educated middle classes, and gradually the law changed to take into account the aspirations of women. During the nineteenth century, women began to be accepted within professions such as medicine. However, during that century, very few had the right to vote in national elections, sue in court, or own property. Married women were seen as the property of their husbands, having made over to him all rights over their own bodies in matters regarding sex, children and domestic work.

At the same time, women were increasingly being employed away from the home, following the industrial revolution, and middle-class women were also very active in charitable work and social welfare.

In 1859 Catherine Booth, the wife of General Booth who founded the Salvation Army, published *Female Ministry: Women's Right to Preach the Gospel* (London, Morgan and Chase, 1859). In it she argued:

> God has given to women a graceful form and attitude, winning manners, persuasive speech, and, above all, a finely tuned emotional nature, all of which appear to us eminent natural qualifications for public speaking. We admit that want of mental culture, the trammels of custom, the force of prejudice, and one-sided interpretations of scripture, have hitherto almost excluded her from this sphere; but, before such a sphere is pronounced to be unnatural, it must be proved either that woman has not the ability to teach or to preach, or that the possession and exercise of this ability un-naturalizes her in other respects; that so soon as she presumes to step on the platform or into the pulpit, she loses the delicacy and grace of the feminine character. (Page 4)

Booth also made the point that women who speak under the influence of the Holy Spirit are not claiming any authority for themselves, but are no more than vehicles for delivering the gospel.

The details of the rise of feminism are beyond what you need to know for the purposes of understanding issues of gender in the Church, but you should be aware that, by the nineteenth century, the situation of women was utterly unlike that of the early years of Christianity and the Middle Ages. The First World War brought further change in the role of women in society as jobs traditionally undertaken by men were filled by women when the men went to war. By 1918, their new role was established in the economy and society. The issue then became how to interpret those passages in the New Testament that appeared to oppose this empowerment of women. This task was aided by developments within biblical scholarship.

The development of biblical criticism: the Bible and the Reformation

Until the Protestant Reformation in the sixteenth century, Christians learnt about their faith from the Church through the teachings of the clergy. The Church's teachings (doctrine) were drawn equally from the Latin text of the Bible and from the traditional teachings of the Church, passed down from generation to generation. Priests, who could read Latin and had studied Church doctrine, taught people what the Bible said.

However, following the Reformation, Protestant Christians were able to study the Bible in their own languages, and to form their own opinions about its meaning. They could then argue that one particular passage of scripture should be interpreted in the light of others, or of the New Testament as a whole. Because of the availability of scriptures and the challenge to the authority of the Church at the Reformation, Protestant Christians claimed the freedom to challenge traditional interpretations of scripture.

Background to the interpretation of scripture

During the Reformation of the sixteenth century, the authority of the Catholic Church was challenged by the reformers; and the Bible, in translation, was becoming more widely available and read. Protestants considered that it was the Bible, rather than the authority of the Church, which should be their principal guide to Christian belief and practice.

During the nineteenth century there were developments in what is generally termed '**Liberal theology**'. This was the attempt to show the relevance of religious ideas to modern life. It also sought to rationalise and present the Christian faith in a way that was compatible with science and with modern thought generally. So, for example, Albert Schweitzer and others tried to get beyond the biblical text in their quest to understand the historical Jesus. Part of that was the development of **biblical criticism**, which was the systematic and critical examination of the biblical text.

Liberal biblical criticism argued that the Bible should be studied like any other collection of ancient documents. Theologians studied the Bible using both 'higher' criticism (examining how different passages and books were written and how they relate to one another) and 'lower' criticism (examining in detail the content, language and meaning of individual passages to identify the precise meaning of the original words).

Key terms

Liberal theology An approach to biblical scholarship and theological thinking that aimed to analyse the Bible and Christian teaching using modern thought informed by reason and science.

Biblical criticism Studying the Bible using a range of different approaches to come to a fuller understanding. Liberal biblical criticism treats the Bible as a text that is subject to analysis just like any other piece of writing.

229

Note that biblical criticism is not 'critical' in the sense of taking a negative attitude towards the text; it is critical in the sense of using all one's critical faculties to try to understand its proper and original meaning.

Some key features of biblical criticism

1 Biblical criticism examines the original languages in which scripture was written, to make sure that the translated words reflect the meaning that their authors intended.

2 Biblical criticism looks at the form of each piece of writing (for example it could be a letter: I Corinthians is a letter giving advice to fellow Christians. It could be liturgical material: Philippians 2:6–11 was probably recited when people gathered for worship) in order to find the context in which it should be understood.

3 Biblical criticism examines the background to each passage of scripture – including the commonly held views of the day, things that the writer would assume his readers would know and therefore did not need to explain.

The intention of biblical criticism was to find the truth expressed through the scriptures, without assuming that a straightforward acceptance of the translated text would be enough. This was certainly not the first time that scriptures had been examined critically or considered to be anything other than a literal account of events. For example, St Augustine in the fifth century considered some biblical narratives to be allegories, designed to inspire religious feelings and morality, rather than factual accounts.

Challenges to liberal biblical criticism

Although liberal biblical criticism was widely accepted as a legitimate tool for theologians, there were those who felt that treating the Bible as an ordinary text that could be analysed this way was wrong. One academic theologian who challenged this form of criticism was Karl Barth. Liberal biblical criticism was completely rejected by those who started the Christian fundamentalist movement in the USA in the early nineteenth century.

Karl Barth (1886–1968)

Barth was a Swiss theologian whose views on the role of scripture became very influential in twentieth-century Evangelical theology.

1 Karl Barth

In 1916, Barth challenged the liberal approach to biblical criticism. He argued that the Christian message in the Bible is not a development of Enlightenment values. Its role was to challenge ordinary human assumptions. It was wrong to say that human reason can be used to judge scripture. In fact, scripture is the judge of human reason. Barth's work lies behind the approach to scripture taken by Conservative Evangelicals.

2 Fundamentalism/literalism

During the first half of the twentieth century, some Protestant groups in the USA developed an emphasis on the 'fundamentals' of faith, including a straightforward and literal interpretation of scripture. They claimed that everyone, inspired by the Holy Spirit, should be able to read, understand and interpret the scriptures, because God's word was clear and straightforward. They believed it was wrong to study it 'critically' because that would undermine the straightforward meaning. For them, the Bible did not need conform to modern critical scholarship or attitudes.

People who follow a more liberal approach say that general features of society today – including gender neutrality and the acceptance of homosexuality – should be considered by Christians in the light of general features of the Christian gospel. For example, Jesus accepted women among his followers and he mixed with those who were social or religious outcasts.

On the other hand, those who take a more literalist or **fundamentalist** approach argue that the rules which applied in first-century Palestine should continue to apply today, because they were accepted by the early Christians. This, therefore, includes the views of early Christians as they engaged with the values and morality of the Roman and Greek cultures within which they developed.

Since the earliest Church, the role of women has been a contentious issue. Biblical criticism can help to identify where the text may support or undermine ideas about gender equality, but arguments based on biblical criticism do not have any force with those who take a fundamentalist approach.

Women play a significant part in the New Testament narrative, including especially Mary, the mother of Jesus, and Mary of Magdala. The different roles of women as followers of Jesus are reflected in the story of Mary and Martha (Luke 10:38–42), where Martha is occupied with household duties and Mary instead listens to Jesus teaching. Women were the first to witness the risen Christ in the garden and to bring news of his resurrection to the disciples.

Some of the key texts used in debates about gender and sexuality come from the New Testament letters. There is some disagreement among scholars about which letters were written by Paul, and show the earliest teachings of the Church, and which letters are from a later date, written under his name but not by him. However, the majority of scholars agree that 1 and 2 Timothy and Titus (the so-called Pastoral Epistles) and Ephesians are later writings by another author, and if this is the case, it is no surprise that they express views different from those of St Paul in his letters to the Romans and the Galatians.

Biblical passages indicating support for gender equality

Some passages in the Bible would seem to support arguments in favour of gender equality.

In Romans 16:1–2, for example, Paul introduces a female deacon to the Church:

> I commend to you our sister Phoebe, a deacon of the church in Cenchreae. I ask you to receive her in the Lord in a way worthy of his people and to give her any help she may need from you, for she has been the benefactor of many people, including me.

Key term

Fundamentalism A movement that started in the early twentieth century which regarded certain things as fundamental beliefs of Christianity. These 'five fundamentals' were: biblical inspiration and the infallibility of scripture; the virgin birth of Jesus; belief that Christ's death was the atonement for sin; the bodily resurrection of Jesus; the historical reality of the miracles of Jesus.

231

Paul then describes Priscilla and Aquila as 'fellow workers', along with Mary, who is described as 'working very hard for you'. He greets 'Tryphaena and Tryphosa', those women who work hard in the Lord, and asks the Church members to greet his dear friend Persis, another woman who has 'worked very hard in the Lord'. This suggests a situation in which women and men equally share in the work of the Church, and deserve to be greeted by name.

This situation is grounded theologically in Galatians 3:26–28:

> So in Christ Jesus you are all children of God through faith, for all of you who were baptized into Christ have clothed yourselves with Christ. There is neither Jew nor Gentile, neither slave nor free, nor is there male and female, for you are all one in Christ Jesus.

In other words, the basis of all forms of equality is being 'in Christ'. Rules and social norms do not apply.

Biblical passages against gender equality

Some passages in the Bible would seem to deny any arguments in favour of gender equality.

In Ephesians 5:22–23, arguing that Christians should submit to one another, the author (traditionally assumed to be Paul, but most scholars today believe that this was not the case) adds:

> 'Wives, submit yourselves to your own husbands as you do to the Lord. For the husband is the head of the wife as Christ is the head of the church ...'

He then emphasises that husbands should love their wives as they love themselves, but adds that wives should respect their husbands.

Also, to put it into perspective, the author goes on to say (6:5):

> 'Slaves, obey your earthly masters with respect and fear, and with sincerity of heart, just as you would obey Christ.'

So the author is accepting existing power relations between slaves and masters, children and parents and wives and husbands, but emphasises that, for Christians, mutual love and respect should guide all those relationships. If this were generally taken literally today, many Christians would therefore accept slavery. In fact, the overwhelming majority of Christians today regard slavery as an evil, and its practice in New Testament days as an example of the way in which Christianity took root in a particular culture whose values were in many respects different from those of the modern world.

In I Corinthians 14:34–35, Paul says:

> 'Women should remain silent in the churches. They are not allowed to speak, but must be in submission, as the law says. If they want to inquire about something, they should ask their own husbands at home; for it is disgraceful for a woman to speak in the church.'

In this passage, Paul is replying to questions asked by the Church community in Corinth. We don't know the exact question, but most scholars agree that this is intended as a response to a specific situation rather than a doctrinal ruling for the whole Church.

▲ First-century Hellenistic woman

A critical examination of 1 Timothy 2:8–15

1 Timothy 2:8–15 is seen as a particularly key passage on the equality of women. We will explore this passage in detail.

An overview

> Therefore I want the men everywhere to pray, lifting up holy hands without anger or disputing. I also want the women to dress modestly, with decency and propriety, adorning themselves, not with elaborate hairstyles or gold or pearls or expensive clothes, but with good deeds, appropriate for women who profess to worship God.
>
> A woman should learn in quietness and full submission. I do not permit a woman to teach or to assume authority over a man; she must be quiet. For Adam was formed first, then Eve. And Adam was not the one deceived; it was the woman who was deceived and became a sinner. But women will be saved through childbearing—if they continue in faith, love and holiness with propriety. (Timothy 2:8–15)

> It is unlikely that the writer here was Paul himself as was traditionally held – scholars are generally agreed that 1 and 2 Timothy and Titus were written after Paul's time.

In the following chapter the qualities required of those who have oversight over the Church (bishops and deacons) are described. Of the many qualities, such as not indulging in too much wine, or seeking dishonest gain, it is clear that they are men and that their wives should be worthy of respect.

Such texts are widely used against the ordination of women, and against women holding other teaching roles in churches – applied both in the Catholic Church, and, mostly, within Conservative Evangelical Protestant Churches.

A critical examination

In examining any ancient text, it is important to consider its original use and context. There may have been a particular issue with the Church in Ephesus that the letter was trying to correct. If so, its advice is specific and may not be universally applicable. Also, it is important to remember that few women at that time were given much formal education, and so were more likely to be led astray by teachings they may not have understood. In other words, even if it was right for the women of Ephesus not to have taken a leading role in the Church, that may not apply today.

1 Timothy is a letter, written in response to some form of crisis in the Church at Ephesus, but we have only one side of the exchange of letters here, so scholars do not know what it was that the writer was replying to. It may have been a very specific local problem. Clearly, there was something wrong with the Church, and the writer is trying to prevent it from further harm.

First of all, the fact that the writer opposes women speaking in Church in Ephesus shows that this was already happening. This perhaps explains verse 8 above, where the men are exhorted to 'lift up holy hands without anger or disputing'. This suggests that the men had been arguing with the women and the women had been answering back, which threatened the habitual power exercised by men over women.

But there is also a problem with a particular Greek word that is used in 1 Timothy. In verse 12, the writer says 'I do not permit a woman to … assume authority over a man'. The word translated as 'assume authority over' is the Greek word *authentein*, but because this is the only time this word occurs in the scriptures we cannot be sure of its meaning.

This way of examining the meaning of words, and the background and possible context of Bible texts had always been used by theological scholars within the Church, but it became more widely accepted in the nineteenth century, as the liberal approach to theology and biblical criticism became established within universities.

Biblical fundamentalists reject the idea that the text can be analysed and set in context. They argue that every word of the Bible is inspired in the sense that God spoke through the writer, and therefore that his words should be universally applied.

Key terms

Christian Egalitarians Those who believe that men and women should be permitted equal roles in the Church.

Christian Complementarians Those who believe that men and women are equal but different, so their roles in the Church are different and should complement one another.

Different responses to the New Testament texts on the issue of gender

There are two broad lines of response to the issue of gender within the scriptures and the Early Church: Egalitarian and Complementarian.

Christian Egalitarians argue that there should be no distinction between men and women when it comes to their roles within the Church. That applies also between racial and social groups – all are to be equal before Christ, and should be treated as such.

Christian Complementarians argue that men and women are of equal importance in the sight of God, but that they have different and complementary roles, in marriage, family life, society, and also in the organisation of the Church.

The Catholic view: equal but different

The Roman Catholic Church believes that philosophy, tradition and the teaching of the Church all point towards a complementarian view of the roles of men and women in the Church.

Natural Law

Within Catholic thinking, Natural Law suggests that people should live in a way that reflects their inherent nature. If men and women have different natures, it follows that they should take different roles in life. This does not mean that one is more valuable than the other, but just that they are different. This follows the complementarian view that men and women should complement one another.

The tradition of the Early Church

We do not know the extent of women's ministry in the Early Church, except for references to them in the scriptures, as set out above, and their opposition by church leaders in the fifth century. One of these, Pope Gelasius I, wrote in 494 opposing women taking part in the celebration of the Eucharist, so it is clear that some were taking on the role that was later reserved exclusively for men.

Discussion point

'Male Headship' is a complementarian view that is widely held among some Evangelicals today. Quakers strongly support egalitarianism. Based on the biblical texts we have considered above, do you think that the Bible supports egalitarianism or complementarianism for Christians today? (This kind of discussion can get very heated, so please try to remain respectful when explaining your views.)

Apostolic Succession

The Catholic and Anglo-Catholic view of the ordained ministry also points to the fact that Jesus appointed only men as his apostles. **Apostolic Succession** is the idea that the bishops of the Church are consecrated in a line of succession that goes unbroken back to the apostles. Therefore, ministry can only be passed on from men to men.

In 1976, the Vatican issued a declaration *Inter Insigniores*, 'On the Question of the Admission of Women to the Ministerial Priesthood'.

Although it recognised the important contribution of women to the Church, on the specific issue of ordination it argued:

1 That the **ordination** of women in the Early Church was limited to minority sects and was condemned

2 That the Church follows Christ himself in choosing only men for this ministry

3 That whilst other Churches, following the Reformation, ordain women, this does not follow the historical tradition of the Church as a whole

4 Jesus chose only men to be his 'twelve', but in his positive dealings with women, he rejected the social convention of his day. Jesus, therefore, showed the model for a high view of women which nevertheless excludes them from leadership in the Church.

Inter Insigniores makes an important point about biblical criticism. Although the Church is founded upon the example and teachings of Jesus as found in the New Testament, it is the Church that decides how those texts should be interpreted.

The Protestant view: the priesthood of all believers

A key feature of Reformation theology is expressed in the idea of '**the priesthood of all believers**'. This was the idea that all are equal before God, and that there is no need for God's grace to be mediated through a priest. All Christians are called to serve God, and no one vocation or activity is any more 'sacred' than any other. Following the Protestant Reformation, people came to recognise the religious significance and importance of everyday life, secular as well as religious.

At the time of the Protestant Reformation, women were seen as in need of protection, either within families or by marriage, but for Protestants, the secular roles of wife and mother were regarded as equal in importance to those of the monastic life. As a result of this, there is no need for a special priestly role in mediating between the two. Ordination as practised by the Catholic Church was not necessary for men, so the question of female ordination did not arise.

Protestant Churches today have varying views on the ministry of women, but these focus on whether or not women may hold a position of leadership rather than on the Catholic view (shared by Orthodox and Anglican Churches) of a specially holy priesthood. The arguments for and against women leaders in the Protestant Churches are, therefore, the same as those for and against gender equality generally.

> **Key terms**
>
> **Apostolic Succession** The passing on of authority from one generation to the next by the laying on of hands at ordination, going back to the apostles.
>
> **Ordination** The religious rite by which a person is made a deacon or priest through the laying on of hands.

> **Key term**
>
> **The priesthood of all believers** The Protestant idea that all human beings can have direct communication with God on their own account, without the need for priests.

Within the Anglican Church, it should be remembered that the Church of England, although separated from the Roman Catholic Church by Henry VIII, remained Catholic in its structure and theology, but was Reformed in much of its thinking. For this reason, the approach to women's ordination in the Anglican Churches is half way between the Protestant and Catholic traditions. The Church of England accepts some of the freedom of the biblical interpretation of Protestantism, but with the hierarchical and priestly structure of Roman Catholicism.

Weighing up the role of women in Christianity

Most people would accept that there are serious gender differences expressed within the New Testament. It is also accepted that, in the world in which the Early Church developed, the role of women was very different from that of today.

In order to get a balance on these issues, you may want to ask yourself:

1 How far are the New Testament references to the role of women just a reflection of society of the time?

2 How and why do the New Testament writers deal with these issues? Are conservative (complementarian) views a necessary attempt to restore balance and authority within the Christian community?

3 If the New Testament texts have to be interpreted in the light of their original context in order to have authority for Christians, how do you decide what is right or wrong today?

4 Should the Church conform to the social norms of today, as it may have done to social norms when it was written? In other words, we might ask: 'How can we reflect the intentions for us now behind what the New Testament writers said then?'

These general questions impact on current debates within the Church, in terms of the ordination of women, homosexuality and the response of the Church to transgender issues.

The social and legal status of women today

▲ Women today have held senior roles in all professions but often still reach a glass ceiling

The social status of women varies greatly in different parts of the world, influenced by the economic situation, culture and religion. Thus, for example, in areas that survive on subsistence farming, women work the land and bring up children as they have always done. In Saudi Arabia, by contrast, women work away from the home and follow careers, but what they can do in society is also controlled by the very strict religious codes followed in that country. For example, they are not allowed to drive a car, and must remain modestly dressed in public.

The place of women within the Church is partly decided on theological grounds, but discussions are influenced by the social and political situation.

In the UK, it is illegal to discriminate against women in terms of employment. If a woman is capable of doing a job, she should be allowed to do it on equal terms with a man. There have been exceptions to this principle. For a long time, women were not allowed to be ordained within the Church of England. This was controversial on theological grounds, but it also created legal problems, since it could be argued that the Church was breaching equal opportunity legislation by forbidding female ordination.

The other social restriction women face on their careers is termed 'the glass ceiling'. Although in theory women are allowed to compete with men at all levels, in practice there are more men than women in senior roles in business and industry. One of the main reasons for this is that women often take a career break to have children. This means they miss out on promotion to more senior positions.

In politics, women have held senior roles – as Prime Minister in the UK, as a Democratic nominee in the 2016 US presidential election, and as Chancellor of Germany, the most influential post within the European Community. Legally and socially, men and women should be treated equally – that is a principle deeply embedded within democratic societies.

Debates about female ordination in the Church of England up to and after 1994 and the continuing debate today

In the Church of England, there is a threefold order of ordained ministry. The first level is deacon, and although there are some permanent deacons, most deacons are then additionally ordained priest within two years. After several years of ministry, some priests are consecrated bishops.

The Anglican Church is one of a number of Churches that makes up the **Anglican Communion**. These are Churches that govern themselves, but share a common Anglican theology, and all pay respect to the Archbishop of Canterbury.

> **Key term**
>
> **Anglican Communion** A worldwide group of Churches which are self-governing, but all share a measure of common theology with the Church of England, and who all pay respect to the Archbishop of Canterbury.

The ordination of women to the priesthood

The first attempt to discuss women's ordination was the Lambeth Conference in 1920. An Archbishops' Commission was set up to consider the matter, but ruled it out.

Florence Li Tim-Oi (1907–92)

Florence Li Tim-Oi was a deaconess in China, who was ordained priest in 1944 because there were too few men available to minister to Anglicans in China during the war with Japan.

The next step was taken in the Far East to meet a particularly urgent need. In 1944, in response to a shortage of men in the Church following the Japanese invasion, Florence Li Tim-Oi was ordained in China. This was temporary, and she resigned her licence after the war. However, when the Synod of Hong Kong and Macao ordained two other women as priests in 1971, she was again officially recognised as a priest.

In the Church of England, the **General Synod** (the Church's governing body) discussed the ordination of women in 1975 and again in 1978. In 1975, it was agreed that there were no 'fundamental objections' to women being ordained. In 1978, it was proposed that barriers to the ordination of women should be removed by changes to Church law. The motion was passed by the House of Bishops and the House of Laity, but lost in the House of Clergy. Since all three houses have to approve changes to Church laws, this effectively blocked progress.

Those opposed to the ordination of women argued that the Church of England did not have the authority to overturn the tradition of male-only ordained ministry in the Apostolic succession. Some felt that it would damage the relationship between the Church of England and the Roman Catholic Church, which is opposed to female ordination. Others argued based on a conservative reading of the biblical references discussed on pages 232–233.

In 1981, the Synod agreed that women could be ordained as deacons. Legislation was passed in 1985 and the first ordinations of women deacons took place in 1987. At that time, men who were deacons would normally then go on to be ordained as priests, but this option was not available for women. In 1988, the proposal to ordain women to the priesthood finally received the required majority in all three houses of Synod in 1992, and on 12 March 1994, the first 32 women were ordained as priests in the Church of England.

The consecration of women as bishops

Within the Anglican Communion, Barbara Harris was elected suffragan (or assistant) bishop of the Episcopal Diocese of Massachusetts in the USA in 1988, and consecrated the following year. In the Church of England controversy continued and its first female bishop, Libby Lane, was consecrated in 2015.

Key term

General Synod The governing and decision-making body of the Church of England. It comprises three houses: the house of Bishops, the house of Clergy and the house of Laity.

Elizabeth Jane Holden 'Libby' Lane (1966–)

Lane became the first female bishop in the Church of England when she was consecrated in January 2015 as Bishop of Stockport.

The debate about female bishops was rather different from that about female priests, and centred on the Catholic view of the Apostolic succession. The role of a Bishop, as overseer of a large number of Church congregations, includes the ordination of priests, and the **sacrament** of confirmation for those who have been prepared to become full members of the Church. Traditionalists considered that any ordination or confirmation carried out by a woman would not be valid, because she could not (as they saw it) continue the tradition of male ordination and **consecration** going back to the apostles. For this reason, some Conservative Churches in the Anglo-Catholic tradition insisted that they would not accept the 'oversight' of a female bishop or of any bishop who consecrated female priests. Arrangements were, therefore, made for them to be cared for by 'provincial episcopal visitors' (or 'flying bishops' as they were called). They were responsible for the care of those who, in conscience, could not accept the ministry of female priests and bishops.

In spite of these provisions, some Anglican clergy felt that the Church of England had ceased to have a legitimate ministry. Some asked to be received into the Roman Catholic Church, and to receive ordination into the Roman Catholic priesthood. This included some married Anglican priests. Catholic priests are normally required to be celibate, but an exception was made for some of those who moved from the Church of England.

The continuing debate today

The Church of England as a whole may have accepted the ordination of women as priests and the consecration of women as bishops, but many individual Christians and congregations, including some priests and bishops, continue to oppose the ordination of women. The Church of England makes allowances for people who feel this way by providing 'alternative episcopal oversight'. This means that parishes which reject the ordination of women are put under the authority of a Bishop who shares their view, in addition to the Bishop of their own diocese.

However, as the number of women priests in the Church of England has risen, the position of Bishops who oppose the ordination of women has become the subject of criticism. In 2017, it was announced that the suffragan Bishop of Burnley, Philip North, was to be the next Bishop of the diocese of Sheffield. As a diocesan bishop, he would have been responsible for all the parishes and clergy in the Sheffield diocese, including many female priests and parishes which welcome the ministry of women. Following criticism from within and outside the diocese, North withdrew his acceptance of the post.

At the same time, those who take a conservative view and reject the ordination of women have sometimes found themselves unable to continue to accept the authority of the Church, and a number of churches have refused to accept any oversight at all from a diocesan bishop who ordains women. At its most extreme, this has led to parishes separating themselves from the Church of England by asking conservative bishops from other countries to provide oversight. In 2017, the parish of Jesmond invited a bishop from a conservative Church in South Africa to consecrate their curate, Jonathan Pryke, as a bishop, totally rejecting the authority of their diocesan Bishop of Durham.

A comparison of the significant ideas of Hampson and Ruether about the patriarchal nature of Christianity

Feminist theology

Feminist theology began in the late nineteenth century, but really challenged the Church in the second half of the twentieth century against the background of the women's movement. Although its arguments reach back into the history of the Church and the place of women in religion generally, feminist theology can also be seen as part of a wider cultural phenomenon, in which women affirm both their distinctiveness and their rights within society.

Feminist theologians argue that Christian theology is **patriarchal** (shaped by and for the benefit of men), and oppresses women. Christian feminist theologians therefore seek to counter patriarchal structures within the Church, and to emphasise the place and value of women in a gender-inclusive way within the Christian tradition.

There are different strands within feminist theology:

1 A **liberal** strand presents the patriarchal system as illogical, denying women the fundamental right to equality with men.

2 A **biblical** strand looks at the idea of God as loving and caring – qualities associated with women. It also points to the importance of women within the accounts of the life and teaching of Jesus.

3 A **radical** strand that has moved beyond Christianity, which seeks to find ways to speak of God which are true to our present day ways of thinking, which will be gender inclusive.

We shall examine the position of two feminist theologians: Daphne Hampson and Rosemary Radford Ruether. In addition to their writing on feminism and theology, in 1986, under the auspices of Catholic Women's Network and Women in Theology, Hampson and Radford debated: 'Is there a place for Feminists in a Christian Church?' (available at **http://ethics.academyconferences.com/index.php/shop**) [Note 3]

Daphne Hampson (1944–)

Daphne Hampson is a post-Christian theologian. She taught at St Andrews University and is now, in her retirement, an associate of the faculty in Oxford. 'Post-Christian' means *post* Christian, not Christian, but also post *Christian* showing the tradition from which it came.

The statement on Hampson's position in Volume 1 that 'the whole Christian story that was "true" in the first century CE must necessarily be true in the twenty-first century CE, which means that all its patriarchal "baggage" has to be accepted in the twenty-first century', can mislead. Hampson simply points out that it has been fundamental to Christian belief in every age that there was a uniqueness to the Christ-event. Therefore, Christians must look back to first century Palestine, with the result that its patriarchal imagery and presuppositions are transported into the present, affecting people not least at the subconscious level.

▲ Daphne Hampson

Hampson holds that Christianity is not true. She defines 'Christian' as a position as the belief that there was a uniqueness about the events surrounding Jesus of Nazareth: Christians have believed that either Jesus was resurrected from the dead, or that Jesus was related to God in a different way to anyone else, or both. Hampson thinks that, since the eighteenth-century Enlightenment, we have known that this is not possible. There could not be a one-off event which breaks the laws of nature, like a resurrection. The idea of one person who has a different kind of relationship to God from all other people does not make sense.

Furthermore, Hampson finds Christianity not moral. Believing that people must take responsibility for themselves, she does not think that people should be referring to a revelation in history, or a transcendent God.

Ideas about revelation and God arise because Christianity is the type of religion it is. Christians believe in a revelation in history, and in a God who is wholly different from human beings, so they obey God instead of exercising moral choices freely. Christians cannot just start from the present because they believe in a transcendent God who has revealed Godself in history, and so they must always take what they think to be God's word into consideration.

Key term

Irredeemably sexist This is a term used to describe the view that Christianity is inevitably sexist, so that it is illogical to be both a feminist and a Christian.

The consequence of such a 'historical' religion which looks to a past revelation is that the outlook and imagery of a past patriarchal age is brought into the present, affecting people at a subconscious level. In other words, Christianity is **irredeemably sexist**. It comes to look only natural that being male should be seen as the norm for humankind, while woman is seen as different, secondary and 'the other'. Any thought system which attempts to make it look as if one part of humanity is the norm can be described as fascist. Insofar as this is the case, Hampson thinks that Christianity is fascist.

▲ A rare medieval image of androgynous Christ, showing him as a man with breasts

Despite this, Hampson credits that the Christian myth has served as a vehicle which has carried people's love of God in the West. She thinks that people should now express that awareness of God in terms appropriate for the present day and age. God should not be seen as 'out there' and anthropomorphic; rather, God is a dimension of the one reality to which humanity also belongs. It then makes sense to speak of 'drawing on God', or 'being open to God'. There is no reason for such a religious outlook to be gendered.

Rosemary Radford Ruether (1936–)

Rosemary Radford Ruether is a feminist, a liberation theologian, and a member of the Roman Catholic Church. She focuses on the message of Christianity as one of liberation, and argues that Christianity is a religious culture which can be re-stated in feminist terms. Now retired, she worked in various American universities and theological schools. She has published widely on feminism and liberation theology.

Ruether considers that past events, present experience and future hopes all contribute to an understanding of Christianity. She describes Jesus

241

as a proclaimer of liberation in his own time. She sees a parallel between Jesus' teaching in the Gospels and feminist critiques of society today. Social injustice and religious hierarchies at the time of Jesus were the result of male domination. Jesus is described as siding with the oppressed and outcasts of society, including women, and was critical of oppressive authority, including the use of religious rules to limit what people do, rather than to liberate them.

An example of this is Jesus' criticisms of the way rules were used to forbid acts of charity on the Sabbath. He concludes 'The Sabbath was made for man, not man for the Sabbath' (Mark 2:27).

Jesus is often presented as understanding both the needs and the strengths of women. Ruether sees Jesus exemplifying female traits of healing and caring, as well as male traits of power and authority. In this sense, Jesus embodies both male and female aspects of human nature. In her book *Sexism and God Talk* she describes this idea as '**androgynous**' Christology. Jesus is seen as struggling to help others, not as an impassive and distant authority figure.

Traditional theology sees Jesus carrying the punishment for sin, as part of a scheme based on authority, rules and punishment in a patriarchal society dominated by a male view of God. Ruether argues that Christianity today is in the process of recognising the female qualities as well as the male qualities in God, so that through the work of the Spirit, Christianity can become a religion of emancipation from patriarchy. She does not claim that this was its original context, but argues that when the Christian gospel stories are interpreted today in the context of women's experience, they can be helpful in developing a feminist culture of emancipation.

Ruether thus implies that in some ways, the female nature is more Christ-like than male nature. According to Ruether, many women are not driven by power, authority, rules and punishment, unlike many men. They do not exclude those who are different, but instead are welcoming and inclusive. Ruether believes that female nature is caring, healing and forgiving, and it is these qualities that make Jesus different from other leaders in history. In her book *To Change the World: Christology and Cultural Criticism*, Ruether says: 'The emergence of women points to a messianic future that will transform the male world of war, conflict and exploitation into the woman's world of peace and reconciliation.' [Note 2]

Ruether also argues that women, by their biological nature and their role in childbearing, are closer to nature than men, and therefore it is natural to look to women to develop a more pure, ecologically-inspired ethics. Nature itself, constantly giving birth and nurturing, may be seen as inherently female in the way it works. Such ideas are expressed as eco-feminism, and bring feminist ideas in line with the basic need for humankind to modify the male-dominated exploitation of the planet.

Key term

Androgynous This word literally means man-woman-like, and refers to the idea that someone or something has both male and female qualities.

A comparison of the views of Hampson and Ruether

Looking at the reality of human experience of religion, and the history and teachings of Christianity, there is a fundamental choice, reflected in the different approaches of Hampson and Ruether:

● *Either* (Hampson) Christian claims could not possibly be true, and because a past patriarchal history is central to Christianity, it is inevitably sexist. Men and women together need to find new ways of speaking of that dimension of reality which is God.
● *Or* (Ruether) there is a measure of female thinking within the New Testament and elements of Christian theology, so that it is possible to remain Christian and yet also experience and express the aspirations of women today, inspired by the Holy Spirit and the example of Jesus' ministry.

Activity

Research the biographies of Daphne Hampson and Rosemary Radford Ruether. Try to identify the reasons why they came to the conclusions they did about Christianity.

Which of the two do you find most convincing? Explain reasons for your choice.

Different Christian views about celibacy, marriage, homosexuality and transgender issues

Celibacy

Celibacy is living life without sexual activity. Christianity traditionally teaches that marriage is a sexual, social and emotional union, so celibacy and marriage are closely related to one another. In the Christian tradition, celibacy is not simply living without sex; it is choosing to live the life of a single person in order to devote oneself completely to God.

In Judaism at the time of Jesus, most people were expected to marry and have a family, the exception being those who wanted to exercise some special ministry for at least part of their lives. The fact that (as far as we know) Jesus did not marry makes him relatively unusual, but not exceptional.

The very early Christians believed that the end of the world was coming in the immediate future. This meant they should prepare for that, rather than having children. In his first letter to the Christians of Corinth, Paul says 'But if they cannot control themselves, they should marry, for it is better to marry than to burn with passion' (1 Corinthians 7:9). He is making a concession to human nature: since sex outside marriage is a sin, those who cannot control their sexual urges should marry. This implies that it is better to control sexual urges and live a life of celibacy. By the time Matthew was writing his gospel, celibacy was seen as a deliberate religious choice. In Matthew 19:12, Jesus teaches 'there are those who choose to live like eunuchs for the sake of the kingdom of heaven'.

But as time passed without signs that the world was coming to an end, the Early Church came to expect that life would continue, and it was also assumed that most Christians (and particularly most Christian leaders) would marry. We have seen above (page 233) that leaders were expected to be married as a sign of their moral responsibility.

From the fourth century, a monastic tradition grew up which celebrated total devotion of one's life to God, and therefore celibacy was seen by some

243

as a higher calling than family life. With the increasingly negative view of sexuality, and of the place of women, celibacy grew in importance, for both men and women. Indeed, for many women, the celibate life of a convent provided an intellectual environment in which they could flourish, freed from male domination and domestic responsibilities. Today, celibacy is widely practised by monks and nuns, and by clergy in the Roman Catholic Church and Orthodox Churches.

The Catechism of the Catholic Church (#1579) says this:

> **All the ordained ministers of the Latin Church, with the exception of permanent deacons, are normally chosen from among men of faith who live a celibate life and who intend to remain celibate 'for the sake of the kingdom of heaven'. Called to consecrate themselves with undivided heart to the Lord and to 'the affairs of the Lord', they give themselves entirely to God and to men. Celibacy is a sign of this new life to the service of which the Church's minister is consecrated; accepted with a joyous heart celibacy radiantly proclaims the Reign of God.**

In the Orthodox Church, priests may be married when they are ordained but they cannot marry after their ordination. Bishops may not be married, so bishops are selected from those priests who remain celibate. Some Orthodox Churches have united with the Roman Catholic Church and in these Churches, the Orthodox traditions about celibacy are respected.

When the Church of England voted to allow the ordination of women, a number of married priests moved to join the Roman Catholic Church. Some of them were ordained to the Roman Catholic priesthood as a special concession.

There is some pressure in the Roman Catholic Church to end the rule of clergy celibacy. There is a severe shortage of people offering themselves for ordination, and many priests leave the ministry in order to marry, so there are not enough priests to care for the worldwide population of Roman Catholics. Allowing married priests would go some way towards solving this problem. In 2017, the Pope said that the church would consider whether married men might be ordained in 'remote communities'.

In contrast, many Protestant Evangelical Churches prefer their clergy to be married with a family, following the advice in 1 Timothy 3: 1–7. They argue that a celibate man fails to live up to the biblical requirements for a church leader to be the husband of one wife, and to have an orderly family life.

Key questions to reflect on here:

- Does the promotion of celibacy as a religious way of life undermine the value of sexuality?

- Given that it is natural for human beings to procreate, is a promotion of the celibate life 'unnatural'? (This does not imply that those who do not have children are in some way unnatural – it may be quite natural for them to remain childless or sexless for all sorts of reasons. But that is not the same as deliberately choosing the celibate life for religious reasons.)

Marriage

From the time of the Early Church, there were only two acceptable life options: celibacy or marriage. At first, it was thought that the Kingdom of God would arrive in the near future, and therefore there was no need for families or care for the next generation. St Paul suggests that marriage is something of a concession to those who cannot remain celibate (1 Corinthians 7:9). However, by the time of the letter to Timothy, it is clear that being married and taking care of a family shows that person to be suitable to lead the local Christian congregation.

Within the Church, marriage became a sacrament, a special means of receiving God's grace. Promoting family life showed links with the Jewish communities from which many early Christians came, and was a contrast to more liberal views of sexuality and relationships in Graeco-Roman society at the time.

Within the Catholic tradition, marriage remained a sacrament, and raising a Christian family a vocation, but it was also seen as inferior to the vocation to a celibate life. In the West, from the fourth century, priests, monks and nuns were required to be celibate, but the Eastern Churches expected most parish priests to marry, and only those who hoped to become bishops remained celibate.

With the Reformation, the balance shifted against celibacy, and in favour of marriage. A family was seen as God's blessing upon the union of husband and wife. For the Protestant reformers, marriage was not a sacrament, but a 'worldly thing ... that belongs to the realm of government' (Luther).

Roman Catholic teaching focuses on the sacramental nature of marriage: it is a physical act which causes a profound change to the souls of the people involved. Since the two individuals become 'one flesh' in marriage, divorce is not possible. If a couple are unhappy, they may live apart, but neither partner is allowed to re-marry because their marriage cannot be dissolved in the eyes of God and the Church. Divorcees cannot re-marry in church, and if they re-marry, they are excluded from Holy Communion because they are considered to be living a life of sin. In certain circumstances, a marriage may be *annulled* (declared never to have happened) if the church authorities have evidence that the marriage was not properly sacramental from the start, for example if one of the partners never intended to have children. People whose marriage has been annulled may re-marry because the Church considers that their first marriage was not a real one.

Protestant Churches in general do not see marriage as a sacrament. This means that a marriage can be dissolved, although most Protestants would agree that the end of a marriage shows that the couple have failed to live up to God's high standards for personal life. Jesus appears to allow divorce only as a result of marital unfaithfulness (Matthew 5:32). Many protestant Churches allow the re-marriage of divorcees in church if there is evidence that they have admitted their failure and intend to live out a marriage as God would wish.

There are problems when Christianity tries to put historical views into the context of modern western societies:

1 Today, marriage is often seen primarily as a relationship offering satisfaction to the partners who enter into it, rather than as a sacrament whose purpose is to establish a family.

2 Since legal registration of marriages does not now require a religious ceremony, the Christian element in marriage can be seen by some as an 'optional extra' over and above the legal and financial commitment of a couple. But this raises the question of whether or not a secular marriage in a Registry Office is a full marriage in the Christian sense.

3 The Christian marriage ceremony states that it is a commitment for life. The problem then becomes what to do with those who divorce. Should they still be able to take full part in the life of the Church if they have taken a deliberate step to exit from a relationship that is seen as a sacrament? Should they be regarded as still married in the eyes of God, even if they are legally divorced? If so, what is the status of any subsequent marriage?

4 And what about those within the Christian community who have entered into single-sex marriages? If they adopt children, or bring children from an earlier relationship into the home, does that have the same standing as a conventional marriage and family setup?

In these and similar issues, the dilemma is whether to emphasise the caring and loving example of Jesus, and therefore to accept into the Church those who enter into second or same-sex marriages as being equally loved by God, or whether to stick to traditional views. Debates for and against allowing same-sex marriages largely depend on arguments over homosexuality (see below). Those Christians who see homosexuality as acceptable are generally inclined to support the idea of marriage between two men or two women. Those who believe that homosexuality is a disorder, and homosexual acts sinful, consider same-sex marriage as invalid. The official position of most Churches is that although same-sex marriage is now permitted by law in some countries, including Great Britain and the Republic of Ireland, ceremonies cannot be conducted in churches or places of worship, mainly because of the many different and disputed views on same-sex relationships. At the time of writing, the only mainstream exceptions to this are Quakers, Lutherans and the Scottish Episcopal Church.

Homosexuality

Background

Until the time of the European Enlightenment, it was normal for religion to be imposed by the state. For example, when Emperor Constantine converted to Christianity in the fourth century, the whole Roman Empire became Christian, even though some people continued to follow pagan beliefs. In the post-Reformation settlement at the Treaty of Augsberg (1555), it was agreed that each state should follow the religion of its leader. The choice of religion for the whole state was, therefore, made for everyone by those in power. However, over the last 300 years or so, religion has largely moved into the private sphere. The Protestant Reformation promoted the idea that each individual had a direct relationship with God, so religious belief and practice became matters of personal choice and commitment.

▲ The Rainbow Flag, designed by San Francisco artist Gilbert Baker in 1978, is now widely recognised around the world as a symbol of gay, lesbian, bisexual and transgender pride.

This idea became the normal way of thinking by the nineteenth century. But in the second half of the twentieth century many people wanted to explore their own spirituality without formal religious systems. This was partly a result of two World Wars, but also of economic and social changes.

This shift towards the individual and their choice of religion and lifestyle is particularly relevant to issues of homosexuality and transgender, for here there has been a major clash between the shifting views of Western society as a whole and the Christian religion. The situation is quite different elsewhere, for example in Africa and the Middle East.

Until the end of the 1950s, Churches of all denominations regarded homosexuality as a sin. Homosexual acts were illegal, and therefore often clandestine and sometimes squalid. Gay people might live together discreetly as housemates, but more casual relationships often involved meeting in secret in public places, such as public lavatories. Gay men were more likely to be picked up by police in these circumstances, and public exposure in a trial was both humiliating and socially damaging.

The gradual process of social and legal change in the UK started with the Wolfenden Report in 1957, which suggested decriminalising homosexual acts carried out in private between consenting adults. Ten years later, this became English and Welsh law through the Sexual Offences Act of 1967.

Contemporary responses

As homosexuality became legal and socially acceptable within much – but not all of – society, the question was how the Church, with its traditional promotion of heterosexual family life, should engage with those practising homosexuals.

Some (particularly within the Catholic tradition) argue that the distinction should be made between 'tendencies' and 'acts'. So someone may experience themselves as gay, for example, but may not choose not to engage in same-sex sexual activity.

Some argue that a person with homosexual tendencies should be required to remain celibate, rather than be allowed to perform homosexual acts. This is an attempt to balance the value and caring nature of homosexuals with the traditional view that homosexual activity is a sin. Equally, it can be argued that a transgender person should simply learn to live with a divided sense of gender, rather than seek a hormonal and/or surgical way to change.

Note that within Catholic theology, homosexual tendencies and feelings are not in themselves sinful, but homosexual acts go against the principle of Natural Moral Law, so are regarded as sins. The Catholic Church, of course, regards the conception of children as the 'final aim' of the sexual act. Thus, every expression of sexuality that cannot, in theory, lead to conception, is condemned. This applies to contraception and masturbation as well as to homosexuality.

The fundamental question is, should Christianity remain fixed in its moral principles in order to be true to its origins? Or should it develop moral principles in an understanding of Jesus as one who accepted, mixed with and valued those who were – to use the modern term – 'socially disenfranchised'? Jesus was certainly unafraid to challenge unequal socio-political structures.

Reinterpreting tradition

Much of the problem faced by homosexuals within the Christian Churches stems from biblical texts that appear to condemn homosexual activity. The big question to struggle with here is whether to start with key ideas about Jesus' attitude towards others, and then evaluate other biblical texts on that basis, or whether to try and understand the biblical text in its original context without interpretation.

The problem of all such interpretation, however, is that as soon as people try to interpret the text, they bring to it their own assumptions and experiences. These are coloured by the society within which they live, and the way they experience themselves as physical beings with sexual natures and a capacity for intimate relationships.

The legalisation of homosexuality was soon followed by the formation of the Lesbian and Gay Christian Movement in the UK in 1961. Within the Churches, the key theme has been whether or not, and how, to recognise and celebrate diversity and difference.

This task may be hampered by the different ways of interpreting biblical texts. Some texts have been interpreted by the LGBT community to illustrate positive aspects of their experience, for example the relationship of David and Jonathan, or Ruth and Naomi, or the Song of Songs in the Old Testament. Others create real problems if taken at face value.

Old Testament passages

The idea of God as Creator is a recurrent one in the Bible (and the Genesis creation stories in particular). Some have seen it as an affirmation that God has made homosexual men and women, bisexual and transgender people just as they are. This means they should be fully accepted by those who have been made differently.

Several texts in the Old Testament appear to oppose homosexuality:

- Leviticus 18:22 – 'Do not have sexual relations with a man as one does with a woman; that is detestable.'
- Leviticus 20:13 – 'If a man has sexual relations with a man as one does with a woman, both of them have done what is detestable. They are to be put to death; their blood will be on their own heads.'

Both of these verses are included in a whole list of prohibited sexual arrangements, which includes various forms of incest, adultery, and sex during a woman's period. In Leviticus 20, capital punishment is also prescribed for other sexual sins, including adultery and incest.

Activity

Use a Bible to find out about the relationship between David and Jonathan, and between Ruth and Naomi. Read the Song of Songs, which uses erotic poetry to describe a heterosexual love affair between a couple who are not married.

Make a list of the ways each of these might be used to illustrate a positive aspect of lesbian, gay, bisexual or transgender experience.

A key text: Genesis 19: Sodom and Gomorrah

(You can read the original in a Bible: the below is a paraphrase.)

Lot, the nephew of Abraham, lives in Sodom, having been welcomed there as a stranger. He sees two angels arrive in the city and invites them to stay with him. At first unwilling, they finally agree. The men of Sodom then come to the house and demand that Lot produces the men, so that they can have sex with them. They act in a threatening and violent manner. Lot is unwilling to hand them over, but offers his two virgin daughters instead, inviting the men of Sodom to do whatever they like with them.

Helped by the angels, who magically cause the men outside to go blind, Lot escapes with his wife and daughters, and is told by the angels that God plans to destroy the city. Contrary to instructions, Lot's wife looks back to see the destruction and is turned into a pillar of salt.

Now in hiding in the mountains with only their father for company, Lot's two daughters are deprived of men with whom to have sex, and therefore conspire to get their father drunk and to have sex with him so that they can get pregnant by him and thus continue the family line.

In the narrative, at the very beginning, the story says that the men of Sodom are wicked, but no homosexual act is described or takes place – it is simply threatened. On the other hand, Lot is willing to hand over his daughters in order to appease the men of the city, and the daughters are prepared to have an incestuous relationship with him in order to bear children.

It is hardly a narrative that establishes a consistent set of moral norms as far as sexuality is concerned. It can be argued that Sodom and Gomorrah's destruction through God's anger was not because of the unspecified male-male genital acts themselves, but that these were threatened in the context of violence and inhospitality.

▲ Lot and his daughters

It is, therefore, far from straightforward to take a passage such as this and use it to condemn specific sexual acts between men. The same passage could equally well be used to illustrate gender violence, when Lot offers his daughters to the crowd. The prophet Ezekiel says (16:49) 'Sodom's sins were pride, gluttony, and laziness, while the poor and needy suffered outside her door.' He does not focus on sexual sin at all.

New Testament passages

In the New Testament, texts to consider include:

I Corinthians 6:9–10:

> 'Do not be deceived: Neither the sexually immoral nor idolaters nor adulterers nor men who have sex with men nor thieves nor the greedy nor drunkards nor slanderers nor swindlers will inherit the kingdom of God.'

The point made by some Bible interpreters is that almost everyone will find themselves on such a list to some degree – all are equally in need of forgiveness. There is some dispute between Bible scholars about the exact meaning of some of the Greek terms in this list, and it isn't clear whether it refers to different kinds of male prostitute, or to homosexual men in general.

Romans 1:26–28:

Having pointed out that people have rejected the truth of God as visible in nature, and have practised idolatry, Paul says:

> 'Because of this, God gave them over to shameful lusts. Even their women exchanged natural relations for unnatural ones. In the same way the men also abandoned natural relations with women and were inflamed with lust for one another. Men committed indecent acts with other men, and received in themselves the due penalty for their perversion.'

This passage continues, and includes gossips, slanderers, the ruthless, and those who disobey their parents, all of whom are said to deserve death. The key feature, however, comes at the opening of the next chapter, namely:

> 'You, therefore, have no excuse, you who pass judgment on someone else, for at whatever point you judge another, you are condemning yourself, because you who pass judgment do the same things.'

Paul is making the point that Christians should not judge others, since all need forgiveness.

Quite apart from the problems concerned with interpreting biblical texts generally, such passages regard heterosexual relationships and family life as the norm. Homosexual acts are included in a whole list of immoral or antisocial attitudes and activities which implicate almost everyone to some extent. The key feature of the New Testament passages, however, is that one should not judge others, because all deserve condemnation and all can receive forgiveness. This is not the same as a claim for equality of sexual preference.

Transgender issues

The Bible has nothing to say specifically about transgender people. The possibility of sex-change surgery was not available, and in first-century Palestine, with its small traditional communities, it would have been impossible for a man to live as a woman, or vice versa. So although there is nothing in the Bible that condemns transgender living, there is nothing specific that supports it either.

Arguments against allowing change of gender

If all people are created by God, it could be argued that God, who does not make mistakes, gave transgender people their body, and so they should be content with the gender God gave them.

The Early Church was strongly opposed to surgery which tampered with sex identity. Eunuchs (men who had been castrated) were not permitted to be ordained as priests. The Church historian Eusebius reports that the theologian Origen castrated himself following a rather too literal reading of Matthew 19:12 (or possibly he was castrated by his enemies), and as a result Origen's ordination was declared invalid.

Those who believe it is wrong to change gender argue that all the passages which relate to homosexuality also apply to those who change their gender, since a surgical gender transition cannot change the sexual nature that a person is born with. If a transgender female sleeps with a man, it is the same as if two men engage in a homosexual act, and is therefore condemned.

Arguments in favour of allowing change of gender

The first creation story says that when God created humankind 'in the image of God he created them; male and female, he created them' (Genesis 1:27). This passage can be interpreted to mean that God's nature, and by extension the nature of all humankind created in God's image, contains both male and female. If this is the case, changing gender is merely a case of emphasising one aspect of God's image over another.

In his letter to the Galatians, Paul says 'There is neither Jew nor Gentile, neither slave nor free, nor is there male and female, for you are all one in Christ Jesus' (Galatians 3:28). Paul seems to be saying that for Christians, gender identity has no importance, and if that is the case, changing one's gender is of no significance in terms of salvation.

Alternatively, a transgender person could claim that God created them as a whole, with the nature of one gender and the body of another, giving them the responsibility of choice about how to live their life.

There is one passage in the apocryphal Gospel of Thomas (a very early text which is not part of the Bible) which appears to encourage a change of gender:

Simon Peter said to them: 'Let Mary go away from us, for women are not worthy of life.' Jesus said: 'Look, I will draw her in so as to make her male, so that she too may become a living male spirit, similar to you. (But I say to you): Every woman who makes herself male will enter the kingdom of heaven.' (Gospel of Thomas, Logion 114)

However, this passage is a problem in terms of gender equality, since it seems to suggest that only men can enter the kingdom of Heaven.

Key questions for interpreting these biblical texts:

1 Do the views expressed reflect the moral and social situation of a particular time and place, or do they apply to everyone and for all time?

2 If they reflect the moral and social situation of a particular time and place, who determines what interpretation is appropriate today?

3 If they apply to everyone for all time, how should the Church treat LGBT people?

The Church of England: a pragmatic approach to ordination

For many years, it was acknowledged that many of those ordained to the Church of England priesthood were homosexual, but it was judged that, provided their homosexual activity was contained within stable relationships and did not interfere with their pastoral ministry, the qualities displayed by the male homosexuals, in terms of sensitivity and acceptance of people in need, made them particularly good pastors. This was a pragmatic approach. It became more problematic with the ordination of those who were openly gay or lesbian. At that point a decision had to be taken about what was expected of such **ordinands**. The general view was that gay or lesbian candidates could be ordained, but would be required to remain celibate. Homosexual Christians argue that this goes against their personal integrity.

Within the Anglican Communion, the first openly gay priest to be consecrated bishop was Gene Robinson, who became bishop of New Hampshire, in the USA, in 2004. The first lesbian woman to be consecrated bishop was Mary Glasspool,

Key term

Ordinand A person who is preparing to be ordained.

251

who became a suffragan (or assistant) bishop in the Diocese of Los Angeles in the USA in 2010. However, some Churches in the Anglican Communion, including the Anglican Church of Australia and most African and Eastern Anglican Churches, continue to forbid the ordination of homosexuals to the priesthood. The issue is so heated that it threatens to split the Anglican Communion.

The general principle in the Church of England is that openly homosexual people may be ordained, provided that they are and intend to remain within a stable relationship, and that – although acknowledging homosexual feelings – they do not actually engage in homosexual sexual acts. In 2005, after a long period of discussion and consultation, the General Synod of the Church of England agreed that people in same-sex civil partnerships could be ordained to the priesthood provided that they remain celibate. This was extended to bishops in 2013.

Key questions:

1 Does this restriction go against the personal integrity of the person in a loving homosexual relationship who seeks ordination?

2 Is it reasonable for the Church to require a couple in a legal committed relationship not to engage in sexual activity?

Technical terms for Christianity, gender and sexuality

Androgynous This word literally means man-woman-like, and refers to the idea that someone or something has both male and female qualities.

Anglican Communion A worldwide group of Churches which are self-governing, but all share a measure of common theology with the Church of England, and who all pay respect to the Archbishop of Canterbury.

Apostolic Succession The passing on of authority from one generation to the next by the laying on of hands at ordination, going back to the apostles.

Biblical criticism Studying the Bible using a range of different approaches to come to a fuller understanding. Liberal biblical criticism treats the Bible as a text that is subject to analysis just like any other piece of writing.

Celibacy The choice to abstain from marriage and sexual relations for social or religious reasons.

Christian Complementarians Those who believe that men and women are equal but different, so their roles in the Church are different and should complement one another.

Christian Egalitarians Those who believe that men and women should be permitted equal roles in the Church.

Consecration 1) To make something or someone sacred; 2) The religious rite by which a priest is made a bishop through the laying on of hands.

Feminist theology An approach to biblical scholarship and theological thinking that aims to analyse and challenge biblical interpretation and Christian working from a feminist perspective.

Fundamentalism A movement that started in the early twentieth century which regarded certain things as fundamental beliefs of Christianity. These 'five fundamentals' were: biblical inspiration and the infallibility of scripture; the virgin birth of Jesus; belief that Christ's death was the atonement for sin; the bodily resurrection of Jesus; the historical reality of the miracles of Jesus.

General Synod The governing and decision-making body of the Church of England. It comprises three houses: the house of Bishops, the house of Clergy and the house of Laity.

Irredeemably sexist This is a term used to describe the view that Christianity is wholly sexist in its view of humanity and society, so that it is impossible to be both a feminist and a Christian.

Liberal theology An approach to biblical scholarship and theological thinking that aimed to analyse the Bible and Christian teaching using modern thought informed by reason and science.

Ordinand A person who is preparing to be ordained.

Ordination The religious rite by which a person is made a deacon or priest through the laying on of hands.

Patriarchal   Literally means 'ruled by fathers', but in the context of feminist theology, it refers to the fact that the text, practices and teachings of religion were produced and passed on by men. This means that they ignore the role of women in the history of the faith and undermine women in the church today.

Priesthood of all believers   The Protestant idea that all human beings can have direct communication with God on their own account, without the need for priests.

Protestant Reformation   The period during the sixteenth century when, as the result of protests against some beliefs and practices of the Roman Catholic Church, new churches were formed that were separate from the Roman Catholic Church.

Sacrament   Physical action which has spiritual meaning and affects the soul of the person who receives it.

Summary of Christianity, gender and sexuality

Development of biblical criticism: The Bible and the Reformation

Christian thinking about issues around gender and sexuality is tied up with ways that the Bible has been read and understood. Until the Protestant Reformation in the sixteenth century, all western Christians were under the authority of the Roman Church, led by the Pope. Few Christians could read the Bible themselves, partly because few people could read at all, and partly because the text of the Bible was only available in Latin, which most people could not understand. During the Protestant Reformation, the Bible was translated into the vernacular (normal spoken language) of the people. At the same time, the Protestant reformers encouraged people to read the Bible for themselves and develop their own interpretation separately from Church teaching.

1 Background to the interpretation of scripture

The Roman Church taught that the Bible needed to be interpreted by scholars who had also studied the traditional teaching of the Church, passed down from the time of the Apostles. When Protestant lay people read the Bible, they developed different ways to understand the texts. Some saw scripture as self-interpreting; others used reason and developments in thought to develop new ways to understand what the Bible was saying. During the nineteenth century, many Christians began to see the Bible as a text to be interpreted by reason, to make it compatible with science and modern thought. Scholars studied the text to identify sources, literary units and ways that the text had been developed by the Early Church. This kind of approach is called liberal biblical criticism.

2 Some key features of biblical criticism

Biblical criticism examines the text in its original language to understand what the original authors intended. It looks at the kind of writing to identify the context needed to understand it. It looks at the background to each passage to help modern readers to see what it meant when it was written. The intention of these processes is to find the truth expressed in the Bible, recognising that it cannot just be read as simple fact or instructions.

3 Challenges to this approach: Barth and fundamentalism

In Barth's view, the Bible was not simply a book which could be fully understood for a modern context by this kind of study. He saw it instead as an inspired text which challenged and confronted enlightenment values of reason and scientific certainty. The Bible is the measure by which science and reason are judged, not the other way around.

A different challenge arose in the early twentieth century from fundamentalists, who rejected liberal criticism in favour of 'the plain meaning of scripture'. They insisted that the text of the Bible was literally true, and that no scholarship or interpretation was necessary to understand it. They also believed that the instructions and moral advice applies directly to Christians at all times and in all places.

4 Key New Testament texts

Gender equality is suggested by:

Paul's letter to the Romans, 16:1, mentions women who are in leadership roles. Galatians 3:26–28, also by Paul, speaks of all social barriers being meaningless 'in Christ Jesus'.

Gender equality is challenged by:

Paul's first letter to the Corinthians, 14:34, 35, seems to say that women may not speak in Church. However, we know that this letter is a reply to a lost letter from the Christians of Corinth, addressing a specific incident, rather than as a general ruling. Ephesians, not written by Paul, places women in a submissive role in society.

5 A critical examination of 1 Tim 2:8–15

The letter to Timothy was written after the time of Paul. When the writer says 'I do not permit a women to teach or to have authority over a man; she must be silent', he is clearly saying that women are not equal to men, in society or in the life of the Church.

However, scholars use liberal criticism to show that the exact meaning of the language is uncertain, and that context of the Church (a problem in the community at Ephesus) and the surrounding society (pagan followers of the Roman goddess Diana) could explain the very negative view of women in this letter.

Biblical fundamentalists reject ideas of textual analysis and context. They argue that God spoke through the writer of the text, and therefore that these words should be universally applied.

6 Different responses to the New Testament texts

- Christian egalitarians argue that men and women are equal before God, and so have equal rights, roles and responsibilities in the Church.

- Christian complementarians argue that they are not equal, but have different qualities that work together for the good of society and the Church. Men are leaders and have authority in Church and the community, while women are carers whose role is to support men in the community.

- The Roman Catholic Church uses Natural Law to argue that men and women are of equal value to God but have different, complementary roles in the world. Jesus appointed only men as apostles, and authority passes from one generation of men to the next through the laying on of hands. The 1976 Vatican declaration *Inter Insigniores* rules out the possibility of women being ordained.

- The Protestant view is expressed in the idea of 'the Priesthood of all Believers'. Protestant reformers argued that each individual has access to God without needing the mediation of priests. The role of women in Protestant Churches depends on their status in society at the time. Some Churches take a literalist view of 1 Timothy, and exclude women from leadership, while others allow women to hold offices in Church on the same terms as men. The Church of England, which is both catholic and reformed, is influenced by both views.

Some Christians argue that it is simply a case of reading and applying the Bible text, while others insist that the Church should reinterpret the text for today's social norms.

Changing roles of men and women in society outside of religion

1 Women in the Church before the nineteenth century

Women may have held positions of authority equal to men in the earliest Church, but their position in society was not equal to that of men. By the fifth century, they were in a secondary position which was theologically justified with reference to Eve as the source of sin and temptation. The rise of monasticism allowed women to study and to hold authority in their (mostly all-female) religious communities. However, in both society and in the Church, with very few exceptions, power, wealth and authority were held, controlled and used by men.

2 Women in the nineteenth century

As Britain became industrialised, women entered the workforce in caring, service and unskilled roles. The role of women was still largely focused on the home and charity work. As education became more widely available to women, some began to enter professions like medicine, and there was a growing women's rights movement. In 1879, Catherine Booth argued a case for women's right to preach because they are better communicators, and in any case, the Holy Spirit guides a preacher.

3 The social and legal status of women today

The social status of women today varies depending on place, culture, economic situation and religious norms. In Britain, their status and roles in the Church depend partly on theology and partly on their social and political role in modern society. In the UK, it is illegal to discriminate against women in employment. When the Church of England refused to ordain women, it was going against the norms of modern society, even though it argued its case on theological grounds.

Developments in Christian thought: Debates about female ordination

1 Female ordination within the Church of England

The Church of England has a threefold order of ministry: bishops, priests and deacons. This ministry was only open to men until the twentieth century.

2 Ordination of women to the priesthood

With the exception of Florence Li Tim Oi, ordained in 1944 because there were no men available during the

War, the Church of England opposed the ordination of women to the priesthood until the 1970s. In 1975, it was agreed that there were no 'fundamental objections' to the ordination of women, and in 1985, women were allowed to be ordained as deacons. In 1988, Synod approved the proposal to ordain women to the priesthood, and in 1994, the first women were ordained as priests in the Church of England.

3 Consecration of women as bishops

In the Church of England the first female bishop, Libby Lane, was consecrated in 2015. Those opposed to the consecration of women as bishops argued that Apostolic Succession meant that no woman could represent the authority handed down through the generations of men from Christ himself. Any confirmation or ordination done by a woman would break the chain of tradition and would therefore be invalid. Some Churches refused the authority and leadership of a woman bishop, so the Church of England allowed them to be overseen by a male bishop. Some people left the Church of England altogether and joined the Roman Catholic Church because they felt that the link with the historic Church had been broken.

Objections to the ordination of women in the Church of England included:

● They did not have the authority to overturn the tradition of male-only ministry

● It might damage the relationship with the Roman Catholic Church

● A conservative reading of the texts discussed on pages 232–233 argues against ordaining women.

4 The continuing debate today

Two key consequences of the continuing debate over the ordination of women in the Church of England are, on the one hand, a growing hostility towards those church leaders who continue to oppose the ordination of women, and on the other hand, a rejection of the authority of the Church among those who oppose the ordination of women.

5 Feminist theology

Feminist theology is an approach to theology which takes as its starting point the hopes and aspirations of women. Its roots lie in the social changes of the late nineteenth century and the growing movement for women's rights.

There are different strands within feminist theology. The **liberal** strand analyses the system as one that

denies women the right to equality. The **biblical** strand sees God in the Bible having traditionally 'female' qualities, and focuses on the importance of women in the life and teaching of Jesus. The **radical or Marxist** strand looks to change society so that women and men are equal.

6 Daphne Hampson

Daphne Hampson is a post-Christian theologian who holds that Christianity is not true. A one-off event which breaks the laws of nature, like a resurrection, is impossible. The idea of one person who has a different kind of relationship to God from all other people does not make sense. She also holds that Christianity is not moral. Christians believe in a revelation in history, and in a God who is different from humans, so they obey God instead of taking responsibility for their moral choices.

For Hampson Christianity makes it look natural that being male should be seen as the norm, while women are seen as 'the other'. In this respect, Hampson believes that Christianity is fascist. Christianity is 'irredeemably sexist'. She thinks people should instead express awareness of God in terms appropriate for the present time. God should not be seen as 'out there' and anthropomorphic. God is a dimension of one reality which everyone is part of.

7 Rosemary Radford Ruether

Ruether is a Roman Catholic liberation theologian and feminist. She sees parallels between Jesus' teaching and practice in the Gospels (care for the oppressed and outcasts, challenging religious authorities) and feminist challenges to society today. She notes that Jesus seems to understand the needs and the strengths of women: he has feminine characteristics. In this way, Jesus shows both male and female aspects of human nature – he is 'androgynous'.

Ruether implies that women can be seen as more Christ-like than men, because women are caring, healing and forgiving, as Christ was.

Ruether also sees women as closer to nature than men, so they have a purer approach to ethics inspired by nature. This idea is described as Eco-feminism.

Different Christian views about celibacy, marriage, homosexuality and transgender issues

1 Celibacy

In contrast to first-century Judaism, the Early Church seems to have had a mixed view about marriage. If the world was to end soon, then Christians were meant to focus on preparing for that. However, by the time of the Pastoral Epistles, Church leaders were expected to be married with families.

As the Church developed, attitudes to women, sex and married life became more negative, and from the fourth century, a monastic tradition developed, where men (and later women) could follow a 'higher' calling, devoting themselves to God and giving up the opportunity to marry and have a family. Celibacy became normal for Catholic clergy. Although in Orthodox Churches, some clergy marry, bishops must be celibate.

After the Protestant Reformation, most Protestant Churches abandoned clerical celibacy. Today, monks and nuns of all traditions practise celibacy, as do Roman Catholic priests and some Orthodox clergy. Clergy in the Church of England may marry. Protestant Evangelical Churches may require their ministers to be married with a family to obey the advice in 1 Tim 3:1–7.

2 Marriage

Celibacy was seen as the ideal in the Early Church as Christians prepared for the end of time. By the time of the letter to Timothy, however, Church leaders were expected to marry and run a well-ordered family. The Church controlled marriage as a sacrament, the means by which God's grace was made present in the family and community. As celibacy developed in the Middle Ages, marriage became seen as a second-best option. In the sixteenth century, the Protestant reformers changed the status of marriage from sacrament to the blessing of what was essentially a legal union between a man and a woman.

In Christianity today, the different Churches continue to have different views. For Roman Catholics it is a sacrament, and for most Protestants it is not. In addition, modern society has different views and expectations. For some, it is focused on the relationship between a couple rather than the basis of a family. For some, the religious aspect of a marriage ceremony has become an optional extra to the legal requirements. Marriage 'till death do us part' looks increasingly meaningless as divorce rates rise. More recently, same-sex marriage has challenged traditional views of what marriage means. The Roman Catholic Church, for example, will not allow re-marriage after divorce, while the Orthodox Churches do.

3 Homosexuality and transgender issues

Some biblical texts seem to condemn homosexual behaviour, most notably Leviticus, which describes it as an 'abomination'. The story of the destruction of Sodom is also used to support this view, although Ezekiel specifically says that the sins of Sodom were pride, gluttony and laziness. The story of Lot actually shows violence against women and incest, but homosexual rape is only suggested, not carried out. The Churches have traditionally, therefore, opposed homosexual relationships, supported by more problematic New Testament texts in I Corinthians 6:9–10 and Romans 1:26–28.

Changes in society and social norms led to a gradual acceptance in society of aspects of sexuality that Churches rejected. Until 1967, homosexual acts between men were illegal. Today, homosexuality and transgenderism are generally accepted in normal society, and same-sex marriage is legal. Many Churches welcome gay, lesbian, bisexual and transgender people into their communities. However, some Churches, including both the Roman Catholic Church and some Conservative Evangelical Churches, continue to insist that same-sex sexual activity is sinful. This raises important questions about how the Bible is interpreted in today's society.

The Church of England: a pragmatic approach

In the past, the Church of England has ordained many homosexual men whose sexual life was discreet to the priesthood, recognising the gifts they brought to ministry. More recently, the Church has had to set out guidelines for those hoping to be ordained. In the Church of England openly gay people may be ordained, provided they are in a stable relationship, and provided they do not engage in homosexual sexual acts. In 2005, General Synod of the Church of England allowed people in same-sex civil partnerships to be ordained to the priesthood provided that they remain celibate. This was extended to bishops in 2013.

Today, many western Anglican Churches ordain gay men and women. However, some Anglican Churches in Australia and Africa continue to forbid the ordination of homosexuals to the priesthood. The issue threatens to split the Anglican Communion.

9

Christianity and science

You will need to consider the following items for this section

1 How and why science has influenced Christianity and how Christianity has responded, with particular reference to: emphasis on evidence and reason in science; specific scientific discoveries; science as a stimulus to Christian ethical thinking.

2 Developments in Christian thought:

- How scientific explanation has challenged Christian belief with reference to the 'God of the gaps'; nineteenth-century responses to Darwin's theory of evolution; and contemporary responses to the Big Bang theory, including reference to creationist views

- The belief that science is compatible with Christianity with reference to the views of John Polkinghorne

- Different Christian responses to issues raised by science: genetic engineering.

Introduction

What we think of as modern science came as a result of developments in thinking that took place between the sixteenth and eighteenth centuries. Although there have been huge changes in science since that time – evolution, relativity, quantum mechanics, neuroscience and the digital revolution – all of these became possible because of the basic principles established in earlier centuries.

There were earlier scientific thinkers, but they lacked the systematic approach to evidence that developed from the sixteenth century and came to shape science as we know it today. Most of the first 'modern' scientists were religious, and did not see their work as conflicting with established Christian teachings.

A key feature of this rise of science was the assumption that human reason could understand the way the world works, without any divine or supernatural influence. This implied a trust in evidence and experiment as a means of acquiring knowledge, and an assumption that the world was both orderly and intelligible. It also required a willingness to challenge and evaluate all claims to truth, setting aside the authority of the Church.

In some ways, this scientific approach was made possible by Christianity. Christianity had presented the idea of a world that was predictable and ordered by God, and also that the world was a positive resource provided for humankind. Previously, however, human reason was seen as giving support for an understanding of the divine order (as for example in the work of Aquinas). With the rise of science, human reason became autonomous – it followed its own agenda, rather than simply serving to endorse religious teachings. This threatened the authority of religion, and challenged the view, found particularly in some Protestant circles, that human reason was 'fallen' and, therefore, incapable of establishing the truth.

This use of reason and the examination of evidence was not entirely new. Aquinas and others had used reason and evidence as a means of supporting religious beliefs (for example his arguments for the existence of God). The authority of the Catholic Church had been challenged at the Reformation. What was new in this science was that it developed a systematic approach to understanding the world that was entirely independent of religious ideas – whether or not the scientists happened to be Christians. The emerging scientific method was clearly successful in making predictions, offering explanations, and developing technologies; its success was, therefore, a powerful argument for its validity.

The emphasis on evidence and reason in science

In the seventeenth century, two approaches to knowledge were developed which would have a profound impact on Christian beliefs: **empiricism** and **rationalism**.

Francis Bacon, Isaac Newton and others insisted that knowledge started with observation and evidence. From this, reason could then deduce the laws of nature, expressing them in scientific/mathematical terms. This claim that all knowledge comes from experience is termed *empiricism*, and it remains at the heart of scientific thinking today. Every scientific claim depends on evidence – either from experiments or by observation. This has become the norm, so that now, in all areas of life (including religion) people tend ask what the evidence is for any claim that is made.

By contrast, René Descartes, often described as the founder of modern philosophy, used the method of systematic doubt to establish what could be known without doubt. Since the senses can sometimes deceive us (for example when mistaking a dream for reality), he doubted all empirical evidence. His only certain knowledge was of himself as a thinking being. This approach, seeing the mind, rather than the senses, as the starting point for knowledge, is termed *rationalism*.

Generally speaking, the world of science since the seventeenth century has been based on empiricism rather than rationalism. It has started with observation and experiment, rather than with pure thought. However, it is clear that our understanding of the world depends upon the way in which we *interpret* the information that comes through the senses. Human mental processes and perceptions have a part to play; no evidence is free from interpretation.

Key terms

Empiricism The view that all knowledge starts from sense experience.

Rationalism The view that all knowledge starts with the processes of human thought.

The scientific method

> [I]t is not what the man of science believes that distinguishes him, but how and why he believes it. His beliefs are tentative, not dogmatic; they are based on evidence, not on authority or intuition. (Bertrand Russell) [Note 1]

There are two fundamentally different processes involved in gaining knowledge: *deduction* and *induction*. We have looked at these in connection with the arguments for the existence of God, in Volume 1. Here is a reminder:

The deductive approach

If one proposition is true, others may be deduced from it. That works well, provided the first proposition is correct. So, for example, the mediaeval view of the heavens was that they were perfect, and the circle was a perfect shape; therefore, the planets had to move in circles. When this piece of deduction conflicted with evidence, astronomers had to find another explanation. They thought that perfect motion *had* to be in circles in some way. Alternative explanations were far too complicated, so the underlying idea of circular motion was challenged. This, in turn, challenged the view that the heavens were perfect.

The inductive approach

The inductive method depends on observation and testing, and was the key feature of the development of science. Scientists:

- observe and gather evidence for what is being examined, seeking to eliminate, as far as possible, all irrelevant factors
- analyse the evidence, and draw conclusions from it in the form of a hypothesis
- devise experiments to test out the hypothesis: if a hypothesis is correct, then certain experimental results should be anticipated
- modify the hypothesis, if necessary, in the light of the experiments
- argue for a theory that will explain the evidence and results
- once there is a theory, use deduction to predict things that should be the case if the theory is correct
- establish tests that can either verify or disprove the theory.

It is sometimes assumed that science delivers certainty. However, the inductive process can yield at most only *a high degree of probability*. It is more true to say that science offers the best available explanation. There is always the chance that an extra piece of information will show that the original hypothesis is wrong, or that it only applies within a limited field. The hypothesis, and the scientific theory that comes from it, may change as a result of more observations.

Theories that are tested out in this way lead to scientific laws. **Scientism** is the view that discovering these laws offers the only route to knowledge; but this is not necessarily true.

What is clear is that science is *naturalistic* – it deals with the natural world as it is experienced. This potentially brings it into conflict with any supernatural claims of Christianity.

> **Key term**
>
> **Scientism** The view that science alone can give true knowledge of reality; that it alone can determine what is meaningful, and that eventually it will explain everything. Such an approach tends to ignore the contribution of the arts or of psychology and the emotions to human self-understanding.

Some Christian responses to the rise of science

One early response to the rise of science was the development of a view of God that we call 'deism'.

Deism

If everything can be explained in terms of physical laws, there is little scope for belief in a personal God who enters into nature and affects its operations – by performing miracles, for example. On the other hand, an ordered universe suggests that it might have been created by an intelligent designer. This led to the development of the idea of Deism – belief in an intelligent but impersonal creator: one who creates the universe then leaves it to its own free devices.

An advantage of Deism is that it offers a religious way of explaining the predictable nature of the universe. However, it cannot easily be challenged by science, because it does not depend on God doing anything in the world. Once God has set the mechanism working, he leaves it to its own devices.

John Polkinghorne is a theoretical physicist, theologian and priest. In *Science and Providence* (1989) he points out a limitation of Deism, in that the Christian God is regarded as personal: someone with whom, through prayer, people can interact, and who is expected to care and provide for people. An impersonal deistic idea of God is just an intellectual idea. It is not the same as the Christian belief in a God with whom people might have a personal relationship.

Existentialism

Existentialism is a philosophy based on the idea that humans create their own personal reality through the choices they make. The world is not fixed and handed to them, but is something that can be shaped by individual commitments and values. This approach is clearly very different to that of science. Many Christians accept the scientific approach to the world, but they are also concerned with key questions about the meaning and purpose of life and about the relationship between every individual and existence itself.

Søren Kierkegaard, the earliest Christian existentialist, saw faith as a matter of personal commitment, not related to scientific facts. Since his time, liberal Christian thinkers, for example Paul Tillich, have suggested that Christian beliefs and symbols need to be understood in relation to existential questions concerning the meaning and purpose of life if they are to be relevant to people's lives. Christianity offers a set of beliefs and symbols that give a sense of meaning and purpose (for Tillich on symbolic language, see Chapter 1 Religious language). The individual then has to decide whether or not to accept those beliefs as a matter of personal commitment. In other words, Christianity is concerned with existential questions rather than with scientific questions. On this view there is no conflict between religion and science, because they are different (and equally valid) ways of looking at the world.

You will see below that John Polkinghorne has no difficulty in combining science with the personal/existential approach to Christianity, so he offers yet another Christian approach to science.

Specific scientific discoveries: Influence on Christianity, and Christianity's response

This section looks at a selection of major scientific discoveries in the past few centuries and their impact on Christian beliefs, together with the way in which Christianity has adapted to the challenges they present.

We shall look at the following discoveries:

● Evolution
● Big Bang
● Quantum theory
● Neuroscience.

Note that whereas evolution and Big Bang are required by the specification, quantum theory and neuroscience are not, so no questions can be asked on them. They are included here as optional extension work, and you could refer to them in your answers where relevant.

Darwin and the discovery of evolution

Charles Darwin (1809–82)

The son of a doctor, Darwin studied medicine at Edinburgh and then went to Cambridge, intending to be ordained. In 1831 he was offered a place on board HMS *Beagle* as a naturalist, to explore wildlife in South America. He returned in 1836, convinced, by the peculiarity of the variety of species he had seen, that one species must develop out of another. He spent the next twenty years gathering evidence and developing his theory of natural selection, publishing *On the Origin of Species by Means of Natural Selection, or the Preservation of Favoured Races in the Struggle for* Life (to give it its full title) in 1859.

Key term

Natural selection One of the basic mechanisms of evolution, where organisms better adapted to their environment tend to survive and produce more offspring.

Darwin's *On The Origin of Species* (1859) was hugely controversial because for the first time, it suggested that a simple natural mechanism – **natural selection** – could explain the appearance of design by God and, therefore, made the idea of a designer God unnecessary.

With hindsight, the theory of natural selection seems remarkably simple. It is this:

● Within any species there are some members whose particular characteristics help them to survive better than others.
● Those who survive to adulthood are able to breed, so they pass on those characteristics to the next generation.
● Through this mechanism, over successive generations, characteristics which improve the chance of survival will be found in more individuals within the species.
● Over time, the characteristics of a species are gradually modified in favour of those that help the species to survive in its particular environment.

261

Darwin starts by pointing out that people had long bred domestic animals to encourage particular characteristics. In nature, animals and plants produce more offspring than can possibly survive. Their numbers would always be controlled by lack of food and/or space. Only those with the best adapted characteristics would survive. This gave him the mechanism (natural selection) he needed to explain the progressive changes in species.

This theory challenged the unique status of the human species, but even more crucially, **it challenged the notion of purpose in creation**. Species flourish or decline depending upon how they adapt to their environment. There is no external *purpose* in their survival. That contradicted the idea of a God who created the world for a purpose, and whose will is being worked out within it.

Darwin's 'religious' views

Darwin eventually lost his religious beliefs because he considered them to be naïve. In his autobiography, he records that even when aboard the *Beagle*, he '… had gradually come … to see that the Old Testament from its manifestly false history of the world, with the Tower of Babel, the rainbow as a sign, etc., etc., and from its attributing to God the feelings of a revengeful tyrant, was no more to be trusted than … the beliefs of any barbarian.' [Note 2]

By the time he was 40, Darwin no longer believed in Christianity either, and although he did not become an atheist, he was certainly an agnostic.

A religious response to the theory of evolution

Nineteenth-century Christian responses to the theory of evolution are dealt with on pages 272–273. Looking briefly at reactions from Christians today, most would see natural selection as the mechanism by which God works. For example, the Catholic theologian **Karl Rahner** (1904–84) argued that human beings are made wholly by evolution, but also – from a religious point of view – wholly by God; so God and evolution are compatible explanations of human origins. There is no need to think of God 'starting off' the process of evolution by *interfering* in the early history of the world. Evolution works by the natural laws and processes of biology, chemistry and physics, and these laws are presumably the design principles by which the universe behaves in the way it does. It is perfectly reasonable for Christians to understand God as the 'author' of the laws of nature, and in that sense as the author of evolution. This kind of approach suggests that the idea of a supernatural God who intervenes and directs what is happening in the world is no longer necessary.

The Big Bang theory

To work out how the universe began, scientists have to observe the way it is now, and use laws of physics to calculate what may have occurred. They observe that galaxies are moving away from Earth and from one another. This suggests that the galaxies were originally closer together and are now flying apart. On that basis, the distance of a galaxy from Earth can be calculated by working out how fast it is moving away. From the speed of expansion, it is possible to calculate the age of the universe.

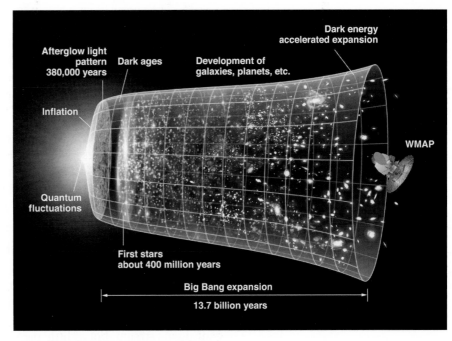

▲ The inflationary Big Bang Universe

Key term

Big Bang Name given to the theory that the universe began from the rapid expansion (not an explosion) of a gravitational singularity, a point of infinite density, some 13.8 billion years ago.

The point at the left of the diagram above shows the point of singularity from which the '**Big Bang**' expansion occurred. The 'cosmic microwave background' is the thermal radiation created at the beginning of the universe, and is the oldest light that we can detect.

It is now generally believed that the universe started about 13.8 billion years ago, and the model that currently has most support is the '**Lambda-CDM**' '**standard model**' **of Big Bang cosmology** associated with dark energy and cold dark matter. According to this model, the present universe expanded out in a sudden burst of enormous energy and heat from a point of close-to-zero size but of infinite density, known as a 'space-time singularity'; all the general theories of physics break down when we approach the singularity.

In an explosion, matter is flung outwards *through* space. The 'Big Bang', however, was not an explosion, it was the *expansion of space itself* – an event in which what we know as 'space' and 'time' were created – a point *from which* space and time have come, not a point *within* space and time.

Although always open to modification, the Big Bang theory is accepted by most members of the scientific community as the best available explanation for the origin of the universe.

The impact of Big Bang theory on Christianity has been mixed. For most Christians, the Big Bang theory suggests that the universe had a beginning, and that this was how God created the universe. The Catholic Church endorses this view (and as a matter of fact, the theory of an expanding universe was first proposed by a Belgian physicist and Roman Catholic priest, **Georges Lemaître (1894–1966)**). However, some accounts of the theory suggest that the Big Bang happened without the need for a Creator, as a spontaneous event where the universe simply came into existence. At the moment, there is no agreement about the origin of the Big Bang. We look in detail at Christian responses to the Big Bang theory on pages 273–276.

Key term

Quantum mechanics Also known as quantum physics/quantum theory – the physics which deals with matter at the smallest scales. The theory was introduced in 1900 by the physicist Max Planck: energy exists in individual units – quanta (from Latin *quantum*, 'amount').

Quantum theory

Towards the end of the nineteenth century it was widely believed that science had already made its most important discoveries and that, from now on, it would simply build systematically upon its existing successes. That was to change radically at the beginning of the twentieth century, seen particularly in Einstein's theory of relativity, and then the development of quantum theory.

The world revealed by relativity and **quantum mechanics** is so far removed from earlier cosmologies, and so difficult for most people to grasp, that the old debates about God and nature need to be revised to take the new perspective into account. However, the key issues in relating Christian faith to science remain similar to those of earlier eras.

The idea that matter is made up of atoms separated from one another by empty space was put forward by the Greek 'Atomist' philosophers Leucippus and Democritus in the fifth century BCE. However, a major new development came about early in the twentieth century with the recognition (following a discovery made by **Max Planck** in 1900) that radiation (for example light, or energy) did not appear to arrive as a continuous stream, but as little packets, or 'quanta' – hence the term 'quantum theory'. Under certain conditions, light can appear as a wave or a particle, a phenomenon known as 'wave-particle duality'.

Until the discovery of the electron in 1897, the atom was thought to be indivisible, and was visualised as a very small but solid portion of physical matter. The atom was then found to have a nucleus consisting of tiny protons and neutrons, with electrons circling round it, like planets in a solar system. Most of the atom is empty space.

Particle physics (the term used for the study of sub-atomic particles) developed from that point. We now know that atoms are made up of many different particles, divisible into smaller 'quarks', which themselves come in different forms. Matter is, therefore, far from simple. It is composed of complex arrangements of nuclear forces, binding together particles, which themselves cannot always be distinguished as independent entities.

Particles seem to change, depending upon how they are observed, and at this level their behaviour appears to be random (unlike the predictable laws of Newtonian physics). This leads to an important feature of quantum theory. *Quantum theory cannot predict the action of individual particles, but describes the atomic world in terms of probabilities, based on the observation of very large numbers.*

Three of the main implications of quantum theory for religion are described below.

1 God perhaps works in the world by influencing events at the quantum level.

Quantum theory takes us even further away from the idea of God running a 'clockwork' universe. **Niels Bohr**, a quantum physicist, held that uncertainty was built into nature. If you think about that, it suggests that what happens in the world has a degree of uncertainty or even randomness. How would God control, or influence, such a world? Einstein himself was upset by this, and had a long-running debate with Bohr, insisting that 'God does not play dice'. Most physicists think that Einstein lost the debate.

In answer to this, when we look at the views of the priest and physicist John Polkinghorne, below, you will see that Polkinghorne argues that God works in the world through influencing events *at the quantum level*. When we get to events at our level of experience, events are no longer random: they can be described by the laws of science, *so God can bring about order from disorder*. Moreover, in this way God can act in the world undetected, and so our moral freedom is preserved (see the Free Will Defence, in Volume 1, pages 62–71). This brings us to the next possibility:

2 Quantum physics perhaps shows that we have some degree of free will.

You will remember that quantum physics is important for the discussion of free will and moral responsibility (Chapter 5, page 147). Most Christians believe that in order to be morally responsible we must have some degree of 'libertarian' free will. Against that, determinists argue that the brain is a physical system, and that all physical systems operate by cause and effect, so we have no free will. Some interpretations of quantum theory are deterministic, but **others suggest that there is a 'niche' for free will in the brain's quantum processes**.

At the moment it is not possible to say definitively that such a quantum 'niche' exists; nevertheless, it is an area for ongoing study and debate in which Christian morality is deeply concerned.

3 The 'Many Worlds' interpretation of quantum physics.

This stems from the 'wave-particle duality' that we referred to in the first paragraph of this section on quantum theory. You do not need to know the detail here – just the implications, which are that there are many possible states of a measured system, and there is no way of telling which ones exist and which do not. Some physicists claim that they *all* exist simultaneously in parallel universes. In other words, there is a multiverse and not just one universe.

When we look below at contemporary reactions to Big Bang theory, the third reaction we discuss there is multiverse theory (see page 273–274). You will see that if some version of multiverse theory is true, then some physicists think that this makes it much less likely that a God is needed to create them, because different universes appear to be created automatically through different choices. Others argue that this is irrelevant to whether or not God exists, since God is still a likely explanation of why anything exists at all, including multiverses. You will need to assess that possibility when you get to that point.

Neuroscience

Since Descartes, dualists have made an absolute distinction between the thinking self and the physical body. This fits with a general sense that I 'am' myself but that I 'have' a body. Until the last fifty years, dualism was regarded as the norm, and that fitted well with the Christian idea of the soul or self – a spiritual entity that inhabited a body, but which would live on after physical death.

More recently, however, many philosophers and scientists have taken a materialist view of the self, and this is illustrated most clearly by the work that has been done in neuroscience. It has always been recognised that brain activity is closely related to thought, emotion, experience and so on. What neuroscience has shown is the way in which emotions and thoughts, and sensory experience such as sight or hearing, are related to particular parts of the brain.

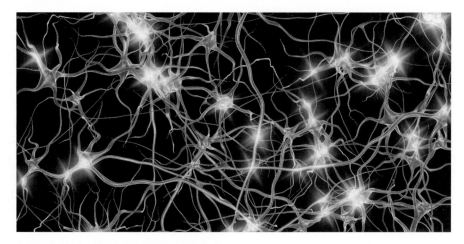

▲ Neurons are the 'data processing' units of the brain. The brain contains about 100 billion neurons.

The challenge of neuroscience to religious belief is that a neuroscientist can claim to show that all human experiences, including religious ones, may be explained in terms of brain activity. This means that they are, in the broad sense, 'natural'. The self or soul is simply a way of describing neural activity when connected to the rest of a living body. If the body dies, the neural activity stops, so the self or soul dies too.

Neuroscience, by showing the working of the living brain, has effectively closed off the largest of the existing gaps in our scientific knowledge. It is only a matter of time before neuroscience can examine the action of individual neurons. If neuroscience succeeds in showing that the self is nothing but an illusion caused by the brain's activity, then this implies that there is no self who is morally responsible to God, no self who can have a personal relationship with God, and no self who can survive death.

However, looking back at Chapter 3 on Self, death and afterlife, the theory of **Dual Aspect Monism perhaps answers these objections**. The self is a combination of mental and physical in one substance, and it is not possible to reduce the human mind to a simple physical description.

We turn, now, to the effects of science on *ethical* thinking.

Science as a stimulus to Christian ethical thinking

Science is not itself a body of knowledge, but is a *method of understanding the world*, based on reason and evidence. Science itself is morally neutral, in that it is simply a form of investigation. Moral questions arise, however, once there are technologies that impact upon people's lives, on other species, or on the environment.

You should bear in mind that issues of human life and death that we looked at in Volume 1, Chapter 5 (embryo research, cloning, designer babies, abortion and euthanasia) all result from science, so you already know that science makes religion think about and respond to issues.

Most Christians argue that, from its creation, the world has been organised by God for the benefit of humankind, and therefore that it is right to understand it and to develop ways of improving the human situation. Medicine was a feature of the Christian community long before modern science. For example, monasteries in the Middle Ages took a lead in caring for the sick. Christians have often been in the forefront of medicine, transport and communications, particularly in terms of using science to care for the sick.

As science and technology have developed, the question arises: are there limits to what medical science should do? The fundamental question, from a Christian perspective, is how far the natural order is God's will, or how much it can be changed using science and technology. For example, should someone be kept alive using medical technology even if they are in a persistent vegetative state? Or is it right to allow the person to die because death is a feature of the natural world?

In extreme medical conditions, one way to tackle this is a Natural Law approach, which seeks to preserve life because of the basic human urge to live. This is the usual approach of the Roman Catholic Church. Alternatively, a utilitarian approach would seek to maximise happiness and minimise pain, and this could lead either to euthanasia or to using every form of technology to prolong life.

Both of the above approaches could be taken by Christians, but for them there are other issues to take into account. If the Bible is the ultimate authority on Christian behaviour, there is no simple answer, since medical technology was not available in Jesus' day. So no one can say what Jesus' attitudes to new technological treatments might have been. One approach would be to draw parallels with situations described in the New Testament. In other words, the person would ask in effect 'What would Jesus do?' This approach is often taken by Protestant evangelical Christians. The danger with this approach is that they simply do not know what Jesus would have done. There is, therefore, a temptation to read into the biblical narrative the answer they wish to find.

Moral issues posed by science

Science has made all kinds of things possible that were not conceived of in the early days of Christianity, some of which have given rise to moral issues. Two key areas of consideration are modern medicine and genetic modification.

Modern medicine

Modern medicine has the potential to cure many illnesses and to prolong the life of those who are sick. But when it is right to turn off a life-support machine and allow a person to die? Should a great deal of money be spent on expensive treatment for one patient if the same resources could be used for simpler treatments that would benefit many patients? Would it be right to perform a brain transplant?

If you look back at Chapter 4.2 on Situation ethics in Volume 1, you will remember that Joseph Fletcher believed that Christianity needs to embrace new technologies where they can improve people's lives, and that this can mean abandoning rule-based ethics such as Natural Moral Law, which he saw as a stumbling block to the ongoing development of Christian ethical thinking.

The potential of genetic modification

Would you want to be genetically modified, if it could make you stronger or healthier? From a believer's perspective, are there limits to what humankind should do to change God's world?

Again, look back at the chapter on Situation ethics in Volume 1, and think about Fletcher's argument that we should consider genetic modification where it would improve the human condition. Space exploration will probably become necessary sooner rather than later in order to relieve the pressure of population size on the environment generally and raw materials specifically. That might require genetic manipulation to allow humans to live in different environments, for example high-gravity or low-oxygen situations.

In Chapter 3 on Self, death and after life, we saw that science has the potential to merge human biology with robotic systems, and potentially to upload a human mind into a computer-environment that could be subjectively immortal. This takes science into the domain of religion. If you were offered life extension by some such technique, would you opt for it? What might that imply about Christian beliefs concerning life after death? **Ethically, would Christians be justified in seeking indefinite life-extension?**

In these and many more ways, science has given humankind possibilities that it did not have before, and these raise ethical issues. The particular challenge for Christian moral thinking today is that it deals with issues that are quite different from those that faced people two thousand years ago. **There is no easy or straightforward way to read the Bible and find clear answers to modern ethical questions**. By raising these new issues, science has stimulated Christian moral thinkers to give a reasoned justification of their moral position.

Science and evolutionary ethics

Modern interpretations of natural selection raise basic ethical questions for both secular and religious ethics. Darwin's theory can be summed up in the phrase, 'survival of the fittest', coined by the nineteenth-century thinker Herbert Spencer (1820–1903). The 'survival of the fittest' became the basis for an ethical view. If the weakest in society were given extra help and survived to breed, then the species would weaken. The logic of this ethical spin on natural selection is that the strong should be encouraged and the weak eliminated in order to secure a better future.

This view of the ethical priorities of humankind could see Christian ethics, with its emphasis on compassion, as weakening the species. This was a view taken, for example, by the German philosopher Nietzsche. In his 1883 book, *Also sprach Zarathustra* (*Also spoke Zarathustra*), he challenged people to see their future in terms of an *Übermensch* (Superman/Overman) who would be the next step in the evolutionary process. A crude and literal interpretation of this was a contributing factor in the Nazi holocaust, but Nietzsche was making a case for providing new answers to old problems, because the world is changing so fast that **without adapting our ethical thinking, Christians and atheists alike will have no answer to where science will take us.**

Discussion point

1 Given that evolution shows, as Herbert Spencer suggested, that only the fittest survive, does Christianity have any effective moral answer to the accusation that its principle for caring for the weakest members of the human race is effectively damaging the wellbeing of those who are fit to survive?

2 If genetic manipulation is a likely way to make humans resistant to disease, do Christians have a duty to adopt a much more open policy to genetic research and development?

Environmental ethics

Scientific advances in agriculture and farming, along with the genetic modification of crops and animals, are arguably having an increasingly negative effect on the world's environment. In Volume 1, pages 322–330, we considered the extent of the damage to the environment caused by the Christian belief that scripture gives humans dominion over the whole environment. Not all Christians accept that interpretation, but many do, with the result that Christianity has contributed significantly to the environmental crisis that the world now finds itself in. Although many Churches have an environmental policy, there is little coordinated effort among Christians to make a major impact on environmental issues.

Activity

As a group, consider and write brief notes on your responses to the following issues:

1 If creation operates by way of natural selection, then God's plan is based on the systematic failure and death of the majority of members of any species, because that is the result of 'selection'. Can this be in any way compatible with a Christian ethic based on compassion?

2 If altruism (acting selflessly for the benefit of others) is no more than a genetic trait designed to promote the success of one's own species, is altruism just disguised selfishness?

3 If, as science suggests, everything is built on the basic laws of physics, and is theoretically predictable, how can Christian ethics be based on personal freedom and commitment?

How scientific explanation has challenged Christian belief

The 'God of the gaps'

The 'God of the Gaps' argument runs as follows.

As scientific knowledge of the world increases, there is less and less scope for 'God' to be used as an explanation for what we do not understand. 'God' then retreats further and further into the gaps in our knowledge. When science knows all there is to know, there will be no place for God at all.

For example:

● In ancient times, phenomena such as lightning, hail and thunder were thought to be the result of supernatural beings/gods expressing their displeasure with humanity, whereas it is now known that these are common meteorological phenomena.
● It was commonly believed that God moved the planets in their orbits, whereas it is now known that planetary behaviour is governed by gravity.
● God was believed to create animal species as we now see them, whereas science shows that all species have evolved from simpler organisms.

Using 'God' to fill in the gaps in our scientific knowledge means that God himself becomes simply an explanatory hypothesis – he becomes part of the scientific explanation. If that is the case, then God should be detectable by scientific means – but looking for God with telescopes, microscopes and other kinds of scientific equipment would be patently absurd, because what is being looked for cannot be God.

The view that God is only an explanatory hypothesis, a being whose existence can be used to explain what we observe in the world, forms the basis of one of the best-known stories in the Philosophy of Religion. In 1955, Antony Flew presented the 'Parable of the Gardener' to illustrate the way in which people hold on to their beliefs in spite of evidence to the contrary. You can check the full text and sources of this parable in Chapter 1 Religious language (pages 11–13). To remind you of the essentials:

> Two explorers find a clearing in the jungle, in which they find a mixture of flowers and weeds. One explorer sees the clearing as a garden and therefore argues that there is a gardener who comes to tend the garden, but the other disagrees. They wait, but no gardener appears, so they set up various checks to see if there is an invisible gardener. Although they find no evidence of a gardener, the first explorer still believes there is one; but the second argues that there is no difference between a gardener who cannot be detected and no gardener at all.

The point of the parable, for Flew, is to show that belief in God is completely unscientific, because: 1) despite all the scientific/empirical tests set up to discover the existence of the gardener (who of course stands for God), no test ever reveals him, but 2) the first explorer, who stands for a religious believer, still maintains his belief in the existence of the gardener. Every time a test fails to reveals the gardener's existence, the believer simply makes an excuse: 'Ah, but he is invisible/he cannot be touched/he has no smell/he cannot be heard.' So for Flew, all religious statements about the existence of God die 'the death of a thousand qualifications'. Every time the explorers fail to detect the gardener, the 'believer' qualifies what he means by his gardener, until nothing is left, and in the same way, every time Christians fail to detect the existence of God, they qualify what is meant by God until nothing is left.

This may seem a very negative view of the scientific method, and of scientific objections to religious beliefs, but it is an extremely useful one. Science is based on reason and evidence. Every scientific claim depends on evidence. If nothing is allowed to count against it, it is invalid.

This issue of considering evidence for the existence of God leads to the 'God of the gaps' problem. As we said earlier, if God is part of the scientific explanation for the world, it should be possible to detect God by scientific means. If there is no convincing evidence, then his existence fails as a scientific hypothesis. This assumes, of course, that God is the sort of entity that exists alongside others in the world. Many religious believers would say that is a faulty way of thinking about God – God is not one thing alongside others.

But, if religious people are going to make **factual** claims about God, then those claims can be tested by science. If science can explain events fully, there is nothing in the event that requires further explanation, so God is not needed as an explanation. As science advances, there are fewer things that need a divine explanation in the absence of a scientific one. Eventually (the argument goes) there will be no gaps left in scientific knowledge for God to fill, so belief in God will become scientifically untenable.

Religious responses to the 'God of the gaps' argument

There are several answers that religious believers can make to the 'God of the gaps' argument:

1 **For example, the theologian Paul Tillich argued that God should be described as 'Being-itself' rather than 'a being'.**

Applied to the 'God of the gaps' dilemma, if God is a being among others, there is indeed less and less room for him. But classical theism is based on the idea that God is both *immanent* (within the world) and *transcendent* (beyond the world). God is not just a thing in the world, **but the means by which the whole world exists**. So the quest for a 'gap' for God is fundamentally mistaken. *Any god found in a gap could not be the 'God' of classical theism!*

2 **John Polkinghorne thinks that God does not intervene in the world 'crudely', but instead influences it at the quantum level.**

Polkinghorne thinks that God acts at the quantum level because such activity there would be undetectable for humans. Since everything in the large-scale universe is affected by what happens at the quantum levels, God is active in the world, so there is no 'gap' to fill. [Note 3] Polkinghorne's views are considered in some detail on pages 276–281.

3 **Maurice Wiles has a different view of God's action in the world which avoids the God of the gaps problem.**

You will remember, from Chapter 2 on Miracles, that for Wiles, God has just one action in relation to the universe, that of creation, but it is on-going and includes everything. For Wiles, God is active, all the time, everywhere, within and beyond the universe.

4 **Perhaps the key question is this: Is any god whose activity is revealed only within the gaps left between scientific explanations an adequate god for Christian theism?**

If the answer to this question is 'no', then the 'God of the gaps' argument is a useful one for Christians to take note of. It prevents 'God' from being seen as a particular and limited being – which is not only bad theology, but was originally condemned as idolatry, since that is the term for treating something limited as though it were God.

Nineteenth-century Christian responses to Darwin's theory of evolution

No modern scientific theory has had a greater influence on Christian theology than Darwin's theory of evolution. Yet, it would be wrong to assume that all scientists at the time agreed with Darwin and that all Christians opposed him. The idea that faith and evolution were in conflict only emerged early in the twentieth century, when the idea of evolution was presented by biblical fundamentalists as a denial of the Book of Genesis and therefore as a rejection of God.

1 Church of England scientific representatives generally ridiculed the theory.

They claimed that it was simply a way of turning humans into beasts, which of course it was, since it is now rather obvious that humans are beasts: genetics shows incontrovertibly that humans are apes, and share a common ancestor with apes. The Scottish missionary and explorer, David Livingstone (1813–73) apparently suggested that he could see no struggle for existence in the plains of Africa. [Note 4]

Not only that, evolution challenges the idea that human beings were literally created in God's image (Genesis 1:26–27) – there is no specifically human image. Moreover, other animals do have rationality and do exhibit moral traits (see the discussion in Volume 1, Chapter 5, on issues of non-human life and death; see also Volume 1, pages 323–324).

2 Conversely, most liberal Anglicans admired the theory, claiming that evolution was the way in which God designed the world.

This is probably the most favoured Christian response in the twenty-first century – that God initiated the evolution of species by means of evolution and natural selection with the specific aim of producing beings such as ourselves. One of the biggest 'fruits' of this view today can be seen in John Hick's Irenaean theodicy, where Hick claims that God produced humanity by evolution so that we would remain at an epistemic distance from God (for Hick's theodicy, see Volume 1, pages 71–76). Any evidence to the contrary, showing that humanity must have come about through divine intervention in nature, would destroy our freedom to accept or deny God.

One of Darwin's most influential Christian supporters was Charles Kingsley, who commented that the idea of a God who created creatures capable of self-development was as noble as the idea of a God who needed to intervene to produce new species.

3 Some Christians, however, did take an 'interventionist' approach.

They argued that natural selection is not needed, because when he wants to, God intervenes directly. Today, most of those who believe this are termed 'creationists'. **Creationism** is discussed below.

4 On the Origin of Species stirred up a debate concerning how the Bible should be interpreted.

Quite apart from Darwin, there was a general recognition among many Christians that Genesis could not simply be taken as a literal account of creation.

5 There was also negative criticism and caricature.

Bishop Wilberforce argued that there was no evidence to show that, even in domesticated animals, there could be any change in their species. At the British Association meeting in Oxford in 1860, there was a debate on this between Wilberforce and T.H. Huxley, who supported Darwin's views. Wilberforce asked Huxley whether it was through his grandfather or grandmother that he claimed his descent from an ape. Huxley apparently responded by saying that he was less concerned about being related to an ape, than to be connected with a man who used his great gifts to obscure the truth and to introduce ridicule into a scientific debate.

In the twenty-first century, many Christians see no incompatibility between evolution and God's role as creator. Although Dawkins is vociferous in claiming otherwise, the simple fact is that **evolution describes a process** that is governed by the natural laws of biology and genetics. As such, that process itself requires an explanation.

Contemporary responses to the Big Bang theory, including reference to creationist views

1 The main point about the Big Bang theory, from the Christian point of view, is that it seems to provide incontrovertible evidence that there was a beginning of the universe.

In Genesis 1:3, the first thing that God creates is light, and many Christians see this as a metaphor for the light-stream from the Big Bang.

Something which has a beginning naturally seems to require something to begin it, since as far as we can tell from physics, all events are caused. If the universe was caused, then there must have been a First Cause, and, of course, we considered this claim in connection with Aquinas' Third Way (Volume 1, pages 36–50), and found it to be a reasonable inductive argument.

2 The 'fine-tuning' argument for the Big Bang suggests to Christians that God caused it to happen.

In the chapter on the Cosmological Argument in Volume 1, we mentioned the fact that in order to produce intelligent life, the 'cosmological constants' (such as the stickiness of gravity, the expansion rate of the universe, and the production of RNA, DNA and proteins) all have to be correct to an impossibly narrow configuration. The fact that we are here, therefore, suggests that something (God?) has fine-tuned the constants, since the odds of their being correct purely by chance are about 10^{180} against, which is also an inconceivably large number. In other words, if this is the only universe, then God must have made it.

3 But, multiverse theory (which holds that there are many universes) suggests that there may be a colossal number of universes – perhaps 10^{500} or more, all of which began with a Big Bang.

If that is the case, then statistically there would be many universes in which the cosmological constants after the Big Bang are set to the same levels as this one, purely by chance, so the 'fine-tuning' argument is not as strong as it looks.

Key term

Multiverse theory Name given to a collection of theories according to which this universe is part of a potentially infinite number of universes.

273

Recent studies have convinced physicists of the stature of **Roger Penrose** (b. 1931; a highly regarded English mathematical physicist) that the **cyclic theory of the universe** is in fact true. Penrose and Vahe Gurzadyan (b. 1955, an Armenian mathematical physicist) claim to have detected evidence for previous cycles of expansion and contraction. Penrose suggests that there could have been a first cycle (preceded, presumably, by a first Big Bang), or else an infinite series of cycles. If the series of Big Bangs is infinite, then do we really need a God to explain any stage of an *infinite* process?

Even if some such theory turns out to be true, however, the fact that something exists rather than nothing still needs to be explained. Either what exists caused itself or was caused. If it was caused, then the existence of a Creator God is a likely candidate to be the cause.

Some physicists reject multiverse theory. They do so generally because other universes are unobservable, so science cannot test them. This is John Polkinghorne's approach. As a mathematical physicist and ordained priest, Polkinghorne accepts the Big Bang theory and the 'fine-tuning' argument, and so sees the Big Bang as brought about by the will of God.

4 The official position of **the Catholic Church** was given in 1951, when Pope Pius XII declared that the Big Bang theory did not conflict with the Catholic idea of creation.

Clearly, an atheist would say that the Big Bang was uncaused or self-caused, whereas Christians (such as Catholics) would argue that it was caused by the will of God. There is no shortage of scientists who accept God as the cause of the Big Bang.

Here is a comment from Francis Collins, Director of the National Human Genome Research Institute since 1993:

> The big bang cries out for a divine explanation. It forces the conclusion that nature had a defined beginning. I cannot see how nature could have created itself. Only a supernatural force that is outside of space and time could have done that. [Note 5]

For an interesting discussion between Francis Collins and Richard Dawkins, have a look at: **inters.org/Dawkins-Collins-Cray-Science**

5 Creationist views:

Those Christians who reject scientific accounts of the origins of the universe are called *creationists*.

Creationist explanations appeal to their own brand of science, which basically refers to the statements in the Bible. When these conflict with the findings of modern science, the latter are seen as false, and the Bible is alleged to be the 'true' science. 'Intelligent design' claims to be properly scientific, but its many critics reject that claim.

There are two main types of creationist explanations: that of six-day (young earth) creationists, and that of 'progressive' (old earth) creationists.

i **Six-day (young earth) Creationism**

● Although scientific evidence shows that the age of the universe is around 13.8 billion years, and that of the earth is around 4.5 billion years, Young Earth Creationism holds that the earth was created by God between 5,700 and 10,000 years ago.

Key terms

Six-day (young earth) Creationism A version of creationism which uses the Genesis timeline to argue that creation occurred in 6 literal days, between 5,700 and 10,000 years ago. All humans descend from Adam and Eve, and all species were created by God, as we see them now, and not through the evolution of species.

- This belief follows a literal reading of Genesis in which God created the earth in six 24-hour days.
- All humans descend from Adam and Eve; there was no death before the 'Fall', and species were created, 'as seen', by God, and not produced through the evolution of species.
- This interpretation is defended for example by Henry Morris, who wrote a series of books in the twentieth century promoting what he called 'creation science'.
- As another example, Ken Ham (an Australian-born fundamentalist Christian living in the USA) dates Noah's Flood at 2348 BC; argues that the ark carried enough species for biodiversity; that dinosaurs co-existed with genetically modern humans; that radiometric and other scientific methods of dating the earth are wrong; and that the only evidence that counts is that of the one who was there – God.
- This view is held by a large number of people, particularly in the USA, where it is taught in some evangelical churches.

  There is no scientific evidence for Young Earth Creationist views. Since (as we saw in Volume 1, Chapter 6) the Genesis narratives of Creation and Flood have a clear dependence on some features of their earlier Babylonian counterparts, it is difficult to see the force of Creationist views beyond the level of simple belief, which some are content to have.

ii Progressive (old earth) Creationism

- This account accepts the view of geology, that the earth is approximately 4.5 billion years old, and of cosmology, that the universe is about 13.8 billion years old.
- The word for 'day' in the Genesis account (Hebrew *yom*) is taken to mean something like, 'creative epoch', so God had bursts of creative activity followed by long periods of equilibrium.
- It rejects Darwinian evolution in favour of the view that God created species uniquely, so there has been no gradual evolution from earlier species or ancestors.
- New arrivals were created by God's intervention as an 'intelligent designer', and these new species appeared fully formed.
- Some accept evolution as an explanation of 'lower' beings, but claim special creation for humans.
- The pre-human hominid species discovered by archaeology are deemed not to have souls. Adam was the first man to be given an eternal soul.
  - The Flood was a local event, and not world-wide.

    Old earth creationism is really no more scientific than the young earth variety. The evidence rejects the idea of God creating species uniquely or specially; the Hebrew word 'yom' does not mean 'creative epoch', and there can be no evidence whatever as to whether or not pre-human hominids had souls. The claim that Noah's Flood was only a local event ignores what the text says (that the whole earth was covered with water and that *all* species died except for those in the ark with Noah). Old earth creationism is another unsuccessful attempt to salvage some kind of literal meaning for Genesis.

iii Intelligent Design

- Intelligent Design argues that certain features of the universe and of living things are best explained by an intelligent cause rather than by an undirected process such as natural selection.

Key terms

Progressive (old earth) Creationism A version of creationism according to which the age of the Earth and of the universe is given correctly by science, but Darwinian evolution is abandoned or modified in favour of God's unique creation of species. The six 'days' of creation are interpreted as six progressive 'epochs' of creation. Adam was the first man to have a soul.

Intelligent Design An attempt to make Creationism respectable by giving it scientific support: for example, from Michael Behe's theory of 'irreducible complexity', which is intended to challenge Darwinian evolution on the grounds that irreducible complexity cannot be produced by successive modifications. The theory is generally ridiculed by 'mainline' scientists on the grounds that its main ideas are not testable.

- Intelligent Design generally does not identify the designer, although some Intelligent Design proponents equate the designer with the Christian God.
- Michael Behe (an American biochemist and proponent of Intelligent Design theory) claims that many biological systems are 'irreducibly complex' at the molecular level, so that the removal of any one part of the system would make it stop working. Behe holds that this challenges Darwinian evolution because irreducible complexity cannot be produced by successive modifications.

Intelligent Design is a more modern attempt to make creationism respectable, but the scientific community is virtually unanimous in rejecting it as pseudoscience, since its scientific claims hardly fill a page of writing, and that page is generally rejected. Moreover, its main ideas are not testable, whereas the hallmark of a scientific theory is that it can be tested. Intelligent Design insists that some structures show evidence of design by a supernatural intelligence, and that structures like the eye cannot be produced by small gradual steps. Biologists/evolutionists argue that Intelligent Design theorists blatantly ignore the evidence.

In discussing Christian opposition to the Big Bang or Darwin, it is important to remember that the fundamentalist interpretation of Genesis is a recent and minority phenomenon. It has grown rapidly, especially in the USA. Fundamentalists claim a traditional approach to Christianity, based on treating an English translation of the Bible as if the words were a key to everything. They claim they are defending God's truth against attack from science.

In fact, that does not reflect the way Christianity has been understood and practised over the centuries. Most religious thinkers have a more sophisticated understanding of the Bible and its language. In the early fourth century, St Augustine wrote that parts of the Bible required interpretation, since they did not fit with observable facts.

The contrasting views are often misrepresented. Many atheists think that all religious people are creationist fundamentalists, and so they dismiss the more intellectually based and balanced views of mainstream Christians.

The belief that science is compatible with Christianity with reference to the views of John Polkinghorne

Science is based on an analysis of evidence, and the framing of hypotheses concerning the fundamental structures and principles upon which the universe is formed. It cannot get *beyond* the sphere of the evidence upon which it is based.

By contrast, religion often makes claims that are not based on empirical evidence. In speaking about God, or an afterlife, it goes beyond the realm of science. This leaves open the question of whether anything can be known outside experience – in other words, whether there is any valid 'supernatural' knowledge.

As long as science keeps to the analysis of empirical evidence, and religion keeps to personal stories and inspirational concepts that are seen as totally 'beyond' the realm of science, then there are few clashes between them. The problems occur when religion makes claims that depend upon evidence that can also be examined by science. If religion claims that the universe displays purpose and direction, or that it shows a special and providential place for humankind, such claims can be checked by empirical evidence.

John Polkinghorne

John Polkinghorne (b.1930)

Polkinghorne is an English theoretical physicist and an ordained Anglican priest. From 1968–79 he was professor of Mathematical Physics at Cambridge University. He resigned that chair and became a priest in 1982. He was knighted in 1997. John Polkinghorne is one of a number of scientists who reject the alleged divide between religion and science.

Science and Creation: The Search for Understanding

This is one of Polkinghorne's most important books, and one of his first statements here is that:

> It is the desire to understand the world that motivates all those who work in fundamental physics. A similar desire is part of the inspiration for the religious quest. [Note 6]

Polkinghorne's main premise is that the world is intelligible (we can understand it by science), when it might easily not have been so. This has (for Polkinghorne) obvious religious implications.

- In Paley's view, the arena for the interaction between religion and science is natural theology, which he defines as '… the search for the knowledge of God by the exercise of reason and the inspection of the world'.
- When we inspect the world by science, we are able to understand it to an amazing extent. Our understanding of general and special relativity, quantum mechanics, and now String Theory, is astounding.
- There is no obvious reason why this should be so:

> That the world is intelligible is surely a non-trivial fact about it … We are so familiar with the fact that we can understand the world that most of the time we take it for granted. It is what makes science possible. Yet it could have been otherwise. The universe might have been a disorderly chaos rather than an orderly cosmos … Our minds have shown themselves to be apt and adequate for the solution of all the problems which the physical world presents to us. [Note 7]

● It is all too easy for those who would dismiss religion to suggest that evolution explains what we are. But:

> [I]t seems incredible that, say, Einstein's ability to conceive of the General Theory of Relativity was just a spin-off from the struggle for survival. What survival value does such an ability possess? [Note 8]

● Not only that, we need to inquire as to why the cosmological constants are so fine-tuned that they have produced beings like ourselves who are capable of understanding the universe. The fact that we are here suggests that there is an 'Anthropic Principle' behind the universe, meaning that the cosmological constants are fine-tuned to produce humans.

● Multiverse theory seeks to trivialise this principle by suggesting that, given enough universes, some (including this one) must be ordered by chance; but if there are other universes, they are completely unobservable, so to base any scientific arguments on their possible existence is pointless (and unscientific).

● Further, natural theology uses the insights of science in order to reach a clearer understanding of the world. It works alongside revelation from scripture and religious experience to give humans a unified world view that comprehends both science and religion. We need to use scientific data to understand ultimate questions. Physical description and theological interpretation must go hand in hand.

● Polkinghorne concludes that the rationality of the universe is a reflection of the rationality of the Creator.

To evaluate this:

● If this is the only universe, then Polkinghorne is almost certainly right: the fine-tuning of the cosmological constants, and the fact that we find the world to be intelligible, would be overwhelming evidence in favour of the existence of God, and of God's intention to create the universe that we experience.

● However, multiverse theory is not as speculative as Polkinghorne thinks. In String Theory, for example, it is a mathematical inference. In some theories, the singularity of the Big Bang is treated as a quantum particle in superposition, meaning (roughly) that it exists in all possible configurations; the implication being that all those configurations are actualised as parallel universes. **Theories such as these are speculative and metaphysical (beyond physics), but 'God' is also speculative and metaphysical.** Polkinghorne's dismissal of multiverse theory therefore looks as if he wants to cut out a rather major objection to his views about God 'fine-tuning' the cosmological constants to produce this (and only this) universe.

● Moreover, we looked above at the suggestions of Penrose and Gurzadyan, that the radiation coming from the Big Bang shows sign of an earlier cycle of the universe. If it turns out that there were earlier cycles, then the number of cycles could be large enough to produce any number of universes (such as this one) in which intelligent life arises simply by chance.

● Polkinghorne has no obvious rationale for assuming that the Creator is the God of Christianity. He makes a strong case for a religious dimension to life, but he makes no compelling case at all for this dimension being Christian. A Christian will of course assume that the God being talked about is the Christian God, but the problem with all natural theology is that it cannot show this to be true. Think back to Aquinas' Cosmological Argument for the existence of God, where he ends each of the 'Ways' with the statement, 'This all men speak of as God', where again it is merely an assumption that such a being would be the Christian God.

Science and Providence: God's Interaction with the World

To look briefly at another of Polkinghorne's books:

- A key concept for most Christians is that of God's '**providence**'. This is the belief that God has in some way chosen to provide for, create, nurture and sustain humankind: that life is something guided by God for his own purpose. Some religious thinkers make this a key factor in their understanding of God, and Polkinghorne is one of their number.
- In *Science and Providence*, he suggests that without special providence, the idea of the *personal* God of Christianity has no content, and by special providence we mean that God seeks to meet people's individual needs in individual ways.
- How does God do this? By influencing events undetectably at the quantum level. Since events at the quantum level influence everything at our level, then God can intervene for us providentially. Polkinghorne suggests that:

> The Christian understanding of providence steers a course between a facile optimism and a fatalistic pessimism. God does not fussily intervene to deliver us from all discomfort but neither is he the impotent beholder of cosmic history. Patiently, subtly, with infinite respect for the creation with which he has to deal, he is at work within the flexibility of its process. [Note 9]

How should we evaluate Polkinghorne's argument that God does act providentially in the world?

- For those who accept the doctrine of God's providence, Polkinghorne makes a reasonable case that God can intervene subtly in the world, at the quantum level.
- Within Christian theology, the problem is exactly what constitutes the 'fussy' intervention Polkinghorne talks about. Does it make sense for God to choose to be patient and subtle, in the face of the Black Death, or the First World War, or the holocaust, or even the death from cancer of a single innocent child? To say that it would have been 'fussy' for God to intervene, raises questions about the nature of God. God is believed to be compassionate. If God is omnipotent and therefore able to stop it, how can God be so subtle and patient that suffering continues unchecked? In other words, Polkinghorne's support for the idea of God's providence does little, if anything, to solve the problem of evil.
- The main problem seems to be one of **evidence**. To say that God could work through quantum processes is one thing. To have any hope of demonstrating that is quite another.

279

One World: The Interaction of Science and Theology

And finally, to look briefly at a third example of Polkinghorne's work.

To pick out two themes here:

1 Religious experience

Polkinghorne refers, approvingly, to A.N. Whitehead's suggestion that:

> The dogmas of religion are the attempts to formulate in precise terms the truths disclosed to the religious experience of mankind. In exactly the same way the dogmas of physical science are the attempts to formulate in precise terms the truths discovered by the sense perceptions of mankind. [Note 10]

Whitehead makes two claims here: first, that there is an analogy between the activities of theology and science, and second, that both are concerned with understanding and ordering of experience. Polkinghorne goes on to say that religious experiences are far more common than most people think, and hints that the different experiences encountered by believers in the world's religions are 'different culturally conditioned responses to the same reality'. [Note 11]

You should refer back to Volume 1, to Chapter 3 Religious experience, to make your judgement on this claim. As with much of what Polkinghorne says, his ideas seem to show that *religion* and *religious experiences* need to be taken seriously, which many would agree with. But if such experiences are 'culturally conditioned', this might imply that all the 'facts' of **Christianity** are nothing more than an interpretation of religion, and do not express facts that can be compared to scientific facts.

2 Jesus

Polkinghorne goes on to suggest that the Christian scriptures are **evidence** for the claims that Christians make about Jesus, and that **this evidence needs to be examined by the use of reason**. In doing this, Polkinghorne claims that:

> This use of scripture is closely akin to the handling of evidence in observational science. [Note 12]

Can we really accept Polkinghorne's view here? Observational science examines repeated instances of specific data. The essence of the claims about Jesus is that they are held to be a unique revelation of God. How much 'kinship' is there in those approaches? Belief in Jesus is precisely that – belief. It can never be a scientific hypothesis.

General conclusions concerning Polkinghorne's views

- We have argued elsewhere that there is probably one (and only one) scientific claim that Christians can make, namely that 'There is a God'. This is a valid scientific hypothesis based on the fact that the universe exists, is intelligible, and arguably has a cause external to itself.
- However, that claim can be made by any religion, not just Christianity. Polkinghorne's attempt to give a more precise scientific basis for Christian claims is an excellent defence of a personal, Christian, point

of view, but does not establish a scientific *basis* for Christianity. Belief in Jesus' resurrection remains a belief, and not a scientific hypothesis.

● Christianity is, nevertheless, compatible with science in so far as most rational Christians (like Polkinghorne) see Christianity and science as different ways of understanding reality. Those who reject science as being unchristian, and those who reject Christianity as being unscientific, are rather missing the point.

Different Christian responses to issues raised by science: genetic engineering

Science is the systematic use of reason and evidence, and the evaluation and refining or replacement of theories. It is, therefore, morally neutral. By contrast, religion is concerned with moral issues. It is reasonable for religious people to comment on the ethical issues raised by science and technology.

Science and technology throw up ethical questions that do not have easy answers. Because science has contributed hugely to human well-being in the past, people assume that it will continue to contribute positively. Where clear harm is not shown, there is a tendency to use a utilitarian ethic (do whatever appears to offer the greatest benefit to the greatest number of people). For example, manipulating the DNA of human embryos is often seen as acceptable because it may benefit many people.

▲ Oncomouse

An oncogene is a gene that has the potential to cause cancer. Oncology is the study and treatment of tumours. Oncomouse (see photo above) was genetically modified to carry an activated oncogene for the purpose of oncology research. For some, this kind of technology oversteps the mark of what is morally acceptable, particularly where it interferes with the 'proper nature' of animals.

Religion does not have a monopoly on moral thought – that can equally well be done from an entirely secular and rational point of view. But science alone does not provide moral guidelines for research or technology. Just because something *can* be done does not mean that it *should* be done. Christianity provides general moral principles, but those need to be applied through reason to issues in modern science. Dame Mary Warnock (an English philosopher and educationalist) argues that whilst Christians may make personal ethical decisions based on the teachings of their faith, they can only extend decisions to wider society if they can justify them using reason and experience available to anyone, religious or not.

Christians agree that human life is a gift from God. Some, therefore, hold that any attempt at **genetic engineering** is an attempt to manipulate a life so that it is different from the way God intended it. This may go against God's will for the person concerned. It also means that humans are trying to take on powers that belong rightly to God.

Other Christians point to science and reason as God-given abilities. Respect for life should lead Christians to use that ability to the greatest extent possible to benefit life. God would not have given humans the ability to engage successfully in genetic engineering if he did not want them to use it.

Key terms

Genetic engineering The attempt to engineer a unique set of genes for the genetic modification of humans, animals and plants. It has the potential to cure conditions such as cystic fibrosis and Down's syndrome, to produce children with 'improved' physical and mental characteristics, and to produce transhumans.

Human Genome Project An attempt to map all the human chromosomes, with a view to isolating the genes responsible for conditions such as cystic fibrosis and Down's syndrome.

Scientific health warning!

You need to know about different Christian responses to genetic engineering, but that does not require you to get bogged down in the scientific details. For a quick glance at the science, see, for example: **www.yourgenome.org/facts/what-is-genetic-engineering**

1 The Human Genome Project is the attempt to map all the human chromosomes.

Once this task is complete (as yet a long way off), this would give us the ability to identify and isolate the genes responsible for conditions such as cystic fibrosis and Down's syndrome. **The problem** is that having such knowledge requires great responsibility in its use, since genetic engineering has the potential to change human, animal and plant structures beyond all recognition.

2 Genetic engineering is not the same as cloning.

Cloning produces exact copies of an organism, and genes are copied within the same species. Genetic engineering aims to engineer a unique set of genes in humans, animals and plants, and to do that, genes can be exchanged between different species.

3 How genetic engineering works.

Enzymes are used to extract pieces of DNA from one organism and to insert them into a gap in the DNA of another organism, so that the organism with the added DNA becomes genetically modified.

4 What is it used for now?

It is used for the genetic modification of humans, animals and plants. For example, you will have read about GM (genetically modified) crops, which have been modified to be resistant to disease and to insect attack, and to produce a much higher yield. With humans, genetic engineering has been used to produce bacteria that make insulin very quickly, for treating people with diabetes. For a more comprehensive survey, look at: **en.wikipedia.org/wiki/Genetic_engineering#Medicine**

Key term

Transhumans Humans genetically engineered to have (when the technology develops) advanced intellectual, physical and psychological powers.

5 What is its potential?

Virtually limitless. Aside from improved and increased animal and plant strains, it has the potential:

- to treat conditions such as cystic fibrosis, Alzheimer's and Down's syndrome
- to engineer children who have certain 'improved' characteristics, such as intelligence and appearance
- to produce **transhumans**, using new technologies to engineer humans who have advanced intellectual, physical and psychological powers. On the physical side, these could include, for example, abilities engineered to work in hostile environments under water, in space, or in high-gravity environments (on other planets), or to use advanced weapons systems linked to the redeveloped brain and body.

6 Different Christian responses to genetic engineering.

The different approaches to genetic engineering among Christians are not particularly denominational. To some extent they are differences of emphasis.

i The Catholic Church has been moving cautiously with regard to its stance on genetic engineering, and the issue is of course complicated by the fact that the science of genetic engineering is still in its infancy, and the ethical issues are not particularly clear, because we are not yet aware of all the risks involved.

- With regard to GM (genetically modified) crops, the Church gives qualified approval, mainly because GM crops are one way in which the poor can be fed. Given the level of malnutrition in the world, this is obviously a main factor in Catholic thinking.
- The Catholic approach to the GM of animals is somewhat more guarded. Some voices within the Catholic Church argue that in terms of natural moral law, altering the genetic code of animals does not allow them to fulfil their final end; their genetic structure was given by God, so it is not obvious that animals such as pigs should be engineered to provide compatible body parts for humans.
- The Catholic Church gives general approval to **therapeutic genetic engineering** where, for example, there is the potential to cure conditions such as Alzheimer's, Parkinson's, cystic fibrosis and muscular dystrophy.
- When it comes to germline therapy, where healthy genes are introduced into the germ cells (sperm, egg, zygotes, etc.) with the aim of correcting gene-variants that will be passed down from generation to generation, the Catholic Church is generally hesitant, because there are many practical difficulties with this approach, and any bad effects (which might not be foreseen or foreseeable) will be passed on to children.
- Genetic engineering has the potential to take humanity into a transhuman state. This is also referred to as 'enhancement therapy', where new technologies are used in order to improve the human 'specification'. Within the next 25 years or so, for example, it is likely that intelligence can be increased exponentially, and that humans can be modified to have extraordinary physical and psychological strength. This, the Catholic Church rejects, because it means that humanity would no longer be in God's image.

Key term

Therapeutic genetic engineering Genetic engineering intended to repair genes in order to correct/eliminate conditions.

ii As might be expected, given their number, the Protestant Churches have a wider range of reactions, although the main concerns echo those of the Catholic Church, giving qualified approval to genetic engineering of crops and of animals, to therapeutic engineering with the aim of curing diseases, and being far more cautious about germline therapy.

- Having said that, there are Protestants who argue that all human potential is given by God, because God is the Creator; so if new technologies are developed which have the potential to improve life for plants, animals and humans, then they should be embraced where the risks are justified.
- This can extend to enhancement therapy, so in Christian Situation Ethics, for example, we saw that Fletcher suggested that Christians should not rule out any procedure because of existing rules or doctrines (Volume 1, page 194). Humans are by nature selectors and designers, so if adequate controls are in place, there is no reason why humans should not be redesigned to improve the species.
- Fletcher is not advocating a genetic free-for-all; rather he is arguing that Christian ethics should not be hamstrung by ruling out any procedure because it is allegedly 'unbiblical'.

iii Some Christian Churches are much clearer on their policies towards genetic engineering than others. For example, in 1995 the Seventh-Day Adventist Church produced an official statement, 'Christian Principles for Genetic Interventions'. This can be read online at: **www.adventist. org/en/information/official-statements/documents/article/go/- /christian-principles-for-genetic-interventions**

This document points out that Christians are given great power by God, and with power comes responsibility, since humans are accountable to God for what they do. It spells out four areas of ethical concern: 1) **the sanctity of human life**: if genetic procedures reduce the meaning of being human to the mechanistic workings of human biology, then there is serious potential for devaluing human life. 2) **the protection of human dignity**: for example, the protection of personal privacy and confidentiality, because knowing a person's genetic profile could be of significant value to potential employers, insurance companies and relatives. 3) **the acceptance of social responsibilities**: for example, should individuals with genetic disorders be allowed to procreate as they wish? Also, how will the benefits and burdens of genetic intervention be shared by rich and poor in society? 4) **the stewardship of God's creation**: what limits to genetic change should there be? Are there boundaries that should not be crossed when transferring genes from one life form to another?

The document concludes with a list of ten ethical principles that Christians should follow for genetic interventions: confidentiality, truthfulness, honouring God's image, preventing suffering, freedom of choice, the stewardship of creation, non-violence, fairness, human dignity and healthfulness. The document finishes with a glossary of terms, and the benefits of such an approach are that individual Christians can be aware of the debate.

Technical terms for Christianity and science

Big Bang Name given to the theory that the universe began from the rapid expansion (not an explosion) of a gravitational Singularity, a point of infinite density, some 13.8 billion years ago.

Creationism Name given to a set of religious beliefs according to which religious accounts of the origin of the world/the universe are to be believed where they differ from scientific accounts. These include 'Young Earth (six-day) Creationism', 'Progressive/Old Earth Creationism', and the theory of Intelligent Design.

Empiricism The view that all knowledge starts from sense experience.

Genetic engineering The attempt to engineer a unique set of genes for the genetic modification of humans, animals and plants. It has the potential to cure conditions such as cystic fibrosis and Down's syndrome, to produce children with 'improved' physical and mental characteristics, and to produce transhumans.

Human Genome Project An attempt to map all the human chromosomes, with a view to isolating the genes responsible for conditions such as cystic fibrosis and Down's syndrome.

Intelligent Design An attempt to make Creationism respectable by giving it scientific support: for example, from Michael Behe's theory of 'irreducible complexity', which is intended to challenge Darwinian evolution on the grounds that irreducible complexity cannot be produced by successive modifications. The theory is generally ridiculed by 'mainline' scientists on the grounds that its main ideas are not testable.

Multiverse theory Name given to a collection of theories according to which this universe is part of a potentially infinite number of universes.

Natural selection One of the basic mechanisms of evolution, where organisms better adapted to their environment tend to survive and produce more offspring.

Progressive (old earth) Creationism A version of creationism according to which the age of the Earth and of the universe is given correctly by science, but Darwinian evolution is abandoned or modified in favour of God's unique creation of species. The six 'days' of creation are interpreted as six progressive 'epochs' of creation. Adam was the first man to have a soul.

Providence The term for the view that God created the universe in such a way as to provide what is needed for life, and especially for human life.

Quantum mechanics Also known as quantum physics/quantum theory – the physics which deals with matter at the smallest scales. The theory was introduced in 1900 by the physicist Max Planck: energy exists in individual units – quanta (from Latin *quantum*, 'amount').

Rationalism The view that all knowledge starts with the processes of human thought.

Scientism The view that science alone can give true knowledge of reality; that it alone can determine what is meaningful, and that eventually it will explain everything. Such an approach tends to ignore the contribution of the arts or of psychology and the emotions to human self-understanding.

Six-day (young earth) Creationism A version of creationism which uses the Genesis timeline to argue that creation occurred in six literal days, between 5,700 and 10,000 years ago. All humans descend from Adam and Eve, and all species were created by God, as we see them now, and not through the evolution of species.

Therapeutic genetic engineering Genetic engineering intended to repair genes in order to correct/eliminate diseases.

Transhumans Humans genetically engineered to have (when the technology develops) advanced intellectual, physical and psychological powers.

Summary of Christianity and science

Modern science is based on the view that human reason can understand the way the world works based on observation, evidence and experiment. Christianity views the world as created and sustained by God. Christians have historically been associated with scientific developments, for example, Isaac Newton and Charles Darwin. However, there have been conflicts between the Church and science. The relationship between religious ways of understanding the world and scientific ways of explaining it is a complicated one.

The emphasis on evidence and reason in science

Modern science is mostly based on a view of the world that arose in the seventeenth century. Scientific knowledge is based on observation and experience – *empiricism* – in contrast to *rationalism*, the idea that human thought is the basis for all knowledge. Rationalists such as René Descartes mistrusted human experience because human senses can be deceptive. Empiricists such as Isaac Newton observed, formulated hypotheses, tested them and then drew conclusions based on the observed results. However, even empiricists must use reason to interpret their observations and draw conclusions.

Science uses both deduction and induction. The inductive method is the basis of modern science. Scientists observe and gather evidence, analyse it, and form a hypothesis. They test the hypothesis using experiments, and either the hypothesis holds, or a new hypothesis is needed. If the theory is correct, deduction can then be used to predict things that should be the case. This offers the best available explanation, not absolute truth. The view that science is the only way to find true knowledge is called *scientism*. Scientific claims are naturalistic, and therefore have the potential to conflict with the supernatural claims of religion.

Christian responses to the rise of science include Deism and Existentialism

Deism is the idea that God created the universe with physical laws, then left it to operate on its own without any further divine intervention. This eliminates a possible conflict between science and religion because it allows for the universe to be explained fully by science without needing to provide evidence for a God who intervenes in the world.

However, the idea of God in deism is different from the God of Christian belief, who has an ongoing personal relationship with humans.

Existentialism argues that humans create their own reality through making choices. The world is shaped by personal decisions. Faith is a personal choice to make a commitment to God, not something with external meaning. Paul **Tillich** developed this to show that people choose to commit to religious beliefs and symbols for a sense of meaning and purpose. He argued that for Christians, God does not exist as a being, but is the source of existence itself – the 'ground of being'. Belief in God expresses existential commitments, so it is not related to empirical fact. Religion is in a different category to science, and there is no conflict between the two.

Specific scientific discoveries

1 Darwin and the discovery of evolution

Charles Darwin's *The Origin of Species* suggested that the simple natural mechanism of natural selection could explain the differences between and within species. This made the idea of a designer God unnecessary. It challenged the idea of *purpose* in creation and the idea that humans are a unique part of creation. We are just what has evolved. Darwin himself seems to have lost his religious beliefs as a result of this. Most Christians today take the view (expressed for example by Karl Rahner) that evolution is the mechanism by which God works to create humanity.

2 Big Bang theory

Big Bang theory suggests that everything we now see came from a space-time Singularity about 13.8 billion years ago. It is theologically interesting because it suggests that this is how God created the universe.

3 Quantum theory

Quantum theory reveals the world of matter at the smallest scales. It shows that there is genuine indeterminacy in the world at this level: we are dealing with probabilities rather than facts. Polkinghorne suggests that *it is at the quantum level that God interacts undetectably with the world*, so our free will is preserved despite the fact that God acts in the world. Some argue that free will is a reality that happens in the brain's quantum processes. The Many Worlds interpretation of quantum theory gives some support to multiverse theory – the idea that there could be an infinite number of universes apart from this one. This may (or may) not suggest that no Creator is needed.

4 Neuroscience

Neuroscience can challenge religious belief because it suggests that all human experiences, including religious experiences, can be explained in terms of brain activity. The concept of a 'soul' is not needed, which suggests that there is no life after death. Against that, Dual Aspect Monism suggests that mind cannot be reduced to a simple material/physical description. Minds are more than just brain activity.

Science as a stimulus to Christian ethical thinking

Science has brought about huge changes in modern medicine. These have forced Christians to consider how far these technologies go against traditional Christian ethics (such as Natural Moral Law) and how far new strategies (such as Situation Ethics) should be developed to deal with them.

Genetic modification is a particular case in point, because it leads Christians to consider what limits there are to changing God's world.

There are several scientific possibilities for **life extension**, some of which might give humans relative immortality. Christians will have to develop ethical approaches to these emerging technologies in response to their concerns about God's control over life and death.

The theory of **evolution**, and Herbert Spencer's doctrine of the 'survival of the fittest', are even more important now, because we have reached the point where we can accelerate and change the course of 'natural' evolution, for example with genetic engineering. Since Christians will have to live with these developments, an ethical framework needs to be developed to do so; but at the moment such frameworks are limited.

Our current **environmental crisis** is in part the result of scientific advances in machinery and biology/genetics, and in part the result of the view held by many Christians that God gave humans unrestricted power over animals and plants. Many Christian Churches are responding to these issues, but there is no central body to coordinate these responses, so at the moment they do not have a major impact on environmental issues.

How scientific explanation has challenged Christian belief

1 The 'God of the gaps'

This is the argument that as scientific knowledge of the world increases, there is less and less scope for 'God' to be used as an explanation for what we do not understand. 'God' then retreats further and further into the gaps in our knowledge. When science knows all there is to know, there will be no place for God. Moreover, if God is used as part of the scientific explanation of the world, then he becomes discoverable by science, which is absurd.

The God of the gaps argument is illustrated well by Flew's *Parable of the Gardener*, where the believer refuses to accept that God does not act in the world, and that there will soon be no gap left for such a role. Christian responses to this include:

- Tillich's argument that God is 'Being-itself', and not 'a being' who acts in the world.
- John Polkinghorne's view that God acts in the world by being active undetectably at the quantum level.
- Wiles avoids the problem by arguing that God's one 'act' in relation to the universe is creation, and that is ongoing.
- For most Christians, a god who is revealed only in the gaps in scientific knowledge would not be God at all, so at least the argument has made Christians consider more sophisticated arguments about God's action in the world, for example that of Polkinghorne.

2 Nineteenth-century Christian responses to Darwin's theory of evolution

- **The scientific wing of the Church of England** derided the theory because it shows that humans are beasts, which is ironic, because that is precisely what they are.
- **Liberal Christians** usually admired it, because they assumed that evolution was God's way of creating humanity. Charles Kingsley thought that the idea of God creating creatures capable of self-development is noble.
- **'Interventionists'** rejected evolution in favour of the idea that God intervenes in nature when he wants to. This view is now taken by creationists.
- Darwin's work produced much debate on how the Bible should be interpreted, and many

Christians concluded that Genesis cannot be a literal account of creation.

- There was also much negative criticism and caricature, for example **Bishop Wilberforce**.

3 Contemporary responses to the Big Bang theory, including reference to creationist views

- Big Bang [BB] theory seemed to show that **there was a beginning** to the universe, and that God was indeed the First Cause.
- **The 'fine-tuning' argument** for the Big Bang has been taken by many to be a proof that God created the universe.
- However, **multiverse theory** defeats the fine-tuning argument.
- Although multiverse theory still does not explain why there is something rather than nothing.
- Moreover, some physicists (for example Polkinghorne) reject multiverse arguments because **multiverses are unobservable**, and so are considered to be unscientific.
- The Catholic Church still endorses the Big Bang argument as being caused by the will of God.
- **Young Earth and Old Earth Creationists** reject all or most of the scientific arguments about the origin of the universe. **Intelligent Design** claims to be a scientific theory, but has almost zero support from scientists.

The belief that science is compatible with Christianity with reference to the views of John Polkinghorne

Polkinghorne has written extensively on this topic, for example in *'Science and Creation'* [SAC], *'Science and Providence'* [SAP], *'One World. The Interaction of Science and Theology'* [OW].

1 SAC

In SAC, Polkinghorne [JP] argues that the world is intelligible when it might easily not have been so. Our minds have an amazing ability to understand the world. The rationality of the universe is a reflection of the rationality of the Creator. Evolution of course is a fact, but it does not explain Einstein's ability to think out the theory of Relativity (which has no survival value). JP also accepts the Anthropic Principle and the fine-tuning argument, largely because he considers multiverse theory to be unscientific, because parallel universes cannot be observed.

JP's strongest point is probably the intelligibility of the world, which to many Christians might suggest the intention of a rational Creator. There are problems with JP's ideas, however. If multiverse theory is speculative because other universes are unobservable, so are all ideas about an unobservable and transcendent God. Moreover, JP cannot show that the Creator is the God of Christianity – that is an article of Christian faith, and not of scientific knowledge.

2 SAP

In SAP, JP analyses the idea of God's providence. He agrees that God does not act 'fussily' (crudely and visibly) in the world, but argues that God can (and does) act providentially in the world at the quantum level, 'nudging its probabilities' (so to speak) so as to produce tangible results in the world at the macro level (the level at which we exist and experience the world).

This seems very vague. If we cannot see these results, how do we know they are there? If we can, then why would God not simply intervene at our level? Moreover, if God can act in the world at all, we are back to the problem of evil: if God acts, then he appears to act selectively. Such a God is not the Christian God of love.

3 OW

In OW, JP claims that there is an analogy between the activities of theology and science, and that they are both concerned with the understanding and ordering of experience. Moreover, religious experiences are more common than most people think, and are different cultural responses to the same reality. This seems an odd argument, since it seems to suggest that the 'facts' of Christianity are not facts at all – just cultural interpretation.

JP goes on to suggest that the Christian scriptures are *evidence* for Christian claims about Jesus, and that this evidence needs to be examined by reason. This is of course true, but JP says that this is like handling the observational evidence of science, which it is not: science deals with repeatable observations of specific data. Christian claims about Jesus are that they are a unique revelation of God.

Different Christian responses to issues raised by science: genetic engineering

Genetic engineering [GE] is not the same as cloning. It involves using enzymes to transfer pieces of DNA from one organism into the DNA of another organism, so the organism with the added DNA becomes genetically modified. Applications include modification of plants and animals in order to increase yields and to increase resistance to diseases and pests; also, in humans to cure conditions such as cystic fibrosis and Alzheimer's, to engineer children with 'improved' characteristics; and to produce transhumans.

The Catholic Church gives qualified approval to GE in plants and animals, not least to feed the hungry, although a Natural Moral Law approach might put a question mark over altering the genetic code of animals so that they cannot fulfil their final end. The Church also approves of therapeutic GE in order to cure human diseases, but is hesitant over germline therapy where unforeseen bad effects would be passed on to children. GE to take humanity to a transhuman state is rejected: humanity would no longer be in God's image.

Protestant Churches have a wider range of views (given the number of different Churches). Much of the Protestant approach echoes the caution of the Catholic Church, but Fletcher's Situation Ethics, for example, does not rule out transhuman GE, refusing to be bound by religious laws or doctrines.

Some Protestant Churches have clear policies on GE, for example the Seventh-Day Adventist Church, which spells out four areas for ethical concern: the sanctity of human life; the protection of human dignity (for example by privacy and confidentiality); the acceptance of social responsibilities (for example sharing out the benefits of GE among rich and poor), and the stewardship of God's creation (particularly the grey area of transhuman GE).

10 Christianity and the challenge of secularisation

You will need to consider the following items for this section

1 The challenge of secularisation: including the replacement of religion as the source of truth and moral values; relegation of religion to the personal sphere (individualisation); the rise of militant atheism: the view that religion is irrational.

2 Developments in Christian thought:

- Responses to materialistic secular values: the value of wealth and possessions.
- McGrath's defence of Christianity in *The Dawkins Delusion*.
- Emergence of new forms of expression, such as Fresh Expressions and the House Church movement.
- Emphasis on the social relevance of Christianity including liberationist approaches such as supporting the poor and defending the oppressed.

N.B. This topic may be studied with exclusive reference to the British context.

Introduction

Today's society is increasingly **secular**, but the process of secularisation is not at all simple. It means many different things, for example:

- Fewer people attend acts of worship or claim to belong to a religion.
- More people claim to be atheist, reject everything to do with religion, and argue that they can lead fulfilled and moral lives on the basis of reason and evidence but without supernatural beliefs or religious authority.
- Fewer features of life (for example health care, education, social welfare) are organised directly by the Church.
- Political and legal decisions are made without reference to religious ideas or to moral views associated with religion.
- People are free to believe, or not believe, as they wish.

People are now free to describe themselves as atheist. They may, for example, affirm that they will tell the truth if they give evidence in court, rather than swearing to tell the truth with a hand on a Bible. But this acceptance of atheism has only gradually come about since the end of the eighteenth century.

Alongside the political and legal aspects of belief, secularisation is seen particularly in the way in which particular spheres of life have been increasingly less religious. At one time, education and health care were largely carried out by the Church. Although religion still has influence over aspects of education (for example faith schools), the way education is organised and funded is largely secular.

▲ A vicar taking assembly in a primary school

With reference to Christianity, this secularisation of the legal and social aspects of life may imply one of two things:

1 Christianity is losing its authority in society, and secular organisations are taking traditional church roles, so Christianity has failed to persuade people of its beliefs or moral values.

2 Christian moral values and attitudes have now become so much part of everyone's thinking that there is no longer any need for a specific religious reference.

The key question here is whether this 'secularisation' of Christian activity is challenging the Churches, or whether the fact that ordinary people see the value of these things, quite apart from their religious context, is a sign that religion has performed its function of giving to society a set of values. In other words, is secularisation a sign that the Christian religion has succeeded or failed?

The broad perspective

Until the Protestant Reformation in the sixteenth century, the Church claimed authority both over people's spiritual lives, and over nations and societies. The distinction between religious and secular was not a matter of personal belief or lack of it. Things were religious if they were related to the Church with its sacraments and hierarchy of leaders. Things were secular if they were concerned with social and political order. But the Church had authority over both religious and secular affairs.

At the Reformation, there were two major social changes. The authority of the Church was challenged by the reformers, and new Churches were formed in which individuals were encouraged to study the scriptures for themselves. Joining the Church became a matter of a personal choice, rather than a routine rite of passage for everyone.

Following the Enlightenment and the development of science, reason and evidence became key to knowledge, and older religious traditions were challenged. For the first time, people could claim to be atheists, or to have no interest in religion. David Hume was a philosopher who took up this very new position, challenging religion from the standpoint of secular reason.

The situation was also different between countries. In Catholic countries, the Church clashed with the new emphasis on reason and evidence. In Protestant countries, the new emphasis on reason and evidence was welcomed as strengthening everyone's right to think through and understand their faith.

Through the nineteenth and twentieth centuries, people gained increasing freedom of belief and religious practice, and many chose not to follow religion at all. This led to fewer people attending organised worship, particularly following the World Wars, and again in the 1960s. This is described as the phenomenon of secularisation.

In this section, we shall be looking at some of the challenges to religion presented by the emphasis on this-worldly concerns by many people in Britain and elsewhere. But you should always keep in mind that this is a limited (if growing) phenomenon, and that a significant number of people globally continue to follow one of the major religions.

The challenge of secularisation

The replacement of religion as the source of truth and moral values

Thomas Aquinas argued that human reason can grasp certain truths, but only as a first step. Doctrine and scripture are needed to see the whole truth. During the Renaissance, people rediscovered classical thought, including the works of Aristotle about Natural Law. People reflected on the role of religion in society. They saw that thirteenth-century thought contrasted with the Dark Ages (fifth–tenth centuries CE), when intellectual life was stifled by the authority of religion. In the Dark Ages, religion seemed to be opposed to rational thought, but in the thirteenth century, religion and rational thought seemed to work together to allow people to develop personal morality.

The authority of the Church was challenged again during the Protestant Reformation, this time by the authority of scripture, interpreted according to individual conscience and understanding. It became possible to hold individual beliefs that did not conform to the national religion. This challenged the idea of one universal truth. In the seventeenth and eighteenth centuries, the rise of scientific thinking led some people to think that belief in God was not necessary.

In the nineteenth century, people came to see faith as a matter of personal commitment, or a way of seeing life as a whole (for example theologians such as Schleiermacher). Philosophers started to see religion as something functional, for example, keeping the working class from fighting their oppressors (Karl Marx) or satisfying a psychological need (Freud). Religion was increasingly seen as personal but optional.

Ludwig Feuerbach (1804–72)

Feuerbach was a German philosopher and anthropologist, whose most well-known book, *The Essence of Christianity* (1841) argued that Christianity was nothing more than the projection of human hopes and aspirations.

Along with Marx and Freud, Feuerbach is generally held to be a detractor of religion, seeing it as a dangerous illusion and merely a projection of aspects of humankind. For Feuerbach, God is no more than a projection of the highest aspirations of humans. He suggests that religion is essentially a matter of cultivating a sense of self within the world in a way that is distinctively human, and that finding peace with God is a matter of becoming at one with one's true nature.

Basing arguments on reason alone removed the need for a religion. But many of the values expressed in secular terms were exactly those that had been promoted by the Church – the sanctity of life, the value of the individual, the right to liberty, to life, and to retain property. In many ways, secular morality followed on from religious traditions, but with the religious elements removed. Moral attitudes were accepted on a rational, rather than a religious, basis.

Modern secular **humanism** is, in many ways, a form of theology without God, with an ultimate belief that humankind improves through reason and evidence. The following extract is taken from the British Humanist Association website (**https://humanism.org.uk/**):

> Humanism is the belief that we can live good lives without religious or superstitious beliefs. Humanists make sense of the world using reason, experience and shared human values. We seek to make the best of the one life we have by creating meaning and purpose for ourselves. We take responsibility for our actions and work with others for the common good.

Key term

Humanism The belief that people can live good lives without religious or superstitious beliefs.

Relegation of religion to the personal sphere (individualisation)

In the fifth century, Augustine saw Christian faith as something that a person commits to in a personal way. Similarly, at the Reformation, there was a more personal challenge and invitation to interpret the scriptures. The Catholic Reformation included elements of personal commitment and dedication, with spiritual exercises to deepen a person's faith. Lutheran theology held that God could be encountered and worshipped through the ordinary family life, not just through the Church. However, historically, religion was not a matter of individual choice. The conversion of the Roman Emperor Constantine effectively committed the whole Roman Empire and its citizens to Christianity.

The post-Reformation agreement in 1555, known as the Augsburg Settlement, ruled that each prince would have the right to decide on the religion of his own state. Later, the Peace of Westphalia (1648) said that those whose religion was not the same as the state religion should be free to practise it in private, and also, to a limited extent, in public. There was a gradual acceptance that people should be free in matters of religion, no matter what society they lived in.

As society became more secular, religion became a set of ideas and values that individuals might choose to follow. This is the key feature of the 'secular' view of religion, but it comes from the history of Christianity itself.

The multi-faith society of the twenty-first century is quite the opposite of the situation in the sixteenth century. The choice of a religion may be seen almost as a consumer decision – it is taken up because it suits one's own self-image, and promises to deliver personal benefits.

So one way to see developments is as a gradual relaxation in matters of religion, starting with the Emperor Constantine adopting Christianity as the official religion of his empire; through the Holy Roman Empire and the power of the popes; through the Reformation and the agreement that each nation should decide its own religion; to the Westphalian acceptance that people should be free to practise their religion in private, whether or not it was that of the state; through to a modern free-for-all in which religion is simply a personal choice. There is a broad, general truth in that view.

The continuing public role of religion

Today, there are two ways in which religion is increasingly being seen as an exclusively personal matter:

1 The number of people who choose not to belong to any religion is rising. Some of these call themselves atheists or agnostics. Others will simply say that they are not interested in religion at all.

2 Those within a religious tradition may insist that it is not enough simply to attend worship, or to accept nominal membership through baptism. Indeed, worship and rites of initiation such as baptism are not even necessary. Instead, a person should be personally convinced and committed to the religion.

Religion is said to be 'relegated' to the personal sphere when it seen as entirely a matter of personal choice and conviction. This would suggest that evangelisation is wrong or immoral, because trying to persuade people to change their views goes against their personal autonomy.

But it is not the whole story. Many people accept and defend many aspects of the Christian religion, for example: preserving church buildings and cathedrals, or having Christian ceremonies for state occasions. Many people agree that religion contributes to culture. An atheist may be inspired by listening to Bach's St Matthew Passion or reading the beautiful language of the King James Bible.

In many ways, religion still belongs to the public sphere. The Church of England remains the established religion in England. Civic occasions, for example, remembering those who are killed in war, or celebrating the life of a monarch or other famous persons, are still mainly religious. After a tragedy, people may attend special memorial services to give them the opportunity to grieve together, or to celebrate the values of the person or people who have died.

Discussion point

▲ The National Anthem is often sung with much enthusiasm at sporting occasions.

The first word of the National Anthem is 'God', and it is difficult to see what a secular alternative might be, and whether or not it could enable the lines to scan. Most people sing the National Anthem without thinking of any of its religious connotations.

Should the National Anthem be secularised, and if so, what should it contain?

To see secularisation as a challenge to Christianity assumes that Christianity is not a secular religion, but one that is based on belief only in a heavenly realm, and with realities that are not those of this present life. This might have been true of some Christianity in the past, but it is not true today. Christianity has a great deal to say about secular behaviour, morality, personal behaviour and community.

The rise of militant atheism: the view that religion is irrational

By the nineteenth century, thinkers including Marx, Feuerbach and Nietzsche had explored secular humanism from many different angles. Equally, through the twentieth century, thinkers within academic theology had explored ideas about God that were very different from the caricature presented by atheism. This came to a head in 1963 with the publication of *Honest to God* by Bishop John Robinson. This argued that the conventional image of God – caricatured by the idea of an old man in the sky – would have to go, since it did not work intellectually or theologically, nor would it help to address the religious needs of the late twentieth century. The book assumes that modern society is secular in nature.

It was translated and discussed worldwide in a way that its author had never expected. It provoked two very different reactions:

1 Within the academic world, many theologians wondered what all the fuss was about. These ideas had long been explored by theologians such as Paul Tillich, and the God Robinson was arguing against had never been taken seriously in any literal sense.

2 For many within the Churches, however, it seemed to be undermining the very basis of Christianity, by arguing against the sort of supernatural

God upon which they assumed their religion was based. Many ordinary Christians never really think about what they mean by the word 'God', so anything that seemed to be attacking any idea of God was seen as an attack on Christian belief in God in general.

In the decade following *Honest to God*, the main area of growth within the Church of England had come from the Evangelical wing, especially when linked to Pentecostal experiences. There were also changes in the wider Church:

- Liberation theology is a movement within Christianity which began in Central and South America. Based on Marxist views about society, it focused on the idea that Christian belief and practice should focus on helping people to gain liberation from oppression caused by poverty and powerlessness. In order to do this, the Church in Latin America became active in social and political reform. Liberation theology applied the gospel in a direct way to secular needs and concerns.
- Reforms in the Roman Catholic Church initiated by the Second Vatican Council, including vernacular [spoken in the language of the region] services and more lay involvement, had strengthened links between the teaching of the Church and personal faith and practice.
- The Church of England focused increasingly on issues of liturgy (with new forms of worship), organisation, gender (particularly in debates about the ordination of women) and sexuality.

So while Western society was becoming more secular in general, theologians and the Churches seemed to be more concerned with their own internal agendas. Meanwhile, people who no longer considered themselves to be Christian were confronted with world events, but no longer used the framework of religion to make sense of them. They had to fall back on their own reason and experience as they looked at war and conflict. Where conflict involved religious ideologies, people who had rejected religion were inclined to be critical of the role of religion in war and terrorism, and by extension, all religion.

We have already seen in Chapter 9 that the rise in scientific thinking can also contribute to a worldview that rejects religious explanations for natural phenomena. Many other things contributed to a disenchantment with traditional religion. The rise of so-called 'New-Age' spiritualities (spiritual beliefs and practices based on ancient, tribal or new religious ideas) in the 1970s offered a more individualised or local framework for people to explore ideas about the meaning and value of life. A number of scandals within traditional churches, including widespread child abuse and financial scandals, undermined confidence in institutional religion and the leadership of the clergy.

'Militant atheism' emerged into this situation. Militant atheism is the general name given to the view that all religion of any kind is a bad thing. They are called 'militant atheists' because they are very hostile to religion – they see it as something they have to fight against. This is in contrast to atheists in general who simply do not believe in God (strong atheists) or who believe that there is nothing to convince them that God exists (weak atheists). Militant atheism argues that belief in the existence of God, life after death, miracles, the virgin birth, resurrection and so on, is neither logical nor based on evidence, and so it is **irrational** to believe in them. People who hold irrational beliefs, according to militant atheists, are either insane or stupid. Militant atheists focus on the 'literal sense' of religious beliefs, seeing any form of religious claim to be the equivalent of believing in fairies or Santa Claus.

Key term

Irrational Adjective meaning 'without reason', which has a generally negative meaning.

Militant atheists also blame religion for wars, for inhumane treatment of other people, and for 'dumbing down' human thought. They see the involvement of religious groups in education and health care as forms of propaganda or brainwashing, and claim that raising children in a religion is a form of child abuse.

Richard Dawkins (1941–)

One of the most prominent militant atheists is Richard Dawkins. A well-known evolutionary biologist, he argues that religion is both a source of conflict (morally flawed) and a justification for belief without evidence (intellectually flawed). (See page 301.)

Responses to militant atheism

The main criticism of new atheists is that they misrepresent mainstream Christianity. By focusing their criticism of God as an 'imaginary being' and on biblical literalism as if these were mainstream Christian beliefs, they challenge the same minority views that mainstream theology challenges. They ignore instances where conflict has been waged by atheist regimes (for example, the Soviet Union), and they disregard the way that religion has contributed to intellectual development and human flourishing.

Others argue that militant atheist views are based on ignorance of theology and a personal distaste for aspects of religion. Militant atheists often define religious beliefs in over-simplified terms, or attribute extreme or minority views to all believers, and then pour scorn upon them. This is a philosophical fallacy known as a 'straw-man' argument. There are indeed extreme and minority views, but in general, mainstream Christianity is complex and intellectually rigorous, and Christian belief is psychologically and morally justified.

Some religious people can be narrow-minded, prejudiced and morally weak. Simple belief in the supernatural and superstition are out-of-date modes of thinking and incompatible with reason and science, but for some people, this is how they choose to exercise their faith. Militant atheism claims that religion makes people unreasonable and unpleasant. But simply recommending that everyone should be reasonable and 'nice' does not start to do justice to human experience, including hope and a sense of purpose, which feed religion.

The view that religion is irrational

Nobody doubts that there are non-rational elements in religion. The richness of religious experience, the emotional and physical engagement in worship or meditation, the act of joining with others in celebration – all these involve people in a way that goes beyond the simple exercise of their reason.

From the Enlightenment to the nineteenth century, people tried to set out religious beliefs in terms of human reason, so that its claims to truth could be acceptable to everyone. In general, these attempts failed. Christianity argues that this is because most people's experience of life is not limited to the rational. That includes the experience of art, music and poetry as well as religion.

However, militant atheists go beyond recognising the non-rational elements in religion. They suggest that religion itself is irrational. In other words, adopting religious beliefs goes against reason.

The first question to consider is whether or not religious beliefs are to be taken literally. If they are, then many beliefs (for example miracles, the resurrection of Jesus, or the virgin birth) are irrational, because they go against the assessment of evidence using reason. See, for example, David Hume's argument about the lack of evidence to prove that a miracle has taken place (See Chapter 4 on Miracles).

But, if they are not taken literally, those who believe them are not necessarily being irrational. So, for example, if a person takes the view that the Resurrection of Jesus is a dramatic way of presenting the idea that the spirit of Jesus is alive and active within the Church, then that is not irrational. It does not depend on any physical evidence about what happened to Jesus' body, but on the sense that people are inspired to live in a way that embodies his life and all that it stood for.

Each cultural expression, whether it is a novel, a poem, a painting or a piece of logical argument conveys some insight or provokes a response. But each should be considered on its own terms. It would be irrational to try to analyse a poem as though it were a set of literal propositions. For example, Wordsworth wrote a poem that begins, 'I wandered lonely as a cloud…', but this is a simile, not a statement of fact. A person who is walking alone is in reality nothing like the floating of a cloud. To dismiss the poem for that reason is to misunderstand completely the nature of poetic imagery.

Religious beliefs and texts are cultural artefacts. They are communicated using human language, with all the limitations and flexibility that language has. Religious beliefs may be helpful or harmful, inspiring or disgusting, but to say that they are irrational is to misunderstand them.

Humanists tend to emphasise the role of reason and evidence, but that may be naïve in terms of human nature. People do not generally, if ever, fully operate on the basis of reason and evidence alone. Intuitions and the range of human emotions go beyond or bypass reason and evidence. Some branches of Christianity place emphasis on the fallen nature of humankind, and therefore the limitations of human reason. Replacing all supernatural ideas with reason and evidence will not bring about universal peace and happiness.

Developments in Christian thought

Christian responses to materialistic secular values: the value of wealth and possessions

The concept of materialistic values involves the idea that status in society is measured by wealth and possessions, rather than by qualities such as wisdom, virtue and intelligence. People who are rich are believed to be successful, whether or not they are wise, good or clever. Materialistic values may be religious if wealth and possessions are thought to be given by God: in the Old Testament, for example, Solomon was rewarded for his wisdom by being given great riches. Materialistic values are secular when wealth is not seen as a gift from God or any other religious power.

In the New Testament, Jesus reversed some of the usual expectations of his day, particularly about wealth and possessions. He argued that the poor were blessed, because their situation was about to be reversed with the coming of the Kingdom of God. In a parable (Luke 16:19–31), he contrasts a rich man with a beggar who is left hoping for scraps that fall from the rich man's table. They both die. The rich man goes to a place of suffering, and the poor man enjoys comfort in heaven beside Abraham.

▲ This image by Jan Luyken and Pieter Mortier illustrates the Parable of the Rich Man and the Poor Man. It shows the rich man feasting while the poor man suffers at his gate.

Jesus appears to deal with rich and poor alike, but also applauds those who are charitable – not because they are keeping a religious rule, but because they choose to share their wealth and care for others. Jesus does not condemn wealth in itself, but argues that it is extremely difficult for a rich man to enter the kingdom of heaven – and therefore that riches can be a distraction from the more important aspects of life. Someone who is rich is concerned to preserve and increase their wealth on earth rather than focusing on building up what Jesus calls 'treasure in heaven' – virtuous behaviour and charitable attitudes.

We know that, in parts of the earliest Church, people shared everything they had with one another in the community, because early Christians believed that the end of the world was soon to come. However, the biblical letters also show communities divided by economic differences. This shows that attitudes to the ownership of wealth varied, even in the earliest Church. There was never a time when all Christians rejected materialistic values.

From the early fourth century a monastic tradition developed in Christianity. Some men and women deliberately gave up their personal wealth and lived in a communal or solitary existence, in poverty and simplicity. This practice continues today in the Church of England and in the Orthodox and Roman Catholic Churches.

In the middle ages, monasticism was seen as a superior spiritual state to that of the householder. With the Reformation, however, the distinction between priests and ordinary lay people was set aside (see page 235 for the 'priesthood of all believers'). Living family life in the secular world meant using and owning money and property. Voluntary poverty no longer offered moral superiority, so there was no spiritual advantage to monastic life. Charity giving and responsible use of wealth, however, continued to be religious duties.

Key terms

Capitalism Political and economic system which allows wealth to be controlled by individuals and businesses for private profit.

Communism A political system in which power, wealth and status are equally shared by all in the community, region or state.

Key terms

Materialism A world view that sees material possessions, money and personal comfort as more important than spiritual beliefs and practices.

Prosperity Gospel A form of Christianity which sees wealth, status and privilege as rewards from God for strong faith and good works.

During the following centuries, the increase in trade as European countries expanded their power into Africa, the Americas and the east led to the development of **capitalism**. This is a political and economic system which allows wealth to be controlled by individuals and businesses for private profit. In the nineteenth century, the industrial revolution further strengthened capitalism, so that business owners and merchants became very rich while many of their workers struggled to survive on low wages and poor working conditions. It was this inequality which Karl Marx challenged when he developed the ideology that he called '**communism**'.

However, there were many examples of wealthy industrialists whose Christian values led them to provide more generously for their workers. Among the most well-known are the Quakers George and Richard Cadbury who built the town of Bournville for their employees as well as providing decent wages, a pension scheme and medical care. Another Christian, Titus Salt, the owner of a huge textile mill, built the village of Saltaire to provide decent housing for the workers in his mill, including a Congregationalist church for the community.

The relationship between religious belief and wealth in modern society

Materialism is a world view that sees material possessions, money and personal comfort as more important than spiritual beliefs and practices. It is often contrasted with a religious world view which sees beliefs and practices as more important than anything else. In modern society, the relationship between religious belief and wealth is complicated.

Personal beliefs, often acquired in childhood, seem to work across all levels of economic well-being. Some of the wealthiest countries have many religious inhabitants. There is little evidence to show that atheism is promoted by wealth. One branch of Christianity gaining popularity in the USA regards prosperity as a sign of God's favour, so this view of Christian teaching is called the '**Prosperity Gospel**'. The majority of mainstream Christians strongly reject the Prosperity Gospel, but is it influential within the heavily capitalistic culture of the USA.

Many Christians see wealth as a gift from God, but they feel an obligation to share the wealth they receive with others. Many churches encourage 'tithing' – that is, the donation of one tenth of a person's income to the church, to be used for the community and to relieve poverty or distress.

It would be wrong to assume that all Christians have enough wealth to give some to others. Those who are not so fortunate may occasionally or regularly depend on services provided by their churches and fellow Christians to help them financially. Many churches operate or work with food banks, and some city churches run services for the homeless members of their community.

Some small Christian communities try to copy the earliest Christians by sharing goods in community and living a simple life that is not dependent on earning wealth. One example of this is the lifestyle of Bruderhof communities. They gladly renounce private property and share everything in common.

McGrath's defence of Christianity in *The Dawkins Delusion*

Richard Dawkins is an evolutionary biologist who is also a militant atheist. In his book *The God Delusion*, he argues the case for militant atheism (see page 295).

Dawkins' key points:

- Religion depends on belief in God (he calls this the God Hypothesis).
- The God Hypothesis is flawed, so God does not exist.
- Religion is a primitive error which has spread like a virus.
- People can be morally good without the influence of religion.
- Religion undermines science and promotes fanaticism and bigotry.
- Religion is a bad influence on society because it causes division.
- Teaching religion by parents and in schools is mental abuse.
- Religion does not answer people's big questions – they should instead turn to science and philosophy.

Dawkins makes a fundamental distinction between supernatural religion – belief in the existence of a God or gods, miracles, life after death and suchlike – and the natural sense of awe and wonder. This distinction depends on a very shallow view of God as a supernatural wonder-worker. In *The God Delusion* Dawkins is attacking very specific beliefs in a supernatural realm and religion based on it. He assumes that most people find meaning in life and aim to develop moral principles without reference to religion or a supernatural God.

However, many Christians share the view that God, understood as the reality within which 'we live, move and have our being' (St Paul) or 'the ground of Being' (Tillich) is in no sense a supernatural magician. This better reflects the view of many of Christianity's greatest thinkers – including Augustine and Aquinas.

The Christian theologian Alister McGrath argues that science is not in a position to adjudicate on matters of religion – whether or not a God exists – and that both science and religion must therefore keep to its own sphere of operation. Science is limited to those things that are discoverable through reason and experience. We shall look at McGrath's views in more detail below.

In the broader context of secularisation, *The God Delusion* raises another important set of issues. These are attitudes to homosexuality, abortion, inclusiveness, and freedom of choice in matters of religion or religious education (particularly of children by their believing parents). Most people now hold the view that individual human beings have rights and should be respected and treated as of valuable in themselves. Dawkins criticises a narrowly supernatural religion, and the unquestioning commitment to a literal understanding of the Bible, because it just does not fit the general assumptions of modern life. In this, he is criticising a minority view that is not shared by most Christians, but he assumes that such views represent Christianity as a whole.

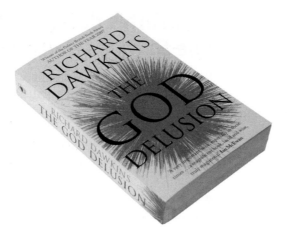
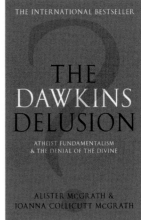

The God Delusion represents a popular twenty-first-century secular viewpoint. Dawkins' outlook is scientific, in that he is committed to reason and evidence. It is also humanistic, in that he criticises events described in the Bible from the standpoint of a humanistic valuation of life. He claims that children might be deprived of a normal education because their parents hold religious views that conflict with a normal educational curriculum.

> The majority of us don't cause needless suffering; we believe in free speech and protect it even if we disagree with what is being said; we pay our taxes; we don't cheat, don't kill, don't commit incest, and don't do things to others that we would not wish done to us. Some of these good principles can be found in holy books, but buried alongside much else that no decent person would wish to follow: and the holy books do not supply any rules for distinguishing the good principles from the bad.
>
> Dawkins, *The God Delusion*, p297 [Note 1]

In *The Dawkins Delusion*, McGrath seeks to counter Dawkins' position by showing that Christianity is compatible with science – not by trying to refute Dawkins arguments point by point, but by exploring the overall viewpoint from which Dawkins writes.

McGrath points out that Dawkins assumes that science leads automatically to atheism. This suggests that scientists who accept the possibility of God, or see value in religion, must be deliberately going against what they know to be the case. By giving examples of distinguished scientists who accept the possibility of God, McGrath shows that Dawkins' view is very narrow.

McGrath also shows that there are limits to what science can demonstrate. Science cannot demonstrate the 'true' nature of reality, because there are no tests or observations that can show where that truth lies.

Stephen Jay Gould has proposed a 'middle way' arguing that science and religion each deal with their own sphere of human experience. Dawkins opposes this by arguing that there is only one sphere, the physical sphere that is understood by science. McGrath opposes both Gould and Dawkins because he thinks that religion and science *do* have some areas of overlap and can therefore enrich one another.

> For there is, of course, a third option – that of 'partially overlapping magisteria' [...] reflecting a realization that science and religion offer possibilities of cross-fertilization on account of the interpenetration of their subjects and methods.
>
> McGrath, *The Dawkins Delusion,* Chapter 2 [Note 2]

McGrath notes that Dawkins deliberately chooses to oppose supernaturalist fundamentalism, which is an easy target for reason and evidence. Dawkins ignores the 'liberal' approach to religion. He complains that supernatural religion is not open to argument, but holds to its beliefs unquestioningly. However, it is clear that he himself holds to some basic atheist views unquestioningly. He refuses to believe that anyone can genuinely come to a different conclusion, even someone with a distinguished background in science. In other words, he opposes one form of fundamentalism with another.

> Dawkins is clearly entrenched in his own peculiar version of a fundamentalist dualism. Yet many will feel that a reality check is appropriate, if not long overdue, here. Dawkins seems to view things from within a highly polarized world view that is no less apocalyptic and warped than that of the religious fundamentalisms he wishes to eradicate.
>
> McGrath, *The Dawkins Delusion*, Chapter 2.

McGrath too, has weaknesses in his arguments. He suggests that atheism may be a response to the human need for 'moral autonomy' and that atheism is an excuse for immorality.

Atheists do argue that humans should take responsibility for their own moral decisions, but that is not primarily the reason why people claim to be atheists.

In general, therefore, McGrath complains that Dawkins suffers from 'cognitive bias'; in other words, he favours evidence that supports the point of view he has already chosen. It is a key feature of science, however, that it attempts to eliminate any such bias. In this respect, Dawkins ceases to think as a scientist when he considers religion.

McGrath does not set out to prove that Christianity is true. What he does argue, effectively, is that Dawkins' attempt to show that belief is a delusion is not persuasive. It is deeply flawed, both from a scientific and a religious point of view.

Overall, therefore, the argument is that Dawkins repeats some well-known criticisms of religion without attempting to present a fair and balanced view. McGrath points out that he is, therefore, simply backing up his prejudice, rather than attempting a serious study.

303

Emergence of new forms of expression

Christianity, both as a whole and as individual Churches and denominations, has continually reinvented itself since the days of the earliest Church, in order to operate effectively in the world of its time. Finding new ways to express Christianity is a completely different way to respond to the challenges of secularisation. Two recent ways that Christianity has been expressed are the *Fresh Expressions* movement and the House Church movement.

Fresh Expressions

Fresh Expressions grew out of a report entitled 'Mission-shaped Church', presented to the General Synod of the Church of England in 2004. It is also active within other British Churches, for example, the Methodist Church and the Baptist Church. Although it comprises many very different groups and activities, Fresh Expressions has a central support team, led by a former Anglican bishop.

The term 'fresh expressions' is used for a variety of ways in which Christian groups operate alongside conventional church membership. They are not thought of as replacements for traditional church communities, but rather supplement them and work with them in what is sometimes called a 'mixed economy' church.

In general, these movements have an evangelical aim. In other words, they seek to work alongside people who would not normally see themselves as belonging to a Christian church. By sharing in the lives and interests of other people, Christians are also able also to share their own Christian beliefs. In some cases, such actions are seen as 'outreach', leading people to become members of a conventional church community, but not always. Sometimes, they are intended to nurture an alternative kind of church community. But they are also seen as having value in themselves, and as an expression of the ministry of Jesus, who mixed with people who were not conventionally religious.

Activity

Look at the Fresh Expressions website **www.freshexpressions.org.uk** and find out about past Fresh Expressions projects. Pick two contrasting projects and answer these questions for each of them.

1 Where was the project, and what people was it working with?

2 What was the project trying to do?

3 How is this different from the normal work of a local church?

4 How does it respond to people's needs and interests?

Now try to imagine what a Fresh Expressions project in your school or local area might look like.

This is very different from the approach to religion criticised by Dawkins and other new atheists. They assume that religion is primarily about believing in the existence of supernatural entities, and therefore that it is illogical and against the norms of modern, scientific thinking. By contrast, the Fresh Expressions approach to religion is to explore the concerns and views of ordinary people, and then to see how Christian ideas and teachings may be relevant.

In this sense, Fresh Expressions is a secular approach to religion – it deals with religious values and expressions in ordinary, secular situations. In particular, the language of Fresh Expressions is very much Jesus-centred. It starts by exploring the life and attitudes of Jesus and how they might be relevant in people's lives today, rather than with beliefs and rituals.

Although the language and approach of the Fresh Expressions movement is quite different from that of the older theological traditions, it has parallels with the theology of Paul Tillich. Tillich described God as 'Being-itself' and our 'Ultimate Concern'. In a secular context, these terms refer to the way people experience the meaning of life – the things that give direction and meaning to life. In this way, Fresh Expressions claims to draw out values and meanings from a situation, rather than trying to impose them from outside.

The mission statement of Fresh Expressions as given in their 'Who are we?' statement on their website (**www.freshexpressions.org.uk**) is:

> **Fresh Expressions seeks to transform communities and individuals through championing, resourcing and multiplying new ways of being church. We work with Christians from a broad range of denominations and traditions and the movement has resulted in thousands of new congregations being formed alongside more traditional churches.**

It is important to recognise that this works *within* the secular rather than *against* the secular. It describes situations in which people with Christian beliefs explore, 'what God is doing' in the world. They are not trying to persuade people that God exists, which can lead people to assume that God is an external supernatural entity. Those who participate in Fresh Expressions are less likely to speak of religion as a pattern of belief and worship, and more as a process of putting the life and teachings of Jesus into practice. Although Fresh Expressions leaders may have their own conventionally religious beliefs, their agenda is to bring people together in a community of shared values and practice, where, by working together with common aims, people can figure out for themselves if or how God might work in their community.

The Fresh Expressions approach addresses the mismatch between those in the UK who claim to be Christian, and those who attend church on a regular basis. It operates in a secular context for those who are not practising members of a church. Although its aim is evangelical, it starts by listening to people's needs and interests, rather than simply preaching to them.

The House Church movement

▲ House Churches' worship in a private home can be more informal than traditional church services.

The House Church movement is another way that some Christians have responded to the pressures of secularisation. It sees modern secular society as largely hostile to Christianity. It aims to re-establish the practices of the Early Church, when Roman society was hostile to Christianity, and people drew strength from worshipping together in private homes.

In the earliest days of Christianity, Christians met in one another's houses. As it became an established religion, the focus of activity shifted towards having separate church buildings, and later to parish churches and cathedrals. This, along with a formal ministry of deacons, priests and bishops, helped to ensure uniformity of worship and teaching. But with this came the sense that Christianity was based on an established set of teachings and practices, imposed upon people by religious authorities. This was challenged at the Reformation, with the Protestant emphasis on personal commitment and the authority of the Bible, and later by the Catholic Reformation within the Catholic Church, with its emphasis on personal and emotional engagement.

Some Christians have met in houses for many years, for example the Plymouth Brethren. In Europe, the House Church movement was developed, first starting in the 1960s, by those who wanted to free themselves from the structures of conventional churches and return to the practices of the Early Church. The intention was that people could meet and worship free from the formal restraints of worship in Church buildings. Although found within most denominations, the House Church movement developed most strongly within the evangelical and charismatic traditions.

In addition to House Church meetings themselves, local and national events were organised to link members of House Churches with one another. Events such as *Spring Harvest*, which began in 1979, draw together members of evangelical churches as well as House Churches. Spring Harvest is a national multi-centre conference which includes worship, bible study and religiously themed activities for people of all ages, based in holiday parks.

Because the House Church movement did not have any central authority to determine doctrines or practices, there were a number of divisions within the movement. Nevertheless, the movement continues to grow. By the end of the 1980s there were over 1,000 House Churches, and by the early twenty-first century, there were over 1,300 (figures from **lausanneowldpulse.com**).

An early split in the House Church movement led to the establishment of the British New Church Movement (BNCM). It was associated particularly with the growth of charismatic worship. Unlike the House Churches associated with other denominations, the BNCM aims to build new communities. Because these may have many members, few BNCM communities meet in private houses.

The focus of the House Church movement and the BNCM is on community and healing. New individuals are welcomed into groups of people to share Christian values and teaching, believing that the community can focus the power to heal. In some ways, it is a secular experience. It is separated from the control, structures and doctrines of organised Churches. There is some focus on religious teachings, but those teachings are acted out in the context of the activities of the community.

The language of these new Churches is very different from that of, say, a discussion within the Philosophy of Religion. In some ways, it is more like a healing therapy. House Church members do not spend time discussing whether or not God exists. They focus instead on individual experience. Many experience a sense that God is calling them to a particular lifestyle or kind of worship. The good feeling they get from being part of the House Church community acts as a confirmation that this experience is real. It makes them feel stronger in themselves, and more able to deal with pain, stress or anxiety. This is, however, firmly based on a specific understanding of the Bible, which includes healing the sick and casting out demons – language which is quite different from that used by secular therapies.

Emphasis on the social relevance of Christianity including liberationist approaches such as supporting the poor and defending the oppressed

Another way that Christians respond to the increasing secularisation of society is to try to demonstrate that Christianity remains socially relevant in today's society. To argue that Christianity is socially relevant, it is necessary to show that:

- the teachings of Christianity can engage with the lives of people in society today
- the actions of Christians can engage with the lives of people in society today
- these teachings and actions can work for change within society.

This implies that Christianity is also politically relevant, since politics is concerned with the way society is ordered and the values that direct its communal life.

Within the Christian community – and particularly within the Evangelical and House Church traditions – there is emphasis on the transforming power of the Christian gospel. In other words, individual lives are changed by becoming Christian and adopting Christian beliefs and values. At an *individual* level people are transformed, whereas at a *social* level, they conform to existing social and political norms. This reflects the change in the status of religion in society, from something imposed by the state to something that is an individual choice.

However, the trend towards individuality has not been uniform. There are many areas where membership of a particular Church has become a mark of political loyalty. This was seen, particularly, during the 'troubles' in Northern Ireland, and in places where Christians are in the minority in society.

Quietist or activist?

▲ Should Christians stick to traditional spirituality, or should they engage in social action, as these Street Pastors are?

If Christianity is primarily about 'another' world, presented as 'The Kingdom of Heaven' and contrasted with what happens in 'this world', then there is a tendency to accept the sinful and distorted nature of the society within which Christians live.

On the other hand, if the 'Kingdom' is regarded as something that Christians are to build within this world, and live out in their individual and communal lives, then there is likely to be far more critical engagement with society, and a direct attempt to change it.

A 'quietist' argues that everything can be left in God's hands, and that Christians should not engage in social or political action. An activist argues that the Gospel and Christian moral order requires individuals and Churches to engage with the world, particularly in terms of helping those who are sick or poor. This may involve direct social and political action on their behalf.

Secular ownership of Christianity

One way the process of secularisation may be measured is by asking people about their attendance at public acts of worship. The percentage of people who attend Church regularly is decreasing, so on that basis, Britain is increasingly becoming a secular country. However, many people who do not attend Church nevertheless feel a sense of attachment to a local church building. It may represent the place where they, or their relatives, were married or buried; it may provide a sense of permanence and continuity in a world where everything else changes; it may also serve as a focus in times of need (as when there is a local tragedy) or celebration. Thus, the sense of ownership of a church building – and sometimes the defence of that building if it is threatened with closure – may indicate that society is less secular than expected.

The same is true in some other countries, where the Church has generally been identified with the state since the time of the Reformation. It is also noticeable that in some places – for example, Finland – there is a sense of the contrast between two religious traditions, with two impressive places of worship in Helsinki, for example, a Protestant Cathedral and an Orthodox Church. Churches can also express national identity, as is the case of Catholicism in Poland, which revived to express Polish identity after a period of persecution within the former Soviet Union.

Religion can, therefore, become a symbol of nationalist identity. For example, the Russian Orthodox Church has grown and become more important in society following the fall of the anti-religious communist regime in the Soviet Union and the new freedoms offered since 1989.

Examining religious claims and their challenge from an atheist standpoint may reflect a growing confidence of atheism in the UK and elsewhere. However, it is not the only way of assessing the relationship between the Church and the secular world. Globally, the situation is far from clear. Religion is growing in some areas, becoming more political in others, and declining in yet others.

Christianity, it can be argued, is a naturally secularising religion. It follows the example of Jesus, who taught that caring for the poor and healing the sick (both secular operations) take priority over obedience to religious rules. Because of this, the secular vocations of teaching and healing, which have now become separated from organised religion, are a form of secularisation that is exactly in line with a radical interpretation of Christianity's earliest message

Liberationist approach

Should the Church remain aloof from the social and political issues of the day, or should it become involved in the secular realm?

Following the example of Jesus, Latin American theologians argued that Christians should act in secular society on behalf of the poor and the oppressed. That might involve becoming active within, for example, education, trade unions and political parties, or even, in extreme circumstances, revolutionary movements. Liberation theologians were inspired by the actions of Jesus as described in the New Testament.

Liberation theology started from a practical engagement with poverty and political action. In this sense, it was a necessary secularising of the gospel in order to make it relevant to the lives of ordinary working people.

▲ Gustavo Gutiérrez (b. 1928) and Leonardo Boff (b. 1938) were both involved in the development of Liberation theology in Latin America.

For liberation theologians, one role of the Church was to educate people to recognise the difference between their own lives and real justice as described in the gospel, and to help them find ways to challenge the forces that oppress them.

The movement met severe criticism, not least from the Pope. He believed that the presentation of Jesus as some kind of political revolutionary was not true to the gospel or the teachings of the Church.

A fundamental split developed concerning the role of the Church:

1 **Liberationists** wanted to change society to promote justice and give power to the poor and powerless. It saw this as the natural and practical application of the teaching of Jesus.

2 Traditionalists believed that the primary concern of the Church was to support the poor by offering spiritual aid to individuals.

In other words, it was fundamentally a question about the Church and secularisation. Should the Church be involved with the secular world of social injustice and politics, or should it offer only spiritual help, bringing individuals into a new relationship with God?

This was never a completely either/or choice. Liberationists did not deny the value of spirituality, nor did the traditionalists deny concerns about exploitation and poverty. It was more a matter of balance, and of methods of working.

> **Key term**
>
> **Liberationist** An approach to theology that starts with an analysis of the situation of the poor and oppressed, and then uses the gospel as a way to challenge the causes of their poverty and oppression.

Óscar Romero (1917–80)

Archbishop Óscar Romero was the Roman Catholic archbishop of San Salvador. He was assassinated while saying Mass at a cancer hospice in San Salvador on 24 March 1980. The previous day, in a sermon, he had called on government soldiers, as Christians, to stop carrying out the government's repression and violations of human rights. Romero had regularly spoken out in favour of the poor in the deteriorating political situation in El Salvador. His death gave worldwide publicity to both the situation in El Salvador, and to the position taken on poverty and injustice by the Church.

Liberationist approaches in a British context

In 1985, the archbishops of the Church of England commissioned researchers to look at the life, conditions and faith, of people in inner cities. Their report, *Faith in the City. A Call to Action by Church and Nation*, showed high levels of poverty in some inner city areas. When a lot of people in one area were poor, the whole community felt that it was powerless. Poverty was measured based on six factors: levels of unemployment, overcrowding, households lacking basic amenities, pensioners living alone, ethnic origin, and single parent households.

The report identified certain areas that it called 'Urban Priority Areas'. These were places where people experienced the highest levels of poverty. The report recommended to the Church of England that parishes in these areas should have more clergy, and give extra attention to training clergy and lay people. Churches were also asked to consider the ways that worship was conducted, and to extend and improve the work they were doing with children and young people. The report also recommended that churches should try to use their buildings more effectively to respond to the secular needs of their communities, rather than using them only for religious services.

At the same time, the report made specific recommendations to the government. These were not religious reforms, but things to do with employment law, housing legislation, income support and social benefits, and access to legal advice and support. By addressing these secular issues as well, the report was engaging with people's whole existence, not just issues in their spiritual life. This is a liberationist approach applied to the context of British inner cities.

Faith in the City was widely welcomed within the Church of England, but had a more mixed reception in wider society. The Conservative government at the time had a largely negative response, seeing the recommendations as politically left-wing. They argued that people should help themselves, not depend on the state to help them out of poverty.

The report led to the founding of the Church Urban Fund, which made grants to groups working in secular as well as religious organisations to tackle inner city poverty and powerlessness. The report was dismissed by one minister in the conservative government of the time as 'pure Marxist theology'.

Faith in the City changed the way that the Church of England worked in cities, especially in areas of inner city poverty. In 1990, a similar report was commissioned into the Church in rural areas, *Faith in the Countryside*, and in 1997, the Methodist Church commissioned their own report, *The Cities*, in 1997. It is now normal for some Churches in Britain to take a liberationist approach in their work. Most parish churches and Methodist churches are used both for worship, but also for secular purposes, which address the needs of their communities. Priests and ministers have a pastoral role that goes much further than just the spiritual care of their people. Many churches run food banks, drop-in centres and community care activities.

This liberationist approach sees the Church responding to the secularisation of society by taking responsibility for the well-being of the community in secular as well as religious matters.

Activity

Research the *Faith in the City* report. You can download a copy of the whole report from the Church of England website if you wish, but there are plenty of other summaries and commentaries available. Write down the key recommendations of the report. See if you can find out what the Church Urban Fund has achieved.

What aspects of the report might need updating since it was written? Write a page or more on what you think liberationist approaches might be concerned with in society today.

Two very different views of secularisation

We have examined several different approaches to Christian theology in response to secularisation.

Much of this chapter has been concerned with the increasing concern of people for life here and now, as opposed to a specifically religious approach – which is sometimes seen as 'spiritual' and therefore not concerned with practical issues.

In this last section, we have examined an approach to Christian theology that argues in favour of the Church taking direct and practical action on behalf of the poor and to counter injustice. This reflects Christianity's 'secular' concern.

In these situations, the secular world is the place where the gospel is to be preached. The theological backing from this comes from a doctrine of the 'incarnation' – namely that in Jesus, God was believed to become fully human as well as fully divine. If God is fully human, he is to be found in the secular world and not just seen as someone outside of space and time. Christian secularisation is a way of looking at and acting out the gospel in terms of the ordinary secular world here and now.

This topic of secularisation, therefore, highlights key features of Christianity:

1 the nature of Jesus Christ as God incarnate

2 the idea of the Church as being the body of Christ on earth

3 the example of Jesus, as recorded in the New Testament, in his dealings with the poor, outcasts and religious outsiders.

Whether secularisation should be seen as a threat to Christianity or a challenge for Christianity to follow its 'incarnational' origins, is a matter of continued debate.

Technical terms for Christianity and the challenge of secularisation

Capitalism Political and economic system which allows wealth to be controlled by individuals and businesses for private profit.

Communism A political system in which power, wealth and status are equally shared by all in the community, region or state.

Humanism The belief that people can live good lives without religious or superstitious beliefs.

Irrational Adjective meaning 'without reason', which has a generally negative meaning.

Liberationist An approach to theology that starts with an analysis of the situation of the poor and oppressed, and then uses the gospel as a way to challenge the causes of their poverty and oppression.

Materialism A world view that sees material possessions, money and personal comfort as more important than spiritual beliefs and practices.

Prosperity Gospel A form of Christianity which sees wealth, status and privilege as rewards from God for strong faith and good works.

Secular Concerned with the affairs of this world, so not concerned with religious or spiritual matters.

Summary of Christianity and the challenge of secularisation

In its most general terms, secularisation is the process by which society becomes less religious. This can be seen by the fact that fewer people belong to a religion, and more people are atheist. Health care, education, and social welfare are no longer organised by the Church, and politics and the law no longer depend on religious teaching.

This secularisation may imply either that Christianity is losing its authority, or that Christianity has become so much part of life today that it is no longer distinguishable from secular society.

The replacement of religion as a source of truth and moral values

Until the Renaissance, Church teaching was considered to be the source of truth and the basis for all moral values. As science developed in the middle ages, some thinkers saw religion as opposing rational thought. During the Protestant Reformation, it became possible to hold individual beliefs different from the national religion, challenging the idea of one universal truth. In the seventeenth and eighteenth centuries, the rise of scientific thinking led some people to think that belief in God was not necessary.

By the nineteenth century, faith was becoming a matter of personal commitment, or a way of seeing life as a whole. Philosophers started to see religion as something functional, for example, keeping the working class from fighting their oppressors (Karl Marx) or satisfying a psychological need (Freud). Religion was increasingly seen as personal but optional.

Basing arguments on reason alone removed the need for religion. But secular morality was largely based on the Ten Commandments, even though morality was expressed in terms of reason rather than religion. Modern secular humanism takes the view that humankind improves through reason and evidence.

Relegation of religion to the personal sphere (individualisation)

Historically, religion was not a matter of individual choice. In 1555, the Augsburg settlement ruled that each prince would decide on the religion of his own state. However, the Peace of Westphalia (1648) allowed people to practise a religion different from the state religion. As society became more secular, religion became a set of ideas and values that individuals might choose to follow.

Today, personal faith is a matter of individual choice. The number of people who choose not to belong to any religion is rising, and some Christian traditions place a heavy emphasis on personal commitment.

Although the practices of religion are now mostly a matter pf private choice, religion does still have a public role in civic occasions. Also, many people value Christian culture, art and buildings, and treat the clergy with respect.

The rise of militant atheism

John Robinson's 1963 book *Honest to God* made explicit the view that God as 'an old man in the sky' did not work intellectually or theologically in the secular society of the twentieth century. At the same time, liberation theology was being developed in South America, the Roman Catholic Church was becoming more relaxed, and the Church of England was concerned with new forms of worship, gender and sexuality.

'Militant atheism' emerged into this situation. Militant atheists see religion as both intellectually flawed and morally flawed. They denounce literalist religious beliefs, equating belief in God with the tooth fairy. They blame religion for wars and cruelty to others. They want to remove religious influences from education and health care and view a religious upbringing as child abuse.

However, militant atheists misrepresent mainstream Christianity. They assume all Christians are fundamentalist literalists, and at the same time they ignore atrocities and cruelty caused by atheists.

The view that religion is irrational

There are non-rational elements in religion, but that does not mean it is irrational. From the enlightenment onwards, religious beliefs were explained in terms of human reason. This was not entirely successful, because people's beliefs do not only depend on reason, but also on emotions and experiences. Militant atheists suggest that religion itself is irrational. To be religious is to be irrational.

Taken literally, many beliefs do *seem* irrational, because they cannot be justified using reason. But if they are not taken literally, they may be considered reasonable because they inspire people to live in a way that shows what Jesus taught. Religious beliefs are communicated with human language, which is both limited and flexible. They may cause good or ill, but is incorrect to describe them as irrational.

People do not operate on the basis of reason and evidence alone. Feelings and emotions are not subject to reason and evidence. One view is that, since humankind is 'fallen', human reason is faulty anyway.

Responses to materialistic secular values: the value of wealth and possessions

1   The value of wealth and possessions in Christianity

In the New Testament, Jesus reversed contemporary views about wealth and possessions. He dealt with rich and poor equally, and commended charity. He argued that riches distract from what matters in life. In the earliest Church, some communities held goods in common as they awaited the end of the world, while others had social and economic divisions. The monastic tradition encouraged men and women to give up personal wealth to live in community, and it is still practised in the Church of England and in the Orthodox and Roman Catholic Churches. After the Protestant Reformation, life in the secular world, with the financial requirements of family life, became equal in status to voluntary poverty. Charity giving and responsible use of wealth, however, continued to be religious duties.

2   Relationship between religious belief and wealth

There is no noticeable difference in wealth overall between atheists and Christians. Although most Christians reject it, the Prosperity Gospel, which teaches that God rewards those who please him, is influential in the USA. On the other hand, many Christians live simple lives and give generously to those in need.

Many Christians are poor, and may depend on services provided by their churches and fellow Christians to help them. Many churches operate food banks, or services for the homeless. Some Christian communities, for example, Bruderhof, copy the earliest Christians by sharing goods and living a simple life.

McGrath's defence of Christianity in *The Dawkins Delusion*

Richard Dawkins is an evolutionary biologist who argues the case for militant atheism in his book *The God Delusion*. He focuses on using science to challenge supernatural religion and literalist beliefs, and assumes that all Christians hold these views. The theologian Alister McGrath argues that science is not in a position to judge on matters of religion. Science can only talk about things that can be assessed using reason and experience.

The God Delusion criticises fundamentalist attitudes as if they were mainstream on matters of homosexuality, abortion, inclusiveness, freedom of choice in matters of religion and religious education. He assumes that such views represent Christianity as a whole. Dawkins ignores the 'liberal' approach to religion. His outlook allows only for reason and evidence, and is humanistic.

In *The Dawkins Delusion*, McGrath counters that Christianity is compatible with science. Dawkins assumes that science leads automatically to atheism, but this means that religious scientists choose to ignore the 'truth' of atheism. McGrath thinks that religion and science have some overlap and can therefore enrich one another.

McGrath over simplifies the ideas of Feuerbach in order to dismiss them, and he suggests that atheism may be an excuse for immorality. McGrath accuses Dawkins of favouring evidence that supports his point of view. Since science should not be biased, Dawkins' views on religion are unscientific. Dawkins' criticisms of religion do not present a fair and balanced view.

Emergence of new forms of expression, such as Fresh Expressions and the House Church movement

1   Fresh Expressions

Fresh Expressions grew out of the report 'Mission-shaped Church' in 2004. It is active in several British Churches. The term 'fresh expressions' is used for Christian groups which operate alongside conventional Churches.

They work alongside people outside traditional Churches. Sometimes, they build an alternative kind of Church; but they also mix with people who are not conventionally religious, as Jesus did.

Unlike the approach to religion criticised by Dawkins, Fresh Expressions explores the concerns and views of ordinary people, and then aims to see how Christian ideas and teachings may be relevant. It deals with religious values and expressions in ordinary, secular situations. Although the language and approach of the Fresh Expressions movement is quite different from that of the older theological traditions, it has parallels with Paul Tillich's idea of God as 'Being-itself'. Fresh Expressions draws out values and meanings from a situation, rather than trying to impose them from outside.

Fresh Expressions works *within* secular life, putting the life and teachings of Jesus into practice. It operates in a secular context for those who are not church members.

2   The House Church movement

Early Christians met in private houses. Later, the Church used church buildings and developed a formal ministry. This started to change during the Reformation, with its emphasis on personal commitment and the authority of the Bible,

Some Christians today have always met in private houses, for example, the Plymouth Brethren. The House Church movement started in the 1960s, to try to return to the practices of the Early Church. It developed particularly in evangelical and charismatic traditions. House Churches tend to meet in private homes, but the British New Church Movement aims to set up new Church communities, and meets in larger building to accommodate numbers.

New Churches focus on the Holy Spirit calling individuals to a way of life or worship, based on a specific understanding of the Bible, which includes healing the sick and casting out.

Emphasis on the social relevance of Christianity including liberationist approaches such as supporting the poor and defending the oppressed

If Christianity is to be socially relevant, it must engage with the lives of people in society today and work for good within society. Since politics is concerned with the way society is ordered, it therefore must be politically relevant.

Politics and social relations are generally defined in terms of power. Christians see the world as good, created by God, but Christians are expected to look beyond the world to the Kingdom of God, where the weak are lifted up and the powerful are put down. One view is that individual lives are transformed by the gospel, although people conform to existing social and political norms. If enough people are changed by religion, that impacts on society as a whole.

1   Secular ownership of Christianity?

Although the number who attend Church is decreasing, many people feel a sense of attachment to their local church. This suggests that society is less secular than expected. Churches can also express national identity, for example, the Russian Orthodox Church in post-Soviet Russia.

Christianity follows the example of Jesus, who taught that secular duties of caring for the poor and healing the sick matter more than religious rules. Teaching and healing have now become separate from organised religion because Christianity is intrinsically secularising – it concerns itself with human well-being.

2   Liberationist approach

Liberation theology developed during the late twentieth century in Central and South America.

Liberation theologians saw the teachings of Jesus as a source of liberation from injustice. That might involve Christians becoming active in social movements for change – secularising the gospel to make it relevant to the lives of ordinary people.

Liberationists wanted secular action to change the structures of society while traditionalists wanted to give spiritual support to the poor. Óscar Romero was a Catholic archbishop who was assassinated during Mass for supporting secular action in El Salvador.

Liberation theology in Britain has focused especially on inner city poverty and injustice. The Church of England archbishops' *Faith in the City. A Call to Action by Church and Nation* considered the state of communities and churches in inner cities in Britain. It identified Urban Priority Areas, where the majority of people were living in poverty, and made recommendations to the Church, calling on them to engage with secular issues such as law, benefits and social support. It also called on the government to address social inequality by changes in the law. As a result of the report, the Church Urban Fund was established by the Church of England to support religious and secular action to tackle poverty and powerlessness.

Two very different views of secularisation

Secularisation can be a concern for life here and now, without religious implications. Alternatively, it can be seen as Christianity moving from a purely religious agenda to a social and political agenda and caring roles, informed by the gospel teachings and actions of Jesus. This approach can be characterised as incarnational: just as God became flesh in Jesus Christ, so the Church works out its humanity in secular action.

11

Christianity, migration and religious pluralism

You will need to consider the following items for this section

1 How migration has created multicultural societies, which include Christianity, with particular reference to the diversity of faiths in Britain today; freedom of religion as a human right in European law and religious pluralism as a feature of modern secular states; the influence of this context on Christian thought.

2 Developments in Christian thought:

● Christian attitudes to other faiths: Exclusivism with reference to John 14:6; Inclusivism with reference to the concept of 'anonymous Christians'; how Christian denominations view each other.

● Pluralism with reference to John Hick; its implications for interfaith and interdenominational relations.

● Christian responses to issues of freedom of religious expression in society.

Introduction: The relative and the absolute

There are different kinds of attitudes with respect to the differing claims of religions. Some people are absolutist when it comes to religious ideas, and some are relativist. An absolute position is one that insists that there is a right view and a wrong view, and the two are mutually exclusive. A relativist position argues that the rightness or wrongness of a view depends on where one stands relative to that view.

An absolute position takes you over. If you believe something absolutely, you cannot do that 'most of the time' – you either do or you don't. It is the same with moral claims – you cannot say 'it is always wrong to steal, sometimes'. If it is always wrong to steal (an absolute principle) then that cannot be qualified without losing the word 'always'. 'It is never right to make absolute claims' is self-contradictory.

Religion has usually tended to be absolute in its claims. People are expelled for 'wrong' beliefs. At one time they would have been tortured and killed for 'wrong' beliefs, on the grounds that wrong doctrine would lead to eternal torment in hell, so a brief time of torture to persuade them back to the right belief would save people from hell, and was really the lesser of two evils. So within each religion there is likely to develop an 'us/them' attitude towards those whose beliefs are different. The more convinced a person is that his or her beliefs are right and all contrary beliefs wrong, the more intolerant they are likely to be, if only in order to persuade those in error and thereby save them.

What then do you do in a world where there are many religions competing for people's attentions, each of which claims to know the truth – can they all be right? Are their claims mutually destructive? That would be too simplistic an answer, for most religions accept that there is a limit to human knowledge. Some agree that it is possible that others will understand an aspect of truth different from their own, but possibly compatible with it. The problem is not incompatibility, but the degree of respect and cooperation that is possible between different religions. This is made possible, to a considerable extent, by seeing the beliefs of each religion as reflecting its own historical and cultural background – a view that, as we shall see later, is expressed as 'multiculturalism'.

How migration has created multicultural societies, which include Christianity

Until the eighteenth century, the only non-Christian religion that most Europeans had come into contact with peacefully was Judaism. In parts of southern Europe, people were familiar with Islam, but general understanding of this was influenced by the conflict of the crusades. By the eighteenth century Europeans knew more about other world religions, so 'religion' became more of a generic term. However, the issue of religious diversity became more immediate in the twentieth century, following immigration and the development of a multi-racial and multi-cultural society.

Through the second half of the twentieth century, significant numbers of immigrants came from elsewhere to settle in Britain, bringing with them their own languages, cultures and religions. Immediately after the Second World War, many people from Eastern Europe migrated to the UK from countries that became part of the Soviet Union. Following Indian independence in 1947, increasing numbers of Indians and Pakistanis entered the UK, peaking in 1972 when they were expelled from Idi Amin's Uganda. In the 1950s, the British government encouraged immigration from the Caribbean countries and from Hong Kong because of labour shortages in the UK. In the 1980s, many people fled the civil war in Somalia and settled in the UK, and there were also immigrants fleeing from the Balkan conflicts of the 1990s.

Some assumed that such immigrants would soon become fully assimilated into British culture – in other words, they would adopt the language, customs, dress and religion of the United Kingdom. But as immigrant groups became established, many retained their own cultural identity. People became aware through the 1960s and 1970s of the need to recognise

Key term

Multicultural Made up of many different cultures, which may include different nationalities, beliefs, values and social customs. This term has a wider scope than *multiracial*, which refers only to race, and *multi-faith* which applies only to religion.

the cultural identity of minority groups. By the 1980s there was a general recognition of what is called '**multiculturalism**'.

Some saw multiculturalism as a threat to core national values and traditions, and therefore destructive to national identity. They argued, among other things, that Britain was a Christian country with values and traditions that had their roots in Christian belief, teaching and practices. Jewish communities had been well established in Britain for many years without causing a threat to national identity (indeed the Prime Minister Benjamin Disraeli was born a Jew), but the influx of Hindus, Buddhists, Muslims and Sikhs after the war made multiculturalism more visible. Of course, many immigrants were Christian too, most notably those from the Caribbean, but their culture and traditions were quite different from the British way of life in the 1940s and 1950s.

The 'Rivers of Blood' speech

In 1968, Enoch Powell, a Conservative Member of Parliament who was opposed to large-scale **migration** into the UK, gave a speech in which he said:

'We must be mad, literally mad, as a nation to be permitting the annual inflow of some 50,000 dependents, who are for the most part the material of the future growth of the immigrant descended population. It is like watching a nation busily engaged in heaping up its own funeral pyre

[...] As I look ahead, I am filled with foreboding. Like the Roman, I seem to see 'the River Tiber foaming with much blood.' [Note 1]

Key term

Migration The movement of substantial numbers of people from one place to another.

However, in general, it was recognised that the culture of each group in a multicultural society should be respected and protected. It was generally hoped that multiculturalism would lead to a rich and beneficial mixing of cultural traditions. Multiculturalism was seen as a way to promote tolerance and equal access and opportunities in employment, education, law and business.

The diversity of faiths in Britain today

There is a diversity of different faiths in Britain today.

At the time of the 2011 Census, the membership of different religious groups was as follows:

Christianity 59.3% (down from 71.8% in 2001)

No religion 25.1% (up 10.3% from 2001)

Islam 4.8% (up 1.8% since 2001)

Hinduism 1.5%

Sikhism 0.8%

Judaism 0.5%

Buddhism 0.4%

All other religious groups (including those who identify their belief as Agnostic or Humanist) make up under 0.1 per cent of the population. All minority religious groups have increased their membership since the 2001 Census.

This balance between religious communities is affected by immigration. In 2011, 11 per cent of Christians and 53 per cent of Muslims were born outside the UK. The biggest change between 2001 and 2011 was the fall in the number of Christians and the rise in the number of people who claimed no religion. This has not been affected significantly by immigration.

The presence of people of many different faiths in the UK is more obvious in some areas than others. When groups of people first migrated to the UK, they tended to settle in places close to one another where possible, so that some areas, especially in industrial cities which already had a more mixed population, attracted a higher population of people from a specific region. This meant that they could build places of worship, open shops to cater to their own tastes, and organise events to keep alive their cultural roots.

One example of this is Manchester's Chinatown, which was originally home to a small number of early twentieth-century laundry workers from China. When immigration from Hong Kong increased in the 1950s and 1960s, Manchester seemed like a natural place for people to settle. There were plenty of employment opportunities, and there was already a small Chinese community. Today, Chinatown is a buzzing cultural centre in a very multicultural city, with churches, restaurants, shops and banks catering to the British Chinese community.

Activity

Print out a map of your local area or your nearest city. Find as many places of worship as you can for that area using the internet – look for churches, chapels, Buddhist and Hindu temples, mosques, gurdwaras and synagogues. Plot them on the map. Can you find any other evidence for multiculturalism in those areas?

You could also look for more detailed census information for the area you are looking at if you wish.

Can you think of any specific reasons for the pattern of multiculturalism and multi-faith in the area you are looking at?

Freedom of religion as a human right in European law

Universal Declaration of Human Rights, Article 18

Everyone has the right to freedom of thought, conscience and religion; this right includes freedom to change his religion or belief, and freedom, either alone or in community with other and in public or private, to manifest his religion or belief in teaching, practice, worship and observance.

Comment 22 of the UN Human Rights Committee clarified that the protection given by Article 18 applies to 'theistic, non-theistic and atheistic beliefs, as well as the right not to profess any religion or belief'.

European Law

The Universal Declaration of Human Rights, Article 18 is confirmed and included in the *European Convention on Human Rights and Fundamental Freedoms*, Article 9.

British Law

The United Kingdom is a signatory to the *European Convention on Human Rights* which, in Article 9 (as above) includes freedom of thought, conscience and religion. This has been included within the *Human Rights Act, 1988*.

It is, therefore, against the law to prohibit or restrict the practice of religion, and this allows **religious pluralism** within British society. It is, however, also against the law to say or do anything that is likely to incite violence or racial hatred, so if a religion preaches hatred towards others, it is no defence to claim freedom of religion.

Historically, religions have been intolerant towards one another, and also between sub-groups within a single religion. This can been seen, for example, in the European wars of religion between Catholics and Protestants, or between some Sunni and Shi'a Muslims within Islam. Some Old Testament passages suggest that religious intolerance is a duty for Jews, for example Exodus 23: 23–24 and 32–33: 'My angel will go ahead of you and bring you into the land of the Amorites, Hittites, Perizzites, Canaanites, Hivites and Jebusites, and I will wipe them out. Do not bow down before their gods or worship them or follow their practices. You must demolish them and break their sacred stones to pieces.'

Religious pluralism as a feature of modern secular states

A multi-faith society inevitably contains people from different cultures who live close to one another as part of the same society. In some parts of the world, this may lead to tension and conflict, but in modern western nations, this may develop into multiculturalism. This idea is the view that all cultures are to be respected, celebrated and understood in terms of their origins. There should be mutual engagement and dialogue, and that society is richer for having cultural diversity. Multiculturalism opposes the idea that any culture should have another culture imposed on it, or that people should be deprived of the opportunity to express their cultural heritage.

Those who oppose multiculturalism argue that it leaves little scope for a society to be held together. There is no agreed scheme of thought with which everyone agrees. They argue that this is dangerous, because it means that society lacks cohesion – there is nothing to hold it together. There is also a danger that immigrant communities which flourish without becoming assimilated into the culture of the host country, can become increasingly isolated and subject to popular discrimination.

There is another problem. Multiculturalism assumes that no single culture can claim to be the best. But religion is based on the conviction that what it offers is the best form of life, superior to that of those who have no religion or follow other religions. That is one reason why religions arise in the first instance; it is that which holds their members together.

> **Key term**
>
> **Religious pluralism** A situation where people of many faiths live in the same society without conflict, respecting one another's views. In some contexts the term can also refer to the view that all religions are equally valid.

> **Key term**
>
> **Secular state** a country where the government, legislature and society are not controlled by, or dependent on, the teachings of a religion.

So there is a multicultural temptation to say that one's own beliefs are not inherently superior to those of others, but a religious temptation to say just the opposite. Religious pluralism is the religious equivalent of multiculturalism. It is a response to a situation where several religions exist alongside one another in the same society. Religious pluralism assumes that all religions are to be respected, celebrated and understood as having intrinsic value for their believers.

There is considerable overlap between multiculturalism and religious pluralism. Since many religions are particularly associated with specific cultural communities, it is sometimes impossible to unpick which traditions and practices are best described as culture and which are specifically religious. Some religions are shared by people with very different cultures (for example, Polish Roman Catholics and Caribbean Pentecostals are both Christian, but Polish culture and Caribbean culture are very different), and some apparently similar cultures may include people of different religions (for example, Manchester's Chinatown includes Christians, Buddhists and people who follow Chinese traditional religion).

Multiculturalism also raises issues for social workers and others. People may be afraid to challenge cultural practices that are harmful or illegal because they do not want to appear racist, or to appear to offend the religious values of a specific community.

Issues of multiculturalism

Two issues have become particularly controversial within the UK:

- female genital mutilation (FGM)
- forced marriage (marriage against the will of one or both of the partners)

FGM is practised in some communities with cultural roots in Africa, the Middle East and Asia.

Forced marriage is the practice of forcing a young person or couple into a marriage without their consent. This is not the same as arranged marriage. It is a common practice in many religions for parents to arrange marriages for their sons and daughters, and the young people have the choice to accept or reject the marriage partner their parents suggest. However, in some families, the young people do not have the option to object, so they are forced into a marriage without their consent.

In each case, society says that such practices are illegal. FGM causes unacceptable suffering to young women and girls, and forced marriage goes against the values of British society, where people have a free choice about whom they marry. A few people argue that both practices are cultural expressions within specific religious communities. They claim that whether or not they should be allowed should be the decision of the particular religious community, not the secular law.

Note that both of these are largely cultural rather than religious practices, so this is really a cultural issue rather than a religious one. The mutilation of women and forced marriage go against the religious teachings of all mainstream religions. However, it is sometimes difficult to separate cultural practices from religious ones. Some people who practise FGM and forced marriage argue that they are required practices within their own branch of religion. They argue that their right to freedom of religious expression (see page 319) means that they should be allowed to continue these practices. However, the law in the UK limits freedom of religious expression if that freedom causes harm to people, or if it breaks another law.

You can find UK government information relating to these issues at the following wesbites:

www.gov.uk/government/collections/female-genital-mutilation

www.gov.uk/stop-forced-marriage

Influence on Christian thought

When talking about culture in terms of food, styles of dress, family traditions, and some religious practices, then it is possible to get a taste for these things by sharing festivals, for example. It gives people a sense of belonging to a world community rather than to a local one only. Christians may share Diwali fireworks with Hindu neighbours, or eat the Passover Seder with Jewish friends, and they may welcome people of all faiths to Christmas parties and Easter egg hunts.

It is less simple, however, to be part of a world community in terms of religious beliefs. Clearly, Christians who live alongside people of other faiths need to examine their own faith, and their attitude towards the faith of others, in order to have a responsible attitude towards others.

One possibility is to use human reason as a judge between religious claims. For example, Religion 1 claims X, and Religion 2 claims Y.

- EITHER a person uses reason to consider both X and Y, and decides that one of them is more 'reasonable' than the other.
- OR a person uses reason to decide that X is the more inclusive belief, and Y is a sub-set of that belief, so both may be held to be true.

The problem is that this assumes that religious people will accept the idea that reason can be used to make a judgement about their beliefs.

The claims of religion have been subjected to reason many times in history. Aquinas' Natural Moral Law points towards a view of Christianity as wholly reasonable. But this kind of reasoning leads to a situation where beliefs, including belief in God, are optional expressions of the value and celebration of human life in the universe. This is possible, since it is the position that Buddhism has traditionally held. It argues that everyone should test out ideas, and only accept them as true if they can be confirmed for each person. But that contradicts the views of major Western religions.

The problem is that humans have a strong psychological need for certainty. Religions are appealing because they offer absolute beliefs and moral principles. This partly explains the recent rise in fundamentalism, a literal acceptance of simply expressed religious beliefs, ignoring all complexities of interpretation. This kind of fundamentalism appeals to those who want religion to give them certainty. It is absolute conviction – whether moral or religious – that leads a person to be a suicide bomber or a martyr. People who do such things act out of an absolute certainty that they are right, not on the basis of *probability* that what they stand for *might* be right.

So a thinking person in a multi-faith world has a dilemma:

- If someone holds religious beliefs with absolutely certainty, could they possibly accept that their views may be open to challenge, or that their perspective may not be the only true one?
- If a person holds no religious beliefs, could they accept that they may be wrong, and that someone else's claim to absolute truth may be correct?
- If someone holds religious beliefs, would they be prepared to consider that their beliefs are open to reasoned scrutiny?
- If a person holds no religious beliefs, but considers that everything should be based on reason and evidence (such as some scientists), could

Discussion point

Christianity teaches that Jesus was God in human form (God Incarnate). Islam teaches that Jesus was a very important prophet, but he was only human. Which view do you think is the more 'reasonable'? Which is the more inclusive? Do you think that reason can always be used to judge between competing beliefs?

that person possibly consider that there might be a source of knowledge that is valid but not subject to reason and evidence?

How do people deal with competing claims from different religions or different religious ideas, for example about life after death/reincarnation/re-becoming/eternal life?

Working from the basis of either experience or authority, each religion is self-validating. It is only possible to consider competing claims on the basis of reason and evidence. But, in that case, there is an assumption that reason takes priority over religious teaching and experience. A religious person may not be willing to accept that assumption.

One way that religions are differentiated from one another is that it is impossible for someone to be a member of both at the same time, without losing something essential. This is supported by the fact that some religions produce creeds, lists of key beliefs which define who is 'in' and who is not.

Chinese religion

Religions and denominations based on specific creeds, doctrinal ideas or practices, in confrontation with one another, are a particularly Western phenomenon. In China, for example, there is a blending of Confucian, Taoist and Buddhist traditions. Individuals use ceremonies and traditions associated with all three of them in different circumstances, without seeing that as a problem.

Christian attitudes to other faiths

Exclusivism and inclusivism

In a situation where there are a number of different religions with different beliefs, there is a dilemma. Can they all be equally true?

- An 'exclusivist' says that his or her religion is the only true one. Other religions are wrong, even if their beliefs appear to be the same as one's own.
- An 'inclusivist' says that another religion may have aspects of belief that are the same as his/her own, and is therefore 'true'. However, most 'inclusivists' still claim that their own religion is unique.

This can be explained from a Christian perspective. Evangelical Christians, for example, believe the goal of human life is salvation from sin and going to heaven. This is only possible through a personal relationship with Jesus, so only Christians, who have a personal relationship with Jesus, can be saved. This is **exclusivism**.

Others may argue that God may choose to forgive the sins of those who have not committed themselves to Jesus because they have lived good lives, so people of other faiths and none can also be saved. This is an inclusivist approach.

Some beliefs are mutually exclusive. For example, it is impossible to accept that Jesus is literally the 'Son of God' and at the same time to uphold the strict monotheism of Judaism or Islam. This means that Christianity and Islam are incompatible when it comes to the status of Jesus. Christians

> **Key term**
>
> **Exclusivism** The view that one religion is the only true one, and that other religions are wrong.

323

believe that Jesus is the Son of God, and Muslims believe that God has no son, and that Jesus (Isa in Arabic) was a wholly human prophet.

Inclusivists hold that their own religion teaches the truth more completely than any other. At the same time, they accept that there may be some elements of truth in other religions. For example, the Second Vatican Council issued a Declaration on the Relation of the Church with Non-Christian Religions, *Nostra Aetate* (Latin: *In our Time*). It declared that 'The Catholic Church rejects nothing that is true and holy in [other] religions', and that they 'reflect a ray of the Truth that illuminates everyone'. The complete text of *Nostra Aetate* is available online at: **www.vatican.va/archive/hist_councils/ii_vatican_council/ documents/vat-ii_decl_19651028_nostra-aetate_en.html**

There are two approaches to **inclusivism**:

- Closed inclusivism – one specific religion has all truth, but others have some of it too.
- Open inclusivism – one specific religion has the best grasp of, but not all of truth, and so it can learn some truth from the teachings of other religions.

Exclusivism with reference to John 14:6

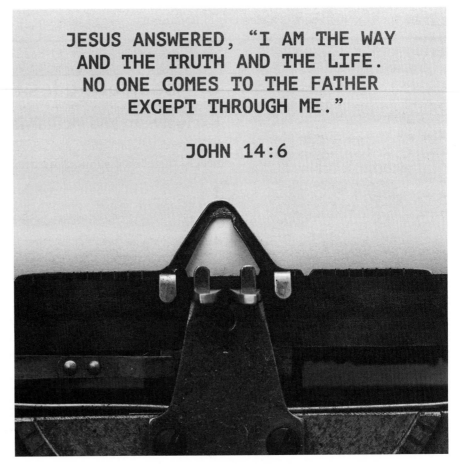

This verse is used by some Christians as a basis for Christian exclusivism. It seems to say that explicit faith in Christ is necessary for salvation. Those Christians who take an exclusivist view may accept two exceptions to this. The first is in the case of children who die before they reach the age

Key term

Inclusivism The view that although one religion is true, other religions may show aspects of the one true religion.

at which they can understand and commit to Christ: the salvation of such children is seen as a sign of God's mercy. The other is the situation where someone has never encountered Christ. One way of assessing the eternal fate of such a person would be to see how they had responded to 'general revelation', the idea that God's law can be seen through nature, both in natural morality and in a sense of wonder.

However, the norm for biblical fundamentalists is that God will condemn all who are not committed to Christ. This makes **evangelism** a priority, since it could save people who would otherwise not be saved. Within a multi-faith situation, people who hold this view hope to convert those of other faiths for a positive reason: to offer them the salvation that comes through faith in Jesus. Others who do not see the Bible as the literal words of God, would not necessarily support the need for conversion, and would be more likely to take an inclusivist approach.

Other Bible verses that are used to support the exclusivist position are as follows:

> For God so loved the world, that he gave his only Son, that whoever believes in him should not perish but have everlasting life. (John 3:16)
>
> For everyone who calls upon the name of the Lord will be saved. (Romans 10:13)
>
> And there is salvation in no one else, for there is no other name under heaven given among men by which we must be saved. (Acts 4:12)

This general view was traditionally expressed in the Catholic idea **extra ecclesiam nulla salus** – *there is no salvation outside the Church.* This view has historically defined the relationship between the Catholic Church and other people, including other Christian denominations and non-Christians. This view has now been modified, but not eliminated, through Vatican II (see page 324).

From a Christian perspective, exclusivism is based on the view that all religion and all salvation is judged in terms of the revelation in Jesus Christ.

In general, an exclusivist points to the idea that nothing other than one's relationship with Christ counts when it comes to salvation. The key question is whether that commitment needs to be made explicitly, or whether it can be seen implicitly in a person's attitudes, actions and values. In some ways this reflects the debate between justification by faith and justification by works that was outlined in Chapter 9 of Volume 1.

If belief in God's salvation through Christ alone is compromised, there may be a decline into relativism, in which all religions may be seen as equally true or equally false. An exclusivist is concerned to avoid this. It goes against the key and distinctive feature of Christian thought, that God is revealed through Christ is a unique way.

Criticisms of exclusivism

A general problem with an exclusivist view is that, if God is free to do whatever he chooses, it is illogical to say that he cannot act through other religions or none. Exclusivism limits God's potential for forgiveness and

---

Key term

Evangelism Spreading Christianity by preaching or by personal witness. Not to be confused with Evangelicalism, which is a branch of Christianity that sees the spreading of the gospel as a primary responsibility for Christians.

Key term

extra ecclesiam nulla salus The Roman Catholic teaching that there is no salvation for those who are outside the (Roman Catholic) Church.

salvation. Exclusivists justify doing so on the basis of Bible texts, but this gives the Bible priority in deciding who is for heaven and who for hell. **This, in effect, binds God to a particular interpretation of scripture**.

A major problem with the exclusivist position, therefore, is that it depends heavily upon a literal and simple interpretation of the Bible text which gives it authority. However, biblical and historical studies have shown that the text of the New Testament went through a process of development and editing which reflects the situation in which the Early Church found itself. It is a product of the Church. The issue becomes not just what is written, but why, and in what context. With those questions, it becomes more difficult to maintain a position in which the Bible can be the basis for any exclusive claim.

It would seem that the standard argument for exclusivism, based on John 14:6 and similar verses, is circular. **It cannot offer an independent justification of exclusivism**. The New Testament texts are the product of the Church, so they reflect the commitment of those who are already members. They express the convictions about Jesus and salvation held at the end of the first century. We cannot even be sure that Jesus said the things attributed to him.

Getting a balance

In any argument about whether salvation is only available to those who are members of the Church, the exclusivist view is just one possible interpretation of the teachings of Jesus. It has to be seen alongside accounts of Jesus' dealings with gentiles, outcasts and those who followed forms of Judaism that were regarded as heretical. The range of Jesus' actions and teachings lead to a view that he was inclusive in his dealings with people of other faiths. It is, therefore, reasonable to conclude that inclusivism has as least as much biblical support as exclusivism.

Any balanced understanding of Jesus needs to take all of the New Testament accounts of his life and teaching into account. To rely only on one or two late-recorded statements (and John's Gospel is generally regarded as the last of the four Gospels to be written down) is unwise, unless one is already committed to them as being key.

Inclusivism with reference to the concept of 'anonymous Christians'

Quite a few biblical texts suggest that God provides for, and plans salvation for, everyone. Here are some:

In Acts 10:34–35 in the account of his meeting with Cornelius, Peter says:

> I now realise how true it is that God does not show favoritism but accepts from every nation the one who fears him and does what is right.

Later, in Acts 14:16–17 Paul and Barnabas announce that God has been showing himself even in the earlier, pre-Christian, era:

> In the past, he let all nations go their own way. Yet he has not left himself without testimony: He has shown kindness by giving you rain from heaven and crops in their seasons; he provides you with plenty of food and fills your hearts with joy.

And, in 17:22–31, Paul makes his speech on the Areopagus based on having seen an inscription 'to an unknown God'. In his speech, Paul notes that they already worship a God whose name they do not know. He, Paul, is proclaiming this very God, so the Gospel is going to bring to completion what has already been started in them.

In general, it can be argued that the author of **Luke/Acts** takes a view of Judaism and of the Roman and Greek religious traditions that are in line with a modern inclusivist view.

Against those who pass judgement on others, this passage emphasises that God has no favourites:

> There will be trouble and distress for every human being who does evil: first for the Jew, then for the Gentile; but glory, honor and peace for everyone who does good: first for the Jew, then for the Gentile. For God does not show favoritism. (Romans 2:9–11)

Discussion point

The exclusivist position makes human choice for or against Christ the deciding factor. The inclusivist position focuses on the idea that God wants all to be saved, whatever their present status.

An exclusivist point of view means that those who are not saved will be damned. Is this compatible with a God who is both omnipotent and loving?

Is an inclusivist position compatible with the idea that Christ offers a unique path to salvation?

Since the term Gentile is used for all non-Jews, this is in effect a comment about judging everyone, whether they have a religion or not. It says that judgement is made on the basis of doing either good or evil, so it shows a clear inclusivist position.

Another approach to the relationship between Christians and others is to see *all* religions as ineffective, so that the only thing that counts is the grace of God. This is the position taken by Barth. This point of view places all people, Christian and non-Christian, in the same position with respect to the grace of God.

The theologian Barth saw revelation in Christ as something that abolishes all forms of religion. Barth opposed the liberal approach which saw Christianity as one religion among many, and instead, he placed both Christianity and other religions under the single judgement of Jesus Christ. He emphasised the absolute sovereignty of God and the ineffectiveness of all religion.

One approach sees some who are outside the Christian community as **'anonymous' Christians**. The Roman Catholic theologian Karl Rahner was the first to use this term.

Key term

Anonymous Christians A view proposed by Karl Rahner, that people who are not Christians in practice, worship or belief are nevertheless able to experience grace and salvation.

Karl Rahner (1904–84)

Rahner was a German priest and theologian. His early writings were considered suspect by the Roman Catholic authorities, but from 1962 he was influential in the way Catholic thinking developed during and after the Second Vatican Council.

> Anonymous Christianity means that a person lives in the grace of God and attains salvation outside of explicitly constituted Christianity — Let us say, a Buddhist monk — who, because he follows his conscience, attains salvation and lives in the grace of God; of him I must say that he is an anonymous Christian; if not, I would have to presuppose that there is a genuine path to salvation that really attains that goal, but that simply has nothing to do with Jesus Christ. But I cannot do that. And so, if I hold [that] everyone depends upon Jesus Christ for salvation, and if at the same time I hold that many live in the world who have not expressly recognised Jesus Christ, then there remains in my opinion nothing else but to take up this postulate of an anonymous Christianity.
>
> Karl Rahner in *Dialogue*, page 135. [Note 2]

Rahner's view is that, without consciously becoming Christian, everyone encounters God's grace and saving purpose. Rahner suggests that people should be confident that the power of God is sufficient to overcome 'the limited stupidity and evil-mindedness of men'.

The implication of this is not that an atheist, or a member of a non-Christian religion, is secretly Christian. That would be to deny their integrity and their commitment to their particular view of the world. It simply says that the saving grace of God, from a Christian perspective, may be working in and through them. It implies that they are saved through works, rather than through faith (Volume 1, Chapter 9), because good moral conduct is not dependent on any underlying belief.

In practical terms, this view replaces confrontation between faiths with the sense that all are on a common quest. Therefore, all religious groups have core ideas in common. However, his 'anonymous Christian' tag is not used for all non-Christians, but only with reference to specific ideas or practices. In other words, he is avoiding any sense that all religions are the same, but he does think they should explore the things they have in common.

Rahner's views have been criticised by those who take a fundamentalist position, but also by those who see his concept of anonymous Christianity as patronising to other faiths. John Hick argues that it is an insult to people born into families of other faiths, because it suggests that the faith they are following is mistaken or faulty. He calls the notion of anonymous Christianity paternalistic. He says:

'The devout Muslim, or Hindu, or Sikh, or Jew can be regarded as an anonymous Christian, this being an honorary status granted unilaterally to people who have not expressed any desire for it.' [Note 3]

Discussion point

Some Christians recognise members of other faiths as being, in some respects, 'anonymous Christians'. Could they also accept that, from a Hindu perspective, Jesus may be seen as an avatar of Vishnu? Could they accept that a Buddhist might see Christians as sharing an indwelling 'Buddha nature'?

How Christian denominations view each other

Toleration

If you tolerate something, you allow it even though you disagree with it. It therefore implies a negative judgement on what is tolerated, while holding that it is worse to be intolerant.

Historical background

There was never a time in the whole history of Christianity when there has been uniformity of religious belief and practice. The letters of Paul in the New Testament show what he saw as errors in the beliefs and attitudes of some early Christian communities. Clearly, there were important issues to resolve, particularly over the terms under which Jews and Gentiles could come together within the Church. By the end of the first century there were at least 40 individual Christian communities.

By the fourth century, there were five main centres of the Church: Rome, Constantinople, Alexandria, Antioch and Jerusalem. Christianity developed slightly differently in each place, and there were disputes between theologians over points of doctrine. In 312CE the Emperor Constantine converted to Christianity, and the following year, the Edict of Milan ended the persecution of Christians. Later, he made Christianity the official religion of the empire, and tried to reach a uniformity of beliefs. In 325, he called a council of Bishops to Nicea in Turkey. One result of this meeting was an agreed statement of faith, the Nicene Creed.

From that time on, those within the Church who disagreed with the official creeds were considered heretics, and were frequently persecuted. However, there was never complete agreement either in matters of religious practice or of formal beliefs. Six further **ecumenical** Church councils over the next 450 years continued to debate and define doctrine before the Great Schism in 1054.

This split in the Church was caused by a number of long-term disputes concerned with doctrine, practice and organisation. These included the exact nature of the Holy Spirit, the wording of the Creed, the use of leavened and unleavened bread in Holy Communion, and a power struggle between the bishops of Rome and Constantinople, each of whom claimed that their **See** was more important. Whereas the Patriarchs (senior bishops) of each of the five main centres had previously exercised authority over his own area, the Patriarch of Rome (the Pope) claimed to be head of the whole Church. At the same time, the Patriarch of Constantinople claimed that his See was the 'first among equals'. In 1054, this came to a head when the two leaders refused to recognise one another's demands, and a series of excommunications marked the start of a formal split. The Western Church from then on was called the Catholic Church. The Eastern Churches are called the Orthodox Churches.

Then, in the sixteenth century, the Reformation split Western Christianity, first into Catholics and Protestants, each of whom persecuted the other. The Church of England remained Catholic, but it too separated from Rome and the authority of the Pope, and was influenced by Reformation ideas. Subsequently there were further splits, with the Free Churches, Methodists, Baptists and others eventually becoming independent denominations, free to meet for worship, although often with legal restrictions imposed upon their members.

Today, there are three broad divisions: Orthodox, Roman Catholic and Protestant. The Anglican Churches, including the Church of England, sit between the Catholic and Protestant traditions and take elements from each.

Key terms

Ecumenism Initiatives to develop relationships between Christian Churches to promote Christian unity.

See A diocese; the region and people under the control of a bishop.

But within those basic divisions there are many different denominations, of which 349 are members of the World Council of Churches. In addition to these, there are independent evangelical churches, non-denominational 'mega-churches' and small house churches, all of whom act autonomously rather than being part of any existing denomination.

Reasons for divisions within Christianity

It is clear that there are certain things that explain the separation between Churches:

1 **Issues of authority.**

   a Should authority belong to one leader? Should all leaders have equal authority, or should there be no leaders?

   b Should scripture be the source of authority? Should authority belong to each individual believer and their relationship with God?

2 **Questions relating to particular traditions or practices.** For example, the Baptist movement emphasises adult baptism as a reminder of Jesus' baptism, whereas Catholic and Orthodox Churches believe in the sacramental baptism of infants.

3 **Questions relating to Church governance and organisation.** For example do local congregations make their own decisions, or is the Church centrally governed by rules and laws?

4 **Questions arising because of particular interpretations of scripture.** Some denominations focus on a literal reading of the plain text of the Bible as the inerrant word of God, and others as the product of fallible human writers who were inspired by the Holy Spirit.

5 **Questions of inspiration and style of worship.** The Pentecostal movement, for example, emphasises the 'gifts of the Spirit' in informal and loosely structured worship, whilst the Catholic Church's worship is usually formal, structured, and mainly focused on the sacrament of Holy Communion.

6 **Questions related to the acceptance of creeds.** From the fourth century, this was taken to be the way of separating heretics from orthodox believers.

[Note that the word 'orthodox' with a lower-case 'o' means 'right-believing'. When written with an upper-case 'O' it refers to the Eastern Churches.]

How Christian denominations view each another

Since different denominations have different doctrinal emphases, the way they view other Churches varies. In this section, we shall look at the way the Roman Catholic Church, Protestant evangelical Churches, and the Church of England see those outside their own denomination in institutional ways. It should be stressed that individual members of these denominations may have their own views.

The Roman Catholic Church

▲ The concept of Apostolic Succession means that authority from Jesus himself, which he gave to the apostles, is passed on from one generation to the other in a physical way by the laying on of hands at ordination

For the Catholic Church, it is essential to maintain continuity with the Faith as taught by the apostles. This is seen particularly in the 'Apostolic Succession' in which authority is passed at ordination from one person to another. Continuity is expressed in the way that people continue to hold the same core beliefs which are expressed by saying the ancient creeds, and by using the same rituals that were used from the earliest days of the Church – the sacraments of Baptism and Holy Communion. This continuity guarantees authority – the same traditions are passed from one generation to another. If the Church is the Body of Christ, and therefore a single spiritual entity, there is no real scope for division. People either belong to that body or they do not. Those who are separated from it may display admirable qualities, and may seek in their own way to follow Christ, but they are nevertheless cut off from the authentic source of Christian teaching and sacraments.

Liberal Catholic thinkers therefore opt for a *closed inclusivist* position with respect to other denominations as well as other religions. They reflect aspects of the Christian faith, but they lack the continuity and authority of Catholicism.

The Catholic approach is seen in *Ut Unum Sint* ('*That they may be one*') – an encyclical issued by Pope John Paul II in 1995. In this document, non-Catholics are referred to as 'separated brethren'. Catholic theologians can and should enter into dialogue with them in a spirit of charity and humility, but are always to stand fast in the teaching of the Church.

331

The unity willed by God can be attained only by the adherence of all to the content of revealed faith in its entirety. In matters of faith, compromise is in contradiction with God who is Truth. [Note 4]

Protestant evangelical Churches

Luther taught that salvation could only come about by the grace of God (*sola gratia*), through faith (*sola fides*). Everything that Christians needed to know could be found in a plain reading of the Bible (*sola scriptura*). Individual Christian believers could communicate directly with God, and did not need priests to mediate (priesthood of all believers). So, from the time of the Reformation, there was a conviction that individuals could, under the inspiration of the Holy Spirit, read and understand the scriptures for themselves, without requiring any authoritative interpretation from the Church. Along with this was Luther's idea that salvation is offered to sinful humankind by the grace of God, undeserved and unrelated to ritual observance. Faith, in this context, is a personal commitment to God in Christ, informed by scripture. The emphasis is on faith, rather than on obedience to tradition or participation in the sacraments.

From this perspective, Protestant evangelical Churches judge other Christians by the way they apply principles from the New Testament, and by whether or not individual members of those Churches declare their commitment to Christ as their personal saviour. For this reason, they see those Churches which teach that specific actions and forms of worship are necessary, as failing to follow scripture.

Protestant evangelical Churches, basing their lives on the Bible, prefer to be self-governing communities without any central or national authority structures. They base this on the New Testament example of the Early Church in the book of Acts, which appears to have been autonomous and self-contained. This means that Protestant evangelicals see the hierarchical authority structures of the Church of England, the Roman Catholic Church and Orthodox Churches, with their bishops, priests and deacons, and central governance, as unbiblical, and therefore as in error.

Because, for them, authentic faith is a matter of personal conviction and commitment, those who choose not to make a commitment remain outside the Church and therefore cannot achieve salvation. This is an *exclusivist* position. Although Protestant evangelicals do not themselves exclude people, they believe that those who have not made a commitment to Christ have excluded themselves from salvation.

The Church of England

After the Church of England separated from the authority of the Pope in the 1530s, it remained Catholic in its theology. During the troubled years that followed, there was a growing influence in the Church from reformation (especially Calvinist) theologians, so that by the time of the Elizabethan Settlement in 1559, the Church of England was described officially as 'Catholic and Reformed'. Over the centuries, the Church of England has held, at various times, a range of views, and still today there are evangelicals, Anglo-Catholics and Pentecostal communities all within the Church of England.

For this reason, it is difficult to identify one single view with relation to other Churches. The official position of the Church of England towards other Churches is non-committal: it recognises other Churches, acknowledging that they are different in matters in worship, in forms of ministry, in structures for decision-making, and in the way they work in the world. Because of the differences within the Church of England, there is a general admission that no Church, including their own, is perfect. This willingness to work with other Churches towards agreement over key issues has led to a number of bilateral conversations and formal agreements with other Churches. These include the **Anglican-Roman Catholic International Commission (ARCIC)** from 1969 onwards, the 'Porvoo Agreement' with Lutheran Churches in 1996 and the 'Reuilly Declaration' with the French Protestant Churches in 2001.

It would be inaccurate to define the position of the Church of England as one, agreed view, but the kind of engagement they undertake with other Churches, and the unwillingness to exclude other Christians from the possibility of salvation, could certainly be described as inclusivist. For example, the Church of England is divided over ordaining women, but it works closely with the Roman Catholic Church, which excludes women from the priesthood, and the Methodist Church, which accepts the ordination of women at all levels of ministry.

Ecumenism

Ecumenism is the word that describes initiatives to develop relationships between Christian Churches to promote Christian unity. The Ecumenical Movement originated in the early twentieth century, and its work is most clearly seen in the work of the World Council of Churches. The emphasis of the ecumenical movement in general is not to deny or explain away differences between Christian denominations, but to suggest that they have plenty in common and can therefore undertake to work together. The approach of the World Council of Churches is practical rather than theological. It is thus very different from the Orthodox and Catholic approach, which starts from the idea that the Church is the Body of Christ, and is, therefore, to be expressed in the sacraments and in assent to the creeds of the Church.

The Roman Catholic Church has not applied to become a member of the World Council of Churches. Nevertheless, it does engage in formal conversations with other Churches: in addition to the ARCIC conversations with the Church of England, it has been in dialogue with the Lutheran Churches since 1964 and has maintained dialogue with Orthodox Churches for many years. These conversations focus on understanding the theological and doctrinal issues over which the Churches have historically disagreed, to see if there is a way to find common ground.

Pluralism with reference to John Hick; its implications for interfaith and interdenominational relations

A key thinker on issues of religious pluralism, from a Christian point of view, is John Hick.

Hick is a **universalist**. Universalists believe that God's salvation will be available to everybody, whatever their religion. Hick starts with facts:

> [W]hether one is a Christian, a Jew, a Muslim, a Buddhist, a Sikh, a Hindu – or for that matter a Marxist or a Maoist – depends nearly always on the part of the world in which one happens to have been born. Any credible religious faith must be able to make sense of this circumstance. And a credible Christian faith must make sense of it by relating it to the universal sovereignty and fatherhood of God. This is rather conspicuously not done by the older theology which held that God's saving activity is confined within a single narrow thread of human life, namely that recorded in our own scriptures.

(John Hick: *God Has Many Names*). [Note 5]

Hick looks at the claims made by religions, and distinguishes between:

1 claims related to historical facts, which are in principle capable of being resolved (for example, was Jesus crucified outside Jerusalem by the Romans?), and

2 trans-historical questions (for example, what happens when you die?), for which there may be fundamentally different answers not settled with reference to facts.

When it comes to conceiving of God, or divine reality, he distinguishes between, on the one hand, the ultimately Real, as it is in itself, and on the other hand, the different views we have of it.

To get beyond factual and superficial differences between religions, it is important to establish what religion is for. For Hick, the crucial feature of religion, and its basic task is 'the transformation of human existence from self-centredness to Reality-centredness' (*God has Many Names*, page 95). Hick thus sees religion as primarily about self-transformation rather than historical or other truth claims. On that basis he argues that the incompatibilities between religions are not of real religious significance.

Hick's views have been challenged by many, including Paul Griffiths. [Note 6] He asks how to deal with religious groups that support extreme actions which other religions see as against the religious spirit, for example murder or suicide. Griffiths says it is unrealistic to say that the differences between some religious groups mainstream religion are superficial. To take an example, Islamic State cannot be considered 'similar' to any major mainstream religion, Islam included, as their beliefs are so fundamentally opposed.

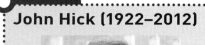

John Hick (1922–2012)

Hick was an English philosopher who had a particular interest in religious pluralism. One of his most popular books is *A Christian Theology of Religions: The Rainbow of Faiths* (1995, SCM).

Key term

Universalism The view that all humans will be saved by God, whatever their religion.

There are also issues for some religious groups whose practices go against the norms of society. Thus, for example, Jehovah's Witnesses reject the idea of having a blood transfusion, even if it is necessary to save life. Some breakaway Mormons engage in polygamy, and it is permitted in Islam, with qualifications and limitations designed to protect women, but mainstream western society does not allow polygamy. This makes it difficult to frame religiously neutral legislation that can accommodate such views. According to the teachings of Islam, for example, people should follow what is taught in the Qur'an and the Hadith, but there may be conflicts with the norms of behaviour and legislation in a western democratic society.

Future opportunities to turn to God

Hick argues that a combination of human freedom and the vulnerability of human life together provide a context for people to learn and grow spiritually. You will remember that in his theodicy (Volume 1 on the Problem of Evil) he describes life as a 'vale of soul-making'.

Because Hick does not accept the idea of hell, he then faces the problem of what happens to those who do evil within this life. His view is that, if a loving God is eventually to allow all to be saved, then there must be other opportunities, beyond this life, to do good, and thus to gain salvation. He therefore suggests that there are other lives, beyond death, during which there are further opportunities to grow spiritually and come to God.

This can be compared with the Roman Catholic doctrine of Purgatory. *The Catechism of the Catholic Church* (1992) [Note 7] says that 'Purgatory is the state of those who die in God's friendship, assured of their eternal salvation, but who still have need of purification to enter into the happiness of heaven.' Hick's view differs from this in that, for him, everyone who dies can achieve 'purification'. Also, Hick seems to focus on future lives in this or other worlds, rather than a single temporary state beyond death.

▲ A sixth-century mosaic from the Basilica of Sant'Apollinare Nuovo, Ravenna. It shows the Parable of the Sheep and the Goats from Matthew's Gospel.

Hick's view is in tension with some passages from the Bible. One example is Matthew's account of the teaching of Jesus known as the Parable of the Sheep and the Goats (Mt 25:31–46). In this, the goats are condemned to eternal punishment. The usual interpretation of this is that some people are not saved. Hick rejects a literal application of this, and instead suggests that the story might be a response to the persecution of Christians in the earliest Church. The early Christians may have wanted to see their persecutors punished, and included the parable to support this. This would make the story less decisive as a basis for Christian belief, but Hick cannot dismiss the fact that it still remains a feature of the early view of judgement.

A key feature of the parable as it now appears in Matthew's Gospel (25:31–46) is that judgement does not depend on the acceptance of Jesus, nor even on the recognition of him at all. Those who are blessed are surprised to find themselves rewarded, because they have not consciously acted for Christ. It is their behaviour towards others that is the basis of judgement. In so far as they helped (or rejected) those in need, they were in fact helping (or rejecting) Christ. This argument based final judgement squarely on ordinary secular behaviour, not on religious commitment. This is a useful biblical basis for the case for universalism: judgement completely ignores or bypasses religious affiliation. However, this is not a conclusive case for inclusivism: there is still a clear indication that those who do not engage in good moral conduct are destined for destruction.

If Hick's views were generally accepted, they might help to build relationships between different religions (**interfaith relations**) and between different churches within Christianity (**interdenominational relations**). The implications of what he says about religion as self-transformation, and about universal salvation could, potentially, bring people of different beliefs together. However, although his positive view of pluralism contributes to understanding between faiths at a community level, the theological ideas that underpin his views are not widely accepted.

For Christians, one major problem lies in his views about life after death. Conventional Christianity teaches that humans live one life, and then die and are judged. Hick's idea that there are other lives beyond death goes against that teaching. Because of this, even most liberal Christians see his universalism as something separate from Christianity.

Different denominations within Christianity have their own specific reasons for finding Hick's views unhelpful. Protestant Evangelicals in particular do not accept his view of universal salvation. Roman Catholics see him as mistaken when he dismisses the importance of specific beliefs and practices and the uniqueness of truth revealed through the Church. His writing and ideas are complex, and appeal more to scholars and theologians than to ordinary churchgoers, in any case.

For members of some other faiths, Hick's view that religion depends on self-transformation rather than truth claims is wrong. Islam and Judaism, for example, depend on specific truth claims about the nature of God. Hick's idea of the 'ultimately Real' cannot do justice to the reality of God as Muslims and Jews understand God to be.

In Islam, Christianity and Judaism, Hick's universalism challenges the claim of each faith to be the one true faith. Hick himself may be universally inclusive, but the monotheistic faiths do not recognise his view of their

Key terms

Interfaith relations
Relationships between different faiths, and between worshipping communities of different faiths, for example, between Islam, Judaism and Christianity.

Interdenominational relations
Relationships between different Christian Churches, for example, between the Roman Catholic Church and the Church of England.

religion, although individuals within these faiths may do so. Hinduism, Buddhism and Sikhism are naturally more inclusive that the monotheistic faiths, and their concept of the ultimately Real is closer to Hick's. However, only Sikhism would generally accept the view that differences between faiths have no significance.

Even for those of no faith, Hick's view that religion is a universal experience is a problem. Atheists such as Dawkins argue that the very idea of God is redundant and that self-transformation is a completely human process. Hick's theodicy is a prime example of how trying to explain the world in terms of religion makes it over-complicated. The simplest, and therefore the obvious viewpoint is that God does not exist and that religion is worthless.

For these reasons, Hick's views have little impact on formal relationships either between faiths, or between different denominations in Christianity.

However, for some individuals, Hick's ideas help to reconcile the different teachings of religions with an inner sense of the one-ness of human religious understanding. Hick views the relationship between humans and ultimate reality as something shaped by culture and history. This makes sense to those who try to see beyond specific contexts to look for a universal understanding.

Christian responses to issues of freedom of religious expression in society

Different views about the role of the Church in the world lead to different approaches to religious freedom.

1 Evangelical Christians in particular emphasise the importance of personal commitment to Christ, the need to be 'born again', and the necessity to become part of the Church, the Body of Christ on Earth.

2 Other Christians may see themselves as called to work for transformation of society. They argue that they should contribute to moral and social debate from their distinctive perspective. They may want to promote civic order, on the grounds that it contributes to the common good.

Those who emphasise the first approach are more likely to prefer the separation of Church and State, and to allow a greater measure of freedom of religious expression (often only for their own religion) within society. They may also claim freedom of expression to strongly oppose (using force if necessary) actions within society they see as contrary to their faith, for example abortion.

A biblically-based, evangelical approach to Christianity emphasises that Christ's kingdom is not of this world (John 18:36), and therefore that secular rules have no relevance to personal salvation. Salvation is entirely a matter of grace through faith in Christ. Since personal choice is key, such a view emphasises the importance of complete freedom in matters of religion. The government has no part to play in the process of salvation. Even if the rules of society are in line with Christian morality, following them or trying to enforce them is irrelevant, because obedience to secular rules is not the same as a personal relationship with God.

Those who emphasise the second approach see it as a Christian responsibility to promote Christian values within society for the benefit of all. This view has generally prevailed in western society since the seventeenth century.

Most Christians now take the view that individual freedom to practise any religion or none is an essential feature of society. Such freedom is needed for genuine moral choice. For example, in the statement *Religious Freedom, the Path to Peace* delivered on 1 January 2011 for the World Day of Peace, Pope Benedict XVI said:

'Respect for essential elements of human dignity, such as the right to life and the right to religious freedom, is a condition for the moral legitimacy of every social and legal norm.' [Note 8]

From both the Catholic and evangelical perspectives, freedom from imposed religious conformity, and freedom to make a personal choice, are necessary requirements for both morality and personal commitment.

Freedom of expression

The Universal Declaration of Human Rights states that 'everyone has the right to freedom of opinion and expression'. The question is whether it is right to have situations where the expression of religious views should be limited or forbidden. We have seen above (page 321) that certain things that people claim are expressions of religion, such as FGM and forced marriages, are not permitted by law. There are situations where the general social good can override the right to express religious convictions publicly. People can be protected by law from speech which incites violence or racial hatred. It is harder to see how they can be protected from being offended. Offence is subjective, and different people are offended by different things.

In Britain, following the **Human Rights Act of 1998** and the **Equality Act of 2010**, there is considerable protection from discrimination on grounds of 'religion and belief'. These two laws changed the situation from one of passive tolerance of religion and belief to one where religious freedom is actively promoted.

Christians see people as created in the image of God, and a person's relationship with God is an essential part of who they are. Any attempt to restrict their expression of the Christian religion is a restriction on them as a person, preventing them from being fully human.

One question about the free expression of religious views is what to do when it appears to conflict with equality legislation. For example, should a Christian running a bed-and-breakfast be free to object to a homosexual couple renting a room, on the grounds that their religion considers homosexuality to be a sin? Equality legislation in this instance has been interpreted as favouring of the rights of the gay couple and their right to be treated equally to others, but this appears to conflict with the religious conscience of those running the hotel.

Freedom of religious expression also gives people the right to express opposition to views on practices that some people justify on the basis of their religious faith, for example, views on abortion, euthanasia, FGM, forced marriage and homosexuality.

Case study: Wearing a cross

In one well-publicised case, a British Airways employee, Nadia Eweida, was told by her employer that she could not wear a lapel cross on her uniform while at work. The case was finally decided by the European Court in 2012 **[Note 9]**. The secularist argument was that displays of religious affiliation should not intrude into the workplace. The religious response was that it was an indication of the person's religion that would cause no harm.

At the same time, the court had to decide whether a nurse, Shirley Chaplin, should be allowed to wear a cross on a chain – something prohibited by the NHS Trust for which she worked.

The European Court overturned BA's ban on Eweida wearing her cross, but supported the NHS in the case of Chaplin. In the case of Chaplin, wearing any necklace was judged to be a health risk in hospital – a purely secular reason for upholding its ban.

Christians might argue that wearing a cross is not a blatant attempt to make converts, or to push religion while interacting with other members of the public, but simply an expression of who they are and what they hold to be of value. On the other hand, in a multi-faith secular society, there is the fear that religious symbols of any sort run the risk of being divisive.

▲ Nurse Shirley Chaplin was not allowed to wear a cross while working

An important consideration in these cases is whether the particular action or belief is central to the practice of the Christian faith, or only peripheral. For example, if Christians were banned from meeting for worship that would clearly attack a fundamental feature of the faith. The question is, is wearing a cross as jewellery attacking a fundamental feature of the faith? Is requiring a Christian registrar to conduct a civil partnership against her convictions about the nature of marriage attacking a fundamental feature of the faith?

The problem is deciding in such cases what is an essential expression of one's Christian faith and what is not. When a registrar refused to conduct a civil ceremony, for example, she argued that the Church's teaching on marriage was a core feature of her faith. The argument against her was that requiring her to conduct the ceremony as part of her job did not interfere with the core feature of her faith, her right to *worship* as she wished.

There are many questions, big and small, that hinge on this distinction. In France, secular society insists that pork should be on school menus, even though it is goes against the religion of Muslim and Jewish children who attend school. Is there a fundamental difference between religious dietary rules, and a secular choice to be vegetarian? Should everyone be forced to eat meat of all sorts if that is the majority view in society?

In these cases, the fundamental question is whether religion should be a personal matter, or whether it should be upheld by public attitudes and institutions. In general, there is an assumption today that society is secular. However, politicians continue to claim that Britain is 'a Christian country' (for example, David Cameron's Christmas message, 2015). This kind of language is also used in more sinister ways by those who want to coerce immigrants to accept social practices which may have Christian origins.

Society in Britain today is, in general, both liberal and plural. People have a right in law to be treated with equal respect, whatever their race, gender, religion or sexual orientation. However, Christianity includes principles and moral teachings that, for historical reasons, or simply because they are based on a narrow interpretation of the Bible, appear to go against this assumption of equality. For example, many Churches disapprove of homosexual acts. Of course, within the Churches, the status of members of the lesbian, gay, bisexual and transgender (LGBT) community varies greatly, and many are welcomed into Christian fellowship. However, it remains difficult for some Christians to work with the assumption of equality that is expected in a secular society, for example, the hotel owners who refused to rent rooms to homosexual couples.

A balance is required. One way to achieve this would be not to attempt to impose one specific set of religious beliefs on others, not to limit or subvert their religious rights in any way, and not to behave in a way that puts others at risk, or prevents the normal exercise of their work.

Technical terms for Christianity, migration and religious pluralism

Anonymous Christians A view proposed by Karl Rahner, that people who are not Christians in practice, worship or belief are nevertheless able to experience grace and salvation.

Ecumenism Initiatives to develop relationships between Christian Churches to promote Christian unity.

Evangelism Spreading Christianity by preaching or by personal witness. Not to be confused with Evangelicalism, which is a branch of Christianity that sees the spreading of the gospel as a primary responsibility for Christians.

Exclusivism The view that one religion is the only true one, and that other religions are wrong.

extra ecclesiam nulla salus The Roman Catholic teaching that there is no salvation for those who are outside the (Roman Catholic) Church.

Inclusivism The view that although one religion is true, other religions may show aspects of the one true religion.

Interdenominational relations Relationships between different Christian churches, for example, between the Roman Catholic Church and the Church, of England.

Interfaith relations Relationships between different faiths, and between worshipping communities of different faiths, for example, between Islam, Judaism and Christianity.

Luke/Acts The Gospel of Luke and the Book of Acts were written by the same author, so when talking about Acts, it is customary to refer to the writer as 'the author of Luke/Acts'.

Migration The movement of substantial numbers of people from one place to another.

Multicultural Made up of many different cultures, which may include different nationalities, beliefs, values and social customs. This term has a wider scope than *multiracial*, which refers only to race, and *multi-faith* which applies only to religion.

Religious pluralism A situation where people of many faiths live in the same society without conflict, respecting one another's views.

Secular state a country where the government, legislature and society are not controlled by, or dependent on, the teachings of a religion.

See A diocese; the region and people under the control of a bishop.

Universalism The view that all humans will be saved by God, whatever their religion.

Summary of Christianity, migration and religious pluralism

The relative and the absolute

When people from different cultures live in the same society, it is called multiculturalism, and one aspect of this is that people of different cultures may also have different faiths. Different religions, and different branches within religions, make competing claims to know the truth. Absolute claims mean that there can only be one truth, and this leads to dissent and conflict. Relative claims to truth risk diluting the basis of people's faith.

Historical background: How migration has created multicultural societies, which include Christianity

Migration has always been a feature of society, sometimes by conquest or for trade, and sometimes for social or economic reasons or to escape war. In the second half of the twentieth century, immigration from Eastern Europe, the Indian subcontinent, the Caribbean and Africa has made Britain a multicultural society. While many welcomed this, some felt that British identity was threatened.

1 Diversity of faiths in Britain today

According to the 2011 Census, nearly 60 per cent of British residents are Christian, 25 per cent claim no religion, 5 per cent are Muslim and the other world faiths together make up 3.2 per cent.

2 Freedom of religion as a human right in European law

The Universal Declaration of Human Rights, Article 18 stipulates that there should be freedom of thought, conscience and religion for theistic, non-theistic and atheistic beliefs. EU and British law also uphold these rights. It is, therefore, against the law to prohibit or restrict the practice of religion.

3 Religious pluralism as a feature of modern secular states

In an ideal multicultural society all cultures are respected and celebrated. Multiculturalism leads to a rich, diverse society. Some people oppose multiculturalism because the lack of common values can lead to a society that lacks cohesion. If immigrant communities do not integrate, this can lead to conflict.

There is a tension between the positive qualities of multiculturalism and the conflicting truth claims of religions associated with different cultures. Where cultural practices claim a religious dimension, there may be problems if the practices are contrary to British law. For example, female genital mutilation is a cultural practice of some Asian and African societies. When immigrant communities mix cultural practice and religious values, they may claim FGM is a religious requirement, even though it goes against all mainstream religious teachings.

Competing religious claims to truth could be measured by using reason to judge between them, but religious believers may not be persuaded by reason, because belief depends on personal experience and commitment. The psychological need for certainty is met by religious beliefs and moral teaching. This partly explains the attractiveness of fundamentalism, which offers clear teaching on belief and moral issues at a time when society in general seems to offer only vague ethical principles.

4 Exclusivism and inclusivism

In a situation where there are a number of different religions with different beliefs, they may relate to one another in an exclusive way (My religion is the only true one) or an inclusive way (Parts of other religions are the same as mine, so parts of them are true). Some beliefs are completely incompatible.

Inclusivists believe their own religion teaches the truth more completely than others, but they recognise some truth in other religions. This view has been the position of the Roman Catholic Church since the Second Vatican Council.

Christian attitudes to other faiths: Exclusivism with reference to John 14:6

John 14:16 seems to claim that faith in Christ is necessary for salvation. Fundamentalists and many evangelicals take this to mean that there is an urgency to convert those of other faiths. The traditional Catholic idea of *extra ecclesiam nulla salus* (there is no salvation outside the Church) expresses a similar position. More recently the Catholic Church has clarified this, to say that there is no *certainty* of salvation outside the Church.

Barth opposed the view of Christianity as being simply one religion among many, and instead argues that all religions come under the judgement of Jesus Christ. This view is both inclusive (all are judged equally) and exclusive (Judgement of Christ).

For exclusivists, salvation is only possible through a personal relationship with Christ. However, this seems to limit God's grace to practising Christians, which makes God seem less powerful.

As an argument for exclusivism, John 14:16 is not conclusive. It appears only in John's Gospel, and all the Gospels were written by the Church long after Jesus' death, so it is unlikely to be an accurate account of the words of Jesus himself. Jesus' actions and other teachings suggest a much more inclusive approach.

1 Inclusivism with reference to the concept of 'anonymous Christians'

A number of New Testament texts suggest that God plans salvation for everyone, but they do not specify how people of other faith are to be saved. Barth's view is that differences between religions are unimportant, because only God's grace matters. This kind of inclusivism could be described as universalism, and is rejected by those who see salvation as something brought about by specific religious commitment.

Another view is that of Rahner, who suggests that those outside Christianity who are under God's grace are 'anonymous Christians'. 'Anonymous Christianity' suggests that people who are not Christians in practice, worship or belief are nevertheless able to experience grace and salvation. This means that people of all faiths and none participate in salvation, and this makes them effectively 'Christian' in terms of salvation.

Fundamentalists oppose Rahner's view because it challenges their exclusivism. Others, for example, Hick, see 'anonymous Christianity' as being patronising to other faiths. Hick prefers to see all faiths as intrinsically worthwhile in their own terms, offering God's salvation directly without any reference to the path of a single faith.

2 How Christian denominations view each other

From the earliest days there have been differences within Christianity. Despite the attempt of Constantine to impose uniformity at the Nicene Council in 325, the Churches in the East and West continued to drift apart until the Great Schism of 1054 saw a formal separation between the Orthodox Churches and the Catholic Church. The Protestant Reformation in the sixteenth century split the western Church. At about the same time, the Church of England also split from the Catholic Church.

Key issues of difference between Churches include: whether or not to have central leadership and authority; practices such as baptism and communion and their importance; the organisation of Churches; biblical interpretation; worship styles; and core doctrines.

The Roman Catholic Church emphasises the role of tradition, and the institution of the Church as preserver of that tradition. It sees Churches which have separated from it as having lost the authority of tradition. For this reason, the Roman Catholic Church views other Churches as 'separated brethren' who may have some of the authentic qualities of the Christian tradition, but have lost the certainty of truth. This is a qualified exclusivist position.

Protestant evangelical Churches focus on the priesthood of all believers, and the idea that each individual Christian has a direct relationship with God. Salvation can only come through God's grace. They measure other Churches by their faithfulness to scripture, and consider rituals and central authority with suspicion. Since anyone who has not made a personal commitment cannot be saved, they consider members of Churches which do not share their views on scripture and commitment as outside the Church. This is an exclusivist position

The Church of England includes a range of views, from quite evangelical to Anglo-Catholic. Officially, the Church of England recognises other Churches even where they are different in matters of organisation, practice, doctrine or worship, and they work willingly with other Churches even when there are doctrinal differences. Although individual Church communities may have views coloured by their churchmanship, in general, the Church of England is inclusivist with respect to other Churches.

Ecumenism is the process of developing relationships between Christian Churches to promote unity. Ecumenical organisations such as the World Council of Churches focus on what Churches have in common, so that they can work together in practical ways. The Roman Catholic Church is not part of the World Council of Churches, but does engage in dialogue with other individual Churches on matters of doctrine and practice, for example, the Anglican-Roman Catholic International Commission.

Pluralism with reference to John Hick; its implications for interfaith and interdenominational relations

John Hick is a key thinker on issues of religious pluralism. He is a Universalist: he believes that 'all religions have an equal claim to share in absolute truth'. He sees religion of all kinds as the way people are transformed from self-centredness to reality-centredness. The differences between faiths are incidental – what matters is this common role they all share. There are problems with Hick's view – it cannot account for religions which teach violence or cruelty, and it is challenged by those whose religious faith separates them from the norms of society.

Hick believes that all human beings come under the care of a loving, religiously neutral God, and all will eventually be saved. If people die without sufficient spiritual growth, he suggests that they will have other lives in which to develop until they are ready for salvation. Although this is somewhat similar to eastern views of rebirth and reincarnation, Hick's view differs because he sees it as a process of spiritual evolution rather than working out the positive and negative consequences of previous lives.

A biblical challenge to Hick's universalism can be found in the Parable of the Sheep and Goats in Matthew 25. Although people are saved based by their actions towards others, and not by their religious beliefs, they are condemned or saved based on this one life alone. Whilst liberals in Christianity and other faiths may see Hick's views as a possible way forward for interdenominational and interfaith relations, in reality, they offer an alternative theology which has limited contribution to make to either.

Christian responses to issues of freedom of religious expression in society

Attitudes to religious freedom vary. If religion is seen principally as a set of beliefs and a relationship with God, Christians argue for separation of Church and state, and for freedom of religious expression for themselves. If it is seen as a role people have in the world, Christians aim to promote Christian values in society, and see freedom of religious expression for all as important.

Evangelicals and Catholics tend to emphasise the other-worldliness in Jesus' teachings, and reject the role of the state or society in matters of religion.

Freedom of expression is guaranteed by Article 19 of the Universal Declaration of Human Rights. However, this does not give people the right to express views that incite racial hatred or violence. British law (the Human Rights Act, 1998 and the Equality Act, 2010) protects people from discrimination on the grounds of religion or belief. There have been several high-profile cases where people have claimed that their right to freedom of religious expression has been violated, and these have generally been decided based on how far a particular 'expression' is a core belief of their religion, in the context of the events.

The fundamental question is whether religion should be a personal matter, or whether it should be upheld by public institutions. Although UK society is largely secular, many still claim it is 'a Christian country', and the Church of England has a position of privilege in society and institutions. Society is, in general, both liberal and plural, and this challenges Churches and other faith communities on issues such as sexual equality and sexuality.

12

The dialogue between Christianity and philosophy

You will need to consider the following items for this section

1 Beliefs and teachings about:

- God
- self, death and afterlife
- sources of wisdom and authority
- religious experience
- the relationship between scientific and religious discourses
- the truth claims of other religions
- miracles.

2 In the process of looking at these beliefs and teachings, you need to consider:

- How far the belief is reasonable – that is based on reason and/or is consistent with reason
- How meaningful the statements of faith are, and for whom
- How coherent the beliefs are, and how consistent they are with other beliefs in the belief system
- The relevance of philosophical enquiry for religious faith, with particular reference to the debate about the nature of faith as 'belief in' or 'belief that'.

First: how to approach Dialogues

1 **By the time you get to Dialogues, you will already have done most of the hard work**. You are NOT required to learn vast amounts of new material for the Dialogues section. Almost all of what you will need you will have covered from your study of Philosophy, Ethics and Christianity.

2 **In 'doing' the Dialogues, you will be automatically revising what you have done on Philosophy, Ethics and Christianity**, and this was intended to be the case, so that you can focus on critical analysis/critical awareness/evaluation.

So: **do not get hung up (so to speak) on memorising content**: it isn't about that. In the past, candidates have often confused critical analysis with making lists of arguments in favour of a point of view followed by arguments against that point of view. That is nothing more than AO1 – knowledge – so you need to get beyond that in order to show your skills of analysis.

3 **The whole ethos of Dialogues is about *broad* questions**: it is not about the nitty-gritty of the specification.

4 **In writing essays, the balance between Christianity and Philosophy or Christianity and Ethics, is up to you.** You do not have to worry about getting a 50/50, 40/60 or any other balance in your answers. You DO have to refer to both Christianity and Philosophy, or Christianity and Ethics in order to answer the questions set.

5 Equally, whether you are writing about the Dialogue between Christianity and Philosophy or Christianity and Ethics, **you can use any material you have studied that is relevant to the question. It does not matter if you have studied it as part of Christianity OR Philosophy OR Ethics, as long as it is relevant to the question.**

For example, questions on God in connection with evil might draw on material from both Philosophy and Ethics.

6 **You get a choice with the Dialogues questions**: you do one of two questions.

7 **All Dialogue questions have the same format**: a statement followed by the rubric of: 'Critically examine and evaluate this view with reference to the dialogue between Christianity and Philosophy' (or 'Christianity and ethical studies' or 'Christianity and the views of a named scholar').

8 **Dialogue questions are 'unstructured'**, meaning that the AO1 and AO2 are not separated.

For example, these are the questions from the first set of Specimen Assessment Materials on the Dialogue between Christianity and Philosophy:
● **'Christian beliefs about the afterlife are reasonable.'**
  Critically examine and evaluate this view with reference to the dialogue between Christianity and Philosophy. **[25 marks]**
● **'Religious experience gives Christians knowledge of God.'**
  Critically examine and evaluate this view with reference to the dialogue between Christianity and Philosophy. **[25 marks]**
Whichever of these two questions you choose to answer, 10 marks are available for AO1 and 15 marks for AO2.
You can either separate the AO1 from the AO2 in your answer, so giving your answer in two parts, **or you can combine them**.
The Dialogues Mark Schemes are published with the AO1 and AO2 given separately, but that is only for the benefit of examiners and of learning centres: again, your answers do not have to separate AO1 and AO2.
9 Note that for Dialogues, as for all A-Level exams, **AO2 is now worth 60% of the total marks available.**

10 **The emphasis is on the word 'dialogue', and not on listing facts** or listing what different Christians, theologians and philosophers have to say.

11 Remember that **where questions have named scholars, the only scholars whose names might appear in questions are those listed in the specification.** The questions will NEVER require more than you have been told to study. You can, of course, include relevant material from other named scholars in your answers: that is up to you.

How to approach the seven dialogue areas for Religion and Philosophy

To repeat what was said above, approaching the Dialogues sections is NOT a case of learning yet more facts. You will have looked at the facts in the units of Philosophy, Ethics and Christianity. Dialogues is about what you *do* with the facts.

Remember that in looking at the dialogue between Christianity and Philosophy:

- It isn't necessarily a case of Christianity being *opposed* to Philosophy. Many of the great philosophers have been Christians, and they have raised the questions to be debated.
- You can draw on the work of scholars who have already been engaged in dialogue, including all those named in the specification.
- You can also draw on the work of other scholars; for example, those referred to in this textbook and in Volume 1.
- You do not have to restrict yourself to the dialogues between scholars: You can have the dialogue with Christians and/or with scholars: for example, you can interrogate Hume on miracles, or Aquinas on the Cosmological Argument, or Stace on religious experiences.

So that you can see the breadth of this dialogue, here is a table of the scholars named in the Philosophy chapters: both those required for study in the specification, and those mentioned by the textbook to illustrate aspects of each area of study:

Table of scholars for the Philosophy chapters		
Specification topic	**Scholars required for study**	**Other scholars referred to**
Design argument	Paley	
	Hume	
Ontological argument	Anselm	Barth
	Gaunilo	
	Kant	
Cosmological argument	Aquinas	Copleston
	Hume	
	Russell	
Evil and suffering	Hick	Mackie
	Griffin	Plantinga

Table of scholars for the Philosophy chapters		
Specification topic	**Scholars required for study**	**Other scholars referred to**
Religious experiences	Otto James Stace Swinburne	St Teresa of Ávila Freud
Religious language	Hick Hare Wittgenstein Tillich Aquinas	Ayer Hume Popper Flew Ramsey Pseudo-Dionysius Maimonides Buber H.H. Price
Miracles	Hume Wiles	Augustine Aquinas Flew Holland Tillich Ward Hick Mackie
Self, death and afterlife	Descartes	Plato, Aristotle, Ryle, Hume, Fox, Penrose & Hameroff, Nagel, Jackson, Campbell, Locke, Parfit, Hick, Price, Swinburne, Stevenson, Dennett, Bohr, C.G. Jung, Whitehead, Griffin

Looking now at the Dialogues topics from which exam questions will be drawn:

God

This is a huge topic, because by definition 'God' gets everywhere into Christianity and the Philosophy of Religion.

For example: in Volume 1, 'God' appears in the following chapters:

- arguments for the existence of God
- the problem of evil and suffering, which is largely about trying to make sense of evil in the face of God's attributes of omnipotence, perfect goodness and omniscience, and God's relation to time (for example a timeless God presumably knows the entire future)
- religious experiences from God, and how God relates to the world
- Christian sources of wisdom and authority: God underpins all of these

Activity

From this (Volume 2) textbook, briefly note down where particular ideas are being made about God in the Philosophy chapters on Religious language, Miracles, and Self, death and afterlife. Also do this for the Christianity chapters on gender and sexuality, science, secularisation, and migration and religious pluralism.

- 'God' in Christianity – Christian monotheism; God as omnipotent Creator and controller of all things, transcendent and unknowable; the doctrine of the Trinity; Jesus as (the) Son of God
- Christian beliefs about God and the afterlife
- Christian moral principles in so far as they derive from/depend upon God.

You can see, then, that you have a great deal of material to draw on in any Dialogues question involving God.

- Remember that Dialogues questions are intentionally broad, so you are at liberty to draw on anything that is relevant to the question asked.
- Remember that it is up to you to decide what to select in answering Dialogues questions. You can use whatever you think is most relevant.
- It would be better to draw on a few themes/ideas, and not to attempt to include too much, otherwise you might end up listing facts rather than answering the question.

Activity

In the two sets of Specimen Assessment Materials published by AQA, there are two Dialogues questions where 'God' is given specific mention:

- **'Religious experience gives Christians knowledge of God.'**

  Critically examine and evaluate this view with reference to the dialogue between Christianity and Philosophy.

- **'Christian statements about God are meaningless.'**

  Critically examine and evaluate this view with reference to the dialogue between Christianity and Philosophy.

For each question, using the textbook, your notes, and Levels of Response AO1 and AO2:

1 Sketch out the evidence and ideas (AO1) that you might use to explain *what the debate in the question is about and what the key facts are*, for example (for the first question), the ways in which Christianity sees religious experience bringing knowledge of God, and what natural explanations there may be for such experiences.

2 Work out how you would tackle the critical analysis and evaluation of the statement: what **case** would you set out to make, and how would you use your AO1 sketch to illustrate it?

3 Write out a 420-word essay covering the AO1 aspects of your answer.

4 Write out a 630-word essay covering the AO2 aspects of your answer.

Note that both word counts are approximate. Try counting the number of words at the end of your essays in order to get used to writing this length of response. The word counts are of course only advisory.

You could consider doing the remaining AO1 and AO2 essays as homework exercises, and/or as timed essays in class.

Self, death and afterlife

The focus here is on the Christianity chapter on Self, death and afterlife (Chapter 8 in Volume 1). For Philosophy, the focus is on the parallel chapter on Self, death and afterlife (Chapter 3, page 70).

You therefore have a ready-made contrast between Christian ideas and philosophical ideas on the subject.

For the Christian ideas, you have sections on the meaning and purpose of life; different Christian understandings of resurrection; some textual material (1 Corinthians 15:42–44 and 50–44); and different interpretations of judgement, heaven, hell and purgatory (including the idea of 'objective immortality' in Process Theology). Also, God has to *exist* in order to grant life after death.

For philosophical ideas, you have sections on: the nature and existence of the soul; Descartes' specific argument for Substance Dualism; the body/soul relationship; and the possibility of continuing personal existence after death. These range from modern forms of Dualism (for example that of Swinburne), to Hick's monist 'replica' theory, to Dennett's functionalist view that human minds could run on a computer platform – for some, there is no God, so this is the only kind of immortality.

You are not, therefore, going to be short of material on which to draw.

Activity

This is one of the essays from the Specimen Assessment Materials:

'Christian beliefs about life after death are reasonable.'

Think of the many opportunities and choices you have here. For example:

- The fact that Christians do not agree as to whether resurrection is bodily or spiritual.
- Hick's attempt to show that resurrection of the body is logically possible ('replica' theory).
- The support for religious ideas from Descartes' Substance Dualism/Swinburne's version of Dualism/Dual-Aspect Monism and objective immortality.
- The rejection of Christian ideas by physicalists/materialists (for example Bertrand Russell; Gilbert Ryle).
- The rejection of Christian ideas by Parfit and Dennett.
- The possible synthesis we find in Dual-Aspect Monism and Panpsychism and Process Theology.

Using the same activity format as described above for **'God'**:

1 Sketch out the evidence and ideas (AO1) that you might use to explain *what the debate in the question is about and what the key facts are* – for example, what Christian beliefs about life after death are and why these are rejected by some philosophers.

2 Work out how you would tackle the critical analysis and evaluation of the statement: what **case** would you set out to make, and how would you use your AO1 sketch to illustrate it?

3 Write out a 420-word essay covering the AO1 aspects of your answer.

4 Write out a 630-word essay covering the AO2 aspects of your answer.

Sources of wisdom and authority

If you look at page 238 of Volume 1, the sources of wisdom and authority are neatly laid out for you in the diagram. For Christians, these sources include:

● God
● Special Revelation (for example scripture, religious experiences, the ongoing work of the Holy Spirit)
● General Revelation (for example reason and conscience)
● The Church (In Catholicism: the Apostolic Tradition stemming from Jesus to the Apostles, to the Church and the Church Fathers; also the Apostolic Succession to the Pope and the Magisterium; in Protestantism: particularly *sola scriptura*, and the authority of the pastor).

For the dialogue with Philosophy, there are a number of ideas and arguments which question the Christian sources of wisdom and authority.

For example, the diagram on page 238 of Volume 1 shows that most religious authority stems from God, since God's authority gives authority to Church, scripture, tradition, reason and religious leaders. Any challenge to the existence (and thereby the authority) of God is a challenge to all other forms of religious authority.

Activity

Using the relevant textbook chapters, together with any other resources, discuss and make notes on how the following might challenge Christian sources of wisdom and authority:

● the problem of evil

● scientific authority

● religious language

● free will and moral responsibility

● Bentham's rejection of Christian moral and political authority.

Remember that you are looking at *philosophical* arguments, so with religious language, for example, think of the Logical Positivists.

Are there any other areas of debate between Christianity and Philosophy that might be relevant?

Religious experience

You will have studied the following aspects of religious experience in Volume 1 and may have drawn on many examples of Christian religious experiences as you did so:

● corporeal, imaginative and intellectual visions
● Rudolf Otto on the numinous
● William James on mystical experiences
● Walter Stace on non-sensuous and non-intellectual union with the divine.

For philosophical analysis of religious experiences, you will have looked at:

- Swinburne's principles of credulity and testimony
- the challenges of *verifying* religious experiences
- scientific challenges (and religious responses).

In addition to the chapter on Religious experience, there are a number of other relevant ideas; for example:

- in the section on Religious language: Christian Religious experiences (for example those in the Bible) are expressed in specific ways (as with visions and mystical experiences). Is the language cognitive or non-cognitive?
- in Self, death and the afterlife, are near-death experiences specifically religious?

To remind you, **the Specimen Assessment question** – 'Religious experience gives Christians knowledge of God' – specifically links religious experience with knowledge of God.

The relationship between scientific and religious discourse

The main chapter for this is Chapter 9 Christianity and science (page 257), which covers a lot of the ground:

- how and why science has influenced Christianity, and Christian responses, with reference to:
  - the emphasis on reason and evidence in science
  - specific scientific discoveries
  - science as a stimulus to Christian ethical thinking.
- developments in Christian thought:
  - scientific challenges to Christian belief: the 'God of the gaps'; Darwin's theory of evolution
  - contemporary responses to the Big Bang theory (and creationist views).
- John Polkinghorne on the compatibility of religion and science
- different Christian responses to issues raised by science: genetic engineering.

In addition, think about the relevance of the following sections:

- Christian appeals to science/observation/experience in the Design Argument (Paley) and the Cosmological Argument (Aquinas).
- Scientific objections to accounts of religious experiences.
- Religious language:
  - the challenges of the verification and falsification principles to the meaningfulness of religious language
- Hume's main *inductive* argument against miracles.
- Scientific accounts of immortality (for example, Functionalism).

Again, depending on the question, there is a lot you could choose from. Remember also H.H. Price's argument about **'belief in' and 'belief that'** (Volume 1, pages 14–15).

Activity

From the Specimen Assessment Materials, we have this question:

'Science is an enemy of Christian faith.'

1 As a group, consider which parts of the material we have picked out on scientific and religious discourse might be used to construct an answer to this question.

2 Select your own route into the question and answer it.

3 Print and share essays.

4 As a group mark them using the 10- and 15-mark Levels of Response for Dialogues questions.

The truth claims of other religions

The material for much of this is in Chapter 11 Christianity, migration and religious pluralism (page 316). It also invites you to consider whether believers can challenge the beliefs of other religions without attacking their own.

For those who would like something extra, R.B. Braithwaite has an interesting take on religious pluralism.

Braithwaite's view is that the problem of the conflicting truth-claims of the world's religions can be addressed by suggesting (for example) that different cultures and different religions respond to and interpret 'God' in different ways. If there is one God, however, how is it that each religion understands God by a different revelation – for example that of Muhammad in Islam, that of Paul in Christianity, and that of Siddhartha Gautama in Buddhism? Also, how is it that each religion has different teachings?

One answer is that their different beliefs are non-cognitive interpretations which nevertheless share a common denominator.

This view is suggested by the work of R.B. Braithwaite. No question can require you to refer to Braithwaite's ideas, but you can refer to them where they are relevant.

R.B. Braithwaite (1900–90)

Braithwaite was an English physicist/mathematician who nevertheless became a Cambridge lecturer in moral sciences in 1928. During October 1946, the Cambridge Moral Sciences Club met in Braithwaite's rooms at King's College, and both Wittgenstein and Karl Popper were present. At one point the argument between the two became so heated that Wittgenstein apparently brandished a poker at Popper before leaving the meeting in a huff. The poker, of course, belonged to Braithwaite. [Note 1]

Braithwaite takes it for granted that religious language is not literal. His main idea follows Wittgenstein's view that the meaning of religious language is found through its use. In his view, religious statements are used **conatively**, meaning that they are to do with your *will*/what you *intend* to do, and this allows them to be empirically meaningful.

This is because (according to Braithwaite) religious statements express a believer's intention to act morally. If someone decides to become a Christian this primarily involves two things:

i   She *intends* to follow the Christian moral code: she puts its moral principles into action.

ii She adopts all the Christian 'stories' by which this moral code is expressed.

For example, a Christian who accepts the Christian belief that 'God is love' will put that belief into practice by adopting an agapeistic lifestyle (as in Situation Ethics). Where a Christian reads that Jesus forgave an adulterous woman, healed lepers and blind people, and fed 5000 people with a few loaves and fish, these stories are taken as commands to forgive others, to look after the sick, and to feed the hungry. Otherwise there is little point in the stories. Christians do not have to believe that these stories are true – some do, some do not – they just need to act on them. Even the story of Jesus' resurrection can be taken in this way: the resurrection brought hope to the disciples when they were in a situation of no hope, so a Christian's moral responsibility is to bring hope to those who have no hope.

Also, this means that the believer's intentions can be tested empirically. If she adopts an agapeistic lifestyle, then we can see that she practises what she preaches.

The same must be true for all religions. Jews, Muslims, Hindus, Buddhists and Sikhs can be judged by whether or not they put the moral principles of their religion into practice. Their ethical beliefs are basically very similar, but they are expressed in different stories. Perhaps the different stories are just different vehicles for expressing the same moral truths. **If so, then the world's religions are different, but equally valid expressions of ethical intention.**

Evaluation of Braithwaite's view

Most believers do not think that their religious views amount to non-cognitive moral intention – they think that their assertions are cognitive/factual. In Braithwaite's favour, however, the world's religions cannot all be factually correct, because some of the facts contradict each other, so some (or, more likely, all) believers must be wrong in thinking that their beliefs are cognitive.

Miracles

There is very little agreement among philosophers or Christians as to the nature or existence of miracles, but the view that the biblical miracles were actual historical events is based on beliefs about the authority of the Bible. Hume rejects miracles because he thinks they can be explained by (gullible) human psychology, and because inductively they must always be, by definition, the least likely explanation of what has occurred. As a Christian, Wiles also rejects them, because otherwise the problem of evil has no real answer. This topic is based on your study of miracles in Chapter 2. You may find it useful to draw on examples of miracles in Christianity in any answer on this topic.

Finally, the specification rubric suggests that in the process of looking at these beliefs and teachings, you need to consider:

- How far the belief is reasonable – that it is based on reason and/or is consistent with reason.
- How meaningful the statements of faith are, and for whom.
- How coherent the beliefs are, and how consistent they are with other beliefs in the belief system.
- The relevance of philosophical enquiry for religious faith, with particular reference to the debate about the nature of faith as 'belief in' or 'belief that'.

Whether beliefs (etc.) are **relevant**, **reasonable**, **meaningful**, **coherent**, and **consistent** with other beliefs are some of the standard words of evaluation, so when you write Dialogues essays, these are the kinds of question to bear in mind. Sometimes the question will specify this in its wording: for example, the Specimen Assessment question on Self, death and afterlife asks whether or not Christian beliefs here are **reasonable**. The second Specimen question on God asks whether statements about God are **meaningless**.

You should recognise that questions about 'meaning' and 'meaningfulness' are looking specifically at the Chapter on Religious Language, since the question: 'Is religious language meaningful?' is of central importance for Christianity.

The fourth bullet point, on 'belief in' and 'belief that', we dealt with earlier. To remind you, it features on pages 14–15 of Volume 1.

Activity

As a group, discuss and write down the links to other chapters in the textbooks, for example on the Existence of God, Evil and suffering, Religious experience, Religious language, and Self, death and afterlife, and Christianity and science.

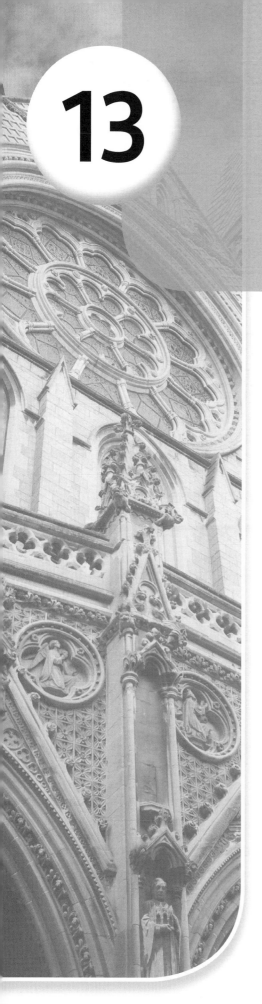

13 The dialogue between Christianity and ethics

You will need to consider the following items for this section

Christian responses to the following approaches to moral decision-making in the light of key Christian moral principles:

1 deontological, with reference to Kant

2 teleological and consequential, with reference to Bentham

3 character-based, with reference to Virtue Ethics

4 How far Christian ethics can be considered to be deontological, teleological, consequential, or character-based

5 Christian responses to:

- the issues of human life and death prescribed for study

- the issues of animal life and death prescribed for study

- theft and lying

- marriage and divorce

- homosexuality and transgender issues

- genetic engineering

6 Christian responses to issues surrounding wealth, tolerance and freedom of religious expression

7 Christian understandings of free will and moral responsibility, and the value of conscience in Christian moral decision-making.

The impact of other ethical perspectives and ethical studies on Christian views about these issues, both past and present. This may include:

8 challenges to and support for Christian views

9 compatibility of Christian views with those of other ethical perspectives

10 the relative strengths and weaknesses of Christian perspectives and other ethical perspectives studied on these issues

11 the implications of criticisms of Christian ethical teaching for the religion as a whole and its sources of authority.

Christian responses to the following approaches to moral decision-making in the light of key Christian moral principles

'Key Christian moral principles' refer primarily to the material in Chapter 9 (Volume 1), in particular:

- the Sanctity of Life Principle: the 'strong' and 'weak' forms of the principle. These are detailed in pages 313–317.

- issues of Dominion and Stewardship over animals and over the environment as a whole. These are detailed in pages 322–329.

Key Christian moral principles also include, for example: obedience to God; following the example of Jesus; the Christian 'cardinal' virtues of: prudence (practical wisdom), justice, fortitude (courage) and temperance (self-control), together with the religious virtues of faith, hope and love (see Volume 1, pages 127–128).

1 Deontological, with reference to Kant and
2 Teleological and consequential, with reference to Bentham

These two sections are placed together here, because they are dealt with in detail in the second section of Chapter 7 Bentham and Kant, under two titles:

- How far is Bentham's Utilitarianism consistent with religious decision-making? (Page 213)
- How far is Kant's Categorical Imperative consistent with religious decision-making? (Page 216)

'Religious' in both these sections means, specifically, 'Christian'.

Bentham is concerned primarily with the consequences of our actions, but his end-goal is the 'greatest happiness for the greatest number'. This means that his Utilitarianism is both a consequentialist and teleological system. His teleology is very compatible with Christian teleology, because it looks forward to the end-goal of eternal life with God in the Kingdom of Heaven. The difference is that Bentham's just, fair and happy society is focused on the 'here and now', since Bentham did not believe in any form of life after death.

In addition to the deontological aspects of Kantian ethics, you might also like to think about Kantian teleology, because there seems no doubt that Kant's idea of the *summum bonum*, the state of the 'highest good', where virtue has its reward, is closer to the Christian teleological aim of heaven, since for Kant, the *summum bonum* is brought about by God as a fair and just reward for fulfilling one's duty.

3 Character-based, with reference to virtue ethics

Clearly there is some compatibility between Aristotelian virtue ethics and Christianity, since the cardinal and religious virtues are firmly embedded in Aquinas' Natural Moral Law.

Since Chapter 4 on Virtue ethics (Volume 1) does not specifically look at the compatibility between Christianity and virtue ethics, here is an overview of the issue:

The compatibility between Aristotle's virtue ethics and Christian ethics

1 The most valuable aspect of Aristotle's virtue ethics for Christianity is its use in Aquinas' theory of Natural Moral Law, since Aquinas' views are a synthesis of Aristotelian ethics with Christian ethics:

- Aristotle's physics has a **teleological** focus, meaning that he assumes that everything has a specific function, end, or purpose; hence he develops his function argument in virtue ethics. Aquinas adopted this teleological focus into Natural Moral Law. Whereas for Aristotle the end of human activity is *eudaimonia*, for Aquinas it is union with God.
- From the virtues listed by Aristotle, Aquinas selected four as the '**cardinal' virtues** (from Latin *cardo*, 'hinge'), which he accepted as the foundation of natural morality: prudence (practical wisdom), justice, fortitude and temperance. The three Christian **theological virtues** are faith, hope and love, and these derive from St Paul in the New Testament. Together, the Catholic Catechism lists these as the '**seven virtues**'. The cardinal virtues are those that can be attained by human ability, whereas the theological virtues are given to humans through God's grace.

2 **Virtues are essential to all Christian views about morality**, and if a Christian focuses on the seven virtues, having those virtues will contribute to the development of the community as a whole. On the other hand, there are many Christians who follow Divine Command Theory, in which God simply decrees that certain actions are right and wrong, which is alien to Aristotle's thinking.

3 Fletcher's Christian version of Situation Ethics is sometimes seen as similar to Aristotelian Virtue Ethics, in so far as both theories are relativist, and are governed by an overriding principle: *agape* love and virtue respectively. The comparison is fair up to a point, but Situation Ethics would allow any action which brought about the most *agape* love, including adultery, theft and murder; whereas in the Nicomachean Ethics Aristotle states explicitly that such actions can *never* be virtuous (see point 4 below).

To be clear about relativism in Virtue Ethics, most modern discussions of relativism refer to cultural and historical differences between people, whereas Aristotle assumed that the virtues are known by reason, and are therefore universal in themselves as qualities. In other words, the virtues of courage, generosity, self-control and truthfulness – in fact all the virtues – are the same for all times and places. Truthfulness does not change over time as a quality: it is relative only in relation to the dispositions of individual people in particular situations.

4 Jesus is often seen as the epitome (the high point) of human virtue, because like Aristotle, Jesus focused on personal disposition rather than on rules and regulations. For example, in the Sermon on the Mount, Jesus says this about adultery:

'You have heard that it was said, "You shall not commit adultery." But I say to you that every one who looks at a woman lustfully has already committed adultery with her in his heart.' (Matthew 5:27–28).

Further, Jesus comments on murder:

> 'You have heard that it was said to the men of old, "You shall not kill; and whoever kills shall be liable to judgment." But I say to you that every one who is angry with his brother shall be liable to judgment.' (Matthew 5:21–22a).

Jesus is suggesting here that people who focus on the rules and consequences concerning murder and adultery are missing the point: morality is about the will, about intention, and about personal dispositions. This emphasis on personal disposition rather than simply on action brings Christian ethics closer to Virtue Ethics. Obedience to the rule is important (5:17 – 'Think not that I have come to abolish the law and the prophets …'), but obedience to the rule is achieved not by actions, but by having a virtuous mind which does not think lustful or angry thoughts.

> In the Nicomachean Ethics, Aristotle says that actions such as adultery, theft and murder can never be virtuous because they do not correspond to anything in a virtuous mind. They cannot be thought about in connection with a mean, and there is no excess or deficient way of committing such actions: one cannot select the right person to murder or to commit adultery with; '... rather, however they are done, they are in error.' [1107a 24] [Note 1]

On the other hand, Jesus' actions are sometimes rather extreme to be compatible with Aristotle's virtue ethics: for example in the same section of Matthew's Gospel referred to above, Jesus says:

> 'If your right eye causes you to sin, pluck it out and throw it away ... And if your right hand causes you to sin, cut it off and throw it away; it is better that you lose one of your members than that your whole body go into hell.' (Matthew 5:29–30)

Even if Jesus is speaking figuratively here, such behaviour would not really be compatible with Aristotle's doctrine of the mean.

4 How far Christian ethics can be considered to be deontological, teleological, consequential, or character-based

The basic distinctions between deontological, teleological, consequential and character-based ethics, are detailed in Chapter 4 (Volume 1).

You might like to think about the following:

1 The chapter on **Aquinas' Natural Moral Law** (Volume 1: 4:1) emphasises that the primary precepts are not deontological rules about specific actions: they are teleological – concerned with our final end, which has three points of focus:

- Our *telos* (goal/purpose/end) on Earth is happiness: what Aquinas calls 'human flourishing'.
- The *telos* of humanity as a whole also has an ultimate focus. Complete happiness cannot be found in something created, but only in the 'beatific vision' of God that is promised in the next life.
- The *telos* for humanity as a whole is the vision of God – union with God; but Aquinas also thought that each person has an individual *telos* based on their natural abilities (or lack of them).

By contrast, the secondary precepts, which are derived from the primary precepts, are deontological/rule-based.

Aquinas also emphasises the *virtues* of character, together with the theological virtues of faith, hope and love, so to that extent Christian ethics is character-based.

2 Situation Ethics is consequentialist: it aims to achieve the most *agape*-love in the situation, which does suggest that we have a duty to love, although legalism by definition lacks love. Some Christians who follow Fletcher's theory have the teleological aim of heaven. Others seek to bring about a loving Christian kingdom in this life.

3 Divine Command Theory is deontological, since all biblical rules must be obeyed. It is also teleological in the sense that the final goal and reward of obeying God's moral commands is heaven.

Activity

This is one of the essays from the Specimen Assessment Materials:

● **'Christian ethics is deontological.'**

Critically examine and evaluate this view with reference to the dialogue between Christianity and ethical studies.

Bearing in mind that *you* can have the dialogue with Christianity, (you do not have to study what a range of scholars think about this) plan out a separate AO2 response to this question (remembering that the AO2 is worth 60% of the overall mark of 25).

5 Christian responses to: the issues of human life and death and issues of animal life and death prescribed for study; theft and lying; marriage and divorce; homosexuality and transgender issues; genetic engineering

Remember to keep this section broad-based.

● For Christian issues of human life and death and animal life and death, you should use the Natural Moral Law and Situation Ethics sections from Chapter 5, Volume 1, Application of ethical theories (pages 209–216).
● For marriage and divorce, and homosexuality and transgender issues, see the last section of Chapter 8 Christianity, gender and sexuality (page 243).
● For genetic engineering, see the final section of Chapter 9 Christianity and science (page 281).

Activity

This is one of the essays from the Specimen Assessment Materials:

- **'Christian understandings of the nature and rights of animals have been undermined by ethical studies into animal rights.'**

Critically examine and evaluate this view with reference to the dialogue between Christianity and ethical studies.

Some 'ethical studies into animal rights' are described, for example, on pages 207–219 (Volume 1), where:

- the 'facts' are presented concerning the use of animals

  - as food
  - in scientific procedures/cloning
  - in blood sports
  - a source of organs for transplants.

Most of these 'facts' pick holes in Christian views on animal ethics (pages 207–209).

- Some Christian views are presented on pages 209–216 (Volume 1, Natural Moral Law and Situation Ethics). You do not need to refer to any other Christian views, but may do so if you wish.

- An alternative ethical view is given on pages 216–219 (Volume 1, Virtue Ethics). One point to note here is that much of Aquinas' Natural Moral Law View of the status of animals is derived from Aristotle.

- You may also want to consider the views of other writers such as Peter Singer and Andrew Linzey.

Bearing in mind that in this question, you might be the one to have the dialogue with Christians (and with Aristotle) on animal ethics: **outline how you might plan out the AO1 and the AO2 parts your response.**

6 Christian responses to issues surrounding wealth, tolerance and freedom of religious expression

For wealth, see Chapter 10 on Christianity and the challenge of secularisation: 'Responses to materialistic secular values: the value of wealth and possessions'.

For tolerance and freedom of religious expression, see Christianity, migration and religious pluralism: 'Christian responses to issues of freedom of religious expression in society'.

7 Christian understandings of free will and moral responsibility, and the value of conscience in Christian moral decision-making

For Christian understandings of free will and moral responsibility, see Chapter 5 in this volume.

For Christian understandings of the value of conscience in moral decision-making, see Chapter 6 in this volume.

Activity

Draw up a Table of scholars for the Ethics chapters along the lines of that given above for the Philosophy chapters (pages 346–347).

The impact of other ethical perspectives and ethical studies on Christian views about these issues, both past and present

8 Challenges to and support for Christian views

For 'challenges to and support for Christian views', don't forget that non-Christian ethics may support Christian views.

9 Compatibility of Christian views with those of other ethical perspectives

For 'compatibility of Christian views with those of other ethical perspectives', 'other ethical perspectives' includes, for example, Virtue Ethics, Bentham's Utilitarianism and Kant's Categorical Imperative.

10 The relative strengths and weaknesses of Christian perspectives and other ethical perspectives studied on these issues

'The relative strengths and weaknesses of Christian perspectives and other ethical perspectives studied on these issues' refers to the strengths and weaknesses of different Christian views, also of Bentham and Kant, on the ethical issues in Dialogues.

11 The implications of criticisms of Christian ethical teaching for the religion as a whole and its sources of authority

'The implications of criticisms of Christian ethical teaching for the religion as a whole and its sources of authority' is asking you: 'How do criticisms of Christian ethical teaching affect Christianity and its sources of authority?' For example:

● Natural Moral Law might be criticised as being out of touch with modern medical ethics
● Situation Ethics might be criticised for being too vague on how people ought to behave
● Divine Command Theory might be criticised for taking a literal view of the Bible's moral authority.

To what extent do such criticisms bother Christians? Do they damage the credibility of the Christian religion as a whole?

The Exam: Specimen Assessment Materials

1 Introduction and review

> **For all the details concerning A-Level exams, please see Volume 1, pages 353–71. What follows here assumes that you have read all of the chapter on the Exams and Specimen Assessment material in Volume 1.**

History is littered with examples of brilliant students who have not read or taken on board the instructions on exam papers.

For ease of reference, the A-Level guide in Volume 1 contains the following:

- Preliminary advice + Specification layout: pages **353–354**.
- General advice of Mark Schemes, Levels of Response, Assessment Objectives, and Specimen Answers: page **355**.
- Sitting the exam after 2 years: pages **356–357**.
- New A-Level AO1 Levels of Response: page **363**.
- New A-Level AO2 Levels of Response: page **364**.
- Specimen AO2 Christianity candidate response + exercise: page **364–366**.
- Some general rules for answering questions: page **366–367**.
- Effective preparation and revision: page **367–368**.

2 Student sample answers for A-Level topics

For A-Level, below are some additional specimen answers to questions from the Specimen Assessment Materials:

Christianity

Note that mistakes in grammar and spelling have not been corrected.

A01

Examine why there are different views in Christianity concerning the issues of:

● Marriage
● Homosexuality.

You should refer to both issues.

[10 marks]

Sample student answer

Different Christian views occur because there are different ways of interpreting the Bible. Conservative evangelicals take the Bible literally for all time, and liberals interpret it in the light of scholars and experience. Also different churches put different emphasis on scripture and tradition. Churches that use tradition a lot rely on church teachings, eg, the Catholic Church. Churches that think scripture is more important, eg Baptists just go straight to the Bible.

Genesis 2 says it is not right for man to be alone, and also that the two shall become one flesh. For literalists this means that marriage is important, but it has to be between a man and a woman because Adam and Eve were male and female. Liberals say that modern experience shows that being gay is OK even though Leviticus says it's wrong, so gay marriage is allowed, and divorce is allowed because our modern experience is different from the Bible writers.

Catholic teachings are in the Bible, but the tradition is the really important thing. There is a whole section of the Catechism about marriage. Catholics believe 'one man and one woman for life'. So marriage can't be between two people of the s ame sex, and divorce can't happen. They can separate but the church won't recognise divorce or let them remarry. Catholicism also teaches that priests, monks and nuns shouldn't marry so they can focus on God. Baptists base their ideas on scripture because of Luther's solar scriptura and don't like same sex marriage, but they allow divorce for unfaithfulness because the Bible says that is OK. They don't agree with celibacy for priests because in 1 Timothy it says leaders should be married to one wife.

Conservatives say homosexual sex is very bad because they read the Bible literally. Leviticus says it's an abomination, so that applies now as well. Liberals interpret the text and say that society and our understanding have changed since then, and we now think it's OK to be gay as long as people show love as Jesus taught. Roman Catholic teaching says that being gay is a kind of physical problem, and it is wrong for gay people to have sex. They base this both on the Bible and on the teachings of their tradition.

Activity

Using the A-Level A01 Levels of Response, what Level would you award this essay? Explain how your decision matches the grade criteria for that Level.

This is best done in pairs, followed by group discussion and agreement.

AO2

'Christian feminism has had little impact on Christianity.'

Evaluate this claim.

[15 marks]

Sample student answer

In some ways Christian feminism has had an impact and in some ways it has not, it depends a bit on how far you think Christianity has a problem with women generally. Some people say that God made men and women different but equal which is complimentary, but others think they should really be equal because God made them male and female in Genesis 1, also Paul said that being male or female doesn't matter in Christ. Feminism only has an impact if you think things need changing, and concervatives and fundermentelists don't think it needs changing because they think male headship is a good thing.

Feminism has made people think about how patristic the church is. Most of the people in the Bible are men, and most of the big theologians were men, so the whole church is dominated by them. Some people say this is OK because God made Jesus a man and all his dissiples were men too, so women don't have anything important to do. They get saved by getting pregnant and having babies instead, as Timothy says. Concervative evangelicles say this sort of thing.

But some people didn't like that much and thought women should be equal to men in the church. After all, there were some women who did things in the Bible like Feebee who was a deaconess somewhere near Paul. But Paul didn't like women speaking in churches and said they should shut up and only talk at home, he didn't let women teach either. Cathlics don't let women teach or preach because they agree with Paul.

There are three kinds of feminist theology. Liberal feminists think it is wrong to be patristic because women and men should be equal in the church, biblical feminists focus on the women in the Bible and what they did to show that women are just as important as men

really, Radicual feminists try to change the structure of the church to be fair to women which means letting women be preists etc. Scholar Daphne Hampson campaigned for women to be able to be priests in the Church of England, but got fed up with the sexism of the church and gave up because she said the church was just too sexist. However, she was a bit successful because women did get ordained in the Church of England in 1994 and there are now even some female bishops, but there are still some people even in the Church of England who are opposed.

Scholar Rosemary Radford Ruther was a Cathlic woman who tried to make Christianity more feminine generally. She said that God had female bits as well as male bits and the church should be able to see that. Jesus was nice to women so the church should be too. She said you could still be Christian and believe that women should be equal. As she was a Cathlic, she didn't really have much impact because the Pope and the tradition of the church is all male. She made a lot of people think about it, but that couldn't really change anything because the Cathlics are not democratic. Women can't be preists or popes but they can help out with arranging flowers or cleaning, that is not equal because arranging flowers dosen't have much impact. Rosemary RR retired and did echotheology instead which is all about women and nature.

In conclusion, feminist theology has had an impact a bit. The church of England lets women be clergy, but it hasn't done anything to the Cathlic church and that's bigger so really the impact is very little. Concervatives don't do feminist theology at all so there's no impact on them, therefore I agree with the statement that Christian feminism has had little impact on Christianity.

Activity

Using the A-Level AO2 Levels of Response, what Level would you award this essay? Explain how your decision matches the grade criteria for that Level.

This is best done in pairs, followed by group discussion and agreement.

Philosophy and religion

AO1

Examine the nature of mystical experiences.

[10 marks]

Sample student answer

Mystical experiences are experiences of God where a person does not have any sense experience of God. Instead God is experienced by the mind's eye. The scholar who described mystical experienced the fullest was William James. James took drugs so that he could understand what it was like to have a mystical experience.

Mystical experiences have four descriptions. 1 they are ineffable, meaning that the person has an intuition about what is going on. 2 they are noetic, so they cannot be described. 3 they are short, and 4 the person is passive, because God takes over their mind. If you have a religious experience with these four characteristics, this means that you have had a real experience of God, because these four characteristics are a common core to when we experience God. They are like a pattern, so if you have all four parts of the pattern, you must have experienced God.

William James said that you can get what you want out of religious experiences. The experience is to an extent what the person wants to see, so if you are a Viking warrior, then you will want to have a warrior's religious experience, because that is what is meaningful to you. If you are like Saint Theresa then you will have a mystical vision of Jesus, because that is what she wanted to see.

Activity

1 Pick out two major problems with this answer, and relate them to the wording in the AO1 A-Level Levels of Response.

2 What would you have included in an essay on this topic that the candidate has not?

AO2

'When the body dies, the person dies too.'

Evaluate this claim.

[15 marks]

Sample student answer

This statement would be the view of a materialist philosopher who argues that persons are nothing over and above their physical body and brain. The idea of a body includes its brain, because a person's body cannot exist without the brain – it would just be a lump of tissue and bone that could not move, eat or think. The view of materialists is based on observation: corpses do not get up and walk. To talk of life after death is an oxymoron, because life and death are opposite terms.

I think that the statement is therefore self-evidently true. Nobody has ever come back from the dead to say otherwise. Christians like to believe that Jesus was resurrected by God, but the evidence for that belief is contained only in the bible, an ancient book written by people who believed in miracles, a flat earth, and the creation of species as we now see them. They cannot be blamed for this but it is ridiculous to think that we should still accept prescientific claims about dead bodies arising from their tombs.

Persons are described in terms of their bodies and brains, and brains have memory and psychology, but these die when the brain dies, so no trace of what a person is like are left after death except what we can see in the children.

John Hick's replica theory is nonsense. God cannot recreate a replica of a dead person so that it is the same person. Persons occupy a unique position in space time and have their own physical structure which dissolves after death. The physical matter in a corpse becomes redistributed among the environment, so how is God supposed to fit the particles of Jim's original body into Jim's resurrected body if Jim died in a fire and his flesh turned to charcoal? If God gives Jim another body, it will not be the same body, so Jim cannot be the same person, whether or not we still refer to him as Jim. If a nuclear bomb wipes out a city, such as Hiroshima, then all the people in the centre of the explosion are obliterated. God would have to give all these people new bodies. Is this really likely, or is it wishful thinking?

The same is true with Hindu beliefs about reincarnation of the soul. Hindus believe that when they die the real person is the soul and this is reborn into another body. This is even worse than the idea of resurrection of the body, because it is not the same body in any way at all – in fact by definition it cannot be the same body, because samsara means that you have to re-embodied after every life. How can the person therefore be the same person?

Derek Parfit shows that when the body dies the person dies as well. He does this by thought experiments, for example the teletransporter. A person is (in the future) teletransported to Mars, where he works. His body is disassembled by the machine and reassembled on Mars in the same atomic order, so he is the same person. But what happens when a new machine is invented that simply creates a copy of the person (Jim) on Mars, so Jim now exists at the same time on earth as on Mars. He looks at and talks to his other self on Mars, and sees the shaving cut he got that morning, and his memories are exactly the same as those of Jim 2 on Mars. But eventually Jim 2 will become a new person for two reasons. (1) Jim 2 is made of different matter (different atoms) from Jim 1, and Jim 2 now has new sets of memories that he picks up on Mars that Jim 1 does not have. They cannot, therefore, be the same person.

In conclusion, when the body dies the person dies is right, because persons cannot be defined without their bodies. Locke's idea that the prince could wake up in a cobbler's body and still be the prince is cobblers.

Activity

1 This is an articulate answer with some strong points in it. What is the major weakness of the essay?

2 Using the A-Level 15-mark Levels of Response criteria, what Level would you put this essay into? Explain your answer by referring to the Levels statements.

Ethics and religion

AO2

'Situation Ethics is not an effective way of making moral decisions.'

Evaluate this claim.

[15 marks]

Sample student answer

To be effective, any method of making moral decisions has, quite simply, to work. How would any ethical theory work? – it could only do so by producing a just and fair society in which there were basic freedoms, respect for life, including that of the environment as a whole, and a general commitment to good inter-personal relationships. People would be well educated and articulate. No ethical theory can do all of that, so ethics has to go hand-in-hand with politics, and that is one of the most sensible claims made by Aristotle, since in all countries it is the politicians who hold the power. If you want something done, therefore, it has to be politically achievable, and this includes having an effective ethical system.

Situation Ethics (the variety suggested by Joseph Fletcher during the 1960s) is one such effective system. Its essential value is its emphasis on individual responsibility. Without that level of responsibility there can be no ethical behaviour as such. That is why Fletcher is anti-nomian – following rules cannot, by itself, amount to effective moral decision-making, because it removes human freedom, and freedom is the essence of morality.

Fletcher's Situation Ethics (SE) has four presuppositions: morality must be pragmatic, maximising agape love in the situation; relative to the situation (so there can be no words like 'never', or 'always', in people's moral statements); positive (affirming Christian belief), and personal (people take precedence over laws). This is a good basis for any theory, and Fletcher uses it through his book ('Situation Ethics') to give possible answers to a variety of ethical dilemmas, such as Bonhoeffer's attempt to assassinate Hitler; the correctness of dropping nuclear warheads on Japan to bring the war in the Pacific to a close with less loss of life; and the case of Mrs Bergmeier's sacrificial adultery'. Fletcher is not claiming that the decisions made here are right; rather they are morally effective, because they are real attempts to do the most loving thing in the situation.

However – is this enough? Normative ethical theories (such as Catholic Natural Law and Bentham's Act Utilitarianism) have for centuries proposed alternative ideas about how we should take moral decisions. Natural Law insists that God cannot be left out of the equation. Fletcher would deny this, but holds that God has given humans moral freedom to choose, so the 'Law' in 'Natural Law' already says too much. Catholics would point out one simple truth – that most people are not capable of

dealing with too much freedom of any kind, which is why we need a criminal justice system.

There is no doubt that if left to their own moral devices, somebody who was a situation ethicist could reach some truly horrendous moral decisions whilst believing that he or she was acting for the good of all. It is a cliché that Hitler believed he was doing the right thing, but presumably it was true, otherwise he would not have murdered so many people in so many appalling ways.

Reviewing Fletcher in a confined essay is not an ideal task, since his ideas are simple, but their application is not. How do we choose between different normative ethical theories? Who is to say that following God's moral commands is any worse or any better in practical terms than giving the greatest happiness for the greatest number, or developing virtues of character so that people are habituated into making good moral decisions? Fletcher's ideas are interesting, but they have not stood the test of time. Fletcher himself abandoned Christianity, although his ethical approach remained much the same, but without the religious bits.

Perhaps the most likely conclusion is that Fletcher's Situation Ethics is an effective way of making moral decisions, but it neither perfect nor the only way to be morally effective. Fletcher wants people to be morally responsible, so this must, in the end, mean that he would be happy for them to abandon Situation Ethics if their moral sense told them that there was a better theory. I would personally argue in favour of Aristotelian Virtue Ethics (updated to twenty-first-century culture), since habitual virtues of character seem to be a better base for effective decision making than leaving what you choose to do until the situation arrives.

Activity

Identify the strengths and weaknesses of this answer.

367

3 Student sample answers for Dialogues questions

For Dialogues, below are some sample answers to questions from the Specimen Assessment Materials:

'Science is an enemy of Christian faith.'

'Critically examine and evaluate this view with reference to the dialogue between Christianity and Philosophy'.

[25 marks]

Candidate's separate AO1 response

(N.B. the numbering is the candidate's.)

People would say this for a number of reasons. I shall examine the following ideas in my essay.

1 Science works by observation and experiment, whereas God cannot be seen or tested in any way, so they are completely different. Also, the scientific method is not like anything religious. The scientific method involves observation, testing, hypothesis, more testing, etc until the hypothesis is shown to be true or false, whereas religion just says that God did it.

2 Science gets results. It makes vacuum cleaners and cars, and makes life easier to live, so people can trust it. Christian faith does none of these things. In fact it can get you killed, depending on where you live in the world.

3 Science criticizes religion in many ways. For example scientists can scan the brain to show that certain areas of the brain light up when a person is having a religious experience, which shows that religious experiences are just things that happen in the brain. Also, people with epilepsy are more likely to have religious experiences than anyone else, so the experience is caused by a condition of the brain.

4 Science criticizes religion about creation and evolution. The bible says that God made the world in seven days, but this is not true. Science shows that the universe began about 13,000,000,000 years ago with a big bang, so God is not needed to create the universe. The bible says that human beings were made as we see them now, and that all species of animals were made in this way. But evolution shows that everything in biology descends from much simpler organisms over millions of years, including humans, so there was no special act of creation, so humans are not special.

5 Science criticizes religion because of miracles. Hume says that miracles are just the way that religious people interpret ordinary events. Hume has a scientific argument which he says disproves all miracles. Miracles are the most unlikely thing to happen, so if someone claims that they have seen or experienced a miracle, it is always going to be true that they were lying or they made a mistake.

6 Science criticises religious language. Religious people believe that their beliefs are facts, so Christians believe that Jesus was God and that Jesus performed miracles and died for our sins. The Logical positivism says that these ideas cannot be verified, meaning that you cannot touch, taste etc any religious facts, so they are not facts at all. The only facts are those which can be shown to be true by sense experience, so science shows that religious statements are meaningless.

Candidate's separate AO2 response

Science is an enemy of the Christian faith because it shows that the religion and its scriptures are no scientific. Christian views are not shown as true or false by observation and experiment. Religious views are show as true by the bible and by the church, so in the Catholic church the Pope and his council law down the rules about what catholics should believe. This cannot work because there is no evidence to back this up apart from what the pope says is true. The Pope condems contraception but this means that people in Africa are getting infected with AIDS and have to be treated with expensive drugs instead of using condoms to prevent the infection in the first place.

Science is an enemy of the Christan faith because it can show that religious experiences are not experiences of God. Instead they are just ways in which the brain works. Parts of the brain give us religious experiences, so we invent them, probably because they are a psychological help to us when trying to face the facts of death and disease (Freud).

Science is an enemy of the Christian faith because it criticizes Genesis and the stories of creation. Big bang theory shows that God could not have created the world, because science shows that the big bang just happened, and Bertrand Russell says that the universe is a brute fact, meaning that it doesn't have an explanation. There are also many Christians who still believe that evolution is false, and that science is their enemy because God's word is greater than any science.

Science is not an enemy of the Christian faith because some scientists argue that God could have started the big bang. John Polkinghourne is a christian priest and a physicist, and he says that the universe cries out for explanation. Also, we can do physics, so God must have created us with that ability. We can use physics to show that there may have been big bangs before this one, so the cycle of big bangs goes on, maybe for ever. We still have to show where the universe comes from, so God is the most likely answer.

Science is an enemy of the Christian faith because it criticizes miracles. God is omnipotent, so an all-powerful God must be able to do what he wants. Science does not tolerate unexplainable acts, and by definition miracles are unexplainable acts. This does not necessarily show that science is an enemy of the Christian faith, because scientific objections have forced Christians to think more deeply about what miracles are, and different scholars have different ideas. Maurice Wyles says that there is only one miracle, which is the act of creation itself, and that is ongoing. Other Christians avoid scientific criticism by arguing that miracles have anti-real force, for example, so Holland's story of the child on the railway line could be used to show that miracles are events that do not contradict scientific laws. This seems to be a better understanding of how science and religion should relate to each other, although perhaps this still doesn't provide a satisfactory response, since many Christians would argue that religion and science are different language games anyway.

Science is an enemy of the Christian faith because it shows that religious language is not factual. If that is the case, then what value does religion have in a scientific world? Facts are things that everybody can check. The facts of religion are just what religious people say are facts, but it would be just as easy to say that UFOs are facts.

Activity

1 Pick out three areas of the candidate's total response which you think contribute well as a response to the question.

2 Pick out three areas of the candidate's total response which you think are weaknesses in the candidate's response to the question.

3 At one point, the candidate does start to use critical analysis. Where precisely does this happen, and what makes it 'critical analysis'?

4 If the candidate's entire response was confined to the separate AO1 material, what Level would you give it, using the 10-mark Levels of Response?

5 As a group, decide what Level the complete response merits.

'Christian ideas of moral responsibility have been undermined by understandings of the nature of free will.'

Critically examine and evaluate this view with reference to the dialogue between Christianity and ethical studies.

[25 marks]

Sample student answer

Debates about free will take three positions. Some are determinists. There are different types of determinists. first of all, scientific determinists hold that the laws of physics are determined, because in physics everything goes back in a chain of cause and effect to the big bang, and if every cause has an effect, then we end up at the present by a determined chain of causes. In that case we can't have free will. It does not exist. We are therefore moral robots, and cannot be morally responsible. Christian ideas about moral responsibility do not therefore work, because we have no free will.

Another kind of determinism is theological. This follows from the belief that God is omniscient, knowing everything. If god knows the future, then God knows exactly what I will do for every second of my life. Again, then, I cannot have free will, because if God knows that I will do something at 4pm tomorrow, then I will do it, whatever I might think. Again, there can be no moral responsibility in the Christian sense because I am not free to choose my actions.

The second position is libertarianism. This means that I have the liberty to do what I want. Not absolutely what I want, but within limits. For example to some extent I am determined by my intelligence, so even if I wanted to solve quadratic equations at 10 a second I could not, because I am no good at maths. Also, to some extent I am conditioned by my upbringing and environment, so these might mean that I am more (or less) likely to go around killing people or robbing them. Apart from that, libertarians think that they are morally free to make their own decisions.

Libertarianism is the view that nearly all Christians take (apart from those who believe in predestination, which I do not), because it allows them to be morally responsible. Importantly, it means that people can be praised for what they do right and punished for what they do wrong. Especially it means that Christians can get to heaven if they choose to obey commands from God, or else they will go to hell. This is a real possibility for Christians, as we see in Jesus parable of the Sheep and Goats, where the goats are the bad guys who get send to hell because they did not do the Christian things like looking after the sick, visiting people in prison, looking after parents, and things like that. If the will is not free, then none of this makes sense. Christians assume that it makes sense, which is why they believe it, and so they assume they are free.

The third position is soft determinism, also called compatibilism, which holds that freedom is compatible with determinism because freedom requires determinism. Hume is the main scholar who defined this position. His argument was that everything we do is carried out within the causal framework of cause and effect, and that has to be true, otherwise everything would be random. People are restrained from doing band acts because they see that the cause of killing someone leads to the effect of being put in prison. Compatibilism (Hume) holds that we are free to follow our desires, so long as there are no other restraining factors working on us. Christians cannot really accept this argument because it is not real freedom. Freedom to act within the restraints of our wishes and desires is not true freedom. Also, soft determinists still believe in causal determinism, so how can we really be free in any sense of the word?

Since most scientists believe that causal determinism is true, otherwise science wouldn't work (there would be mayhem if the laws of science changed from day to day), science would say that we do not have the moral freedom that we think we do. For Christians, this means that moral responsibility is a mistake.

Some Christians believe that the mind is free in some unknown way, perhaps because quantum theory shows that the mind is not causally determined even though the brain is. Scientists see this as grasping at straws; Christians say that it isn't, otherwise life would not make sense. We feel we are free, so we are free.

Activity

Write a short critique/review of this essay: What are its strengths and weaknesses? How far does it answer the question? Is it sufficiently detailed? Does it show skills of critical analysis? Does it examine its facts and theories?

How would you have improved on this answer?

'For both Christianity and Virtue Ethics, voluntary euthanasia is wrong.'

'Critically examine and evaluate this view with reference to the dialogue between Christianity and ethical studies.

[25 marks]

Sample student answer

Voluntary euthanasia is where people want a good death because the pain of living is unbearable and they are going to die soon anyway. It is requested because the person cannot die without help from a doctor. Many people believe that people have a right to die as well as a right to life, and that if they wish to end their lives that is nobody's business but their own. Others don't agree, because they think that a dead person cannot change their minds, and the effects of allowing voluntary euthanasia on society would be terrible.

Voluntary euthanasia would be wrong for followers of Aquinas's natural law theory because people have a natural tendency towards life and not towards death. VE goes against the primary precept of preserving life, because once you are dead your life cannot be preserved. According to the Catholic Church today, VE is a sin because it rejects God's gift of life.

For other Christians, VE is not wrong, because to Situation Ethics Christians it all depends on the situation. There are no rules that have to be obeyed in SE, apart from the rule of love, and how love is applied always depends on the situation. If the person is in unbearable pain, and he has chosen to die without being pushed into it by others, then there is no obvious reason why VE should not be allowed. Joseph Fletcher said that prolonging life uselessly attacks a person's moral status. Some would say that there are too many risks with VE, but for Fletcher, moral decisions are about taking risks, because we have to make a judgment based on what we can see of the situation. If the judgment is wrong, then we are not morally to blame. In the same way a utilitarian works for the greatest happiness for the greatest number of people, but this also involves guessing what will happen in the future. All we can do is to take decisions according to what we believe will probably be the case. We cannot be blamed for not knowing the future.

This means the title is wrong, because SE Christians would accept VE in some situations but deny it in others, and Catholic Christians would always reject it. Other Christians would probably decide what to do on other grounds. For example, some Christians follow divine command theory, which is the theory that

God is all powerful and all knowing, so God must know best morally. On his theory we have to follow God's commands, and these are found in the bible. This is a position held by many protestant Christians who live by the sola scriptura rule. The problem with this is that there are no specific rules about voluntary euthanasia in the bibel, so what do we do? Most divine command Christians think that you should use the rules in the bible that are closest to the action you want to perform, so the most obvious rule is the commandment which says 'Thou shalt not kill', VE is killing, so VE is against the bible's rules. Another rule in the bible is that he who sheds somebody's blood will have his own blood shed. The bible says that God has a plan for every person for their life. Some Christians believe that your life is predestined, because if God is all knowing, he must know what you will do. If your life is planned out then God cares for every individual, so VE must be against God's wishes. In Jeramiah, God tells jeramiah that he knows him even when he was in his mother's womb, so if God cares that much about every individual then any form of VE must be wrong, however painful the person's situation is.

I think that the real problem with this question is that it assumes that all Christians think the same, whereas obviously they do not. Our vicar tells us all sorts of things that we should believe, including that God listens to your every words and sees your every thought, which worries my father lots. But surely God would have something better to do with his time. To think that God creates humans so that they spend 70 years or more doing what he wants them to do seems pointless – we would be nothing more than moral robots, whereas the essence of being a morally good person is that you do what you do from free choice. If you do what you do from fear of punishment in hell or reward in heaven, then you are just like a child who takes sweets when they're offered.

If the Bible reveals God's moral will, how is it that the Bible contradicts itself in so many places? In the Christian part of scripture, Paul says that everything is love, so the greatest thing a Christian can have and must do is love. In the old testament, however, God commits murder in a way that makes most generals seem tame by comparison. Why would *God* kill all the first-born children of people and animals in Egypt in order to make the king let the people go? I have forgotten virtue ethics.

In virtue ethics it depends on what counts as being the most virtuous action. The Greeks valued courage above most things, so one of the most courageous things would be to accept voluntary euthanasia rather than live on because you were scared of dying. The whole purpose of life according to Aristotel was to achieve well-being, and if you are suffering from some incurable disease or if you are dying from some wound, then the most courageous thing would be for somebody to put an end to your life at your request.

There are many cases in the textbooks about medical ethics where people are suffering from dementia and are also in pain, so there are cases when husbands kill wives and wives kill husbands as an act of love or virtue. To kill somebody in these circumstances might be considered a vice, because unless they asked to be killed beforehand, if dementia is set in, they may not be able to give an opinion. For most people, though, it would be seen as a virtue, because it involves the virtues of compassion for suffering, sympathy with the sufferer, honesty in telling yourself that you have to do this, love for the person involved, and mercy. The virtues outway the vices in such cases, so virtue theory would probably allow VE.

For Aristotle, one sign that you have acted virtuously in a difficult situation is where you feel regret at what you have done. He gives the example of a ship owner who has to get rid of his cargo in a heavy storm in order to save the lives of everybody on board. In the case of VE, a husband who killed his wife from virtuous reasons (not because he wanted her money) would feel a sense of regret because he is killing the person he loves, despite the fact that it relieves her suffering.

I have to conclude that the statement is wrong, since neither virtue ethics nor all Christians would see VE as being wrong. Probably, for most people, this would be an individual decision to make rather than one dictated by ethical theories, because VE is deeply personal, and depends on many things, such as your love for the person you might help to kill. Situation ethics probably says it best – it depends on the situation and on your motive for what you do, and in any particular situation, only you can assess those things.

Activity

The candidate made the important (but not uncommon) mistake of not reading the question properly, hence the startled announcement that virtue ethics had been 'forgotten'. Do try to read the question thoroughly.

1 Do you think that the candidate planned the essay (either part of it) before writing it?

2 Which is the best section of writing, and why?

3 Assess the Level of this essay in terms of the 10- and 15-mark Levels of Response indicators for Dialogues questions. Show how you reached your decision. How does it compare with the decisions of others in the group?

As a concluding comment to Volume 2, when you write essays, particularly those for Dialogues questions, try to be bold in the sense that you use all your critical faculties to reason out an answer. Thomas Aquinas says that if the highest aim of a captain were to preserve his ship, he would keep it in port forever, so push the boat out and see how far you can go.

Notes

1 Religious language

Note 1 www.iep.utm.edu/rel-lang/ (The explanatory comments in square brackets are not part of the quotation.)

Note 2 You can read an English translation of the *Tractatus* online, for example: http://archive.org/stream/tractatuslogicop05740gut/tloph10.txt

Note 3 Ayer, A.J.: *Language, Truth and Logic*, London, Victor Gollancz Ltd, FP 1936, p.115.

Note 4 Ayer, A.J.: *Language, Truth and Logic*, London, Victor Gollancz Ltd, FP 1936, pp.107–108.

Note 5 Ayer, A.J.: *Language, Truth and Logic*, London, Victor Gollancz Ltd, FP 1936, p.116.

Note 6 Ayer, A.J.: *Language, Truth and Logic*, London, Victor Gollancz Ltd, FP 1936, p.36 (quoting from Bradley's *Appearance and Reality*).

Note 7 Popper, Karl: *The Logic of Scientific Discovery.* (First published 1935), London, Routledge Classics, 2002, p.316.

Note 8 Flew, Antony: 'Theology and Falsification', in: *New Essays in Philosophical Theology*, ed. Antony Flew and Alasdair MacIntyre, London, SCM Press, 1955, pp. 96–97. Flew's account of the parable is reprinted from pages 13–14 of Chapter I, 'Theology and Falsification', in *The Philosophy of Religion*: (Oxford Readings in Philosophy) edited by Basil Mitchell, Oxford University Press, 1971.

Note 9 Flew, Antony: 'Theology and Falsification', In *The Philosophy of Religion*: (Oxford Readings in Philosophy) edited by Basil Mitchell, Oxford, Oxford University Press, 1971, p.14.

Note 10 Flew, Antony: 'Theology and Falsification', in *The Philosophy of Religion*: (Oxford Readings in Philosophy) edited by Basil Mitchell, Oxford, Oxford University Press, 1971, p.15.

Note 11 Flew, Antony: 'Theology and Falsification', in *The Philosophy of Religion*: (Oxford Readings in Philosophy) edited by Basil Mitchell, Oxford, Oxford University Press, 1971, p.15.

Note 12 Hick, John: 'Theology and Verification', Chapter III in *The Philosophy of Religion*: (Oxford Readings in Philosophy) edited by Basil Mitchell, Oxford, Oxford University Press, 1971, pp.59–60. [Article reprinted from: *Theology Today*, 17 (1960), 12–31].

Note 13 In: *A John Hick Reader*, edited by Paul Badham, Macmillan, 1990 (FP in *Talk of God*, ed. G.N.A. Vesey for the Royal Institute of Philosophy, London: Macmillan; New York: St Martin's Press, 1969.

Note 14 Hick's argument is in *The Philosophy of Religion*: (Oxford Readings in Philosophy) edited by Basil Mitchell, Oxford, Oxford University Press, 1971, pp 56–58. Hick's example is the claim that 'There are three successive sevens in the decimal determination of *pi*'. At the time Hick was writing, the solution of *pi* did not contain three successive sevens, but Hick argued that such a series could always occur at some point, because the decimal solution of *pi* is infinite, so the claim could at some point be verified if true, but could never be falsified if false.

There are two problems with this: 1) Three successive sevens have turned up in the decimal solution of *pi*, so the claim has been verified. 2) The solution of *pi* is a matter of mathematical *logic* and not of factual *experience*, so the argument fails anyway.

Note 15 Hare, R.M.: in *The Philosophy of Religion*: (Oxford Readings in Philosophy) edited by Basil Mitchell, Oxford, Oxford University Press, 1971, p.15.

Note 16 Flew, A.: in *The Philosophy of Religion*: (Oxford Readings in Philosophy) edited by Basil Mitchell, Oxford, Oxford University Press, 1971, p.22.

Note 17 Hick, John: *An Interpretation of Religion. Human Responses to the Transcendent,* Macmillan, 1989, page 348.

Note 18 Hick, John: *An Interpretation of Religion. Human Responses to the Transcendent,* Macmillan, 1989, p.349.

Note 19 Hick, John: 'Religion as Fact-asserting', pp. 15–33 in: *A John Hick Reader*, edited by Paul Badham, Macmillan, 1990.

Note 20 Hick, John: *Faith and Knowledge*, Second edition, Ithaca, Cornell University Press, 1966 (1957), p.195.

Note 21 Hick, John: *God and the Universe of Faiths.* Essays in the Philosophy of Religion, Macmillan Press 1988 (1973), pp.22–23.

N.B. For those who wish to get to closer grips with Hick's ideas, the first three chapters of this book are a rewarding read.

Note 22 Aquinas: *Summa Theologica* I, Qu.13.

Note 23 Vardy, Peter and Arliss, Julie: *The Thinker's Guide to God*, MediaCom Education Inc., pp.50–51.

Note 24 Hick, John: *Philosophy of Religion*, Second edition, New Jersey, Prentice-Hall, 1973 (1963), pp.69–71.

Note 25 Hick, John: *Philosophy of Religion*, Second edition, New Jersey, Prentice-Hall, 1973 (1963), p.71.

Note 26 Ramsey, Ian: *Religious Language: An Empirical Placing of Theological Phrases.* London, SCM Press, 1957.

Note 27 Taken from: Brian Davies: *An Introduction to the Philosophy of Religion*, Oxford, Oxford University Press, 1982, p.10 (quoting from: Moses Maimonides, *The Guide for the Perplexed*, transl. m. Friedlander (London, 1936), p.86ff. The text of the latter can be read online, for example at: www.teachittome.com/seforim2/seforim/the_guide_for_the_perplexed.pdf

Note 28 Davies, Brian: *An Introduction to the Philosophy of Religion*, Oxford, Oxford University Press, 1982, p.12.

Note 29 Tillich, Paul: *Dynamics of Faith*, New York, Harper & Row, 1957, p.42.

Note 30 Hick, John: *Philosophy of Religion*, Second edition, New Jersey, Prentice-Hall, 1973 (1963), p.73.

Note 31 Hick, John: *Philosophy of Religion*, second edition, New Jersey, Prentice-Hall, 1973 (1963), pp.73–74.

2 Miracles

Note 1 Ward, Keith: *Divine Action*, Collins, 1990, p.174.

Note 2 See, for example, the account at: www.snopes.com/luck/choir.asp

Note 3 Mackie, J.L.: *The Miracle of Theism. Arguments for and against the Existence of God*, Oxford, Clarendon Press, 1982, p.21.

Note 4 Badham, Paul: 'The Philosophical Theology of John Hick'; Chapter 1 in: *A John Hick Reader, ed. Paul Badham.* Macmillan, 1990, p.5.

Note 5 Ward, Keith: *Divine Action*, Collins, 1990, pp.171–172.

Note 6 Tillich, Paul: *Systematic Theology*, Volume 1, London, SCM, 1978, p.117. (quoted from Beverley Clack & Brian R. Clack: *The Philosophy of Religion. A Critical Introduction*, London, Polity Press, 1998, p.143.)

Note 7 Ward, Keith: *Divine Action*, Collins, 1980, Chapter 10.

Note 8 Ward, Keith: *Divine Action*, Collins, 1980, p.177.

Note 9 Hick, John: *God and the Universe of Faiths. Essays in the Philosophy of Religion,* Macmillan Press, 1988 (1973), p.51.

Note 10 Holland, R.F.: 'The Miraculous', in: *American Philosophical Quarterly*, Volume 2, Number 1: January 1965, pp.43–51 (University of Illinois Press).

Note 11 Hume, David: *Enquiries Concerning Human Understanding and Concerning the Principles of Morals:* Third Edition, revised by P.H. Nidditch, Oxford, Clarendon Press, 1975, Section X, 'Of Miracles', §87, p.110.

Note 12 Hume, David: *Enquiries Concerning Human Understanding and Concerning the Principles of Morals:* Third Edition, revised by P.H. Nidditch, Oxford, Clarendon Press, 1975, Section X, 'Of Miracles', §90–91, pp.114–116.

Note 13 Hume, David: *Enquiries Concerning Human Understanding and Concerning the Principles of Morals:* Third Edition, revised by P.H. Nidditch, Oxford, Clarendon Press, 1975, Section X, 'Of Miracles', §90, p.115.

Note 14 Hume, David: *Enquiries Concerning Human Understanding and Concerning the Principles of Morals:* Third Edition, revised by P.H. Nidditch, Oxford, Clarendon Press, 1975, Section X, 'Of Miracles', §90, p.115.

Note 15 Hume, David: *Enquiries Concerning Human Understanding and Concerning the Principles of Morals:* Third Edition, revised by P.H. Nidditch, Oxford, Clarendon Press, 1975, Section X, 'Of Miracles', §90, p.115, Note 1.

Note 16 Mascall, Eric, quoted by Antony Flew in: 'Miracles': pp.346–353 in: *Encyclopedia of Philosophy*, Volume 5, New York, Macmillan and Free Press, p.346.

Note 17 Hume, David: *Enquiries Concerning Human Understanding and Concerning the Principles of Morals:*

Third Edition, revised by P.H. Nidditch, Oxford, Clarendon Press, 1975, Section X, 'Of Miracles', §98, p.127.

Note 18 Hume, David: *Enquiries Concerning Human Understanding and Concerning the Principles of Morals*: Third Edition, revised by P.H. Nidditch, Oxford, Clarendon Press, 1975, Section X, 'Of Miracles', §93, p.117.

Note 19 Hume, David: *Enquiries Concerning Human Understanding and Concerning the Principles of Morals*: Third Edition, revised by P.H. Nidditch. Clarendon Press, Oxford, 1975, Section X, 'Of Miracles', §94, page 119.

Note 20 David Hume: *Enquiries Concerning Human Understanding and Concerning the Principles of Morals*: Third Edition, revised by P.H. Nidditch, Oxford, Clarendon Press, 1975, Section X, 'Of Miracles', §101, p.131.

Note 21 Hume, David: *Enquiries Concerning Human Understanding and Concerning the Principles of Morals*:

Third Edition, revised by P.H. Nidditch, Oxford, Clarendon Press, 1975, Section X, 'Of Miracles', §100, p.130.

Note 22 Wiles, Maurice F.: *Faith and the Mystery of God*, SCM, 1982, p.28.

Note 23 Wiles, Maurice F.: *God's Action in the World. The Bampton Lectures for 1986*, Xpress Reprints, 1993 (FP 1986), p.66.

Note 24 Wiles, Maurice F.: *God's Action in the World. The Bampton Lectures for 1986*, Xpress Reprints, 1993 (FP 1986), p.67, referring to Brian Hebblethwaite: *Evil, Suffering and Religion*, Sheldon Press, 1976, pp.92–93.

Note 25 Wiles, Maurice F.: *Faith and the Mystery of God*, SCM, 1982, p.71.

Note 26 Ward, Keith: *Divine Action*, London, Collins, 1990, Chapter 10: 'Miracles as Epiphanies of the Spirit.'

Note 27 Ward, Keith: *Divine Action*, London, Collins, 1990, p.181.

3 Self, death and afterlife

Note 1 Aristotle: *De Anima (On the Soul)*, written 350 BCE. Online at: http://classics.mit.edu/Aristotle/soul.1.i.html (Translated J.A. Smith), Book 1, Part 1.

Note 2 Aristotle: *De Anima (On the Soul)*, page 657: Translated J.A. Smith: file:///C:/Users/John/Downloads/Aristotle%20De%20Anima%202015.pdf

Note 3 Descartes, René: *Meditations on First Philosophy, with Selections from the Objections and Replies*; translated and edited by John Cottingham, Revised ed., Cambridge, Cambridge University Press, 1996 (FP 1986), p.3.

Note 4 The full title is: *Discourse on the Method of Rightly Conducting One's Reason and of Seeking Truth in the Sciences.*

Note 5 Descartes, René: *Meditations on First Philosophy, with Selections from the Objections and Replies*; translated and edited by John Cottingham, Revised ed., Cambridge, Cambridge University Press, 1996 (FP 1986), §85–86, p.59.

Note 6 Ryle, Gilbert: *The Concept of Mind*, Penguin Books, 1963 (FP Hutchinson, 1949), p.17.

Note 7 Ryle, Gilbert: *The Concept of Mind*, Penguin Books, 1963 (FP Hutchinson, 1949), pp.17–18.

Note 8 Hume, David: *The Immortality of the Soul*: from PDF: www.qcc.cuny.edu/SocialSciences/ppecorino/PHIL_of_RELIGION_TEXT/CHAPTER_7_SOULS/Hume-OnImmortality-Soul.htm

Note 9 Nagel, Thomas: *What Is It Like to Be a Bat?* Source: *The Philosophical Review*, Volume 83, Number 4 (October 1974), pp.435–450 (p.436); published by: Duke University Press on behalf of *Philosophical Review*. Stable URL: www.jstor.org/stable/2183914

Note 10 'Complementarity' was a term coined originally by William James, but taken up by the physicist Niels Bohr (1885–1962).

Note 11 See, for example: http://askanaturalist.com/do-we-replace-our-cells-every-7-or-10-years/

Note 12 Campbell, C.A.: *On Selfhood and Godhood* (The Gifford Lectures: 1953–1954 and 1954–1955), George Allen & Unwin, 1957, pp.76–77.

Note 13 The term 'TTS' is borrowed from H.P. Grice: 'Personal Identity', pp.73–95, in: John Perry (editor): *Personal Identity* (University of California Press), 1975.

Note 14 Derek Parfit: *Reasons and Persons*, Oxford, Clarendon Press, 1984. Parfit's thought experiments on brain fission and fusion appear in Part Three, on 'Personal identity'. This begins with a discussion of teletransportation (pp.199–201).

Note 15 Russell, Bertrand: *Why I am not a Christian*, 1957: taken from: www.personal.kent.edu/~rmuhamma/Philosophy/RBwritings/deathFinalEvent.htm

Note 16 Hick, John: 'Theology and Verification': Chapter III in *The Philosophy of Religion*, edited by Basil Mitchell (Oxford Readings in Philosophy), Oxford, Oxford University Press, 1971. (FP in *Theology Today*, 17 (1960), pp.12–31).

Note 17 For more details on this, see, for example: Michael Sudduth: *H.H. Price's Model of Disembodied Survival*: http://michaelsudduth.com/wp-content/uploads/2016/01/HHPrice.pdf

Note 18 See: Richard Swinburne: *The Evolution of the Soul* (Revised Edition), Oxford, Clarendon Press, 1997, p.299ff.

Note 19 Swinburne, Richard: *The Evolution of the Soul* (Revised Edition), Oxford, Clarendon Press, 1997, pp.309–310.

Note 20 Swinburne, Richard: *The Evolution of the Soul* (Revised Edition), Oxford, Clarendon Press, 1997, pp.310–311.

Note 21 In Richard Swinburne's contribution ('An Afterlife') to a Humanist Philosophers' Group conference at King's College, London, October 2002: 'Death: a Live Issue'; published in *Thinking About Death*, ed. Peter Cave & Brendan Larvor, London: British Humanist Association (2004), pp.38–42. Online transcript: D.H. Mellor: 16.8.04 – http://people.ds.cam.ac.uk/dhm11/Swinburne.html

Note 22 Swinburne, Richard: *The Evolution of the Soul* (Revised Edition), Clarendon Press, Oxford, 1997, p.311

Note 23 You might like to scan the *Bhagavad Gita* in English, for example at: www.dlshq.org/download/bgita.pdf

Note 24 Taken from *The New York Times* obituary article on Stevenson, 18 February 2007: www.nytimes.com/2007/02/18/health/psychology/18stevenson.html

Note 25 Stevenson, Ian: *Twenty Cases Suggestive of Reincarnation*, University of Virginia Press, 1966.

Note 26 Stevenson, Ian: *The Evidence for Survival from Claimed Memories of Former Incarnations* (reprinted from the *Journal of the American Society for Psychical Research*, Volume LIV – April 1960 – Number 2).

Note 27 Fox, Mark: *Religion, Spirituality and the Near-Death Experience*, Routledge, 2003, Chapter 5: 'Second sight? NDEs and the blind', p.224.

Note 28 Fox, Mark: *Religion, Spirituality and the Near-Death Experience*, Routledge, 2003, p.341.

Note 29 See, for example, www.near-death.com/science/experts/susan-blackmore.html

Note 30 For example, in the *New Statesman*, 22 December 2011: www.newstatesman.com/blogs/the-staggers/2011/12/richard-dawkins-issue-hitchens

Note 31 Dennett, Daniel: *Consciousness Explained*, Allen Lane, The Penguin Press, 1991, p.431.

Note 32 Dennett, Daniel: *Consciousness Explained*, Allen Lane, The Penguin Press, 1991, p.430.

Note 33 Taken from www.nybooks.com/articles/1995/12/21/the-mystery-of-consciousness-an-exchange/

Note 34 Griffin, David Ray: *Reenchantment without Supernaturalism. A Process Philosophy of Religion*, Ithaca & London, Cornell University Press, 2001, p.240.

4 Introduction to meta-ethics: the meaning of right and wrong

Note 1 Calvin, John: *The Institutes of the Christian Religion*, Book III, Chapter XXIII, section 2 (Translation as in: Janine Marie Idziak, *Divine Command Morality*, The Edwin Mellen Press, 1979, p.101).

Note 2 Barth, Karl: *Church Dogmatics*: Volume II, Part 2, Chapter VIII, section 36 (Translation as in: Janine Marie Idziak, *Divine Command Morality*, The Edwin Mellen Press, 1979, p.106).

Note 3 Barth, Karl: *Church Dogmatics*: Volume II, Part 2, Chapter VIII, section 36 (Translation as in: Janine Marie Idziak, *Divine Command Morality*, The Edwin Mellen Press, 1979, p.120).

Note 4 For example, in 1 Samuel 15 God commands King Saul to destroy the Amalekites, down to the last man and woman, infant and suckling, ox and sheep, camel and ass. Most people today would see this command as completely immoral; moreover, reason says that it is completely immoral; so it should not be obeyed.

Note 5 Bentham, Jeremy: *An Introduction to the Principles of Morals and Legislation*, FP 1789, Chapter 1, 'On the Principle of Utility', in: John Stuart Mill: *Utilitarianism*, Fontana, 1962, p.33.

Note 6 See: Attfield, Robin: *Ethics. An Overview*, Continuum, 2012, pp.172–173.

Note 7 Moore's *Principia Ethica* can be read online, for example at: http://fair-use.org/g-e-moore/principia-ethica

Note 8 The Trolley Problem was first devised by Philippa Foot: 'The Problem of Abortion and the Doctrine of the Double Effect': *Oxford Review*, Number 5, 1967. The original form of the problem concerned a judge considering whether or not to frame an innocent person in order to avoid a rioting mob taking bloody revenge on a particular section of the community.

The 'problem' has since been stated in many forms, including the one used here.

Note 9 Ross, W.D.: *The Right and the Good*, 1930. Taken from PDF: www.ditext.com/ross/right2.html

Note 10 Attfield, Robin: *Ethics. An Overview*, Continuum, 2012, p.173.

5 Free will and moral responsibility

Note 1 Laplace, Pierre-Simon: *A Philosophical Essay on Probabilities*, Chapter 2: taken from PDF: http://bayes.wustl.edu/Manual/laplace_A_philosophical_essay_on_probabilities.pdf

Note 2 Biographical information from: https://en.wikipedia.org/wiki/B._F._Skinner

Note 3 Chomsky's review of Skinner can be read on Chomsky's own website: https://chomsky.info/ which contains a large number of interesting articles.

Note 4 See, for example, the article by Michael Egnor: www.evolutionnews.org/2014/01/do_benjamin_lib/ See also the article in the *New Scientist*: www.newscientist.com/article/dn22144-brain-might-not-stand-in-the-way-of-free-will/

Note 5 This is the view of MT.

Note 6 Hume, David: *Enquiries Concerning Human Understanding and Concerning the Principles of Morals*, Third Edition, Oxford, Clarendon Press, 1975, Section VIII, 'Of Liberty and Necessity', §64, p.82.

Note 7 Hume, David: *Enquiries Concerning Human Understanding and Concerning the Principles of Morals*, Third Edition, Oxford, Clarendon Press, 1975, Section VIII, 'Of Liberty and Necessity', §69, p.89.

Note 8 Hume, David: *Enquiries Concerning Human Understanding and Concerning the Principles of Morals*, Third Edition, Oxford, Clarendon Press, 1975, Section VIII, 'Of Liberty and Necessity', §73, p.95.

Note 9 McAdoo, Oliver, in: Mike Atherton, Chris Cluett, Oliver McAdoo, David Rawlinson, Julian Sidoli, ed. Martin Butler: *AQA Philosophy (AS)*, Nelson Thornes, 2008, p.325.

Note 10 Skinner, B.F.: *Beyond Freedom and Dignity*, 1971: PDF at: https://archive.org/stream/Beyond_Freedom_and_Dignity/Beyond%20Freedom%20&%20Dignity%20-%20Skinner_djvu.txt – pp.26–27.

Note 11 Skinner, B.F.: *Beyond Freedom and Dignity*, 1971: PDF at: https://archive.org/stream/Beyond_Freedom_and_Dignity/Beyond%20Freedom%20&%20Dignity%20-%20Skinner_djvu.txt – pp.68–69.

Note 12 Hume, David: *Enquiries Concerning Human Understanding and Concerning the Principles of Morals*, Third Edition, Oxford, Clarendon Press, 1975, Section VIII, 'Of Liberty and Necessity', §77, p.99.

Note 13 Hume, David: *On the Immortality of the Soul*, 1777: PDF from: www.earlymoderntexts.com/assets/pdfs/hume1757essay4.pdf – p.28.

Note 14 Hume, David: *Enquiries Concerning Human Understanding and Concerning the Principles of Morals*, Third Edition, Clarendon Press, Oxford, 1975, Section VIII, 'Of Liberty and Necessity', §78, p.99.

6 Conscience

Note 1 Shakespeare: *Hamlet*, Act 3, Scene 1.

Note 2 *Psychological Reports*, 1993, 73, 1399–1402. Mark W. Durm and Shane Pitts, http://journals.sagepub.com/doi/pdf/10.2466/pr0.1993.73.3f.1399

Note 3 Langston, Douglas C.: *Conscience and Other Virtues: From Bonaventure to Macintyre*. Pennsylvania State University Press, 2001, p.89.

Note 4 Roubiczek, Paul: *Ethical Values in the Age of Science*, Cambridge, Cambridge University Press, 1969, p.154.

Note 5 Schleiermacher, Friedrich: *The Christian Faith*. Third edition (intro. Paul T. Nimmo), Bloomsbury, T & T Clark, 2016, §83, pp.341–42.

Note 6 Langston, Douglas, L.: *Conscience and Other Virtues: From Bonaventure to Macintyre*. Pennsylvania State University Press, 2001, p.39.

Note 7 Butler, Joseph: *Human Nature and Other Sermons*, ed. Henry Morley, [eBook #3150], Transcribed from the 1887 Cassell & Co. edition by David Price; Sermon 1, 'Upon Human Nature.' www.gutenberg.org/files/3150/3150-h/3150-h.htm

Note 8 Butler, Joseph: *Human Nature and Other Sermons*, ed. Henry Morley, [eBook #3150], Transcribed from the 1887 Cassell & Co. edition by David Price; Sermon II, III, 'Upon Human Nature.'

Note 9 Butler, Joseph: *Human Nature and Other Sermons*, ed. Henry Morley, [eBook #3150], Transcribed from the 1887 Cassell & Co. edition by David Price; Sermon III, 'Upon Human Nature.'

Note 10 Nietzsche, Friedrich: *Beyond Good and Evil. Prelude to a Philosophy of the Future.* Translated & Edited by Marion Faber, Oxford, Oxford University Press, 1998 (FP as *Jenseits von Gut und Böse: Vorspiel einer Philosophie der Zukunft*, Leipzig, 1886), pp.12–13.

Note 11 Fletcher, Joseph: *Situation Ethics. The New Morality.* Louisville, Kentucky, Westminster John Knox Press, (Introduction by James F. Childress), 1997, p.53.

Note 12 Langston, Douglas C.: *Conscience and Other Virtues: From Bonaventure to Macintyre.* Pennsylvania State University Press, 2001, p.22.

Note 13 *Catechism of the Catholic Church*, Part III, Sect. I, Chapter 1, Art.7, 1809 (Augustine: *De moribus ecclesiae catholicae*, 1,25,46:PL 32,1330–1331).

Note 14 Fletcher, Joseph: *Situation Ethics. The New Morality.* Louisville, Kentucky, Westminster John Knox Press, 1966, pp.154–165.

Note 15 Cordón, Luis A.: *Freud's World. An Encyclopedia of His Life and Times*, Greenwood, 2012, p.75.

Note 16 Freud, Sigmund: *An Outline of Psycho-Analysis. International Journal of Psychoanalysis* 21:27–84 (1940), p.29. From PDF: http://icpla.edu/wp-content/uploads/2012/10/Freud-S.-An-Outline-of-Psychoanalysis-Int.-JPA.pdf

7 Bentham and Kant

Note 1 Biographical details taken from: https://en.wikipedia.org/wiki/Jeremy_Bentham

Note 2 Bentham, Jeremy: *An Introduction to the Principles of Morals and Legislation*, FP 1789, Chapter 1, 'On the Principle of Utility', in: John Stuart Mill: *Utilitarianism*, Fontana, 1962, p.33.

Note 3 Bentham, Jeremy: *An Introduction to the Principles of Morals and Legislation*, FP 1789, Chapter 1, 'On the Principle of Utility', in: John Stuart Mill: *Utilitarianism*, Fontana, 1962, §3, p.34.

Note 4 Baron, Peter, http://peped.org/philosophicalinvestigations/revisting-kant/ 'Philosophical Investigations' is a very useful website resource.

Note 5 Russell, Bertrand: *The Problems of Philosophy*, Oxford, Oxford University Press, 1980 (1967), FP 1912, pp.2–3.

Note 6 Mill, John Stuart, in: 'Utilitarianism', Chapter 2, pp.268–269 in: *John Stuart Mill: Utilitarianism, On Liberty, Essay on Bentham, together with selected writings of Jeremy Bentham and John Austin*, ed. Mary Warnock, Fontana Press, 1962 (Utilitarianism FP 1861).

Note 7 Mill, John Stuart, in: 'Essay on Bentham', Chapter 2, p.99 in: *John Stuart Mill: Utilitarianism, On Liberty, Essay on Bentham, together with selected writings of Jeremy Bentham and John Austin*, ed. Mary Warnock, Fontana Press, 1962.

Note 8 Taylor, Vincent: *The Gospel According to St. Mark. The Greek Text with Introduction, Notes and Indexes*, Second edition, Macmillan: St Martin's Press, New York, 1966, p.488.

8 Christianity, gender and sexuality

Note 1 Ruether, Rosemary Radford, Sexism and God-talk: Towards a Feminist Theology, 1983

Note 2 Ruether, Rosemary Radford, *To Change the World: Christology and Cultural Criticism*, New York, Crossroad Publishing, 1981, p.46.

Note 3 Hampson, Daphne and Ruether, Rosemary Radford, 2017, 'Is there a place for Feminists in a Christian Church?' See http://ethics.academyconferences.com/index.php/shop

9 Christianity and science

Note 1 Russell, Bertrand: *The History of Western Philosophy*, George Allen & Unwin Ltd, 1961 (FP 1945), p.514.

Note 2 You can read this online at: http://darwin-online.org.uk/content/frameset?viewtype=text&itemID=F1497&pageseq=1

Note 3 Polkinghorne discusses such ideas in, for example: *One World. The Interaction of Science and Theology*, SPCK, 1986, Chapter 3, 'Order and Disorder'.

Note 4 See https://en.wikipedia.org/wiki/Reactions_to_On_the_Origin_of_Species – which contains an interesting cross-section of views.

Note 5 Collins, Francis: *The Language of God: a Scientist Presents Evidence for Belief*, Simon & Schuster, 2007, p.67.

Note 6 Polkinghorne, John: *Science and Creation. The Search for Understanding*, SPCK, 1988, p.11.

Note 7 Polkinghorne, John: *Science and Creation. The Search for Understanding*, SPCK, 1988, p.20.

Note 8 Polkinghorne, John: *Science and Creation. The Search for Understanding*. SPCK, 1988, p.21.

Note 9 Polkinghorne, John: *Science and Providence. God's Interaction with the World*, Templeton Foundation Press, 2005 (FP 1989), p.44.

Note 10 Polkinghorne, John: *One World. The Interaction of Science and Theology*, SPCK, 1986, p.28 (quoting from: A.N. Whitehead: *Religion in the Making*, Cambridge University Press, 1926, p.57).

Note 11 Polkinghorne, John: *One World. The Interaction of Science and Theology*, SPCK, 1986, p.29.

Note 12 Polkinghorne, John: *One World. The Interaction of Science and Theology*, SPCK, 1986, pp.30–31.

10 Christianity and the challenge of secularisation

Note 1 Dawkins, Richard: *The God Delusion*, (10th Anniversary Edition) Black Swan, 2009.

Note 2 McGrath, Alister: *The Dawkins Delusion*, SPCK, 2007.

Note 3 Martin, David: *On Secularization: Towards a Revised General Theory*, Routledge, 2005 p.186.

11 Christianity, migration and religious pluralism

Note 1 Text of 'Rivers of Blood Speech' from: www.telegraph.co.uk/comment/3643823/Enoch-Powells Rivers-of-Blood-speech.html

Note 2 Rahner, Karl, Imhof, Paul and Biallowons, Hubert: *Dialogue: Conversations and Interviews 1965–1982*. Crossroads Publishing Co., 1986

Note 3 Hick, John: *God has Many Names: Britain's New Religious Pluralism*. Westminster John Knox, 1980, p.50.

Note 4 *Ut Unum Sint: On Commitment to Ecumenism*. §18. This may be read online at: http://w2.vatican.va/content/john-paul-ii/en/encyclicals/documents/hf_jp-ii_enc_25051995_ut-unum-sint.html

Note 5 Hick, John: *God Has Many Names*, Macmillan, 1980, p.44.

Note 6 Griffiths, Paul: *Problems of Religious Diversity*. Blackwell, 2001.

Note 7 Roman Catholic Church: *Catechism of the Catholic Church*. Vatican, 1992.

Note 8 Pope Benedict XVI: *Religious Freedom, the Path to Peace*. Vatican, 2011.

Note 9 Bowcott, Owen: 'Cross ban did infringe BA worker's rights, Strasbourg court rules' in *The Guardian*, 13 January 2013 (online at: www.theguardian.com/law/2013/jan/15/ba-rights-cross-european-court)

12 The dialogue between philosophy and Christianity

Note 1 If you would like to read a series of attempts to reconstruct the real saga of Braithwaite's poker, visit: www.theguardian.com/books/2001/mar/31/artsandhumanities.highereducation

13 The dialogue between ethics and Christianity

Note 1 References to Aristotle's Nicomachean Ethics are from: *Aristotle's Nicomachean Ethics, translated, with an interpretative essay, notes, and glossary*, by Robert C. Bartlett and Susan D. Collins, Chicago and London, The University of Chicago Press, 2011.

Text and photo credits

The publisher would like to thank the following individuals, institutions and companies for permission to reproduce copyright illustrations for this book:

Photo credits

Index

Index